Remaking Berlin

Infrastructures Series

edited by Geoffrey C. Bowker and Paul N. Edwards

Paul N. Edwards, *A Vast Machine: Computer Models, Climate Data, and the Politics of Global Warming*

Lawrence M. Busch, *Standards: Recipes for Reality*

Lisa Gitelman, ed., *"Raw Data" Is an Oxymoron*

Finn Brunton, *Spam: A Shadow History of the Internet*

Nil Disco and Eda Kranakis, eds., *Cosmopolitan Commons: Sharing Resources and Risks across Borders*

Casper Bruun Jensen and Brit Ross Winthereik, *Monitoring Movements in Development Aid: Recursive Partnerships and Infrastructures*

James Leach and Lee Wilson, eds., *Subversion, Conversion, Development: Cross-Cultural Knowledge Exchange and the Politics of Design*

Olga Kuchinskaya, *The Politics of Invisibility: Public Knowledge about Radiation Health Effects after Chernobyl*

Ashley Carse, *Beyond the Big Ditch: Politics, Ecology, and Infrastructure at the Panama Canal*

Alexander Klose, translated by Charles Marcrum II, *The Container Principle: How a Box Changes the Way We Think*

Eric T. Meyer and Ralph Schroeder, *Knowledge Machines: Digital Transformations of the Sciences and Humanities*

Geoffrey C. Bowker, Stefan Timmermans, Adele E. Clarke, and Ellen Balka, eds., *Boundary Objects and Beyond: Working with Leigh Star*

Clifford Siskin, *System: The Shaping of Modern Knowledge*

Lawrence Busch, *Knowledge for Sale: The Neoliberal Takeover of Higher Education*

Bill Maurer and Lana Swartz, *Paid: Tales of Dongles, Checks, and Other Money Stuff*

Katayoun Shafiee, *Machineries of Oil: An Infrastructural History of BP in Iran*

Megan Finn, *Documenting Aftermath: Information Infrastructures in the Wake of Disasters*

Ann M. Pendleton-Jullian and John Seely Brown, *Design Unbound: Designing for Emergence in a White Water World,* Volume 1: *Designing for Emergence*

Ann M. Pendleton-Jullian and John Seely Brown, *Design Unbound: Designing for Emergence in a White Water World,* Volume 2: *Ecologies of Change*

Jordan Frith, *A Billion Little Pieces: RFID and Infrastructures of Identification*

Morgan G. Ames, *The Charisma Machine: The Life, Death, and Legacy of One Laptop per Child*

Ryan Ellis, *Letters, Power Lines, and Other Dangerous Things: The Politics of Infrastructure Security*

Mario Biagioli and Alexandra Lippman, eds, *Gaming the Metrics: Misconduct and Manipulation in Academic Research*

Malcolm McCullough, *Downtime on the Microgrid: Architecture, Electricity, and Smart City Islands*

Emmanuel Didier, translated by Priya Vari Sen, *America by the Numbers: Quantification, Democracy, and the Birth of National Statistics*

Andrés Luque-Ayala and Simon Marvin, *Urban Operating Systems; Producing the Computational City*

Michael Truscello, *Infrastructural Brutalism: Art and the Necropolitics of Infrastructure*

Christopher R. Henke and Benjamin Sims, *Repairing Infrastructures: The Maintenance of Materiality and Power*

Stefan Höhne, *New York City Subway: The Invention of the Urban Passenger*

Timothy Moss, *Remaking Berlin: A History of the City through Infrastructure, 1920–2020*

Remaking Berlin

A History of the City through Infrastructure, 1920–2020

Timothy Moss

The MIT Press
Cambridge, Massachusetts
London, England

Printed with the generous support of the Gerda Henkel Foundation, Düsseldorf.

This book was set in Stone Serif by Westchester Publishing Services. Printed and bound in the United States of America.

Names: Moss, Timothy, 1959– author.
Title: Remaking Berlin : a history of the city through infrastructure, 1920–2020 / Timothy Moss.
Description: Cambridge, Massachusetts : The MIT Press, [2020] | Series: Infrastructures series | Includes bibliographical references and index. | Summary: "The first carefully researched historical analysis of the co-evolution of Berlin and its infrastructure services"—Provided by publisher.
Identifiers: LCCN 2020000803 | ISBN 9780262539777 (paperback)
Subjects: LCSH: Berlin (Germany)—History. | Berlin (Germany)—Politics and government. | Berlin (Germany)—Social conditions—20th century. | Berlin (Germany)—Social conditions—21st century. | Public works—Germany—Berlin—History.
Classification: LCC DD879 .M67 2020 | DDC 943/.155087—dc23
LC record available at https://lccn.loc.gov/2020000803

10 9 8 7 6 5 4 3 2

To Uli
in deepest gratitude

Contents

List of Figures

List of Tables

Abbreviations

AL	Alternative Liste (Alternative List)
Bewag	Berliner Städtische Elektrizitätswerke (Berlin electricity utility)
BKL	Berliner Kraft- und Licht (Bewag) (partially privatized Berlin electricity utility)
BOD	biochemical oxygen demand
BRD	Bundesrepublik Deutschland (Federal Republic of Germany)
BUND	Bund für Umwelt und Naturschutz Deutschland (Friends of the Earth Germany)
BWB	Berliner Wasserbetriebe (Berlin water and wastewater utility)
BWW	Berliner Wasserwerke (Berlin water utility)
CDU	Christlich-Demokratische Union (Christian Democratic Union)
CHP	combined heat and power
COD	chemical oxygen demand
CWI	Charlottenburger Wasser- und Industriewerke (a private water utility)
DDP	Deutsche Demokratische Partei (German Democratic Party)
DDR	Deutsche Demokratische Republik (German Democratic Republic)
DG	Deutsche Gasgesellschaft (a private gas utility)
DNVP	Deutschnationale Volkspartei (German National People's Party)
DAF	Deutsche Arbeitsfront (German Labor Front)
DVP	Deutsche Volkspartei (German People's Party)
ERP	European Recovery Program
ESA	Elektrizitätswerk Südwest (a power utility)
EU	European Union
FDGB	Freier Deutscher Gewerkschaftsbund (Free German Trade Union Federation)
FDP	Freie Demokratische Partei (Free Democratic Party)
GARIOA	Government Aid and Relief in Occupied Areas

Gasag	Berliner Städtische Gaswerke (Berlin gas utility)
GBI	Generalbauinspektor für die Reichshauptstadt (Inspector General for Buildings in the Reich Capital)
IBA	Internationale Bauausstellung (International Building Exhibition)
ISA	Institut für Städtebau und Architektur (Institute for Urban Planning and Architecture)
IWW	Institut für Wasserwirtschaft (Institute for Water Management)
KPD	Kommunistische Partei Deutschlands (Communist Party of Germany)
KWB	Kompetenzzentrum Wasser Berlin (Berlin Center of Competence for Water)
LDP	Liberal-Demokratische Partei Deutschlands (Liberal Democratic Party of Germany)
LTS	large technical systems
MEW	Märkisches Elektrizitätswerk (an electricity utility)
MLP	multi-level perspective
NSBO	Nationalsozialistische Betriebszellenorganisation (National Socialist Factory Cell Organization)
NSDAP	Nationalsozialistische Deutsche Arbeiterpartei (Nazi Party)
SED	Sozialistische Einheitspartei Deutschlands (Socialist Unity Party of Germany)
SERO	Sekundärrohstoffe (secondary raw materials)
SPD	Sozialdemokratische Partei Deutschlands (Social Democratic Party of Germany)
StEP V+E	Stadtentwicklungsplan Ver- und Entsorgung (Urban Development Plan on Utility Services)
StEW	Städtische Elektrizitätswerke (Berlin electricity utility)
STS	science and technology studies
SVZ	Sekundärrohstoff-Verwertungszentrum (material recycling center)
USPD	Unabhängige Sozialdemokratische Partei Deutschlands (Independent Social Democratic Party of Germany)
VEB	Volkseigener Betrieb (state-owned enterprise)
VVB	Vereinigung Volkseigener Betriebe (association of state-owned enterprises)
WAB	Wasserversorgung und Abwasserbehandlung (East German water and wastewater utility)
Wassag	Berliner Städtische Wasserwerke (Berlin water utility)
WEW	Groß-Berliner Wasser- und Entwässerungswerke (East Berlin water and sanitation utility)

Preface

Big projects often need a nudge to get going. In this case, it was a call for papers to an international conference held in July 2004 in Deutschlandsberg, Austria. The conference title was "Urban Infrastructure in Transition: What Can We Learn from History?" At that time, I had been working for over a decade on contemporary transitions to urban infrastructure in a reunited Germany, exploring the impacts of unification, deindustrialization, privatization, and liberalization on energy and water services. Although a trained historian, I had been drawn to the study of the dramatic events following the fall of the Berlin Wall. Living in Berlin in the early 1990s, history in the making had a stronger appeal than history itself. The call for papers in 2004, building a bridge between historical and contemporary research, was, for me, a call for reflection on how I could connect my ongoing research to what had inspired me into scholarship in the first place. It created an opportunity to study something that had always puzzled me, but which I had never had the chance to investigate in depth: the impact of the political division of Berlin in 1948–1949 on the city's infrastructure systems. On the basis of some hurried research, I penned an abstract for the call which, eventually, developed into an article entitled "Divided City, Divided Infrastructures: Securing Energy and Water Services in Post-War Berlin." I am very grateful to Harald Rohracher and the organizers of the event in Deutschlandsberg for giving me what turned out to be that nudge over the edge.

The idea of writing a book on Berlin's infrastructure history since the creation of Greater Berlin germinated at this time. Initial steps were made possible with a partial sabbatical from my post as department head at the Leibniz Institute for Regional Development and Structural Planning (IRS), Erkner, in 2007. A number of journal articles emerged from this initial foray into the field. The breakthrough came, though, with a fellowship awarded for this purpose by the Gerda Henkel Foundation (GHS) in 2017–2019. Preceded by a one-year guest professorship at the Humboldt University of Berlin, where I head a research group at the Integrative Research Institute for Transformations of Human-Environment Systems (IRI THESys), this gave me the time to conduct the in-depth archival research, literature analysis, and expert interviews essential for the book. I am greatly indebted to IRS, GHS, and IRI THESys for making this possible.

If the institutional setting provided the necessary space for researching and writing this book, the ideas informing it have emerged from discussions with many colleagues over the years. First and foremost, I thank Simon Marvin and Simon Guy. Since our first European Union project in 1996, both have inspired me immeasurably with wisdom and insight, strategic vision and friendship. It is no exaggeration to say that, without them, my career would have taken a very different path and this book would never have been conceived. Then, it was the roundtable events on urban infrastructure held in Autun, Burgundy, that provided an exquisite setting for testing out my findings in the company of leading historians and geographers. I would like to say a huge thank you to Olivier Coutard and Jon Rutherford for organizing these unforgettable events and for their patience with my obsession for Berlin.

I would like give a special thanks to all my former colleagues in our department at IRS Erkner. For thirteen years we worked closely together on fascinating research into contemporary environmental governance in Germany and the European Union, ranging from water resources management and infrastructure policy to the energy transition. Ludger Gailing was a constant source of support and intellectual sparring partner throughout. At IRS I found huge inspiration on infrastructure issues from Matthias Naumann, Ross Beveridge, Sören Becker, Jochen Monstadt, Frank Hüesker, and Markus Wissen, as well as—more widely—from Andrea Bues, Natàlia Garcia Soler, Ute Hasenöhrl, Kristine Kern, Katharina Krause, Andreas Röhring, Frank Sondershaus, and Carsten Zehner. Thanks go also to Martina Leppler for keeping things going.

Since moving to IRI THESys in 2016 I have benefited hugely from the supportive and stimulating scholarly environment of this interdisciplinary venture. I would like to give special thanks to Jörg Niewöhner and Patrick Hostert for giving me the break and encouraging me since. Other people at the institute who have helped me greatly are Gretchen Bakke, Anne Dombrowski, Kathrin Klementz, Sebastian van der Linden, Axel Klie, Olof Krüger, Tobias Krüger, Ourania Papasozomenou, and Dimitris Zikos.

I am very grateful to the Manchester Urban Institute of the University of Manchester for granting me a guest professorship there in 2017. Stefan Bouzarovski, Saska Petrova, James Evans, and Kevin Ward were very supportive in what proved to be a formative time. The book's structure was, indeed, conceived in the hallowed tranquillity of the John Rylands Library. Matthew Gandy provided invaluable advice in devising the book concept. The staff at Berlin's State Archive (Landesarchiv Berlin) have been very helpful in dealing with my enquiries over the years. I would like to thank especially Andreas Matschenz, Monika Bartzsch, and Bianca Welzing-Bräutigam. I have been very well supported by the staff at the Gerda Henkel Foundation, in particular Angela Kühnen and Anna Kuschmann. I am indebted to the Foundation also for providing financial support for this book and funding a series of short films about my research, freely available on its scientific portal L.I.S.A. (https://lisa.gerda-henkel-stiftung.de/das_unsi chtbare_berlin?nav_id=8405&language=en). Stephan Zengerle and Martin Pogac made a great job of producing these films. Many thanks also to go the many practitioners and researchers of Berlin's infrastructure who kindly agreed to be interviewed for this book. Respect for their anonymity prohibits me from naming them, but their contribution has been hugely valuable. The staff at the MIT Press have been highly supportive throughout the production process, in particular, Justin Kehoe, Katie Helke, María García, and Susan Clark. I thank also Sherry Gerstein and Michael Durnin for excellent copyediting.

In addition to those mentioned above, the following people are also due thanks for the varied ways in which they have assisted and improved my work over the years: Dana Abi Ghanam, Christoph Bernhardt, Christine Bichsel, Dorothee Brantz, Vanesa Castán Broto, Harriet Bulkeley, Morten Elle, Harald Engler, Maria Francesch Huidobro, Itay Fischhendler, Kathryn Furlong, Frank Geels, Günther Grassmann, Håvard Haarstad, Jan Hansen, Conor Harrison, Lior Herman, Mike Hodson, Joseph Hoppe, Jonathan Hummels, Andy Karvonen, Astrid Kirchhof, Jens Libbe, Andrés Luque Ayala, Will Medd, Martin Melosi, Jan-Henrik Meyer, Peter Mollinga, Susanne Balslev Nielsen, Julia Obertreis, Rob Raven, Gillad Rosen, Siddharth Sareen, David Saurí, Dieter Schott, Elizabeth Shove, Adrian Smith, Philipp Späth, Erik Swyngedouw, Joel Tarr, Helmut Trischler, Bernhard Truffer, Eric Verdeil, Gordon Walker, and Pia Wolffram.

I thank all these people for the various ways they have supported this venture. All the remaining errors are, of course, mine.

Last but not least, I am hugely indebted to my wife, Ulrike Grassau, for all the love and sustenance she has provided along this journey.

Berlin and Hayton, March 2020

Note: All translations from the German original into English are by the author.

1 Introduction: Berlin's Invisible Infrastructures

When you are next in Berlin take a 109 bus to the bridge over the River Spree. Instead of following the tourists toward the famous Charlottenburg Palace, walk east along the leafy river bank, passing the city's characteristic mix of turn-of-the-century and postwar apartment blocks until you reach the Charlottenburg power station, dominating the waterfront. There unfolds before you a panorama of electricity-generation technology through the ages. It begins with the original power plant dating back to the Kaiserreich, easily identifiable with its ornate brick decoration. Further to the left is a building housing a control room from the Weimar era in typical modernist style. Wedged between them is a boiler hall built in the 1950s and to the far left a huge denitrification plant dating from the 1980s. This roll-call of energy architecture is a material testimony to the history of municipal electricity provision in the city once renowned as the "electropolis" of Europe. Its visual appearance evokes a powerful imagery of adaptive continuity, with each new building representing a more modern way of transforming raw fuel into electrical current. From this vantage point, on the bank of the Spree, the history of Berlin's electricity supply appears as a continuous story of technological progress. This is the narrative that has been told and retold by generations of civil engineers engaged in building, operating, or studying these edifices to urban modernity.

If you then cross the river over the aptly named Siemens footbridge and go to the back of the power station on Quedlinburg Street, the impression is strikingly different. Instead of architectural icons jostling for attention, you are faced with a disorderly collection of buildings of uncertain function. Some are being dismantled, others appear no longer in operation or are being used for purposes other than power generation. A high, white wall around the complex obscures your vision and lends an aura of secrecy. In contrast to the front of the power plant that calls out to be looked at, the back is a statement of concealment. The certainty and confidence exuded by the power plant's facade is challenged by the ambiguity and disorderliness of its rear.

These contrasting impressions gained from a stroll around a power station are a metaphor for this book. Taking a fresh and unusual look at something we all take for granted is what the book is all about. It is a history of Berlin's infrastructures, certainly, but one that differs hugely from the familiar perspective of civil engineers and urban planners. While they have presented impressive accounts of technological advances to the city's infrastructures, I direct attention toward the less visible, but equally significant ways in which urban technology has acted as medium and manifestation of political aspirations.[1] This political dimension to infrastructure is largely invisible in popular narratives. Revealing this hidden underbelly of the city's energy and water systems and subjecting it to critical scrutiny is central to my venture. Metaphorically speaking, you need to explore the back as well as the front of a power station if you want to appreciate how infrastructure works and how it is made to work.

Conduits of Modern Urbanism

This book interprets Berlin's turbulent twentieth-century history afresh through the lens of its networked infrastructures. It reveals how the policies, plans, and practices surrounding the city's energy and water/wastewater services changed (or did not change) in response to the regime diversity, geopolitical interventions, and socioeconomic volatility that have pitted Berlin's recent history and what this says, on a more fundamental level, about the relationship between a city and its infrastructure. Exploring how infrastructure systems, generally renowned for their obduracy, were affected by dramatic regime shifts—from the Weimar Republic, the Nazi dictatorship, socialist East Berlin, capitalist West Berlin to the reunified city—reveals attributes of sociotechnical configurations hidden in other cities by the patina of familiarity. Taking Berlin as an exemplar, the book demonstrates what infrastructure history can tell us about a city: in terms of how it was envisioned, structured, and governed in the past and what these legacies can mean for urban and infrastructure transitions today.

Berlin's infrastructures have, at different times over the past 100 years, been myth, model, and medium of the modern city. By the 1930s, Berlin had come to symbolise *the* networked city in Europe. Mythologized on film and paper as the "electropolis," by virtue of its pioneering role in electricity technology and supply, Berlin enjoyed a public image as the "technological city through and through."[2] This is powerfully reflected in contemporary films, such as *Metropolis* or *Berlin: Symphonie einer Großstadt*. After the war, other myths came to shroud Berlin's infrastructures. Local power plants and gas works came to symbolize the resilience of West Berlin against enclosure and intervention by the Soviet Union and East Germany. Integrated infrastructure plans promised the materialization of a truly socialist modernity in East Berlin. While these myths often failed to live up to expectations, the models which Berlin represented to other cities had a far-reaching impact. In the 1920s, cities from across the globe looked to Berlin for ideas on how to provide public services to a growing metropolis.[3] It was termed the "training ground of modernity" (*Exercierfeld der Moderne*), a hothouse for innovations in urban infrastructure.[4] In the late 1980s, West Berlin became a pioneer of urban environmentalism, inspiring energy efficiency and water conservation technologies in cities worldwide. Today, the re-municipalization of the city's water and energy utilities, accompanied by popular pressure to render them more transparent, environmentally sustainable, and socially equitable, is attracting global attention as an alternative model to corporatism. No history of Berlin, however, can highlight the positives while ignoring the negatives. The iconic status which Berlin enjoyed at several times during the twentieth century contrasts sharply with the city's image as the nerve-center of National Socialism, symbol of wartime devastation, and victim of Cold War division.[5] The Nazi era, in particular, is rife with instances of abuse, rather than use, of the networked city. Here, infrastructures became harbingers of impending destruction and oppression.

This book sets out to tell the history of Berlin through the prism of its infrastructures with four core objectives in mind. First, it analyses the coevolution of Berlin and its piped infrastructures over a period of 100 years, spanning five highly diverse political regimes. Second, it examines how municipal, national, and international politics and policies have manifested themselves in Berlin's infrastructures since 1920. Third, it explores the tensions between obduracy and change to the city's infrastructures across a century witnessing multiple political ruptures and dramatic socioeconomic transformation. Fourth, it reveals the distinctive trajectories of, and interdependencies between, five infrastructure sectors—electricity, gas, district heating, water, and sanitation—in a single city.

The book's ambition, therefore, is to tread new ground in the study of urban infrastructures in Berlin and beyond by covering a long time period (from the creation of Greater Berlin in 1920 to the present day), encompassing diverse political regimes (from democratic to socialist and fascist), and comparing multiple infrastructure sectors (from energy to water). Alongside this empirical originality it also aspires to enrich ways of conceptualizing the multiple temporalities and spatialities of urban infrastructures. To this end, three overarching research questions guide the narrative: First, in what ways does Berlin's infrastructure history raise our understanding of how the city was envisioned, structured and governed in the past? Second, what can this history tell us about the nature of change and continuity to sociotechnical systems and of relations between a city and its infrastructure? Third, what do these legacies from the past mean for urban and infrastructure transitions today?

This story is about how urban infrastructures have helped "remake" Berlin over the past 100 years. The book's title—"Remaking Berlin"—draws on a popular meme of the city's fluidity and malleability that has fascinated commentators from the 1920s to the present day. Writing in 1929, Franz Hessel spoke of Berlin being "always on the move, always on the point of turning into something different."[6] Echoing this sentiment in 2006, Allan Cochrane wrote that "Berlin's histories past and present are always in the process of being made, always provisional, never finalized."[7] In this volatile and ephemeral history, what role did infrastructures play? Did energy and water infrastructures act as a stabilizing force in the face of so much volatility? Was there, to quote Dirk van Laak, "a striking discrepancy between the discontinuity of political history [of Germany] on the one hand and the continuity in building and expanding infrastructures on the other"?[8] Or did infrastructures mirror, and even reinforce, regime change and geopolitical intervention? This book sets out to uncover the various ways in which infrastructures have contributed to the "remaking" of Berlin over the past century, enabling and limiting options for shaping the city. The "remaking" at stake has never been purely physical, but also social. It has involved the propagation through infrastructure of, for instance, new political entities, social compacts, or urban imaginaries. Networked infrastructures, I will argue throughout, were conduits not merely of water and energy, but also, more fundamentally, of modern urbanism.

This is, essentially, a political history of Berlin's infrastructures. It targets primarily how energy and water services were planned and provided, rather than how they were used. The principal (human) actors in the narrative are, therefore, utility managers, city politicians, municipal government officials, and—more recently—civil society organizations. It is important to note that the book does not aspire to being a cultural history of infrastructure. It does not explore the user's perspective.[9] Nevertheless, issues of infrastructure use and resource consumption are considered when they had a particular impact upon service provision. Three user/consumer aspects recur throughout the book: first, how consumption patterns adapted to socioeconomic trends and political interventions; second, what criticism of utility services was voiced by users; and, third, how the energy and water utilities perceived of, and engaged with, user communities to shape demand.

A second caveat is required in mapping out the scope of this venture: the book does not treat infrastructures of transportation, waste disposal, or communication. This is not because these sectors are less significant, but because studying more than five infrastructure sectors over a whole century would have posed serious limits to the depth of analysis. It was important, therefore, to focus on a group of technical infrastructures that have much in common. The five sectors selected—electricity, gas, district heating, water, and sanitation—are all piped infrastructures, in that they are characterized by networked pipes, cables, and ducts that distribute material flows or currents across space. This distinguishes them from transportation or waste disposal. In Berlin they have been owned and operated primarily by municipal utilities, unlike communication networks, with substantial influence by city administrations. These similarities offer fruitful ground for exploring interdependencies, mimicry, and competition between the five sectors. A further factor influencing the selection has been to rectify the bias toward transportation that has characterized most treatments of infrastructure in the city's historiography. There already exist a number of works that tell the history of Berlin's rail, road, and air transport systems, whether as forces of urbanization, expressions of political instrumentalization, or symbols of urban identity.[10] Its piped infrastructures, by contrast, have received little attention in the city's histories.

The book deliberately targets an audience of diverse disciplinary backgrounds, challenging monodisciplinary approaches and stimulating cross-disciplinary debate between science and technology studies, urban studies, and urban history. On the one hand, it encourages historians of technology and urban historians to rethink how networked infrastructures shape, and are shaped by, urban structures and processes over a long time period and across shifting contexts. On the other, it provokes geographers and political scientists to consider in a more nuanced way where today's urban energy or water transitions are coming from, historically speaking. The book aspires also to reach beyond the academy to professionals working in the fields of urban planning, infrastructure management, and the urban environment who are interested in learning about the relevance of Berlin's infrastructure history for modern-day transitions. Given the powerful appeal Berlin exerts on the public imagination, it is hoped the book will strike a chord with the general reader fascinated by the turbulent past and contested, yet liveable, present of this unique city.

Histories of Berlin and Its Infrastructures

Why does Berlin matter? How can a city with such an unusual past deliver insight that is relevant to academic and professional debates? These are questions which have been raised in the wake of a veritable hype surrounding Berlin in the reunification era. Since 1989, social scientists have been drawn to the city as a melting pot of West and East in a globalizing world, producing a rich tableau of scholarship on the post-unification period. Berlin has become, in the words of Andreas Huyssen, "a prism through which we can focus issues of contemporary urbanism."[11] This has prompted warnings of "exoticizing Berlin's situation"[12] and generated an intriguing debate on whether Berlin today constitutes an "exceptional case"[13] or an "ordinary city."[14] The charge of exceptionalism is even more pertinent to an historical analysis covering the past 100 years. During this period of time Berlin has experienced a greater diversity of political rule, a greater intensity of economic disruption, and a greater vulnerability to geopolitical intervention than, arguably, any other city in the world. Of course, it is these extremes which make Berlin's story so captivating. Yet, while these can generate powerful narratives, their wider relevance to scholarship needs justifying.

The core argument made by scholars in favor of studying the unfamiliar is that atypical or extreme cases can reveal phenomena otherwise concealed by routinized practices, institutionalized procedures, and taken-for-granted structures.[15] Referring to infrastructures in particular, Jane Summerton's exhortation to focus on times and places of radical disruption is worth quoting in full: "It is well known that analyzing extreme situations—system failure, periods of rapid growth or structural transformation—often help [*sic*] us to elucidate 'the normal' in different expressions of technology. By studying phases in which technical systems undergo radical change, we might expect to gain new insights into basic dynamics and properties of these systems."[16]

This applies to Berlin not simply for one particular event, but—to a greater or lesser degree—throughout the past century. During this period Berlin has witnessed multiple critical junctures, including the hyperinflation of 1923, the Nazi seizure of power in 1933, wartime destruction, political division in 1949, the building of the Wall in 1961 and reunification in 1990. It has experienced highly diverse political regimes, ranging from democratic to fascist and state-socialist, as well as military occupation. To quote Huyssen once more: "There is perhaps no other major Western city that bears the marks of twentieth century history as intensely … as Berlin."[17] It is precisely this rich diversity and continuous instability which can deliver such fresh insight into the relationship between a city and its infrastructure. As Erik Swyngedouw has demonstrated in his history of water in twentieth-century Spain, fascist rule and geopolitical interventions reveal properties and dynamics of hydropolitics "in a clear and unambiguous manner."[18] Berlin is interesting, therefore, not because it is a representative case, but because it is such an insightful one.

Given the recent scholarly interest in Berlin, it is extraordinary how incomplete and fragmented the city's historiography remains. Astonishingly, there exist very few book-length urban histories that cover the entire period from the creation of Greater Berlin in 1920 to even the recent past.[19] Some periods of Berlin's history have been subjected to intense study, while others languish untouched or under-researched. Best studied from a political history perspective is West Berlin between political division and reunification.[20] Municipal politics in the Weimar era has also received significant attention.[21] By contrast, we know very little at all about how the city government operated in East Berlin under state socialism. Even the Nazi era has, surprisingly, not received the attention it deserves. Recent publications on Berlin under National Socialism lament the lack of systematic studies of this period and the absence of any history of the city government at this time.[22] Historical research of Nazi Berlin has focused instead on dramatic or harrowing stories, such as Goebbels's campaign to control Berlin, the persecution of the city's Jews, Speer's plans for Germania, the local Nazi Party, and the resistance movement. This book represents an attempt to redress these imbalances in the city's political historiography, providing fresh insight into how municipal government operated under fascist and state-socialist, as well as democratic, regimes. It represents an initial foray into a long-term, cross-regime analysis of the city's history, using infrastructure as the lens of choice.

In the histories of Berlin that do exist, piped infrastructures are largely invisible.[23] A recent edited volume on Berlin under Nazi rule characteristically addressed infrastructure only in terms of transportation.[24] A pioneering study by Otto Büsch of Berlin's municipal enterprises—with detailed analysis of the city's electricity, gas, and water utilities—was written in 1960 and is limited to the Weimar era only.[25] Thomas Hughes's seminal book on the emergence of electricity systems in Germany, Britain, and the United States does include a case study on Berlin, but only for the period 1880–1915.[26] An edited collection on Berlin's industrial heritage, published in 2020, dedicates at least some chapters to urban infrastructures.[27] While political histories of urban infrastructures have recently been published for Hamburg and Munich, nothing comparable exists for the German capital.[28]

This has meant that the history of Berlin's infrastructures has been left, largely, to civil engineers and urban planners. Their contribution to our knowledge of the technical design, capacity, and performance of the city's energy and water systems is highly valuable. Hilmar Bärthel, an engineer and long-standing employee of the East Berlin planning department, has produced a series of volumes documenting the detailed history of the city's gas works, power stations, water works, and sewage treatment plants from their early beginnings to the present.[29] Heinrich Tepasse has written several books on the relationship between urban technology and urban planning in Berlin's history from an engineering perspective.[30] Thorsten Dame has studied Berlin's electricity industry through its architectural history.[31] Other works, by Shahrooz Mohajeri and Christian Eiden, focus on the formative period of Berlin's water and sanitation systems in the late nineteenth and early twentieth century.[32] These works are dedicated to mapping technological trajectories in Berlin from innovation to consolidation. They present a powerful imagery of linear progress to urban modernity and continuity. The politics of infrastructure, if addressed at all, is characterized largely as an external disturbance.[33] This book, in sharp contrast, foregrounds the politics of Berlin's infrastructures. It sets out to challenge the notion of infrastructure being somehow apart from political discourse and contestation, arguing that urban, national, and even international politics were played out and, indeed, manifested themselves in the fabric of the city's energy and water systems.

In doing so, the book draws on recent research about today's transformations to Berlin's infrastructures. Since reunification, the city's energy and water utilities have acquired a new visibility. Initiatives to privatize them in the 1990s to help offset the city's chronic debt and then to re-municipalize them since 2010 following popular protest have spawned high-profile debates on the purpose and future of infrastructure in the city. Together with climate change, these pressures are challenging long-standing assumptions, logics, and practices underpinning infrastructure policy and management. They have brought infrastructure out into the public domain, revealing quite how political it can be. Urban scholars are today uncovering the contestations over Berlin's infrastructures and the alternative visions they are generating.[34] This book acknowledges the way they are opening up the city's infrastructure to critical social science perspectives and makes the case for extending this politically sensitive analysis to a 100-year history of the city's infrastructures. The fundamental argument is that exploring how the city's energy and water systems got enrolled in, resisted, or sustained five hugely diverse political regimes can shed important new insight on the dynamic relationship between a city and its infrastructures. The very uniqueness of Berlin's crisis-ridden twentieth-century history can, it is argued, reveal dimensions to this relationship concealed elsewhere by the veil of routinized processes and path-dependent structures.

Histories of Urban Infrastructure

Inspirational to this work is a veritable "infrastructural turn" in the social sciences and humanities today.[35] Infrastructures are being used in recent research as a window on human-environment relations in general, and the urban condition in particular. They have become a medium of choice for scholars working on the history or anthropology of technology, urban or climate governance, and environmental history. It is at this intersection of science and technology studies (STS), history of technology, and human geography that new understandings of infrastructures have emerged that reach far beyond the technical bounds of civil engineers. Today, infrastructures are perceived in the social sciences as complex and dynamic networks that always comprise both the social and the technical. This is well expressed in a recent definition of infrastructures as "socio-technical assemblages of materiality, discursive, fiscal, and organizational forms and relations."[36] Their value to society is regarded as pivotal, despite their general invisibility. Infrastructure, in the words of Paul N. Edwards, "is the invisible background, the substrate or support, the technocultural/natural environment, of modernity."[37] Their invisibility, indeed, conceals deep-rooted embeddedness in society, as Jörg Niewöhner argues: "Infrastructure seeps into the background, it sediments out and disappears from view. And with it disappear all the technical, social, political, and ethical choices that are necessarily made during the design, construction, implementation and maintenance of any infrastructure."[38]

This book is about revealing these kinds of choices made in the past that have shaped Berlin's infrastructures and have rendered them largely invisible to public scrutiny until very recently. It seeks to unpack the visions underpinning infrastructure policy and strategy, their materialization in technical networks, and the functions performed by infrastructure for the city.

Today's scholarly interest in infrastructures was pioneered in large measure by historians. The importance of infrastructures to state building and state hegemony has been acknowledged since the work of Karl Wittfogel on "hydraulic civilizations" in Oriental societies and Donald Worster on "rivers of empire" in the American West.[39] Since then, historians of technology have demonstrated the multifarious ways in which infrastructures become imbued with power relations in industrial, colonial, and postcolonial societies.[40] Today, the coevolution of large technical systems and the societies they serve has become a popular meme for historical analysis.[41]

Urban and environmental historians applied this approach to cities, generating powerful insight specific to urban infrastructure. An early example was the work of Joel Tarr, Gabriel Dupuy, and others about the effects of technology on urban form and of urban politics on technology.[42] William Cronon set a milestone in 1991 by illustrating how Chicago and its natural hinterlands were coproduced by means of new technologies that mobilized physical substances essential for the city's growth.[43] Martin Melosi's book *The Sanitary City* of 2000 traced the trajectories of wastewater technologies and the institutions that supported them in US cities from their municipal beginnings to the present day.[44] In Germany, Dieter Schott revealed the contested relationship between urban technology and urban politics in three medium-sized cities prior to the First World War.[45]

Urban scholars have since drawn on debates in human geography to enrich the conceptual and critical framing of infrastructure politics.[46] Pathbreaking monographs on urban infrastructures include Stephan Graham and Simon Marvin's *Splintering Urbanism* on the coproduction of liberalized utility services and urban fragmentation, Matthew Gandy's *Concrete and Clay* on the urban governance of natural resources in New York City, and Maria Kaika's *City of Flows* on the celebration and subsequent concealment of water infrastructures in Athens.[47] Interestingly, all three books, although written by human geographers, are powerfully historical in their scope and argument.

As will be revealed in more detail in the following chapter, this rich literature at the interface of STS, human geography, and the history of technology is generating a new genre of scholarship on the co-constitution of cities and their infrastructures. This book is positioned precisely at this intersection of disciplines and is designed to enrich ongoing debates on this complex relationship. Its novel contribution is, essentially, fivefold. First, the book represents a long-term study of urban infrastructures that is not limited to past eras of emergence and stabilization or present phases of reconfiguration, but spans 100 years of sociotechnical history. It thereby addresses mature infrastructure systems that have received little attention by infrastructure historians in the past.[48] Second, the book does not assume that infrastructures are inherently stable or obdurate, but focuses rather on the ways in which infrastructures are made or become obdurate and how they get destabilized. Particular attention is paid here to the nonlinearity of sociotechnical trajectories, the layering of old and new technologies, and alternative pathways that presented themselves during the course of Berlin's 100-year history.[49] Third, the book compares and connects multiple infrastructure sectors in a single city. This is still unusual in infrastructure studies, representing a significant gap in the literature.[50] The dimensions of connectivity to be covered will include physical interdependence, as between wastewater treatment and electricity supply, common governance arrangements, and competition between different utilities, for instance between electricity and gas utilities over district heating. Fourth, the book explores the multi-scalar politics of infrastructure, ranging from disputes over local air pollution and municipal strategies for infrastructure expansion to national policy interventions and geopolitical constraints. How these factors on different scalar levels interacted and manifested themselves in systems of energy and water provision is of prime interest. Finally, the book eschews simplistic notions of the city as a single, bounded entity. Just as it understands infrastructure as a sociotechnical configuration, so too does it conceive of the city in relational terms, with multiple geographies emerging out of heterogeneous associations.[51]

Researching Berlin's Infrastructures

The interdisciplinary thrust of the book, encompassing both historical and contemporary analysis and drawing on a wide range of scholarly debates, has posed particular challenges in conducting the research. The overarching task has been to access diverse sources of empirical material and to interpret this data with the help of different, but complementary, conceptualizations of urban infrastructure history. The risk has always been, in terms of theory, to avoid combining the incompatible and, with regard to the empirics, to resist writing a history that traces back the present.

Conceptually, the book is framed by sociotechnical approaches to the study of urban infrastructure, as indicated above and elaborated in the following chapter. This has required in-depth analysis of secondary literature on ways of theorizing the relationship between continuity and change to sociotechnical systems as well as the relationship between cities and their infrastructures. Sources have been sought within the fields of STS, history of technology, and urban studies. They have been assessed in terms of their contribution to each of these key relationships, identifying gaps in research for this book to fill. This has demanded sensitivity toward the epistemological roots of each field of scholarship.

The empirical research has needed to be extensive by virtue of the long period under study, the intensity of Berlin's recent history, the range of infrastructures studied, and the dearth of secondary literature on certain periods of time. The empirical chapters which form the backbone of this book derive from the analysis of a wide variety of published and unpublished material, as well as oral history. Secondary literature on the political and economic history of Berlin since 1920 has provided background knowledge on how each of the five political regimes were constituted, how they worked, to what ends and by what means. This has been essential to contextualize infrastructure politics in each era. General literature has also been drawn on to reveal important socioeconomic trends and crises of relevance to utility service provision and use. The available secondary literature on the city's infrastructures, written largely by civil engineers and planners, has been gleaned to provide details on the technologies applied, infrastructure built, and resources used in each service sector over the 100-year period. Particularly valuable has been the published primary literature dating from the early 1920s to the present day. For the purpose of this book all relevant professional journals for electricity, gas, heating, water, and sanitation published in Germany since 1920 have been searched for articles relating to Berlin, written primarily by utility directors, prominent civil engineers, and municipal officers. This has produced a rich source of data that has been supplemented with statistical reports, policy documents, and local newspapers also dating from the whole period of study.

The principal source for primary data has been unpublished material deposited in archives. Above all, the State Archive of Berlin (Landesarchiv Berlin) has proved a treasure trove of documents and correspondence relating to the period between 1920 and 1990, housing some 250 files of direct value to the book. The principal files used are those of the city government (Magistrat until 1949, then senate in West Berlin and Magistrat in East Berlin until 1990). The archive of the municipal gas utility Gasag is deposited at the State Archive. Unfortunately, the archive of the water utility Berliner Wasserbetriebe was not accessible during its current transfer to the State Archive. Nor was the archive of the municipal power utility Bewag (now Vattenfall) accessible to the author, despite repeated requests to the utility. These limitations did not prove serious, however, since the correspondence and documentation of all the city's utilities are well represented in the city government files for most periods. Additional material on environmental nongovernmental organizations (NGOs) in East Berlin was acquired in the archive on opposition in East Germany run by the Robert Havemann Society.

For first-hand accounts, interviews were held with around forty stakeholders of infrastructure policy and management. These interviews were conducted between 1993 and 2018 with former as well as active utility managers, city government officials, consultants, researchers, and environmentalists operating in Berlin—East and West—since the 1970s.[52] The interview partners were selected to provide insight on recent developments not covered by archival material, to yield diverse perspectives on Berlin's infrastructure systems, but also to reflect on the city's infrastructure history with the benefit of hindsight.

Structure of the Book

The book is structured around a largely chronological analysis of Berlin's infrastructure history over the past 100 years, introduced by a conceptual chapter that frames the research and concluded by a chapter drawing out the key findings. Chapter 2 positions the book within the rich literature on urban infrastructures and their histories, and develops a framework to guide the analysis. It sets the scene by challenging superficial impressions of obduracy and linearity to Berlin's infrastructure history before elaborating on what it means to treat infrastructures as sociotechnical configurations. The chapter then sets out the analytical framework of the book, structured around the value of taking infrastructural, long-term, political, cross-sectoral, and ecological perspectives on Berlin's history and—by extrapolation—cities in general. These themes are used to interpret findings in the subsequent empirical chapters and guide the conclusions in the final chapter.

Chapter 3 sets the scene for the empirical research by introducing Greater Berlin as a territorial entity created in 1920 by a new democratic alliance to unify the metropolitan area and promote equitable living conditions. It demonstrates how, from the earliest days of the enlarged city, urban infrastructures were enrolled in a municipal quest for unitary and affordable services in the face of hyperinflation. Chapter 4 explores how, following currency stabilization in 1924, the city's electricity, gas, water, and sanitation utilities—as major players of Berlin's municipal economy—were used to weave the fabric of a networked municipalism. It assesses how far the utilities were able to deliver on the political agenda of unifying and improving service standards across the city and to enrol consumers in this venture. The chapter concludes by revealing how the expansionist plans for urban infrastructures became the target of criticism in and beyond the city, contributing to the destabilization of the democratic order.

Chapter 5 presents an unfamiliar history of Nazi Berlin: one viewed through the lens of its energy and water services. It explores how Nazi rule changed the way Berlin's infrastructure systems were managed and owned, the political goals they pursued, the roles ascribed to their consumers, and the resource flows they mediated. It describes how, after 1933, the "networked city" became gradually and insidiously enrolled in national agendas of repression, racism, autarky, and militarization. Chapter 6 addresses the impact of wartime destruction, military occupation, and political division on the city's infrastructures, spanning the decade between the beginning of the war in 1939 and the creation of two separate German states in 1949. It analyses how resilient Berlin's infrastructures proved in the face of urban vulnerability, but also how infrastructural vulnerability and resilience were used as political tools in the increasingly divisive climate of postwar Berlin.

The following two chapters study the experience of political division from an infrastructure perspective in East and West Berlin, respectively. Chapter 7 describes how East Berlin's municipal utilities became subordinated to a state-socialist planning and management regime and how this affected services for energy and water/wastewater. It addresses the thorny relationship with West Berlin, exploring different realms of interdependence and how East Berlin authorities dealt with them. Above all, it highlights the gap that emerged between an emergent socialist infrastructural ideal and the poor performance of under-resourced infrastructures. Chapter 8 explores the urban and geopolitical contexts within which West Berlin strove to sustain its insular existence, assessing how the city's infrastructures were enrolled in a strategy of urban autarky. It reveals how this strategy needed adapting to suit the sociotechnical constitution of each infrastructure sector and how it affected utility management, consumerism, and the urban environment. When the limits to urban autarky became increasingly apparent from the 1970s onward, alternative strategies of regional cooperation and resource efficiency gained credence.

Chapter 9 takes Berlin's infrastructure odyssey up to the present day. It traces a volatile period which began with the euphoria of reunification in 1990 and the enrollment of the city's infrastructure systems in Berlin's aspiration to regain world-city status. This gave way to despondency as Berlin's economy collapsed, its public debt soared, and the city's electricity, gas, and water utilities were privatized during the late 1990s. The chapter explores how privatization affected infrastructure services and their urban governance. It concludes by describing the emergence of social movements campaigning to re-municipalize the city's infrastructures and assessing their impact on the form and substance of infrastructure governance today.

The final chapter reflects upon the legacies of Berlin's infrastructure history for research and policy. Looking across the whole book, it interprets the findings in terms of the objectives formulated in chapter 1 and the conceptual framing of chapter 2. It revisits the five analytical themes developed in chapter 2, illustrating them with examples taken from across the 100-year panorama and highlighting their implications for research on urban infrastructure history. Particular attention is paid to what the Berlin case can tell us about the relationship between sociotechnical continuity and change, as well as between a city and its infrastructure. The chapter concludes with observations on the value of Berlin's infrastructure history for urban sociotechnical transitions today.

2 Trajectories of Technological Urbanism

The technical infrastructures serving Berlin today look, at first sight, very much like they have done for decades. If Berlin's utility managers from the 1920s could be transported forward in time to the present they would, by and large, recognize the structures and functions of the city's energy, water, and sanitation systems. Electricity is provided, as it has been since the 1920s, via a network of cables of varying voltage connected to power stations within and beyond the city that are still fired, largely, by fossil fuels. The district heating system powered by urban cogeneration plants and the gas supply grid would also be familiar to them. The water supply and wastewater disposal networks are largely unchanged physically, following the same conduits—and, in some cases, even using the same sewers—since their creation in the mid to late nineteenth century. The technologies enrolled in converting and treating the city's energy and water flows have changed, of course, and the sources of energy have become more varied with the emergence of natural gas, biogas, wind, and solar power. Nevertheless, the degree of physical continuity of Berlin's infrastructures is striking. It would have been a source of some surprise and, certainly, pride for the founding fathers of Berlin's utility systems to see their infrastructures continuing to drive the city in the twenty-first century.

This prompts the question why the history of Berlin's infrastructures is worth revisiting at all. If nothing appears to have altered substantially, why bother to look for what might be only minor modifications? Are the generations of civil engineers who have related the story of the city's infrastructure in terms of a linear trajectory of technological progress perhaps right, after all? If there are any changes to consider, can they not be limited to the realm of politics that, at certain moments in Berlin's turbulent history, interfered in the routinized running of its urban technologies?

This book argues, conversely, that Berlin's infrastructures are more dynamic than meets the eye. Impressions of physical obduracy are deceptive. They hide the intensive work involved in keeping infrastructures going. They hide the multiple ways in which technical artifacts are given meaning and purpose through political strategies, cultural norms, and social practices. They hide the shifting functions and values attached to urban infrastructures over time. They hide, above all, the relationship between what changes and what does not change in such complex systems. Understanding what components of Berlin's infrastructures altered, when, and why is what this more nuanced and ambitious story of urban infrastructure is all about.

Such an undertaking needs points of orientation to guide the reader through the labyrinthian twists and turns of Berlin's infrastructure history. Before embarking on the narrative, therefore, this chapter sets out an analytical framework that structures the line of argument underpinning the empirical chapters that follow. For although the book is essentially empirical, it aspires also to enrich conceptual scholarship on urban infrastructure histories. The analytical framework developed below is designed to fulfill three functions: first, to highlight what is original about the book; second, to guide interpretation of the data and findings in each chapter; third, to structure analysis of the book's novel contribution to scholarship, especially in the concluding chapter. The framework is devised, therefore, to speak to both the empirical detail of Berlin's own history and conceptual debates on urban infrastructures, as conducted by historians of technology, urban studies scholars and those engaged in STS. It comprises five themes, elaborated in the remainder of this chapter. The first theme, *infrastructural traces of Berlin*, explains what can be revealed by taking an infrastructural perspective on Berlin's history. The second, *conjunctions of continuity and change*, demonstrates the value of taking a long-term perspective on urban infrastructures. The third, *urban politics through infrastructure*, explores the benefits of studying infrastructure politics under widely divergent political regimes. The fourth, *infrastructural interdependence*, explains what can be revealed through attention to multiple infrastructures. The fifth and final theme, *infrastructured metabolisms*, targets the multiple geographies enrolled in the transformation of natural resources through urban infrastructures. In the following sections, each analytical theme is presented in turn, highlighting its novel contribution to existing scholarship on urban infrastructures and its particular value for studying the Berlin case.

Infrastructural Traces of Berlin

Berlin continues to generate huge interest, in both the public realm and academia, as a site and symbol of ideological struggle across the twentieth century. What drives this magnetic appeal today is not simply the degree of turbulence and range of political regimes the city has endured, but fundamentally also the way in which the city is tussling with its past. Following reunification of Germany in 1990, a plethora of work has been published on how the city—primarily its political representatives, opinion makers, and engaged citizens—has been trying to come to terms with the dark episodes of its recent history and integrate them into a narrative of a new, self-critical, and democratic society. One of the prominent contributors to this debate, Karen Till, describes Berlin as a stage on which the drama of history is being performed before our eyes.[1] She and others, such as Brian Ladd and Andreas Huyssen, talk of the ghosts from the past that pervade any discussion of Berlin's future.[2] They highlight how certain ghosts get invoked, while others remain neglected, to advance particular visions of the city. Intriguingly, these authors all focus on how this historical sensitivity and selectivity manifests itself in material form.[3] Buildings and monuments of powerful historical symbolism—such as the Jewish Museum, the Reichstag building or the Palace of the Republic of the German Democratic Republic (DDR)—are used to explore how Berliners, and Germans more generally, are grappling with their past.

What is striking about this debate in and beyond academia is that it is restricted almost exclusively to those urban structures that are visible above ground. It is, essentially, a dispute over architectural form and urban design conducted by practitioners and researchers of these fields. The role played by underground structures, or infrastructures more generally, in reflections upon Berlin's past is largely neglected. This is perhaps not surprising given the invisibility of piped infrastructures in the public domain. As noted in the introductory chapter, urban technology is so often taken for granted by the body politic, general public, and media alike that its presence is seldom noticed and its political purchase barely acknowledged. The first theme of the analytical framework explores, therefore, what novel insight on Berlin's history an infrastructure lens can reveal. It asks: what are the infrastructural traces of Berlin's recent history and why is it important to study them?

To address these questions, I turn to a rich body of literature taking a social science perspective on infrastructure in general and the relationship between a city and its infrastructure in particular. Infrastructure has in recent years become a prism of choice for the study of the human condition, with contributions coming from a wide range of disciplines, notably STS, geography, history, anthropology, and sociology. This body of scholarship is today exploring the experimental, symbolic, temporal, and political dimensions to infrastructure systems popularly regarded as purely technical artifacts.[4] This wave of interest is rooted in the affordance of infrastructure to reveal the "infra" (meaning below or beneath) and the "structural" (meaning fundamental or constitutive) to society.[5] From this perspective, infrastructures underpin modern life in a figurative as well as a literal sense. What makes them special—and intriguing for research—are a number of distinctive properties, which Susan Leigh Star has characterized as their embeddedness in physical structures and social arrangements, their extensive spatial and temporal reach, their taken-for-grantedness, their high degree of standardization, their evolution out of existing structures, and their high visibility on breakdown.[6]

Reducing technical infrastructures to their material components alone, as presented in many existing accounts of Berlin's infrastructures, completely misses their rootedness in, and relevance for, society. The fundamental contribution of social scientists to infrastructure research over the past thirty years has been to demonstrate how the energy and water systems that make everyday life in the modern world possible are not just material artifacts. They also comprise organizational arrangements, institutional rules, economic resources, cultural values, user preferences, and the physical environment, to name just a few indicative components.[7] It has become commonplace among social scientists to conceive of urban infrastructures as sociotechnical configurations. This means that, in any infrastructure system, the technical is always also social and the social always also technical. Thus, the technical specifications of a power station cannot be meaningfully interpreted without reference to the political debates over plant emissions that influenced its design. Similarly, public protests against increased water bills are unlikely to make sense without consideration of the cost-intensive physical structures built to supply the water.

Social studies of infrastructure have highlighted two distinctive and important features of such sociotechnical configurations: what Penny Harvey and colleagues have helpfully termed their "compositional" and "recursive" qualities.[8] A "compositional" take on infrastructure explores the emergence of, say, an energy or water system through the interaction of its component parts. This perspective opens research up to the processes "whereby certain actors, materials, standards, ideas and images get *folded into* infrastructures, whereas others get denigrated."[9] A "recursive" view on infrastructure looks rather at the relations between infrastructure and society. In this relational understanding of infrastructure, "technologies are shaped by society at the same time as they shape society."[10] Research espousing both perspectives—compositional and recursive—does not take any sociotechnical configuration or relation as a given, but as an object of analysis in which neither the technical nor the social is privileged a priori.

This goes a long way to explaining the current appeal of infrastructures in the social sciences and humanities. Infrastructures are attractive because of the relational work they perform.[11] They act as an interface between humans and nature in transporting and transforming natural resources.[12] They interconnect different spatial scales, from the home to the globe.[13] They are a medium between the past, present, and future by virtue of their durability and the planning culture this has generated.[14] At the same time, infrastructures are valued because of their composite constitution. Understood as sociotechnical configurations, they permit the exploration of social and material worlds in conjunction, thus transcending simplistic distinctions between "nature" and "society."[15] They represent manifestations of power relations and political rule in material form.[16] In the words of historian Paul N. Edwards, infrastructures are nothing less than "the connective tissues and the circulatory systems of modernity."[17]

Turning to cities, many social scientists are studying infrastructure to provide novel insight on the urban condition.[18] Indeed, much of the pioneering work on conceptualizing infrastructures is, today, coming from the field of urban studies. This was not always the case. Only twenty years ago Stephen Graham and Simon Marvin, in their seminal book *Splintering Urbanism*, referred to infrastructure as the "Cinderella of urban studies."[19] Today, Cinderella has very much come of age. In the words of the geographer Ash Amin, "[we] are seeing the rise of a new genre of thinking that narrates the social life of a city through its material infrastructure."[20]

There are several roots to this recent "infrastructure turn" in urban studies.[21] First, as physical, organizational, and social vulnerabilities of infrastructure are being revealed, the reliance of cities on functioning sociotechnical systems is regaining the recognition it enjoyed in the past.[22] Lewis Mumford's exaltations in the 1930s to think together the surface and the subterranean city are being echoed by today's scholars when they talk of urban life resting on hidden infrastructures.[23] Second, the "geographical naïvety" of early generation transitions research has goaded many geographers into investigating the hidden spatial dimensions to sociotechnical change.[24] Criticism that transitions studies have overlooked the importance of place, sociospatial dynamics, the Global South, the role of cities, and the scalar politics of energy or water infrastructures has generated fresh knowledge on the multiple ways in which space matters.[25] Third, the "material turn" in both human geography and urban history has brought infrastructures into the limelight.[26] Scholars interested in biophysical systems not simply as objects of social construction and production but as agents themselves are turning to infrastructures as powerful expressions of socio-material relations, by virtue of the material flows they mediate and physical inertia they exude.[27] Infrastructures have become a favored medium for scholarship on "rematerializing cities."[28] Finally, infrastructures are being studied today for how they reflect and reinforce broader trends of urban governance. The "splintering urbanism" thesis of Graham and Marvin has launched a wave of research into the ways in which infrastructures can exacerbate urban fragmentation, materialize unequal power relations, shape urban well-being, mediate urban natures, or structure territorial control.[29]

Over the past twenty-five years, urban scholars have engaged fruitfully with STS to develop a nuanced perspective on city-infrastructure interactions that Jon Rutherford has termed "relational technological urbanism."[30] This line of research combines what STS is good at, fine-grain analysis of the interaction between actors, artifacts, and institutions in technological development, with what human geography is good at, theorizing the multiple spatialities underpinning socioeconomic, political, and environmental processes.[31] This literature regards cities and infrastructures as co-constitutive: cities shape infrastructures, just as infrastructures shape cities.[32] It demonstrates how sets of processes, policies, and practices come together differently in specific places and at particular times.[33] It emphasizes the situated and dynamic nature of urban infrastructure configurations.[34]

That this research on the sociotechnical constitution of urban infrastructures bears a huge relevance to the study of Berlin is self-evident. It opens up promising avenues for critiquing conventional notions of urban infrastructure, offers novel ways of conceptualizing infrastructures and their relationship to broader societal phenomena, and provides important pointers for the empirical analysis. What infrastructural "traces" can be revealed from the application of this perspective to Berlin's recent history? First, the book explores how Berlin got "infrastructured": that is, how infrastructure has shaped the urban condition over the past century. The modes of "infrastructuration" addressed will be wide-ranging, encompassing physical, institutional, economic, social, and symbolic effects.[35] Second, the book investigates, conversely, how Berlin's infrastructures reflected, enabled, or constrained urban development and politics. Again, this will cover a broad range of human and nonhuman factors. Third, the notion of "traces" is used to identify the infrastructural legacies from the past that continue to influence energy and water systems in Berlin. Their history of municipal provision, sectoral separation, regional exploitation, and political division reverberates through infrastructure policy and practice to this very day.

Conjunctions of Continuity and Change

The second theme of the analytical framework introduces a novel understanding of the temporality of urban infrastructures. It sets out to explore what can be revealed by taking a long-term perspective on the relationship between continuity and change. The temporal dimension to infrastructure has fascinated historians of technology and STS scholars for decades.[36] The overarching interest has been to establish how infrastructures develop into particular sociotechnical configurations in the first place and why they prove so persistent once enacted. "For most of us," Jane Summerton wrote twenty-five years ago, "technical systems conjure up images of stability and permanence."[37] How, then, do they change, if at all? This remains today a hotly contested issue. There exists a plethora of theories and concepts across the social sciences and humanities that aspire to explain sociotechnical change, as documented in a recent survey by Benjamin Sovacool and David Hess.[38]

Looking across the history of a city's infrastructure systems for a period spanning 100 years clearly sets this study apart from the powerfully "presentist" approach to sociotechnical change that is characteristic of much research in urban studies. For many human geographers conducting this work, history is merely a backdrop to what they find far more interesting: the policies, projects, and practices changing infrastructures today. The treatment of the past in their studies tends to be cursory and instrumental, setting the scene for the substance of their (contemporary) analysis.[39] The assumption by many urban geographers, indeed, is that infrastructure history has been conclusively "done" by historians of technology and needs complementing now with greater attention to spatial, rather than temporal, issues.[40] This, as will be argued, is a very narrow reading of infrastructural temporality.

The long-term perspective taken by this book also distinguishes it from historically rooted approaches more familiar to historians of technology and the broader STS community. Two approaches have been particularly formative since Thomas Hughes's pioneering work on large technical systems (LTS) in the 1980s.[41] They are, firstly, path dependence and, secondly, sociotechnical transitions.

The theory of path dependence uses history to explain the obduracy of sociotechnical systems. Drawing heavily on the LTS literature, path dependence ascribes the durability and stability of large technical systems, as for energy or water provision, to the self-reinforcing mechanisms that, over time, establish "lock-in" to a particular sociotechnical configuration. The historian Martin Melosi uses the concept of path dependence in his book *The Sanitary City* to help explain why choices in American cities over water supply, waste water, and solid waste taken in the early to mid-nineteenth century constrained the choices available in the late twentieth century.[42] Dirk van Laak talks of how past infrastructural visions, manifested in material form decades ago, continue to frame options in the present.[43] This is the essence of path dependence: relatively insignificant events in the past can substantially reduce the options for development in the future by generating a dominant sociotechnical configuration resistant to change.[44] Although the temporal range of these works is certainly long term, the approach cannot capture adequately Berlin's experiences over the past 100 years. There are definitely elements of Berlin's infrastructure that reveal strong path dependence, such as the physical structures referred to in the introduction to this chapter. However, path dependence alone falls well short of explaining the shifts, reversals, and hybridity of the city's sociotechnical systems that occurred across its turbulent recent history. The orientation toward large, centralized systems precludes the study of other, alternative infrastructures competing with, or coexisting alongside, the dominant configuration. A focus on path dependence alone would also have difficulty in accommodating political regime change and the enrollment of Berlin's infrastructures in supporting fascist, socialist, and liberal ideologies.

Transitions theory, as the name implies, directs attention toward change, rather than continuity, in sociotechnical systems. Championed by innovation and STS scholars, it draws on historical examples to explain how these complex systems have transformed in the past and how they might be reconfigured today.[45] History is used by transitions scholars to reconstruct transformative junctures of technological innovation as an explanation and inspiration for the present. The transitions literature has attracted huge attention over the past two decades. Key to its success has been the ambitious conceptual framework it has produced and refined over the years to explain the complex dynamics of sociotechnical change: the so-called multi-level perspective (MLP).[46] With this single model transitions scholars aspire to capture the coevolution of new technologies, shifting markets, multiple actors, and institutional reforms that in the past have enabled radical change and, by inference, have the potential to do so in the future.[47] MLP has proved a useful heuristic for structuring usually messy accounts of dynamic sociotechnical systems.[48] It orders forces for continuity and change within a framework of three arenas: sociotechnical "regimes" working to sustain the dominant system, "niches" where innovations and experiments take place and "landscapes" of broader, contextual circumstances.[49] The MLP framework has been used to analyze dozens of historical case studies of sociotechnical change in diverse domains.[50] These include several addressing past transitions in the energy and water sectors, for instance from coal to gas or from wells to piped water systems.[51] The transitions approach, however, is also an inadequate model for relating Berlin's infrastructure history. Although better equipped than path dependence theory to explore moments of transformation, it is far less suited for analyzing change and continuity over such a long period of time. As has been criticized by others, transitions research is oriented toward the transition from one sociotechnical system to another, ignoring the diversity of trajectories in real-life situations.[52] It also tends to sideline political contestation and power struggles over sociotechnical transitions.[53] Finally, it lacks sensitivity to the spatial dimensions of sociotechnical change, as many geographers have noted.[54]

The limitations of each approach discussed above are rooted less in the uniqueness of the Berlin case than in the dearth of studies taking a long-term perspective on infrastructure.[55] Because few scholars have analyzed a city's infrastructures across a long period of system maturity, there exist no conceptual frameworks wholly suited to a study of this kind.[56] A longitudinal study spanning a 100-year period and multiple shifts in political governance, as in this case, cannot be framed in terms of path dependence, system transition, niche experimentation, or incremental change alone. It requires a conceptual framing that is sensitive to the interaction of *both* long-term trends and short-term shocks, *both* radical transformation and gradual adaptation. It needs to avoid a priori assumptions about continuity and change embedded in many conventional narratives, putting these, rather, to the empirical test in an open-ended manner.

This book calls for a rethinking of the temporalities of urban infrastructures. Such an approach should not restrict attention to the emergence of a recognisable system, transition from one system to another or reconfiguration to accommodate current pressures for change. Rather, it should be mindful of the multiple ways of theorizing sociotechnical trajectories as well as combinations of obduracy and adaptation that are empirically identifiable over time. For these reasons the book prefers to conceptualize sociotechnical temporality as conjunctions of continuity and change. The term "conjunction" has the advantage of meaning both the act of conjoining events or circumstances and the state of being conjoined.

This approach builds on recent research that is describing how urban infrastructures unfold in messy ways.[57] The sociotechnical change described and theorized by these urban studies scholars is contested, incremental, hybridized, and spatially grounded.[58] They are challenging the notion that sociotechnical systems are monolithic, homogeneous, and universal, arguing that past interest in the stability and durability of these systems has only served to "black-box" infrastructure studies.[59] The popular vocabulary of lock-ins and regimes, they argue, has blinded research to the rich and dynamic entanglements revealed in more inductive empirical work.

Many of these scholars have been turning to assemblage theory to provide conceptual orientation for the different ways in which diverse social and material elements are brought into alignment (assembled) or destabilized (disassembled).[60] The assemblage concept, drawing on actor-network theory, envisages reconfiguration as an ongoing process of forming and sustaining associations between diverse components.[61] It is increasingly being used in social science research to connote indeterminacy, emergence, and turbulence in the study of socio-material relations.[62] Applied to infrastructures, it does not privilege stability as the assumed norm, but seeks to reveal the considerable work—by human and nonhuman actants—required to stabilize or adapt a particular sociotechnical configuration.[63] Significantly, the assemblage concept embraces agency not only of a whole configuration, but also of its constituent parts, such that "one and the same assemblage can have components working to stabilize its identity as well as components forcing it to change or even transforming it into a different assemblage."[64] This is reflected in Anne Maassen's findings on the heterogeneity of lock-in, relating to some, but not all, components of a configuration, as well as in Antina von Schnitzler's study of continuities over water metering in South Africa during and after apartheid.[65] By treating the agency of "things" not as an intrinsic property but as a product of association, this relational understanding of materiality is revelatory from a temporal perspective for providing—in the words of Karen Bakker and Gavin Bridge—"a way to unpack apparent permanencies and stabilities."[66]

The book draws on this nuanced, contingent understanding of sociotechnical continuity and change, but adds to it what Stephen Collier has coined a "historicity of assemblages."[67] Assemblage thinking, for all its strengths, does scant justice to long-term historical developments.[68] Its applications have generally been limited in temporal scope. The assertion made in this book is that the techniques used in assemblage studies to map often hidden processes of change and continuity do not need to be limited to sociotechnical phenomena on a small spatial scale or within a narrow temporal frame. They can be usefully applied to analyze meso-level processes of dis- and reassembling infrastructural configurations at the urban scale over a long time period. Sebastián Ureta's work on the emergence and disruption of policy assemblages in Santiago de Chile demonstrates how the assemblage concept can be usefully applied to analyze urban politics.[69] The "invisible Paris" invoked by Bruno Latour and Emilie Hermant represents a temporal assemblage of multiple beings, each one of which "is linked to a history whose pace and tempo differ entirely."[70]

What conjunctions of continuity and change are likely to emerge from an analysis of "historicized assemblages"? Taking this perspective, the book explores five novel understandings of temporality to urban infrastructures.

First, it embraces the tensions between pressures for continuity and pressures for change *at any one time*.[71] Rather than conceiving of infrastructure systems as being either in a state of obduracy or a state of transition, this nuanced approach draws attention to forces continually pulling in both directions.[72] As Erik Swyngedouw has argued, both path dependence and radical change characterized Spain's twentieth-century history of "hydro-social cycles."[73] Harriet Bulkeley and colleagues, similarly, exhort social studies of urban infrastructure to reveal "the ways in which obduracy and flux in urban systems is created, maintained and contested."[74] The Berlin case will demonstrate how elements of a sociotechnical configuration that are destabilizing the system coexist and interact with elements that are working to stabilize it. This requires attending not only to the degree of instability and change exhibited by the constitutive elements of an infrastructure system, but also to how these elements "unfold at different speeds, at diverse registers, and at an uneven pace."[75]

Second, the chosen perspective draws attention to the nonlinear trajectories and hybrid enactments of urban infrastructure. In popular narratives of linear progress around a dominant LTS, deviant, alternative, and complementary technologies are often dismissed or ignored.[76] Matthew Gandy has criticized how histories of urban infrastructure tend to orientate toward "ideal types" rather than the variety often encountered in the field.[77] Kathryn Furlong challenges the common assumption that "the inherent trajectory of infrastructure is toward stability and invisibility as it 'matures.'"[78] As the Berlin case will illustrate, not only do competing or complementary systems exist alongside the dominant one, but sociotechnical trajectories can, under certain circumstances, be derailed. Challenging assumptions of linearity to sociotechnical trajectories involves exploring reversals, stagnation, and decay to systems generally renowned for their durability.[79]

Third, it follows from this that urban infrastructure is always a combination of the old and the new. Thinking of infrastructures as palimpsests, in which new elements are layered over existing ones, rather than replacing them, is a helpful way of conceiving this relationship. This is what Stephen Graham and Nigel Thrift mean when they discuss "infrastructural palimpsests."[80] The meme of the palimpsest has also been used by Matthew Gandy to conceive of the contemporary city, in which "remnants of the past are juxtaposed with new elements."[81] It has also been mobilized by Andreas Huyssen to characterize Berlin itself, as a montage of multiple historical forms.[82] It is only through historical analysis that this multi-layeredness of infrastructure can be made truly visible.[83]

Fourth, a "historicized assemblage" approach helps reveal the coexistence and interaction of multiple timescales and their implications for conventional periodizations. Karen Till encourages us to consider Berlin as a city "where temporalities collide in unexpected ways."[84] Translated to its infrastructure, this concern addresses how a sociotechnical configuration is always having to cope with multiple timelines. The time required to plan a new power station can differ wildly from the duration of a municipal government, the speed at which a pollutant can enter a watercourse or the rate of change to consumption patterns. Nikhil Anand and colleagues have made the point that infrastructures, by combining different temporalities, can mediate historical processes.[85] Antina von Schnitzler has used this insight to challenge conventional periodizations and explore continuities in infrastructure practices across political regime change.[86]

Finally, this approach helps deconstruct the popular notion of the past, present, and future being three distinct eras. Analyzing what changed to sociotechnical configurations when, how, and why can reveal how much of the past is embedded in the present as well as how much of the future is envisioned in the past. It sensitizes us to "present pasts," describing the selective and instrumental way in which certain pasts are privileged in contemporary narratives.[87] It highlights also the "past futures": that is, the sociotechnical imaginaries of earlier generations that have had a formative influence on the design and symbolism of urban infrastructures.[88]

Urban Politics through Infrastructure

This third theme of the analytical framework explores infrastructures as conduits of urban politics. Here, again, the book draws on a rich vein of scholarship—in this instance on what is broadly termed "technopolitics"[89]—but adds a novel perspective afforded by the Berlin case. This revolves around the city's unique experience of widely divergent political regimes over the past century. Berlin is a microcosm of twentieth-century political ideology, encompassing fascism, state socialism, Cold War politics, and various enactments of capitalist democracy. How were infrastructures used, abused, or neglected by each political regime? In what ways have infrastructures resisted enrollment in political projects?

Over twenty years ago the anthropologist Susan Leigh Star coined the much-cited phrase: "Study a city and neglect its sewers and power supplies (as many have) and you miss essential aspects of distributional justice and power."[90] Today, it is widely acknowledged in the academy that infrastructures are fundamentally political. While earlier research in this field targeted the enrollment of infrastructure as tools or symbols of state control, more recent work has opened up the debate to regard infrastructures as a political terrain of contestation, resistance, and circumvention involving both human and nonhuman agents.[91] In essence, this body of scholarship asserts that material artifacts, such as water resources or a power station, are neither external to politics nor passive and stable. On the contrary, as Andrew Barry argues, the unpredictability and instability of built and natural environments are integral to the conduct of politics.[92] In his study of disputes over a transnational oil pipeline, he develops the concept of "material politics" to direct attention "to the specificity of materials, to the contingencies of physical geography, the tendencies of history and the force of political action."[93] While his work demonstrates how world politics is done through energy infrastructures, Antina von Schnitzler uses her history of the prepaid water meter in South Africa to show how technopolitics can reach down into household practices of everyday life.

Building on a relational understanding of sociotechnical systems, the political significance of infrastructures is treated in this literature not as a given, but emerges out of contingent practices of interaction between their human and nonhuman components. Through these practices political actions manifest themselves in technical form.[94] Ideological ambitions and acts of resistance become inscribed in an energy or water network.[95] At the same time, the materiality of an infrastructure system or the environmental resources it depends upon can influence political issues and shape the bounds of political possibility. Infrastructures—it has been noted—often prove less malleable to those in power than is widely assumed.[96] The material components of infrastructure, for instance, can resist enrollment in a political project, as demonstrated by Karen Bakker over the privatization of water in England and Wales, and by Stephen Collier over the persistence of district heating in post-Soviet Russia.[97] This dual meaning of technopolitics opens up the study of Berlin not just to the political appropriation and instrumentalization of infrastructure, but also to the ways the city's sociotechnical systems have resisted, constrained, or even guided political action.

Moving from the generic to the urban, many urban scholars agree that the relationship between cities and infrastructures is deeply political.[98] Human geographers, in particular, have been effective in demonstrating how infrastructures are shaped by, but also shape, power relations in and beyond a city. Works by Erik Swyngedouw, Matthew Gandy, and others have established that infrastructures are both a product and a medium of the political economy of a locality.[99] Three strands of critical geography have enriched this line of thinking. The "splintering urbanism" thesis of Graham and Marvin has revealed how the unbundling of infrastructure networks via liberalization and privatization since the 1980s was inextricably linked to the emergence of new configurations of urban space.[100] It has inspired a generation of urban scholars to study how neoliberal agendas for infrastructure have reinforced uneven urban geographies across the globe. "Urban political ecology," coined by Swyngedouw and colleagues, has been equally influential in arguing that infrastructures have been central to capitalist appropriation of urban "socionatures" and the marginalization of the underprivileged.[101] Postcolonial research on cities has used infrastructures to reveal the inequities embedded in former colonial rule and to discuss their legacies for urban transitions in the Global South today.[102] Together, this urban scholarship has highlighted the geographies of connection and separation facilitated by infrastructure, spanning multiple scales and socio-spatial contexts.[103]

While few scholars would today deny that urban infrastructure is inherently political, some challenge the soft determinism implicit in many accounts of technopolitics. Olivier Coutard and Simon Guy argue that the powerful narrative of neoliberalism and its roll-out in infrastructure reconfigurations across the globe can blind research to empirical phenomena which do not fit the model.[104] This is illustrated by Stephen Collier's study of post-Soviet Russia that demonstrates how neoliberalism did not transform the country's district heating system along market principles, but could only selectively reconfigure inherited material structures and social norms.[105] Closer to home, Ross Beveridge has revealed how, in post-reunification Berlin, neoliberal agendas were not rolled out according to a global script, but were enacted in the city's water utility in a very place-specific and contingent way.[106]

Historians, although generally apart from this debate on technopolitics, have long sought to the highlight the political dimensions of infrastructure. Early work by Karl Wittfogel on the power of dams in "hydraulic civilizations" and by Thomas Hughes on the "networks of power" involved in electrification set the scene for later historians of technology to unpack the political appropriation of infrastructures.[107] Dirk van Laak has demonstrated how imperial infrastructures enrolled in state projects of modernization and colonial control often failed to perform as planned.[108] Per Högselius, Arne Kaijser, and Erik van der Vleuten have analyzed the role of infrastructures in the machinery of war.[109] Of particular interest to the study of Berlin is the recent work by environmental historians on the relationship between infrastructures and authoritarianism. Drawing on seminal works by Frank Uekötter on environmentalism under National Socialism and by David Blackbourn on the taming of nature in modern Germany, this growing body of scholarship is exploring the particular ways in which authoritarian regimes of the right and left have treated the environment and used infrastructures as vehicles of sociotechnical control.[110]

Exploring urban politics through infrastructure in this book builds on these pillars of scholarship and contributes to them in the following innovative ways. First, the book explores the extent to which changes in political regime induced shifts in Berlin's technopolitics. The ability to study the impact of shifts from democratic to authoritarian regimes (of the political right and left) and back in a single city creates an unprecedented opportunity to unpack the distinctive features of liberal capitalist, national socialist, and state-socialist rule with regard to infrastructures. This can provide a deeper, comparative understanding of how infrastructures become enrolled as symbols of ideology and targets of contestation in different political systems. Second, Berlin's continuous embroilment in national and international politics permits—indeed, requires—a study of urban infrastructure that is not limited to the city alone. However strong Berlin's "networked municipalism" proved to be, it was always subject to a greater or lesser degree to national government policy (especially under National Socialism and the DDR) and to geopolitics (especially during the Second World War and the Cold War). This unique positioning will generate insight into the relationship between municipal, national, and international technopolitics. Third, given the local embeddedness of Berlin's utility services, organizationally as well as materially, the case is particularly suited to an analysis of the impact of infrastructure on urban politics. How the city's energy and water systems frustrated or facilitated political ambitions in and beyond the city provides fascinating insight into the agency of sociotechnical assemblages of this kind.

Infrastructural Interdependence

The fourth theme of my framework draws attention to an aspect that has been largely ignored in infrastructure studies: the relationships between different infrastructure sectors. For all the criticism of "siloed" thinking and inadequate integration in designing and implementing policy on energy and water, there is an astonishing dearth of research by social scientists on the interfaces and interplay between different branches of piped infrastructure. The vast majority of infrastructure studies focus on one sector only and overlook interdependencies with other sectors.[111] Thematic specialization and the risk of overcomplexity have probably meant that research has addressed either electricity or gas or district heating or water supply or sanitation. While a few social studies do treat the heavily interdependent fields of water supply and sanitation, virtually none address the energy-water nexus from an infrastructure perspective.[112] This is all the more surprising today, given the growing recognition of the importance of interfaces between water resources and hydropower, between wastewater and heat provision, or between biogas and electricity generation in combatting climate change.[113]

In an urban setting scholarship on the topic is currently barren. One hopes this will change in the wake of a recent special issue in *Urban Studies* on cities in an era of interfacing infrastructures, edited by Jochen Monstadt and Olivier Coutard, that includes an exciting range of case studies.[114] In their introduction to the special issue, the editors identify four major research gaps on infrastructural integration in cities. These relate to: (1) the tensions between pressures for unbundling and re-bundling urban infrastructures; (2) the boundary work involved in bringing fragmented urban infrastructures together; (3) the politics required to align this work with urban change; (4) the uneven geographies at play in reconfiguring infrastructural interfaces.[115] In the absence of other systemic assessments of the research agenda on this topic, there is less for this book to draw inspiration from than for the other four themes of the analytical framework.

By encompassing five infrastructure sectors in a single city, the book is designed to make an original and substantive contribution to this emergent topic. Apart from addressing the research gaps identified by Monstadt and Coutard, it is well positioned to set cross-sectoral analysis in an historical context in order to identify significant changes in relations between sectors over a whole century. Three dimensions to these relations are given special attention. The first is interdependency between different sectors, as expressed, for instance, in their common dependence on coal in the early decades and on electricity since the 1950s. The second is competition between sectors, especially within the field of energy, where the city's power and gas utilities have been bitter rivals over the provision of energy for street-lighting, cooking, and room heating. The third is knowledge transfer between sectors, in particular with regards to their ownership, organizational structure and institutional relationship with the city authorities. Berlin provides an excellent case for studying all three dimensions by virtue of the five sectors being run not by an integrated urban multi-utility (*Stadtwerk*), as is common in most German cities, but by separate utilities in municipal ownership for most of the period under study.

Infrastructured Metabolisms

The fifth theme of the book's analytical framework targets the relationship between urban infrastructures and the natural resources they transform within and beyond the city. Sociotechnical systems mediate our use of the natural environment in far-reaching ways. Electricity generation has relied heavily in the past on the extraction and combustion of coal, destroying landscapes and polluting the atmosphere. Wastewater disposal generates environmental degradation in rivers and lakes, as well as depositing toxic substances into the oceans. The technical structures used to provide utility services—whether water works, wastewater pumping stations, or pressurized gas pipes—all consume massive amounts of energy. The very embeddedness and essentiality of these sociotechnical networks lock modern societies in to high levels of energy and water use. Urban infrastructures, consequently, have a massive impact on resource flows and environmental quality that reach far beyond the city limits. These "infrastructured metabolisms" and their spatial relations are particularly well revealed in the case of Berlin's recent history. Over the course of the past 100 years the urban metabolism of Berlin has been reframed territorially on many occasions, with infrastructures being enrolled in projects to advance municipal integration, subjugate the city to ambitions of national autarky, and sustain an insular West Berlin. It is to the metabolic relationship between the city, its surrounding region, and the wider environment that this final theme speaks.

The historian William Cronon was a trailblazer in this field with his seminal book on Chicago as "nature's metropolis."[116] His detailed analysis of commodity flows between the emergent city and the wider Great West region enabled Cronon to demonstrate powerfully how urban and rural landscapes transformed each other.[117] What made this work so original at the time was how it described the relationship between a city and its surrounding countryside in a unified narrative.[118] This challenged urban historians to look beyond a city's limits and environmental historians to consider urban as well as rural environments. Cronon emphasized, intriguingly, how these urban-regional metabolisms were mediated by infrastructures: in his case, railways and waterways.

Just as Cronon debunked popular divisions between the "city" and the "countryside," so recent research by environmental historians and human geographers has challenged deep-rooted ontological distinctions between the "city" and "nature." Martin Melosi, in his historical study of waste and energy in the USA, made the case for overcoming rigid categorizations of the "natural" and the "built" environment, presenting cities as very much part of physical nature and its social constructions.[119] However, it is critical geographers, particularly from the field of urban political ecology, who have made the most emphatic and theoretically grounded case for presenting the production of cities as a continuous process of socio-environmental changes that generate ever new urban "natures."[120] What makes this body of work so pertinent to the study of Berlin is that it treats infrastructures as mediators of social and biophysical relations, and emphasizes how these relations are historically shaped.[121] This is exemplified in the historical thrust to Matthew Gandy's study of New York's water supply, Maria Kaika's book on dams in Greece, and Erik Swyngedouw's work on water and modernism in twentieth-century Spain.[122] They all unpack processes of "infrastructuring" nature as constitutive of the urban condition. Following this line of thinking, other scholars have demonstrated how infrastructures shape not only metabolic flows in and through the city, but also urban landscapes, whereby particular patterns of resource consumption become "built in" to the physical form of the city.[123] With this kind of research, infrastructure studies are today branching out from their sociotechnical roots to embrace social-ecological perspectives that put the environment center stage.[124]

In the book this crucial relationship between infrastructures, the environment, and spatial relations is explored with particular regard to the following issues. First, Berlin is treated here not as a spatially bounded entity, but as a city deeply embedded in wider regional and national contexts. The metabolisms of its energy and water systems cannot be studied, it is argued, without reference to how they were shaped by, but also shaped, social-ecological factors reaching far beyond the city. For this reason, the relationship between Berlin and the surrounding state of Brandenburg has always been fraught. Second, the book demonstrates how modes of extracting, transforming, and using natural resources via infrastructures have been the objects of contestation across

Berlin's history. Controversies over existing or envisioned sociotechnical configurations of these metabolisms have raged at times between utilities and city authorities, between service providers and users, as well as within the fraternity of infrastructure planners. Berlin's political and socioeconomic volatility lent these disputes a particular ferocity. Third, it is shown how environmentalism has increasingly become the focus for a fundamental critique of the "build and supply" paradigm that has for so long dominated infrastructure management in Berlin, as elsewhere. Since the 1970s the city's energy and water infrastructures have become targets of political opposition that has spawned alternative visions, technologies, and practices of urban metabolism. Today, it is argued, protests against privatization and campaigns to remunicipalize Berlin's electricity, gas, and water/wastewater utilities are challenging conventional logics of the networked city and creating very different sociotechnical imaginaries of socially inclusive and environmentally sustainable urban infrastructures.

An Urban History of Technopolitics

This analytical framework is designed to demonstrate that there is more to infrastructure history than one linear trajectory, just as there is more to its geography than being located in one city. Uncovering and connecting the multiple temporalities and geographies of urban infrastructure are fundamental to this book, both in guiding the empirical research and framing its contribution to the wider academy.

A study of Berlin's infrastructures needs to consider histories that are not just evolutionary or retrospective. In addition to the path dependencies and critical junctures that have always attracted attention, the analysis has to consider the nonlinear trajectories, discarded alternatives, and legacies from the past that have also shaped city-infrastructure relations. A time-sensitive analysis of technological urbanism needs to look beyond infrastructure as a monolithic and universal system to contemplate competing, complementary, and hybrid infrastructures. It should seek to reveal infrastructural palimpsests, in which old and new components are juxtaposed in continuous processes of realignment. It should also be attentive to the processes by which different components of a sociotechnical configuration change, or do not change, at different times. How configurations from the past continue to frame infrastructure practices and policies in the present—whether as objects of veneration or of censure—is of critical importance.

A study of Berlin's infrastructures, equally, needs to embrace geographies that are not just physical or city-bound. The geographies at work in urban infrastructures are also institutional, environmental, political, socioeconomic, and cultural. How elements from these diverse arenas became assembled into very place-specific configurations of energy and water provision at particular times is a core concern of this book. A spatially sensitive analysis of infrastructure also needs to consider the multi-scalar dimensions of a city's sociotechnical systems, whether acknowledging their dependence on the surrounding region or exploring their embroilment in geopolitical contestation. In the case of Berlin, this means being attentive, for instance, to household use of utility services, the spatial reach of technical networks, environmental flows in and out of the city, the impact of national policy agendas, and globalization. It means appreciating the existence of various "technological urbanisms" even within a single city.

On the basis of this conceptualization of urban infrastructures and with the guidance of the five themes of the analytical framework, we can now turn to the empirical narrative of Berlin's own history of technopolitics. While this narrative is structured in the following chapters around core issues characterizing each respective era, the analytical themes are used throughout to highlight points of generic interest and interpret the findings in terms of broader scholarship. They are revisited in the final chapter, structuring the overall conclusions of the book and its contribution to research on urban infrastructure histories.

3 Unitary Services for a Greater Berlin

> The spirit of the new Berlin is a world-metropolis spirit and so must transcend the local focus of old-style civic loyalties. And this world-metropolis spirit it is that must define the content and form of the urban setting in which it will dwell.
>
> —Martin Wagner and Adolf Behne, 1929

The territory of the Berlin we know today was a creation of early Weimar democracy. Before 1920 the municipality of Berlin was tiny, encompassing a mere 70 square kilometers. It extended only from the Zoological Gardens in the west to the Ostkreuz junction in the east, from Schiller Park in the north to Viktoria Park in the south. Many of today's inner-city districts, like Charlottenburg, Schöneberg, Neukölln, and Lichtenberg, were, until then, independent Prussian cities. The boundaries between Berlin and its surrounding municipalities had, in the wake of rapid urbanization, long since become invisible, yet they had been fiercely protected by conservative forces fearful of subordination to the metropolitan core. Their resistance to any plans to extend the city limits prior to the First World War was, under imperial rule, always effective. The three-class electoral college that restricted representation in Prussia's state parliament ensured the protection of conservative interests over calls for change.[1] Only after the November 1918 revolution and the election of a democratically constituted Prussian state assembly in 1919 were the reformers able to fulfill their ambition. On April 25, 1920, a narrow majority comprising social democrats, independent social democrats, and pro-republican democrats voted to pass the Law on the Creation of Greater Berlin that came into force on October 1, 1920.[2] Just how close Berlin came to remaining a disunited conurbation became apparent when, within a year, fresh elections to the Prussian parliament ended this majority. It is salutary to reflect that the territory of Berlin familiar to us today was the product of the most fleeting of political alliances.

The Prussian government may have been entrusted with the final decision, but the question of how large the new Berlin should be was one contested largely in and around the city itself. In March 1919 the mayor of (old) Berlin, Adolph Wermuth, sent a circular to all his municipal departments, requesting them—in a refreshing expression of post-revolutionary openness—to make suggestions for the territorial extent of the new city. One of these circulars landed on the desk of Carl Kühne, the head of the city's water utility. Kühne seized this opportunity to overcome once and for all the long-standing opposition from surrounding communities to his plans to improve Berlin's water services by incorporating all the relevant areas within the new city. His idea was, simply, to design the new city around its water resources and infrastructures. In his written response to the mayor, he set out four principles for the enlarged Berlin, which should include: all groundwater catchment zones needed for current and future water supply, all areas through which Berlin's water mains passed, all areas served by the Berlin water utility and a major private water supplier, and all sewage farms used to treat the city's wastewater.

For illustration, Kühne included a map on which he had drawn the perimeter of this vision for Berlin in his characteristic green crayon (see figure 3.1). The result was a huge city of some 20 kilometers in radius. Kühne justified his ambitious territorial claim, cannily, with political rather than technical arguments. Only by following his design principles, he argued, could unitary water services and tariffs be provided across the whole urban area and could surrounding communities be prevented from blocking Berlin's future development. Unsurprisingly, Kühne's original design for Berlin was not the model selected. However, through his persistent interventions during the subsequent process of negotiation he managed to ensure that the Greater Berlin created in 1920 did incorporate the major groundwater catchment areas and mains pipes serving the city.[3] We owe the shape of today's Berlin, in part at least, to the individual foresight of a water utility director and the collective acknowledgment of the significance of water for the city's future.

Infrastructures for the New World-Metropolis

The creation of Greater Berlin in 1920 was a phenomenal act of territorial aggrandizement. Amalgamated into the new municipal entity were, besides the old city of Berlin, no fewer than seven other cities, a further fifty-nine smaller municipalities, and twenty-seven landed estates (*Gutsbezirke*).[4] The territory of the city increased over twelvefold (see figure 3.2). At 878 square kilometers, Greater Berlin became overnight the world's second largest city, after Los Angeles. In terms of population it now ranked third, behind New York and London, with 3.8 million inhabitants, double the figure for the old city.

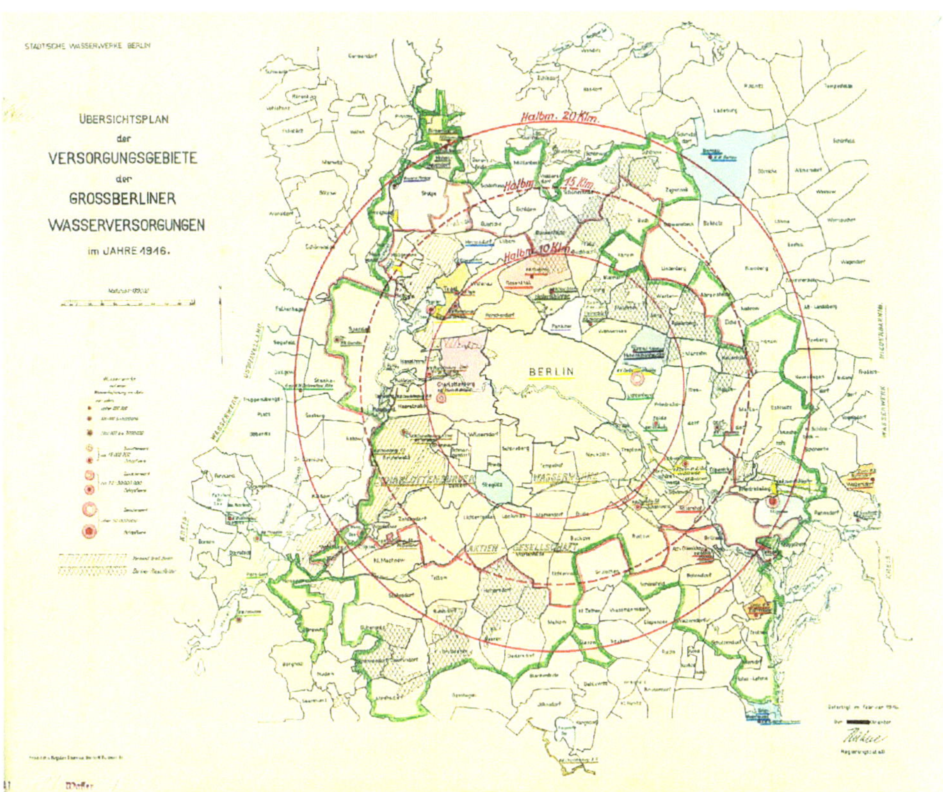

Figure 3.1

Carl Kühne's vision of a Greater Berlin, March 28, 1919

Source: Landesarchiv Berlin (LAB) A Rep. 255, no. 93.

The motivation for creating a unitary Berlin was only marginally about rectifying a long-standing territorial misfit between the conurbation and its administrative jurisdiction. Far more significant was the deeply political purpose to make the whole urban territory more equitable and efficient. Massive disparities of income, welfare, and service quality existed across the metropolitan area. Prior to 1920, wealthier municipalities had been able to keep local tax rates low while enjoying huge tax revenues, enabling them to invest in major projects of municipal modernization. While the city of Charlottenburg could spend 120 Marks per head of population in 1913, poorer municipalities like Neukölln, Lichtenberg, or Köpenick had only 56–58 Marks at their disposal and struggled to maintain the most basic services.[5] This severe imbalance, in the eyes of many postwar reformers, called for a major redistribution of benefits and costs across

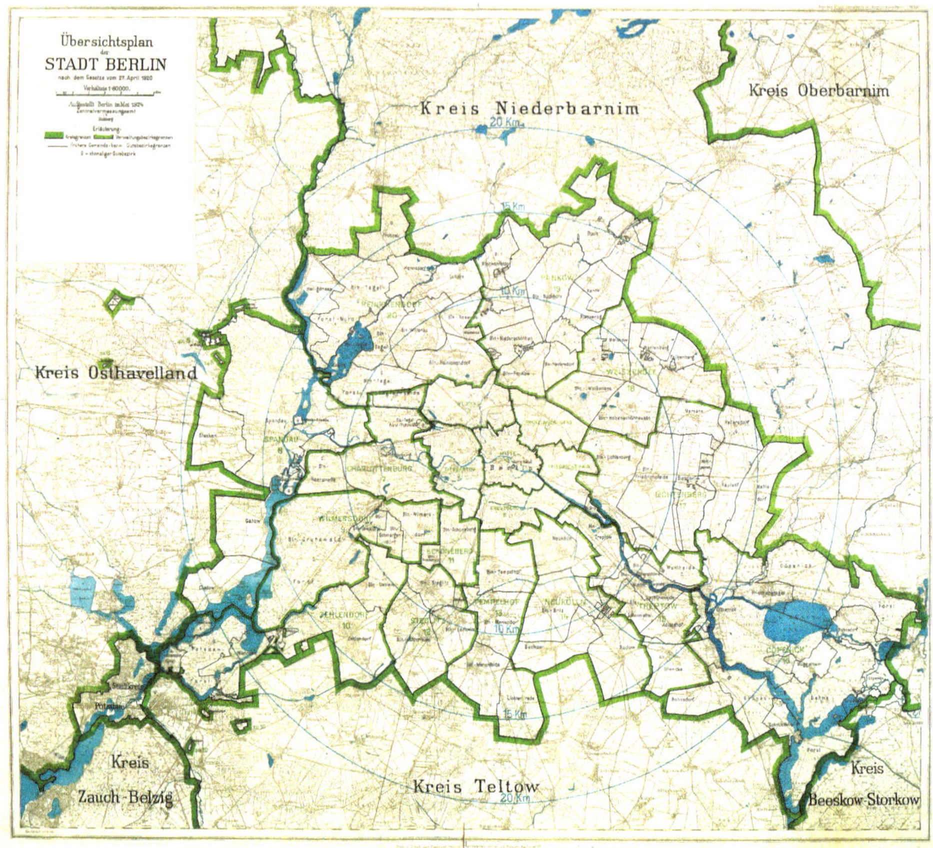

Figure 3.2
Map of Greater Berlin, 1920
Source: Landesarchiv Berlin (LAB) F Rep. 270, no. A 175.

the whole city. The first mayor (Oberbürgermeister) of Greater Berlin, the democrat Gustav Böß, spoke of generating "equal burdens and services for all citizens of Berlin" as the core rationale of the new unitary city.[6] In this he was supported in the city parliament by the Social Democratic Party (SPD), the Independent Social Democratic Party (USPD), and most of his own German Democratic Party (DDP). A second motive was to create a more efficient administrative machinery to address the pressing challenges of a burgeoning metropolis. Having municipal services across one conurbation provided by ninety-four self-dependent administrative entities had resulted in not only massive inequalities but also excessive costs and bureaucracy. A Greater Berlin would, it was hoped, enable much-needed administrative rationalization and modernization.

Given the radical nature of this political agenda, it is not surprising that the creation of Greater Berlin was bitterly resisted by those who had lost their privileged status within the unitary city. Political parties of the right—in particular the anti-republican German National People's Party (DNVP) and the German People's Party (DVP)—began a series of protests against this incarnation of municipal socialism on three fronts.[7] Some wealthy districts on the periphery of the new city campaigned to be removed from Greater Berlin. This "Leave Berlin" movement was active in the early 1920s but gradually subsided as the benefits of being part of the unitary city became increasingly apparent.[8] Rural municipalities outside of Greater Berlin continuously expressed their concern about further expansionist ambitions of the metropolis. The political right exploited these fears to justify repeated attacks on Greater Berlin and defend the integrity of the Province of Brandenburg that surrounded the city.[9] Within Greater Berlin, those boroughs run by bourgeois parties were keen to protect their authority against centralizing tendencies of the citywide government. For although Greater Berlin was a unitary city, its constitutional status envisaged a significant degree of decentralization in the form of twenty borough administrations, each with its own council, elected assembly, and administrative departments. Relations between the central city government and the borough administrations were to remain fraught throughout the Weimar Republic, acting as a touchstone for political sensitivities and retributions.

By contrast, there was broad political consensus that utility services for electricity, gas, water, and sanitation were ideal instruments for promoting the redistribution and rationalization agendas of Greater Berlin. No one disputed that past jurisdictional fragmentation had generated massive inefficiencies in service provision and unnecessary competition between municipalities. Infrastructure networks had been designed to serve individual entities without regard for the city as a whole, resulting in costly duplication and diseconomies of separation. The city of Schöneberg, for instance, had built a sewer system to fit its political boundaries that was regarded as hydraulically and financially irresponsible.[10] Worse still was rampant rivalry. As Mayor Böß lamented, "The municipalities used every opportunity to outmaneuver their opponent. Their utilities competed ruthlessly with each other—at the expense, in the end, of the tax payer."[11]

The creation of Greater Berlin was viewed by the vast majority of its thirty city councillors (Stadträte) and 225 elected deputies (Stadtverordnete) as a golden opportunity to set the city's infrastructures on a fresh footing appropriate to its world-metropolis ambitions. These municipal leaders—most of whom were new to their posts in 1920—held high expectations of energy and water services in the enlarged city. Urban infrastructures could be reconfigured to match the new citywide administration, competing utilities could be amalgamated into unitary enterprises, inefficient plants could be decommissioned, mains networks could be extended out to areas not previously connected, and uniform tariffs could be established across the whole city. Significantly, these aspirations were not limited to how Greater Berlin could enable change to urban infrastructures. What really interested the reformers was, conversely, how energy and water infrastructures could help implement the city's social, economic, and fiscal policy objectives.[12] This entailed enrolling the utilities in improving living standards across the city, keeping service fees affordable, modernizing housing for lower income groups, acting as model municipal employers, offsetting budget deficits, and stimulating local business, to mention only the most prominent claims. Greater Berlin's new political class looked to urban infrastructure to provide more than just uniform services of energy and water/sanitation across the city. The ambition was to use municipally owned utilities as multifunctional instruments of urban policy in a context of postwar reconstruction, reorientation, and reform. This challenge was willingly taken up by the directors of Berlin's electricity, gas, and water utilities, who recognized how this agenda would strengthen their own hand immeasurably. It also enjoyed the support of the city's civil servants responsible for infrastructure policy.[13]

This chapter explores how those responsible for Berlin's energy and water systems—in the city administration, parliament, and utilities—enrolled public infrastructures and services in pursuing municipal objectives, focusing on the period from the creation of Greater Berlin in 1920 to the stabilization of the German Mark in 1924. Although covering only a short time-span, this period was highly volatile yet also hugely formative in setting out the structures and agendas for the future. It was characterized by massive political uncertainty, unrest, and protest in these early years of Weimar democracy. It culminated in the iconic hyperinflation of 1923 that destroyed the last vestiges of stability. How did Berlin's infrastructure systems cope with these unprecedented challenges? How were they reorganized to meet the needs of a unitary city? These questions are addressed in the following sections in terms of five core strategies pursued by the city government. These relate to: unifying the urban networks, harmonizing services and tariffs, municipalizing utilities across the city, enrolling infrastructures in the urban political economy, and unfettering the utilities from bureaucratic control.

Unifying Urban Networks

The immediate task in October 1920 was to reorganize the existing infrastructure systems around the new unitary city. This entailed, on the one hand, amalgamating the various municipal utilities in operation across the conurbation and, on the other, reconfiguring the physical networks around the enlarged territory. Many of the former municipalities incorporated into Greater Berlin in 1920 possessed their own water works, gas works, and sewage departments that now needed to be integrated into unitary utilities owned and run by the new jurisdiction. For the larger former cities this act of amalgamation was experienced as a painful loss of what were regarded as key manifestations of municipal self-dependence. For this reason, attempts by the city government to centralize utility management in the early 1920s were resisted by the boroughs keen to retain at least some modicum of influence over their former infrastructures.[14] Less controversial, but just as challenging, was the physical reordering of these infrastructure systems to overcome outdated political boundaries and establish the structures for territorial uniformity.

Unifying the electricity sector was, in Mayor Böß's opinion, the very first challenge awaiting the new city government in 1920.[15] Electricity services were characterized by a patchwork of different utilities, different grids, different voltages, different tariffs and different modes of fee collection.[16] Prior to 1920 the territory of Greater Berlin had been served by twelve electricity utilities, including the municipally owned Berliner Städtische Elektrizitätswerke (StEW), operating sixteen power stations within the conurbation as well as importing electricity from external sources. Some of the amalgamated municipalities had their own power stations; others had supply contracts with electricity utilities. While the municipal power plants were readily incorporated into the enlarged StEW, the long-term concessionary agreements with third-party utilities could not be altered. As a result, Greater Berlin was served after 1920 not only by its own StEW but also by three other electricity utilities operating largely in the wealthier south and west of the city (see figure 3.3). These were: Elektrizitätswerk Südwest (ESA), a public-private company supplying Schöneberg, Schmargendorf, and Wilmersdorf; Märkisches Elektrizitätswerk (MEW), a public enterprise owned by provincial, district, and local authorities that served parts of Weißensee and (via its subsidiaries) most of the southwest of the city; and Elektrizitätswerk der Stadt Potsdam, a municipal utility that supplied the areas closest to Potsdam.[17] A complete and immediate universalization of Greater Berlin's electricity system was, therefore, not feasible.[18]

Establishing unitary government even over the amalgamated municipal power stations proved difficult. Between 1920 and 1922 there was effectively no citywide electricity system in operation, merely regular meetings of power plant directors discussing ways to better coordinate types of electricity, service standards, and electricity tariffs.[19] Only in August 1922 were the electricity departments, power stations, and electricity grids of the former municipalities formally incorporated into StEW. On this basis StEW was able to begin its program of centralizing and rationalizing the urban electricity system. It closed down all the power stations of the amalgamated municipalities—with the exception of those in Charlottenburg and Steglitz—for being outdated and

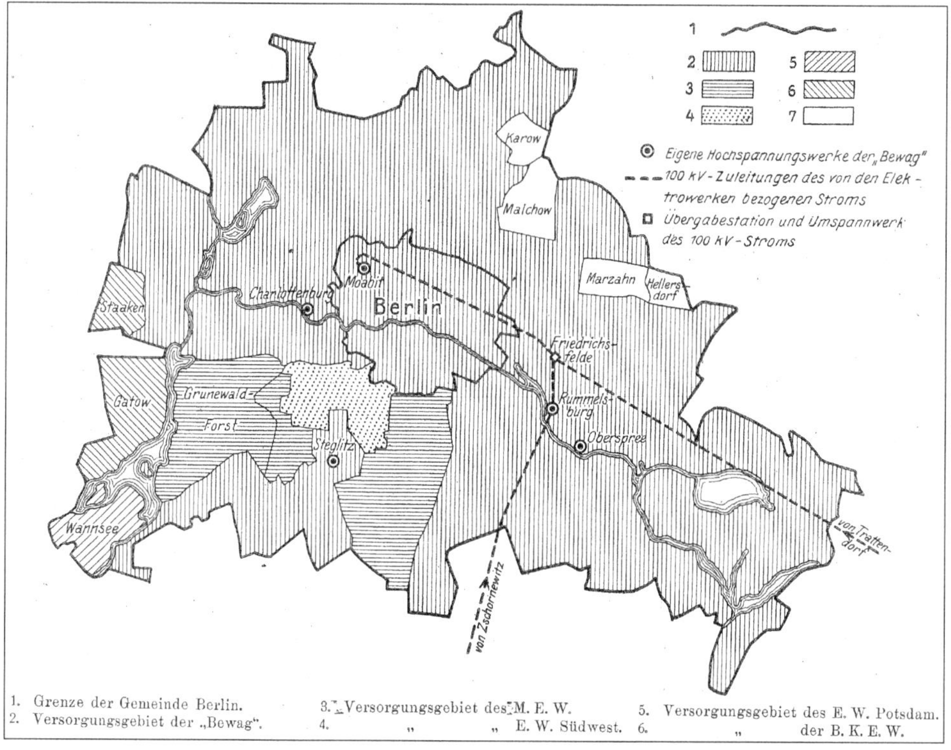

Figure 3.3

Map of electricity utilities serving Greater Berlin, 1925

Note: The area served by StEW is marked in vertical lines: "2" in the key.

Source: Thierbach, "Die gegenwärtige Versorgung der Stadt Berlin," 1465.

inefficient.[20] It also developed a new 30,000-volt ring grid to connect power stations across the city. These measures were made possible by the growing dependence of Berlin on imported electricity from the mining region of Lusatia, reducing the need for local power generation. Long-distance electricity supply to Berlin had only begun in June 1918 to avoid a supply crisis in the armaments industry.[21] In 1918, when only 6 percent of households in (old) Berlin were connected to the electricity grid, imported electricity had made up only 11.3 percent of that sold in the city.[22] By 1920, however, with rapid growth in demand for electricity by industry, households, and the public sector, over half of the electricity sold in Greater Berlin was imported. This figure peaked at 71.5 percent in 1923.[23] Such dependence on imported electricity was highly uncharacteristic of German cities at the time. It can be attributed essentially to three factors: first, the inability of Berlin to generate sufficient amounts of electricity at affordable prices;

second, the economic interest of the Reich's own electricity utility, Reichselektrowerke, to sell electricity generated by its new power stations at Zschornewitz and Trattendorf; and third, political pressure in the early Weimar years to nationalize Germany's electricity industry, using the capital Berlin as a pioneer.[24]

Gas supply in Berlin was, by contrast, entirely local, using town gas produced in gas works distributed across the city. Greater Berlin in 1920 owned sixteen gas works that served, largely, insular gas networks designed around former municipal territories.[25] Those gas works belonging to the amalgamated municipalities were initially responsible to their respective borough administration. This created new problems of urban coordination and undermined early attempts to unify gas supply structures.[26] Wherever possible, the united municipal gas utility, Städtische Gaswerke, closed down inefficient, small-scale gas works: at Tegel-Dorf, Wittenau, and Niederschöneweide in 1921; at Heiligensee, Gitschiner Strasse II, and Rahnsdorf in 1922; and a further six by 1927.[27] It also set about constructing a central gas main connecting the separate networks into one with a uniform pressure. As with electricity, the city's gas utility did not hold a territorial monopoly, but had to share supply with two private gas utilities: Gasgesellschaft Niederbarnim, in which Berlin held a 10 percent share, and Gasbetriebsgesellschaft (Deutsche Gasgesellschaft [DG]), the former English Gas Company appropriated during the war, in which Berlin had a 30 percent stake.[28] In 1920 almost three-quarters of the territory of Greater Berlin was supplied by the city's own Städtische Gaswerke, the remainder by these two private utilities (see figure 3.4).[29]

Greater Berlin's water supply was reliant primarily on groundwater abstracted locally. The city was fortunate in being able to source over 90 percent of its water supplies from groundwater aquifers, relying for the remainder on treated surface water.[30] Thanks to the intervention of Carl Kühne, the director of Berlin's municipal water utility, in 1919 the enlarged territory of Greater Berlin encompassed water protection areas critical for this supply. These groundwater abstraction zones were located along the banks of the River Spree in the east and center of the city and the banks of the River Havel in Tegel and Spandau. In November 1920, just one month after the creation of Greater Berlin, Kühne was clearly delighted by the prospects, yet keen to draw the organizational consequences: "The water supply of the new municipality of Berlin is based not on the boundaries of the ... boroughs, but on the groundwater and surface water resources shaped by nature and serving the common good, covering the entire city territory. Because it serves the whole community it should be centralized and placed under the authority of the city council."[31]

Creating a uniform water supply system was to prove harder than Kühne had hoped, with strong parallels to the cases of electricity and gas. The unification of the various

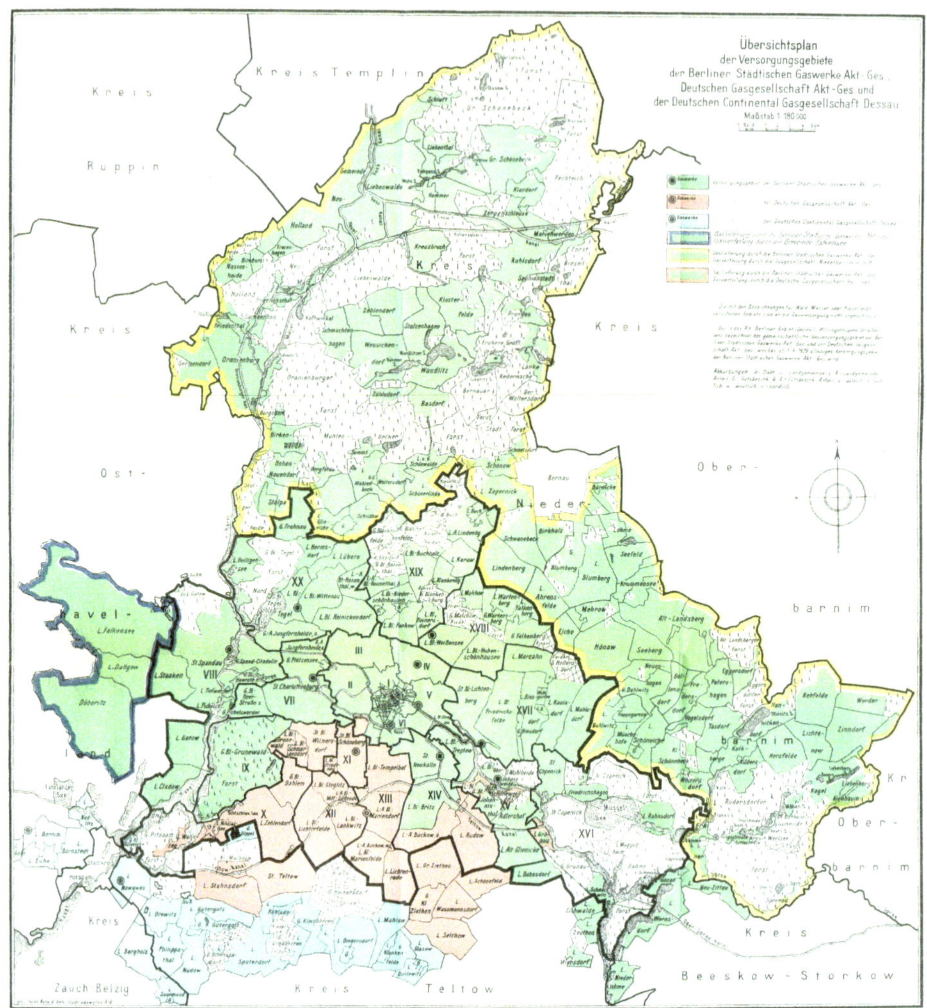

Figure 3.4
Map of gas utilities serving Greater Berlin, 1920
Source: Landesarchiv Berlin (LAB) A Rep. 259, no. 340.

municipal water utilities of Greater Berlin was only complete in July 1922, when they were all formally amalgamated into Berlin's water utility, Städtische Wasserwerke.[32] This gave Berlin's water utility full control over eighteen water works spread across the city.[33] Smaller, inefficient water works were then taken out of service, water mains were conjoined in order to provide uniform quality of service across the whole city, and the mains network was extended to outlying areas not previously connected.[34] Nevertheless, integrating and modernizing the hugely diverse water supply systems across the city, many of which were in a poor state of repair, proved a major challenge throughout the 1920s.[35] In addition—and again reminiscent of electricity and gas services—Berlin's water utility did not serve the whole city, but had to tolerate a private competitor that served the south and west of the city, Charlottenburger Wasser- und Industrie-AG (CWI) (see figure 3.5).[36] This company—colloquially known as Charlotte

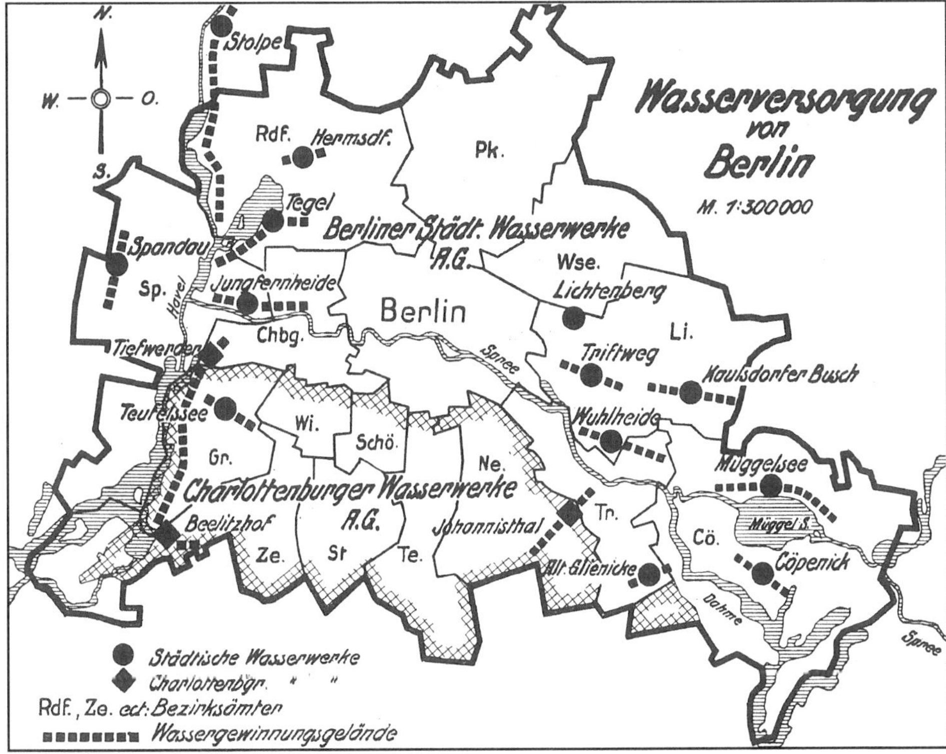

Figure 3.5
Map of water utilities serving Greater Berlin, 1926
Source: Kühne, "Gegenwarts- und Zukunftsprobleme," 427.

Wasser—supplied water to around one-quarter of Greater Berlin's inhabitants in the early 1920s.[37] Another, much smaller, utility, Wasserwerk Buch, served a sanatorium complex in the northeast. The water mains of these two companies were not connected to the Berlin utility's network and used different water pressures.[38]

The sanitation sector proved the most intractable of all, in organisational terms. Prior to 1920 over fifty different administrative entities across the Berlin metropolis were responsible, in one form or another, for wastewater collection, transportation, treatment, and disposal.[39] These ranged from local sewer departments and offices of hygiene to irrigation units and sewage farms using wastewater for agricultural production. All the eight cities as well as most of the fifty-nine smaller municipalities incorporated into Greater Berlin in 1920 were served by public sewers. However, only nine of these were connected to Berlin's sewer system.[40] There existed over eighty sewer systems that operated in isolation, even when running under the same street.[41] Integration was further hampered by the existence of diverse technical designs. Whereas (old) Berlin, Charlottenburg, Schöneberg, and Friedenau used a combined sewer system (transporting wastewater and rainwater together), other boroughs, such as Köpenick and large parts of Wilmersdorf and Lichtenberg, had separate wastewater and rainwater systems, while others had both combined and separate systems.[42]

As sanitation was not organized around self-dependent utilities but the responsibility of municipal departments, the city of Berlin was able to take over the entire network of sewers, pumping stations, pressure pipes, sewage farms, and sewage treatment plant that belonged to the incorporated municipalities (see figure 3.6).[43] The statistics speak volumes, literally and metaphorically. Greater Berlin now operated 4,145 kilometers of mains sewers, eighty-three pumping stations, and 27,207 hectares of land for irrigating sewage.[44] Berlin's chief civil servant responsible for sanitation, Fritz Langbein, announced in August 1920 that Greater Berlin would produce 160 million cubic meters of wastewater annually.[45] This, he calculated for effect, was like filling an area of 20,000 hectares 80 centimeters deep, without even accounting for rainwater (another 60 centimeters).

The unitary sanitation authority for Greater Berlin (Berliner Stadtentwässerung) proved successful between 1920 and 1923 in closing down a number of small, inefficient sewage treatment plants, sewage farms, and pumping stations deemed redundant.[46] It also managed to redirect wastewater flows in a more rational manner by connecting existing sewers and reconfiguring the hydraulic pumping systems. Organizationally, however, Langbein's efforts to create a new, central directorate for wastewater collection, treatment, and disposal ran up against severe opposition from the boroughs.[47] They campaigned for the retention of their own civil engineering departments, pointing to the need to respect the diversity of sewage systems across the city.[48]

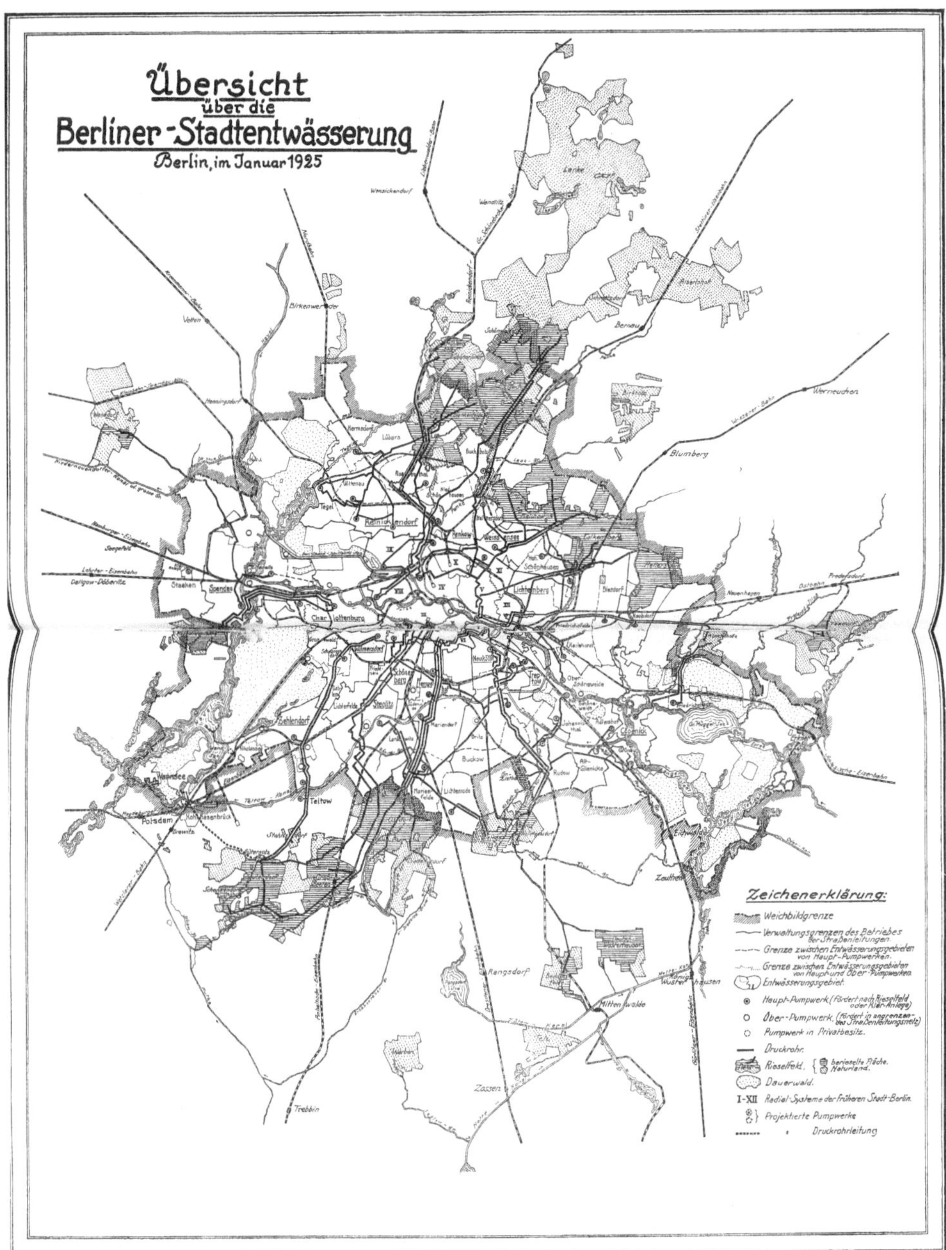

Figure 3.6

Map of sanitation system of Greater Berlin, 1926

Source: Langbein, "Die Stadtentwässerung," 360–361.

Alongside this scalar divide between the city and its boroughs was another, equally problematic sectoral one between the city sanitation department and the municipal enterprise responsible for managing the sewage farms, Stadtgüter GmbH.[49] On the thirty-one farms run by this company in 1920, some 8,440 hectares were dedicated to irrigating Berlin's largely untreated sewage as a source of water and nutrients for horticulture and livestock farming.[50] This was not always of mutual benefit. Whereas the sanitation department needed the sewage farms to take up and irrigate Berlin's sewage at all times, Stadtgüter was interested in using Berlin's sewage only when this served the needs of agricultural production and the irrigation capacity of the land.

Harmonizing Services and Tariffs

The city authorities and utility directors could not wait until this process of organizational and physical restructuring of the urban networks initiated by the creation of Greater Berlin was complete. The new unitary city needed to demonstrate positive achievements and to do this fast, if critics were to be silenced and economic volatility mitigated. Since the city leaders could not amalgamate all service providers in Berlin, they aspired at least to harmonize services and tariffs across the city by setting a good example with their own utilities and negotiating with their competitors.

Harmonization of services and tariffs was a clarion call for all Berlin's infrastructure sectors. The slogan for the electricity system at the time was "uniform current, uniform voltage, uniform price."[51] The aim for gas was "equal costs and equal supply for all inhabitants."[52] In the sanitation sector the ambition was for "a uniform system of wastewater disposal that meets the highest hygienic, but also economic, requirements."[53] The implementation of this common goal, however, differed hugely between sectors. Uniform services and prices were easiest to achieve in the sanitation sector for the simple reason that Berlin's sewer system, as noted above, was the responsibility of a municipal department, not several utilities. Having multiple organizational entities for sanitation services did not affect the central city government's powers to determine common tariffs and service conditions across the city. The situation in the water sector was very different. In June 1922 the city government was able to introduce a unitary fee for water supply in the territory served by all the former municipal water works.[54] This marked a major achievement. However, there remained huge price differentials between the areas served by Berlin's own water utility and those served by CWI. The coexistence of this profit-driven utility supplying water to a quarter of all Berliners at relatively high prices and with low performance standards was a thorn in the side of Greater Berlin that the city government persistently sought to remove.

Agreements were more readily made between the various utilities supplying electricity across Berlin. This was undoubtedly because the competitors of Berlin's own electricity utility (StEW) were also owned largely by public entities—whether the surrounding Province of Brandenburg, its districts (*Landkreise*), or municipalities—thus minimizing the need to provide shareholders with regular profits. StEW quickly reached agreement with MEW to exchange supply territories. This entailed StEW taking over some areas inside Berlin previously served by MEW in exchange for giving up areas outside the city that it had supplied in the past.[55] Creating uniform tariffs for electricity was achieved immediately in the territory served by StEW. Negotiations with the other power utilities over extending this tariff model across the whole city proved lengthy, but were ultimately successful. ESA agreed to adopt StEW's tariffs in the areas of Berlin it supplied in 1927 and MEW followed suit in 1928.[56] This left only Wannsee, in the southwest tip of Berlin, with a different tariff system set by Elektrizitätswerk der Stadt Potsdam.[57] In addition to creating a uniform tariff across virtually all the city, the Berlin city government simplified the tariff system substantially in January 1921. The huge variety of tariffs existing beforehand were replaced by four categories: (1) a basic, uniform tariff for households and small businesses (1.20 M/kWh); (2) a special, sliding tariff for low-level users (under 1,600 hours a year); (3) a tariff for lighting (2.00 M/kWh); and (4) a tariff for industry and commerce (1.20 M/kWh).[58]

Besides tariffs, uniformity was urgently needed with regard to electricity type and voltage.[59] In 1920 the inner-city areas, which had received electricity first, operated with direct current (DC), while those parts of the city that had experienced electrification later had alternating current (AC).[60] There existed also a patchwork of diverse voltages across the city, with networks of 65, 110 and 220 volts reflecting the fragmented nature of electrification in the conurbation.[61] The decision was made to replace these with a uniform system of AC at 380/220 volts. Implementation took time, inevitably, but was complete by 1927 in the urban center and by 1934 in the city as a whole.[62]

Municipalizing Infrastructural Territory

As Otto Büsch established in his 1960 study of municipal enterprises in Weimar Berlin, there existed broad political agreement in the city government throughout the 1920s that utility services in Greater Berlin should be placed under municipal ownership as far as possible.[63] While the municipalization of services beyond this field became one of the most contested issues of party-political debate, extending municipal ownership to all energy and water infrastructures operative in Berlin was always supported by huge majorities in the city parliament (Stadtverordnetenversammlung) and the city council.

Socialists and democrats were adamant that providing stable municipal ownership of the city's water, gas, electricity, and transportation services was essential as a means of offsetting the volatile postwar economic situation, improving living standards, and creating a fairer city.

It was only in 1915 that the city had acquired the electricity utility serving (old) Berlin from AEG when the existing concessionary agreement terminated.[64] This municipal takeover of one of Germany's pioneering power utilities was of huge significance. As Mayor Böß later explained: "Electricity utilities under municipal control can orientate their expansion in accordance with the needs of urban planning, public transport, hygiene, and housing far easier than private enterprises."[65] The city's own StEW (later, Bewag) provided the lion's share of electricity in Greater Berlin, supplying 80–85 percent of its territory and 88–90 percent of total electricity sold in the city by 1927.[66] In order to increase its influence over its competitors, Berlin raised its shareholding of ESA to 46.4 percent during the 1920s.[67]

In the gas sector, where the municipal gas utility held a lower share of supply to Greater Berlin (ca. 75 percent), the pressure to municipalize private competitors was greater.[68] In 1920 the city acquired automatically the 35.35 percent of shares in DG that had belonged to the former cities of Schöneberg and Wilmersdorf. Lengthy negotiations between Berlin and DG resulted in a contract signed on March 31, 1924, that set out the conditions for future cooperation. In return for the city renewing the supply contract with DG until 1975 and granting the chairman of DG a seat on the Berlin gas utility's supervisory board, Berlin acquired the gas supply to the whole city center (old Berlin), the right to buy all DG plant and property in the southern boroughs of the city, shares in DG to the tune of 16 million Marks, and nine seats on the supervisory board of DG.[69] The city also bought up the gas works of Oberschöneweide and Weißensee I and II from the district of Niederbarnim in 1925, and of Holtzmarktstrasse from DG in 1930. This left only two gas utilities operating in Berlin.[70]

If the process of municipalizing the electricity and gas sectors was relatively consensual and successful, the attempt to increase the city's influence over CWI stands out as an instance of virulent contestation.[71] This emanated partly from the differing business logics of the private and municipal utilities and partly also from the diverse tariffs and service standards referred to earlier. The conflict was enflamed, however, by the deep personal animosity between the director of the Berlin water utility, Carl Kühne, and his counterpart at CWI, Alfred von Feilitzsch. While Kühne was keen to pursue what he termed the "socialization" of all Berlin's water works following the municipalization of the Berlin water utility in 1915, von Feilitzsch was determined to resist intrusion into ownership of CWI.[72] In 1920 the city of Berlin had acquired some shares in CWI that had belonged to incorporated municipalities, but these represented less than a 2 percent shareholding and were thus insignificant.[73]

The opportunity for the city to challenge CWI's territorial monopoly over one-quarter of the city emerged in the hot summer of 1925, when CWI proved unable to meet rising demand for water. Inhabitants of the boroughs of Tempelhof, Schöneberg, and Steglitz supplied by CWI protested strongly about low water pressure or no water at all during the summer.[74] By September the situation had become so serious that it was debated in the city parliament, prompting calls by the SPD and DDP for the supply contract with CWI to be terminated and by the Communist Party of Germany (KPD) for immediate municipalization of the private company.[75] On December 17, 1925, a contract was signed between the two utilities in which it was agreed that the Berlin water utility would take over the supply of Schöneberg and Steglitz from 1928 onward in return for paying CWI 2.5 million Reichsmark.[76] This did not put an end to the controversy, as there followed a two-year dispute over the issue of access rights to CWI's water mains in Steglitz.[77]

When Berlin's water utility did eventually take over the supply of Schöneberg and Steglitz, director Kühne could not resist a jab at his arch rival. In a press statement he presented the takeover not only as a "first great step towards the municipalization of Greater Berlin's entire water supply system," but also as a major blow to CWI, which had lost at one stroke a third of its supply territory.[78] Von Feilitzsch retaliated with a strong rebuttal, accusing Kühne of a gross misrepresentation of facts and going on the offensive himself. He raised doubts about the Berlin water utility's ability to meet the water needs of Schöneberg and Steglitz and criticized the utility for planning to supplement its groundwater sources with less hygienic surface water drawn from the River Oder and Lake Tegel.[79] Kühne responded by dismissing the criticisms raised by von Feilitzsch and accusing him of hypocrisy over the water quality issue, pointing out that CWI had no qualms about using water drawn from a source close to the bathing beach at Wannsee frequented by 80,000 people on a hot day.[80] Given this degree of public mud-slinging, it is not surprising that further agreements between the two companies were not reached in the coming years. Only in October 1935 was a contract signed between the two utilities which, for the first time, established uniform water tariffs and supply conditions across the whole city. CWI was eventually incorporated into the Berlin water utility in August 1945—not, as was widely claimed at the time, by decree of the occupying allied forces, but by means of buying up shares in CWI that had belonged largely to Jews.[81] Municipalization came in many guises, as the chapter on the Nazi era will reveal.

Utility for the Urban Political Economy

Greater Berlin's utilities were expected to provide more than just uniform services at affordable prices for all Berliners. They possessed, in the eyes of the city administration and the governing parties, enormous leverage power as model employers, sources of public revenue, and enablers of modern living standards. If the expectations were high, so too were the challenges in this postwar era of political disruption and rampant inflation. This section explores how the city's utilities performed under such adverse circumstances and what role they played in sustaining the urban political economy.

Berlin's electricity, gas, and water utilities were significant, first, as major employers in the city. Otto Büsch calculated that between 17,000 and 18,000 people were employed at these three utilities during the inflation years.[82] These numbers marked an increase over the prewar years, largely as a result of the introduction of the eight-hour working day and six-hour shifts following the revolution. The gas utility employed the largest number, peaking at 11,375 employees in 1923. By comparison, the water utility employed a mere 1,773 people at the end of that year.[83] As the inflation began to bite, pressure within the city government grew to cut expenditure by reducing staff levels, as reflected in the debate on the city budget in May 1921.[84] Generally, however, redundancies were avoided during the hyperinflation so as not to exacerbate an already fraught employment market. It was only after the stabilization of the currency that staff levels were cut back, in the case of the gas utility by 2,000 employees between November 1923 and January 1924.[85]

Maintaining a high level of employment during the hyperinflation did not make the utilities immune from industrial protest. All three were caught up in the waves of strikes that swept Berlin between 1919 and 1923. In 1923 alone, the city's statistical office calculated, Berlin witnessed seventy-six strikes, involving 457,000 strikers and costing over two million lost working days.[86] The Prussian government was particularly keen that the city's electricity, gas, and water utilities should not stop operating. The Prussian interior minister warned the city in August 1923 against strikes in these essential sectors; a warning that became an order following a decree by the local army headquarters in October 1923.[87]

These interventions reflected how far Berlin's electricity utility StEW had become a focal point for radical strike action.[88] Electricity workers at StEW went on strike a dozen times between early 1919 and late 1923, primarily for better wages and working conditions, but also as part of broader political protests and for revolutionary change.[89] On each occasion electricity supply was interrupted, causing major disruption and disaffection across the city. Alfred Döblin captured the effects of Berlin's strikes in a poignant piece written in November 1922: "you try the electric lights: no luck with the switch; the gas on the cooker flickers feebly: an hour later it has gone. The water taps are open: no water; no water to wash, to drink, to cook; for the WC: misery. The human hand lies behind all these things."[90]

Strikes at StEW came to epitomize the political rift within the labor movement after the war. Its strongly unionized workforce revealed a growing split between a pro-SPD union and a left-wing union close to the KPD.[91] The split came to a head on November 5, 1920, just one month after the creation of Greater Berlin, when electricity workers went on strike for higher wages against the will of the SPD, USPD, and unions at StEW. This was hugely embarrassing for the new city government that was then controlled by the SPD and USPD. The strike was terminated by presidential decree a few days later.[92] However, StEW's inept handling of the strike provoked further unrest that was only quelled when the entire executive board of the company resigned in early 1921. The drama reignited in April 1921 when the popular leader of the works council at StEW, Wilhelm Sült, was shot in police custody and subsequently died.[93] Sült, who had enjoyed cult status in the Berlin labor movement during the revolution, is quoted as saying: "electricity utilities are the lever over the entire economy; we must retain control of this lever."[94] In the eyes of Sült and many of his followers, StEW was no model municipal employer.

A second key function of Berlin's utilities lay in the financial support they provided to the city's beleaguered budget. Berlin, like most other German cities, was suffering from a substantial loss in revenue combined with a sharp increase in costs for unemployment and welfare benefits.[95] The Reich government's tax reforms of 1920 had removed the municipal surcharge to income tax, making municipalities heavily dependent on transfers from the Reich and state governments. This gave Berlin not only less tax revenue, but also less control over its revenue.[96] As social expenditure rose to over a quarter of the city budget in the following years, the city resorted to increasing the minor taxes it could control—for instance, on dogs, amusements, and hotels—in an increasingly desperate attempt to balance the budget. These minor taxes, which had contributed a mere 6 percent of Berlin's budget before the war, made up a third of all revenue in the immediate postwar years.[97] It is against this backdrop of fiscal stringency that the city's municipal enterprises—and the three utilities in particular—offered attractive respite. The city authorities were largely free to levy tariffs and use the revenues from the utilities as they pleased. As the revenues for electricity, gas, and water services were collected monthly, tariffs could be adapted to the rate of inflation, thereby proving more immune from devaluation than taxes set a year in advance. As a result, surpluses from the three utilities covered up to 17 percent of the city's total budget in any one year.[98] Without this cash injection, Berlin would have been far less able to maintain the welfare payments that were the lifeline for so many Berliners impoverished by unemployment and hyperinflation.

At the same time, thirdly, the city authorities were keen not to create new hardships by increasing utility tariffs beyond what was deemed affordable. As these tariffs could never keep pace with hyperinflation fully, costs for utility services were constantly low, by prewar standards, providing relatively cheap gas, electricity, and water to Berliners at a time of intense hardship. Increases to electricity, gas, or water tariffs, nevertheless, always sparked contestation in the city parliament. While the SPD argued for tariff increases to meet the fiscal needs of the city, the KPD accused the city government of increasing everyday living costs for consumers.[99] Here, it is important to note that tariff increases did not hit all consumers equally hard. Whereas increases in electricity tariffs tended to affect industry and trade, owing to the low number of households with electricity, and increased water prices fell primarily on homeowners, thanks to rent controls, poorer households were hit first and foremost by increases in gas tariffs.[100] The debate on the city budget in 1921 proved a watershed moment in utility tariff policy. There it was decided, against strong opposition, to increase tariffs rather than freeze them. The argument of treating the utilities as a lever of municipal economic, fiscal, and social policy took precedence over protecting them as model socialist enterprises.[101]

As inflation began to rocket from 1922 onward, the utilities found themselves increasingly unable to finance even basic services. During the hyperinflationary period all modernization and extensive repair work was stopped; only essential maintenance was permitted.[102] As the economy struggled and unemployment soared, consumption of water, gas, and electricity dropped sharply.[103] In 1923 the average Berliner used only 94 liters of water a day, compared with 106 liters in 1920.[104] As consumption rates declined, so did utility revenues. The utilities found themselves caught in a rat-race of spiraling costs that could only inadequately be covered by belated tariff increases. Sudden hikes in the price of coal, in particular, prompted numerous electricity blackouts. In 1922 two-thirds of Berlin's gas lamps remained switched off.[105] In 1923 electric street lighting was reduced to 25 percent of prewar levels.[106]

By late 1923, hyperinflation was making a travesty of conventional modes of utility service funding. On October 20, 1923, a cubic meter of gas cost 440 million Marks.[107] In mid-November a kilowatt hour of electricity cost an astronomical 420 billion Marks.[108] By then, tariffs were being set on a daily basis and collected as fast as possible. As these revenues were virtually worthless by the time they arrived, the utilities had to resort to selling off or pawning what material they could to stave off insolvency. StEW managed to pay for coal in the last months of hyperinflation only by selling its accumulator batteries for the valuable lead they contained.[109] A most graphic description is given by one of the directors of Berlin's electricity utility, Martin Rehmer, recollecting those last days of absolute turmoil:

> On Friday morning the cashier's office didn't know what they were going to pay the wages with. When they sent a messenger to the Reichsbank to collect the wages, he came back requesting a furniture van to transport all the notes. When we sent him with a furniture van, he came back with a small briefcase full of notes of such huge denominations that they were useless for paying the wages.... Paper money collected would be sorted at night; we had up to 60 people just counting money, night after night. Notes that had become worthless were packed into sacks and sold for one dollar per hundredweight. Laundry baskets full of paper money were transported to AEG to pay for small electrical motors.[110]

For all the difficulties encountered by the utilities during the inflation there was one consolation: Berlin never found itself required to sell off these jewels in the municipal crown, either whole or in part. It was counted as one of the greatest achievements by the city government at the time that it had managed to rescue all the utilities into an era of stability and growth.[111] With the introduction of the Rentenmark on November 20, 1923, limited in number and valued at one trillion paper Marks, prices quickly stabilized. Utility tariffs were calculated afresh, according to the cost of living index. On January 1, 1924, electricity cost 36 Rentenmark-Pfennig per kWh, gas 18 Pfennig per cubic meter, and water 18 Pfennig per cubic meter.[112] The nightmare was over; normality had returned.

Unfettering the Utilities

The debilitating effect of hyperinflation on Berlin's utilities had been exacerbated by their inability to respond rapidly to changing circumstances. The directors of the city's electricity, gas, and water utilities may have come to lead some of Germany's largest municipal enterprises, but the process of creating unitary infrastructure systems after 1920 was, as noted earlier, incomplete and contested. It was only in 1922 that all municipally owned utilities were removed from the control of the separate boroughs and placed under the central supervision of citywide administrative departments (Deputationen). Even then, all decisions of significance required the approval of three city government bodies: the respective Deputation, the city council and the city parliament. This procedure for gaining the required approval was criticized by utility directors and city councillors alike for being lengthy and bureaucratic, but also for allowing—in their eyes—excessive influence by party political interests.[113] Even the Deputationen comprised politically appointed representatives, many of whom—it was claimed—lacked the knowledge and competence to make well-founded decisions affecting the utilities' future.[114]

In May 1922 the city council published a fifteen-page report to counter public criticism at the lack of progress in improving gas, electricity, and water services since the creation of Greater Berlin.[115] It asserted that unifying the many utilities of the amalgamated municipalities was one of the most important tasks of the city government, but acknowledged that expectations in the new utilities had yet to be fulfilled. It went on to explain what had been achieved since 1920 and what steps were needed to enable the utilities to provide the multiple functions expected of them. There arose a heated debate over the following eighteen months about how to reform the city's utilities. The crux of the issue was how far political control should be limited and commercial decision-making delegated to the utilities. An expert committee commissioned by the city government came up with a proposal, in July 1922, for transforming the electricity, gas, and water utilities into share companies in full municipal ownership.[116] With this organizational status, it was argued, the utilities could act relatively free from the bureaucratic hurdles and financial constraints that were severely limiting their ability to invest in infrastructure. Since the committee comprised mainly utility directors, their desire to be liberated from such "external influences" should come as little surprise. More worrying was one of their key demands to "remove the new organization of the city's utilities from the municipal atmosphere as far as possible."[117] By this was meant making the utilities immune to political interventions from the democratically elected or legitimized entities of city government. Director Kühne of the Berlin water utility expressed his enthusiasm for the committee's reform proposals in a memo dated September 4, 1922.[118] Predictably, he welcomed also the recommendation that the private CWI be incorporated into his public utility, but rejected the committee's idea of creating one unitary company for electricity, gas, and water services.

The reform proposal unleashed intense debate in the city parliament and city council. Proponents, such as Mayor Böß, argued that the utilities would be able to make everyday business decisions without constant reference to supervisory municipal bodies and gain access to foreign and domestic loans essential for investments in their infrastructure.[119] Social Democrats were worried that the utilities, if transformed into share companies, would be vulnerable to any future attempts to privatize them. Communists criticized the proposal for undermining political control of the utilities by elected city representatives and, thereby, their own ability to influence infrastructure policy.[120]

The decision finally made was to transform the utilities into three separate share companies. On November 24, 1923, within days of the introduction of the Rentenmark,

StEW became Berliner Elektrizitätswerke AG (Bewag), the city's gas works Berliner Städtische Gaswerke AG (Gasag), and the water utility Berliner Städtische Wasserwerke AG (Wassag).[121] The share capital of each new organization was owned by the city of Berlin. Each concluded fifty-year lease agreements with the city for their respective infrastructures that required them to operate "in the interest of the common good" and to levy tariffs that respected the "economic circumstances of everyone."[122] Municipal supervision was henceforth exercised not by the triad of Deputation, city council, and city parliament, but by a supervisory board for each utility that comprised four representatives from the city council, eight from the city parliament, two from the works councils, and two external experts. Overall, this institutional reform was to prove hugely significant for three reasons. First, it liberated the utilities from the fetters of overly bureaucratic procedures. Second, it restricted direct political intervention in their activities by the city's representative bodies, which now exercised influence largely via the supervisory boards.[123] Third, it heralded the commercialization of Berlin's infrastructures, a process involving the utilities acting increasingly as independent market players. Only the sanitation sector was exempt from this reform. As a non-commercial operation, wastewater removal and treatment remained an entity of the city administration supervised directly by the Deputation of civil engineering.[124]

Siloed Sectors and Territories

For all the rhetoric around the creation of unitary services and all the effort made to pursue this core objective, the management of Berlin's utilities after 1920 was in two important respects characterized by trends toward disintegration, rather than integration. These relate to cross-sectoral coordination and collaboration with the wider region.

It is a curiosity of Berlin's infrastructure history that the city has not embraced the model of the municipal multi-utility (Stadtwerk) so prominent in Germany. While most German cities and towns amalgamated several of their utility services—whether electricity, gas, water, waste, or transportation—into one, cross-sectoral municipal utility, Berlin has always operated its services in separate entities. This can be attributed historically, in part at least, to the belated municipalization of Berlin's electricity and water utilities. What had just been created for (old) Berlin during the First World War was not subjected to further organizational change in 1920. Interestingly, several of those municipalities incorporated into Greater Berlin had previously run their utilities under the umbrella of a Stadtwerk. After 1920, these multiutilities had to be unbundled into separate companies that could be then amalgamated into single-sector utilities following the model operative in the city center. This act represents the supremacy of territorial integration over sectoral integration that epitomized Greater Berlin's infrastructure policy. Although the expert commission report of May 1922 recommended the amalgamation of Berlin's electricity, gas, and water utilities as part of their organizational reform, this opportunity was not taken up. By rejecting the creation of a multi-utility, Berlin was to perpetuate "siloed" thinking in its infrastructures. Rivalry between the electricity and gas utilities over the city's energy market was to flare up at various times throughout the twentieth century, hindering a coordinated approach to urban energy policy.[125]

Far more significant, however, was the lack of cooperation between Greater Berlin and the surrounding region of Brandenburg. For the new metropolis Brandenburg was a true hinterland, literally and figuratively. The Law of Greater Berlin effectively internalized the regional coordination problems of the past within an enlarged municipal territory. After 1920 Berlin was too engrossed in implementing internal integration of its own highly diverse entities to take any serious interest in the outlying region.[126] Planning in Berlin became strictly urban in orientation.[127] This proved hugely problematic for regional coordination, given the accentuated imbalance between the enlarged metropolis and the largely rural, residual province of Brandenburg.[128]

In terms of utility services, the surrounding region was source and sink for the resources needed to drive the city. Electricity was imported from the Lusatian lignite fields, which also supplied substantial brown coal resources to all Berlin's utilities. The city's water was drawn from wells situated largely within the city boundaries, but these water resources originated from river catchments and underground aquifers that stretched far into the surrounding region. As Berlin's thirst for water grew, the region's water resources became seriously depleted. In 1921 water in the River Spree flowed at the dangerously low level of 5–6 cubic meters per second, instead of the required rate of 15 cubic meters.[129] Mayor Böß, a strong proponent of the unitary city ideal, conceded that cooperation between Berlin and the Province of Brandenburg was poor, pinpointing gas, water, and electricity services as issues in particular need of improved regional coordination.[130]

Regional imbalances were most virulent, however, in the field of sanitation. The creation of Berlin's sewage disposal system in 1873, following plans by James Hobrecht and others, had radically reordered the relationship between the metropolis and its hinterland.[131] Henceforth, Berlin's wastewater was pumped out to sewage farms located well outside the conurbation, where it was used to irrigate fields used partially for the production of food and fodder. These sewage farms, although on the territory of other municipalities, were owned by the city of Berlin and managed by its own municipal agency. Even after the creation of Greater Berlin most of these sewage farms remained outside the city limits. The agency managing them, having incorporated the land belonging to all amalgamated municipalities in 1920, became a commercially constituted enterprise, Stadtgüter GmbH, in April 1923.

Those responsible for Berlin's sanitation system did not tire of singing the praises of Hobrecht's legacy.[132] From their Berlin-centered perspective the sewage farms were models of modern multifunctionality. First, irrigation of wastewater helped decompose its harmful substances, enabling the naturally filtered water to reenter local waterways. Second, the nutrients and water in sewage enriched agricultural production on these farms, improving their cost-effectiveness. Stadtgüter boasted that it could provide Berlin with all the vegetables the city needed if it was prepared to accept only regionally grown varieties.[133] Third, the sewage farms benefited not only consumers in Berlin, but also around 8,000 small farmers who leased land there, in addition to the 2,500 people employed directly by Stadtgüter.[134] Fourth, the creation of sewage farms had turned hundreds of hectares of what was termed "wasteland" into valuable farming land.

What Berlin's politicians and administrators lauded as a green belt of irrigation farms encircling the city was experienced by close residents more often as a "belt of stench."[135] Those communities not benefiting economically from the sewage farms were constantly complaining to the authorities about the smells and damage emanating from them. For as the volume and toxicity of Berlin's wastewater increased, so did the pollution of the soil and watercourses in and around the sewage farms. Christoph Bernhardt has argued convincingly that the publicly produced sanitary city devised by Berlin caused environmental injustices on a regional scale that were continuously ignored by the metropolis.[136] Wide-ranging political agreement in Berlin, obligatory connection to the sewer network, and the financial security that this enabled all combined to ensure the effective funding and functionality of Berlin's sanitation system, but at the expense of residents subjected to pollution and disturbance at the sewage farms and of the urban poor struggling to afford the costs of centralized wastewater disposal. The vision of connectivity that motivated sanitation engineers and municipal reformers proved, in other words, highly selective, prioritizing the metropolis of Berlin over the Mark of Brandenburg. Berlin's metabolisms of water and energy were inextricably bound to the wider region, but this was not reflected institutionally or politically.

The Imperfect Networked City

The immediate postwar period may have been marked by political instability, economic disruption, and administrative reform that remained incomplete, but the initial years of Greater Berlin's existence proved pivotal for the city's future and the role utility services were to play in it. The overarching aspiration for a unitary city found its most tangible expression in the determined attempts to create territorially integrated material infrastructures and organizational entities capable of delivering the same services to all Berliners across the whole metropolis. This powerful agenda of socio-spatial redistribution and organizational rationalization enabled the amalgamation of the various municipal electricity, gas, and water utilities—as well as sanitation departments—that had existed prior to 1920 and the enforcement of uniform service tariffs for most of the utility sectors and much of the urban territory, as well as the reconfiguration of infrastructure networks to reflect the new political geography of the city. The world-metropolis spirit invoked by Wagner and Behne in the introductory quotation found a fitting replication in the sociotechnical imaginaries that inspired Berlin's pro-republican and reformist politicians, administrators, and engineers. They successfully enrolled an assemblage of material networks, institutional obligations, modernist imagery, environmental resources, and financial revenues to create utilities capable of providing the essential services needed by the enlarged city. More than this, the utilities of Greater Berlin helped sustain the city throughout the inflationary period by providing surpluses for the city budget, maintaining high levels of employment, and keeping tariffs relatively low. Here was urban politics enacted through infrastructure.

At the same time, the infrastructural ideal of a unitary city proved elusive. On many fronts those responsible had to accept imperfections to the networked city they envisioned. Modest successes in municipalization could not mask the existence of private competitors servicing large parts of the city with electricity, gas, and water. Investments in infrastructure could cover little more than essential maintenance. Internal disputes between city and borough authorities compromised plans for centralization. External dependencies on Brandenburg, Prussia, and the Reich—whether environmental, financial, or political—were a constant reminder of the limitations to city-centrism. However, the stabilization of the currency and gradual recovery of the economy from late 1923 onward gave cause for hope that the enactment of a modern Berlin through infrastructure might have been only delayed, and not derailed. With the three utilities now reconstituted as independent municipal companies, expectations in their ability to shape the city's future emerged once more with renewed vigor.

4 Weimar's Networked Municipalism

In 1960 the Historical Commission of (West) Berlin launched its new book series with a scholarly work on the history of Berlin's municipal enterprises in the Weimar era.[1] The choice of topic for the first volume was odd. Looking back to the Weimar Republic for inspiration in reconstructing German democracy was already an established meme of postwar West German historiography. Drawing on municipal enterprises as a vehicle for this line of argument was certainly not. The Historical Commission was, understandably, concerned that the book might appear too specialized for the wide readership it craved for this flagship publication. The book opened, therefore, with prefaces by the commission's chairman, Hans Herzfeld, and the Mayor of West Berlin (and later chancellor of the Federal Republic), Willy Brandt, justifying the topic. The core argument of both was that municipal enterprises had been key instruments of local self-government in Weimar Berlin, enabling progressive economic and social policies through difficult times. Brandt was particularly keen to draw out parallels to the challenges he himself was facing in 1960: "Today, as then, finding the right use of municipal enterprises is a problematic issue at the intersection between administration and economy, politics and society, posing difficult questions about public finances as well as challenges for municipal social and economic policy."[2]

It is this political mission of Otto Büsch's book that makes it historically so intriguing. His work set out to show how Berlin's municipal enterprises during the Weimar era were important not merely in providing basic services for a growing metropolis, but in making democracy real, both in terms of urban policies enabled and political aspirations contested. What fascinated him was the relationship between Germany's first democracy, municipal self-government, and Berlin's own enterprises.[3]

This chapter explores how the city's electricity, gas, water, and sanitation utilities—as major players of Berlin's municipal economy—were used to weave the fabric of a networked municipalism. It assesses, first, how far the utilities were able to deliver on the political agenda of urban development and integration once the currency had stabilized in 1924. This is the era popularly known as the "Golden Twenties" in Berlin, a brief but intense period of economic growth, social consumerism, and cultural experimentation of a city relishing liberation from ten years of hardship. Municipal politicians were very much part of the new modernist mood. With the shackles of war and hyperinflation removed, they grasped the opportunity provided by rapid economic recovery to push with vigor the policies devised for a Greater Berlin. Many icons of municipalism were created in the second half of the decade, including a municipal transport company, major social housing developments, and numerous public parks. More significant politically than these individual achievements was the integrative approach taken by municipal government. Leading municipal politicians and officials never tired of emphasizing how only by planning and running the city in an integrated way could the overarching goals of economic growth and social advancement be achieved with the limited means available.[4]

This "networked municipalism" was predicated upon effective urban services. Utility services for electricity, gas, heating, water, and sanitation, now largely under municipal control, were regarded by city leaders as vanguards of modernization. These infrastructures were thus "networked" not only in the physical sense of their weblike structures, but also in a political sense of being integral components of an urban modernist ideal. In the eyes of those responsible for them—whether in the city parliament, council chambers, or utility headquarters—the vision for these infrastructures was very much about building up supply capacity, drawing on technological innovation, and rationalizing processes of provision. In this sense Berlin's "networked municipalism" echoes the "municipal managerialism" identified by Matthew Gandy for New York City.[5]

The fascination with urban infrastructures was not, though, limited to the agenda setters. The Berlin public appears to have shared their enthusiasm. The popularity of trade fairs devoted to urban infrastructure, such as the exhibition "Gas und Wasser Berlin 1929," testifies to the huge appeal of the topic to the general public. When the Reich Association for German Technology (Reichsverband Deutscher Technik) organized a series of public lecture evenings in early 1930 on technology in Berlin, entitled "Berlin at Work" ("Berlin arbeitet"), it was astonished at the response.[6] The lecture series, which included evenings dedicated to electricity, gas, water, and wastewater, attracted on some evenings over 4,000 people. The chapter explores, therefore, not only what infrastructures and services were provided, but also how they were used and shaped by consumers in Berlin.

The latter years of the Weimar Republic fundamentally challenged this modernist infrastructural ideal on several fronts.[7] Economically, the Depression that followed the

Wall Street Crash in October 1929 devastated industry and commerce in Berlin, engendering mass unemployment but also a major drop in utility revenues. Socially, rampant poverty created immense pressure to reduce tariffs for essential utility services at a time when the city budget, ravaged by declining tax revenues, increasingly relied on the utilities to meet the growing deficit. Politically, the broad consensus that had sustained infrastructure expansion throughout the 1920s began to erode as the political climate grew harsher. The chapter concludes, consequently, with a study of how networked municipalism was unraveling well before the Nazi seizure of power.

Expansionist Urban Imaginaries

With the city emerging from the doldrums of hyperinflation, the directors of Berlin's electricity, gas, water, and wastewater utilities were, in early 1924, well prepared to take advantage of the economic recovery. The expansionist plans they devised were founded on three fundamental assumptions: that Berlin's population would increase significantly, that its economy would boom, and that per capita consumption would rocket.

The population of Greater Berlin passed the symbolic four million barrier in 1925. That same year the municipal planning department produced a development plan for the city that envisaged a future population of 7.5 million inhabitants by 1954 and a staggering twelve million by the end of the century.[8] This plan was often cited by the utilities to justify their expansionist schemes.[9] The water utility director, Carl Kühne, could draw on these population projections to calculate future infrastructure investments without having to defend them: "It is not up to the water utility to discuss whether [a population of twelve million] is desirable or ever likely. Our job is, rather, to calculate for the long term whether and how we can meet the demands made of us, even the most extreme."[10]

Councillor Hahn similarly based his 1928 strategy for Berlin's sanitation system on a future population of six to seven million inhabitants.[11] Even though these population scenarios were admittedly long-term in perspective, they nevertheless proved singularly inaccurate. Berlin's population did grow in the late 1920s, but only by an annual average of approximately 1.5 percent, peaking during the Weimar Republic at 4.33 million in 1930.

A more accurate assumption was that national economic recovery would strengthen Berlin's role as Germany's economic powerhouse. In 1925 Berlin was home to one in fifteen of Germany's inhabitants, but one in twelve of its businesses and one in ten of its employees.[12] The city was the largest center of production—and consumption—in the country. The electrical industry alone employed nearly 175,000 people in the city.[13]

As industrial production increased sharply after 1924, so did demand for power, light, water, and heating.[14]

By far the largest growth was anticipated in per capita consumption rates, particularly for electricity. As more people got connected to the networks, living standards increased, and sales of household appliances grew, it was expected that consumption rates would rise exponentially. The points of reference in this numbers game were, significantly, not past experiences in Berlin or other German cities, but the figures emerging from cities elsewhere, especially in the United States. A report produced by the power utility Bewag in October 1927 cited annual per capita consumption rates of 472 kWh of electricity in the United States, Canada, and Switzerland as the probable future for Berlin, where the figure stood at a mere 194 kWh.[15] Even per capita gas consumption in Berlin—widely regarded as a saturated market losing out to electricity in the competition over lighting—was expected to rise from 30 cubic meters per annum to be more in line with the much higher rates in Britain (160 cubic meters) and the United States (360 cubic meters).[16] Director Kühne predicted in 1926 that Berliners would be consuming 207 liters of water a day by 1954, representing an increase of some 30 percent over 1923 figures (see figure 4.1).[17] The 1928 sanitation strategy, cited above, envisaged wastewater increasing from 162 liters per person per day to 225 liters.[18]

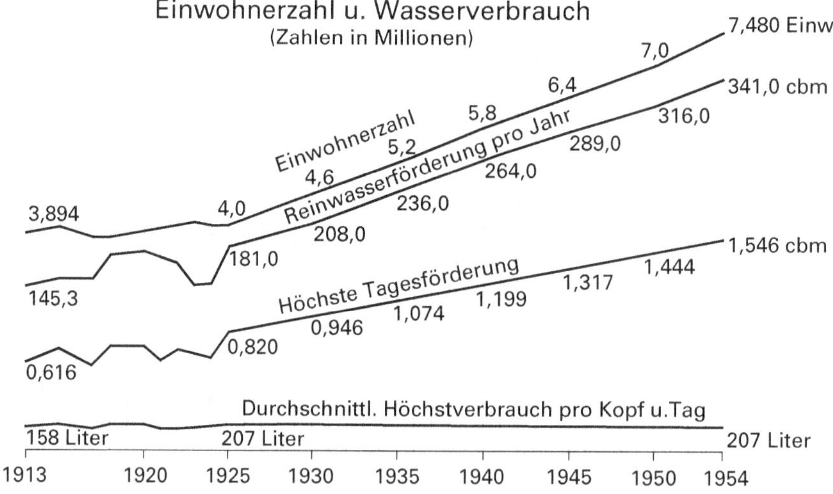

Figure 4.1
Water demand predictions of 1926
Source: Kühne, "Gegenwarts- und Zukunftsprobleme," 432.

In the post-inflationary period, consumption rates for electricity and water did indeed rise sharply within a very short time. Electricity consumption in Berlin trebled between 1923 and 1929, increasing each year by a massive 25 percent.[19] Most of this can be attributed to growing demand in industry and commerce, which made up 65 percent of electricity consumption in 1928–1929.[20] Although electrification of households was growing apace, only 14 percent of Bewag's electricity was sold to private consumers at that time. Particularly challenging were the peak evening loads, which in 1924 were 50 percent higher than in the previous year.[21] The peak load that year, reaching 208 MW, exceeded the capacity of the city's power stations of 198 MW.[22] It continued to grow by an average 52.5 MW each year between 1924 and 1926 as more electricity was used for street lighting, advertising, and extended shopping hours.[23] The increase in water consumption was not quite as dramatic, but equally challenging. Whereas up until 1920 water use had largely kept pace with population growth, after the inflation it rose much faster, increasing by 16 percent each year between 1927 and 1929.[24] In 1925 the Berlin water utility had supplied around 130 million cubic meters of water. By 1929 this figure had risen to over 187 million cubic meters—an increase of almost 44 percent in just four years.[25] That year Berliners were on average using far more water each day (231 liters) than director Kühne had predicted for 1954.[26] Even sales of gas increased by nearly 16 percent—from 364 million to 422 million cubic meters—between 1924 and 1929.[27] If utility directors may be accused of exploiting growth scenarios to the full, they cannot, therefore, be blamed for extending and modernizing their networks to meet the very real surges in demand.

The issue at the time, then, was not whether service capacity should be expanded, but how. A key strategic consideration was the degree to which Berlin should rely on imported energy in line with a general trend toward the centralization of electricity generation and gas production. In the mid-1920s the energy market in Germany was characterized by a national drive for the provision of power and gas via long-distance supply lines from large production plants located at coal or lignite mines.[28] Influential economists and energy engineers created a powerful discourse at the time around the need to centralize energy provision as a means of enhancing national security, eradicating regional disparities in supply, and removing polluting power plants from urban centers.[29]

Berlin, which untypically for a major German city had imported around 70 percent of its electricity in 1923, might have been expected to increase its dependency on outside sources in line with the new Reich policy. This was not the case. On the contrary, the city's power utility Bewag set out to maximize self-generation of electricity.[30] In a strategic report produced in 1925, Bewag's director Martin Rehmer laid out his plans to reduce the level of electricity imports while at the same time increasing local generating capacity to meet rapidly growing demand.[31] The arguments for this dramatic change of tack are illuminating. Long-distance power supplies, Rehmer argued, had proved unreliable in the past, with around 180 breakdowns and twenty-five interruptions of power supply from the Zschornewitz plant in Lusatia in 1924 alone. Second, self-generation was calculated to be 25 percent cheaper than imported electricity. Third, Bewag anticipated no difficulties in acquiring foreign loans for its infrastructure investment program. Under these circumstances the Berlin power utility saw no reason to kowtow to pressure from Reichselektrowerke and accept electricity from the national grid.

This self-confident, city-centered strategy was reflected also in the case of gas supply. Gas producers in the mining region of the Ruhr were keen to develop a lucrative market in Berlin and made repeated offers from 1926 onward to supply the capital. These offers by Ruhrgas AG often came with state endorsement, in the form of support by the governor of the Province of Brandenburg and Berlin.[32] They were steadfastly resisted by the city and its gas utility Gasag, who argued that the production of town gas in the city was considerably cheaper, beneficial for employment at the local gas works, less vulnerable to external intervention, and perfectly adequate to meet demand scenarios.[33]

The trajectories for infrastructure envisioned by those responsible in Berlin were, in other words, oriented toward maximizing self-dependence in supply. In their eyes the city was a focus not only of the consumption, but also the production of utility services. For electricity generation the planned solution was to build two large power stations in the east and west of the city, as well as power storage facilities to meet peak demand. This plan was elaborated and refined in three reports by the power utility Bewag produced in 1925, 1927, and 1928.[34] If Berlin's electricity system was not to collapse, the 1925 report argued, the city had to build a brand new power station at Rummelsburg with an initial capacity of 216 MW by the summer of 1927, extending to 400 MW by the winter of 1929–1930.[35] The price tag for this alone was over 56 million Reichsmark. In addition, a second power station of initially 200 MW and subsequently 400 MW would be required in the west of the city by 1931. To help address the critical problem of peak loads, two power storage facilities were planned in the 1927 report: a Ruths storage plant, in which power was converted to steam, and a water storage power plant.[36] The latter was dropped in the 1928 report as being not economically viable.[37] Any additional peak load would be met with electricity from Reichselektrowerke amounting to a relatively modest 50 MW.[38] To avoid relying on others for any more electricity, Berlin's mayor Gustav Böß was speculating as early as 1929 about building power plants for the city along the Elbe and Oder rivers.[39]

Plans for expanding Berlin's system of water provision were on a similarly grand scale. In his 1926 report on the future of Berlin's water supply, director Kühne set out an ambitious program to exploit available water resources in the city and meet any shortfalls with water imports from neighboring river catchments. Assuming a city of 7.5 million inhabitants in 1954 (see figure 4.1), he calculated Berlin would need to double its existing supply capacity by then, corresponding to a maximum daily supply of 1,546,000 cubic meters and an annual supply of 341 million cubic meters.[40] To maximize use of available groundwater sources in and around the city, the Berlin water utility Wassag had already acquired some 10 kilometers of land along the River Upper Havel between Stolpe and Heiligensee as well as around 6 kilometers on the south bank of Lake Müggel to serve groundwater wells.[41] Its investments in 1926 alone were designed to increase the daily supply capacity of the utility's water works from 575,000 cubic meters to 740,000 cubic meters.[42] If these local sources proved insufficient, Kühne advocated intervening in the Spree and Havel rivers upstream of the city so as to increase the throughflow of water serving bank infiltration for its water works. The options considered in the 1926 plan were either to retain water in winter by damming Lake Schwieloch (and possibly also Lake Scharmützel), thereby creating a reservoir of 70 million cubic meters, or to transfer water from the River Oder via the Oder-Spree Canal into the River Spree, generating an additional 500,000 cubic meters of water a day.[43] In the event of Berlin's population growing to twelve million, requiring an estimated 3.6 million cubic meters a day, Kühne envisaged drawing on massive water transfers from even further away.[44]

Hydraulic hubris of this kind was not the reserve of the Wassag director. City councillor Hahn, responsible for water resources management, produced a plan two years later which presented very similar alternatives for ensuring enough water reached Berlin.[45] The focus here may have been on maintaining minimum water levels in the rivers flowing through the city, rather than securing public water supply, but the water transfer projects discussed were designed to meet both challenges. Hahn came out in favor of transferring water from the River Oder via the Hohenzollern Canal and a new North Canal, as this would not only be cheaper than the reservoir project but also more flexible in dealing with shortfalls in the public water supply system.[46]

Rapid growth of water use posed a huge challenge to sewage disposal as well. In this case, simply providing more of the same technology was not a viable option. Councillor Hahn, in a second report of 1928 addressing sanitation, set out the limitations of sewage farms in dealing with an estimated 225 liters of sewage per capita per day.[47] He calculated that 100,000 hectares of land would be needed to irrigate this amount of sewage, representing eight times the inner-city area within the suburban rail ring.[48]

Berlin would need to buy an additional 45,300 hectares of land surrounding the city for this purpose, destroying countless weekend homes and costing an estimated 170 million Reichsmark.[49] The alternative he proposed was to build sewage treatment plants capable of producing water that could be fed into local watercourses or—if needed—used on existing sewage farms. Overall, six sewage treatment plants were planned, at a total estimated cost of 67.2 million Reichsmark.[50] The sewage treatment was to be biological, based on the activated sludge process developed by Karl Imhoff that involved large quantities of oxygen being added to sewage to assist the bacterial decomposition of organic substances.[51] This plan was approved by the city government in 1930 and was subsequently included in a joint report by Hahn and the director of the Berlin wastewater utility, Langbein, in 1932, following the positive experiences made with the first biological treatment plant at Stahnsdorf.[52]

All these plans can be interpreted as ambitious "sociotechnical imaginaries," in Sheila Jasanoff's sense.[53] They embodied not merely growth scenarios of grandiose proportions, but visions of infrastructural and urban futures that exuded a powerful public service ethos, prioritized the city over the surrounding region, and mapped out investment programs for decades to come. Their sheer boldness prompts questions about their viability. How far, then, did these sociotechnical imaginaries become a reality?

Infrastructural Enactments

The Klingenberg power plant in the east of the city was without doubt the flagship of Berlin's new infrastructural landscape. Built in just over one year, it was the largest and most modern power station in Europe at the time (see figure 4.2). It was widely admired for its architectural design and technological innovation, for instance using coal dust as a fuel.[54] When it became fully operational, in July 1927, the Klingenberg plant generated 270 MW of electricity for the local grid, representing 38.5 percent of all Berlin's own power generation.[55] Visitors to the plant were suitably impressed, with one commenting in 1928: "What first strikes me about this major generating station is the invisible nature of the work being done to create its unimaginably vast amount of power."[56]

Not everyone admired the new facility. Local residents protested so strongly about the air pollution of fine ash emanating from the fired coal dust that filters had to be retrofitted to the chimneys. Most importantly, though, the Klingenberg plant enabled the city's power stations to meet peak load in April 1927 without electricity imports for the first time for years. Figure 4.3 illustrates quite how important the new power station was in meeting total demand. By 1930 growing self-generation capacity had reduced the proportion of imported electricity from 70 percent to a mere 30 percent.[57]

Figure 4.2
The Klingenberg power station
Source: Landesarchiv Berlin (LAB) F Rep. 290-02-01, no. 0000130. Photo by Erich O. Krueger, 1950.

This trend was reinforced when the second new power station, West, began generating power in early 1931 and became fully operational in 1933.[58] Indeed, Berlin had by 1933 increased its own electricity generation to such an extent that, especially during the Depression, local supply exceeded demand, resulting in some power stations operating well below capacity.[59]

The Ruths battery, storing steam generated at the Charlottenburg power station, proved a major attraction for experts at the World Electricity Conference in 1930.[60] Built in 1929, it was designed to provide rapid electricity to cover for power failures or peak demand, requiring only 30 seconds to be fully functional (see figure 4.4). With the capacity to provide 50 MW for a duration of three hours, it was ten times the size of existing Ruths batteries.[61] Despite its novelty, the Ruths storage facility experienced no operating difficulties and was successfully used to cover for failures in power supply in Berlin on forty-eight occasions between 1929 and 1933.[62]

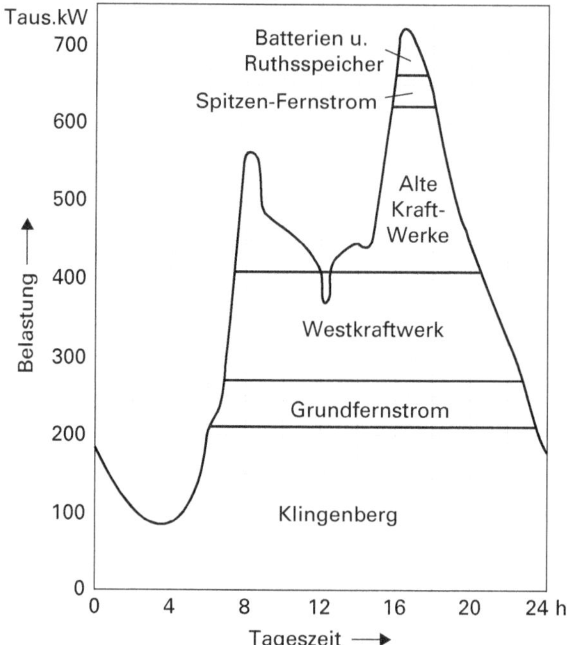

Figure 4.3
Meeting daily electricity loads, as planned in 1928
Source: Rehmer, "Die Stromversorgung der Reichshauptstadt Berlin," 280.

Besides generating and storing electricity on an impressive scale, Berlin modernized its power grid to cope with rapid growth in demand. The city's high and low voltage power lines were extended dramatically: from around 9,000 km in 1923 to 12,000 km in 1926 and 20,000 km in 1933.[63] More significantly, a new group circuit enabled Berlin's power plants to be interconnected and managed by a load distribution center. This increased the grid's resilience against disruption, as each supply area could now be served by two independent sources of electricity—another first in Europe.[64]

Berlin's gas supply infrastructure was also extended significantly, if not on such a scale. The city utility Gasag increased production of town gas at its gas works by one-third between 1924 and 1930, from 355,444,325 cubic meters to 478,344,600 cubic meters.[65] As with electricity, the gas supply network became interconnected with a 120 km ring pipeline that linked all the city's gas works. The total length of Gasag's gas pipes increased to 4,148 km, which—as the utility's director Friedrich was proud to announce—represented the distance between Lisbon and the Ural Mountains.[66]

Figure 4.4
The Ruths steam storage facility
Source: Landesarchiv Berlin (LAB) F Rep. 290 (07), no. 0019330. Photo by Willi Nitschke, April 8, 1952.

Pursuing this exercise in visualizing the invisible, the water utility director, Kühne, boasted that his water mains, if laid out in a line, could span the Atlantic Ocean.[67] Between 1924 and 1929 these urban water mains were extended by some 900 km, as the utility connected many outlying communities of the enlarged city.[68] Wassag's water works were enlarged and modernized, pumping stations installed, and the supply network restructured. Between 1924 and 1928 the capacity of these water works increased by 45 percent, reaching 900,000 cubic meters per day in 1929.[69] This was sufficient to meet the peak demand of 807,868 cubic meters on July 23, 1929, with some reserve. Significantly, the water utility was able to avoid water shortages without having to resort to the regional water retention or transfer projects outlined in Kühne's 1926 report, cited above.[70] Neither of these grandiose schemes was ever put into practice. As Kühne proudly informed the city parliament on September 29, 1930, the utility's infrastructure building program was almost complete and, with a daily capacity of 1 million cubic meters, it would be able to provide enough water for a population of up to 6.4 million.[71]

Berlin's wastewater infrastructures were also enlarged, modernized, and reconfigured in a major way. Over 400 hectares of land were bought for sewage irrigation at sites in Münchehofe, Ruhleben, and Groß-Ziethen.[72] Four sewage pumping stations and two rainwater collectors were built.[73] Sewers had to be reconstructed to accommodate the new underground lines.[74] The sewer network was enlarged from 4,300 km in 1925 to 4,912 km in 1929—the distance of a return journey between Berlin and Constantinople, as Mayor Böß proudly pointed out.[75] Most significant, however, was the construction of the new sewage treatment plants. Of the six originally envisaged (see above), only one was completed and one planned during the Weimar era. The biological treatment plant at Stahnsdorf became operational in August 1931, with a capacity to treat 110,000 cubic meters of wastewater per day (see figure 4.5).[76] It was designed deliberately as an experimental facility with the aim of testing a variety of innovative technologies on a large scale.[77] Besides the biological treatment of wastewater, technologies were installed to reuse and compost sludge, generate sewage gas, irrigate crops, and reuse water in fishponds. This variety gave the plant the flexibility to treat wastewater to different degrees, depending on the needs of the neighboring, crop-producing sewage farms.[78] The drawback was the high cost of this experimental approach and inexperience in building such an unusual plant—points seized upon by the city government's critics.[79] When the second plant, at Waßmannsdorf, was completed in July 1935 it proved as cost-effective as originally planned, thus vindicating Hahn's original plan of 1928.

Figure 4.5
The sewage treatment plant at Stahnsdorf
Source: Bärthel, *Geklärt!*, 155.

Looking across these sectors, we can conclude that the Berlin city government and its utilities did go a long way in materializing their imaginaries of an urban infrastructural ideal. In a remarkably short period of five years, infrastructures for electricity, gas, water, and wastewater were dramatically extended and, in some cases, radically reconfigured. As a result, it was possible to raise the quality of service provision across the city and to provide access to these services for those previously not connected: two core objectives of the municipal agenda in Weimar Berlin. This infrastructure perspective, however, has addressed only aspects of supply. It now needs complementing with additional aspects that explore the role of resource flows, the wider political economy, and consumption patterns. These are considered in the following sections.

Urban Metabolisms

How did Berlin's infrastructures affect metabolic flows through the city? Conversely, how were they framed by the opportunities and constraints these flows provided? The relationship between the physical structures of urban technical networks and the material flows they mediate is multifaceted and bidirectional, as argued in chapter 2. Three vantage points illustrate these relations in the Weimar years: regional water resources, coal consumption, and the by-products of electricity generation and sewage treatment.

Berlin's water supply system had a far-reaching impact on the region's water resources. Huge amounts of groundwater were extracted within the city's own boundaries. It was estimated that in addition to the approximately 200 million cubic meters of water extracted by the city's water utility each year, a further 50 million cubic meters was extracted by private businesses (such as breweries) and another 50 million cubic meters in connection with building work owing to Berlin's high water table.[80] This scale of water abstraction had a damaging effect on both groundwater and surface water resources. Contrary to the popular assertion that Berlin's groundwater resources were unlimited, hydrologists had long warned of the detrimental impact of declining groundwater levels in the city on buildings with wooden foundations, vegetation in the parks, and the operability of fire hydrants.[81] A groundwater monitoring system, set up to measure water levels back in 1869, provided regular evidence of the impact of excessive abstraction. As most of the groundwater extracted in Berlin originated, via bank infiltration, from the rivers that flowed through the city, water abstractions had a negative effect on river flow rates too. Water in the River Spree flowed at an average 3.7 cubic meters per second between 1921 and 1929—a far cry from the 15 cubic meters per second that was the recommended minimum flow.[82]

Various plans had been tabled to address the problem of low river flows in Berlin since 1916. The schemes to retain water in an upstream reservoir or to transfer water from the River Oder, referred to in Hahn's 1928 report (see above), were just two of the options under discussion.[83] In the late 1920s prominent hydrologists, such as Julius Denner, called for a major program of groundwater replenishment that involved retaining water in upstream reservoirs, constructing percolation basins, or using large natural ponds to replenish groundwater with river water, and designing parks and unsealed surfaces to percolate rainwater.[84] This integrated approach to surface and groundwater would, they argued, benefit the water balance of the whole region, groundwater levels in the city, and not just the water supply system. While Denner and Mösenthin spoke of the need to see "Berlin's surface and groundwater resources as one interconnected hydraulic unit," however, the Wassag director Kühne was far more concerned about "where we are going to get the huge amounts of water that the metropolis needs to survive without transgressing the boundaries set down by water legislation to protect by law the interests of others."[85]

Issues of water quantity were deemed the most pressing by contemporaries, but river water quality was often a cause for concern for residents, and not only in the vicinity of sewage farms. The few studies of river water quality conducted during this period pointed to a dramatic worsening of biological and chemical parameters as the River Spree passed through Berlin.[86] A river that boasted a rich fish population and vibrant angling community where it entered the city in Köpenick was, by the time it reached the River Havel in Spandau, devoid of large living organisms. An analysis of river water quality conducted in the winter of 1931 identified untreated wastewater from sewer overflows after flooding events as the prime source of river pollution in the city.[87]

The energy source that kept all Berlin's infrastructure systems going was coal. For all the talk about increasing levels of self-dependence in generating local electricity or producing town gas, Berlin could not run a single power plant, gas works, or water works without coal from elsewhere. The power, gas, and water utilities consumed huge quantities of coal imported from Britain, Westphalia, and Upper Silesia that was transported by rivers and canals into the center of the city.[88] It was calculated that in 1928 Berlin's municipal enterprises together consumed 1.9 million metric tons of coal.[89] Of this, the lion's share went to producing town gas.[90]

The generation of electricity at the city's power stations also created a marketable by-product: heat. District heating was already known on an experimental scale in Berlin. The Technical University of Charlottenburg had been heating its campus from a central heating plant since 1884 and Charlottenburg's town hall had been heated by a local power plant since 1912.[91] In 1926 Bewag tentatively entered the heating market, converting its existing power stations at Charlottenburg and Steglitz to provide steam and hot water, respectively, to surrounding residential neighborhoods. The Charlottenburg facility began operation in October 1926, supplying 33 buildings, with 100 properties served by the Steglitz plant in 1927. The combined heat-and-power plant in Steglitz hit the headlines in 1932 when it supplied the first housing estate "without flame or smoke"—that is, with full central heating and hot water supply—to wide acclaim.[92] By then, Bewag had become an enthusiastic supporter of the technology, advertising its potential to improve air quality in the city.[93]

One of the most innovative technologies of resource reuse developed at this time was the generation and use of methane gas from Berlin's sewage treatment plants. When an initial, mechanical treatment plant was built at Waßmannsdorf in 1927, it was fitted with a facility to extract methane from sewage sludge. This technology had shown promising results in the United States and Britain, as well as in the German cities of Essen, Erfurt, and Nuremberg.[94] By 1929 the Waßmannsdorf plant was producing about 1,850,000 cubic meters of sewage gas a year.[95] This gas was used on site to drive the pumps of the treatment plant, rake solids from the raw sewage, heat the greenhouse, cook in the canteen, and heat the baths for the plant workforce. Initial plans to feed the gas into the Gasag network had to be abandoned owing to the cost of connection to the distant gas grid. At its inauguration, the plant was heralded in the press under the headlines: "A Novel Gas Works for Berlin" and "Sludge as a Source of Power and Light."[96] The plant operated without any notable interruptions, prompting the director of the wastewater utility, Langbein, to calculate that if the planned sewage treatment plants were all equipped with a similar technology, they could deliver 110,000 cubic meters of sewage gas per day to Berlin—enough to meet the needs of 275,000 inhabitants.[97] The first of the new biological treatment plants, built at Stahnsdorf in 1931, produced 10,000 cubic meters of sewage gas per day.[98] This gas was sufficient to cover the entire energy demand of the treatment plant, including generating its own electricity.

Berlin's utilities, in short, did not simply supply the electricity, gas, and water, and treat the wastewater as required of them. They mediated a whole range of material and energy flows involved in serving the metropolis. Some of these were essential inputs to the services provided, such as water from the region's rivers and aquifers for water supply or coal to drive the machinery needed to generate electricity, produce town gas, or pump water across the city. The volumes involved in these metabolic processes were huge, having a major impact on water and air quality in the city, as well as wider environmental implications at the source locations. Other mediated flows were voluntary, in the sense that they were developed as creative ways of reusing energy or marketing by-products from the transformative processes involved. The ways in which Berlin's utilities used heat from power generation and gas from sewage treatment is indicative of their highly innovative approach to essentially basic tasks of service provision. These innovations were, in very different ways, to prove highly formative in Berlin's later infrastructure history.

Serving City and Citizen

The impact of Berlin's infrastructures reached far beyond the resource flows they channeled and into the homes, offices, shops, and factories they serviced. The following section analyzes the multiple ways in which the electricity, gas, water, and wastewater utilities served city and citizen. It looks at how utility services improved living standards, supported local industry and commerce, operated as major employers, and sustained the municipal budget.

By the mid-1920s almost all of Berlin's households were serviced by public water mains and sewers and most by the gas network, but relatively few had access to electricity. This changed dramatically during the Weimar era. Whereas in 1925 only 27.5 percent of households in Berlin were connected to the electricity grid, by 1928 the figure had increased to 54.8 percent and by 1933 to 76.0 percent.[99] During the summer of 1926 Bewag was receiving between 600 and 800 applications a day for connection to the grid.[100] Significantly, electricity in homes was used not just for lighting, as in the early years of electrification, but increasingly for powering a whole new generation of household appliances. These devices to wash and iron clothes, heat water and rooms, or process food were marketed as time-saving devices and symbols of consumerist modernity targeted primarily at the middle-class housewife. As Dieter Schott has argued, electricity utilities cooperated with housing reformers, public health activists, and advocates of women's emancipation to spread the "electric gospel."[101] In 1930 the first "fully electric" housing estate, providing lighting, power, and heating with electricity, was completed in the Siemensstadt district.[102]

Just as electrical appliances were revolutionizing the kitchen, so hot water appliances, showers, and flushing toilets were turning bathrooms—if they had existed at all—into places of enjoyable hygiene. Bathrooms were made a standard feature of all new homes and nearly all of these were connected to public sewers. Since Berlin built a staggering 170,000 new dwellings between 1925 and 1932, this represented a major advancement in living standards.[103] Many of the dwellings were built as social housing designed to be affordable for those with relatively low incomes. For those without employment or who had lost their savings to the hyperinflation, however, such homes were generally out of reach, as were their electrical appliances and hygienic comforts. In a working-class borough like Wedding the 40 percent of homes with electricity in 1928 may have represented a rapid increase from the mere 10.7 percent only three years previously, but it paled in comparison with wealthier boroughs like Charlottenburg, where the connection rate was 71.5 percent.[104]

Berlin's utilities contributed significantly to the local economy in various ways. In the first instance, of course, they provided basic services for industry and commerce. It is interesting to observe that industrial enterprises in Berlin generated very little of their own electricity, but relied on Bewag for their power. In 1928 the proportion of electricity generated in Berlin by industry was only 9.3 percent, compared with the national average of 38.6 percent.[105] Second, the investments in infrastructure made by Berlin's utilities benefited private contractors hugely. For example, in a typical year in the late 1920s Bewag was placing over 34,000 orders at a value of around 232 million Reichsmark with nearly 3,000 contracting firms.[106] Many of the beneficiaries were small businesses, as 27,000 of these orders were for less than 100 Reichsmark. Third, all the utilities helped to alleviate unemployment in the city by conducting emergency job schemes (*Notstandsarbeiten*), mainly on construction sites for new sewers, power stations, and water mains.[107] For example, the wastewater utility provided around 500,000 days of work for the unemployed on extending the sewers in 1925 and 1926 alone.[108]

As a fourth contribution to the local economy, the utilities were themselves major employers in the city. At the peak of prosperity, in 1928–1929, Gasag employed 7,475 people, Bewag around 7,400, Wassag over 1,900, and the sanitation utility over 2,500.[109] Otto Büsch estimated that around 5 percent of Berlin's population lived directly off the salaries and pensions paid by the city's own enterprises.[110] Employees at Gasag, Bewag, and Wassag were covered by generous labor agreements struck between management and the free trade unions, which included a works pension, twenty days' holiday for those employed longer than twelve months, and sickness benefits for three months at 90 percent of regular salary.[111] It should be noted that the number of employees on the utilities' payroll during the late 1920s, although substantial, was significantly lower than at the height of the inflation.[112] Once the responsibility for creating employment under conditions of hardship ended in 1924, the utilities pursued a staffing policy oriented toward improving productivity—that is, increasing the ratio of production to employees.[113]

The wide-ranging benefits for the city engendered by its utilities came, of course, at a price. How the massive costs of infrastructure improvements and maintenance were paid for, and by whom, is of crucial significance. The capital investment figures were vast. The electricity utility Bewag's investment program for the period 1928 to 1932 totaled 317.8 million Reichsmark.[114] Of this, 98 million were earmarked for the new power stations, 168 million for the transmission and distribution grid, and the rest for such costs as land acquisition and interest payments. The wastewater utility invested between 1924 and 1930 a total of 127 million Reichsmark, half of which (65 million) was spent on sewers, rainwater collectors, emergency outlets, and drainage pipes, and the remainder on new sewage treatment plants (18 million), pumping stations (15 million), and sewage farms (29 million).[115] Over the same period the water utility Wassag invested 75 million Reichsmark.[116]

Sums of this size could clearly not be funded out of the utilities' regular revenue streams, but called for loans. Given the limited availability of capital in Germany in the post-inflationary period, most of these loans came from abroad. Berlin's utilities evidently presented highly attractive investment prospects for international bankers, as they were able to acquire significant sums of foreign money at competitive rates. Taking Bewag as the most prominent example, the utility acquired the following loans during this period: 30 million Swiss francs (fifteen years at 7 percent interest) in 1925, 20 million US dollars (twenty-five years at 6.5 percent interest) in 1926, 15 million US dollars (thirty years at 6.5 percent interest) in 1929, and 15 million US dollars (25 years at 6 percent interest) again in 1929.[117] By 1930 Bewag had long-term loans totalling 224 million Reichsmark.[118] Not only did foreign bankers see Berlin's utilities as a sound investment, even foregoing state guarantees for the loans they gave, but the city's elected representatives were keen to support the investment programs and loan applications of their utilities. The bills submitted to the city parliament for approval of the infrastructure investment programs were invariably approved, generally by huge majorities and often unanimously.[119] No political party there wanted to appear to resist the advance of modern urban services.

The main reason for this widespread support for such massive investment programs was that the utilities all proved perfectly capable of servicing the loans themselves. The city budget was never called upon to subsidize either loan repayments or interest payments. All Bewag's foreign loans were serviced by the utility itself without support from the municipal budget.[120] This was certainly not the case with other municipal enterprises, such as the transportation utility BVG, which ran heavy losses that required continuous public subsidy. The electricity, gas, and water utilities, by contrast, were each able to generate enough revenue to afford the costs of heavy loans. The city clerk Friedrich Lange (SPD), no friend of the utility directors, was impressed that Wassag should have a debt of only 14 million Reichsmark in 1930 having invested 75 million Reichsmark since the end of inflation.[121]

All the more astonishing is that the utilities could achieve this with tariffs for electricity, gas, and water supply that were among the lowest in German cities.[122] As described in the previous chapter, these tariffs had to satisfy multiple functions: to enable the utilities to operate without subsidies, to minimize the financial burden on consumers—in particular low-income households—and to contribute to the city budget. For social reasons the tariffs were lowered significantly during the post-inflationary period. Between 1924 and 1926 the base household price for water fell from 21 to 15 Pfennig per cubic meter, for electricity from 22 to 16 Pfennig per kWh, and for gas from 19 to 16 Pfennig per cubic meter.[123] Nevertheless, even these lower tariffs generated enough revenue year by year for the utilities to balance the books and service their loans. More than this: the electricity, gas, and water utilities were able to deliver substantial annual contributions to the city budget (see table 4.1). These payments were made up of three components: a fee for the lease of infrastructure, a 10 percent dividend on shares, and

Table 4.1
Financial contributions of Berlin's utilities to the city budget, 1926–1932 (in million Reichsmark).

	1926	1927	1928	1929	1930	1931	1932
Bewag	17.0	20.1	23.4	26.3	58.7		
Gasag			14.4		18.1	16.3	15.0
Wassag				5.4	13.0	18.0	19.0

Sources: Berliner Kraft- und Licht(Bewag)-Aktiengesellschaft, *75 Jahre Berliner Stromversorgung*, 25; Büsch, *Geschichte der Berliner Kommunalwirtschaft*, 169, 172, 174.

special levies. Otto Büsch calculated that Berlin's municipal enterprises together contributed between 5 and 10 percent of the total city budget during this period.[124] With this additional money the city was able to fund expenditure in other fields, especially housing and social welfare. Cross-subsidization of this kind was not frowned upon by the city's political elite. Rather, it was welcomed as a mainstay of municipal finances in the context of reduced tax transfers from the Reich.[125] The flexibility afforded by the freedom to change tariffs and fees to suit budget requirements reflected the utilities' instrumental significance in pursuing urban policy objectives. For this reason, Otto Büsch termed them "the backbone of the entire municipal economy."[126]

Consumer Control

The predominance of a "build and supply" logic to Berlin's infrastructure management prompts the question of how consumers fitted into the equation. As recent social studies of technology are revealing, practices of consumption influence strategies of supply in important ways.[127] The title of this section is, therefore, deliberately ambiguous. It is suggestive of the power of the consumer to shape demand for utility services and, thus, the design of urban infrastructures, but also of the utilities to manage consumption along pathways conducive to their existing and future capacity to deliver. Both dimensions are explored here.

The rapid increase in demand for electricity, water, and gas—both in absolute and per capita terms—during the post-inflationary era reflected the emergence of new practices and new consumers. As demand grew, Berlin's utilities became increasingly interested in understanding who these consumers were and how they were using their services. This was not out of idle curiosity, but out of a vested interest in grasping how their markets were changing in scope as well as scale. The regular monitoring of in-house meters was proving an inadequate source of information (see figure 4.6). In 1928 Bewag and

Figure 4.6
Reading the water meter
Source: Kühne, *Die Berliner Städtische Wasserwerke*, 60.

Gasag, in collaboration with the privately owned Gasbetriebsgesellschaft, conducted a unique and extensive survey of electricity and gas use in households across the city.[128] Bewag was interested in finding out how far households were using electricity for more than just lighting.[129] Gasag was keen to discover what prospects lay in store for gas use in the home in the wake of electrification.[130]

The results revealed that of the 423,000 households with electricity, about 44 percent had no electrical appliances at all and used electricity only for lighting. Of all households with electricity, 55.9 percent had an electric iron (cf. USA: 76.1 percent),

27.5 percent a vacuum cleaner (USA: 30.4 percent), 5.9 percent an electric cooker (USA: 18.3 percent) and only 0.5 percent a washing machine (USA: 26.2 percent).[131] Unsurprisingly, distribution of electrical appliances varied hugely between the city's wealthier and poorer boroughs.[132] The relatively low dissemination of electrical appliances overall, in comparison with the United States, prompted Bewag to promote sales of such appliances and build up its capacity to generate and store electricity. The decision to build the Ruths storage facility, referred to above, was attributed directly to the lessons learned from the 1928 survey.[133] The results for gas use were markedly different. They revealed that the vast majority of homes with over two rooms had a gas connection and that, of these, just 3.5 percent used gas only for lighting. Another 49.8 percent had gas boilers or cookers, while the remaining 46.7 percent also had gas appliances, such as irons.[134] The conclusions drawn by Gasag were that the home market was largely saturated in all but the poorest of households still relying on coal for cooking and that gas was likely to lose out to a rapidly growing market for electrical appliances. This pessimistic assessment of the home gas user was one factor behind Gasag targeting industrial consumers as a market with development potential. Industry accounted for only about 13.5 percent of Gasag's sales in 1928.[135] The utility therefore set about trying to encourage more factories, restaurants, and launderettes to use gas as a substitute for solid fuel in heating processes.

What the responses of Gasag and Bewag reveal is growing competition between the two municipal utilities for custom and customers in all sectors: households, businesses, and the public sector. Their rivalry became particularly pronounced over water heating and lighting in homes as well as street lighting, with Gasag trying to fend off market intrusion by Bewag.[136] An initiative was launched to amalgamate the two utilities so as minimize such divisive competition and develop a more coordinated municipal energy policy but, despite the support of Mayor Böß, it came to nothing.[137]

Beyond trying to understand these consumers better, the electricity and gas utilities set out to influence household energy use in a variety of ways.[138] The purpose was twofold: to increase revenues through higher sales and to guide demand for energy along trajectories that suited their infrastructures. Private consumers, previously treated as passive and grateful recipients of a basic service, were increasingly regarded as significant market players with diverse and often unpredictable desires.

Initially, this interventionist approach was targeted at increasing energy consumption per se. Advertising electrical and gas appliances for the home became a key marketing strategy for Bewag and Gasag (see figure 4.7). Both utilities set up showrooms across the city, demonstrating and selling new technologies for the kitchen and bathroom.[139] Cookery schools and courses were offered by Bewag to encourage housewives to switch

Figure 4.7

Bewag advertisement for electrical appliances

Source: Brennert and Stein, *Probleme der neuen Stadt Berlin*, 575.

from gas to electric cookers. Gasag organized house visits by female staff, advising housewives on how to make their homes more comfortable and convenient with modern gas appliances. In 1930 19 percent of all gas consumers used this service.[140] The campaigns did not challenge gender roles, but promised relief for housewives from tedious chores so as to dedicate more time to bringing up their children and, only secondarily, earning their own income.[141]

By far the most effective way of promoting energy consumption was the hire purchase scheme for household appliances that was set up by Bewag in 1926.[142] The scheme, termed Elektrissima, proved a breakthrough (see figure 4.8). It was, basically, a low-cost and low-risk hire purchase arrangement. Bewag paid the retailer for the electrical appliance bought by a customer, who subsequently repaid Bewag in monthly installments along with their electricity bill without any interest payments. Customers

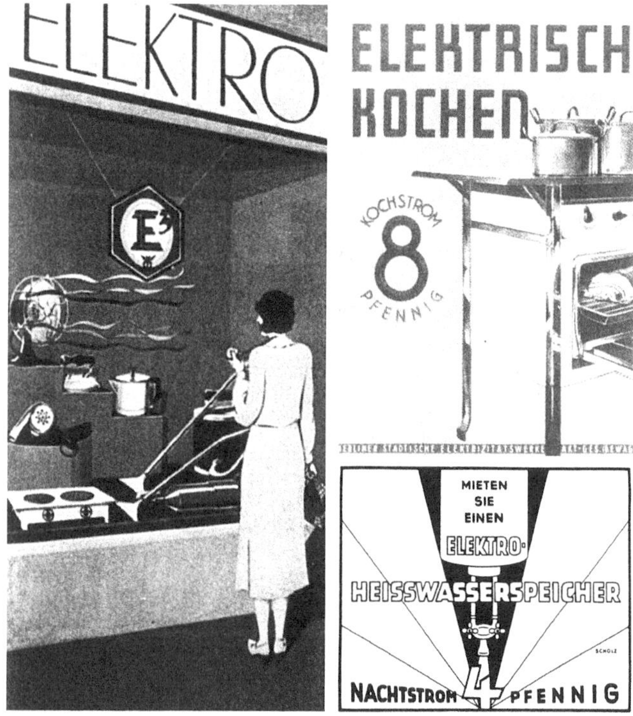

Figure 4.8
Advertisement for the Elektrissima scheme
Source: Berliner Kraft- und Licht(Bewag)-Aktiengesellschaft, *100 Jahre Strom für Berlin*, 1932. Copyright: Bewag/Vattenfall.

could select the duration of repayment and the size of their down payment.[143] In addition, Bewag offered subsidies for connecting to the local grid, if necessary. The Elektrissima scheme was hugely successful. Introduced in the autumn of 1926, by the end of the year already 18,000 appliances had been sold at a value of 1.4 million Reichsmark.[144] In 1927 the number of hire purchase agreements had risen to 112,000 and by 1929 to 171,000, when the value of goods sold totalled 13.7 million Reichsmark.

Not surprisingly, retailers were delighted with this boost to sales, switching overnight from being diehard critics to enthusiastic supporters of the municipally owned utility.[145] Such positive publicity among the business community was politically significant. More important, though, was how the Elektrissima scheme made electrical appliances affordable to far greater numbers of people. In Beate Binder's words, the scheme marked the "democratization of electricity consumption" in Berlin.[146] To Mayor Böß, providing cheap appliances and electricity in this way was fundamental to achieving "social and hygienic progress."[147] Elektrissima's popularity prompted Gasag to introduce a similar hire purchase scheme for gas appliances in 1927. This also proved highly successful, funding the sales of 194,916 household appliances by 1930.[148]

The original purpose of Elektrissima, for Bewag, had been simply "to create a significant increase in the consumption of electricity."[149] This changed in the late 1920s, as Bewag sought increasingly to direct electricity consumption away from peak load times so as to relieve pressure on its limited generating capacity. As evening peak loads began to threaten the stability of the grid, Bewag switched its sales strategy: "It can no longer be the aim of Bewag to sell electricity under any circumstances. We must rather try to promote very particular forms of electricity demand that can gradually improve the load management of our power stations."[150]

To guide electricity demand away from peak times, Bewag introduced in 1926 a lower night tariff of 8 Pfennig per kWh, instead of the regular 16 Pfennig, monitored with a separate meter.[151] Since installing additional meters was expensive, the utility put more effort into promoting electricity use at times when the power stations were underutilized, such as at night, on Sundays, and during the summer, and avoided advertising consumption at peak times, such as for cooking or for lighting rooms and shop windows.[152] Promotional schemes for electricity, like Elektrissima, were consequently reoriented toward the sale of appliances like night storage heaters and hot water storage tanks.[153] For the same reason Bewag sought to expand its network of electric street lamps. Intriguingly, electric batteries for vehicles used, for instance, for postal delivery, street cleaning, and waste disposal were regarded by the utility as having the greatest potential for increasing nighttime electricity consumption.[154] Together, these initiatives mark an extraordinarily sophisticated form of demand-side management for the time.

The Unraveling Web

This complex assemblage of consumption growth, infrastructure investment, social tariffs, and rising revenues began to unravel as Germany and its capital were sucked into a global economic depression of epic proportions in the wake of the Wall Street Crash of October 1929. Just as the economic boom following the stabilization of the currency had heralded a sharp rise in energy and water consumption, so the collapse of the economy was reflected in a dramatic drop in demand for utility services. The amount of water supplied by Wassag declined between 1929 and 1932 by 12.8 percent, to just under 164 million cubic meters.[155] The largest drop was, significantly, among large industrial consumers. Those consuming over 100,000 cubic meters a year used 27 percent less water between 1930 and 1931.[156] Gas sales by Gasag fell by 19 percent between 1929 and 1932, despite an increase in the number of customers.[157] Figure 4.9 reveals how dependent gas sales were on households (marked in red). It was demand for electricity, though, that witnessed the full force of the Depression. Between 1929 and 1931 Bewag's sales to the machine industry plummeted by around 44 percent, and fell by 25 percent to the electrical industry and 16 percent to the metal industry.[158]

As the bottom dropped out of demand in the industrial sector, Bewag increasingly looked to the household sector to offset the shortfall in revenue.[159] Observing that private electricity consumption was relatively immune from the recession, the utility adapted its tariffs and advertising once again to boost electricity use in the home. As one of Bewag's senior employees put it: "If electricity utilities are paying increasing attention to households, this is because the demand from households not only has huge potential but also represents a market that is almost entirely unaffected by shifts in the economy and can therefore provide a valuable basis for the efficiency of power stations in times of economic depression."[160]

Price cuts were used to stimulate demand for electricity among households. For instance, the tariff for home heating was reduced to 8 Pfennig per kWh and a special tariff, also of 8 Pfennig per kWh, was introduced for fully electric homes, covering heating, lighting, and cooking.[161] The Elektrissima scheme now targeted sales of hot water boilers, electric cookers, and fridges.[162] These measures proved successful in actually increasing electricity sales overall, from 144.1 million Reichsmark in 1929 to 155.9 million Reichsmark in 1930.[163]

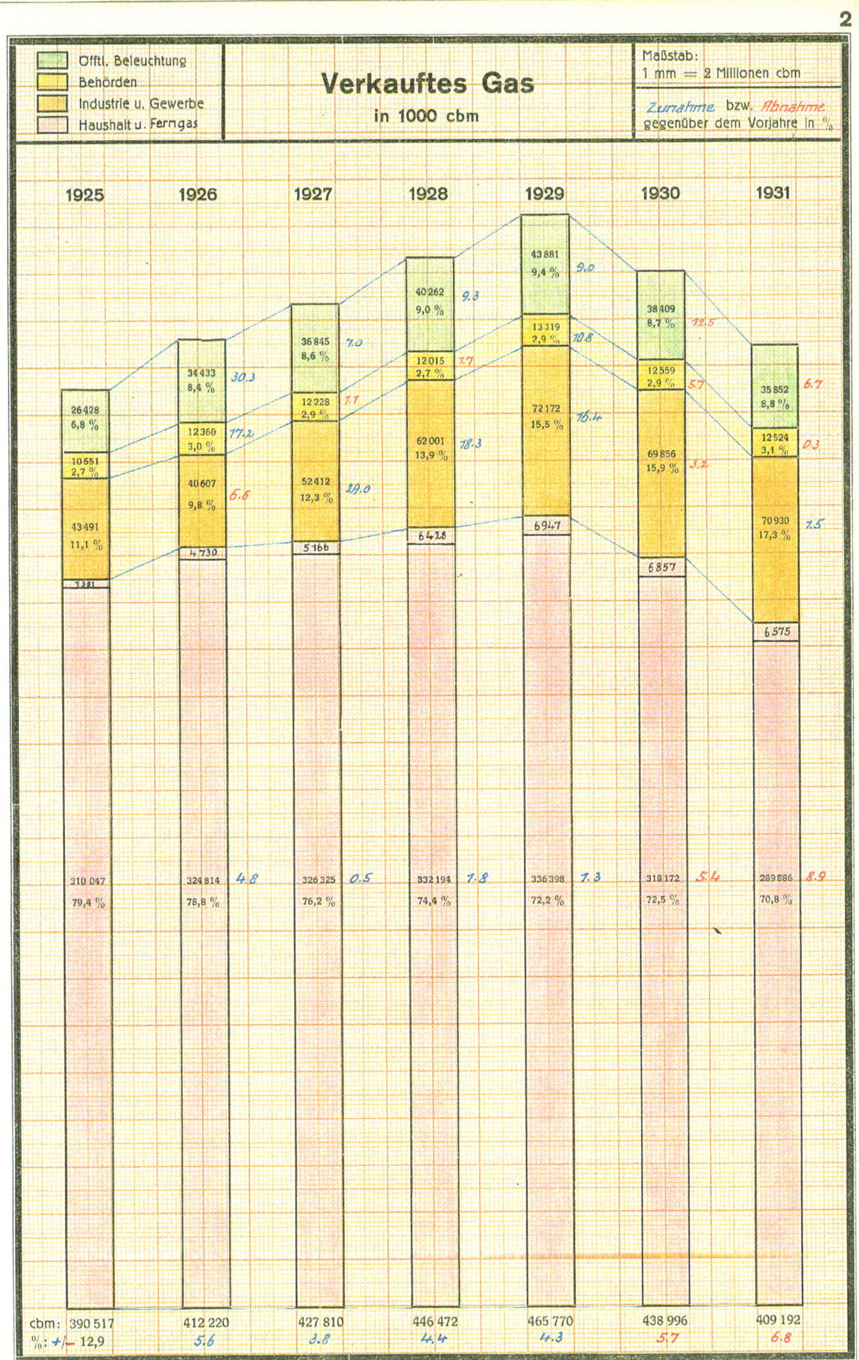

Figure 4.9

Gas sales in Berlin, 1925–1931

Source: Landesarchiv Berlin (LAB) A Rep. 259, no. 258.

Despite the incentives, many impoverished households found it increasingly hard to pay their utility bills. In the event of continuous nonpayment of charges, only the wastewater department was prohibited by regulation from terminating services. This was an option for the electricity, gas, and water utilities, but one they tried to avoid at all costs, for political reasons. As a proxy indicator of the hardship endured by low-income or unemployed consumers, the use of prepaid meters increased rapidly. The proportion of prepaid meters for gas supply in Berlin grew from 4.2 percent in 1926 to 12.8 percent in 1930.[164]

Apart from trying to shore up their revenue, the utilities pared back expenditure. The water and wastewater utilities stopped all major building projects, focusing on network maintenance and repair rather than expansion. Even construction on the sewage treatment plant at Waßmannsdorf was temporarily halted.[165] It was precisely these construction sites, though, that offered the best chance for the utilities to provide temporary jobs for the growing number of unemployed in Berlin. Primarily for this reason building bans were soon lifted. Bewag continued its building program through the Depression, earmarking 23.8 million Reichsmark for new infrastructure in 1931.[166] An emergency job scheme to provide 142,000 work days on Berlin's sewers for the unemployed, at a cost of 4.3 million Reichsmark, was approved by the city parliament after a lengthy debate in November 1932.[167] While cheap temporary jobs were being created on construction sites, more costly permanent ones were being cut. The labor force of Berlin's utilities was trimmed to reduce expenditure, albeit on a modest scale compared with the private sector. Between 1928 and 1932 the workforce of Bewag fell by 15 percent and of the wastewater utility by 25 percent.[168] At the same time, though, the number of people employed by Wassag actually increased by 7 percent.[169]

The most significant impact of the Depression on Berlin's utilities was the pressure they came under to increase their financial support of an increasingly beleaguered city budget. The city's finances were in a treble bind: as tax revenues declined sharply, expenditure on welfare rocketed and access to long-term loans was no longer available. The reduction in tax revenues was only partly due to the economic downturn. Reich and Prussian governments had consistently sought to consolidate their own finances at the expense of municipal budgets. While in the financial year 1924 Berlin had received 100.8 million Reichsmark of the total Reich and Prussian income and corporation tax revenue of 2.5 billion Reichsmark, in 1931 it received only 85 million out of the much increased total of 3.2 billion Reichsmark.[170] Second, the welfare budget became destabilized because support for the unemployed became the responsibility of the municipality once their eligibility for unemployment benefit expired. As a consequence, the number of unemployed claiming welfare benefits from the city rose from 32,000 in 1929 to over 300,000 in 1932.[171] This prompted an explosion in social welfare spending, from 54 million Reichsmark in 1924 to around 375 million in 1932.[172]

The third critical factor for Berlin's budget was that it was not able to convert the short-term credits needed to balance the budget into long-term loans. This was a product less of banking prudence than of a concerted national campaign against the spending policies of Germany's major cities. Since 1926 the right-wing press and political parties had been criticizing cities for allegedly living beyond their means. The underlying sentiment driving this campaign was anti-urban, anti-socialist, and often anti-republican. Berlin and its municipal government, so symbolic of all three, became a prime target. High expenditure by municipal enterprises was subjected to particular criticism, especially by those keen to reverse what they saw as unacceptable intrusions of the public sector into private markets. This campaign would not have had such political impact had it not been championed by the president of the Reichsbank, Hjalmar Schacht. In a well-publicized speech held in Bochum in November 1927 Schacht launched a massive attack on cities and their expenditure, leveling particular criticism at their practice of raising foreign loans for what he decried as "luxury spending."[173]

In Berlin's city council and parliament Schacht's speech was roundly rebuffed for damaging Berlin's credit and standing abroad. Schacht's core critique that foreign loans were being used to fund extravagant excesses of municipal socialism was rejected not only by the socialist SPD and KPD but also by the moderate DDP and Center Party and even the business-friendly DVP and Wirtschaftspartei.[174] They all shared the view, as expressed by Mayor Böß in a memo dated November 23, 1929, that foreign loans had been acquired only for "productive purposes," to fund expenditure on power stations, water works, and underground lines that were essential for Berlin's economic development.[175] How, Böß asked, did the Reichsbank president expect Berlin to meet demand for electricity that was increasing at an annual rate equivalent to the total electricity consumption of Munich? How did he envisage dealing with wastewater in Berlin that had increased in volume by 50 percent in just three years? Böß accused Schacht of ruining the municipal lending market and undermining the relationship between cities and business. Both proved true, with the Reichsbank blocking foreign loans to German cities and the domestic banking sector after 1928 no longer willing to convert Berlin's short-term debts into long-term loans.[176]

Given the financial strictures of this treble bind, Berlin's city council and a majority in parliament felt they had no option but to raise utility tariffs and introduce a surcharge on the utilities to help bail out the city. Without doing so, it was calculated, would result in the city's municipal enterprises contributing 26 million Reichsmark less to the 1930 budget than originally planned.[177] The debates on the tariffs and surcharges in the city parliament were fraught, as it was clear to all that any such additional burdens on the utilities would translate into increased hardship for already impoverished households. A growing rift emerged on the role of the utilities in the crisis, with the parties of the Weimar Coalition advocating increased tariffs in the interest of budget stability and the KPD and the Nazi Party (NSDAP) opposing what they decried as taxes on the poor.[178] The increases—ranging from 12.5 to 25 percent—were all approved in December 1929.[179] Even after these substantial price hikes Berlin's utility tariffs were still lower than in many German cities, as a diagram showing what money could buy in Germany's five largest cities in 1930 illustrated (see figure 4.10).

Together with an emergency surcharge, these tariff increases resulted in a sharp rise in the financial contributions made by the utilities to the city (see table 4.1 above). As these figures reveal, Bewag and Wassag more than doubled their financial contribution to the city budget from one year to the next at a time when demand for their services was declining sharply. Wassag's annual contribution was to even grow throughout the Depression, peaking at 19 million Reichsmark in 1932.[180] Taking into account the fiscal deficits of many other municipal enterprises, such as BVG, the net gain from all

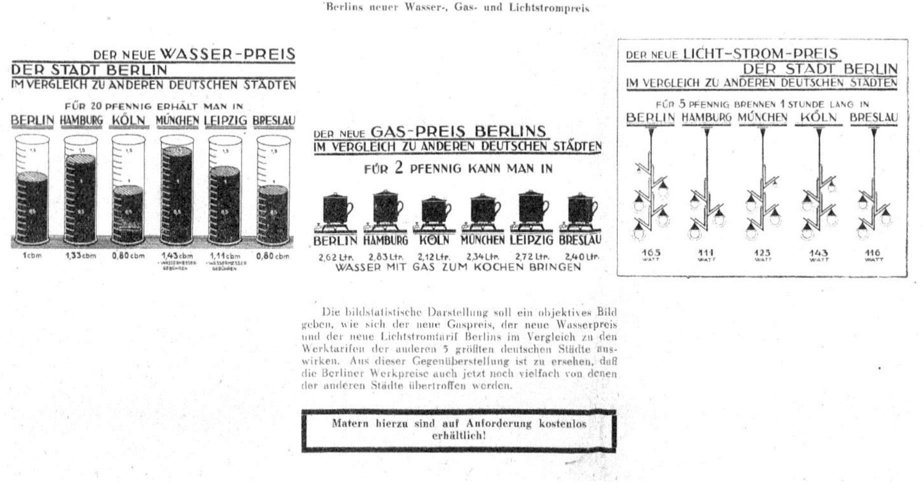

Figure 4.10
Comparison of tariffs for water, gas, and electricity in German cities, 1930
Source: Landesarchiv Berlin (LAB) A Rep. 255, no. 122.

these enterprises was large enough to cover 14.5 percent of the city's colossal budget deficit in 1930.[181] In Otto Büsch's words, "The revenues from the municipal enterprises remained throughout all the crisis years up to the end of the Weimar period a stabilizing factor for the city budget of the capital."[182]

While Berlin was being stabilized financially by its utilities, it was being destabilized politically by two other events in late 1929: the Sklarek scandal and municipal elections. The scandal began with the revelation of corrupt practices involving a clothing business, run by the Sklarek brothers, and a municipal enterprise that purchased goods from them for the city administration.[183] What turned an instance of malpractice into a political crisis was the response of the city government, and Mayor Böß in person. Böß was with a delegation from Berlin on a tour of cities in the United States at the time of both the Sklarek scandal and the Wall Street Crash. In hindsight, it was bitterly ironic that the principal purpose of their visit was to persuade US investors to grant loans to Bewag and BVG as a way of stabilizing the city budget. Owing to the limitations of communication and travel at the time, Böß failed to grasp the severity of the emergent crisis back home. There his political opponents were exploiting his absence to hype the scandal into a symbol of mismanagement in the Berlin administration and the whole "Böß system."[184] When it was revealed that Böß's wife had acquired a fur coat from the Sklareks at a very low price, there was no holding back the calls for Böß to resign. On his return from the United States in October, having been six weeks away, his position was untenable. A broken man, he was suspended from office with immediate effect and spent the remainder of the following year trying to get his name cleared.[185]

With the city reeling from the effects of the Sklarek scandal and the Wall Street Crash, elections to the city parliament were held on November 17, 1929. Given the charged political atmosphere, it was no surprise that the parties of the far left and right were the principal beneficiaries. The KPD's share of the vote increased by 6 percentage points to 24.6 percent and thus within striking distance of the SPD, at 28.4 percent, while the NSDAP increased its share from 1.5 percent in 1925 to 5.8 percent. This gave the Communists fifty-six and the National Socialists thirteen seats in the 225-seat assembly.[186] The parties of the Weimar Coalition (SPD, DDP, and Center) could muster only eighty-seven seats and, even with the sixteen seats of the right-liberal DVP, found themselves well short of a majority. The first sessions of the new city parliament were an augur of things to come. They ended in uproar and police interventions as representatives of the KPD and NSDAP, emboldened by their popular endorsement, sought to outdo each other in their vitriolic attacks on the city government.[187]

Sacrificed for the Indebted City

It was against this backdrop of a leaderless and beleaguered city government that an onslaught was made on the municipal ownership of Berlin's utilities. An early indication was the sale of Berlin's 46 percent shareholding in the private utility Elektrizitätswerk Südwest, which supplied electricity to parts of the city. This was proposed by the city council in March 1930 and resulted in Berlin receiving 25 million Reichsmark for all its shares plus 32 million Reichsmark compensation for loss of revenue.[188] In December 1930 a similar deal was being discussed behind closed doors for the gas sector. The original idea, vented by the privately owned Deutsche Gasgesellschaft, was for Berlin to sell its shares in this company that supplied, via its subsidiary Gasbetriebsgesellschaft, the southwest of the city.[189] Gasag protested strongly against the scheme, which—in the eyes of its director Alexander—would undermine efforts to unify gas services in Berlin.

By January 1931 the private sector was exploring options for privatizing Gasag itself, at least partially.[190] Carl Westphal, director of Thüringer Gasgesellschaft, discussed a form of public-private partnership for Gasag with the director-general of the energy conglomerate Preußen-Elektra, for whom he acted as chief negotiator with Berlin.[191] This model involved the sale of Gasag shares into a new holding company alongside Preußen-Elektra in return for a lump sum paid to Berlin. In this way Westphal hoped that political protest against the full privatization of Gasag could be avoided, while easing the path for a later amalgamation of the new holding company into Deutsche Gasgesellschaft.[192] By March 1931 the city council, unaware of this risk, was resigned to accepting the model, in which the city would have retained a 40 percent share of the operating company and a third of the holding company.[193] The prospect of getting a 90–100 million Reichsmark windfall from the sale was proving too tempting.[194] Then the whole deal got overshadowed by a much bigger fish—the sale of Bewag—and was subsequently shelved.

Bewag was by far the most lucrative of Berlin's utilities, returning handsome dividends to the city as electricity consumption blossomed. When the city ran into dire financial straits in 1930, Bewag, valued at 560 million Reichsmark, ranked top of the disposable assets list. Selling shares in Bewag could, in the eyes of a desperate city government, provide major relief to the city budget at a stroke.[195] Buying shares in Bewag could, for private investors and major power utilities, represent the most significant transaction in the history of the German electricity market.[196] In early 1931 a consortium of interested parties emerged that was led by the state banks of Prussia and the Reich and two of Germany's leading power utilities, Reichselektrowerke and

Preußen-Elektra. At an initial meeting with representatives from Berlin on February 28, 1931, the city clerk, Friedrich Lange, was informed "with a cold smile" that the consortium was prepared to lend Berlin an interim credit of 75 million Reichsmark if the city was willing to enter into negotiations over the sale of Bewag. As Lange reflected realistically in his diary that day: "We may not have taken on any obligation for the planned transaction, but we are powerless to resist strangulation by the Reich and Prussia, who had clearly reached agreement on the method beforehand."[197]

When the same offer was made formally to the city council on March 18, the condition was that the council had to agree by 12 o'clock the following day to enter into negotiations on selling Bewag to the consortium. When the council agreed to these bullying tactics, it was met by a wave of protests in the city parliament.[198] Representatives of all political parties were angry at the short notice given by the consortium, frustrated at the disrespect of the city parliament by the council, and appalled at the unfavorable conditions of the proposed loan and sale deal. Strong criticism of the sale plans came not only from the KPD and NSDAP, but from the otherwise loyal Center Party and even the national conservative DNVP, which was usually in favor of any initiative to privatize municipal enterprises. Only the SPD representative came out in favor of the city council, defending the sale as an act of fiscal necessity, but he criticized the high interest payments on the loan, the low valuation of Bewag, and the lack of protection from tariff increases.

The contract for the sale of Bewag was submitted by the consortium to the city council on May 2, 1931.[199] Drawing on the earlier model for Gasag, it envisaged the creation of a new holding company—the Berliner Kraft- und Licht (Bewag)-AG (BKL/Bewag)—into which Berlin would bring all its Bewag shares, as well as all of Bewag's plant and property for generating and distributing electricity in Berlin. This company had a total shareholding of 240 million Reichsmark. This was divided into a group of public shareholders with double voting rights, comprising the city of Berlin—with 38 million Reichsmark—Reichselektrowerke (21 million), and Preußen-Elektra (21 million) and a group of private investors with shares totaling 160 million Reichsmark. As figure 4.11 illustrates, half the shares of the new company were owned by foreign investors. Berlin retained a mere 15.8 percent shareholding, which even with its double voting rights effectively ended any significant decision-making power over the utility. In return the city received a one-off payment of 208.5 million Reichsmark. The conditions of the contract were hugely damaging to all the policies of networked municipalism that Berlin aspired to. The city was prohibited from setting up its own power utility and obliged to buy electricity only from the new company BKL/Bewag. Any later acquisition of shares by the city would not give the city any additional seats on the advisory

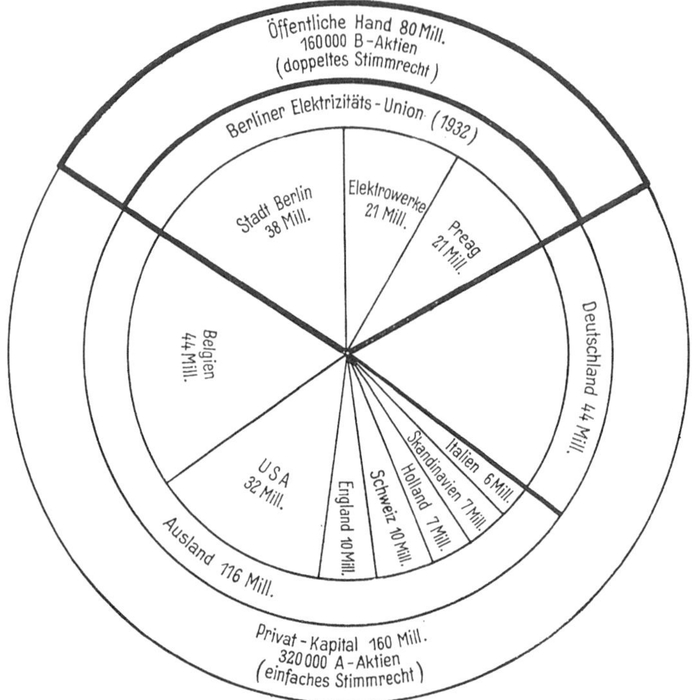

Figure 4.11
Shareholdings in the electricity utility BKL/Bewag, 1931
Source: Matschoß, Schulz, and Groß, *50 Jahre Berliner Elektrizitätswerke*, 67.

board. An option was granted for Berlin to buy back all shares after twenty-five years, but only on condition that it compensated the shareholders by paying them 110 Goldmark for each 100 Reichsmark share plus annual interest of 10 percent. There were no guarantees of employees' rights written into the contract. In paying out revenues from the new company, priority was to be given to shareholders over the concession fee for the city. Berlin would receive its concession fee of 22.4 million Reichsmark a year only if, after the deduction of the shareholder dividend, taxes, interest, and loan repayments, there remained a "sufficient surplus."[200]

Confronted with this offer, the city council was given a week—until 1 p.m. on May 9—to consider whether it accepted or rejected it.[201] The contract, it was made clear, was not negotiable. Since the original offer of a loan in March 1931, the city government had changed. A new mayor, the conservative Heinrich Sahm, had been appointed to replace the long-absent Gustav Böß, as had a new city treasurer, the social democrat

Bruno Asch.[202] More significantly, a reform of Berlin's municipal constitution, initiated by the Prussian state government, came into force on March 30, 1931, that strengthened the powers of the city council, and especially the mayor, whilst reducing the influence of the city parliament. Mayor Sahm made it clear at a press conference on May 2 that if the city parliament voted against the sale of Bewag, he would invoke his new powers and force the sale by decree. To substantiate the threat, he pointed out that the governor of the province of Brandenburg and Berlin had already approved the sale.[203]

The decisive debate in the city parliament took place on May 7–8, 1931.[204] Mayor Sahm presented the sale of Bewag as a painful, but unavoidable, measure to help offset the city's short-term debt of over 500 million Reichsmark at a time when tax revenues were rapidly declining. Delegates of the SPD, Center Party, Deutsche Staatspartei (formerly DDP), and DVP all expressed their huge reluctance, but agreed to support the bill out of fiscal necessity. The parliamentary leaders of the DNVP, Steiniger, and the NSDAP, Lippert, relished the opportunity to portray the sale as a symbolic failure of the governing alliance. The harshest criticism of the deal came, though, from the KPD and its delegate Schwenk: "Under the mask of municipal socialism you have in reality promoted the interests of a capitalist society based on exploitation and now we stand before the result, the fruits of your municipal policy."[205] The bill in favor of the sale was narrowly passed in the city parliament, by 104 votes to 100. The city council and the Bewag general assembly agreed to the sale the following day.

The Bewag sale had a profound impact on the key functions performed by the utility for the city. It is difficult to assess the significance of the financial windfall from the sale, given the dramatic dynamics of rising welfare spending and declining tax revenues. The fact that Berlin's total debt actually declined slightly between March 31, 1930, and December 31, 1932—from 1,201 million Reichsmark to 1,134 million—despite the ravages of the Depression suggests that the money from the privatization deal alleviated the fiscal crisis to some extent, but failed to resolve it, even temporarily. In the longer term, the sale proved damaging even for the city budget, as Berlin's revenue from the utility halved between 1930 and 1932, from 46.8 million Reichsmark to 21.4 million.[206] The effect on staff was dramatic: between 1931 and 1933 the number of employees at BKL/Bewag was reduced by 8 percent, wages and salaries were cut by an average of 16.5 percent, and staffing costs fell as a result by 23 percent.[207] Most significant, however, was the erosion of municipal control over electricity supply. The supervisory board of the utility was now dominated no longer by representatives of the city council and parliament, but by bankers and investors. Of the forty-six members only ten represented the city. The private investors were largely content to allow proceedings to be determined by delegates from the two major power utilities, Reichselektrowerke and Preußen-Elektra, backed by representatives of the Reich and Prussian state banks. Reichselektrowerke used its newfound powers to oblige Bewag to increase the proportion of imported electricity from 28 percent in 1929 to around 40 percent in 1932.[208]

The Bewag sale reverberated even into historiography. After the Second World War it became a cause célèbre of capitalist exploitation for commentators in East Berlin, meriting a monograph of meticulous research and Marxist interpretation by Martin Schmidt in 1957.[209] Otto Büsch's book on municipal enterprises of 1960 refuted this kind of critique, defending the Bewag sale without reservation as a necessity to save Berlin's budget from collapse.[210] Writing with the benefit of considerably more hindsight, Heinrich Tepasse has the last word: "After just sixteen years the city returned the flourishing Bewag utility to private ownership, receiving mediocre compensation in return and being downgraded to a second-class shareholder."[211]

Feeding and Housing the Impoverished City

For those who had lost their jobs, incomes, or even homes as a result of the Depression, the sale of shares in Bewag must have appeared a peripheral distraction. In December 1932 the number of registered unemployed in Berlin peaked at 636,000 people. Including their dependents, at least one third of the city's population was reliant on unemployment benefits of one form or another. Many responded by leaving the city in search of cheap land on the outskirts where they could eke out a living in informal, often illegal, settlements. It has been calculated that over 100,000 people moved out of Berlin from the late 1920s onward.[212] By 1933 these "wild settlers" occupied an estimated 120,000 plots of land, of which 50,000 lay within and 70,000 beyond the city's boundaries.[213]

Necessity on this scale became, for some, the mother of invention. During the early 1930s the urgent need to house and feed so many destitute people became embroiled in the long-standing debate over the future of Berlin's sewage farms. Those in favor of utilizing sewage to maximize food production saw in the Depression a golden opportunity for sewage farms to be revamped as sources of food, housing, and occupation for the unemployed. Their most prominent spokesman was the landscape architect Leberecht Migge.[214] Migge had collaborated in the 1920s with leading urban planners and architects, such as Bruno Taut and Martin Wagner, on major housing projects and was to shock them all later when he joined the NSDAP.[215] His passion in the early 1930s, though, was to demonstrate how people could live off their own land using urban waste and wastewater. The city council was interested enough in Migge's ideas to commission a report from him on how this thinking could be scaled up to deal with Berlin's mass unemployment crisis.

In 1932 Migge produced this report under the title "A Metropolis Colonizes! Berlin Feeds Itself! One Million Berliners Evacuate!"[216] Migge's point of departure was that Berlin's economy was unsustainable. Mass unemployment, economic decline, the limits of technological progress, and a collapse in moral standards were indicative, in his eyes, of the need to return to nature and, specifically, to the soil. He termed his solution "internal colonization," meaning, basically, meeting human needs with local resources. In the report he presented pages of calculations to demonstrate that the Berlin region could, theoretically, feed itself with vegetables, fruit, and meat and thereby avoid importing food from abroad. Key to these calculations was the productive use of solid and liquid wastes from the city. This is where the sewage farms and treatment plants came in. Neither, in Migge's opinion, was using resources effectively: the sewage farms were prone to failure from sewage overload and the sewage treatment plants allowed valuable nutrients to be lost to watercourses. What Migge proposed was to develop Berlin's sewage treatment works into factories of food production, using the nutrients in sewage as fertilizer. He calculated that up to one million settlers could live off 60,000 hectares of land extending in a 25 km radius around the city, producing annually 320,000 metric tons of produce for their own consumption and 280,000 metric tons for sale.[217] Berlin's existing and planned sewage treatment plants, surrounded by greenhouses, gardens, and settlements, would become "modern engines of municipal colonization" (see figure 4.12).[218]

Migge's monumental scheme of resource reuse and human resettlement may have been couched in a rationalist logic of resource efficiency, but the underlying sentiments were deeply dismissive of the people it was meant to benefit. Migge wanted to replace the emerging "wild settlements" with a highly ordered metabolic machine. The "constant stream of half-witted urban migrants" was to make way for a "trained army of convinced colonists."[219] Getting the "plebs" (*Proleten*) to grow their own food would go a long way, he argued, to solving "the social question of our time."[220] In order to prepare the land and buildings for mass settlement he thought it perfectly justifiable to demand sixty-three million man-days of mass labor.[221] Intriguingly, the initial response of the city council was not wholly dismissive. Indeed, in a pre-final version of the plan on the future of Berlin's wastewater treatment of September 1932, cited above, director Langbein of the wastewater utility included a lengthy, positive appraisal of Migge's idea of using the new treatment plants as settlement hubs for the urban poor.[222] In the final version, however, all references to Migge's scheme were removed.

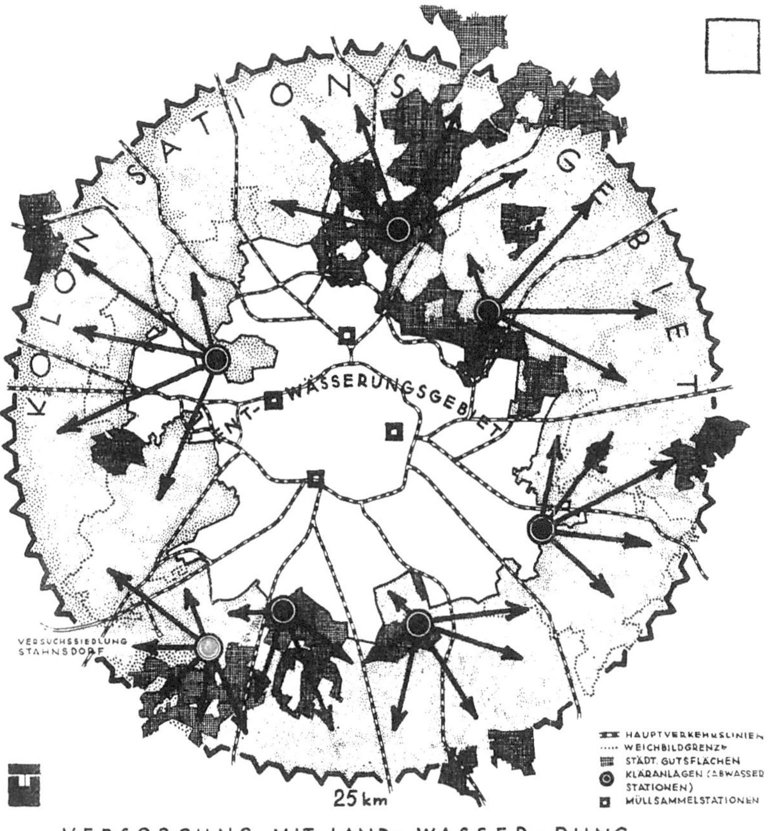

Figure 4.12

A vision for feeding the metropolis from recycled sewage settlements, 1932
Source: Migge, "Eine Weltstadt kolonisiert!," 50.

Politicizing the Networked City

If the privatization of Bewag represented an assault on everything that municipal infrastructure policy had stood for since the creation of Greater Berlin, Migge's scheme to relocate up to a million Berliners around giant nutrient recycling factories marked the transition from the rationalities of Weimar democracy to the irrationalities characteristic of the Nazi era. The period between 1924 and 1929 had been one of optimism that unleashed massive programs of expansion and modernization for all the city's infrastructure systems. Only in retrospect did this optimism appear naïve. At the time, there was ample evidence to justify the decisions taken and investments made by the city government and its utilities. The "networked city" of electricity, gas, water, and wastewater infrastructures was put, overall, to good use in improving living standards, supporting the local economy, and supplementing the municipal budget. Berlin was, in short, maximizing political utility from its utilities. This continued after 1929, but under radically different circumstances and with new priorities. The Depression plunged hundreds of thousands of Berliners into abject poverty and reaped havoc with city finances. This was, arguably, the finest hour of the city's utilities. Themselves struggling with falling demand and declining revenues, the electricity, gas, and water utilities increased substantially their financial support of the city from 1930 onward, ensuring that vital welfare payments were maintained to the burgeoning number of unemployed. Their relative stability during the economic crisis, however, attracted the interest of private investors at home and abroad. Berlin's growing municipal debt provided an excellent opportunity for competitors of the city's energy utilities to gain ownership of, and control over, them. In return for a one-off payment and paltry revenues, the city sacrificed the jewel in its crown—Bewag—to national energy conglomerates and foreign banks.

Meanwhile, the self-governing powers of Berlin's body politic were being undermined by a succession of state intrusions. In July 1930 the emergency decrees of the Brüning government imposed budgetary restrictions and obligatory taxes on the city.[223] Interventions by state commissars to control public spending became commonplace. In 1931 public banks were prohibited from lending money to local authorities. The new municipal constitution for Berlin of March 1931 effectively emasculated the city parliament by delegating debate to a new municipal committee (Stadtgemeindeausschuss) designed to depoliticize municipal government.[224] It also strengthened the powers of the mayor over the city's utilities. Tight controls were introduced to monitor their performance and limit their independence.[225] The stage was set for the future abuse of the networked city.

5 Subjugation to National Socialism

On June 12, 1933, the supervisory board of Berlin's electricity utility, Bewag, met fully for the first time since the Nazis had come to power four months earlier. It was always going to be a tense event. The supervisory board comprised not only municipal officers from Berlin and representatives of Prussian and Reich power utilities, but also delegates of leading international banks holding shares in the utility. Some of these bankers—as city officials had been keen to highlight in advance of the meeting—were Jews.

The meeting began innocuously enough with presentations by Bewag's two directors, Johannes Adolph and Martin Rehmer, on the historical development of electricity in Berlin and the city's power generation and distribution system.[1] Neither made any reference whatsoever to what had happened since January 1933. Then a Herr Plüer took the floor to talk about "staff issues." He launched into a diatribe against the way the utility had been run in the past and on how it was already changing under the new regime. He began by venting his frustration at the result of the works council elections held on March 1, 1933, in which only 520 of Bewag's 6,400 employees had voted for candidates of the Nazi Party. He reported how, at the first meeting of the new works council, this unfavorable result had prompted police to arrest its members and search its offices. Plüer and a Nazi colleague, he officiously stated, had subsequently taken over leadership of staff administration at Bewag and begun sacking what he termed "Marxist elements." At the time of the supervisory board meeting 129 workers and 163 administrative staff had been dismissed, including twenty-eight Jewish employees. As their dismissal was for "political" reasons, they were to receive no compensation. Plüer concluded by warning that this was just the beginning: a plan was currently being implemented to occupy all units at Bewag with National Socialists. We can only imagine how the international board members reacted to this shocking speech. According to the minutes it was followed by two further presentations by senior Bewag employees on electricity tariffs and advertising that also failed to mention the Nazi seizure of power, or indeed what they had just heard. To add a truly surreal touch to the event, the whole procedure was framed by a cooking demonstration, conducted by a nameless "lady" (the only woman present, according to the minutes), to show that it was possible to bake with electricity.

This charged meeting reveals so clearly the juxtaposition of the old and new politics shaping Berlin's electricity system. At this turning point in June 1933 we see the Bewag directors in a state of denial—acting as if nothing had changed—and Nazi insurgents relishing their new-gained powers over the utility. This chapter explores how far Nazi rule altered Berlin's infrastructure systems. In what ways did the new regime set out to shape the city's utilities in its own image? What continuities in infrastructure policy and management can be detected across the shift from democracy to dictatorship? How was Berlin—as a metropolis and a municipal entity—enrolled in National Socialist rule via infrastructure policy and what does this say about the role of cities in the Nazi scheme of things? This chapter explores how Nazi rule changed the way Berlin's infrastructure systems were managed and owned, the political goals they pursued, the roles of their consumers, and the resource flows they mediated, as well as their enrollment in state violence and preparations for war. First, though, some political context is needed to set the scene.

Nazi Rule in Berlin

Taking control of Berlin had always been a prime ambition of the National Socialists. This was partly, of course, because it was the nation's capital and seat of government. Presiding in Berlin meant presiding over Germany. Just as significant, however, was the symbolism attached to overpowering a city that represented so much that Hitler and his cohorts detested. To Nazis, Berlin epitomized the culturally "degenerate" metropolis, rampant economic liberalism, and powerful Marxist laborism.[2] It was also home to more than one in four of Germany's Jews. Exorcizing Germany's capital of these behemoths was, for Nazi leaders, an obsession long before Hitler came to power.

When Hitler appointed Joseph Goebbels—aged only twenty-nine—Gauleiter of Berlin in October 1926 it was with the intent of breaking the bastion of the "red" capital and rallying the extreme right around a reinvigorated local NSDAP.[3] Entering "the lion's den" was how Goebbels described his arrival.[4] His strategy was to provoke opponents with spectacular, violent actions designed to attract media attention. He used his own local party newspaper, *Der Angriff*, to incite hatred and built up a network of Nazi thugs in SA uniform to terrorize working-class neighborhoods.[5] Berlin's municipal government was a favorite target for attack and ridicule. Electorally, the NSDAP made a significant impression with these antics, but failed in its core objective to break the socialist block. In the last democratic elections of the Weimar Republic, held for the Reichstag in November 1932, it got 26 percent of the vote in Berlin, thereby overtaking the SPD (23.3 percent) but trailing the KPD (31 percent).[6]

Hitler's appointment as Reich chancellor on January 30, 1933, released a wave of political repression and violence targeting all opponents of the Nazi Party. It was in this context of hatred and fear that elections were held for the Berlin city parliament on March 12, resulting in a narrow majority for the NSDAP and its coalition partner, the neo-imperialist Scharz-Weiß-Rot alliance.[7] The very next day, Hermann Göring, in his new function as Prussian interior minister, summarily dismissed all the members of Berlin's city council with the exception of the mayor, Heinrich Sahm. Sahm survived in office only thanks to his close friendship with Reich president Hindenburg, whom the Nazis were reluctant to offend so early into their rule. Not trusting Sahm to toe the party line, Göring appointed Julius Lippert, who had led the NSDAP group in the city parliament since 1930, as state commissioner for Berlin.[8] As was made clear in a letter from the Interior Ministry of June 13, 1933, this new post was created to ensure that Berlin's administration was run "wholly according to the principles and spirit of the government of national upheaval."[9] Lippert was granted comprehensive powers to control and veto decisions made by the mayor. He effectively took over the city government, setting up his own units to mirror municipal departments.[10] Sahm, a firm believer in Prussian values of duty and loyalty, offered no resistance to being disempowered in this way and even joined the NSDAP in December 1933, thus lending a veneer of civility to the Nazi seizure of power in the city hall.[11] Only in December 1935 did he resign from office when, with Hindenburg now dead, the Nazis launched a campaign against him for buying at Jewish shops.

The Nazi purge of the city administration reached well beyond the city hall. Over the following months sixteen of the twenty borough mayors were sacked as part of the "political cleansing" campaign. Following the euphemistically termed national Law Restoring the Professional Civil Service of April 7, 1933, around 1,200 civil servants employed in the central and borough administrations of Berlin lost their jobs because they were Jews or members of the political opposition.[12] This figure represented 5.5 percent of all the city's civil servants. The proportion of those sacked for political and racial reasons was considerably higher for municipal laborers and public employees: around 10 percent and 22.4 percent, respectively.[13] Lippert, who had instigated the wave of dismissals, demanded in future utter loyalty to the National Socialist movement from all the city's civil servants.[14] Jewish employees who had survived the initial wave of dismissals lost their jobs following the racial Nuremberg Laws of 1935.[15]

The freshly elected city parliament played no role at all. It met for the last time on June 27, 1933, and was dissolved three months later. By then the socialist parties had long been banned, the liberal parties had been dissolved, and the conservative DNVP and Catholic Center Party had merged with the NSDAP.[16] The city parliament was replaced by a fig-leaf chamber, called the Stadtgemeindeausschuss, that comprised forty-five members proposed personally by Goebbels, as local Gauleiter. It was purely advisory and proved in practice irrelevant.[17] In an amendment to Berlin's municipal constitution, dated June 29, 1934, the powers of the city mayor over the district mayors were strengthened and the city acquired the status as Reich and state capital.[18] Overall, though, the debilitation of municipal self-government that Berlin experienced in 1933 was not unique, following a pattern detectable across the whole country.[19] The last vestiges of local self-government were formally removed with the German Local Authority Decree of January 30, 1935, which effectively enshrined core principles of National Socialist rule in local government.[20]

The vacated posts in Berlin's municipal administration were quickly filled with loyal party members or sympathizers. The fresh city and borough councillors were not all members of the NSDAP, so as to maintain a semblance of inclusivity. Many were, though, being recruited largely from among the 102 NSDAP deputies elected in either the 1929 or 1933 elections.[21] It was such veterans (*alte Kämpfer*) of Nazi organizations that were the prime beneficiaries of the job windfall. It is estimated that 8,000 local NSDAP members received posts in Berlin's municipal administration in reward for their loyalty to the cause.[22] Selected by virtue of party allegiance rather than professional skills, their impact on the competence and orientation of public administration in the city can be readily surmised. Finding Nazi Party members to fill jobs was, within a few months, not an issue anyway. Following Hitler's appointment as Reich chancellor, thousands of Berliners joined the NSDAP out of conviction or expediency. By January 1, 1935, the Berlin party boasted 138,117 members.[23]

The leadership of municipal affairs in Berlin was in no way resolved by the departure of Mayor Sahm in 1935. Competition over the power to shape the city—de facto or de jure—was fierce, as might be expected for the Reich capital. In the years up to the war it manifested itself in ways that illustrate well the contradictions involved in pursuing the so-called führer principle in a municipal context. Personal rivalries combined with party prerogatives, interministerial bickering, and proximity to Hitler to render Berlin's city government particularly prone to the vagaries of Nazism.

Lippert was able to strengthen his authority over the city government in the Law on the Constitution and Administration of the Reich Capital Berlin of December 1, 1936.[24] This law amalgamated his existing office of state commissioner for Berlin with that of the city mayor into a new office entitled Stadtpräsident, transforming what had been a temporary post into a permanent one. It also created a legal quandary by unifying a supervisory state entity with a subordinate municipal one.[25] Constitutional affronts of this kind were taken in their stride by senior Nazis in pursuit of self-aggrandizement. Lippert, however, was not the only leading Nazi to have his finger in the pie. The 1936 law also granted Goebbels, as party Gauleiter for Berlin, extensive new powers over the city government.[26] Henceforth, all senior appointments required his approval and all major decisions had to be vetted by him. This curious construct institutionalized the duality of party and state in running the city and perpetuated the existing rivalry between Gauleiter Goebbels and Stadtpräsident Lippert.[27] This rivalry was weighted heavily in favor of Goebbels. His power as Reich propaganda minister and confidante of Hitler ensured that Lippert always remained in his shadow in Berlin.

Within weeks of Lippert being made Stadtpräsident, his authority—and that of the municipal government—was undermined on a second front. On January 30, 1937, four years to the day since becoming Reich chancellor, Hitler appointed Albert Speer as Inspector General of Buildings in the Nation's Capital, granting him exclusive powers over urban planning in Berlin. Speer was entrusted with the monumental task of rebuilding Berlin in Hitler's image. Hitler had become obsessed with transforming Berlin into a new "world capital," called Germania, as a fitting demonstration of German might.[28] He saw in the young architect, who had previously designed his new Reich chancellery, the requisite combination of personal devotion and ruthless ambition to put this fantasy into practice. To guarantee Speer a free hand in the venture, Hitler decreed that Speer's staff should not be answerable to either a government agency or a municipal council. The Inspector General for Buildings (GBI) was granted special powers as the supreme planning authority for all Berlin, effectively eliminating municipal autonomy over issues of urban development.[29] In the words of Martin Kitchen, "Berlin's town planning was no longer a municipal affair, but was solely in the hands of Professor Speer."[30] The GBI could determine building zones by decree, confiscate property, and commission demolition without consulting the city government. Speer's approval was required for all new buildings in Berlin with a volume of over 50,000 cubic meters and any building in areas scheduled for redevelopment that cost more than the paltry sum of 5,000 Reichsmark.[31] This, however, was not enough for Speer. In practice, his actions as inspector general "showed a sovereign disregard for the law and established institutional practice."[32] He expanded his authority over Berlin on an almost weekly basis, causing massive disruption to procedures.[33] Any attempt by authorities—state or municipal—to circumvent the GBI was met with reprisals.[34]

The *Gleichschaltung* of Berlin's Utilities

How did this so-called enforced conformity (*Gleichschaltung*) of political and administrative life in Berlin as a whole translate into the management and operation of its energy and water/wastewater utilities? The immediate impact, in March 1933, was the dismissal from their respective supervisory boards of those councillors and deputies who belonged to socialist or liberal parties.[35] By June, only representatives of the NSDAP, DNVP, or sympathizers with the new regime sat on these supervisory bodies of Berlin's electricity, gas, and water utilities. In the case of the partially privatized BKL/Bewag, "political cleansing" of the supervisory board meant dealing with potential opposition among its foreign shareholders. That some foreign shareholders were deeply disturbed by events was revealed in a meeting of the board on June 29, 1933, where a row erupted between one of them and a Nazi representative over the future trustworthiness of Bewag.[36] Correspondence between Bewag and city officials in 1936 reveals how the draw for future board members was to be rigged so as to avoid the appointment of members of the Belgian Sofina consortium or of people of non-Aryan descent.[37]

The dismissal of utility directors was, by contrast, less common initially, with experiences varying between sectors. In the case of the gas utility Gasag, there is clear evidence of politically motivated dismissal of senior staff on a major scale. One of Gasag's three directors, Adolf Schmidt, was dismissed without cause on March 25, 1933, and subsequently charged with corruption after the deputy mayor requested his arrest by the Gestapo.[38] The other two, Rohde and Alexander, were relieved of their posts in December 1933, following the arrest of Alexander in July 1933 for allegedly "spreading horror stories and supporting communist insurgency."[39] One of Gasag's plant managers, Hohmann, was sacked in July 1933 for his "political views and character."[40] At the electricity utility Bewag, its director responsible for sales, Robert Kauffmann, was arrested in March 1933 and forced to resign his post for being a Jew and a member of the national leadership of the liberal DDP.[41] He received no pension and only part of the agreed compensation.

Otherwise, continuity of leadership was the order of the day, at least for the time being. Those willing to work with the new regime were allowed to stay on, especially if they were nearing the end of their careers. The director of the wastewater utility, Fritz Langbein, remained in office until his retirement in April 1936, having joined the NSDAP in the meantime.[42] Carl Kühne, director of the Berlin water utility since 1914, also left only when he reached retirement age, in December 1937. His praise of the "national uprising" of 1933 in several documents attests to his having, at the very least, accommodated the Nazi regime.[43] At Bewag, the two directors encountered in the introductory story to this chapter had different fates. Martin Rehmer died after a prolonged illness in February 1935, while Johannes Adolph remained in office, according to the records, until at least 1940.[44] Evidence suggests that he, too, could find favor in Nazi ideology.[45]

A notable case of cross-regime continuity was within the city administration itself. The senior officer responsible for supervising Berlin's municipal enterprises, Bruno Ziethen, who had served Berlin since the early 1920s, remained in office, adapting with apparent alacrity to his new political masters. Already in April 1933 he was expressing his concern about the need to increase the number of National Socialist delegates on Bewag's supervisory board in a confidential memo to the deputy mayor, advising him on how to proceed.[46] Ziethen was also the officer who, in preparation of the supervisory board meeting of June 12, 1933, profiled in the introduction to this chapter, pointed out for internal eyes only which of the foreign bankers attending were Jews. Such enthusiasm for the Nazi cause within municipal administrations—and not merely by new Nazi appointees—is a phenomenon that has been highlighted in recent research of Nazi rule in cities.[47]

With support in the city government and administration assured, the local Nazi leadership could tolerate utility directors who were not party members.[48] When these posts did become vacant, however, the opportunity was usually seized to appoint loyal National Socialists. New appointments to Bewag's board of directors were all members of the NSDAP: Carl Krecke (May 1, 1934), Richard Fischer (April 1, 1939), and Erich Nain (April 1, 1939).[49] When the water utility director Kühne retired, he was replaced in 1937 by a prominent Berlin party member, Karl Kasper. Kasper was typical of a local Nazi careerist, having joined the party in 1925, been elected to the city parliament in March 1933, and appointed by Goebbels as one of the representatives to the Stadtgemeindeausschuss in 1934.[50] Trained as an engineer, he was selected to sit on the supervisory boards of several of Berlin's municipal enterprises, positions he used to influence staff appointments in the utilities.[51] He was, therefore, well placed to acquire for himself the post of director of the water utility when it became vacant, thereby increasing his monthly salary from 500 to 2,800 Reichsmark.[52] The new directors of the city's gas utility, Walter Hoffmann, and wastewater utility, Otto Pallasch, were both at least strongly sympathetic to the Nazi cause.

Despite replacing vacant posts of utility directors with its supporters, the local Nazi leadership was clearly not satisfied with its control over Berlin's utilities. To the outside world the utilities presented themselves as loyal cogs in the grinding wheel of National Socialist rule. The "gifts" made to the Adolf Hitler Donation Fund, set at 5 percent of gross annual wages, were a visible symbol of this subservience to the regime (see figure 5.1).[53] Internal correspondence suggests, however, that Bewag continued to cultivate a

Adolf-Hitler-Spende der deutschen Wirtschaft

Bescheinigung

D Nr. 134530

Berliner Städtische Elektrizitätswerke
Akt.-Ges.

Berlin NW 7

ist an der »Adolf-Hitler-Spende der deutschen Wirtschaft« mit einem Betrag von

---------------111.815,00--------------- Reichsmark beteiligt.

Berlin, im Juni 1934

Sammlungen bei dem Inhaber dieser Bescheinigung sind allen Angehörigen, Dienststellen und Einrichtungen der NSDAP von der Parteileitung der NSDAP verboten, wenn der Inhaber der Bescheinigung die entsprechenden Zahlungsbelege (siehe Sammlungsverbot) vorlegen kann.

Das Kuratorium

Verbindungsstab der N.S.D.A.P. Berlin

Reichsdruckerei, Berlin

Figure 5.1
Certificate of payment to the Adolf Hitler Donation Fund by Bewag
Source: Landesarchiv Berlin (LAB) A Rep. 256, no. 183.

degree of self-dependence from the city administration, owing largely to its broad and international shareholding. In December 1936 deputy Gauleiter Görlitzer accepted a request by State Commissioner Lippert to become a member of Bewag's supervisory board in order to see for himself how foreign and domestic shareholders were blocking their political leadership of the company.[54] When Lippert became Stadtpräsident the following month he ensured that he became chairman of the supervisory board. Clearly, this did not have the desired effect, for in August 1937 he was complaining to Bewag director Krecke, himself a prominent Nazi ideologue, about the unwillingness of the company's external investors to accept the altered political circumstances. He called on the company's board of directors to explore how "the current significant differences of opinion could be straightened out."[55]

How far the Nazi regime was able to influence the internal organization and work environment of Berlin's utilities is difficult to ascertain, but the picture that emerges from the available sources is an ambivalent one. We know that the workforce of Berlin's municipal enterprises was initially not receptive to the new regime at all. Elections to works councils in early March 1933 gave the National Socialist Factory Cell Organization (NSBO) only 5 percent of the total vote in all municipal enterprises. The figures were even lower for works council elections in Bewag (2 percent) and Gasag (3.8 percent).[56] Reprisals came in the form of dismissals of political opponents in the utilities, although figures are hard to come by. As cited above, 292 members of staff at Bewag had lost their jobs this way by June 1933. By September 1934, twenty-nine workers at Gasag had been dismissed for political reasons.[57]

Huge efforts were made by the Nazis to win over the labor force in the utilities. Following the immediate prohibition of trade unions and dissolution of works councils, the NSDAP inserted its own labor organizations to promote loyalty to the new regime and attract support for its ideology with a combination of educational and recreational activities. The best documented of these organizations is the works association (*Werkverein*) at Bewag. It was set up in October 1933 as an after-work club for all Bewag employees, offering them a huge range of activities designed to train the body and mold the mind to National Socialist ideals. Apart from attending regular events for around a dozen types of sport, employees were encouraged to become members of groups dedicated to dancing, painting, music, photography, walking, or the theater. In this way, it was claimed, they would overcome the class differences, party political disputes, and individualist behavior of the past and become part of a "community of the people" (*Volksgemeinschaft*) dedicated to restoring Germany's position in the world. Major sports events were organized to strengthen the spirit of national and racial destiny. The Bewag works association had its own monthly magazine, called *Der Stromkreis*, which, in its own words, was dedicated to inspire its readers "with the spirit of true comradeship and inner solidarity demanded by our chancellor Adolf Hitler" (see figure 5.2). Articles on military preparedness, communist sabotage, and eugenics left no doubt as to the political mission of the publication.

Other articles in *Der Stromkreis* indicate that the works association was not fulfilling expectations. In 1935 an editorial under the title "Where Are the Others?" complained that turnout was unacceptably low at events organized by the works association as well as the Nazi German Labor Front (DAF). Compulsory attendance was suggested to make up for an obvious lack of comradeship. At around the same time, however, Nazi members at Bewag were reporting that the workforce had become politically indifferent or even pro-Nazi following the strategic placement of National Socialists across all units of the utility.[58] Repression was, clearly, cowing any opposition. Those who acquiesced to the regime could be rewarded with secure employment. The electricity and water utilities increased their workforce significantly during the course of the 1930s.[59] Those

Figure 5.2

Title page of the first edition of the Bewag newsletter *Der Stromkreis*

Source: *Der Stromkreis* 1 (1933), title page. Copyright: Bewag/Vattenfall.

who actively supported it could hope for promotion or privileges. Although figures on membership of the NSDAP within each of Berlin's utilities are not available, statistics on postwar denazification do provide some proxy evidence. Between April and December 1945, 1,426 Bewag employees and 1,027 Gasag employees were dismissed for having been members of the Nazi Party or its organizations.[60] As a proportion of 1938 employment data, these figures represent approximately 17 percent of the workforce at both Bewag and Gasag: a high rate of party membership for municipal enterprises that had prided themselves on their pro-republican credentials.

Subordinating Municipal to National Interests

The most visible change to infrastructure policy in Berlin after 1933 lay in the subordination of municipal interests to those of party and state. Serving the German *Volk*, rather than Berliners, became the new raison d'être for the city's utilities. This tectonic shift manifested itself in four ways: first, the enrollment of Berlin's infrastructure systems in acts of national symbolism; second, the fusion of municipal and national functions by key utility directors; third, the absence of clear strategic direction for Berlin's utilities; and fourth, the submission of municipal to national energy policy.

If the public image of urban infrastructure during the Weimar Republic had been fashioned by ceremonial openings of power stations and other icons to modernity, in the Nazi era it was shaped by celebratory acts of homage to Hitler and the German nation.[61] Berlin's utilities hit the news when serving the "führer." The first opportunity presented itself on May 1, 1933, when Hitler spoke to a mass audience on Tempelhofer Feld, a public space so full that it was described by an eye witness as "black with people."[62] Bewag was entrusted with providing the lighting for this special occasion, requiring 3,600 meters of low-voltage cables and costing some 25,000 Reichsmark.[63] The effect was clearly dramatic, as Heinrich Hauser reported: "The field was transformed into a completely different landscape. High above the sea of heads rose gigantic floodlighting gantries, which looked like ancient war machines, like the movable towers used to assault cities."[64] The military metaphor was to prove prophetic. At the time, though, the floodlighting display was a source of marvel that heralded Hitler's speech.

A second speech by Hitler, this time a radio broadcast given on November 10, 1933, presented Bewag with a further opportunity to demonstrate its technical proficiency in serving the dictator.[65] The issue at stake here was not providing electricity for the radio broadcast itself, but coping with the severe shifts in electricity demand that it entailed. As Hitler's radio speech was obligatory listening in all places of work, machines across the country stood still at exactly the same time during the broadcast. The massive drop

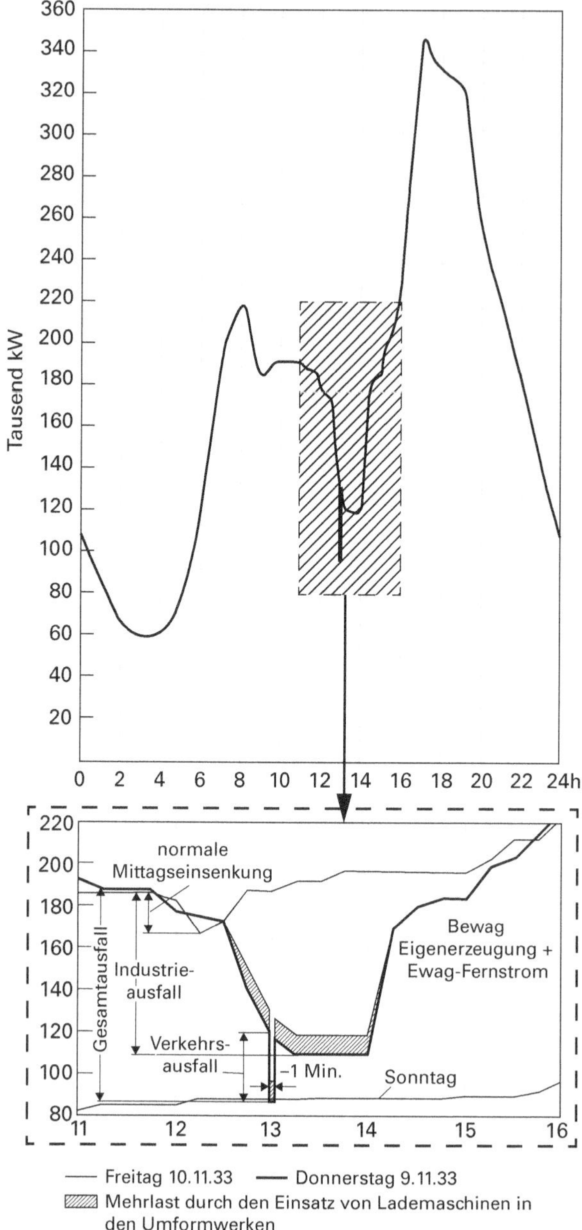

Figure 5.3

Diagram illustrating drop in electricity use during Hitler's speech, November 10, 1933

Source: Matschoß, Schulz, and Groß, *50 Jahre Berliner Elektrizitätswerke*, 206.

in electricity use in Berlin is illustrated by the graph in figure 5.3.[66] Judging by the publicity accorded to this achievement, Bewag was hugely proud of being able to shut down and subsequently power up its generators before and after the speech without any disruption to service.

The Olympic Games in Berlin in the summer of 1936 posed an even greater challenge to load management. Although many had expected electricity consumption to drop sharply during the sports events, Bewag was proved right in predicting more differentiated shifts in demand curves, involving less consumption in the workplace, but much more for rail transport to and from the sports stadia and for street lighting to impress the international visitors. Bewag was again in self-congratulatory mode for mastering the sharp shifts in demand involved in powering the Berlin Olympics and thereby showcasing German prowess on and off the field (see figure 5.4).[67] Gasag was also keen to advertise its contribution to the Berlin Olympics, involving a major investment program for gas lamps to light the new streets around the Olympic stadium. Pride of place, though, was the huge Olympic flame in the Lustgarten, measuring 1.8 meters in diameter, which Gasag fired using an extraordinary 200 cubic meters of gas per hour.[68]

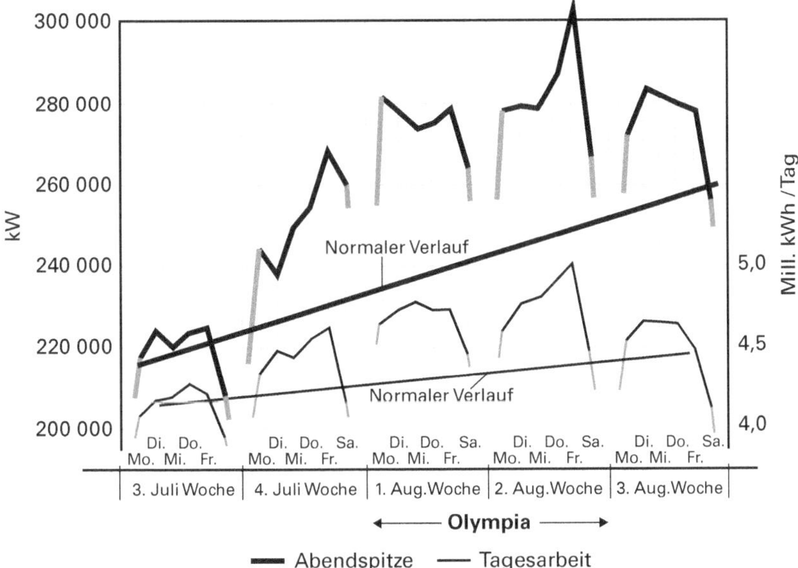

Figure 5.4
Electricity demand curves during the Berlin Olympic Games, 1936
Source: *Der Stromkreis* 3, no. 9 (1936), 246–247. Copyright: Bewag/Vattenfall.

A final example of Berlin's utilities supporting an event of national celebration in the city was the official inauguration of the east-west axis designed by Speer as part of the Germania project, on April 21, 1939. Bewag was heavily involved in providing the electricity required for the new street lighting (see figure 5.5). The tribute paid to this event by Bewag in its works magazine is unwittingly indicative of the shift in priorities from the municipal to the national: "What will remain in our memory is the inimitable achievement for our führer and his national capital, the trusted comradeship and common effort involved in the work, and, not least, a new chapter in the development of public lighting in Berlin."[69]

The second dimension to the intrusion of national politics into the management of Berlin's utilities lay in the national functions performed by several of their directors. Combining offices of party and state, or between local and national governments, is a familiar feature of the Nazi dictatorship.[70] What is distinctive about Berlin's utilities is

Figure 5.5
Festive lighting of the east-west axis in Berlin
Source: *Der Stromkreis* 6, no. 5 (1939), title page. Copyright: Bewag/Vattenfall.

how this common practice of personal union in leadership roles of party and state was extended to include municipal enterprises in the capital. Senior Nazis came to run the city's utilities while simultaneously leading important national or regional organizations of the NSDAP and civil engineering.

One of these figures was Carl Krecke, director of Bewag since May 1934 and later chair of the board of directors. Krecke, a Nazi party member, was appointed head of the Reich Group for Energy (Reichsgruppe Energiewirtschaft) the following month, acquiring for himself the grandiose title "Führer of German Energy."[71] The Reich Group for Energy was an umbrella organization for the energy sector, rather than a state body, yet it possessed supervisory powers over energy companies.[72] This structure of obfuscation allowed the NSDAP, personified by Krecke, to set national policy agendas in the party's image. What these policy priorities were was initially far from clear. The NSDAP had no coherent policy on energy when it came to power.[73] Krecke himself favored centralization of the energy sector as a prerequisite of Germany's future. This became the dominant argument during the early Nazi years, culminating in the Energy Act of 1935 that enshrined concentration as the leitmotiv of electricity generation in large-scale power plants, institutionalized the national grid, and relegated municipal utilities to supplementary actors of national energy policy.[74] Krecke portrayed the Energy Act as a triumph of order over chaos, replacing the patchwork structures of the past with unified leadership and uniform organizations for electricity and gas provision.[75] Although himself the director of a municipal electricity utility, he made no bones about prioritizing national over municipal models of energy provision. In his many speeches and publications he presented the centralization of the German energy market as an essential precondition for maximizing energy provision in times of peace and war. Krecke was able to direct national energy policy along these lines until his death in September 1938. His successor as Bewag director, Richard Fischer, was made head of the Reich Unit for the Electricity Industry, a subordinate body of the Reich Group for Energy, thus perpetuating the union of the capital's electricity utility and national energy agencies under the aegis of the NSDAP.[76]

Karl Kasper, who succeeded Carl Kühne as director of the Berlin water utility in December 1937, had previously held office not only in leading municipal bodies, as already described, but also in the local NSDAP organization.[77] Within the Gauleitung for Berlin he headed both the local Office for Technology (Gauamt für Technik) and the municipal economy department of the Office for Municipal Policy (Amt für Kommunalpolitik).[78] This made him responsible for implementing the four-year plan of 1936 in Berlin's utilities. Drawing on his additional position on the supervisory boards of all three utilities, he aimed to turn them, in his own words, into "National Socialist model enterprises."[79] As part of this venture he was entrusted by Fritz Todt, the head of the party's Central Office for Technology (Hauptamt für Technik), with restructuring Berlin's energy sector. This envisaged, essentially, stronger integration of local electricity and gas systems into national grids and national resource planning. A similar line was taken in the field of water resources management. Kasper was a strong proponent of schemes to introduce comprehensive national planning of water resources around river basins.[80] He viewed this as essential for maximizing use of available water resources and for planning new settlements, also in Berlin. In July 1943, while still running the Berlin water utility, he was made deputy head of the national Economic Group for Gas and Water Supply (Wirtschaftsgruppe Gas- und Wasserversorgung) within the Reich Chamber of Economics and commissioner for water conservation for the entire country.[81]

The accumulation of posts in party, business, and administration at local and national levels, as exemplified by Krecke and Kasper, was characteristic of Nazi rule and marked a significant break with past practices. Such proliferation of offices in party and state has been interpreted by some historians as undermining effective government, creating an "organized chaos" distinctive of the Nazi regime.[82] This view has come in for criticism recently for overlooking the ideological consensus that often existed across party, business, and administration agencies and that could inspire activism around a common cause.[83] For engineers, in particular, the call to serve the common good of the people (*Volksgemeinschaft*) had a strong appeal.[84] The National Socialist ethos of subordinating individual gain to the benefit of the German people ("*Gemeinnutz vor Eigennutz*") resonated with engineers' aspirations to use technology to advance society as a whole.[85] Moreover, engineers had been underrepresented in key administrative posts before 1933.[86] Following the emasculation of their professional organizations and subordination to National Socialist agencies, many engineers looked to the new regime to gain the political and societal status denied them in the past. They were encouraged in this view by Nazi organizations, such as the Combat League for German Architects and Engineers (Kampfbund Deutscher Architekten und Ingenieure) and the Nazi engineering journal *Deutsche Technik*, as well as by the charismatic figure of Fritz Todt.[87] The message transmitted by these mouthpieces of dictatorship was that the new regime would herald the era of engineers.[88]

For all the talk about the importance of infrastructure to the national cause and the need to bring municipal utilities into line, it is highly revealing that, in Berlin at least, no strategic reorientation took place. This marks the third dimension to the subordination of municipal to national priorities. While the Weimar era had witnessed a raft of strategy documents setting out the future development of the city's electricity, gas, water, and wastewater services, during the twelve years of Nazi dictatorship there were none. Any shifts in infrastructure management took the form of ad hoc schemes inspired by national policy, such as the four-year plan or Speer's plans for Germania, addressed below. This was, of course, characteristic of National Socialist rule, which favored interventionist activism over considered deliberation. It was also, though, indicative of the lack of any clear development strategy for Berlin's utilities. Most investments in the city's infrastructure during the Nazi era followed the plans devised in the late 1920s. Work on the new sewage treatment plants or the water supply network continued as originally planned. Despite the criticism heaped on Berlin's utilities by the Nazis prior to 1933, when they actually took control they clearly had no alternative vision for them, beyond kowtowing to national energy and water policy and otherwise following the existing development pathway.

The fourth, and final, dimension relates to the contractual obligations required of Berlin's utilities with national energy providers. The national power utility Reichselektrowerke used its shareholding of Bewag to ensure its electricity delivery contract was extended in 1936 for twenty years, to 1956.[89] This guaranteed that one-third of the electricity distributed by Bewag was imported from the national energy provider. Intrusion into Berlin's gas market required greater persistence and coercion. A renewed initiative by Ruhrgas to supply Berlin with gas via a long-distance pipeline after the Nazi seizure of power revealed a massive split in opinion. Gasag and the city government were both, as in the past, adamantly opposed to the scheme. They argued that long-distance supply from the Ruhr would make Berlin hugely dependent on a single pipeline, increase the price of gas by 40 percent, require investment costs of 12.7 million Reichsmark for the city, and lose 1,300 jobs in the city with the closure of three of the city's five gas works.[90] The Ruhrgas offer was so disadvantageous that the Office for Technology of the Berlin Gauleitung, run by Kasper, felt obliged to produce a scathing report, published in 1934.[91] In it, the local NSDAP accused Ruhrgas of trying to offload overcapacity in gas production and offset losses incurred in constructing its gas pipeline around Hanover. Building on the arguments of Gasag, the report pointed out that Berlin's gas works had contracted out work to local businesses to the tune of 1,338,000 Reichsmark in 1933 and were therefore instrumental in tackling mass unemployment in the city.[92] The prime argument made against the Ruhrgas proposals, though, was that the pipeline would be vulnerable to any French attack on German soil. In such a scenario, "the Berlin population would be without any gas at all after just two days."[93] This kind of opposition ensured that, in the short term, the scheme was shelved, as both sides acknowledged, in a joint commission, that the cost in terms of jobs lost would be too high politically.

By 1936, however, Gasag director Hoffmann was coming under considerable pressure from Krecke and his Reich Group for Energy to agree to a long-distance gas connection to Berlin.[94] The principal argument used by the party now was that, under the new regime, energy resources were a national public good which could no longer be left to local energy utilities serving the particular interests of municipal governments. In 1939 the order was given by the national government for Ruhrgas to build a pipeline from Reichswerke Hermann Göring in Watenstedt, near Salzgitter, to Berlin, to secure gas supply for the munitions industry in the capital.[95] The contract with Berlin was signed on August 22, 1939, despite protests by Gasag at the unfavorable terms, and supply began on October 24, 1940. On January 16, 1943, the pipeline's transfer station at Spandau was destroyed during a bombing raid, leaving the city without imported gas for weeks.[96]

Consumption as a Duty to the *Volk*

Interest in the consumer as a vital component of a well-functioning infrastructure system did not subside under Nazi rule, but took on new significance in line with shifting political priorities.[97] Measures to manage demand for electricity and gas were applied initially to stimulate employment and generate a sense of well-being, subsequently to combat resource waste, and during the war to free up energy for the armaments industry.

Experience during the Depression had shown how household consumption could bolster sales of electricity suffering from industrial decline. In 1933 a national alliance of manufacturers and retailers of the electrical sector, called Elektrofront, was formed to promote electrification in homes and the sale of electrical appliances.[98] In Berlin, the hire purchase scheme Elektrissima, originally introduced in 1926, was pursued with renewed vigor, promoting the sale of electrical household goods.[99] Among the appliances advertised was the infamous Volksempfänger radio, of which 200 were sold a day in December 1933.[100] Bewag's monthly magazine, *Der Stromkreis*, was full of articles in the mid-1930s advertising electrical appliances and calling on Berliners to use more electricity in the national interest (see figure 5.6).[101] The Bewag workforce was even encouraged to give electrical appliances to their family and friends as Christmas gifts in acts of national solidarity, including oddities like tie presses, foot warming plates, and beer warmers.[102] The gas sector followed the same logic, with Gasag setting up a program in 1933 to stimulate demand for new gas connections and the sale of gas appliances, such as water heaters.

Mass advertising campaigns appear to have generated a surge in sales of household appliances in Berlin, as opposed to elsewhere across the country.[103] As Martina Heßler

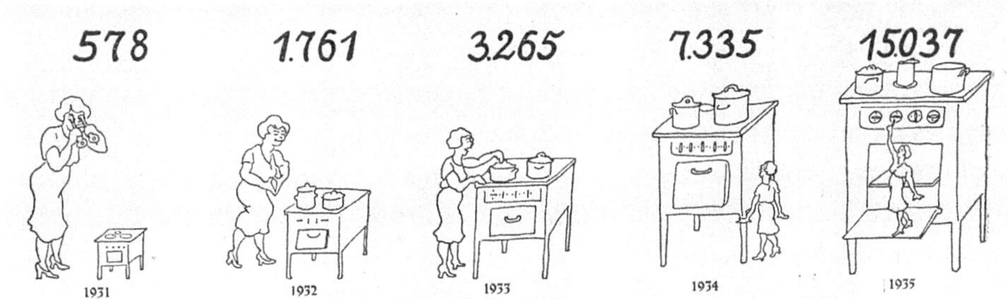

Figure 5.6
Cartoons advertising electricity use in the national cause
Source: *Der Stromkreis* 2, nos. 6/8 (1935), 98. Copyright: Bewag/Vattenfall.

has argued, though, the success of Nazi consumer politics in the field of electricity lay less in disseminating new technologies or stimulating significant energy demand and more in helping to stabilize the regime with positive imagery surrounding the consumption of electricity. The modern German—and the modern German woman, in particular—was encouraged in this way to play her part in the nation's economic recovery.[104] Consumption was, first and foremost, not a pleasure but a duty.

In 1936, with the implementation of the four-year plan, demand management activities shifted from promoting consumption to conserving energy. With the economy recovering fast, electricity use was booming once more. Electricity sales in Berlin to low-voltage customers rose between 1935 and 1938 from 400.3 million kWh to 574.5 million kWh.[105] Gas sales had risen too, though less sharply, from 322 million cubic meters in 1933 to 382 million in 1938.[106] Under the auspices of a national autarky drive, the priority was henceforth to prepare Germany for war by reducing its dependence on imported resources. Advertising for household goods now targeted those that helped prevent waste, such as refrigerators. Under the slogan "Fight the Mold," mass-produced fridges were presented as appliances that could enable people to save food and thereby do their own bit to reduce imports and strengthen national autarky.[107] Once again, consumption practices were framed as a duty to the *Volk*.

Alternative Urban Metabolisms

The four-year plan of 1936 reached far beyond consumer policy. The quest for national autarky embodied in the plan challenged conventional logics of resource use and, indeed, existing metabolic flows coursing through the country. Infrastructure systems for energy, water, and waste were necessarily instrumental to this venture. This section explores what role Berlin's utilities played in developing and practicing alternative urban metabolisms around the principles of reusing or conserving natural resources.

In public the four-year plan was presented by Göring as a means of reducing dependency on foreign markets and securing food and resources for Germany's future.[108] Confidentially, it had been instructed by Hitler in a secret memo of August 1936 as an instrument for preparing the economy and army for what he envisaged as an inevitable war with the Soviet Union. The plan set out a framework for the centralized planning of resource use, the increased exploitation of nationally available resources, such as coal and lignite, and the search for substitutes for essential imported products, such as oil.[109] Engineers were called upon to rise to the challenge and help develop new ways of optimizing production processes, reducing waste, and creating synthetics. Although many of the technologies targeted had already been developed during the 1920s—in both Germany and abroad—and thus pre-dated the Nazi era, they received an enormous boost through the political support and research funding that became available after 1936.[110] The material impact of this resource efficiency drive is, today, generally regarded as having been a failure, at least on a national scale.[111] The emotive appeal of the autarky idea, however, was powerful, as Anne Berg argues in her study of Nazi waste politics: "Notions of a closed energy cycle and the total eradication of waste and wastefulness nurtured the delusional fantasies of the regime to self-heal, regenerate power, infinitely extend limited resources, and ultimately perpetuate itself in the process of wreaking unfathomable destruction."[112]

In Berlin, all the utilities were enrolled in implementing the four-year plan, and did so largely with enthusiasm. Bewag established programs to eliminate resource waste, optimize fuel use, and reduce transportation of coal.[113] Gasag began to extract benzene at its gas works as a substitute vehicle fuel. It also sought to market the gas it produced for the same purpose, setting up coal gas filling stations in the city and providing mobile gas filling trucks (see figure 5.7).[114] The water utility responded by reducing the thickness of water pipes to save material, substituting asbestos for cast iron and seeking alternative materials for its manhole covers, faucets, and road signs.[115]

The utility at the vanguard of the autarky movement in Berlin was without doubt, though, the wastewater department. Its directors, Fritz Langbein and Otto Pallasch, as well as city councillors Adolf Heilmann and H. Kölzow, became enthusiastic advocates of the reuse of substances found in wastewater and other waste liquids.[116] In Heilmann's own words, "[t]he wealthy Germany of the future will not be a country of waste.... Avoid all waste, reuse any unavoidable waste!"[117] There were three prongs to this strategy: first, deriving fuel and lubricants from used oils and fats; second, using

Figure 5.7
Truck of the Berlin gas utility Gasag supplying coal gas as a vehicle fuel, 1936
Source: Bärthel, *Die Geschichte der Gasversorgung*, 93. Copyright: GASAG.

gas from sewage treatment to power vehicles; and third, applying nutrients in wastewater to enrich agricultural production.

As its contribution to fuel recycling, Berlin's wastewater utility set up a local collection system for used oils (primarily gasoline, diesel, turpentine, and lubricating oil) at some 8,500 garages across the city.[118] The purified oils were then used by the utility itself, for instance as fuels for its own vehicle fleet. The financial savings made here covered most of the costs incurred, including all costs for the collection vehicles and local separation appliances, as well as those for running the purification plant. Just the running costs of the collection itself needed subsidizing by the utility. Used fats and grease were collected in Berlin by one company alone from some 500 restaurants and 2,000 butchers, as well as fifty canteens, twenty barracks, and thirty-five hospitals.[119] Once purified, the fat was used primarily for soap and industrial lubricants, but also as a fuel substitute. The effective collection of waste oils and fats, of course, says little about the performance of the purified products as vehicle fuels, which may have been limited.[120]

Berlin was also a pioneer in using methane gas extracted from sewage, as observed in the previous chapter. Writing after the Nazi seizure of power, director Langbein of the wastewater utility remained an ardent supporter of the technology, demonstrating how the biogas derived from Germany's sewers and treatment plants could provide 130 million cubic meters of methane per year—over 5 percent of the country's total gas production.[121] Used as a substitute for gasoline or diesel, this gas, he calculated, could fuel 10,000 cars and save 14 million Reichsmark. In Berlin, methane gas derived from wastewater was used to run the wastewater utility's vehicle fleet and heat its buildings.[122] During the war, under conditions of severe fuel shortages, gas derived from wastewater became a significant vehicle fuel, although, as one expert wryly noted, the poor nutrition of the population had a negative impact on the gas production potential of wastewater.[123]

Most significant—but also most controversial—was the use of wastewater to increase agricultural production.[124] Well before the four-year plan, ministerial decrees of January 1934 and February 1935 proclaimed a reorientation of priorities in wastewater management.[125] Instead of treating sewage to remove harmful substances, wastewater systems were to be redesigned to utilize the valuable nutrients contained in sewage. Already in 1934 a senior official in Berlin's wastewater utility, Weise, was following this lead and making the connection between local nutrient recycling and national autarky policy: "We need to be aware that our neighbors, armed to the teeth, are in a position today to, at any time, destroy a large part of our crops, especially from the air, using fire, poison, or explosives.... Under these circumstances we should be in no doubt that everything must be done in future to retain the nutrients in wastewater in order to use them to increase crop productivity."[126]

Weise outlined ten guiding principles for future wastewater management in Berlin, prioritizing wastewater use over treatment and disposal. According to these principles, biological treatment—the mainstay of sanitary innovation in the late 1920s—was to be permitted only where sewage exceeded the needs of agriculture or where wastewater was strongly polluted. City councillor Kölzow, a member of the NSDAP, was similarly explicit about this shift in strategy that he claimed would increase harvests at least fivefold: "[w]hereas earlier the task was to dispose of wastewater adequately and efficiently, today attention is focused on how to derive the greatest economic benefit for the country from it."[127]

When Mayor Sahm opened Berlin's annual agricultural trade fair, the Green Week, on January 26, 1935, this was the issue he chose to highlight.[128] Framing the policy shift in terms of a new synthesis between city and countryside, he argued unashamedly that hygiene was no longer a priority of wastewater management, which should in future be dedicated to maximizing agricultural production for Berlin and the nation. He concluded his speech with a rhetorical salvo that revealed the depths of municipal subservience to the Nazi cause: "The capital Berlin can no longer by guided by narrow-minded municipal politics. The city gladly subordinates itself to the interests of the nation and the leadership of the new German Reich in devoted loyalty to the Führer of the German people and Chancellor of the German Reich."[129]

Berlin's wastewater utility followed up on these political interventions with a study on ways of adapting its treatment system so as to increase yields on the city's sewage farms.[130] Its director, Langbein, offered no resistance to the reversal of the sanitation strategy of biologically treating all sewage that he himself had co-devised in the 1920s. On the contrary, he became a leading advocate of reusing sewage in and beyond Berlin.[131] When the four-year plan was launched, therefore, it fell on fertile ground and was taken up by wastewater managers and regulators to promote a reorientation of Berlin's urban metabolism around waste reuse in the cause of national autarky.

However, as Frank Uekötter has pointed out, the application of "biodynamic agriculture" in the Nazi era proved turbulent, becoming the object of a long-standing controversy in professional circles that influenced wastewater management practices.[132] Once it had been widely agreed across Germany that wastewater should be used primarily for increasing agricultural production, the issue at stake became whether or not sewage should be biologically treated prior to its use on sewage farms. While hardliners argued that any treatment, beyond the physical removal of solids, would reduce the proportion of nutrients in used wastewater, a majority of sanitary engineers advocated prior biological treatment in order to, at least, minimize risks to hygiene.[133] In this way, well-respected engineers, like Karl Imhoff and Berlin's utility directors Langbein and Pallasch, tried to strike a compromise between the production priorities of Nazi ideologues and the sanitary standards of the Weimar era.[134]

In Berlin, a resolution of this dispute was sidestepped, resulting in the coexistence of diverse and contradictory practices in a manner typical of Nazi rule. On the one hand, the construction of the biological treatment plant at Waßmannsdorf planned during the Weimar years was not halted, but completed in June 1935. Henceforth, biologically treated wastewater from this plant was used for irrigation. Elsewhere, on the other hand, Berlin's wastewater was used for food production after only minimal sludge removal. The extensive irrigation of untreated sewage in increasing quantities around the city aroused concerns relating to the adverse effects on water quality. Complaints by anglers' associations about fish dying in the city's rivers as a result of untreated sewage entering local watercourses met with a stiff rebuttal from the chief chemist of the wastewater utility, Böttcher.[135] Protests by residents about the stench emitting from the sewage farms received equally short shrift. Böttcher, an NSDAP member since 1935, dismissed their claims as shameful, arguing that anybody who had given a minute's thought to what agricultural production on the sewage farms meant for Berlin would never complain about any bad smells they produced.[136]

On the contrary, sewage farms were being set up as suitable sites for mass settlement.[137] With arguments strongly reminiscent of Leberecht Migge's proposals of 1932, described in the previous chapter, city councillor Weise foresaw sewage farms as places where thousands of unemployed people from Berlin would practice self-subsistence in an orderly manner with the support of the Nazi movement.[138] A water management plan for the catchment of the Elbe, Havel, and Spree rivers of 1934 envisaged a green belt of land providing fresh vegetables to the city in a fifty-kilometer zone around Berlin, focused on its sewage farms. This ambitious scheme, it was claimed, would provide 30–40,000 unemployed with many years work and create jobs for 15,000 gardeners and 3,000 farmers. Imaginaries of this kind epitomize how attempts to reconfigure Berlin's material metabolisms during the Nazi era were deeply permeated with fetishisms of social control as well as paranoias of national vulnerability.

Municipalization, Nazi-Style

It might be assumed, given the Nazi's past record of lambasting Berlin's municipal enterprises, that, once in power, they would seek to reverse the pre-1930 policy of municipalization by stealth. This was not the case. With resistance within the utilities stifled, they could be strengthened, if not as urban pioneers, then at least as loyal vassals of the National Socialist cause. Municipal ownership of the electricity, gas, and water utilities did not, therefore, decline, but actually increased during the course of the Nazi era. What was markedly different, however, was the motive for municipalization. This was no longer to increase municipal influence over essential services per se, but primarily to rid the capital's utilities of owners who were foreigners or Jews.

The rhetoric behind this form of municipalization, Nazi-style, was that Berlin's utilities needed to be in full public ownership in order for them to serve the new, national cause. It was in the interest of National Socialism, Karl Kasper claimed, for the electricity, gas, and water services to be publicly owned.[139] An early step in this direction was taken in June 1933, when the new Nazi leadership of Berlin began exploring ways of taking over the privately owned Charlottenburger Wasser- und Industriewerke (CWI). Deputy Mayor Maretzky made no bones about the political agenda behind this move, describing it as the *Gleichschaltung* of a company known to have many Jews among its shareholders.[140] In February 1935 CWI agreed to a contractual arrangement with the city government that ensured unitary water tariffs across the city, granted the city the right to buy the company after thirty years, and required CWI to pay Berlin an annual dividend of 1 million Reichsmark.[141] It is clear from the documents surrounding this deal that CWI agreed to it only under the threat of forced expropriation.[142] During the late 1930s the city bought up shares in CWI, mainly from Jews forced to relinquish or sell up their shareholding following the Nuremberg Race Laws of 1935.[143] By 1942, the city held a 51.4 percent majority share in the company, enabling it to appoint Kasper, by then director of the Berlin water utility, as chairman of the board of directors of CWI. Amalgamation of the two utilities was being prepared in 1943–1944 but did not come to fruition until after the war.

In the gas sector, closer relations between the city government and the national energy sector—as personified by the utility directors and Nazi careerists Kasper and Krecke—enabled a public takeover that had always eluded Weimar municipalism. In March 1940 the city acquired from the district of Teltow all its remaining shares in Deutsche Gasgesellschaft and its subsidiary, Gasbetriebsgesellschaft. Berlin now owned the entire company, worth 80 million Reichsmark. This transaction completed the municipalization of gas in Berlin, enabling Gasag to supply the entire city for the first time.[144] Revealingly, the deal was made in conjunction with the connection of Berlin to the long-distance gas pipeline from Reichswerke Hermann Göring, described above. It was presented to the public as a way of securing Berlin's gas supply in the context of increased national connectivity to strengthen the war effort.[145]

Similarly, in the electricity sector Berlin's utility Bewag took over Elektrizitätswerk Südwest on January 1, 1938, having bought back many of the shares it had sold during the Depression (see figure 5.8).[146] When the concession agreement with the other privately owned power utility, Märkisches Elektrizitätswerk, expired on June 30, 1938, Bewag took over supply of the areas in the south of the city previously served by this company. For the first time in Berlin's history, the city was powered by one single utility. The remaining irritant to the Nazis was, however, that Bewag was owned primarily by private investors, some of whom were foreigners or Jews. Attempts to cleanse the company's supervisory board of foreign and Jewish representatives, as already noted, was an initial indicator of how remunicipalization was likely to pan out.[147]

By 1938, Berlin had bought up Bewag shares from private investors to the nominal value of around 64.5 million Reichsmark.[148] This still left shares worth almost 100 million Reichsmark in private hands. The remaining private investors steadfastly resisted all attempts to grant Berlin additional voting rights on the supervisory board with its increased shareholding, infuriating the city government and reinforcing its determination to rid the company of foreign influence.[149] In early 1939 Berlin's mayor approached the Reich economics minister for assistance in acquiring the 36 million Reichsmark of Bewag shares still held by the Sofina group, based in Belgium.[150] The sticking point was that Sofina insisted on being paid in foreign currency, rather than Reichsmark, and this required setting up a triangular trading deal involving exports from the electrical

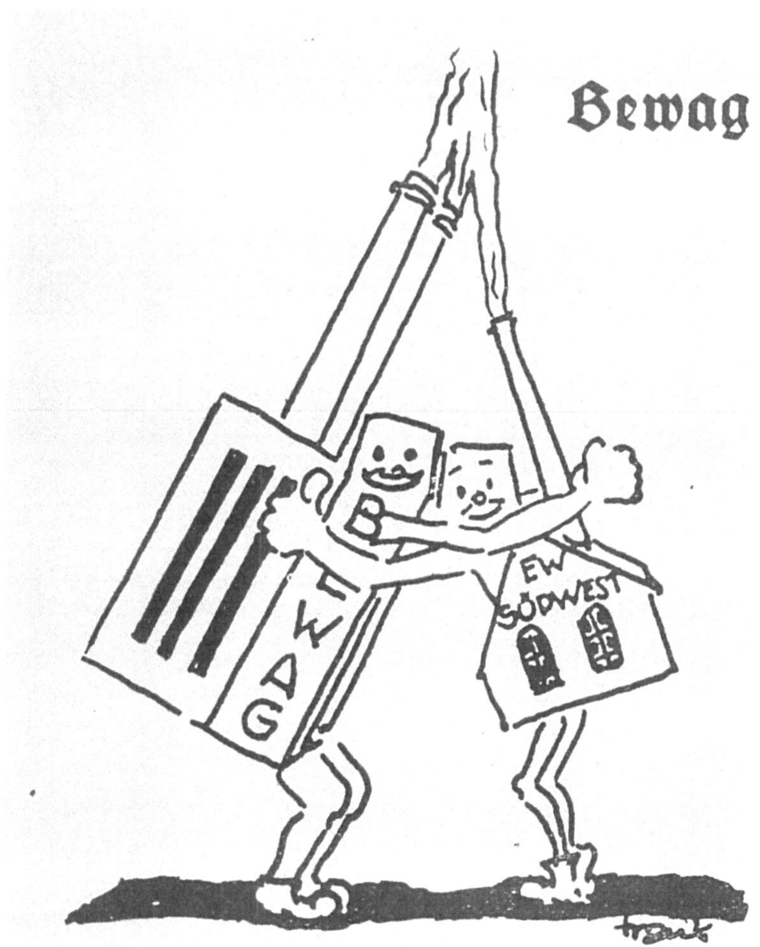

Figure 5.8
Bewag takes over Elektrizitätswerk Südwest, 1938
Source: *Der Stromkreis* 6, no. 1 (1939), 15. Copyright: Bewag/Vattenfall.

conglomerate AEG with the blessing of the economics ministry. Lippert was explicit to Minister Walther Funk about the political and military advantages for Germany of buying up the shares of the principal foreign shareholder and thereby encouraging others to follow suit. The issue at stake, he argued, was the repatriation (*Heimführung*) of the capital's electricity utility to German ownership, but also the liberation of this utility from being tarnished a Jewish business.[151]

This strategy failed, but the beginning of the Second World War presented altogether new options for acquiring Bewag shares owned by foreigners. On May 10, 1940, the very day that the German Wehrmacht launched its attack on the Netherlands, Belgium, and Luxembourg, the administrative officer responsible for Berlin's municipal enterprises, Bruno Ziethen, wrote a memo recording a request by the city treasurer to explore whether shares held by nationals of these countries could now be confiscated as enemy property.[152] Ziethen set down the legal case for confiscating shares held by Belgian and Dutch investors in time of war and highlighted the strategic significance of taking full municipal control of the electricity utility. He warned that if Berlin did not react fast enough it might lose out to the utilities Reichselektrowerke or Preußen-Elektra, who would similarly be keen to get hold of these shares. Over the following months Ziethen sought to clarify the legal claim to the shares while impressing upon the Reich economics minister the importance of returning Bewag to German ownership. As he himself put it: "It is appropriate now for the opportunity created by recent political and military events to be exploited so as to strengthen the city's influence over its electricity supply and thereby restore its pre-1931 status."[153]

In order to confiscate the shares, however, the shareholders needed to be identified and found.[154] As this proved impossible from Berlin, Ziethen commissioned one of Bewag's directors, Nain, to travel to Brussels to research the whereabouts of Sofina and its representatives. When Nain reported back that the two principal representatives of Sofina had fled to the United States and Portugal, respectively, Ziethen instructed him, in October 1940, to enrol consular assistance in Lisbon to get the Sofina headquarters transferred back to Brussels and thereby enable the confiscation to proceed as planned.[155] The last entry in the file, dated April 24, 1941, records Ziethen negotiating with the Reichsbank about reacquiring Bewag shares held in the United States and enemy countries.[156] This unashamed attempt to regain shares in the city's power utility as war booty by the chief administrative officer for Berlin's municipal enterprises is illustrative of how Nazi policies were actively advocated not only by loyal party members appointed to leading posts of city government, but also by long-standing members of the municipal civil service. Ziethen, who had been instrumental in promoting utility municipalization throughout the Weimar era, clearly felt no compunction about switching his allegiance to the new regime and pursuing a perverted version of municipalization that was explicitly racist and aggressively nationalistic.

Instruments of Germania

If there was one project of the Nazi regime that symbolized the subjugation of Berlin to the Reich better than any other, it was Hitler's dystopian idea to "restructure" the city into a world capital, to be called Germania, and its brutal application by his chief architect, Speer.[157] The sole purpose of reconstruction was to provide material expression to Germany's prowess and power. In Martin Kitchen's words, it was "an architectural expression of boundless ambition that bore no relation whatsoever to Berlin's immediate needs or future requirements."[158]

The plan for a new Berlin developed by Speer following his appointment as Inspector General of Buildings in the Nation's Capital in January 1937 envisaged a city of eight million inhabitants.[159] The centerpiece was a north-south axis of truly monumental dimensions, measuring 7 kilometers long and 120 meters wide.[160] This vast parade ground was to be framed by two new railway stations, lined by government buildings and dominated by two iconic structures: a victory arch in the south and a domed hall in the north that—with a height of 117 meters—dwarfed the neighboring Reichstag building. At this point the north-south axis was to be crossed by a second, east-west axis that passed through that symbol of military supremacy, the Brandenburg Gate. To plan and implement this monstrosity Speer was given a blank check by Hitler. The costs of the enterprise were, at the time, unknown and subsequently estimated by Speer at lying somewhere between 16 and 24 billion Reichsmark.[161]

Presented to the public as a reconstruction project, it was experienced in practice, largely, as one of destruction. Building a new city on such a scale meant first destroying those parts that stood in the way. Overall, Speer estimated the number of homes needing to be demolished at between 100,000 and 150,000.[162] This was at a time when Berlin already lacked around 190,000 homes to house its growing population. There is a bitter irony to the cartoon of Bewag laborers that was intended to demonstrate how they were contributing to the reconstruction of Berlin in Speer's image, laying power cables, but actually shows them hacking the city to bits (see figure 5.9).[163]

The destruction wreaked by Speer in Berlin was not only physical. Forced labor by inmates of concentration camps on a massive scale was an integral part of the reconstruction program. Following an agreement between Speer and Himmler in July 1938, some 10,000 camp inmates were used for producing the stone and brickwork to rebuild Berlin.[164] By the time work finally stopped in February 1943, some 130,000 laborers from across Europe had been, to a greater or lesser degree, forcefully enrolled in reconstructing the city.[165] Speer was instrumental not only in the forced labor, but also in forced evictions. Even before the November 1938 pogroms Speer was calling for measures to evict Jews from their homes in order to relieve the housing crisis exacerbated by his own destructive scheme. When the deportation of Jews from Berlin began in August 1941, Speer's organization was a prime beneficiary, seizing 23,765 apartments occupied by Jews by the end of October 1942.[166]

The role of Berlin's infrastructure systems in the Germania project is difficult to ascertain, given the absence or unavailability of sufficient documentation. There is little

Figure 5.9
Cartoon of Bewag workers laying cables for Germania
Source: *Der Stromkreis* 6, no. 1 (1939), 15. Copyright: Bewag/Vattenfall.

known, in particular, about the enrollment of the energy utilities beyond anecdotal evidence. This shows that Bewag was actively involved in constructing the lighting system along the east-west axis, still visible today, appointing a special representative to Speer's GBI.[167] By October 1940 it had laid electricity cables, built transformer stations, and completed heating systems in buildings along the north-south axis.[168] Other sources reveal the outlines of a plan for expanding and reordering the wastewater system to accommodate the enlarged city.[169] This envisaged building four large sewage treatment plants on existing sewage farms to the south of the city and a further four to the north, so as to free up land for new settlements. Beyond the autobahn ring a whole new network of sewage farms was to be constructed, where wastewater reuse cooperatives would farm on a massive area of 200,000 hectares. The costs were estimated at 832.5 million Reichsmark. This wastewater plan is indicative of Nazi rule in two ways. First, it reflects the coexistence of biological treatment and wastewater reuse for agricultural production, as discussed above. Second, it was drawn up not by the city's wastewater utility, but by the GBI. Indeed, representatives from the utility were excluded from discussions at the GBI unit dedicated to wastewater issues. The scheme—described by the utility after the war as "boundless and unfeasible"—was finally stopped in 1942.[170]

Sources on the water sector permit better insight into how Berlin's utilities were enrolled in the Germania project. Correspondence of the water utility reveals much of the euphoria, but also disruption and concerns that accompanied the reconstruction of the city. In the words of the utility director, Kasper, what was required were new plans for the entire water mains system, adapted to the new radial thoroughfares and ring roads.[171] The extension of the conurbation well beyond existing city limits called for a water infrastructure capable of supplying a much larger population spread over a far greater area.[172] All water works were called upon to deliver additional water to meet the anticipated surge in demand. Test drilling was conducted in increasingly distant locations to tap the necessary groundwater resources.[173] At the same time, the water utility was concerned that Speer's plans for the city would involve land use that jeopardized groundwater protection in and around the city. In a letter to Speer, dated April 19, 1940, directors Kasper and Poth warned him urgently against designating water protection zones as suitable areas for bathing and water sports for reasons of hygiene.[174]

A particular curiosity at this time—and one connected, in all probability, to the plans for Germania—was an intervention by Hitler himself in the water supply system for Berlin. It appears to have been the only time that the dictator took a personal interest in Berlin's utility services. On September 30, 1940, Speer sent a letter to the Berlin mayor informing him that Hitler was dissatisfied with the quality of Berlin's drinking water and demanded that it should be restructured along the model of Vienna, Rome, and Athens (see figure 5.10).[175] What Hitler meant by this, it subsequently transpired, was supplying water from mountain springs. This letter sent shock waves through the city administration, landing at the water utility, as it called for a written response to Speer not on whether, but on how this ludicrous idea was to be put into practice. Hitler's intervention was founded on a series of misconceptions. First, water from mountain springs is not inherently superior in quality to that extracted from groundwater aquifers, as was well known at the time. Second, Berlin was envied by water specialists across Europe for the documented quality of its drinking water. Third, the huge distance between Berlin and any elevation that could merit the term mountain would require water transfers on a massive scale along large, expensive pipelines. Fourth, it was not at all clear which mountain sources would be large enough to satisfy the thirst of the growing capital. Clearly, none of these challenges was considered by Hitler, who was probably captivated rather by the fanciful notion of using Alpine springs to cleanse

Abschrift

Der Generalbauinspektor
für die Reichshauptstadt

Berlin W.8, den 30.September 1940
Pariser Platz 4
Ruf: 11 7661

An den
Herrn Oberbürgermeister der
Reichshauptstadt

B e r l i n C. 2

Klosterstr.

Es ist zu untersuchen, durch welche Maßnahmen eine Wasserversorgung für Berlin mit einem einwandfreien Trinkwasser erreicht werden kann. Der Führer hat sich über das Trinkwasser von Berlin Vortrag halten lassen und wünscht, daß Pläne vorbereitet und ihm von mir vorgelegt werden, die für Berlin ähnlich wie für Wien, Rom und Athen ein gesundes,frisches Trinkwasser garantieren.
Ich bitte Sie, mir geeignete Vorschläge zu machen.
Ich werde danach einen Ausschuß zusammenstellen, der die planerische Seite dieser Angelegenheit zusammen mit den anderen außerhalb Berlins in Frage kommenden Stellen klärt.

Heil Hitler!

gez. S p eer .

La.

Figure 5.10
Letter from Speer informing the Berlin mayor of Hitler's dissatisfaction with the city's water supply, September 30, 1940
Source: Landesarchiv Berlin (LAB) A Rep. 015, no. 146.

the degenerate city. Speer, who should have known better, allowed the idiotic idea to take its course.

The Berlin water utility was not in a position, of course, to dismiss the idea out of hand, but felt obliged to commission no less than four separate reports from leading experts explaining, in as guarded a way as possible, why it was advisable to stick to the existing, proven system of water supply.[176] These reports, produced over the following fifteen months, argued that mountain-sourced water was not necessarily better than groundwater, that Berlin had enjoyed very low rates of water-borne diseases with its current system, and that the quality of Berlin's water was actually far superior to that of Vienna, Rome, or Athens. Having written letters to water utilities in mountainous regions situated in the Bavarian Forest, Upper Silesia, the Sudetenland, and the Viennese Alps, the Berlin utility was able to report back that sufficient water resources for Berlin from these areas were simply not available. For added effect, it pointed out that the long-distance pipelines required would be highly vulnerable to enemy attack from the air. It took until February 1942 for the directors of the Berlin water utility to draft their carefully worded response to Speer.[177] In May that year the city's mayor decided not to forward this response to Speer, assuming that he had, by then, far more pressing concerns.[178] The whole episode is highly revealing about how urban infrastructure was (dis)regarded by the Nazi leadership and how infrastructure strategy was informed more by spontaneous intervention than measured deliberation.

Militarizing Urban Infrastructure

Preparing for war demanded increasing attention by Berlin's utilities as the 1930s progressed, but had been a significant issue since the early days of Nazi rule, permeating all debates on infrastructure futures. The military preparedness of Germany's energy systems quickly became an obsession.[179] As early as the autumn of 1933, Subdivision IIIB of the Political Central Commission of the NSDAP declared that national defense was "an open wound in the body of the electricity industry" and that making the energy sector "capable of war" had top priority (see figure 5.11).[180] In Berlin the same year, Bewag responded by setting up an air-raid unit to provide protection for its plant and workforce from aerial bombardment.[181] By September 1933 the utility had already trained 130 employees in air-raid protection, built a bomb-proof shelter at the Klingenberg power station, and identified some seventy cellars for air-raid protection purposes.[182] Building air-raid shelters for the workforce, making infrastructure more resilient to bombing, and creating a rapid response capacity in each plant represented one form of military preparedness practiced by all of Berlin's utilities. By 1939 Gasag

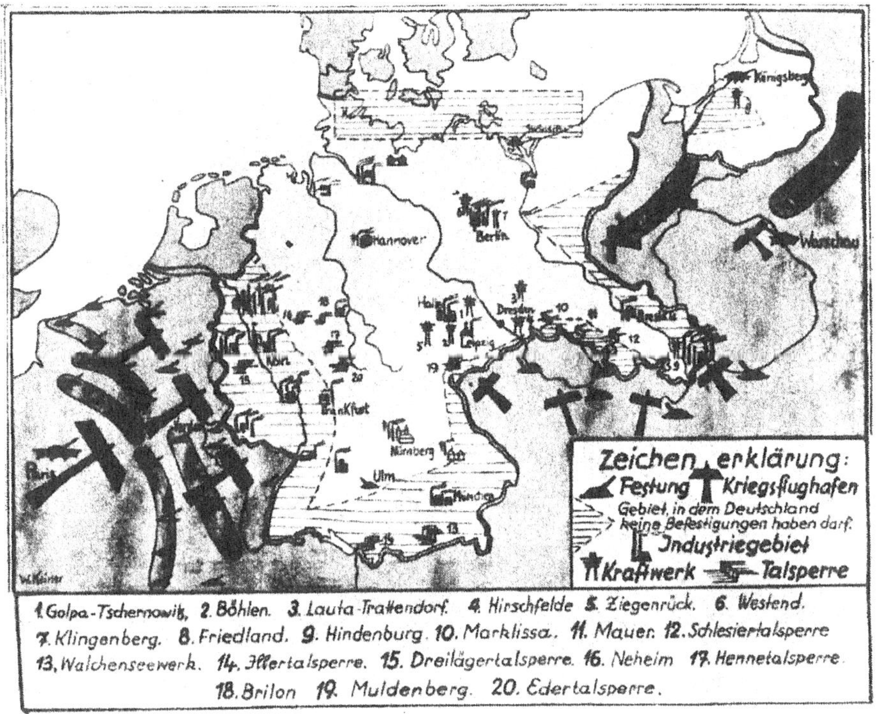

Figure 5.11
Stylized map of German power plants under threat
Source: *Der Stromkreis* 1, no. 1 (1933), 16. Copyright: Bewag/Vattenfall.

was spending 732,000 Reichsmark on air-raid protection measures alone.[183] Meanwhile, at the wastewater utility, plans were afoot to ensure the wastewater in Berlin's sewers could be used for fire-extinguishing purposes, if necessary.[184]

A second form of militarization was to create military-style organizations within the utilities that were entrusted with protecting the plant from any kind of threat—from inside or out—and instilling a sense of comradeship in the workforce. To this end, Bewag created a unit in uniform, called Werkschar, designated as "stormtroopers for National Socialism at the workplace."[185] Groups like this were encouraged to be particularly vigilant against spying and sabotage, an issue of growing concern to the utilities in the late 1930s.[186] A third component to militarization was serving the specific demands of the armaments industry. Providing plentiful and uninterrupted supplies of electricity, gas, and water was critical to the production of military hardware and Berlin was a center of this industry. Bewag was called upon to deliver increasing amounts of electricity to heavy industry, becoming a key component in armaments production.[187] Electricity use by high-voltage customers almost doubled between 1933 and 1938, rising from 452 million kWh to 846 million kWh.[188]

Using and Abusing the Networked City

In the epilogue to his study of municipal enterprises in the Weimar era, Otto Büsch dismisses Nazi rule as having had little impact on these pillars of municipalism. In his assessment, apart from the politically motivated removal of some employees and some tinkering with organizational structures, Berlin's utilities had been impervious to Nazi dictatorship.[189] The services they provided and the functions they fulfilled, he argued, remained a constant across regime change. The picture that Büsch painted in 1960 can be interpreted today as an attempt to build a bridge of continuity spanning from the Weimar to the West German republics. In this narrative, the Nazi era was all too often portrayed as an aberration. Areas of life apparently immune from National Socialist influence—such as urban services—were celebrated as building blocks for postwar Germany.

This chapter has revealed that the real picture is far more complex, even for infrastructures generally reputed to be heavily path-dependent. Dimensions of continuity coexisted with elements of radical change. So, in some respects, Büsch was right. The four utilities continued to provide basic services for the city, using largely the same technologies and material infrastructures. The environmental sources and sinks of these urban infrastructures—whether coal for electricity generation, groundwater aquifers for water supply, or sewage farms for wastewater disposal—did not change substantially under Nazi rule. No new strategy documents emerged for any of the city's utilities during this period. Many of the existing plans—for the construction of sewage treatment plants, for instance—were implemented without significant alteration. In terms of the physical structures and flows, in other words, little did change.

What was radically different, this chapter has demonstrated, were the symbolic purposes to which Berlin's utilities were put after 1933 and their enrollment in quintessentially national agendas of repression, racism, autarky, and militarization. This shift from using to abusing the networked city did not happen overnight. It was a gradual, insidious process deliberately designed to maximize acquiescence and minimize disruption. Thus, not all utility directors were removed from their posts following the Nazi seizure of power. Those regarded as political enemies were rapidly replaced by local National Socialists; those willing to go along with the new regime were permitted to remain until retirement. Schemes to influence demand for electricity and gas by households were not discarded after 1933, but significantly adjusted to suit the new regime. What had been introduced in the 1920s to help stimulate demand and balance load curves was reconfigured first to combat unemployment, then to minimize waste, and finally to save energy for the armaments industry. Similarly, municipalization of urban services was not abandoned in 1933, but reinvented as a means of ridding Berlin's utilities of foreign or Jewish shareholders. None of the alternative technologies for converting waste to energy or reusing wastewater were new to the Nazi era, but the political purposes to which they were put certainly were.

Two phenomena of this period stand out for permeating the narrative constantly. The first is the subjugation of urban to national interests. Under the Nazi regime Berlin's utilities were required to serve, first and foremost, not Berliners but the German *Volk*. This can be detected in a plethora of issues, ranging from the subordination of urban metabolisms to national autarky concerns, the enforced imports of gas and electricity from national utilities, to enrollment in acts of national symbolism and plans for Germania. The municipal service logic that had so characterized the Weimar era was overridden by the rhetoric of sacrifice for a racially purified and politically sanitized notion of the German nation.

The second distinctive theme emerging from the analysis is the widespread willingness of many to follow this new line of infrastructure governance. This echoes the argument of Richard Evans and others that many ordinary Germans internalized those strands of Nazi policy most amenable to them.[190] Although differences of opinion on infrastructure futures—as over sewage farms—did emerge at times, opposition to National Socialist fundamentals did not. Berlin's utilities may have entered the Nazi era with strong representations of anti-Nazi parties and organizations, but by 1935 at the latest the workforce appears to have been completely cowed. Those utility directors who were not members of the NSDAP pursued the new line with often surprising vigor. Continuity of senior staff in the city administration also proved no source of resistance, or even moderation, as the attempt to confiscate Bewag shares from foreigners during the war so starkly reveals. Understanding how Berlin's infrastructure systems came to be enlisted in Nazi rule in these multiple ways is deeply instructive about urban life and politics under the dictatorship.

6 Vulnerability and Resilience during War and Division

In 1946 a study was commissioned by the Berlin city government on the degree of damage to the city's underground infrastructure incurred by wartime bombardment. The subsequent report by Professor Ernst Randzio, entitled *Underground Urbanism* (*Unterirdischer Städtebau*), established that the vast proportion of the city's water mains, sewers, electricity cables, and gas pipes had survived the onslaught of war intact.[1] The resilience of this "invisible city," as documented in the report, became a powerful image not only to inspire postwar reconstruction but also to avert modernist experiments in urbanism. In the politically divisive mood of post-1945 Berlin, conservative urban planners around Walter Moest used the continued existence and functionality of the city's underground infrastructure as a key argument to refute the plan of Hans Scharoun and others to redesign Berlin along socialist-inspired principles. Karl Bonatz, who succeeded Scharoun as Berlin's chief urban planner in late 1946, followed Moest's line of argument that a defeated, war-stricken Germany could not afford to disregard the largely intact fabric of its energy, water, transportation, and communication infrastructures. In doing so, he drew explicitly on Randzio's study. The well-documented survival of Berlin's underground infrastructure became, indeed, the decisive argument behind retaining the city's prewar urban form and rejecting the new urban landscape advocated by modernists. Rarely has the power of infrastructure to shape urban development been so starkly revealed.

This chapter addresses issues of resilience and vulnerability in the face of wartime destruction, military occupation, and political division. It spans a decade of hugely disruptive forces impacting upon Berlin's infrastructures, commencing with the declaration of war in September 1939 and ending with the creation of two separate German states in 1949. These politically motivated forces affected infrastructures in very physical ways, in the form of destruction by aerial bombardment, confiscation by the occupying powers, and truncation of energy networks following political division.

Maintaining essential urban services in the face of such disruption was a constant concern of infrastructure managers throughout this tortuous decade. The chapter explores how resilient Berlin's infrastructures really proved in the face of urban vulnerability, but also how infrastructural vulnerability and resilience were used as political tools in the increasingly divisive climate of postwar Berlin.

The narrative begins with the outbreak of war in 1939 and the ways in which Berlin's utilities became enrolled in the military effort. This involved seconding staff to the armed forces, supplying energy and water to the armaments industry, and intensifying campaigns for resource efficiency. Attention then turns to the destruction caused to infrastructure by aerial bombardment from 1943 onward and the increasingly desperate attempts by the local Nazi leadership to maintain essential services and a sense of urban resilience in the face of impending defeat. The end of the war heralded military rule by the wartime Allies in Berlin and tentative steps to restore local self-government. The chapter explores how this dual leadership and the growing tensions between the Soviet and Western occupying powers became reflected in the way utility services were gradually restored across the city. It discusses the recruitment of infrastructures in fledgling plans for the postwar city, but also the extent of denazification to Berlin's utilities. As the Cold War became enacted in the increasing division of the city into pro-Western and pro-Soviet halves, the chapter explores how its infrastructures were affected by the Berlin blockade of 1948–1949 and the subsequent establishment of separate municipal governments for West and East Berlin.

Supplying the Military Machine

On September 3, 1939, the very day that France and Britain declared war on Germany following its invasion of Poland, the post of National Load Distributor (Reichslastverteiler) was created to regulate electricity supply on a nationwide scale.[2] The new body was entrusted with ensuring that the national grid prioritized the war effort and especially the armaments industry. It could instruct electricity utilities to supply particular customers and impose rationing on power use by consumers deemed nonessential to military preparedness.[3] The organization was headed by Richard Fischer, who had replaced Carl Krecke as director of Berlin's power utility Bewag and as head of the Reich Unit for the Electricity Industry on April 1, 1939. In line with previous practice under National Socialism, municipal and national functions were merged in the hands of a single person loyal to the Nazi cause.

Quite how important electricity and water services were regarded for the war effort was reflected in the creation of another office, that of Inspector General for Water and Energy (Generalinspektor für Wasser und Energie), by Hitler on July 29, 1941. Officially, the new post was justified as essential to coordinate planning of energy and water provision across Greater Germany. In reality, it served to transform both sectors into instruments of warfare and territorial aggrandizement.[4] This was self-evident, since the office was headed by none other than Fritz Todt, the Reich Minister for Armaments and Ammunition. Todt acquired the powers of the Reich economics ministry over energy and of various Reich and Prussian ministries over water in a typical act of organizational rigging tailored around one of Hitler's favorites. On his death he was replaced in February 1942 by Albert Speer, who pursued the policy of centralizing energy provision with greater vigor, increasing his own powers and those of the Nazi Party over municipal energy supply in the process.[5]

In Berlin, the beginning of the war heralded a renewed boost to electricity supply. The reduction in demand for lighting following the enforced blackout from September 1939 was more than offset by the rapid growth in electricity sales for the armaments industry. Bewag's board of directors was able to report in October 1940 that the war had, indeed, had a positive effect on load management by reducing demand for lighting at the peak time of early evening and extending demand into the night with round-the-clock industrial production.[6] Electricity sales by Bewag continued to grow between 1940 and 1942, from 1,644 million kWh to 2,045 million kWh.[7] The proportion of this electricity generated in Berlin rose from 70 percent to over 75 percent, despite all the talk about centralizing power generation.[8]

Water consumption in Berlin declined slightly in the early war years, from 140 liters a day per inhabitant in 1938 to 138 liters in 1940.[9] What these relatively stable total consumption figures conceal, however, was a massive shift from civilian to military use. By 1940 water consumption in homes without warm water supply stood at only 71 percent of 1938 levels; in homes with warm water the decline was even larger, at 61 percent.[10] Over the same period industrial consumption of water supplied by the Berlin water utility rose by 136 percent. Even this sharp increase understated the growing demand for water, as many larger industrial and military users in the city were supplementing water bought from the municipal utility with groundwater extracted from their own wells.[11] The huge growth of self-supply under wartime conditions became, indeed, a bone of contention for the municipal utility, which complained—in vain—about its loss of revenue and the damage to the city's water resources.[12] Calls for coordinated water management planning were, clearly, disregarded when it came to meeting the needs of powerful players in industry, government, and the military.

Berlin's gas supply illustrates well the contradictory forces at play in regulating energy provision for the national war effort. In 1942 production of town gas by the municipal gas utility peaked at 610 million cubic meters.[13] By 1944, however, bombing damage to local gas works and the new long-distance gas pipeline resulted in restrictions to armaments production in Berlin. In October 1944 the National Load Distributor for Gas, now based at the Inspectorate General for Water and Energy, instructed his counterpart in Berlin to exempt the steel industry in Spandau from a 15 percent cut in gas supplies, given its critical importance for armaments production.[14] Only one month later, problems in supplying coal to the gas works of Reichswerke Hermann Göring prompted the Inspector General for Water and Energy to announce drastic restrictions to all consumers of the gas it provided.[15] Berlin, which had only agreed to long-distance gas supply under political pressure in 1938, was allocated a mere 350,000 cubic meters per day. This meant either shutting down steel production in Spandau completely, thereby jeopardizing future armaments production, or prioritizing steel production at the expense of arms manufacturing in the city.[16]

Additional electricity, water, and gas supplies were not the only demands made by the war on Berlin's utilities. Many of their employees were enlisted for military service. The electricity utility Bewag had to release 2,600 employees—around a third of its total staff—for military service during the course of the war.[17] By the end of 1940, 400 employees of Berlin's water utility had been called up to the Wehrmacht, representing around 20 percent of its workforce.[18] Further staff losses were incurred through war-induced deaths and evacuations. Records relate that 311 Bewag employees were killed in action and a further fifty-one in bombing raids on the city.[19] During the war the gas utility lost around 1,000 members of staff, who were either killed by air raids or did not return after fleeing the bombardment.[20] Labor shortages were compensated for by internal restructuring during the early war years.[21] Indeed, the principal concern among Bewag's directors in May 1940, as the German army swept across Northern Europe, was how to prepare for the anticipated further loss of staff following victory. Germany's dominance of the world economy, they mused, would require trained staff to manage energy provision in newly conquered countries, leaving Bewag with even fewer engineers than it had in wartime.[22]

Saving Energy, Sacrificing Services

For consumers, the most immediate and tangible impact of war on public services was the blackout imposed on the city to hinder aerial bombardment. Eye witnesses spoke of the initial blackouts as an urban attraction.[23] People would gather at night to experience the shrouded metropolis. Some romanticized the blacked-out capital as a "city of dreams" bathed in a soft half-light. More prosaic were the restrictions on energy and water use that were gradually introduced as the war progressed. Initially, the authorities were skeptical about the impact of energy saving in households and anxious to minimize disruption to everyday life. A circular distributed by the national Economic Group for Electricity Supply in October 1939 pointed out that saving electricity in households would account for only 2 percent of national power generation and was, therefore, only called for when there was a danger of overloading the grid.[24]

By the winter of 1941, however, national supplies of coal were falling seriously behind demand for power generation, gas production, industrial processes, and room heating. In November 1941 the coal allotted to Bewag was reduced by 10,000 metric tons, requiring the utility to cut its electricity generation by around 5.5 million kWh a month.[25] The following month gas rationing was imposed by the city's gas utility on large companies only, in an attempt to avoid hitting the general public.[26] By February 1942, however, the Inspector General for Water and Energy, Todt, was instructing regional load distributors for electricity and gas to present energy rationing as a sacrifice to the national cause. Safe from having to face the consequences, he was able to argue: "A Gauleiter can inform a whole city to limit gas and electricity consumption within the space of a few hours. An appeal by the party [NSDAP] to people's political conscience will assure success."[27]

In 1942 a national campaign to save energy, launched by Minister Göring, made no bones about the military purpose behind encouraging consumers to use less energy and respect rationing of electricity and gas. "Now electricity and gas must serve the production of armaments," the campaign declared.[28] Germans became enrolled rhetorically into a military compact around energy conservation: "This is the value of the energy saving plan: an initiative of the whole *Volk*, which causes a minimum of inconvenience to restore favorable conditions for producing more weapons."[29]

Todt's successor Speer required power and gas utilities to reduce peak loads and factories to report and reduce energy consumption.[30] Bewag took up the cause by advertising the importance of saving energy to help the war effort. An exhibition it organized in October 1942 argued that no less than 80 percent of the electricity it generated needed to be earmarked for armaments production.[31] Under the slogan "the electricity you save is working for victory," the city's electricity utility called upon its customers to avoid luxuries such as electric heating, as an advertisement of December 1942 illustrates (see figure 6.1).[32] Gender role models were used to indicate who was likely to be acting in an irresponsible manner (the housewife) and who needed to take corrective control (the husband).

Apart from reducing the amount of energy used for nonmilitary purposes, efforts were intensified to use substitutes for imported oil products and limited coal resources.

Figure 6.1
Advertisement to stop using electric fires in the home
Source: Bezirksamt Charlottenburg von Berlin, *Stadt unter Strom*, 48. Copyright: Bewag/Vattenfall.

In Berlin the various alternative energies developed in the late 1920s and promoted under the four-year plan of 1936 were pursued with vigor under wartime conditions. This applied in particular to the use of gas, instead of gasoline, to power motor vehicles. Hitler, in one of his many decrees, had prohibited the use of liquid fuel for vehicles unless essential for the war effort. What was presented as a necessity was recognized by Berlin's gas utility, Gasag, as a business opportunity. In May 1942 Gasag decided to produce methane from town gas as a substitute fuel for vehicles and to build a network of methane gas filling stations across the city.[33] To this end a new enterprise was formed—the Berlin Methane Distribution Company—as a joint venture between Gasag and a private company specializing in fuel technologies, the Coal Derivatives Corporation.

The original plan envisaged the production of around 100,000 cubic meters of methane a day, enough to fuel 3,000 vehicles at 30 filling stations. A year later, in June 1943, the new company was able to report that it had begun selling methane to 250 converted vehicles at a new filling station in Danziger Strasse.[34] The plan now was to produce, by 1944, 310,000 cubic meters of methane a day at three of Gasag's gas works, but also to use a further 16,000 cubic meters of sewage gas a day produced by the city's wastewater utility at its sewage treatment plants at Stahnsdorf and Waßmannsdorf.

The reality paled by comparison. Sales of methane gas in Berlin in 1943 averaged a meager 7,639 cubic meters a day.[35] Shortages of material and labor, as well as disruption to transportation and production processes, were blamed for the poor performance. By September 1944 the amount of methane produced at the three gas works had risen to 27,000 cubic meters a day and the two sewage treatment plants were contributing an additional 5,000 cubic meters a day.[36] However, this still represented just 10 percent of the figure boasted in June 1943.

The problem would not have become so virulent if the Berlin Methane Distribution Company had not been so effective in converting vehicles to methane gas. While it successfully converted 1,076 vehicles in 1943 and a further 1,500 by April 1944, the company was unable to provide sufficient fuel to drive them.[37] This impasse was made painfully clear to Gasag's chief director, Hoffmann, over an incident at one of its methane gas filling stations. On September 29, 1944, a senior civil servant from the Reich propaganda ministry, a Herr Dominik, flew into a rage when informed that there was no gas available at the Schlossplatz filling station to fuel his car.[38] Although the pump attendant offered to drive him to an alternative source, Dominik cursed the methane company as a fraudulent business and threatened to inform his minister, Joseph Goebbels. Thus elevated to a political dispute, the incident demanded a response from Gasag's director. Hoffmann retaliated in a letter to the Reich propaganda ministry by pointing out that the Berlin Methane Distribution Company had been founded on the personal order of Reich Minister Albert Speer and in cooperation with an enterprise whose supervisory board was headed by the managing director of Reichswerke Hermann Göring.[39] The incident is revealing, therefore, not only about real supply problems surrounding the promotion of alternative technologies, but also about how petty bickering could become politically charged, with each side enrolling Nazi grandees to back its cause.

Destruction and Disruption

The vulnerability of urban infrastructures to aerial bombardment had been a matter of concern since 1933.[40] Upon the outbreak of war in 1939, measures to protect power stations, water works, and gas works became a high priority for Berlin's utilities. Smaller plant components were given additional protection by reinforced concrete casing, wastewater pumps were relocated underground, and prominent gas tanks were camouflaged to avoid detection (see figure 6.2).[41] Beyond physical concealment, steps were taken to render the technical networks more resilient to air attack. Parallel water pipes and additional storage units were built to minimize the effect of bombing on water supply.[42] A new water mains ring was created, incorporating the network of the privately owned Charlottenburger Wasser- und Industriewerke (CWI), so as to enable a rapid response to localized destruction. Street water pumps—barely used since the advent of a mains water service—were reactivated and fire hydrants connected to high-pressure water pipes.

Up until late 1943 Berlin had been largely spared from major aerial bombardment, allowing its infrastructures to operate with only minor disruption. This changed dramatically on November 18, 1943, when the bombing offensive on Berlin began. Between November 1943 and March 1944 sixteen major attacks were launched by the Royal Air Force and a further three by the US Air Force. During these few months 8,709 aircraft dropped 29,804 tons of bombs, killing 7,400 people and making over 800,000 homeless across the city.[43] The bitter irony is that this onslaught began in the year that Berlin's population reached its historical peak of almost 4.5 million inhabitants.[44] The air raids resumed in earnest in October 1944. The heaviest air raid on Berlin occurred on March 3, 1945, when over 1,000 bombers killed 1,688 people and rendered 120,000 homeless in a single day.[45] By the end of the war over half a million homes had been destroyed, representing 32 percent of Berlin's housing stock.[46] By then, an estimated 2.1 million Berliners had evacuated the city: around 45 percent of the total population.[47]

It is today acknowledged that energy and water infrastructures were not prime targets of Allied bombing raids. National power provision was barely affected by aerial bombardment in the early years of the war.[48] This was a point made by Speer in captivity after the war, when he ingratiated himself to the Allied occupying forces by indicating how they might have won the war sooner. In the words of the historian Richard Overy: "His personal preference was for a systematic serial assault on the electricity-generating industry, which Speer believed might quickly paralyse production."[49]

Even if the British and US air forces did not target energy and water supply facilities explicitly, any attacks on urban conurbations were bound to have a destructive impact on urban infrastructures.[50] In the case of Berlin, the infrastructure that lay protected underground may have survived the war to a large extent intact, as the opening to this chapter revealed, but the infrastructure above ground was subjected to the same degree of destruction as other physical structures. What mattered, when it came

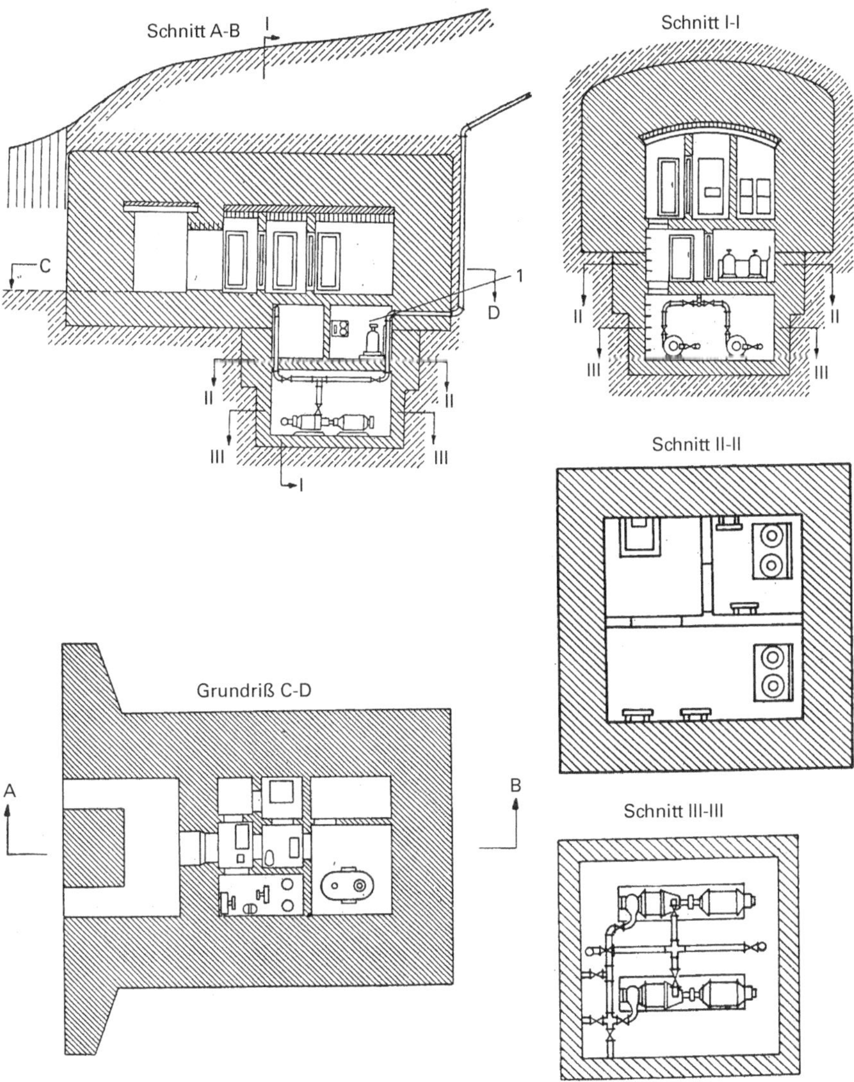

Figure 6.2
Air-raid protection for underground water pumps
Source: Pohl, "Der Luftschutz von Wasserversorgungs- und Entwässerungsanlagen," 304.

to maintaining essential services, was not the amount of physical damage caused by bombing, though, but the vulnerability of particularly critical parts of each technical network.

In the case of the wastewater system, the weak link in the chain was the pumping stations. Of the eighty-seven stations pumping sewage out of Berlin to the sewage treatment plants and irrigation farms, eight were totally destroyed in the war, twelve were badly damaged, another twenty were inoperable, and thirty-three partially damaged.[51] The pressure sewer mains used to pump sewage from these stations was also particularly subject to destruction. The sanitation utility tried to minimize the impact of this destruction, continuously sending out teams to repair the sewers day and night. It was a Sisyphean task, though, given that between 3,500 and 4,000 parts of the sewer network were damaged during just eighteen months of heavy bombardment.[52] As toilets had been destroyed along with the homes they served, many Berliners had little option but to empty their own excrement into the streets. By the end of the war, nearly 200,000 cubic meters of raw sewage was flowing untreated into the city's rivers each day.[53] The result of this collapse of the sanitation system was a public health disaster: death from typhus reached levels not seen since the introduction of public sewers to Berlin in 1870.[54] It could have come much worse. As part of the military defense of the city, plans had been made to destroy all Berlin's walk-in sewers, with catastrophic implications for sewage disposal and public health. Fortunately, these plans—bar some isolated exceptions—were never implemented.[55]

The water supply system also sustained significant damage to its plant and network. By the end of hostilities one of the city's water works had been completely destroyed (Triftweg I) and four others had incurred substantial damage, as had one of the water pumping stations (Lichtenberg) (see figure 6.3).[56] The water supply plant was not, however, the most vulnerable part of the system. The spatial distribution of water works across the city and the connectivity of its water mains gave the supply system the flexibility needed to respond rapidly to the temporary disabling of any of its parts. As a result, the city as a whole was never without water up until the final battle for Berlin in April 1945.[57] Only parts of the network suffered a temporary lack of water. The Achilles' heel of the water system was, rather, the loss of water caused by the destruction of end-points of consumption. When a bomb destroyed a house, and its water appliances with it, water spewed out uncontrollably until the nearest functioning mains valve could be shut off. On the night of November 23–24, 1943, in the most damaging air raid for the water supply system, it was recorded that water was discharging from 3,000 points across the network.[58] In the final four months of the war the municipal water utility alone lost 45 million cubic meters, which represented a third of the year's total water supply.[59]

Figure 6.3
Wartime damage to water works at Wuhlheide in Berlin
Source: Bärthel, *Wasser für Berlin*, 183.

The most vulnerable component of Berlin's gas system proved to be the long-distance gas pipeline. Just as the city government and its gas utility had warned in the late 1930s, this pipeline was highly susceptible to bombing damage with devastating consequences for the city's gas supply. On January 16, 1943, well in advance of the major bombing offensive, the gas transfer station at Spandau took a major hit and was completely destroyed, resulting in a complete halt to all gas imported from Reichswerke Hermann Göring at Watenstedt until it could be repaired.[60] Gas supply to Berlin from this external source dropped between 1942 and 1944 from 261 million cubic meters to a meager 153 million cubic meters as a consequence of repeated damage from aerial bombing.[61] By comparison, the production of town gas at the city's own gas works declined over the same period by a far smaller degree, from 610 million to 541 million cubic meters.[62] By the end of the war, however, none of Berlin's gas works was operative.[63] Of the city's thirty-eight gas tanks, used for storing locally produced town gas, only one had avoided any damage at all (see figure 6.4).[64] The most visible sign of wartime damage to the network in Berlin's streets was the total destruction of 36,000 of the city's 84,000 gas lamps.[65]

Figure 6.4
Wartime damage to a gasometer, 1945
Source: Landesarchiv Berlin (LAB), F Rep. 290-06-06, no. 385.

By comparison, electricity supply was less affected by wartime destruction. Of Berlin's nine power stations, only one (Schöneberg) was rendered inoperative by aerial bombardment.[66] Another two were working at marginally reduced capacity when the war ended: at Moabit (–19 percent) and Upper Havel (–10 percent). Writing in November 1945, Bewag director Wissell expressed his surprise that electricity-generating capacity of all Berlin's power stations had remained high, at 637 MW, prior to the Soviet invasion of the city.[67] The more pressing problem appears to have been the supply of coal in sufficient quantity and quality to fire the boilers. It was this, in combination with damage from land bombardment, that precipitated the only total power blackout that Berlin experienced during the whole war, on April 27, 1945.[68] Wissell spoke of his admiration for the dedicated staff at the power stations for making it possible for electricity supply to be restored the very next day.[69]

The damage caused by enemy bombing to Berlin's infrastructures brought with it huge costs to the utilities, in the form of damaged stock, loss of revenue, and continuous repair work. The loss of value incurred by the electricity utility through wartime damage between 1943 and 1945 was claimed, by Bewag itself, to total 99.6 million Reichsmark. The Berlin water utility Wassag set the value of physical damage to its infrastructure at 26 million Reichsmark and of water losses at 14.8 million Reichsmark. These figures do not include losses incurred by the other water utility in Berlin, CWI, for which there are no surviving records. The wastewater utility estimated total losses through wartime destruction at a staggering 700 million Reichsmark.[70] All these sums, it should be noted, were calculated after the war when the utilities were keen to underline the sacrifices they had made to keep the city operating.

The question of who should foot the bill for wartime damage was a thorny one. The archival files on wartime damage to the electricity and water utilities are full of detailed reports to the authorities on war damage incurred, accompanied by claims for compensation.[71] These claims ranged from damaged technical appliances and office furniture to water used to extinguish fires. Although on paper compensation was to be provided in full by the Main Office for War Damage (Hauptamt für Kriegsschäden), it was often difficult for the utilities to register their claims when incurring several hundred instances of damage after a single aerial attack, especially when it was unclear whether the building owner or the utility was the legitimate claimant. Uncertainties of this kind gave the office responsible for paying compensation ample opportunity to challenge claims and delay payments.[72] The payments made do not appear to have covered anything like the total cost of wartime damage. Of the 22.7 million Reichsmark claimed by the Berlin water utility for damage to property and water losses during the war, only 9 million Reichsmark were paid in compensation by the Main Office for War Damage.[73] The costs of war, for Berlin's utilities, were, therefore, financial as well as physical.

Coercive Resilience

Another form of compensation sought by the utilities was for the demands on their labor force made by the war. In this, they showed no scruples in employing forced labor, in various guises, wherever this was possible.[74] Acquiring reliable data on wartime forced labor by Berlin's utilities has proved difficult, partly owing to missing documentation.[75] The files on the gas utility Gasag do, however, give some indication not only of the levels of employment of foreign workers, prisoners of war, and inmates of concentration camps, but also of the circumstances of these forms of forced labor in Berlin's utilities generally.

The gas utility found itself facing a classic conundrum of National Socialist rule soon after the commencement of hostilities. It was expected to increase production of gas to supply the local armaments industry while at the same time relinquishing a significant proportion of its labor force to military service and sacking members of staff deemed to be of non-Aryan descent. In April 1940 Gasag was lamenting the loss of employees to the Wehrmacht and calling on the Labor Exchange (Arbeitsamt) to provide it with unskilled workers from occupied Czechoslovakia.[76] Just one month later it was recording that all foreigners had been sacked at the start of the war, announcing proudly: "Non-Aryans are not employed in our company."[77] Getting Germans to fill the colossal gap in the labor force was, however, not a viable option. By April 1941 Gasag was employing 100 French prisoners of war and sixty-eight "free" foreign workers, primarily from Holland.[78] These foreign workers from occupied countries received a wage, could move relatively freely in the city, and were permitted a short holiday in their home country. However, their payment was well below what Germans earned, they often had to pay inordinately high rents for basic accommodation in barracks, and they were encouraged not to mingle with the local population. The Dutch people working at Gasag under these conditions were, it appears, not keen to prolong their employment. The principal complaint voiced by the utility was that many of them did not return from their trips home.[79] In October 1941 only twenty of the 183 Dutch workers originally employed were still at Gasag.[80] To add to the dilemma, Gasag found itself being squeezed out of an ever more fiercely contested local labor market. In July 1941 it had to relinquish its 100 prisoners of war for work on farms.[81] The same month the utility was required to find alternative accommodation for its foreign workers, as the municipal camps it had previously used were now requisitioned by Speer's Inspectorate General for Buildings to house prisoners of war working for him.[82]

As the stakes of war rose in 1942, so did the degree of coercion over forced labor. The pressing need for workers to conduct menial, but essential tasks in the city's utilities directed attention toward people from occupied countries in Eastern Europe. A principal reason given for not employing these people before was that they were deemed unreliable and prone to sabotage. Ever since the start of the war, Gasag and the other utilities had become obsessed by the potential risks of sabotage and spying by enemy agents.[83] One of Gasag's directors, Kiesel, had given a speech to the workforce in July 1939 in which he warned his staff against talking to foreigners, encouraged them to report any suspicious activities, and concluded with the exhortation: "Trust the Führer. Protect the German *Volk*. Death to the traitor."[84] A confidential letter from the office of the Stadtpräsident to Berlin's energy and water utilities of May 29, 1942, summarized the concerns that Russian laborers were particularly liable to sabotage, but conceded that the utilities had no option but to employ large numbers of them rapidly, albeit under certain restrictions.[85] These included preventing foreign workers operating in any sensitive facility wherever possible, ensuring round-the-clock supervision by a German, having separate toilets and wash rooms, and housing them in barracks preferably on site.

A circular from the Berlin office of the Gestapo of August 1942 replaced these already debilitating restrictions with draconian rules for the "employment" of laborers from Eastern Europe.[86] It called for Germans to exercise utmost discipline against these people, many of whom would be—it was claimed—saboteurs and agents of the Soviet Union. They were to be kept in camps and transferred to their places of work under strict supervision. They were not permitted to come into contact with other foreign laborers or with prisoners of war. The camps were not to be encircled with barbed wire or have barred windows, but escape from the camps was to be prohibited, as was access to them by Germans. In line with racist ideology, sexual relations between a Russian and a German were strictly taboo, punishable with death for the Russian male or concentration camp for the female. Under these conditions, in October 1942, Gasag "employed" ninety Soviet Russian men and eighty-four women, primarily to transport coal and coke at its gas works.[87] At that time it was also using 102 Ukrainians, thirty-eight Belgians, twenty Dutchmen, and one Frenchman as foreign laborers, in addition to sixty-eight French prisoners of war. What happened to these people is not known. After 1942, traces of them in the historical records of the utility disappear. What is clear is that Berlin's gas utility, and presumably its other utilities too, had no qualms about drawing on forced labor to help shore up its operations and render its infrastructures resilient in the face of war.

Municipal Government under Military Rule

The war ended in Berlin with a dramatic struggle for control of the city between the advancing Soviet army and the hopelessly outnumbered and under-resourced German forces. This iconic Battle for Berlin lasted from April 16 to May 2, 1945, and cost the lives of an estimated 170,000 soldiers and tens of thousands of civilians.[88] The physical destruction of the city left behind by aerial and land bombardment was immense. Over a quarter of all buildings in the huge city were either destroyed or damaged.[89] Of the 1.5 million homes in Berlin, only 370,000 were habitable at the end of the war.[90] It was estimated at the time that 75 million cubic meters of building debris littered the inner-city area alone. Little wonder that a US military commander described Berlin shortly afterward as "the world's biggest heap of rubble."[91]

The termination of hostilities and capitulation of the Wehrmacht on May 8, 1945, placed Berlin under occupied rule according to an interallied agreement reached long before the first Soviet soldier set foot in the city. In September 1944 the Soviet, US, and

British governments had signed a protocol in London specifying how Berlin should be governed following the impending military victory.[92] They agreed to administer Berlin jointly via an interallied "Kommandatura" comprising the military commanders of the three victorious powers. The agreement was later amended to include the French military command as a fourth occupying power. This Allied Military Command was entrusted with ruling the city in its entirety. Its orders were binding on all levels of municipal government. It could veto any decision made by the local authorities.

Beneath this veneer of unitary rule, however, the seeds for political partition had been sown in the London Protocol. Each occupying power was made responsible for one sector of Berlin (see figure 6.5). The Soviet Union was accorded a segment covering 45 percent of the urban territory, the United States 24 percent, Britain 19 percent, and

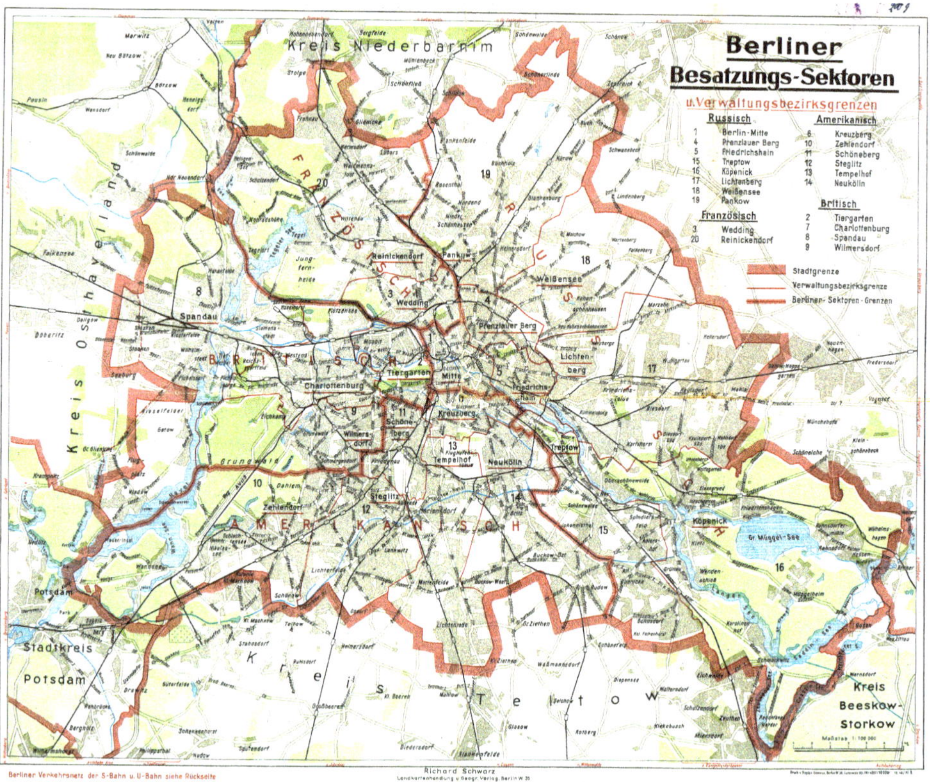

Figure 6.5

Map of occupied sectors of Berlin

Source: Landesarchiv Berlin (LAB) F Rep. 270, no. A 8149.

France 12 percent.[93] In terms of population the Soviet sector comprised 37 percent of the city's inhabitants. Partitioning the city into four sectors, each under the tutelage of one occupying power, paved the way for the "municipal fragmentation of Berlin."[94] Only twenty-five years after the creation of the unitary city, Berlin was confronted with fresh forces for segregation. In addition to internal partition, the sectors governed by the United States, Britain, and France were separated economically from their respective hinterland. The Soviet Union had successfully insisted that each sector of Berlin should be supplied with food and goods only from its respective zone in Germany.[95] This meant that while the Soviet sector of Berlin could be supplied by its immediate surrounding region, the three Western sectors needed to import all supplies from their own occupied zones in the West of Germany. Having to cross the Soviet occupied zone to reach Berlin, they became hugely dependent on the Soviet Union for land access to the city.[96]

What was written on paper was one thing; what was happening on the ground quite another. The Soviet forces used their early entry into Berlin to strengthen their own position before the Western powers arrived. By creating a fait accompli in advance of the power-sharing regime they hoped to maximize Berlin's political dependence on the Soviet Union. Even before the fighting had ended a group of German communist émigrés returned from Moscow to Berlin on April 30, 1945, entrusted with helping the Soviet military set up a postwar administration. The group was led by Walter Ulbricht, who later was to head the East German government for twenty years as First Secretary of the Socialist Unity Party.[97] He is cited as describing the group's mission in early postwar Berlin as follows: "it must look democratic, but we must retain control of everything."[98] On Ulbricht's recommendation a politically inexperienced architect, Arthur Werner, was appointed mayor of Berlin by the Soviet authorities on May 17, 1945.[99] The selection of the "rather naïve" Werner would appear to fit Ulbricht's intention to maintain the appearance of democracy in a postwar city administration otherwise strong in pro-communist representatives.[100] The city council appointed by the Soviet city commander General Nikolai Bersarin on May 19 comprised eighteen councillors, nine of whom were members of the KPD. It was these KPD members who initially called the shots in this first postwar city council, where the SPD was poorly represented.[101] While Mayor Werner performed largely representative functions, real power in the council was exercised by his nominal deputy, Karl Maron, a member of the Ulbricht group.[102]

By the time the Western powers arrived in Berlin and the joint Allied Military Command met for the first time on July 11, 1945, the Soviet authorities had already established a system of local government very much in their image. In the early months the Allied Military Command altered little to the structures and practices initiated by the Soviet commanders.[103] Over the course of the next three years it met ninety-three times, until the Soviet representatives left in June 1948.[104] Although the military authorities intervened frequently in the day-to-day running of the city and borough administrations, relations between the Allied Military Command and the city council appear, overall, to have been cooperative.[105]

In August 1945 a temporary constitution for Greater Berlin, based on historical precedents from 1920 and 1931, marked the first step in the restoration of local self-government. Over the following months four political parties emerged, either as reincarnations of the Weimar parties (KPD and SPD) or as new denominations: the conservative Christian Democratic Union (CDU) and liberal Liberal Democratic Party of Germany (LDP).[106] Hotly debated was whether the KPD and SPD should merge to form one single socialist party. Many in both parties were initially sympathetic to an alliance that could overcome the disastrous division that had mired resistance to Nazism.[107] A majority of SPD members in the three Western sectors of the city, however, voted in a referendum to resist efforts by the KPD to amalgamate with the SPD. As a result, the merger of the KPD and SPD into the Socialist Unity Party of Germany (SED) on April 24, 1946, was restricted to the Soviet sector only, where the referendum had been prohibited.[108] The Soviet military authorities insisted, however, that the SED be recognized in all four sectors.

It was only after October 1946, in the first democratic elections to the city parliament, that Soviet influence on Berlin's municipal government received a major rebuttal.[109] The election campaign of the SPD, CDU, and LDP, highlighting the SED's domination of the city council, proved highly successful. The SPD achieved a resounding victory, gaining 48.7 percent of the vote across the whole city. The CDU got 22.1 percent of the vote and the LDP 9.4 percent. The clear loser of the election was the SED, which received fewer votes than the CDU in the city as a whole (19.8 percent) and managed only 29.9 percent in the Soviet sector. The city council elected on December 5, 1946, was radically different in political complexion to its predecessor: seven councillors belonged to the SPD, three to the CDU, and two each to the SED and LDP. An SPD councillor, Otto Ostrowski, was appointed mayor alongside three deputy mayors, Ferdinand Friedensburg (CDU), Heinrich Acker (SED), and Louise Schroeder (SPD).

A straight switch in municipal leadership, however, failed to happen. The elections were followed instead by a series of stand-offs between the Soviet-backed SED and the Western-oriented SPD.[110] First, the SED sought to use the Soviet veto to prevent its loss of power. The city council appointed in 1945 refused to resign prior to approval of the 1946 elections by the Soviet military command; approval that was not granted for some time. Then the SPD disavowed its own mayor, Ostrowski, when he tried to negotiate directly with the SED to resolve the stalemate over membership of the city council.[111]

He resigned on April 17, 1947, after losing a vote of confidence in the city parliament. This marked a shift in the SPD toward a more confrontational stance against the SED that came to be epitomized in the figure of Ernst Reuter.[112] Reuter had been a former KPD functionary during the 1920s, but by the 1940s had become a hard-line opponent of Soviet communism. When he was elected to replace Ostrowski as mayor of Berlin in 1947 the Soviet military command refused to confirm his appointment. Since no agreement could be reached over Reuter's appointment in the Allied Military Command, Berlin's municipal government was led until its political division in late 1948 by an acting mayor, Louise Schroeder.[113]

Restoring Services under Duress

Against this backdrop of mounting distrust and confrontation between pro-Soviet and pro-Western forces, essential services needed restoring to make Berlin a functioning city once more. This was acknowledged as a top priority by occupying powers, municipal government, and utilities alike. The very first order issued by the Soviet commander of Berlin, General Bersarin, on April 28, 1945, required the city's energy and water utilities to restore their services urgently and called on all their employees to return to work.[114] While the battle for Berlin was still raging, the occupying powers were exerting their authority on the city through its infrastructure. This order no. 1 was followed by another (no. 8) on May 8, 1945, obliging the water utility to repair the principal water mains and pumping stations and to monitor the hygienic quality of drinking water.[115] A further order (no. 20) was issued on June 25, 1945, restricting the provision of electricity in the city to 1.8 million kWh per day and banning the use of electrical appliances by households between 9 a.m. and 7 p.m.[116]

When the Allied Military Command became operational in July 1945 it instated for each utility service a subcommittee of four contact officers (one from each occupying power).[117] These contact officers negotiated with Berlin's utilities on an almost daily basis. Their control of decision making was exercised via progress reports they demanded from the utilities on the state of their infrastructure—initially every day, then every week, and later every month. On the basis of these reports repair and maintenance work was agreed and applications for materials submitted. Acquiring the simplest of materials and apparatus for repairs to damaged plant proved hugely challenging in the initial postwar weeks, not least because—following the agreed Allied protocol—each occupied sector of Berlin could be supplied with goods only from its respective occupied zone in Germany.[118] If, for instance, a water pumping station located in Spandau needed a replacement flange, this had to come from the British occupied zone over two hundred kilometers away. Taking a piece of equipment from a neighboring sector of the city ran up against military protocol and risked affronting an occupying power. Although utility staff complained repeatedly about these restrictions, they found their contact persons—and the Allies in general—usually very supportive in providing essential materials for repairs.[119]

Far less conducive to restoring utility services was the practice by the Soviet military of requisitioning infrastructure as a form of war reparations.[120] It has been estimated that the Soviets removed some 80 percent of Berlin's machine-tool production and 60 percent of its light industrial capacity in the first months after the end of the war, marking the end of Berlin as a great industrial city.[121] Between 1945 and 1946 the Red Army instructed the dismantling of plant at power stations, in particular, that was then transported to the Soviet Union. Articles confiscated in this way ranged from whole turbines to chairs, mirrors, and bolts, as was meticulously documented in a 336-page list compiled by the power utility Bewag.[122] The Soviet authorities took care to ensure that the most valuable infrastructure dismantled came from the Western sectors of the city in advance of the arrival of the US and British forces (see figure 6.6).[123] Whereas in the Soviet sector only 10 percent of the existing boilers and 4 percent of the turbines were removed, in the three Western sectors the figures were 53 percent and 60 percent, respectively.[124] Electricity-generating capacity in the American, British, and French sectors fell dramatically as a result, from 361 MW at the end of the war to a mere 117 MW by late 1945, most of it coming from outdated power stations.[125] The Soviets also dismantled the entire equipment of the connecting station for the long-distance gas pipeline in Spandau, which was removed to hinder gas supply to the Western sectors of Berlin from the British occupied zone of Germany.[126]

Given all the wartime destruction, postwar requisitions, and shortages of materials it is astounding how fast basic services were restored in the city.[127] Most impressive was the achievement of the Berliner Wasserwerke (BWW). In May 1945 the water utility had supplied around 6 million cubic meters of water to the city—approximately 40 percent of the average monthly figure in 1938.[128] Just two months later, in July 1945, it delivered 13.4 million cubic meters and by December 1945 actually surpassed the prewar monthly average of 14.5 million cubic meters. By 1947 BWW was able to meet a summer peak of 1 million cubic meters a day—the highest recorded in Berlin.[129] The principal reason behind this success story was the effective repair of war-damaged water mains. A report by the utility to the British military authorities in August 1946 documented the repair of 99.3 percent of all damaged trunk water mains (with a diameter of 300–1500 cm) and 99.7 percent of all damaged minor water mains (with a diameter of 80–250 cm) across the city.[130]

Figure 6.6
Dismantled power turbines in a West Berlin power plant, 1948
Source: Landesarchiv Berlin (LAB) F Rep. 290 (07), no. 0006259. Photo by Otto Martens, September 8, 1948.

Repair of Berlin's sewage disposal system was almost as swift. The Allied Military Command, in one of its early meetings, had set the massively ambitious target of repairing the city's sewer network by October 31, 1945.[131] This deadline was not actually met, but the wastewater utility was able to report to the American High Command on October 26 that around 1,600 damaged sections of the sewer network had already been repaired, leaving 1,000 still to repair.[132] Just as significant, seventy-seven of the eighty-seven sewage pumping stations serving the city were operable by that time. This was an extraordinary achievement given the arduous circumstances under which the sanitation department—like all the utilities—was operating after the war. These were characterized by a serious shortage of staff, the need to employ unskilled female labor, the chronic undernourishment of the workforce, and, hence, frequent absenteeism to forage for food and coal.[133] Despite improvements to the mains sewage system, poor sanitation remained a serious concern for public health. This was primarily because the toilets of many dwellings had been destroyed and could not be readily replaced. To stop residents dumping their feces in damaged buildings the wastewater utility opened manhole covers to sewers at specific times of day to allow people to dispose of their waste in a more hygienic manner.[134] Personal hardship in the war-stricken city caused other problems to the sewer system. In the absence of proper toilet paper, people resorted to using newspaper and other hard paper as a substitute, thereby causing major blockages to the sewers.

The gas supply network was, in the utility's own words, "in chaos" at the end of hostilities, with most of the technical plant destroyed or damaged and none of the gas works operative.[135] Reconstruction began immediately and, by May 19, 1945, town gas was being produced at three of the city's gas works.[136] Four more went into production by early July. Between May 1945 and December 1946 some 2,700 damaged gas mains were repaired, in addition to around 12,000 gas lamps.[137] By the end of 1946 only 6 percent of the city's gas mains were not yet in use.[138] Gas supply increased rapidly as a consequence, from a mere 1.8 million cubic meters in May 1945 to 17.1 million cubic meters in December 1945.[139] This still represented only 44 percent of the 1938 monthly average of 38.8 million cubic meters. By 1946 the monthly average had risen to 27.5 million cubic meters and by 1947 to 33.1 million cubic meters, a little short of the prewar figure.[140]

Restoring electricity supply was, by contrast, far from a success story. For over two and a half years Berlin struggled to secure sufficient electricity for its inhabitants, businesses, and occupying powers. Several factors characteristic of the postwar era combined to prompt draconian restrictions on electricity use for two successive winters: dismantled generating plants, severe coal shortages, interventions by the occupying powers, inept crisis management by the power utility, and the machinations of an incompetent councillor. Initially, the signs were positive. On August 1, 1945, Bewag's director Hans Witte was able to report proudly that the entire city had full electricity supply.[141] In the course of 1945 the utility's electricity sales rose from a meager 5.4 million kWh in July to 72.8 million kWh in November.[142] The dramatic recovery of peak demand is illustrated in figure 6.7. In the following years, though, consumption figures never even approached the prewar level of 149 million kWh per month. In 1946 electricity consumption averaged at 92.1 million kWh per month; in 1947 it actually declined to 84.5 million kWh.[143] This poor performance was partly a problem of generating capacity, which recovered only slowly after wartime destruction and Soviet requisitioning. Over a space of three years, between January 1946 and January 1949, the installed capacity of Bewag's power stations in all sectors of the city increased by only 16 percent, from 356 to 412 MW.[144] More disruptive, however, was the coal supply crisis during the winters of 1945–1946 and 1946–1947. Following the loss of

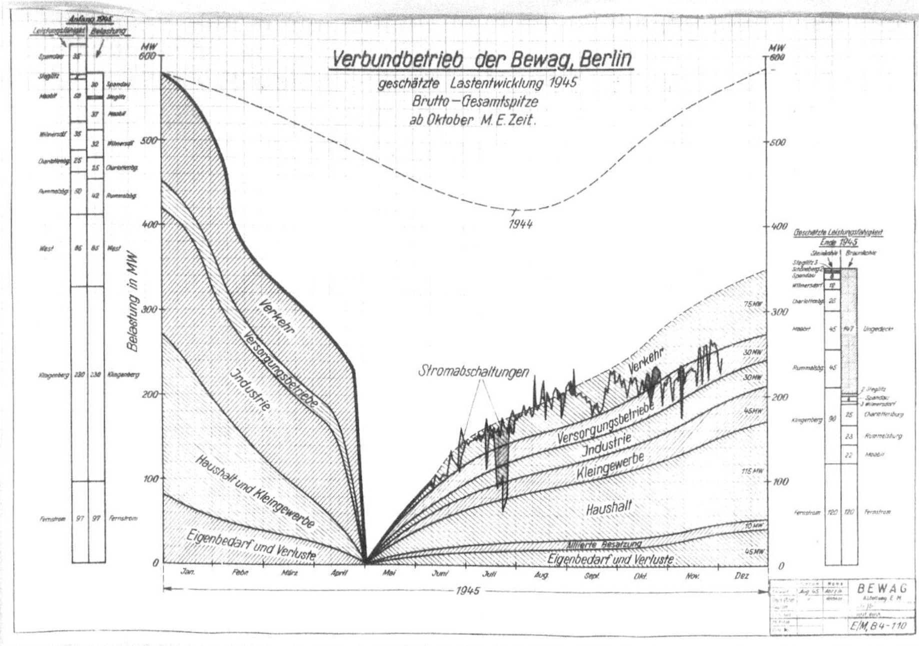

Figure 6.7

Restoration of power supply to Berlin, 1945

Source: Landesarchiv Berlin (LAB) C Rep. 101, no. 1185.

Upper Silesia and its rich coalfields to Poland after the war and difficulties in accessing and transporting alternative sources, supplies of coal to Berlin collapsed at the end of August 1945. Of the meager 3,600 metric tons per day reaching the city, 2,000 went straight to the power stations, 700 to the gas works, 300 to the water works, and the remaining 600 to sustain essential services, leaving nothing at all for home heating.[145]

Under such dire circumstances, restrictions on the use of electricity in homes were introduced on September 1, 1945, by the city council at the behest of the Allied Military Command.[146] These clearly did not have the desired effect, as the Electric Subcommittee of Allied Command ordered electricity provision in Berlin to be cut drastically to 2.2 million kWh per day on September 19, 1945.[147] There followed a series of emergency council meetings and heated correspondence in which the Bewag directors accused the Allies of overreacting, the mayor appealed to the Allies for clemency, the city's consumers ignored or circumvented measures to reduce electricity use, and the councillor responsible for municipal enterprises, Walter Jirak, heaped blame on all but himself. Jirak told the council on December 13, 1945: "The Berlin population has utterly failed; the people glibly continue to exceed their quotas. Where there are no meters the power cables are tapped anyway. Consumption with electric heaters is massive."[148] The next day the city council approved a harsh package of prohibitions of electricity use.[149] Factories were permitted to work only between 7 a.m. and 3 p.m. Shops, restaurants, and bars were not allowed to use lighting. Cinemas, theaters, and concert halls were closed from Monday to Thursday. Use of warm water boilers, vacuum cleaners, and room heaters was strictly prohibited. In municipal departments and enterprises all electric heaters were to be rounded up and stored in a locked room.

The following winter saw a repeat performance of the electricity supply crisis. In the winter of 1946–1947 Berlin's coal reserves fell at one point to just 30,000 metric tons, barely enough to cover essential requirements for a week (see figure 6.8).[150] The blame game re-emerged with vigor. In August 1946 Councillor Jirak was put on permanent leave after an investigation concluded he had been grossly negligent in his supervision of the municipal enterprises.[151] Bewag's director Witte was subjected to massive criticism for the utility's handling of the crisis at council meetings on August 31 and October 12, in particular for unannounced brownouts and misleading press statements playing down the problem.[152] Witte himself blamed the poor quality of coal and the lack of materials, for which the Allies were largely responsible.

When the city's electricity supply threatened to collapse on November 6, 1946, draconian measures were announced at a joint press conference of the council and Bewag.[153] Electricity rationing was to be supervised by energy control centres created in each of the city's twenty boroughs. These centers employed 163 people, who by January

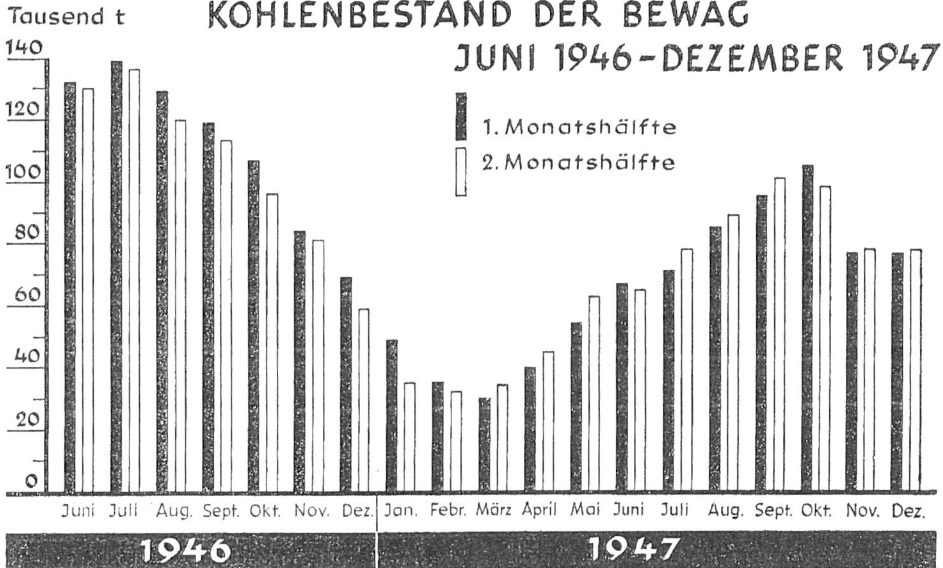

Figure 6.8
Monthly coal reserves of Berlin, 1946–1947
Source: Magistrat von Groß-Berlin, *Berlin 1947*, 134.

1947 had recorded 69,337 instances of electricity rations being exceeded, resulting in 41,643 appliances being switched off.[154] By March 1947 criminal charges had been brought against offenders in 48,000 cases, resulting in fines totalling 34 million Reichsmark.[155] The problem was, as Bewag complained to the city council, few consumers were either willing or able to pay the high level of fines imposed by the Allied Military Command, set at 100 times the regular electricity price. Consequently, only a fraction of the fines imposed were actually paid and the disciplinary effect was undermined.[156] Besides electricity rations not being respected, electricity theft became a major cause for concern. Using electricity without it being metered was possible either by short-circuiting the system or by running the meter backward with the help of capacitors colloquially known as "Little Gustavs."[157] The number of reported instances of electricity theft was put at 1,100 in March 1947 and 2,649 in February 1948.[158]

Given Bewag's inability to provide sufficient power to the city, electricity imports grew in significance. However, these were dependent on Allied approval and on electricity produced elsewhere being available. The proportion of Berlin's electricity imported from the national Elektrowerke actually exceeded that generated by Bewag in 1946.[159] It was only after December 1947, when the Allies finally reached an agreement on imported electricity between the occupied zones and Berlin, that the city's power supply crisis subsided.[160] On March 2, 1948, with the situation under control, the Electric Sub-committee of the Allied Military Command was dissolved.[161] The following month the city council received the order from the US and British command—without the backing of the Soviets—to reconstruct the main power station in the Western sectors as rapidly as possible.[162]

Underground Urbanism

The significance of infrastructure to Berlin's recovery after the war reached far beyond restoring essential services of electricity, gas, water, and sanitation to its beleaguered inhabitants. As indicated in the introduction to this chapter, the very form of the city was decisively shaped by the survival of much of its "underground urbanism." Berlin was not unique in this respect. In many German cities existing urban infrastructures constituted key assets that, according to Jeffry M. Diefendorf, "exerted a great influence on the shape of reconstruction."[163] What was special in the case of Berlin was how underground infrastructures became instrumentalized in a politicized debate about the remaking of the postwar city.

Within a few months of the cessation of hostilities two groups of urban planners and architects had begun to develop very different visions of the city.[164] The first was a group initially led by the chief architect Hans Scharoun that envisaged a city reordered around the principle of functional spatial segregation. It was strongly influenced by ideas of social reform and socialist planning. The second group was based at the Zehlendorf branch of the city council's Central Planning Office under the aegis of Walter Moest, who had earlier served at Speer's Inspectorate General for Building. The so-called Zehlendorf Plan developed by this second group prioritized transport and roads as key levers of urban planning, but also championed the existing underground infrastructure in reconstructing the city.[165] These two urban plans were diametrically opposed, in terms of their basic approach (visionary vs. pragmatic), thematic foci (living conditions vs. transport infrastructure) and political allegiance (socialist vs. conservative).

In the midst of this highly politicized debate on the future of Berlin, Ernst Randzio presented his report on the status of the city's underground infrastructure. Randzio was a professor at the Technical University of Berlin who was commissioned by the city council after the war to calculate the extent and value of damage to the city's entire underground structures, including its electricity cables, water pipes, gas mains, district heating pipes, and sewers, as well as subsurface communication and transportation lines. He presented his findings in a talk to the building committee of the city parliament on May 16, 1946, and a written report submitted to the council the following year.[166] His astonishing conclusion was that only 2–3 percent of Berlin's entire underground infrastructure had suffered damage in the course of the war. In marked contrast to infrastructure above ground, that had been badly destroyed, the city's "underground space" (*U-Raum*) had survived almost entirely intact (see figure 6.9). Randzio's detailed report documented significant differences between infrastructure sectors. Loss of value, as a percentage of 1938 figures, was only 1.1 percent for wastewater infrastructure (sewers, rainwater pipes, culverts, etc.) and 2.0 percent for gas mains, but higher for district heating pipes (5.4 percent), electricity cables (6.1 percent), and, in particular, water mains and house connections (19.2 percent).[167] What this meant overall, Randzio emphasized, was that Berlin still possessed underground assets worth a total of 4.3 billion Reichsmark—almost 40 percent of the value of all surviving infrastructure above ground.[168] Of this impressive sum, the sewer network constituted 800 million,

Figure 6.9

Berlin's intact underground infrastructure, 1947

Source: Randzio, *Unterirdischer Städtebau*, inside back cover.

the electricity grid 300 million, the water mains 254 million, and the gas pipes 146 million Reichsmark.[169]

Randzio claimed that his study was not intended to preempt, but only inform, urban planning in postwar Berlin. The way he opened his report, however, makes it clear that there was never any doubt for him about the conclusions that had to be drawn from it: "The work presented here arose out of recognition that urban planning and reconstruction will remain piecemeal if supply and transportation systems, along with their requisite facilities, are not given sufficient consideration."[170] He concluded by calling for special plans to be drawn up to map Berlin's underground infrastructures, providing examples for select areas in the city. Prioritizing infrastructure in this way and giving it a catchy name—*Unterirdischer Städtebau* ("underground urbanism")—was enthusiastically welcomed not only by civil engineers.[171] Scharoun's successor as Berlin's chief urban planner, Karl Bonatz, was keen to avoid experiments and build on existing structures in reconstructing the city.[172] In the autumn of 1947 he presented two revised versions of the Zehlendorf Plan, that were subsequently combined into the so-called Bonatz Plan of 1948, all based on prevailing street and infrastructure networks (see figure 6.10). In making the case for this approach to urban reconstruction Bonatz drew heavily on Randzio's findings and praised his study explicitly.[173] It is, as a consequence, no exaggeration to claim that the urban form of Berlin was retained in large measure in acknowledgment of the hidden value of its underground infrastructure.

At the same time as underground infrastructures were being revealed as positive assets for urban development, another underground phenomenon associated with the war was having a distinctly negative impact. This was not unexploded bombs or polluted soil, but rising groundwater. Problems caused by rising groundwater levels were, indeed, the principle issue of concern in articles published on water management in Berlin at the time. For decades, incessant construction work and increasing water abstractions had caused groundwater levels in the city to decline to levels prompting concern among hydrologists and urban planners, as discussed in chapter 4.[174] The war, however, had brought an end to almost all building work requiring deep foundations. Once the aerial bombardment began in earnest, prompting the evacuation of industry and population, water consumption collapsed. Consequently, water abstractions from the city's groundwater aquifers dropped sharply. It was this combination of a dormant construction sector and a major drop in water demand that—in addition to the destruction of water infrastructure—caused groundwater levels to rise sharply, reaching levels not experienced since 1885 (see figure 6.11).[175]

This became problematic only because Berlin had been built, since then, on the assumption that groundwater levels would remain low. As groundwater levels rose to

Figure 6.10
Bonatz Plan of 1948
Source: Werner, *Stadtplanung Berlin*, 107.

within a meter of the surface in some areas, cellars became permanently flooded, damp damaged walls, cesspits overflowed, and fruit trees—essential under postwar food shortages—died from waterlogging. A leading hydrologist employed at the city's planning department, Julius Denner, was commissioned to produce a report on the problem in Berlin's inner-city areas. He and his colleagues documented flooding and damp as a result of rising groundwater on a huge scale, especially in low-lying areas of the borough of Lichtenberg.[176] Little could be done to alleviate the situation in the short term, since any water pumped out of cellars was immediately replaced by fresh groundwater rising. Efforts to require the Berlin water utility to abstract more groundwater than it needed proved unsuccessful, as the utility was unwilling to cover the additional costs. As Denner pointed out, the long-term solution was to wait for economic recovery

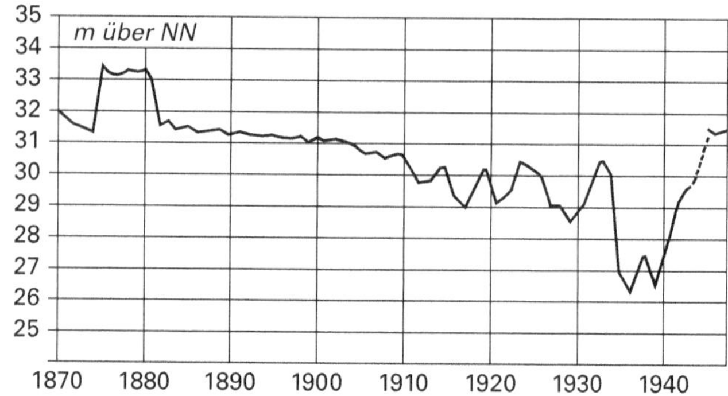

Figure 6.11
Graph showing rising groundwater levels in Berlin after 1940
Source: Medon, "Das Grundwasser von Groß-Berlin," 42.

and the growth of water demand. This is, indeed, what resolved the issue from the early 1950s onward. However, the postwar experience generated important insight into the close relationship between groundwater levels and economic development in the city. Denner revealed, perceptively, that Berlin's groundwater levels were a mirror image of its economic performance, rising when the city was in decline and falling when it prospered.[177] Once again, the underground city was inextricably bound up with the one above ground.

Legacies of Nazism

The leadership of Berlin's utilities and, to a lesser extent, also their workforce took on a new complexion in the wake of denazification after the war. In Berlin the process of excluding former members of the NSDAP and its organizations from municipal office began on June 30, 1945, with an order by the Soviet Military Command.[178] Already by July 9 the city council was able to report that 15,795 NSDAP members had been dismissed from public office since the end of hostilities.[179]

Most, though not all, the directors of the city's utilities were dismissed owing to their party membership or sympathy to the Nazi cause. Gasag's two directors (Hoffmann and Lessel) as well as their deputies (Kiesel and Lähr), who had all been appointed under Nazi rule, lost their posts in 1945.[180] The influential director of the water utility and prominent Nazi Karl Kasper was arrested and imprisoned by the Soviets in May 1945. At Bewag, the new works council identified twenty-one of the thirty people in senior management as having belonged to NSDAP organizations and singled out three directors—Fischer, Adolph, and Krohne—for having supported the Nazi regime with particular enthusiasm.[181] Fischer and Adolph succumbed to pressure to resign. Krohne was actually cleared in the subsequent denazification procedure, despite having been a member of the NSDAP and Gestapo, but was dismissed from the utility in September 1945 on the grounds of having sabotaged power generation equipment.[182] The fourth Bewag director, Erich Nain, was retained initially for being allegedly indispensable to business operations, especially regarding the utility's foreign shareholders.[183] Despite his being supported by the company's supervisory board, the Allied Military Command prohibited him from retaining his director's post. Under these circumstances Nain decided to resign in June 1946.[184] After the division of the city, however, he returned to Bewag in West Berlin, being elected a member of its supervisory board, a post he held until 1962.

Denazification also affected the workforce of Berlin's utilities significantly. Between April and November 1945 1,426 employees of Bewag were dismissed for being members of Nazi organizations, 124 of whom were subsequently reinstated.[185] The number dismissed at Bewag rose to about 2,000 by the end of 1946.[186] By the end of 1945 Gasag had sacked 1,027 employees for having been members of the NSDAP or its subsidiary organizations.[187] Dismissals on this scale produced fresh labor problems for the utilities that were already having to cope with absent staff still detained in prisoner-of-war camps and an undernourished workforce.[188]

National Socialist rule left behind not only tainted biographies but also unfinished business regarding ownership of the city's utilities. The newly instated municipal government seized the opportunity of postwar reordering to complete the re-municipalization of the power utility Bewag and the takeover of the water utility CWI. Within two weeks of the city council being constituted in May 1945 it agreed to explore the prospects for buying up all remaining Bewag shares under the fortuitous circumstances of the postwar settlement.[189] At a council meeting of August 20, 1945, it was decided to buy back shares in Bewag belonging to the Reich and Prussia first.[190] The calculation here was that the Allied Military Command might well be sympathetic to a share transfer that weakened the discredited entities of Prussia and the German Reich and benefited a municipality under its own tutelage. The arguments made at the meeting for bringing electricity back into full municipal ownership were partly familiar—such as the need to control tariffs—but partly also reflective of the postwar situation. Re-municipalizing Bewag would, it was argued, help coordinate infrastructure reconstruction with urban planning and reassert political control over a utility whose directors were regarded as "economic reactionaries" by the communist-dominated council.[191] Approaches to the Allied Military Command did not, however, prove as fruitful as anticipated. By June 1946 Berlin still owned only 47.5 million of the 100 million Reichsmark shares in public ownership.[192] Buying up shares owned by private companies proved just as difficult as it had been for the Nazis. In July 1947 Bewag reported that research into the whereabouts of the shares owned by foreigners, administered by the Sofina consortium and Schröder Bank, had revealed little, since all records of transactions had been destroyed in the war.[193]

While efforts to increase control over Bewag proved laborious and unsatisfactory, other opportunities for re-municipalization fell into the city's lap. When electricity supply to the borough of Wannsee by the neighboring power utility Elektrizitätswerk der Stadt Potsdam ran into difficulties in 1946, Bewag was able to argue convincingly to the occupying American forces there that it would not be in the United States' interest to be dependent for part of its electricity on a utility based in the Soviet zone.[194] It was subsequently agreed that Bewag would take over power supply of Wannsee from July 1, 1946, and the Potsdam utility would terminate its concession agreement with Berlin prematurely, transferring all its assets there to Bewag.[195]

Far more significant was the amalgamation of CWI into the Berliner Wasserwerke (BWW). This long-standing goal of municipal policy was finally achieved on August 30, 1945. The dissolution of CWI that day was long believed to be on the orders of the Allied Military Command. It has since been revealed that this was not true, but rather a convenient argument used by the city and its water utility to conceal the ill-gotten nature of their gains.[196] Berlin had been acquiring shares in CWI since the mid-1930s, principally from Jewish shareholders placed under duress by Nazi rule. This was well known to the municipal administration and the Berlin water utility. At a meeting of the supervisory board of the Berlin water utility in December 1954, its director, Albert Uter, conceded under cross-examination from an SPD delegate that over half of all shares in CWI had been held by Jews prior to 1937 and that the city had acquired many of these shares since that time.[197] He claimed, unconvincingly, that these had been bought legally. This view was clearly not shared by many former shareholders, who challenged the legality of their share "sales" in the courts during the 1950s. Given the duration of these cases, it was only in June 1962 that CWI could finally be wound up. The final episode in Berlin's long-standing attempt to gain full control over its water supply reveals uncomfortable continuities and selective reframings as the city moved from an authoritarian to a democratic regime.[198]

Divided City, Divided Infrastructures

The ten years of disruption that began with the outbreak of war culminated in the blockade of Berlin, the political division of the city, and the creation of two separate states of West and East Germany in 1949. As relations between the Soviet and Western powers soured in the late 1940s, the geopolitics of the Cold War emerged as the defining frame of governance in Germany, but also Berlin. Following the failure to reach agreement at the London Conference of Allied Foreign Ministers in November and December 1947, positions on Berlin between the two sides hardened.[199] While the Western Allies insisted on their right to access all sectors of the city, the Soviets argued that Berlin as a whole was part of the Soviet zone of occupation. Cooperation in the Allied Military Command ended de facto in June 1948 when the Soviets left, never to attend again. What precipitated the blockade of the city by the Soviet authorities was the decision in the Western-occupied zones of Germany to introduce a new currency, the Deutschmark, on June 20, 1948.[200] That this step would provoke a strong reaction from the Soviets must have been anticipated, for it posed an immediate question about whether the new currency would be adopted in the Western part of Berlin, thus dividing the city economically. The Soviet authorities tried to prohibit transfers of the Deutschmark to Berlin and campaigned for a new currency for the whole city, but had to concede defeat when the Deutschmark was introduced to West Berlin on June 24.[201] The very next day they began blocking all land and water routes between Berlin and the Western-occupied zones of Germany.[202]

Berlin's infrastructures were an immediate and significant conduit of the blockade.[203] One of the first acts of physical separation was the truncation of all electricity supplies between the Western sectors of Berlin and the surrounding territories of East Berlin and the Soviet zone. This plunged West Berlin into a power supply crisis more severe than anything experienced during or after the war. West Berlin possessed only small, outdated power stations with a generating capacity of just 148 MW, while East Berlin boasted modern plant with a capacity of 215 MW in addition to potentially vast quantities of imported electricity from the Soviet zone.[204] The Western Allies imposed strict rationing of electricity in their sectors, requiring households to reduce consumption by 75 percent and factories by 25 percent.[205] A three-person household was permitted per month only 9 kWh for lighting and 37 kWh for cooking.[206] West Berliners struggled to light and heat their homes (see figure 6.12). Meanwhile in the Soviet sector, electricity quotas were actually relaxed during the blockade: to 33 kWh for lighting and 132 kWh for cooking. While street lighting was banned in West Berlin, the Eastern sector of the city "was bathed in the brightest of lights."[207] Clearly, the Soviets and their East Berlin allies were keen to make the most of their structural advantage in electricity supply.

Ironically, the situation for gas supply was the reverse, with gas production focused in the Western sectors of the city. There, four gas works produced 1 million cubic meters of gas per day, compared with two gas works producing only half that amount in the

Figure 6.12
A West Berlin family experiencing a power cut during the blockade, 1949
Source: Landesarchiv Berlin (LAB) F Rep. 290 (02), no. 0001142. Photo by Helga Kusche, January 5, 1949.

Eastern sector.[208] It came as no surprise, therefore, when the Western Allies retaliated on June 26, 1948, by instructing the cessation of all gas supplies to East Berlin. As a result, sixty-five gas mains from West to East were cut off, prompting a gas supply crisis in the Eastern half of the city.[209] The water and wastewater infrastructures, by contrast, were not disconnected at this time.

The core challenge posed by the blockade to Berlin's utility services lay, however, in the supply of coal needed to operate the infrastructure, whether power stations, gas works, or water pumps (see figure 6.13). Whereas in East Berlin Bewag held coal reserves of around 47,000 metric tons in July and increased them to nearly 145,000 in December 1948, the utility had in West Berlin just 13,000 metric tons in July and only 17,000 in December.[210] The figure for July was enough to drive the power stations in West Berlin for just ten days, according to Bewag's technical director, Rudolf Wissell. The situation was similar at the gas works. The Western Allies limited the amount of coal that could be used to produce town gas in West Berlin to just 300 metric tons a day.[211] Gas rations were reduced by 50 percent for all customers.[212] Owing to the lack of coal and electricity cuts sewage could no longer be pumped out of West Berlin to the surrounding sewage treatment plants and sewage farms.[213] As a result, it had to be released untreated into the city's rivers, posing a major risk for public hygiene, as at the end of the war.

Accessing coal to drive the city's infrastructures became a core priority during the blockade of Berlin. Out of sheer desperation the West Berlin authorities conducted test drilling for coal in the borough of Reinickendorf, where a seam had been identified at a depth of 40 meters.[214] The only effective response to the blockade in general, and the coal shortage in particular, though, was the airlift of essential goods from Western Germany to the beleaguered West Berlin. This extraordinary project to keep a city going by air transportation alone is today viewed as a masterclass in logistics, but was at the time regarded as a massive risk, politically and technically. Over the course of the following eleven months, US and British forces made 277,000 flights to West Berlin, transporting over 1.8 million metric tons of goods.[215] Significantly, 62.8 percent of this tonnage was coal, much of which went straight to the power stations and gas works to provide energy for the city.[216] Even parts to reconstruct West Berlin's flagship power plant were flown in by plane.[217]

Figure 6.13
Schoolchildren lining up for water from a tanker, 1948
Source: Landesarchiv Berlin (LAB) F Rep. 290 (02), no. 0264837. Photo by E. Schwab, 1948.

The Berlin airlift is seen today as the turning point in the Allies' attitude to Berlin. Prior to the blockade the Western Allies treated Berlin as an occupied city of no long-term significance.[218] The experience of solidarity between occupying forces, municipal government, and the people of West Berlin engendered by the airlift created a powerful commitment to protecting the half-city as a symbol of Western democracy.[219] Occupiers came to be seen as defenders; the defeated city as a bulwark of freedom. The attempt by the Soviets to sow disunity between the Western Allies and the Berlin populace backfired stupendously.[220] Their hopes that the Allies would abandon West Berlin were dashed by the emblematic lifeline of the airlift.

The price of the airlift's success and the solidarity generated within West Berlin was lasting political division of the city. In the course of the blockade the governance of Berlin, and its infrastructures, gradually separated into a bipolar system. For several months the utilities continued to operate across the whole city, but faced growing difficulties. Having to work with two currencies in one city, for instance, posed a massive problem of accounting.[221] People who worked in the East but lived in the West were required to pay in Deutschmark but earned the Reichsmark, which was valued at only a tenth of the Western currency.[222] Infrastructure investments made in one part of the city needed to be billed in the currency operative there. Political interventions in the running of its utilities increased on both sides of the city. The Soviet authorities dismissed one of Bewag's directors, Wissell (SPD), the day after the blockade commenced, accusing him of sabotaging their order to reduce coal consumption and electricity generation.[223] The Western Allies declared the move illegal and refused to recognize the Soviet replacement, director Witte, in their sectors.

The political division of Berlin began to take shape in early September 1948 when the Berlin city parliament split, following disruption by communist demonstrators. Representatives from the West set up a new city parliament in the British sector while the SED group remained in the rump parliament.[224] On November 30 a "provisional democratic city council" was formed in East Berlin, comprising twenty-three representatives from the SED and organizations close to the party. It appointed Friedrich Ebert (SED) as the new mayor with the backing of the Soviet authorities. The following day, the acting mayor, Friedensburg, was prevented from entering his office by police, prompting the emergence of a separate administration for West Berlin.[225] Elections to the city parliament were held in the three Western sectors on December 5, 1948, resulting in a resounding victory once more for the SPD, which received 64.5 percent of the vote with an 86.3 percent turnout.[226] Division of the legislature and executive of Berlin was completed on December 7, 1948, when Ernst Reuter was elected mayor and a fresh city council (henceforth termed senate) was appointed with jurisdiction over West Berlin only.

Parallel to these developments in municipal government, control over the city's utilities was also being separated. The power utility, always the most sensitive to urban politics, was divided first. On December 4, 1948, the Soviet authorities dismissed a second Bewag director, Strassmann, on account of his close association with former director Wissell.[227] Two days later, at a meeting of the Bewag board, director Witte resigned as head of the board and accepted the post of director of Bewag operations in East Berlin.[228] Management of operations in West Berlin moved to a new headquarters in the British sector shortly afterward. Gasag was not divided until March 26, 1949, following the occupation of its headquarters by the police and the arrest of its technical director, Herbert Bausch.[229] That same day the senate of West Berlin created its own Gasag with new offices in the West. The East Berlin Gasag remained responsible to the city council in that half of the city. Also on March 26, the city council in East Berlin established a separate water company there and dismissed both directors of the existing municipal water utility, Wilhelm Steppler and Albert Uter.[230] West Berlin responded by moving the headquarters of its own, new water utility to where CWI had been based.

The abrupt division of Berlin's electricity, gas, and water utilities created fresh problems of service provision. Workforces found themselves employed by different companies overnight, utility headquarters lacked adequate infrastructure plans or data on their customers, and physical connections became subject to tight monitoring of intersectoral flows. Water mains and principal sewers were not initially disconnected. The water works at Johannisthal in the East of the city, for instance, continued to supply water to the Western boroughs of Neukölln and Tempelhof. Consumption, though, was charged to the other side, resulting in bitter disputes over payments.[231] Deals were tentatively made whereby, for instance, work conducted by employees of the AEG factory in the West on the Klingenberg power station in the East was made dependent on the free passage of parts for West Berlin's new power plant by land.[232]

When the blockade was lifted, on May 12, 1949, the rationing of coal in the three Western sectors was lifted and Bewag (East) resumed supply of electricity to Bewag (West) the very same day.[233] An agreement was subsequently reached, on July 18, between the two Bewags for the Western sectors to be supplied with 1 million kWh per day, increasing to 1.4 million kWh in the winter.[234] Figure 6.14 shows that electricity supply remained heavily weighted in East Berlin's favor. Meanwhile, West Berlin's new power station—West—was being constructed at a rapid pace with the help of significant funding out of the European Recovery Program (44 million Deutschmark)

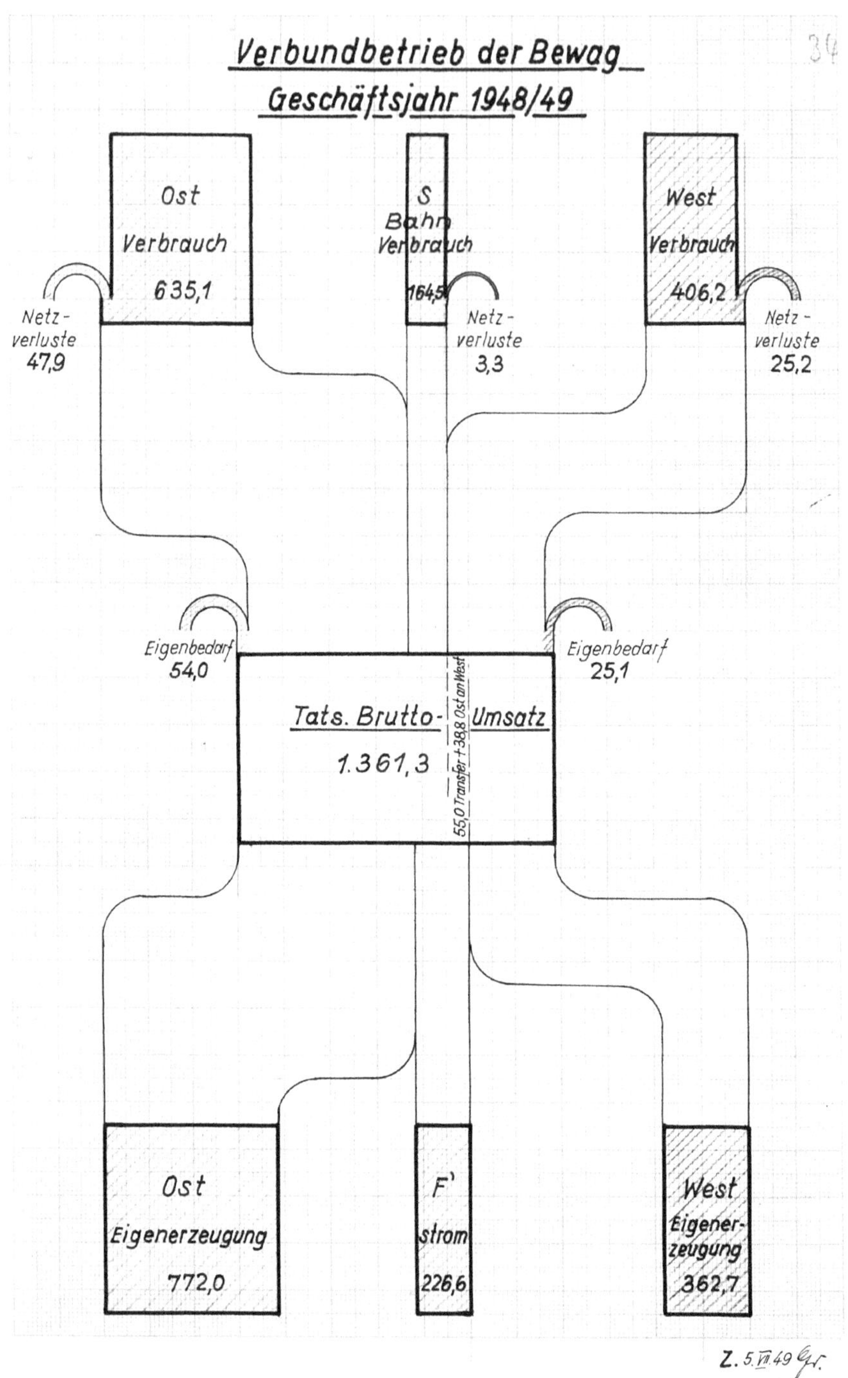

Figure 6.14

Flow diagram of Bewag East and West, July 5, 1949

Source: Landesarchiv Berlin (LAB) C Rep. 752, no. 104.

and the German Bank for Reconstruction (11 million Deutschmark). It was opened on December 1, 1949, in the presence of the American, British, and French commanders, providing the Western sectors immediately with an additional 108 MW of electricity-generating capacity.[235] By that time, two new German states had been established: the Federal Republic of Germany (BRD) on May 23, 1949, and the German Democratic Republic (DDR) on October 7, 1949.

Lessons on Infrastructural Resilience

Looking back across this decade of destruction and division, the resilience of Berlin's infrastructure systems is the most striking constant. The speed with which war damage was repaired and basic services restored in 1945–1946 is truly astounding. The adaptability of the city's energy and water utilities to geopolitical interference and political division commands huge respect. Keeping these huge sociotechnical systems going at all odds and in the face of diverse disruptions was a top priority for utility managers, municipal governments, and occupying powers alike. Each infrastructure sector had its particular vulnerabilities to physical destruction that were revealed during the war, whether the pumping stations of the sanitation system, the end points of the water supply network, or the long-distance gas pipeline. The weakest link in the chain of service provision for all utilities, though, was the supply of coal. Shortages of coal during and after the war, as well as during the blockade, revealed the massive dependence of all machinery driving Berlin's infrastructures on coal, either directly or indirectly, via coal-fired power generation and gas production. Destruction and division exposed the reliance of Berlin's mid-century metabolism on coal.

A sociotechnical approach reveals system vulnerability and resilience, though, to be about much more than the material constitution of urban infrastructure. Notions of infrastructural vulnerability were used as argumentative ploys throughout this decade to make the case for particular resilience strategies, whether to promote energy saving by households during the war, protect sensitive plant from bombardment, or minimize dependence on a political opponent. The infrastructural resilience pursued by diverse political regimes often involved the coercion of others, whether it was foreigners forced to work at the city gas works or utility directors dismissed for their political sympathies. Berlin's infrastructures themselves became instruments of urban vulnerability and resilience, as witnessed by the targeting of electricity supply in the blockade of West Berlin and the formative influence of the city's underground structures on postwar urban planning. The disruption of war and division reveals in stark relief how social and technical elements got assembled in novel infrastructural configurations to defend the city from threats, real and perceived.

On August 30, 1949, the Allied Military Command returned control over Berlin's utilities to the municipal authorities.[236] Henceforth, only imports of electricity from occupied zones of Germany were subject to approval by the former Allies. This act marked the rebirth of municipal control over Berlin's utilities, but also the end of all attempts by the former Allies to supervise municipal decision-making jointly. Berlin's utilities were to be governed, for the next forty years, by two separate political systems framed by the Cold War divide.

7 In Pursuit of the Socialist Infrastructural Ideal

In May 1970 the city government of East Berlin produced an extraordinary urban plan. Entitled the General Plan for Urban Infrastructure Services, it was a civil engineer's dream. It had been developed in an impressive collaborative effort involving the city's planning authorities, the East Berlin utilities for electricity, gas, water, and sanitation, and the city councillor responsible for municipal enterprises.[1] It was masterminded by a unit within the city planning department specially commissioned to coordinate infrastructure and urban planning in preparation for a major housing development program. The plan itself comprised thirty-seven pages of text and numerous commented maps that set out future demand and supply options for each infrastructure service until the year 2000. What made the plan so striking was its aspiration to shape urban development along and around underground infrastructures. Echoing Randzio's postwar plea for "underground urbanism," it elevated the slogan of "*Tiefbau vor Hochbau*" (i.e., prioritizing civil over building engineering) to a principle of urban planning acknowledged by the responsible authorities.[2] This in itself was a remarkable achievement. Equally impressive, given the history of rivalry between several of the city's utilities, was the plan's integrated approach to infrastructure planning. Not only did it cover all piped infrastructures, from electricity, gas, and district heating to water supply and sanitation, but it described how these could be more systematically coordinated across the city. This integrated approach was epitomized, most radically, by the proposal to serve new urban developments with huge, walk-in infrastructure channels housing multiple underground conduits. Here was civil engineering at its boldest: replacing the chaos of individually laid pipes and cables with a single, accessible duct that would ease maintenance and—to quote the plan itself—"rationalize use of the urban underground."[3] This systematic, integrated plan presented a socialist infrastructural ideal that would, it was argued, demonstrate the superiority of socialist planning over the fragmentation and competition characteristic of capitalism.

For all its ambition and originality, the 1970 infrastructure plan was very much the product of a flawed political regime. Indeed, it reflects many of the challenges of providing utility services in East Berlin, and East Germany in general, that will be encountered throughout this chapter. First, the plan served to reconfigure infrastructure spatially around the territory of East Berlin only. In line with urban planning directives, it prioritized infrastructure services in the new development zones on the urban periphery and around the Alexanderplatz area, reorienting development away from the border with West Berlin. Tellingly, the plan was never discussed with the authorities in West Berlin.[4] Second, the scenarios for energy and water provision underpinning the plan bore little relation to the ability to meet them. The massive growth in demand predicted by the plan was founded on an extrapolation of existing trends in resource use, anticipated improvements to living standards, and the desire to keep up with the West. Neither the funding nor the material resources were available to see the infrastructure plan implemented as designed. Third, infrastructure investment and maintenance never acquired the requisite recognition in either East Berlin or the German Democratic Republic (DDR) as a whole. The boldness of the 1970 infrastructure plan was born not out of confidence, but rather out of desperation. What happened when its rhetoric came up against reality is the underlying theme of this chapter.

The story begins with an appraisal of socialist aspirations to showcase East Berlin and the head start, in infrastructural terms, that the DDR's capital had over West Berlin in the early 1950s. There follows an analysis of how East Berlin's municipal utilities became subordinated to a state-socialist planning and management regime and how this affected services for energy and water/wastewater. The chapter then addresses the thorny relationship with West Berlin over the period of division, exploring different realms of interdependence and the strategies developed by the East Berlin authorities to deal with them. It is then shown how securitization against threats from the West colored the everyday management of the East Berlin electricity utility and its attempt to cultivate a socialist workforce. Looking beyond the city, the chapter subsequently analyzes how East Berlin's infrastructure services became increasingly subjugated to national infrastructure policy in the DDR. The urban infrastructure plan of 1970 is then discussed as a meeting point of emergent critical reflection and persistent self-delusion in city-infrastructure relations. The chapter concludes with an appraisal of the environmental legacies of supply-driven and under-resourced infrastructure management in East Berlin and the widening gap in service standards compared with the West by the 1980s.

Serving the "Better" Berlin

Following the political division of Berlin in 1948–1949, the Eastern sector of the city possessed a number of strategic advantages over its Western counterpart. First and foremost was its continued function as a national capital. Legally, East Berlin was not part of the DDR, but one of the four sectors of a Greater Berlin still operating under occupied rule. Representatives of East Berlin had only advisory status in the East German People's Assembly (Volkskammer); East German laws needed approval by the city council (Magistrat) to be valid in East Berlin.[5] In practice, however, the Soviets permitted East Berlin to become the capital of the DDR, in violation of the Potsdam Agreement of 1945. By retaining capital status for at least the Eastern part of Berlin, they reinforced their claim that the DDR represented the "true" Germany and that West Berlin was a postwar construct merely tolerated within the DDR.[6] Throughout the period of division East Berlin was presented, by Soviet and East German authorities alike, as a showcase for socialism in Germany.[7] It housed national ministries and party organizations, retained access to its hinterland, witnessed ambitious urban projects, and was always privileged in the territorial distribution of resources. As a result, East Berlin was not noticeably poorer than West Berlin during the early 1950s.[8]

Political posturing of this kind was substantiated by the head start East Berlin had over its rival in terms of infrastructure capacity and connectivity. In 1950 the largest power station and principal groundwater resources were located in the Eastern sector of the city. Whereas West Berlin that year had only 267 MW of electricity-generating capacity at its disposal to serve 2.15 million inhabitants, East Berlin could boast nearly double the capacity—499 MW—to supply just 1.19 million inhabitants.[9] Without having to supply parts of West Berlin, the East Berlin utility was able to provide much-needed electricity to the national (DDR) grid in the winter of 1952–1953.[10] Emboldened by such surplus resources, East Berlin's infrastructure managers flaunted their advantageous position as an expression of the superiority of socialist means of production (see figure 7.1). Its water utility could boast household consumption rates of 250 liters per person and day in the new apartments along the Stalinallee.[11] The district heating network installed there was heralded as a model for cleaner, modern heating systems across the DDR.[12] The political agenda underpinning infrastructural achievements was made explicit in the contribution by the city's electricity utility, Bewag (East), to the DDR's second five-year-plan in October 1956. The document opened with the statement: "In planning Berlin's energy supply priority must be given to the role of Berlin as the capital of a reunified Germany and the need to supply the whole city with electricity in the most efficient and advanced manner. West Berlin's pursuit of bridgehead

Figure 7.1

Poster "More Electricity to Build up Socialism," 1952

Source: Landesarchiv Berlin (LAB), F Rep. 260–02, no. A 0173.

politics with regard to its electricity supply results in high energy bills for the West Berlin population without guaranteeing full security of supply. This must be replaced by the rational alternative of connection to the [DDR] grid."[13]

It was this access to a hinterland of resources, as emphasized in the quotation, that gave a further strategic advantage to East Berlin's infrastructure potential. While West Berlin had to negotiate use of extraterritorial energy and natural resources or environmental sinks from a weak position of dependence, East Berlin could continue to use existing infrastructural conduits that reached out into the surrounding region. It had control over most of the sewage farms and the two sewage treatment plants serving the city. Most of Berlin's surface water passed first through the Eastern part of the city, feeding its groundwater aquifers and water works. Ready access to the East German power grid meant that East Berlin could—like other cities—import an increasing proportion of its electricity needs, allowing it to decommission polluting inner-city power plants. Greater availability of water and electricity and significantly lower prices for utility services were held up as illustrations that the socialist variant was the "better" Berlin.

Utilities under State Socialism

East Berlin's utilities became enrolled not merely in a new political ideology, but in a complete restructuring of the political economy. During the first fifteen years of DDR rule, they were transformed from relatively self-dependent municipal enterprises into state-socialist organizations following national and party, rather than urban, policy directives. This process was enacted through the emasculation of municipal self-government, the dominance of the SED, and the institutionalization of a hierarchical regime of state planning.

The independence of East Berlin from the DDR government, as enshrined in the Potsdam Agreement, was rapidly revealed to be a fiction. Within the territorial system of government established in the DDR, East Berlin had the equivalent status of a district (*Bezirk*). The role of a district was to implement policies of the state. State policy was determined effectively not by the formal organs of government, such as the People's Assembly (Volkskammer) or the Council of Ministers (Ministerrat), but by the SED. The supreme power of the SED was justified by virtue of representing the working class, in whose name the DDR had been established.[14] The highest national decision-making body was, consequently, the SED party conference, which took place every four years. Decisions made at the party conference were implemented by government bodies at all levels—from national to local—that were mirrored by parallel SED party organizations.[15]

The most powerful person in the city administration of East Berlin was, therefore, not the mayor (Oberbürgermeister), but the first secretary of the local SED. The elected city parliament (Stadtverordnetenversammlung) was entrusted merely with transposing national laws and plans into municipal decrees.[16] It comprised preselected candidates and met only around four times a year. The city council (Magistrat) held more powers than the city parliament, but these were limited largely to implementing decisions taken by the SED and central state bodies.[17] Since a majority of its councillors always belonged to the SED, deviation from the national party line was effectively blocked.[18] Urban planning in East Berlin was strongly influenced by national entities, primarily the Politburo of the SED, the Council of Ministers, and the Ministry of Construction.[19]

State socialism reverberated through East Berlin's utilities in a number of ways (see figure 7.2). De-municipalization was an early feature of DDR infrastructure policy, embedded in a process of mass nationalization that lasted until the early 1960s. A

Figure 7.2
Party publicity for the SED on Klingenberg power station, 1966
Source: Bärthel, "Anlagen und Bauten der Fernwärmeversorgung," 304. Copyright: Bewag/Vattenfall.

Soviet decree of June 1949 amalgamated most municipal and cooperative energy utilities in the DDR into one of four so-called energy districts (*Energiebezirke*), offering no compensation to the municipalities.[20] These energy districts were subsequently placed under the authority of the State Secretariat for Coal and Energy.[21] East Berlin's electricity utility, Bewag (East), posed a dilemma here, since it was still owned in part by foreign shareholders whom the Soviets were wary of upsetting. For several years Bewag (East) remained a municipal enterprise within a system geared to state-socialist structures. This created huge problems for the utility, which had to operate in a socialist economy while it was still, legally, a share company. In December 1953 the utility directors appealed to the mayor of East Berlin to transfer Bewag (East) into a state-owned enterprise (*volkseigener Betrieb*, or VEB).[22] The problems they listed were indicative of the transition from capitalism to socialism. These included the inability to raise loans from banks to fund investments in infrastructure, the burden of expenditure required by the state that could not be covered by revenue, and the dependence on decisions made by the general assembly of Bewag held in West Berlin.[23] Although steps were taken to enable the utility to operate under state-socialist conditions, it was only in 1978 that Bewag (East) was finally transformed into a state-owned enterprise, VEB Energieversorgung.

By contrast, the transformation of East Berlin's other utilities was more straightforward. A national decree on reordering water management of August 1952 created fifteen VEBs responsible for water supply and wastewater treatment, replacing existing municipal utilities as well as local water associations.[24] The previous year, East Berlin's water utility had been amalgamated with the sanitation department to form a joint municipal enterprise, Groß-Berliner Wasser- und Entwässerungswerke (WEW). This entity subsequently became VEB Wasserversorgung und Abwasserbehandlung Berlin. Initially, VEB WAB Berlin, as it became known, remained part of the city administration of East Berlin. However, on April 1, 1963, following a decision of the sixth SED party conference, it was removed from formal municipal control and placed under the authority of state water management.[25] The same happened to the gas utility, Gasag (East), in January 1956, when it was transformed into VEB Gasversorgung Berlin and removed from the aegis of the city council.[26] On January 1, 1979, in a further act of organizational concentration, East Berlin's electricity and gas utilities were amalgamated into a single energy utility, VEB Energiekombinat Berlin, that provided power, gas, and district heating to the half-city.[27] State socialism was used, therefore, to overcome not only the municipal governance, but also the organizational fragmentation of utility services that had long characterized Berlin's infrastructure landscape.

The state planning system contributed further to the centralization of infrastructure policy in East Berlin. The city's utilities, like all productive entities, were subject to the targets and measures set out in the five- or seven-year plans designed to structure the national economy and prioritize key development issues. The first five-year plan, of 1951–1955, effectively subordinated the urban economy to national economic planning.[28] Henceforth, the city budget was the product of discussions between the national finance ministry and the city treasury, based on decisions made by the Politburo on how best to implement the current plan.[29] Coordination of infrastructure planning was entrusted to the spatial planning division (*Territorialplanung*) within the central planning authorities.[30] The planning unit responsible for East Berlin, the Bezirksplankommission, was initially part of the city council but—as with the utilities—was taken out of municipal hands in 1964 and placed under the responsibility of the state planning commission.[31] This left little room for maneuver at the local level, as the state planning commission determined the distribution of financial and material resources to implement each plan.

The advantages of the socialist planned economy, its proponents claimed, lay in being able to set production targets, prioritize improvements, justify investments, and standardize performance on a national scale.[32] This was something that a market economy based on private enterprise could not achieve and, therefore, a source of much pride in the DDR. The targets set out in national plans for, say, electricity or water supply were subsequently translated into regional and then local objectives that were passed down to the utilities for implementation.[33] The targets set were invariably ambitious, emerging as they did from political desire rather than a realistic assessment of demand and supply. They were based, as Stephen Collier has demonstrated for the Soviet Union, less on past experience of demand than on politically determined norms of "need" for an undifferentiated mass of consumers.[34] For instance, average water consumption in East Berlin was expected, according to a contribution to the third five-year plan, to double between 1959 and 1980 to a staggering 312.5 liters per person per day.[35] The utilities had to deal with often hugely optimistic targets emerging not only from the regular planning regime, but also from SED party conferences. These national events were not averse to passing resolutions of a highly specific nature. The ninth party conference in May 1976, for instance, required the construction of 600 mm and 900 mm sewers to transport treated wastewater from the sewage treatment plant in Falkenberg to sewage farms to the northeast of Berlin.[36]

The state-socialist model envisaged implementation of national plans by means of a combination of controls, incentives, exhortations, and sanctions. These, it was considered, would more than compensate for the absence of the exploitative profit motive that drove capitalism. Control was exerted by a chain of targets that, within a utility, reached down to each unit of operation. For instance, the collective works contract devised for the gas utility VEB Gasversorgung Berlin in 1963 required the director, among other activities, to develop business and operational plans, run socialist competitions, improve the quality of coal used at the gas works, develop new methods of assessing the sulphur content of gas, and set up a new conveyor belt for transporting coke.[37] It also included sections on funding SED organizations operating in the utility, the provision of educational activities for employees' children, and the advancement of women in leadership roles. Targets like these were subject to detailed and regular monitoring that resulted in reports sent back up the planning hierarchy. To avoid sanctions for the nonfulfillment of targets, it was not uncommon for performance to be exaggerated. This, of course, required collective collusion within the workforce over the deliberate misrepresentation of data. Since the targets were often deemed unrealistic anyway, few had qualms of conscience about massaging performance data to avoid reproach. Financial sanctions on underperforming businesses were, besides, often too low to act as effective incentives to change established practices. This applied, particularly, to factories that regularly exceeded their quotas for energy use and chose to pay the fine rather than endanger production by conserving electricity. A survey of factories in East Berlin in June 1981 revealed that of the 313 required to report on their electricity use, 117 had exceeded their allotted quota and eighty-three had been fined a total of around 10 million Marks.[38]

Where controls and sanctions failed, exhortations to raise performance in the interest of a higher, socialist good became a standard response to under-fulfillment of planning targets. A particularly socialist form of competition was institutionalized, in which units or whole utilities would compete to raise production, improve efficiency, or promote innovation. In a competition involving all power plants in the DDR, the Klingenberg power station in Berlin won in the first quarter of 1953 by achieving an implementation rate of planning targets of a preposterously precise 104.86 percent.[39] Within Bewag (East) a competition was launched in mid-1954 to save the utility 5 million Marks by the end of the year (see figure 7.3).[40] Reportedly, over 90 percent of the workforce took part, concluding some 800 "competition contracts" that achieved the target savings, which were subsequently transferred to the city council. The rewards for the participants were sometimes pecuniary. Bewag (East) paid out almost 1.5 million Marks in bonuses for brigades successful in internal or external competitions between 1951 and 1955.[41] The incentive for many, though, was to help strengthen socialism in the DDR. The names of some of the brigades formed at the Klingenberg power plant during the 1970s—W. I. Lenin, 1st May, 8th Party Conference—are a testimony to the continued appeal of the socialist ideal, for all its shortcomings.[42]

This appeal was, it should be noted, not restricted to manual laborers. As Dolores Augustine has argued, many engineers in the DDR were drawn by the technocratic

Figure 7.3
Poster for a socialist competition of Bewag (East) "Fighting for Technological Progress," 1956
Source: SED-Betriebsparteiorganisation Bewag, *Unsere Kraft. Betriebsgeschichte der Bewag, 2. Teil*, 94.

managerialism characteristic of state-socialist planning.[43] Those employed by East Berlin's utilities would have shared the state's confidence in the transformative power of technology. This encouraged many of them to identify with the overall objectives of state planning, if not its specific manifestations.

Infrastructure Services between Plans and Practice

Enthusiasm for the technological thrust of state socialism did not prevent leading engineers from voicing concern over huge gaps between the rhetoric of infrastructure planning and the reality of service provision.[44] Particularly in the early years of the DDR, the directors of East Berlin's utilities protested strongly about exaggerated planning targets and inadequate resources to implement them. Bewag's technical director, Witte, a stalwart of the Soviets during the blockade, informed city councillor Hintze in November 1950 that requirements to produce an additional 200 million kWh a year were "a sheer impossibility."[45] At the same meeting his colleague Fried from the water utility criticized the council for failing to provide the funds it had promised to buy machinery essential for maintaining water supply. Two years later the Bewag (East) directors were again protesting against an excessive target for electricity generation imposed by the state planning commission.[46] Critical feedback did not, however, stem the constant stream of directives to increase output passed on by the national energy agency (VVB Energieversorgung) from a plethora of state and party organizations.[47] Senior managers at the water utility lodged repeated complaints that targets for water supply in East Berlin were not being met owing primarily to a shortage of funding.[48] Investment levels in the city's water infrastructure dropped dramatically from 7.88 million Marks in 1952 to 4.59 million Marks in 1953 and 3.50 million Marks in 1954.[49] Urgent demands by the sanitation utility to include, for instance, the electrification of its steam-driven pumping stations in the five-year plan were regularly ignored by the state planning commission.[50] Without adequate state funding and without the authority to levy tariffs high enough to finance investments, the utilities had to make ends meet as best they could.

The effects of underinvestment became quickly apparent in service quality, especially in the water sector. A report compiled by the joint water and sanitation utility WEW in February 1962 on water leakage and wastage highlighted the severity of the problem it was facing.[51] As a result of poor maintenance and repair water losses from the mains had increased in just one year, between 1959 and 1960, from 6.8 percent to 8.0 percent. Meanwhile, water consumption was rising, from 96.5 million cubic meters in 1960 to 103.7 in 1962.[52] The utility did not possess the materials to repair leaking valves and pipes, while spare parts and equipment from the West were prohibitively expensive. Many of the 67,000 water meters in East Berlin were malfunctioning, allowing huge quantities of water to be used without payment. Besides, the report continued, the water tariff was so low that it encouraged wasteful use of the precious resource while socialist production prohibited price increases to regulate consumption.[53] In September of the same year WEW produced a plan for reconstructing the water and sanitation networks to address these problems.[54] It described how, in the immediate aftermath of political division, water services had benefited from the capacity freed up from supplying West Berlin, but that this had since been more than taken up by the sharp increase in water consumption. Peak demand was estimated to reach 590,000 cubic meters a day by 1965, exceeding maximum supply capacity by at least 55,000 cubic meters.

Neither the original report nor the subsequent plan produced the desired improvements. Indeed, capacity at East Berlin's water works actually dropped by over one-quarter between 1949 and 1970 (see table 7.1).[55] Owing to poor maintenance of an ageing infrastructure, the number of burst mains increased from 225 in 1965 to 480 in 1970.[56] In outlying areas of the city the utility was struggling to maintain basic water pressure even under normal weather conditions. During the hot summer of 1970 these areas received no water at all as demand exceeded supply capacity by one-tenth.[57] When a similar supply crisis occurred the following summer, the city council agreed a number of measures to alleviate the situation, such as a public campaign to save water, quotas for factories, modernizing the water works at Friedrichshagen, and groundwater enrichment.[58] Few of these measures were actually implemented. It was only in the late 1970s that water supply capacity was significantly increased (see table 7.1).[59] During this time, the water mains were extended considerably to service new housing estates located on the urban perimeter.

The situation with wastewater treatment was deemed "significantly more alarming" in the plan of September 1962.[60] Most of the pumping stations were not working to full capacity and many of them were deemed too dangerous to operate at all,

Table 7.1
Capacity of East Berlin's water works, 1949–1989.

Year	Capacity (cubic meters per day)
1949	715,000
1970	525,000
1980	810,000
1989	940,000

Source: Bärthel, *Wasser für Berlin*, 233.

besides being highly inefficient.[61] The two sewage treatment plants—at Stahnsdorf and Waßmannsdorf—were operating at only 11 percent of capacity.[62] Later in the decade it was acknowledged, in the five-year plan of 1971–1975, that wastewater exceeded total treatment capacity by some 177,000 cubic meters a day.[63] In the absence of effective sewage treatment plants the existing sewage farms were proving hopelessly inadequate, having to deal with quantities of wastewater between two and nine times the legal limit.[64] As a result, groundwater aquifers were being massively polluted, public hygiene was being seriously compromised, and agricultural production on the sewage farms was declining sharply.

The decision to build a new biological sewage treatment plant at Falkenberg had been taken originally in 1956, but only in 1963 was its construction included in the state economic plan.[65] It was opened, finally, in 1968 and later extended. A second sewage treatment plant, at Münchehofe serving the east of the city, took a similar amount of time to progress from the initial decision in 1965 to completion in 1976, this time owing to difficulties in accessing building materials and labor.[66] When a third treatment plant was built at Schönerlinde in 1987, East Berlin had increased its capacity to treat wastewater to some 720,000 cubic meters a day.[67] This represented an impressive fourfold increase over the 168,000 cubic meters a day treated biologically in 1971.[68] The belated implementation of these major infrastructure projects was motivated not just by recognition of a sanitation crisis, but also out of a desire to free up land used by sewage farms for the city's massive house construction program. In an intriguing illustration of the connectivity between urban and infrastructure development, constructing new sewage treatment plants—it was acknowledged—was a precondition to meeting urban housing targets.

In the field of energy, the principal challenge was to keep up with the sharp increases in demand for electricity, gas, and district heating experienced in East Berlin across the four decades of DDR rule. As table 7.2 illustrates, electricity distributed by the East Berlin power utility increased by around 50 percent each decade. These growth rates might appear impressive, but they were a far cry from the anticipated doubling of electricity demand every ten years that underpinned DDR energy planning, in line with West German models.[69] The principal source of growth in consumption was primarily in the household sector, especially during the 1960s (see table 7.2).

Sales of gas in East Berlin also rose continuously, from 178.6 million cubic meters in 1950 to 865.6 million cubic meters in 1985 (see table 7.3).[70] A huge increase in the number of gas central heating systems as well as access to natural gas from the Soviet Union prompted a surge in gas consumption in the late 1980s.[71] Nothing compared, however, to the explosion in the use of district heating. Sales in East Berlin rocketed

Table 7.2
Electricity provision in East Berlin, 1955–1985.

Year	Electricity distributed by Bewag (East) (GWh)	Proportion generated in East Berlin (%)	Electricity consumption per household in East Berlin (kWh)
1955	1,111	100	
1960	1,420	85	580
1965	1,737	80	811
1970	2,271	55	1,236
1975	2,794	24	1,444
1980	3,392	6	1,754
1985	4,188	31	2,039

Sources: SED-Betriebsparteiorganisation Bewag, *Unsere Kraft. Betriebsgeschichte der Bewag, 2. Teil*, 85, 101; VEB Energiekombinat Berlin, *40 Jahre Deutsche Demokratische Republik*, 10, 12, 18.

Table 7.3
Gas and district heating sales in East Berlin, 1950–1985.

Year	Gas sales (million cubic meters)	District heating sales (TJ)
1950	178.6	82
1955	212.2	162
1960	257.1	283
1965	336.7	1,966
1970	368.4	4,613
1975	387.0	11,010
1980	549.5	16,572
1985	865.6	23,787

Source: VEB Energiekombinat Berlin, *40 Jahre Deutsche Demokratische Republik*, 10, 11.

from a paltry 82 terajoules (TJ) in 1950 to a staggering 23,787 TJ in 1985 (see table 7.3). Demand for district heating grew by a factor of 3.5 in the 1950s, 16.3 in the 1960s, and 3.6 in the 1970s. The proportion of homes in East Berlin served by district heating rose to 37 percent by 1989, representing one of the highest levels in Central Europe.[72]

The sharp growth in demand for electricity, gas, and district heating heightened the challenge of providing sufficient infrastructure to keep pace. Internal reports of the utilities constantly highlighted their inability to satisfy growing needs fully. In April 1969 Bewag (East) noted that the district heating network was lagging seriously behind the urban development projects being rolled out for the capital.[73] A report by the gas utility VEB Gasversorgung of 1973 warned that both its gas works were operating at high risk.[74] Three years later the energy association VVB Energieversorgung described the gas works at Lichtenberg as being "unstable" and "worrying," and air pollution from the other gas works, at Dimitroffstrasse, as being the object of "massive criticism" in the neighborhood.[75] The Energy Commission of Berlin produced several reports in 1970 and 1971 setting out the challenges posed by electricity demand outstripping supply and by massive energy wastage in many factories, offices, and homes.[76]

When early appeals to the public to save electricity at peak times failed to have the desired effect (see figure 7.4), restrictions on energy use became the fall-back option throughout the forty years of state socialism. On October 30, 1953, the city council passed a decree on energy use introducing energy inspectors to monitor electricity and gas use in factories.[77] Their specific task was to ensure that all factories reduced their peak time demand by 30 percent. The following winter witnessed similar shortages of electricity. This time the target of the energy inspectors was electric room heaters in offices and factories. Unannounced visitations by a fifty-man brigade of inspectors on October 11–12, 1954, to 155 public buildings and eighty-nine factories across East Berlin identified 205 room heaters being used illegally. The real number was clearly much higher as, it was ruefully reported, "many of the venues had a well-organized system of people warning of our approach that made identifying room heaters impossible."[78] In later years, despite increasing reliance on electricity imported from the national grid—discussed in detail below—restrictions on electricity use exceeded those imposed in the early 1950s. In January 1971, for instance, street lighting was reduced, all advertising lighting banned, industrial production shifted to off-peak hours, and heating reduced in public transport, while energy inspectors were reintroduced.[79]

Energy shortages were astutely concealed from the outside world. When the four Allied foreign ministers met in East Berlin on January 19, 1954, instructions were given by the Ministry of Heavy Industry to ensure maximum security of electricity supply in the capital. Precautionary measures for the duration of the conference included prioritizing supply to East Berlin and autobahn service stations along the route to West Germany, prohibiting visits to power stations, and—in a revealing nod to the primus inter pares—building an especially secure double circuit to the residence of the High Commissioner of the Soviet Union.[80] In the spring of 1972, following an agreement to ease travel permits to East Germany that was expected to attract thousands of West Germans to East Berlin, the Ministry for Coal and Energy and the city council arranged for restrictions on public lighting to be lifted during the Easter and Whit holiday periods.[81] Lighting was to be switched on along the main thoroughfares and in centrally located shops, as well as on public transport, in theaters and museums, and on representative buildings, such as the Lenin memorial.

Figure 7.4
Poster "More Electricity, Nice ... but Think of the Plan!," 1952
Source: Landesarchiv Berlin (LAB), F Rep. 260–02, no. B 0032.

Dealing with "Westberlin"

The elephant in the room for East Berlin was always the other half of the city. The relationship with West Berlin—or "Westberlin" as it was belittled in DDR-speak—was a complex one. Imagery of division and confrontation engendered by sudden interventions such as the Berlin blockade and the building of the Berlin Wall in 1961 belies an ambivalent and vacillating association between the two sides in practice. A broad spectrum of relations, ranging from complete disconnection to negotiated agreements, played out not only on the political stage, but also across the city's infrastructures between 1949 and 1989 (see figure 7.5). Interdependencies of a material, economic, technical, social, or even personal nature that had built up over generations could not be eradicated by any political intervention. They demanded strategies that recognized mutual interests while emphasizing difference. "Dealing" with West Berlin meant for the East Berlin authorities both coping with its existence and doing deals with the class enemy.

The initial strategy, epitomized by the blockade, was to envelop West Berlin in a socialist embrace. This approach exploited West Berlin's geographical isolation from West Germany and encirclement by East Germany and the Soviet military. By making life in West Berlin difficult, so the thinking went, its residents would come to appreciate the benefits of a reunited city. The aggravating grain of sand that was West Berlin would, in the clasp of the oyster shell of Soviet protection, over time become a socialist pearl. Idealized thinking of this kind found expression in the urban plans for a Greater Berlin that continued to be produced until the mid-1950s.[82] Plans by the East Berlin authorities for electricity, water, and sanitation infrastructures, similarly, retained the fiction of a united city in these early years, at least as an overarching orientation.[83]

An obvious way of putting pressure on West Berlin was to cut off its infrastructure connections. This was, as we have seen, instrumental to the blockade of 1948–1949. Between 1950 and 1955 a number of infrastructures linking the two halves of the city were disconnected by the East, including telephone lines, bus and tram services, water pipes, and electricity cables. The fact that many of these disconnections proved not to be permanent, but subject to negotiation, indicates that the motive was less about enforcing separation than about extracting maximum advantage from the superior geopolitical leverage at East Berlin's disposal. Temporary agreements were reached between East and West Berlin in the early 1950s to supply the West with water and electricity in return for hard currency or valuable goods. Some of these agreements involved special deals to avoid the transfer of funds. One example was West Berlin paying for water from the East in kind, in the form of water provided to the East German Reichsbahn

Figure 7.5
"DDR" blazoned on a water tower on the border with West Berlin, 1961
Source: Landesarchiv Berlin (LAB), F Rep. 260 (02), no. 0080426. Photo by Horst Siegmann.

that continued to operate suburban trains in West Berlin.[84] Another instance involved West Berlin receiving electricity from the East German grid in return for power supplied to East Germany by the Hamburg electricity utility that was recompensed by Bewag (West). East Berlin also sold electricity to West Berlin in exchange for much-needed machinery produced there by AEG.[85]

Deals of this kind were lucrative for East Berlin, in desperate need of hard currency, but only so long as prices were kept high and cross-border resources continued to flow. The vulnerability of these relations to sudden interruptions, protracted negotiations, and disputes over payments prompted West Berlin, however, to seek alternatives to infrastructural dependence on the East, described in detail in the following chapter. As West Berlin built up its own infrastructure, East Berlin's strategic advantage diminished and its cross-border revenues declined. Whereas the balance of water transfers between East and West had stood at 17.6 million cubic meters in East Berlin's favor in 1950, just one year later it had fallen to 4.1 million cubic meters, and in 1952 actually reversed into a deficit of 1.6 million cubic meters.[86] Similarly, when West Berlin became self-dependent on electricity generation by the late 1950s, it no longer needed to draw on power from the East and all cross-border transfers and payments ceased.

The case of wastewater was different, however. Blocking off the sewers at all points where they crossed the border between West and East was not feasible without causing sewage to overflow onto the streets. Besides, so long as most of Berlin's wastewater was irrigated on sewage farms, rather than cleaned in biological treatment plants, East Germany relied on West Berlin's wastewater to sustain essential agricultural production on this land. For these reasons, wastewater treatment became an object of successful cross-border cooperation that lasted the entire period of political division. An agreement reached between the directors of the two sanitation utilities—West and East—on December 12, 1950, for West Berlin's wastewater to be treated by the East in return for a lump sum of 1.3 million Deutschmark a year set the model for later deals dependent on the volume crossing the border. The price tag took into consideration not only the costs incurred by the East in treating the wastewater, but also the benefits it accrued in using it for sewage irrigation and gas production.[87] The interdependence between metabolic flows of wastewater and agricultural produce sustained a degree of regional cooperation not witnessed in other infrastructural sectors.

When West Berlin built its own sewage treatment plants from the 1960s onward, thereby reducing dependency on even this relatively balanced arrangement, the Politburo of the SED responded by reconfiguring its sewer network away from the border to West Berlin.[88] With the decline in wastewater flows from the West, cross-border sewers lost their pecuniary value for the East. To avoid a negative balance of sewage flows, pumping stations were installed along the inner-city border so as to redirect East Berlin's sewage to its own sewage treatment plants. This corresponded to a broader strategy of spatial circumvention of West Berlin pursued in other infrastructure sectors much earlier. Soon after political division the East German electricity grid had been restructured in order to circumvent West Berlin, followed in 1970 by a 110 kV network that connected East Berlin better to the national grid.[89] As part of a deliberate policy of territorial unbundling in 1970 the water mains, rainwater, and wastewater networks were reconfigured away from the border with West Berlin and toward the new city center at Alexanderplatz and the housing estates on the urban perimeter (see figure 7.6).[90] This strategy was reflected in numerous infrastructure plans for East Berlin. Infrastructures that had helped make Berlin a unitary city now became conduits of urban estrangement.

One cross-border flow that had not been stopped during the 1950s was the passage of people. While the border between East and West Germany had been sealed off in May 1952, the border between East and West Berlin remained permeable until 1961. Border controls and identity checks had been introduced and access to either side was gained only by suburban railway, on foot, or by bicycle, but people could still move relatively freely between the two halves of the city.[91] Some employees of West Berlin's utilities continued to live in the East, and vice versa. The problem of this permeable divide lay not only in the geopolitical tensions surrounding the postwar Berlin question, but in the increasing asymmetry of living standards and costs between the two sides. In the West salaries were considerably higher and consumable goods more widely available; in the East rents, utility bills, and food cost much less, thanks to state subsidies. The inclination of many Berliners was, consequently, to earn their money in West Berlin, but to live and buy food in East Berlin.[92] The widespread practice of "border hopping" on a daily basis placed an intolerable burden on East Berlin, which was not benefiting from the work conducted by many people whose living costs it was subsidizing at great expense to the national economy. Efforts to limit border crossing with special passes, detentions, or public advertising campaigns had little effect.

More serious still, the unpopularity of the SED regime was prompting thousands of East Germans to leave for the West. After the erection of the inner German border in 1952, Berlin was the only available exit route. In May 1961, 17,791 East Germans fled through West Berlin; in June the number rose to 19,198, and in July to a staggering 30,444 people.[93] As a result of this ex-migration East Berlin's population declined by 154,000 between 1946 and 1961, during which time West Berlin grew by 200,000 inhabitants.[94] To stop this hemorrhaging of its people to the West, the DDR

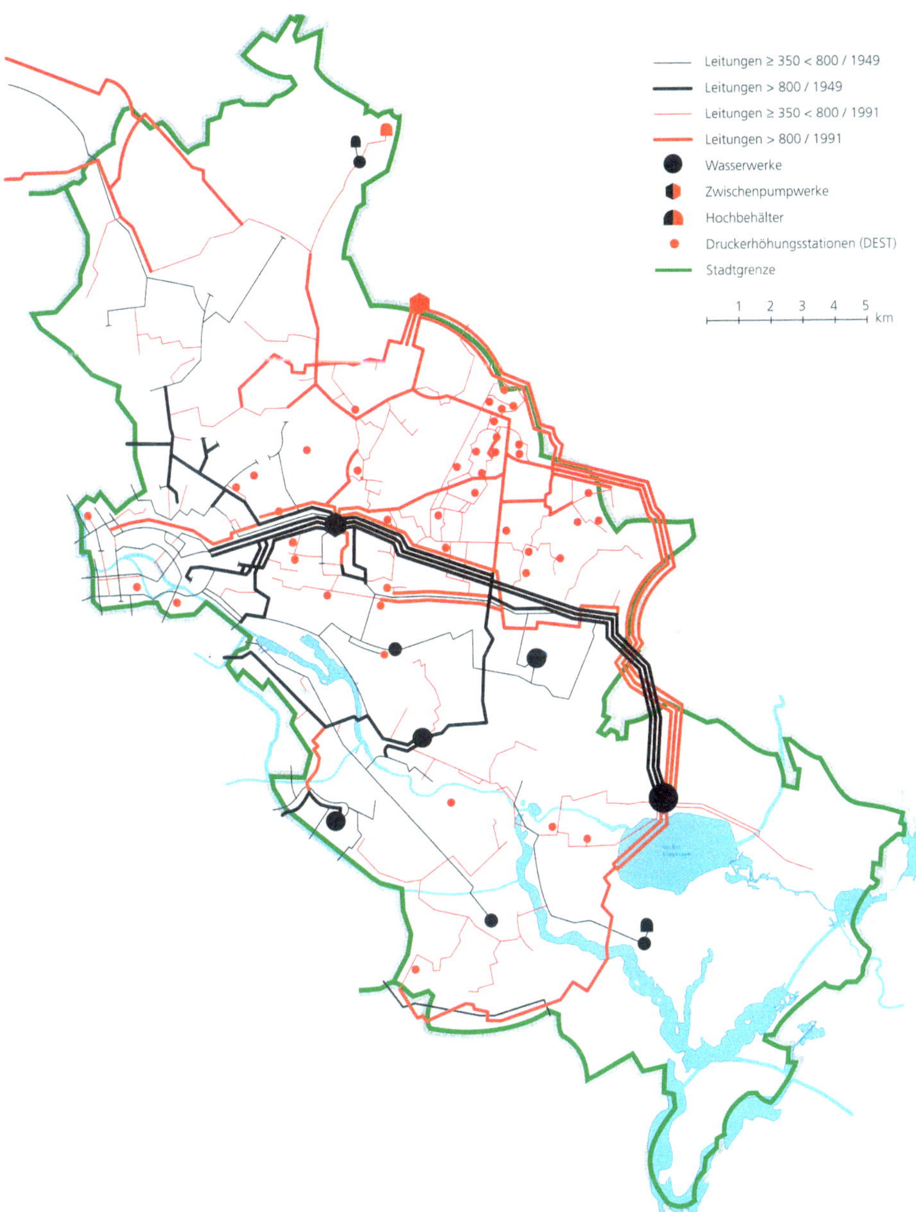

Figure 7.6

Map of water mains in East Berlin, illustrating (in red) pipes built after 1949

Source: Bärthel, *Wasser für Berlin*, 228.

regime—in consultation with its Warsaw Pact allies—took the dramatic step of building a barrier around the entire city of West Berlin in a single night, on August 13, 1961 (see figure 7.7).[95]

The erection of what became known as the Berlin Wall had a devastating effect on the city's inhabitants, separating families, cutting off sources of employment, and destroying livelihoods. The utilities on either side of the divide lost valued employees overnight. The East Berlin water utility, for instance, had to replace its works manager and business manager who lived in West Berlin.[96] Otherwise, the city's energy and water infrastructures were not substantially affected by the building of the Wall.

Figure 7.7
Two armed guards at an open manhole cover, August 1961
Source: Bärthel, *Geklärt!*, 200.

This was because, as already noted, Berlin's utilities had been divided since 1949. Even the sewers between East and West that were to become the legend of daring escape attempts in the following years had already been barricaded at around thirty-five key locations since the mid-1950s.[97] Figure 7.8 shows hand-drawn sketches of iron barriers to be erected in the sewers at Potsdamer Platz and other border crossings that date back to January 1955. These barricades were originally constructed, allegedly, to prevent the movement of spies and criminal gangs smuggling contraband across the inner-city border.[98] After 1961 they were used to block the underground passage of any escapee and became, as a consequence, the responsibility of the Ministry of State Security, better known as the Stasi. By November 15, 1961, all forty-one cross-border sewers over 60 cm in diameter had been sealed off in this way (see figure 7.9).[99]

Recent historiography on the divided city has queried whether the building of the Berlin Wall marked the end of all meaningful interaction between East and West. Pointing to the exchange of ideas, goods, and technologies, some scholars prefer to talk of a permeable "nylon curtain," rather than the solid iron variant.[100] They use the example of urban design in Berlin to demonstrate how ideas did travel across the inner-city border, if usually without acknowledgment. Others dispute that this was a widespread phenomenon. Astrid Kirchhof takes the case of environmental groups in East and West Berlin to demonstrate that cooperation was the exception rather than the rule, since each side focused on issues specific to its own locale and operated within its own cultural milieu.[101] As we have seen, although Berlin's utilities in East and West increasingly went their separate ways after political division, there was much that continued to require collaboration, even in the shadow of the Wall. Wastewater flows between the two halves needed monitoring, water valves at border crossings needed opening in emergency situations, negotiations over flows and payments needed conducting. For these reasons, a minimum of official interaction was maintained between representatives of each utility, although this was not openly acknowledged in East Berlin.[102] With the thaw in relations between East and West in the early 1970s and the accompanying relaxation of travel restrictions for people from the West, informal exchanges between former colleagues did take place, but these were by then of little consequence for the strategic orientation of each utility around the geopolitical priorities of its own political regime, whether East or West.[103]

Nurturing a Socialist Workforce

External and internal pressures on the DDR made it imperative to harness domestic support behind the state. Key to this strategy of internal consolidation was to provide

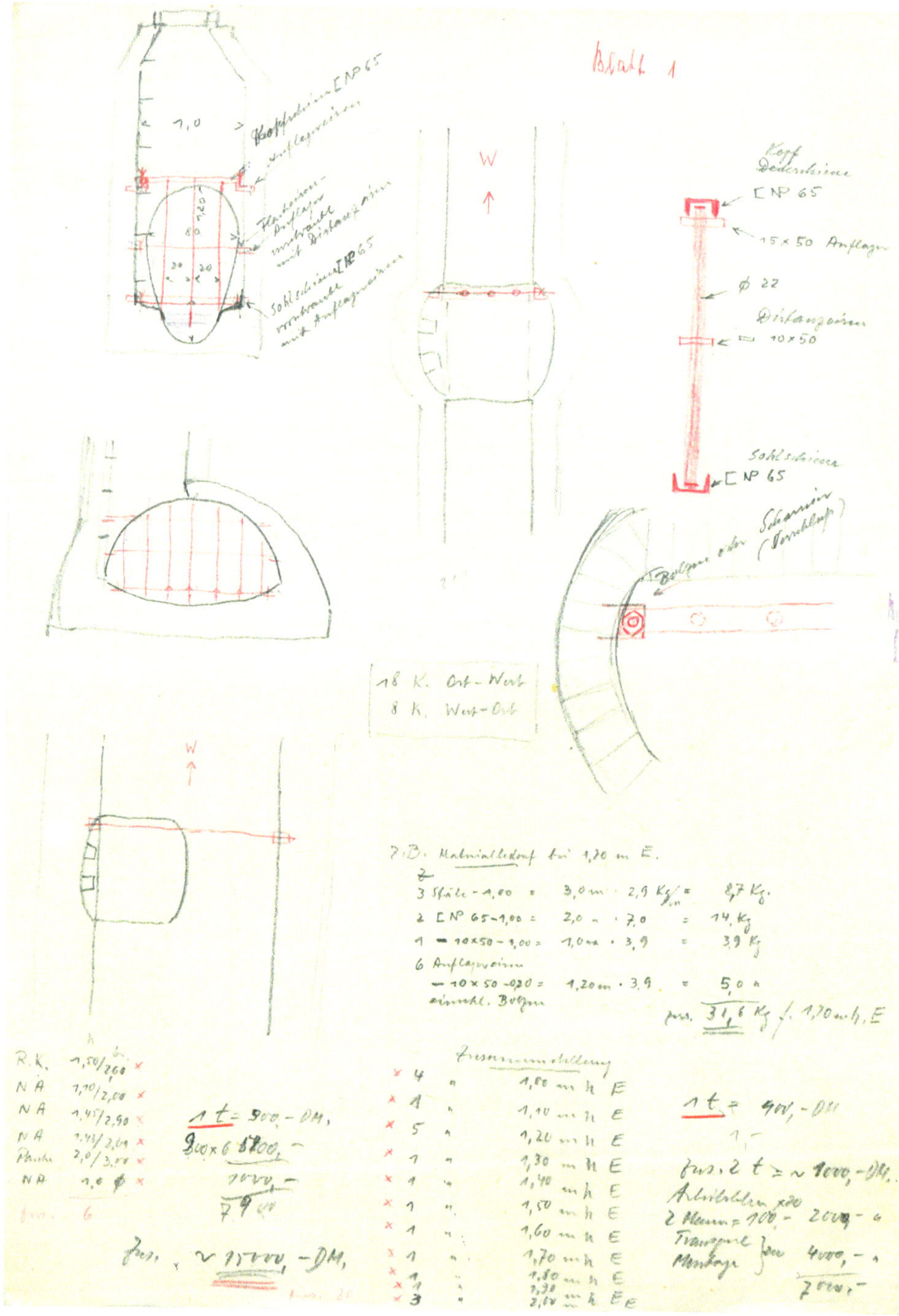

Figure 7.8

Sketches of iron barriers blocking border sewers, 1955

Source: Landesarchiv Berlin (LAB) C Rep. 124, no. 345.

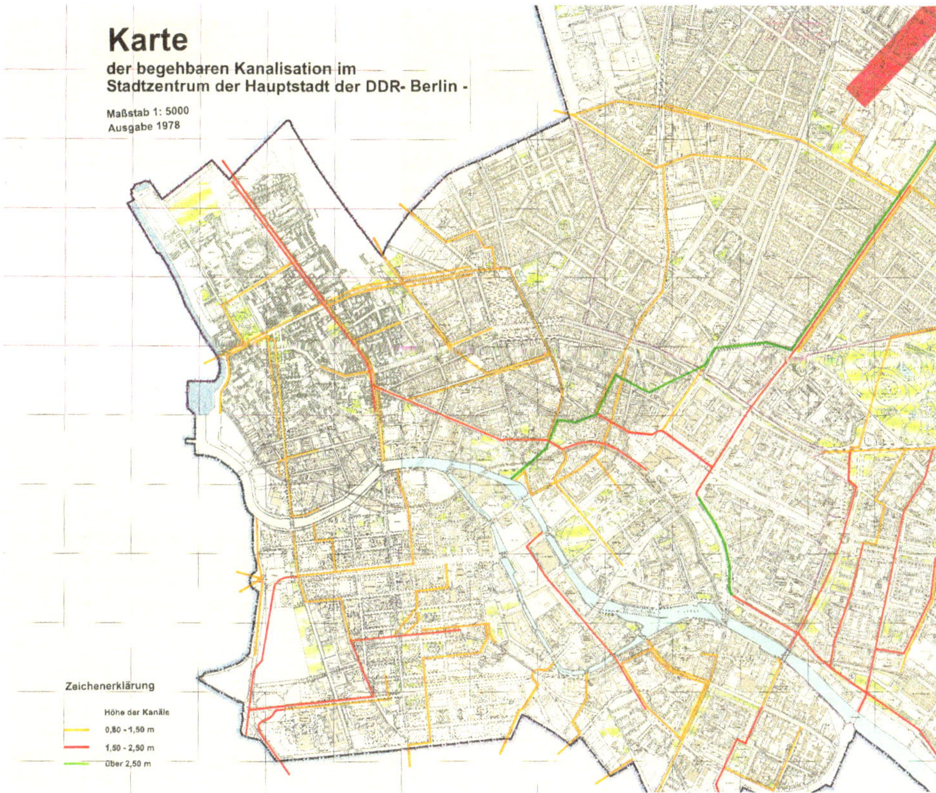

Figure 7.9
Map of accessible sewers in the center of East Berlin, 1978
Source: Landesarchiv Berlin (LAB) C Rep. 303, no. 14.

cradle-to-grave services at low cost to its citizens and to convince them that this could only be sustained by a workforce dedicated to socialism. Besides the state itself providing free health care, subsidized rents, and other benefits, employers were required to offer exemplary services to their staff as well as to educate them in the socialist image. Nurturing a socialist workforce was, consequently, a core function of the country's utilities. Energy utilities, in particular, were expected to maintain "strict socialist order and discipline" among their employees, since "energy provision intervenes in all phases of production and citizens' lives."[104]

East Berlin's utilities resurrected and developed many of the features that had made their Weimar predecessors model employers. Jobs were secure, wages were index-linked to living costs, housing associations provided homes for staff, and a plethora of activities were organized to care for employees and their dependents. To take Bewag (East) as an example, staff levels were maintained at around 4,000 between 1950 and 1977, despite the decommissioning of several labor-intensive power plants and machinery during this time.[105] Average wages at the utility more than doubled between 1950 and 1975, to 787.40 Marks a month, rising to 1,252.20 Marks by 1989.[106] A workers' housing cooperative of all four urban utilities offered affordable flats for many of their employees. By 1989 Energiekombinat Berlin—as it was now called—was planning to spend 13.3 million Marks annually on social and cultural activities.[107] These ranged from free meals, sports events, and child care to free vacations for employees and their families at its own holiday homes. The utility did much to promote women's careers in the production process, in the face of some resistance by the male workforce. The appointment of Hertha Bauer as a head of department at Bewag in December 1949 represented the first woman to achieve a leadership position in any of Berlin's utilities.[108]

Generous employment conditions alone were not enough to convince many in the workforce of the superiority of socialism. Disaffection with planning procedures and party patronage within the utility, as well as concern over political repression in the country at large, prompted various forms of resistance. One was defection to the West. Between 1953 and the autumn of 1956 Bewag (East) lost 115 members of staff to the West, primarily for political reasons.[109] Another was reticence or opposition at the workplace. Labor representation under the DDR changed from a grassroots model of works councils in each production unit to an externally managed system of party works' organizations under the auspices of the state trade union (FDGB) and the local SED.[110] In Bewag (East) an SED works organization (Betriebsparteiorganisation) comprised twelve units operating in the utility's various locations across the city that were each directly responsible to the district party leadership.[111] It was this organization that was tasked with securing loyalty in the workforce to the socialist regime.

A publication presenting the activities of the SED works' organization at Bewag (East), dated 1975, is illustrative of the venom and hyperbole commonly used to dramatize the political conflict between East and West. The authors talked of fighting a "class war" in Bewag (East) against attempts by the SPD to undermine the SED's influence over the utility.[112] Bewag, it was claimed, had always been a "bastion of opportunism" (a typical taunt of the SPD), conveniently ignoring the left-wing roots of Bewag in the 1920s so as to justify their own organization's significance in eradicating opposition.[113] This opposition could take the form of sabotage of critical installations, such as the Klingenberg power plant, by "terror organizations" in the pay of West Berlin.[114] The publication concluded with an unveiled threat: "Enemies and hired stooges will be unmasked and brought to justice or handed over to the relevant state agencies."[115]

Threats of this kind were contrasted with acts of heroic defense of the DDR by the workforce. The publication proudly announced that on June 17, 1953, during what it termed counterrevolutionary insurgency by Western agents, electricity generation at Klingenberg did not stop for a minute, with police, the SED, and workers uniting in preventing entry to the plant by opponents.[116] In response to the general strike, two paramilitary units (Kampfgruppen) were set up at Bewag (East) to defend vulnerable facilities from future political subversion. They were to be active again during the construction of the Berlin Wall in 1961, guarding the sector border and the Klingenberg plant.

Persuasion, as well as threats, was used to form the workforce in the socialist image. Political education was central to the activities of the party works organization and took up significant amounts of an employee's training. A course on electricity distribution for trainees at Bewag (East) in 1956 dedicated twenty-eight of the total sixty-six hours to political education, covering such themes as: introduction to the class struggle, class and the nature of the West German state, and the role of the DDR in the struggle to secure peace.[117] Subsequent internal reports by utility and party suggest that the message was not getting through. In March 1968 a leadership concept paper appealed for greater efforts of political propaganda and socialist education to combat reactionary ideology at Bewag (East).[118] In September 1974 the SED's urban technology unit within the city council complained that progress in advancing socialist consciousness among staff was falling behind what was required by the seventh party conference, criticizing some party comrades for lacking initiative and failing to conduct themselves like good communists.[119] In August 1981 it was noted by this unit that only 27 percent of those employed at the urban technology department of the city council were members of the SED—significantly lower than the proportion in the mayor's office (79 percent) or the transport department (54 percent).[120] The organs of urban technology, whether inside the municipal administration or the electricity utility, proved poor conduits for state socialism, it seems.

Subordination to National Infrastructure Policy

The urban thrust of infrastructure policy in Berlin during the 1920s had already given way to national subversion under the yoke of National Socialism. This orientation toward national, rather than municipal, priorities continued under the East German regime, albeit under a very different ideological banner. We have already demonstrated how the method of state planning undermined municipal control of East Berlin's utilities. Here, we investigate how the content of national infrastructure policy shaped the provision of energy and water services in the capital of the DDR. Four interconnected policies are addressed: the growing dependence on electricity and gas produced beyond the city, the impacts of national autarky policy, socialist resource "rationalization," and the revival of wastewater reuse.

In 1960, the city's power utility was generating 85 percent of the electricity it sold. By 1970 this figure had dropped to 55 percent, and by 1980 to just 6 percent (see table 7.2 above). Within the space of twenty-five years self-sufficiency of East Berlin in electricity generation had been transformed into almost total dependence on power from the national grid. The trend away from local generation and toward centralized electricity production was, of course, familiar across the developed world at the time. Nevertheless, the speed with which East German cities lost control of their generating capacity was remarkable, especially in comparison with West Germany. It was prompted by a policy priority of the DDR government to concentrate electricity production in areas where lignite could be mined on a massive scale.[121] East Berlin was fed increasingly by electricity supplied from power stations in the Lusatia mining region.[122] During the course of the 1960s and 1970s several of East Berlin's power plants were decommissioned or—if they were needed for the district heating network—restricted to producing heat only.[123] It was ironic that, at a time when East Berlin was rapidly expanding its district heating network, the opportunity for producing heat in combined heat-and-power (CHP) plants was effectively undermined by a national policy dedicated to reducing local electricity generation. Virtually all of East Berlin's district heating was, thus, produced in heating plants without cogeneration.[124] These "sausage boilers," as they were pejoratively known in the West, represented a highly inefficient way of using energy.[125]

It was a similar picture with gas production. East Berlin had possessed considerably less gas production capacity than West Berlin in 1950, but was still able to produce most of the town gas it used. A new gas pipeline enabled the city to import gas from the national gas network.[126] By 1978 the city's two remaining gas works were producing just 15 percent of gas consumed there.[127] Overlapping this process of centralization was a planned switch from town to natural gas and, thereby, a new form of dependence on an energy source provided by the Soviet Union. Plans to supply East Berlin with natural gas had been included in the third five-year plan for initial implementation in 1962–1963 but were delayed until the 1980s.[128] The agreement over gas delivery from Czechoslovakia was concluded only in 1971.[129] It took the Politburo until 1977 to decide on supplying East Berlin fully with natural gas. Despite plans to complete conversion to natural gas by the mid-1980s, this was achieved only in October 1990.[130]

The national energy policy that determined the source of electricity for East Berlin rapidly became circumscribed by the need to minimize imports of primary energy sources. Imported fuels like coal and, increasingly, oil cost hard currency the DDR could ill afford. For this reason East Germany turned to its only significant endogenous fuel source: lignite. This low-grade brown coal became the linchpin of the country's drive for national autarky of electricity and gas production.[131] Burning lignite on the required scale, however, entailed extensive open-cast mines and huge power stations. The price of maximizing energy autarky was, consequently, massive landscape deformation and staggering levels of air pollution.[132] National emissions of sulphur dioxide reached six million metric tons in 1985 according to even the DDR's own statistics, generally renowned for downplaying environmental hazards.[133]

In view of the difficulties involved in producing electricity and gas in East Germany, it is not surprising that the government was keen to minimize energy use. During the 1980s the Minister for Coal and Energy, Wolfgang Mitzinger, repeatedly spoke about the need to reduce the total amount of primary energy used. He couched his exhortations in ideologically charged language, arguing that the "rational" use of energy was a principle of socialist economics and, thereby, a national duty.[134] Asserting that the efficient and frugal use of energy was a core feature of East German energy policy was, however, so blatantly inaccurate that interventions of this kind had little impact. Planned energy savings were rarely enacted in practice.[135] East Berlin's Energy Commission, comprising representatives of the city council, utilities, and planning bodies, developed work programs to institutionalize the "rational" use of energy during the supply crises of 1970 to 1972, referring also to the socialist principle to use resources sparingly.[136] However, the measures envisaged were more about setting electricity quotas, mobilizing energy inspectors, and devising controls of energy users than tackling the structural deficits under which these users had to operate.

Meanwhile, the Minister for Environmental Protection and Water Management, Hans Reichelt, was calling for a similar "rationalization" of water provision and use as a national quest.[137] Shortages of water supply in cities across the country prompted appeals throughout the 1970s and 1980s for a more efficient use of water. Rather than questioning the need for, or causes of, high levels of water consumption, this policy was targeted at optimizing production processes and reducing wastage so as to be able to meet the high water demand expected of a modern society.[138] Water resource use was to be intensified, not reduced, with the help of technological progress, long-term planning, tight controls, and competitions for water efficiency.[139] These "socialist methods" of water resources management set great store on techno-managerial interventions and reflected the conviction that socialism could master nature. This confidence proved misplaced, however, for the DDR struggled to match demand with supply throughout its existence.

One intriguing strand of national infrastructure policy that combined the efficiency drive with technological creativity targeted the reuse of natural resources. The recycling of solid waste as "secondary raw materials" (SERO) for production processes came to be a symbol for the national cause of resource autarky and proved significantly more successful than recycling schemes in West Germany. Less well received in professional circles was the attempt by government, party, and academic organizations to revitalize wastewater reuse in the Berlin region. Using only mechanically treated wastewater to boost agricultural production on sewage farms had been a controversial technique ever since the 1920s, as we have seen. In the 1950s a powerful agricultural lobby in East Germany convinced many national agencies of the need to maximize use of nutrients in wastewater as a contribution to food autarky.[140]

At a conference on July 9, 1953, attended by the mayor of East Berlin, the sanitation utility, the local SED leadership, and the city council, agronomists from the Humboldt University made the case for using untreated wastewater on the city's sewage farms and attacked standards of public hygiene for being prohibitively high.[141] The following year the national Institute for Water Management (IWW) came up with a report that was highly critical of the city authorities and their plans for the biological treatment of sewage. Instead of wasting a valuable economic resource with expensive and "wholly inappropriate" sewage treatment plants, it argued, new sewage farms should be built on 42,000 hectares of land capable of feeding up to 130,000 people.[142] The parallels to the wild plans of Nazi ideologues in the 1930s to feed Berlin with products grown with untreated sewage are unmistakable. The East Berlin council and sanitation utility put up strong resistance, though, developing a counterplan describing the critical overload of existing sewage farms and the necessity of replacing them with sewage treatment plants. They proffered the compromise of using treated wastewater from these plants to irrigate sewage farms, just as their predecessors had done in the late 1930s. Nevertheless, relentless opposition by agricultural groups ensured that the city council's plans to build sewage treatment plants were delayed repeatedly. Only an epidemic of dysentery that affected 40,000 people in April 1962 persuaded the national Council of Ministers to prioritize the construction of the sewage treatment plant at Falkenberg.[143] In this instance, concerns for urban hygiene did win over national production targets for agriculture.

A Socialist Infrastructural Ideal for East Berlin

It was against this backdrop of nationalized infrastructures, state-socialist planning, and a fraught relationship with West Berlin that the idea for an integrated and systematic plan covering all East Berlin's piped infrastructures emerged. The origins of the 1970 plan discussed at the start of this chapter go back to the early 1960s. In 1962 combined infrastructure channels were discussed at the Building Academy of the DDR as a comprehensive solution for multiple piped infrastructures in areas of high population density.[144] Based on historical models from nineteenth-century London and, more significantly, Moscow in the 1930s, these walk-in channels were seen as a way not only of coordinating civil engineering structures, but also of organizing the built underground.

It was this ambition to order the subterranean city and, from this, to pre-structure the urban fabric above ground that fascinated Hilmar Bärthel, who integrated the combined infrastructure channels into a much broader urban plan encompassing all piped infrastructures. Bärthel was, in the 1960s, head of the Department of Transportation and Technical Infrastructure at the Institute for Urban Planning and Architecture (ISA) of the Building Academy. In the 1970s he led a group specializing in long-term civil engineering within the Office of Civil Engineering of the East Berlin city council.[145] After German reunification he went on to produce several books describing the technological trajectories of Berlin's water, sanitation, and gas infrastructures in West and East.[146] In 1969 Bärthel wrote a report for the ISA on the significance of existing infrastructure for urban development in the DDR that resonated powerfully with Randzio's arguments of the late 1940s.[147] In it, Bärthel estimated the value of the country's existing underground infrastructures and called on urban planners to assess available infrastructures prior to producing any development plan. This, clearly, was not the norm at the time: "Practice shows that decisions on how to structure cities in the DDR do not take into any consideration whatsoever the problems of underground networks."[148]

Plans to build major new housing estates on the perimeter of East Berlin in the early 1970s provided Bärthel and his team with a golden opportunity to demonstrate what a comprehensive, integrated plan of urban infrastructures could really look like. By then, East Berlin's population was gradually growing, as the Wall prevented emigration and the city, as the nation's capital, attracted in-migration.[149] In the absence of effective refurbishment to existing housing stock, it became a top priority for the DDR government to implement a massive house-construction program for the capital. Land for these large housing estates was provided in large measure on decommissioned sewage farms.[150] East Berlin's flagship urban housing program from 1973 onward was, thus, directly dependent on the construction of sewage treatment plants at Falkenberg, Münchehofe, and Schönerlinde.

The General Plan for Urban Infrastructure Services of May 1970 was coordinated by Bärthel's group at the city council in close collaboration with city planners and utility managers (see figure 7.10). In the words of a group member, a "partnership of trust" was built up among representatives of the city's electricity, gas, water, and sanitation

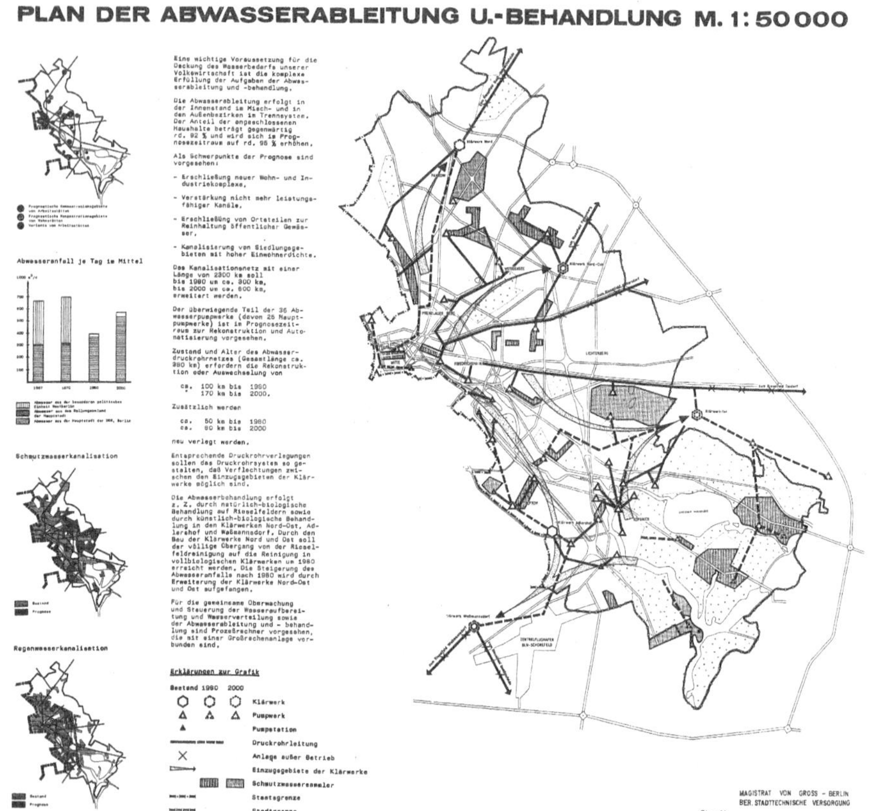

Figure 7.10

Map of sewers from the General Plan for Urban Infrastructure Services, 1970

Source: Landesarchiv Berlin (LAB) C Rep. 107, no. 811.

utilities, civil engineers employed by the city, and planners responsible to the planning commission.[151] Their common intent was to provide city planners with an instrument to assess which future developments in East Berlin were, and which were not, feasible from an infrastructure perspective. The plan began by setting out the significance of reliable utility services for improving productive capacity and "generating socialist working and living conditions for the population."[152] Playing to ideological aspirations was essential for gaining approval by party and state. The overarching justification for the plan was, consequently, expressed in typically turgid DDR prose: "The necessary complex ordering of the material-technical structure of the territory will thus become an ever more important part of the structural policy of the socialist state."[153]

There followed prognoses of demand for electricity, gas, district heating, water, and wastewater services, all envisaging massive growth trends even by 1980.[154] Electricity demand in East Berlin was predicted to grow by a factor of 2.3 by 1980, 5.4 by 1990, and a breathtaking 12.9 by 2000. Gas consumption was expected to increase by a factor of 2.6 by the year 2000 and water consumption to rise by 55 percent over the same period. The plan set out the new infrastructures the city would need to provide that proportion of demand not imported from outside. This included large district heating plants, additional sewage treatment plants, and modernized water works. Even a district cooling system was envisaged that would provide air conditioning for offices and homes across the city. In order to provide spatial coordination for all the infrastructure pipes, cables, and ducts crisscrossing the city, the plan advocated the construction of combined trenches and walk-in channels in densely populated parts of the city (see figure 7.11). In future, repairs to a faulty conduit would not require streets to be dug up every time, but could be conducted via readily accessible entry points.

This plan may have emerged from a position of weakness, but it did not lack ambition. It provided a wake-up call to planners responsible for East Berlin that they could not continue to disregard urban infrastructure if they wanted to provide adequate services to the city and avoid embarrassing failures to their model housing projects. Given the official recognition granted to the plan by the responsible state and municipal agencies, the message appears to have got through. This was no mean feat under the circumstances. In practice, the plan managed to establish its "threshold method" as a means of calculating urban development projects according to the capacity of urban infrastructures, existing or planned.[155] It also enabled planners to coordinate multiple infrastructures in specific spatial contexts. Even some of the more experimental features of the plan got built, such as the combined infrastructure channels, although far less than originally planned (see figure 7.12).[156]

Many of the ideals of complex, integrated planning espoused by the infrastructure plan of 1970, though, failed to gain traction.[157] Representing a socialist infrastructural ideal rather than a realistic portrayal of future possibilities, the plan inevitably ran up against funding shortfalls, institutional fragmentation, and planning bureaucracy that limited its implementation severely. It did not attempt to reduce demand for services to suit the available infrastructure, but propagated growth curves for energy and water far in excess of what was actually consumed in later years. In this respect it perpetuated traditional infrastructure logics of "build and supply" witnessed in the Weimar and

Figure 7.11
Construction of a combined infrastructure channel in Berlin-Marzahn
Source: Tepasse, *Stadttechnik im Städtebau Berlins. 20. Jahrhundert*, 145, citing SAKA Sammelkanal- und Service GmbH.

Nazi eras, reflecting an important dimension of sociotechnical continuity. It proposed investments, such as the walk-in infrastructure channels, that were far too expensive and resource-intensive for the DDR.[158] Most important of all, it failed to significantly improve infrastructure provision in East Berlin in the long term: its key objective. Problems of under-capacity and overuse continued to plague the water supply and wastewater disposal systems, in particular, as Bärthel himself later acknowledged.[159]

On April 8, 1982, the technical infrastructure unit in the local planning commission produced a damning report on the state of East Berlin's piped infrastructure.[160] The litany of structural deficits was debilitating. Utility services in the capital of the DDR were deemed "not consistently reliable," with regular shortfalls in supply at times of peak demand. This was attributed to the age of much infrastructure and poor levels of

Figure 7.12
A combined infrastructure channel in Berlin-Marzahn, 2018
Photo: Timothy Moss.

maintenance. Electricity provision was so overstretched that in half the city no new connections to the grid could be made and improvements were not envisaged before 1990. There was inadequate pressure in the gas mains; the district heating network in Friedrichshain was described as "utterly overloaded." Large areas of the city had low water pressure during the summer, while water protection zones were not being respected. Around 12,000 properties still had no access to public sewers, resulting in a large proportion of their sewage seeping into the soil. Despite recent investments in the city center and the new housing estates, the city's sewers were suffering from frequent leakages attributable to bad materials and poor workmanship. Two of the city's sewage treatment plants could not cope with the amount of wastewater directed to them, with little prospect of immediate relief. It was all bitter testimony that the high-flying visions of the bold 1970 infrastructure plan had come crashing down to earth.

Environmental Degradation

The nemesis of East Berlin's infrastructure manifested itself not just in poor service quality, but also in severe environmental degradation. For all the talk of resource "rationalization," the DDR was one of the most profligate users and polluters of natural resources of its era. Its primary energy use per capita was the third highest in the world, after the United States and Canada.[161] In SO_2 emissions per capita it was the world leader. Water consumption reached 256 liters per person across all consumer groups in 1990, at a time when West Germany was using "only" 193 liters.[162] Pollution of the country's rivers and lakes was notoriously high. In 1989 only 19 percent of East Berlin's surface watercourses were deemed suitable as a source for drinking water, 41 percent were declared fit for irrigation and cooling purposes only, and 40 percent were graded classes 4–6, meaning that they were usable only for shipping.[163]

Technical infrastructures were key to this impasse. The energy and water they transported and treated mediated resource use in most processes of production and consumption. Infrastructural neglect, therefore, sent negative shockwaves through the entire economy.[164] Massive inefficiencies of infrastructures were reflected in the fact that the DDR had the highest primary energy consumption per capita in Europe—at 218 GJ in 1985—but its electricity consumption per capita was only 70 percent of the West German figure.[165]

East Berlin, as a center of national production and consumption, experienced untenable levels of pollution. Internal reports by national agencies repeatedly documented that East Berlin had become one of the most air-polluted regions in the DDR, despite its increasing reliance on electricity generated far away from the city.[166] Initial responses by the authorities in the 1960s—to build higher chimneys and convert more buildings to district heating—had only a limited effect.[167] Since the city's district heating network was increasingly fired by lignite, any environmental benefits of replacing individual, coal-fired systems were offset by the emissions from large heating plants located in the city.[168] A number of reports were compiled and decisions taken by the city council right up until the late 1980s, but since they did little more than list past achievements and reiterate planned projects their impact was minimal.[169] In 1989 emissions were still intolerably high in East Berlin, with levels per capita at 53.3 kg for sulphur dioxide, 20.8 kg for dust particles, and 94.7 kg for carbon monoxide that year.[170]

Neglect and underfunding of wastewater infrastructure had a devastating effect on the aquatic environment. Harmful emissions from the chemical and electrical industry upstream of the city, as well as poor treatment of household wastewater, polluted the region's rivers and lakes, as well as its groundwater aquifers.[171] In September 1965 the deputy chairman of the district planning commission of Berlin spoke of an "alarming situation" for water management in Berlin, requiring "drastic measures" by industry to prevent further pollution of surface and ground water.[172] This compromised further East Berlin's already limited capacity to supply enough drinking water. By 1989, with 40 percent of Berlin's groundwater resources deemed potentially at risk, eighty-two of the 420 wells serving East Berlin's principal water works had been closed down owing to high levels of contaminants.[173] Yet over two-thirds of household wastewater produced in East Berlin was still entering the watercourses without any treatment, even after the construction of several sewage treatment plants.[174]

The water supply problem was compounded by the absence of institutional incentives to conserve water. Thanks largely to the negligible cost to consumers, water was widely treated as a limitless resource. This was lamented by the East Berlin water utility in a report of February 1962: "Since the water price is far too low to encourage conservation of water and since price increases to regulate consumption are prohibited under socialist means of production, the only option is to educate the consumer."[175] Even this was not pursued with enthusiasm. As a consequence, "the issue of water conservation," in the words of a contemporary infrastructure planner, "was simply not on the agenda."[176]

The reluctance to conserve water in response to this environmental crisis had deep ideological roots. Accepting the limits of nature was regarded by many stalwarts of the DDR regime as anathema to socialist ideology.[177] For them, as David Blackbourn has argued, nature was there to be controlled and enrolled by heroic technologies of the socialist state.[178] From this perspective, saving water would have meant capitulating to the forces of nature, which a socialist society was meant to master. Indeed, only socialism, the ideologues argued, could muster the combination of state control, complex planning, and scientific progress needed to harness water resources to the benefit of all. This ideological blinker posed a structural impediment to environmental protection throughout the DDR. The socialist use of natural resources was not submitted to critical scrutiny by party or state.[179] Environmental concerns were consistently trumped by economic interests to increase production. Sensitive data on environmental pollution and overexploitation of natural resources were concealed as a matter of principle.[180] The reports documenting environmental degradation were compiled by state agencies for internal use only.

This is not to say that the DDR was inactive in legislating against environmental pollution. A notable early landmark was the National Culture Act (Landeskulturgesetz) of May 14, 1970, the DDR's first legal framework for environmental protection. This law set down requirements for providing a safe and reliable supply of water for households and industry as well as preventing water pollution.[181] The Water Act of July 2, 1982, aspired to secure the DDR's long-term water resources by increasing the effectiveness of state regulation over water use, minimizing water leakage, and optimizing water use in industry.[182] The emphasis was, however, always on maximizing supply capacity rather than minimizing demand. Water consumption in the DDR continued to rise—by a third—between 1970 and 1990.[183]

Besides passing legislation the DDR also sought to improve environmental quality via agreements with the Federal Republic. The first major inner-German agreement of this kind targeted wastewater treatment in the Berlin region. In 1982 the West German government agreed to pay East Germany 68 million Deutschmark to fund the upgrading of three sewage treatment plants serving Berlin to eliminate phosphorus from wastewater.[184] With this money the DDR authorities were able to introduce this technology successfully to the treatment plants at Stahnsdorf and Waßmannsdorf in 1988–1989.

By the late 1980s complaints by residents about localized environmental hazards had elevated to collective criticism and even to organized opposition, albeit of a clandestine nature and on a small scale. Environmental protests in East Berlin had their roots in the late 1970s, when small groups of people met to debate the environment, peace, and democracy, often under the auspices of church organizations.[185] They produced underground publications—samizdat—circulated from hand to hand in which they drew attention to problems of air pollution, electricity generation, and wastewater treatment affecting the city.[186] These clandestine documents contained forthright criticism of fundamental tenets of DDR energy and water policy, such as assuming a doubling of electricity consumption every ten years despite evidence to the contrary.[187] Their authors drew on publications from the West to outline what, for instance, an alternative energy policy might look like: modernizing power plants, saving energy in homes, and promoting renewable sources.[188] They even collaborated occasionally with environmental NGOs in West Berlin.[189] In 1988 environmental groups from both sides of the divide sent a letter to the city council of East Berlin and the senate of West Berlin appealing for joint action to monitor air pollution and develop a citywide smog alarm system.[190]

Mind the Gap!

By this time, in the late 1980s, East Berlin and the DDR at large were struggling to deal with yawning gaps on two fronts: the gap between rhetoric and reality of life under state socialism and the gap between living standards in East and West. Economically, the country was on the brink of bankruptcy. Low productivity, decaying infrastructure, declining markets in the Eastern bloc, and costly social welfare made the DDR increasingly reliant on borrowing from West Germany.[191] Ironically, the heavily subsidized tariffs for utility services that had been symbolic of socialist superiority were now being sustained with help from the capitalist adversary. In the absence of effective incentives for factories, offices, or households to use energy and water resources sparingly or mitigate against pollution and without the means to fund investments in improved production and consumption processes, the DDR constantly struggled to achieve elusive economic growth targets with outdated technologies and underperforming equipment.

As Eastern bloc countries began opening up to political and economic reform and the Soviet Union under Mikhail Gorbachev grew increasingly reluctant to support the East German regime, people in the DDR found their voice to protest against the injustices of the system in the autumn of 1989. Others took the opportunity provided by the newly permeable borders in Central Europe to leave the country. The exodus accelerated when, on November 9, 1989, the Berlin Wall was momentously opened. Within the month of November 1989 over 130,000 East Germans—almost 1 percent of the population—moved to the West.[192] Whether protesting from within or voting with their feet, the DDR's citizens were reacting against the gap between what they had been promised and what they had experienced, as well as the gap in living standards between East and West.

The quality of utility services was certainly not uppermost in their mind as they considered their future at this time. The dire state of infrastructure in East Berlin can, however, be seen as emblematic of the state-socialist dilemma as the Eastern bloc crumbled. The city's energy and water infrastructures had initially been heralded as conduits of a socialist ideal characterized by technological progress at a low cost to consumers. Emerging economic constraints and shifting political priorities soon left them, though, without the investments needed for maintenance and modernization. Political neglect and planning intransigencies resulted in physical decay and operational inefficiencies. The victims were, on the one hand, the users having to cope with inadequate utility services and, on the other, the environment exploited as source and sink for ever increasing targets of energy and water provision. The legacies of these sociotechnical interdependencies were to resonate for years across the reunited city.

8 Sustaining the Insular West Berlin

On June 11, 1970, two directors of West Berlin's gas utility, Hans-Werner Krentz and Kurt Restin, found themselves on a mission to Moscow. They had come, with the backing of the West Berlin senate, to do a deal with the Soviets over the supply of natural gas to the isolated half-city. Since the blockade in 1948–1949, West Berlin had always resisted the idea of being dependent on a gas supply that passed through East Germany. Fear of political vulnerability to the East German regime was being tempered, though, by new developments of a material and political kind. First, limits to the growth of town gas production were becoming self-evident, in the form of overwhelming air pollution and excessive costs. Second, geological tests had revealed that West Berlin could store up to one billion cubic meters of gas within the city limits in natural underground cavities, thus making it less dependent on a continuous gas supply. Third, geopolitical rapprochement between West and East was opening doors to joint trade agreements. If the municipal gas utility Gasag could come to an agreement with the Soviet Union, the East German regime—so the thinking went—would never dare to interrupt Soviet gas transported across its territory.

The Cold War novices from West Berlin were, however, no match for the seasoned negotiators in Moscow.[1] When Krentz and Restin appeared at the Foreign Trade Ministry building that day, they were met at the door by armed guards and a flat denial that any appointment had been made. After repeated pleadings they were given a slot the following day, only to endure the same humiliating procedure once again. When they did finally get an audience with the vice president of the Soviet export company, Sojuznefteexport, they were told they would have to give an immediate written guarantee of how much gas they intended to buy, without knowing the price tag. They returned to Berlin empty-handed and smarting with indignation. Negotiations on the West German side were subsequently transferred to the gas companies Salzgitter and Ruhrgas.

This brief encounter with the harsh realities of Cold War geopolitics is indicative of West Berlin's predicament. The city was trying to survive while surrounded by political powers hostile to its existence as a bastion of Western democracy and capitalism. In order to do so, it needed a secure supply of energy, water, and other resources. The experience of political division in 1948–1949 had made it painfully obvious how dependent West Berlin was on East Berlin, East Germany, and—ultimately—the Soviet Union for essential utility services. The vulnerability of West Berlin that emanated from its geopolitical and physical isolation, indeed, was manifest in its infrastructure systems. Power lines to the half-city had been disconnected, cross-border water mains were subject to sudden interruptions, and sewage passing from West to East was billed at a high cost. From this position of strategic weakness, the West Berlin authorities and utilities sought to render their infrastructure systems more resilient to isolation, intervention, and political blackmail. Initially, the strategy of infrastructural resilience focused on minimizing dependence on the East and maximizing capacity for self-supply. Latterly, when the limits to urban autarky were becoming ever more visible, regional cooperation was tentatively pursued in the wake of improved East-West relations. As Gasag's mission to Moscow indicated, however, hardwiring geopolitical rapprochement into cross-border infrastructures was a complicated process. Ironically, it was only shortly before the fall of the Berlin Wall in 1989 that agreements were finally reached with the Soviet Union to supply natural gas and with East Germany to supply electricity to West Berlin.

This chapter explores the urban and geopolitical contexts within which West Berlin strove to sustain its insular existence, assessing how the city's infrastructures were enrolled in strategies of urban resilience. The story begins by setting out the political and economic frameworks within which the insular city operated throughout the period of division. It then explicates the nature of infrastructural isolation emanating from political division and exacerbated by the building of the Berlin Wall in 1961. The subsequent sections investigate how urban autarky became a guiding principle of infrastructure policy and how this manifested itself in distinct ways in each of the five service sectors under analysis. The narrative covers a spectrum ranging from full self-generation of electricity and the spatial fix of district heating, via ambivalence over local gas production, to the closure of urban water cycles and mutual dependencies over wastewater treatment. The chapter then analyses how these geopolitical contexts and policy responses impacted upon the internal management of the utilities, consumerism, and the urban environment. It concludes by exploring the growing criticism of urban autarky and the emergence of alternative imaginaries to the "build and supply" logic that continued to underpin infrastructure policy in West Berlin.

Protected and Pampered

West Berlin's vulnerability during the Cold War was tempered significantly by the determination of the three Western Allies to defend its territorial sovereignty and the dedication of West Germany to sustain its beleaguered economy. Without either, West Berlin would have ceased to exist as an independent political entity. For all the uplifting bravado around the defense of the "island city" and the impressive self-reliance enacted by its inhabitants every day, the legendary resilience of West Berlin was dependent, ultimately, on a well-oiled life-support system. The protection accorded to West Berlin from the outside was in no way assured following political division in 1948–1949. Indeed, in the early 1950s it was a cause of great concern in Berlin, as well as Bonn, the provisional capital of West Germany. What evolved over the years was a shift in support roles. While the Allies gradually relaxed their controls over the everyday running of the city, the West German government increasingly drew West Berlin into its political orbit and provided it with financial sustenance.

In May 1949, in an initial statement of trust, the Western Allies revised the occupation statute for West Berlin, increasing the self-governing powers of the city authorities (senate and house of representatives) and minimizing interventions by the occupying powers.[2] Further concessions were made by the Allies in March 1951, after which time they no longer intervened in the everyday running of the city administration but agreed to restrict their prerogative to the geopolitical security and status of the city. This allocation of powers was formalized in the Declaration of Berlin of May 5, 1955, which governed relations between West Germany and the Allies over Berlin until the city regained sovereignty in 1990.[3] Henceforth, the West Berlin government could manage its internal affairs—including urban development and infrastructure services—but had to accept Allied control over its external affairs as well as over air traffic and transport links to the West. Despite all these concessions, West Berlin's domestic policies remained imbued with geopolitical sensitivities toward the Allies. Their background influence over strategic decisions of urban infrastructure was always apparent. They were insistent, for instance, that West Berlin should always retain sufficient coal reserves to keep the city going for at least three months in order to avoid a repeat of the blockade.[4] In the words of a former power plant manager who served during the 1970s, "the Allies always had the last say" in any dealings with the city government.[5]

In return for Allied presence, West Berlin enjoyed protection from any intrusions by the Soviet Union or East Germany. As was revealed in a series of geopolitical crises over Berlin, the three Western Allies were determined to guarantee West Berlin's post-division status. Whether during the uprising of June 1953 in East Berlin, the

Khrushchev ultimatum of October 1958 calling for the Allies to withdraw, or the building of the Berlin Wall in August 1961, the pattern was always the same. The Allies were not prepared to risk offending the Soviet Union by offering support to those opposing the East Berlin regime, but drew the red line on interventions in West Berlin.[6] This umbrella of political protection was complemented by financial support provided in large measure by the United States. US aid to West Germany and West Berlin took three forms: emergency relief under the so-called GARIOA program; the European Recovery Program (ERP), popularly known as the Marshall Plan; and special loans for West Berlin within the ERP.[7] These special loans alone had, by 1985, contributed 16.1 billion Deutschmark to the city.

Nevertheless, it was made clear to the West German government that the Allies did not envisage supporting West Berlin economically beyond immediate emergency aid. Deprived of its status as national capital, cut off from its immediate hinterland, and losing business investors and qualified employees to West Germany, West Berlin was in dire economic straits immediately following division. In 1950 its factories were working at only 40 percent capacity, the unemployment rate peaked at 31.2 percent and the city, consequently, ran up a massive budget deficit.[8] While West Berlin was being heralded as a showcase of Western capitalism, it was, in truth, a basket case.

The legal capacity for the Federal Republic of Germany (BRD) to intervene in support of the beleaguered city was constrained by the postwar settlement, whereby West Berlin was not formally part of the BRD. However, West Berlin's constitution of October 1, 1950, was modelled on the BRD's Basic Law, the city used the same currency as the BRD, several federal agencies were relocated to the city, and the West German government incorporated West Berlin in international agreements wherever possible.[9]

These forms of support paled in comparison with the financial subsidies and incentives that were to flow from Bonn to Berlin.[10] As early as March 14, 1950, the federal parliament declared West Berlin an emergency area and granted an initial tranche of 60 million Deutschmark in aid. In 1952 regular economic aid to the city was institutionalized with the innocuously termed Third Transition Act (Drittes Überleitungsgesetz). This law aligned West Berlin's laws with those of the BRD, giving the city the rights and obligations—though not the formal status—of a federal state. One of these rights was to receive financial support to help balance the city budget. Alongside continuous budget support, West Berlin also benefited hugely from incentives for local business and employees, such as tax breaks, and perks for its inhabitants, such as subsidized transportation, postage, and cultural activities. Together, these three funding streams from the government in Bonn amounted to a staggering 200.5 billion Deutschmark between 1952 and 1986.[11] The lion's share was taken up by budget aid (155.8 billion Deutschmark), followed by tax incentives (17.9 billion Deutschmark).

By 1960 the incentives had proved so successful in stimulating economic growth that West Berlin could boast full employment.[12] However, after 1961, in the shadow of the Berlin Wall, the urban economy again suffered, as people left the city, the population declined, and companies relocated to safer shores.[13] In the 1970s around 40 percent of West Berlin's city budget was being covered by West German taxpayers.[14] This figure rose to 51 percent the year the Berlin Wall fell, in 1989.[15] By then, Bonn was pumping around 500 million Deutschmark a year to West Berlin in direct subsidies alone and a further 8 billion Deutschmark a year in tax breaks, business credits, salary bonuses, and so on.[16] In West Germany this massive level of support was widely resented, but tolerated as a political and economic necessity. In West Berlin financial aid from Bonn became an essential part of life in the insular city that reached out into the materiality of urban infrastructure and the management culture of its utilities, as will be revealed.

Cold War Confinement

The provision of security and succor by the West that sustained West Berlin throughout the Cold War was a distant dream in the early 1950s, as West Berlin's utilities struggled to provide basic services under geopolitical duress. The confinement of the half-city to its own territory was made most palpable through sudden disconnections to its urban infrastructures and tenuous agreements to reopen them in these early years of division.

Energy was the most vulnerable service of all.[17] West Berlin, clearly, did not possess the fossil fuel resources needed to power a postwar city. All sources of energy had to be imported via the DDR: whether coal in barges, oil in tankers, gas in pipelines, or electricity along the grid. This made West Berlin's electricity and gas services massively dependent on transportation capacity, weather conditions, and, above all, the willingness of the East German government to permit passage uninterrupted. The Soviet and East German authorities were clearly prepared to use electricity supply as a pawn in the Cold War game. Disconnecting the power lines to West Berlin without warning became a continuous reminder of the isolated city's dependence on the East, but also an instrument for blackmailing the West into paying more for its energy.[18] Between 1950 and 1955 several power supply agreements were concluded, only to be broken when it suited the Soviet authorities. By 1955 West Berlin had become an "electricity island," a truncated territory cut off from the national grid (see figure 8.1).[19]

Access to gas supplies was less critical initially, given West Berlin's more favorable production capacity for town gas. The two largest and most modern gas works were located in the Western half of the city. Between 1950 and 1953 West Berlin's gas utility Gasag was even able to supply small settlements in the DDR close to the border, in return for gas to areas traditionally supplied from gas works in the East.[20] The supply

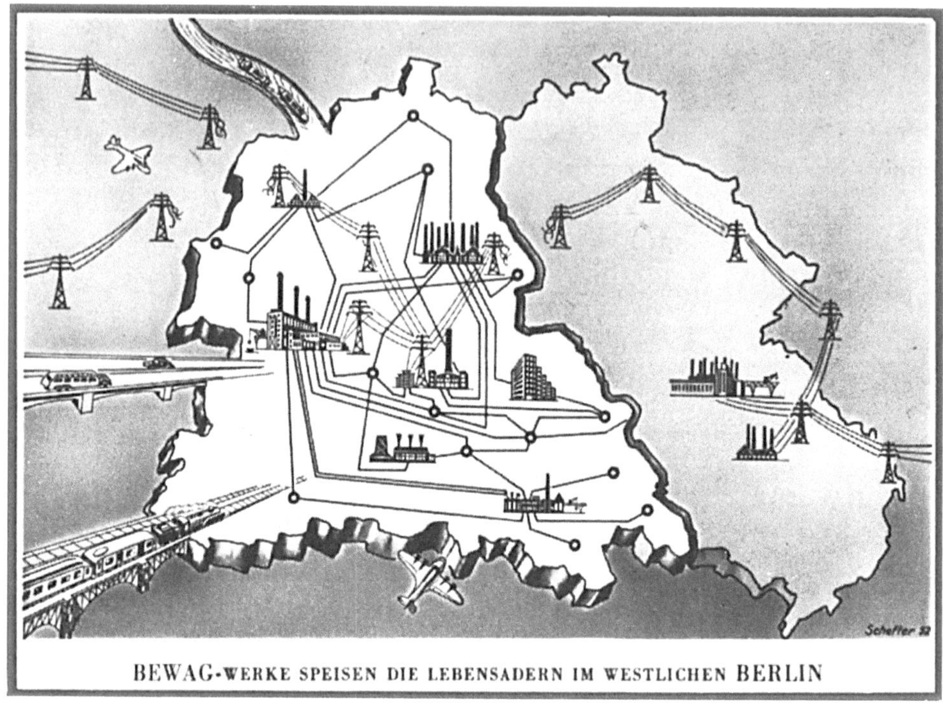

Figure 8.1
West Berlin as an "electricity island"
Source: Berliner Kraft- und Licht(Bewag)-Aktiengesellschaft, *100 Jahre Strom für Berlin*, year 1952. Copyright: Bewag/Vattenfall.

problem confronting gas production was, rather, access to coal, the principal fuel used.[21] Gasag, like the power utility Bewag, required huge amounts of coal. Its annual coal consumption rose from 424,725 metric tons in 1950 to 664,693 metric tons in 1953.[22] Little wonder, then, that any politically motivated interruptions to supply were an immediate cause for alarm. On January 12, 1951, the canal lock at Rothensee near Magdeburg was deliberately blocked, bringing shipping deliveries to West Berlin to a complete standstill.[23] Around 100 barges of coal from the Ruhr had to be unloaded onto trucks, at great inconvenience to West Berlin. The lock was reopened in November 1951 but subject to repeated closures by the East German authorities subsequently.[24] To minimize vulnerability to such interventions, huge reserves of coal were stored at West Berlin's power stations (see figure 8.2).

Unlike electricity or gas, water was far less amenable to long-distance transportation. Any shortages tended to be highly localized. This created problems in areas vulnerable

Figure 8.2
Coal reserves in West Berlin, 1951
Source: Landesarchiv Berlin (LAB) F Rep. 260 (07), no. II13758. Photo by Erich T. Middendorf, September 27, 1951.

to supply shortages, but also, intriguingly, opportunities for cross-border deals. Talks over water transfers across the Berlin divide broke down in 1950, heralding a game of Cold War cat and mouse over water supply that went on for years.[25] When a disagreement blew up over payments from the West, the East Berlin authorities responded on July 3, 1950, by shutting off the mains valves at three border crossings, prompting a water supply crisis in the district of Neukölln. Standpipes were reactivated, tankers distributed water, the local brewery set up hoses to supply water from its own wells, and the West Berlin police even put its three water cannons at the utility's disposal. After three weeks an agreement was reached and the valves were reopened, though this did not stem criticism in West Berlin about how poorly the situation had been handled by its own utility's directors.[26]

A second emblematic incident occurred during a heat wave in 1953, when the West Berlin water utility was forced to appeal to the East for help. On July 7, 1953, the directors of the two water utilities met on the Späth Bridge, where—in the presence of a large press contingent—they opened the valve supplying West Berlin.[27] This meeting on the bridge connecting East to West was to provide an iconic image of cross-border

Figure 8.3
Water directors from East and West meet at the Späth bridge, July 7, 1953
Source: Landesarchiv Berlin (LAB) F Rep. 290 (02), no. 0026487. Photo by Gert Schütz.

collaboration (see figure 8.3). It was all the more significant since it took place just a few weeks after the violent suppression of opposition on East Berlin's streets on June 17. The critical importance of basic services overrode the heightened political sensitivities of the day. The two water directors agreed to meet again in the future.[28] Out of this interaction emerged a deal in August 1955 for each side to supply vulnerable areas in the other half with 120,000 cubic meters of water a month.[29] This more balanced exchange arrangement did not, however, prove immune from disputes over payments, which re-erupted in the summer of 1957.[30]

West Berlin's dependence was greatest over wastewater treatment. Only around 10 percent of its wastewater was treated on its own territory—on a sewage farm at Karolinenhöhe—and thirty of the thirty-six pressure sewers transporting its wastewater crossed into East Berlin or East Germany. Any border blockages to these sewers would have had catastrophic effects. Moreover, unlike water supply, the East was not reliant at all on West Berlin to treat its wastewater. In such an apparently unfavorable position, West Berlin had no alternative but to press for a rapid solution. An early agreement was reached between the two wastewater utilities in December 1950, setting out payments for services rendered, and was renewed in 1954 without difficulty.[31] What made wastewater less prone to contestation—apart from the financial returns—was the dependence of East Germany itself on wastewater from West Berlin to sustain agricultural production on its sewage farms. In this case, interdependence helped reduce service vulnerability.

Whereas cross-border energy circuits and water flows were disrupted by political division in 1948–1949, the passage of people between East and West Berlin was halted by the building of the Berlin Wall on August 13, 1961. The erection of the Wall had no direct impact on the distribution of electricity, gas, water, or wastewater, therefore, but rather on the utilities' staff. The night the Wall was built, 172 employees of West Berlin's electricity utility Bewag found themselves on the other side and were unable to return to their jobs.[32] The same fate befell 124 employees of Gasag.[33] As a token of solidarity and sympathy, both companies posted these stranded employees parcels of food. Gasag sent 135 parcels in September 1961, each containing 250g of coffee, 250g of cocoa, 500g of rice, 250g of bacon, three bars of chocolate, and twenty cigarettes. The city archive contains a number of letters of thanks from these unfortunate victims of the Wall. Written by hand and in a simple, personal style, they make for disturbing reading (see figure 8.4). All the letters express their gratitude to their former colleagues and their desire to see them again soon. They all bear a heavy sense of foreboding, however, that this will not be possible in the near future. Many of the writers report that, owing to the stress of separation, they have become seriously ill and are unable to work.

Urban Autarky

The vulnerabilities of West Berlin's utility services revealed so painfully by the blockade and subsequent disruptions to cross-border agreements were formative in the emergence of a long-term strategic vision of urban autarky. The experiences made in the early 1950s convinced politicians, government officers, and utility directors alike that they had to maximize self-dependence in order to minimize the risk of disturbance by the East. Striving for autarky in service provision became the hallmark of West Berlin's infrastructure policy throughout the period of division. Bewag's directors celebrated their ability to sustain the only urban "electricity island" in the industrialized world.[34] Gasag's directors drew on the self-generation of electricity as a model for local gas production and as an argument against importing gas from West Germany or the Soviet Union.[35] The wastewater utility director and Senator for Transport and Enterprises used the same argument to justify plans for five sewage treatment plants on West Berlin territory, thereby reducing dependence on treatment facilities in the East.[36] As late as 1981 the water utility director was aspiring to "full autarky in water supply" for the city.[37]

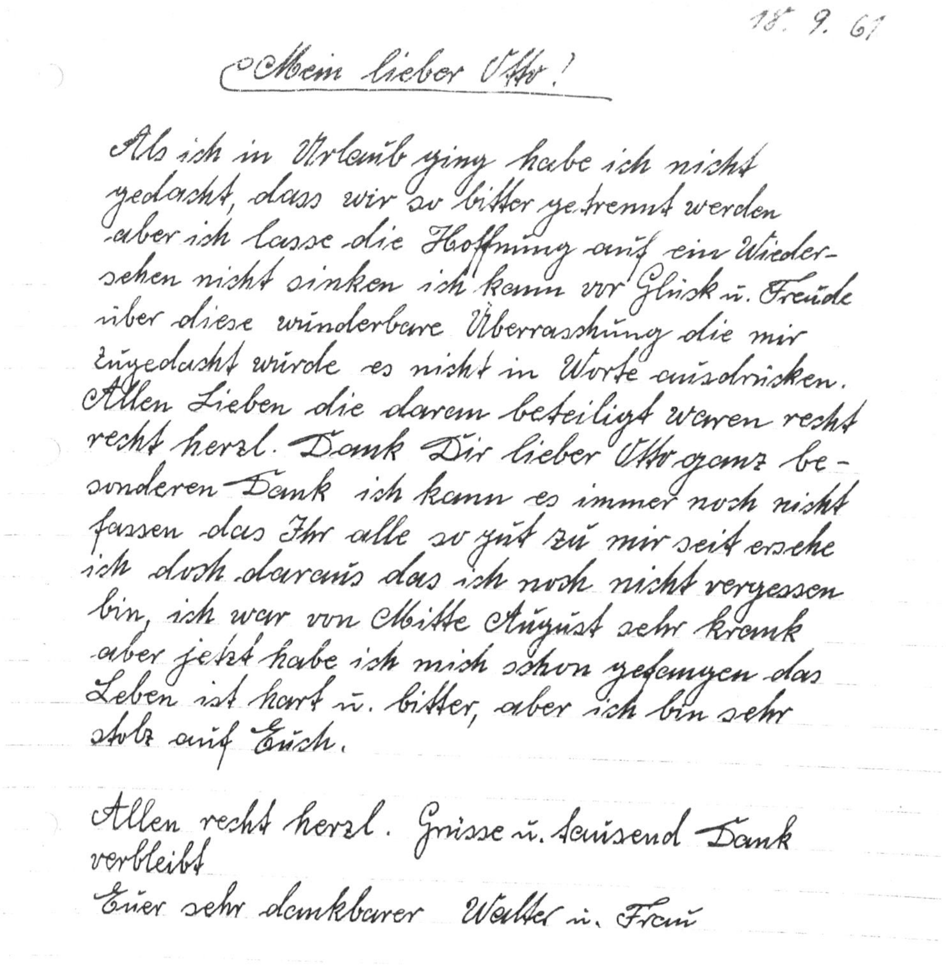

18. 9. 61

Mein lieber Otto!

Als ich in Urlaub ging habe ich nicht gedacht, dass wir so bitter getrennt werden aber ich lasse die Hoffnung auf ein Wiedersehen nicht sinken ich kann vor Glück u. Freude über diese wunderbare Überraschung die mir zugedacht wurde es nicht in Worte ausdrücken. Allen Lieben die daran beteiligt waren recht recht herzl. Dank Dir lieber Otto ganz besonderen Dank ich kann es immer noch nicht fassen das Ihr alle so gut zu mir seit ersehe ich doch daraus das ich noch nicht vergessen bin, ich war von Mitte August sehr krank aber jetzt habe ich mich schon gefangen das Leben ist hart u. bitter, aber ich bin sehr stolz auf Euch.

Allen recht herzl. Grüsse u. tausend Dank verbleibt
Euer sehr dankbarer Walter u. Frau

Figure 8.4
Letter from a Gasag employee caught on the Eastern side of the Berlin Wall
Source: Landesarchiv Berlin (LAB) B Rep. 011, no. 145.

Translating the rhetoric of urban autarky into practice was inevitably problematic, but the task was pursued with vigor. West Berlin's strategic response to Cold War confinement entailed several components, summarized here and described in more detail for each infrastructure sector in the following sections. First, massive investments were made in the half-city's energy and water infrastructures so as to increase capacity to a level as close as possible to self-sufficiency. Second, huge reserves were built up that were capable of sustaining supply even in the event of political disruption or plant failure.

Third, a sufficient quantity of raw materials—in particular, coal and oil—was stockpiled to survive a repeat of the blockade. Fourth, the networks of cables, pipes, and sewers mediating flows of water and energy were spatially reoriented to suit the territory of West Berlin, rather than the whole city.[38] Finally, West Berlin embraced technological experimentation as a source of innovative responses to spatial confinement. Revealingly, the option of minimizing demand for energy or water—thereby reducing pressure on limited resources—was not pursued until the 1970s and only then half-heartedly.

Urban autarky came, however, at a price. It required huge financial expenditure on investments in infrastructure, maintenance of surplus capacity, transportation of raw materials, and the staff required to operate multiple plants. These costs could generally be passed on to the federal government, sweetening the pill for West Berlin at least. Urban autarky also nurtured inefficiencies, for instance in the form of underutilized reserves or local conversion of fossil fuels. This was detrimental to the urban environment and the quality of life of residents. Furthermore, spatial orientation around the half-city of West Berlin removed the need to consider the implications for Greater Berlin as a whole, with or without political reunification. Ultimately, urban autarky could always only be an aspiration, never a full reality. The limits to autarky—such as dependence on imported coal for electricity generation or the gravitational force pulling water and sewage beyond the city border—were ever-present, requiring modifications to the ideal in tune with material necessities and political opportunities. In none of the five infrastructural sectors analyzed here was full autarky ever achieved. Each one followed a particular hybrid of autarky and dependence that, intriguingly, shifted in emphasis between the early 1950s and late 1980s. In the following five sections these sector-specific trajectories are traced to reveal the complex and dynamic realities of living the urban autarky ideal.

The "Electricity Island"

Within an extraordinarily short space of time West Berlin became fully self-sufficient in electricity generation. From 1956 onward it was a true "electricity island." This achievement was all the more incredible against the backdrop of continuously rising electricity demand. Electricity supplied by Bewag more than doubled between 1950 and 1958, then nearly trebled by 1973 (see table 8.1).[39] If growth rates did decline during the following two decades, by 1989 Bewag was supplying West Berlin with 10,327 GWh of electricity single-handedly, independent of external imports.[40] For the utility to manage this without any major power outages over the entire period of political division is a tribute to the dedication of all those involved to make self-reliance a working reality at all costs.

Table 8.1
Electricity provision in West Berlin, 1950–1989.

Year	Electricity supplied by Bewag (GWh)	Proportion generated in West Berlin (%)
1950	893	67
1954	1,409	95
1958	2,112	100
1967	3,419	100
1973	5,895	100
1980	7,539	100
1989	10,327	100

Sources: Statistisches Landesamt Berlin, *Statistisches Jahrbuch 1952*, 291; Statistisches Landesamt Berlin, *Statistisches Jahrbuch 1955*, 283; Statistisches Landesamt Berlin, *Statistisches Jahrbuch 1959*, 322; Presse- und Informationsamt des Landes Berlin, *Energie 1*, 2; Deutsches Institut für Wirtschaftsforschung, *Entwicklung des Elektrizitätsverbrauchs*, 8; Statistisches Landesamt Berlin, *Statistisches Jahrbuch 1990*, 251.

Self-reliance was made possible, first and foremost, by expanding local generation capacity. The flagship power station of the 1950s, West (later Reuter), was opened in December 1949 and, by the end of 1953, was already meeting 82 percent of West Berlin's total electricity demand (see figure 8.5).[41] It was, at that time, the largest coal-fired power station in Germany and one of the most modern in Europe, designed—significantly—to use coal efficiently and thus minimize coal imports.[42] There followed capacity extensions to existing power stations at Moabit, Charlottenburg, and Steglitz during the 1950s and the construction of a new power plant on the Upper Havel in Spandau in 1961–1963.[43] This massive program of infrastructure expansion required investments by Bewag totalling 405 million Deutschmark between 1949 and 1959 for the power stations alone.[44] Most of this was funded out of loans under the ERP program, paid back in regular instalments by the utility.[45] Expansion to generation capacity continued in later years, most notably with the construction of the city's largest power stations at Lichterfelde in 1974 and Spandau (Reuter West) in 1987–1989.[46] By 1989, Bewag was generating over 10 billion kWh a year in eight power stations for around 1.3 million customers.

Generation capacity was calculated on the basis of two criteria: anticipated growth in demand and a security reserve. For most of the period 1949–1989 it was widely assumed that demand for electricity in West Berlin, as in West Germany, would double every ten years.[47] This meant increasing generation capacity by 11 percent every year. As noted above, electricity sales did indeed increase tenfold in the 1950s and again in the 1960s.

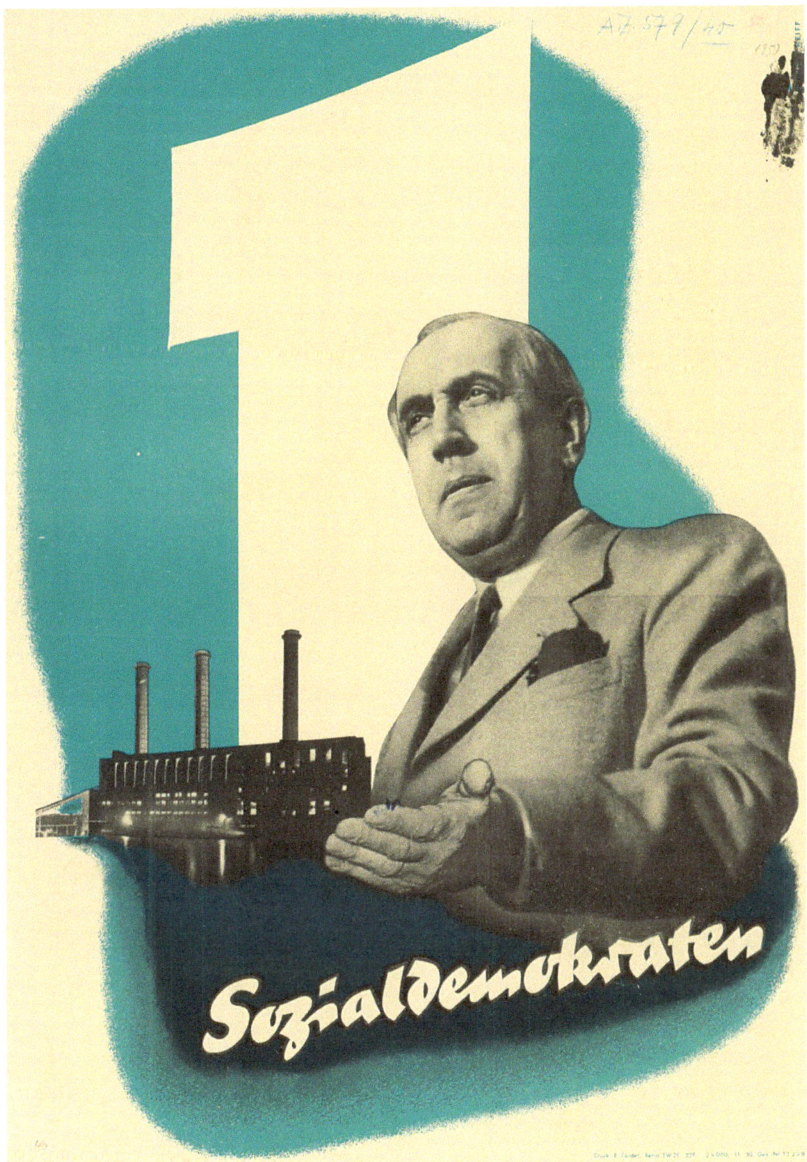

Figure 8.5
SPD poster with Ernst Reuter and the West power station, 1950
Source: Landesarchiv Berlin (LAB) F Rep. 260–03, no. C 0158.

Even more significant when planning generation capacity was the need to meet peak loads without access to an external grid. West Berlin had to construct a system that was capable of managing evening demand peaks that could be ten times higher than low demand at night, owing to the low levels of industrial production in the 1950s.[48] To accommodate sharp peaks and unexpected hikes in demand, an additional reserve was calculated on top of regular supply capacity. During the late 1950s a figure of 17 percent became established as the minimum reserve capacity required to avoid any failure of supply. It was to remain the yardstick for Bewag throughout the Cold War.[49] The logic underpinning this figure was that the security reserve had to cover for the failure of the largest power generation block in the city at any time as well as peak load (calculated at 3 percent of total capacity) and severe weather conditions (a further 3 percent).[50]

Not just capacity, also flexibility was instrumental behind the infrastructure expansion program. Because Bewag could not draw on the external support of a national grid, the sudden failure of a power generation block required an emergency system capable of preventing a drop in frequency (brownout) or a power outage (blackout) in any part of the city.[51] The first component to kick in upon detection of a supply problem was the steam storage plant located at the Charlottenburg power station. This facility, built in 1929, could within minutes be driving turbines generating 40 MW for approximately one hour.[52] By then, several gas turbines, which needed about thirty minutes to warm up, would be feeding electricity into the local grid. If neither of these steps was sufficient to meet demand, then a shutdown plan was enacted according to a strict hierarchy of consumer groups.[53] In 1986 this cascade of emergency measures was front-ended with a huge battery plant located at the Steglitz power station. This electricity storage facility—the largest of its kind in the world at the time—could supply only 17 MW of power for fifteen minutes, but it could do this within ten seconds.[54] With it, Bewag could respond to a problem with even greater flexibility and fine-tune the frequency in the local grid as well. Connectivity between generating facilities within West Berlin was made possible via a new 110 kV power line encircling the city.[55] In practice, the steam storage and battery facilities were used quite frequently. By contrast, the gas turbines reserved for more persistent supply interruptions were, by many accounts, barely used at all.[56] This was the flip side of assuring maximum supply security: generating capacity that stood idle for most of the time. Massive redundancies were built into the system sustaining West Berlin's insular power supply.

The strategy of maximizing capacity for electricity generation was, by the 1960s, running into difficulties. Building ever more coal-fired power stations within the narrow confines of the city was simply not feasible, for a number of reasons. First, space was at a premium and suitable sites for power plants were rare, not least owing to Allied air traffic restrictions. Second, the storage of enough coal to fire these plants and meet the required reserve was proving a real headache. Occasionally, in hot weather, these coal heaps would self-ignite, creating huge fires that officials tried to conceal from the public for fear of arousing panic.[57] Third, residents were growing increasingly critical of the air pollution imposed upon them by inner-city power stations. Yet demand for electricity continued to grow rapidly.[58] In 1970, peak demand in West Berlin reached 1,200 MW, coming close to Bewag's total capacity of 1,292 MW.[59] Maintaining self-sufficiency of power generation within the bounds of the city was posing a challenge.

One solution adopted to tackle the problem of coal storage was to convert some of the coal-fired power stations to oil.[60] Following a pioneer 25 MW plant at Steglitz in 1960, oil-fired gas turbines were subsequently constructed at the power stations at Moabit (34 MW in 1972), Charlottenburg (210 MW in 1976), and Wilmersdorf (277.5 MW in 1978).[61] Between the late 1970s and mid-1980s around a quarter of all West Berlin's electricity was generated this way.[62] By comparison, West Germany was using oil for only around 2 percent of its power generation.[63] West Berlin's insularity and its decision to switch to oil just before the first oil crisis rendered the costs of producing electricity there between 25 percent and 60 percent higher than in the BRD.[64]

A second, tantalizing alternative was to go nuclear. The big attraction of nuclear power for the city authorities was that it required far less storage space for fuel and would have zero onsite emissions of sulphur dioxide and flue ash. In the mid-1950s Bewag set up a unit to investigate the possibility of building a nuclear power plant in West Berlin. By 1957 it had come up with plans for a 150 MW facility on the River Havel.[65] In October 1959 the mayor (Regierender Bürgermeister) Willy Brandt held talks in Brussels about the possibility of building a nuclear power plant of this size in West Berlin as part of the Euratom program.[66] These initiatives did not come to fruition, and by the early 1970s the Berlin senate and Bewag were weighing up the pros and cons of the nuclear option. On one hand, they recognized the security risk of having nuclear rods passing through DDR territory and the low efficiency of running a relatively small plant.[67] On the other hand, a nuclear power plant was seen as a key to resolving the problem of air pollution and coal storage associated with existing electricity generation. If only one-third of West Berlin's power could be provided by locally generated nuclear power, it was estimated, this would reduce SO_2 emissions by 80,000 metric tons a year and coal consumption by 200,000 metric tons a year.[68] A further study, in 1975, argued that a nuclear power plant in West Berlin could be a valuable source of district heating, owing to what it called—without irony—the "favorable population density and distribution."[69] After the emergence of antinuclear protests in West Germany in 1976, support for the nuclear option in West Berlin declined dramatically. While the Bewag management—and works council—continued to toy with the idea, the Berlin senate, federal government, and Allies agreed to ditch it for fear of popular protest.[70]

Renewable energies were a third option that became the object of some research and publicity from the mid-1970s onward, but they had no impact on the city's energy provision. In 1978 the first house in West Berlin was installed with solar collectors for room and water heating, and electrical heat pumps were subsidized to the tune of 1 million Deutschmark.[71] In 1979 Bewag put on an exhibition in Steglitz entitled "Energy from the Environment—Used by Electricity" that advertised heat pumps, solar collectors, and energy roofs.[72] But these initiatives never came to much until shortly before the fall of the Wall.

A fourth option—to influence demand for electricity—was applied only in a very selective manner. A commission set up in 1973 to investigate possibilities for reducing demand for energy in West Berlin was highly skeptical of energy conservation. Comprising representatives of senate departments, Bewag, Gasag, and independent experts, it dismissed various ideas for saving energy—such as extending the school holidays in winter, limiting the opening hours of public baths, or promoting public transport on the underground railway network—for being unrealistic or ineffective.[73] A major report on energy supply in West Berlin compiled by the senate in September 1977 expressed the need to explore all possibilities for saving energy, but reached similarly pessimistic conclusions. Prospects for saving electricity were deemed "limited"; past experience made the authors "not optimistic" about reducing consumption via publicity campaigns.[74] During subsequent deliberations by similar commissions it became apparent, according to insiders, that neither of the energy utilities was willing to entertain energy-saving activities that would only reduce its revenue.[75] For all the talk of saving energy as a response to local supply shortfalls and emergent environmental crises, the city government was ultimately unwilling to force Bewag or Gasag to take energy conservation seriously.[76] All that the energy utilities were prepared to do was to manage demand away from peak load times.[77] This strategy had the advantage for them of reducing pressure on the supply system while avoiding any loss of revenue. "Rational energy use"—a clarion call of the era—meant to Bewag not using less energy, but using it more efficiently and at more favorable times.

The only other option available involved relinquishing the long-held strategy of self-reliance in electricity provision. This had become politically viable following a rapprochement in East-West relations and the Berlin Agreement of 1971. Already in 1972 the Senate Department for Economics was talking of a connection to an external electricity grid as the only satisfactory solution for West Berlin's supply problems.[78] The senator, Karl König (SPD), described grid connection as an urgent necessity in a parliamentary committee meeting of October 7, 1974.[79] There he explained that, under current circumstances of autarkic supply and a doubling of demand every ten years, West Berlin would need to build fourteen new power stations over the next ten years and twenty-eight by 1994. "Everybody wants electricity," he bemoaned, "but nobody wants a power station."[80] His party colleague Alexander Voelker (SPD) went so far as to call the electricity island status of Berlin "an unacceptable anachronism."[81] The following month an agreement was reached between Federal Chancellor Helmut Schmidt and Soviet leader Leonid Brezhnev for West Germany to build a nuclear power station on Soviet territory that would supply both West Germany and West Berlin with electricity.[82] Acceptance of this expression of geopolitical détente in Berlin hinged on the technical issue of whether West Berlin should be connected to this power source directly or via a spur line accessible to the DDR. While the East German authorities insisted on the right to access a cable passing through their territory, the Economics Senator in West Berlin was adamant that "we want no switch in the DDR."[83] The East German veto on the plan agreed between the Soviets and West Germans brought the idea to a halt. When the DDR offered, instead, to supply West Berlin with electricity from its own lignite mining fields in 1980, this was firmly declined.[84]

By the mid-1980s, therefore, West Berlin found itself in an impasse largely of its own making. Unwilling to consider lower capacity needs, skeptical of demand management, distrustful of East Germany, and resentful of public criticism, Bewag resorted to its default setting: building more coal-fired power stations. Only in March 1988 was an agreement finally signed between the DDR, Preußen-Elektra, and Bewag for a grid connection to West Berlin, but only by 1992.[85] Ultimately, the fall of the Berlin Wall in November 1989 and, with it, the end of urban autarky saved West Berlin from the consequences of an electricity supply strategy that had become insular in more ways than one.

The Spatial Fix of District Heating

One distinct advantage of West Berlin generating its own electricity was the opportunity this created for district heating on a grand scale. The location of the city's power stations close to densely populated settlements made them ideal for the cogeneration of heat and power. Initially, Bewag was reluctant to expand its existing small district heating network, preferring to sell electricity for home heating, in the form of night-storage or electric fan heaters.[86] The Berlin senate, though, was keen to provide its new housing estates with district heating, as a visible improvement over lignite-fired stoves. It encouraged Bewag to provide more heating from its centrally located power stations, sweetening the pill of the costly investments with credits and cheap loans.[87] In 1958 the Hansaviertel estate was supplied with heating from the power stations at Moabit and Charlottenburg, in 1963 a heating plant was built for the Gropiusstadt estate, and in the late 1960s Bewag created a heating network that connected its CHP plants. Almost all its new power stations were designed for cogeneration. Within the space of just ten years, between 1960 and 1970, the amount of heating sold by Bewag leapt from 2,680 Terajoules (TJ) to 9,150 TJ, as the surface area served by district heating networks rocketed (see figure 8.6).[88] By 1980 the figure stood at 13,650 TJ.

With political and financial backing from the city government Bewag was soon singing the praises of district heating along with the senate. A number of arguments were used to justify the expansion of district heating.[89] First, cogeneration of heat and power represented a more efficient use of energy, exploiting the heat produced in the generation of electricity. Second, district heating replaced individual coal-fired stoves that were responsible for considerable air pollution in the city. Third, district heating was a cleaner and far easier way of heating homes than traditional coal or lignite stoves. After the oil crisis in 1973 a further argument was marshaled in favor of the technology: district heating from coal-fired CHP plants helped reduce dependency on oil. In many ways, therefore, district heating seemed the perfect answer to West Berlin's insular predicament.

As the 1970s progressed, however, criticism grew over the performance, cost, and exclusivity of the district heating program in West Berlin.[90] Several energy specialists in the city argued that the claim to be reducing air pollution was true on only a very localized level, for district heating also produced high emissions of SO_2 that were simply redirected elsewhere by tall chimneys. Since district heating was billed according the size of a home, rather than the amount consumed, there was no incentive to save energy. They also challenged the cost-effectiveness of district heating, pointing out that connection to the district heating network obliged consumers, unable to influence their heating bills, to pay far more for heating their homes than with coal or, later, gas.[91] A further criticism was that district heating was undermining the prospects for more energy-efficient, small-scale CHP units. A number of so-called block-type CHP plants that had existed since the 1960s were closed down to make way for district heating schemes in several urban development districts.[92]

The future of district heating came to a head in 1978 with the development of a heating concept for West Berlin. A working group comprising several senate departments, Bewag, Gasag, and external advisors had the remit to explore ways of improving energy efficiency and reducing energy imports relating to the field of heating.[93] It became clear from the working group's proceedings that this task was interpreted by most participants primarily as a way of promoting Bewag's plans for expanding its district heating market and Gasag's ambitions to service other areas with gas heating. The concept was, on paper, about optimizing the economic needs and technical facilities of district heating providers.[94] Effectively, though, the city was being divided up into territorial monopolies for Bewag, Gasag, and other heating providers in a spatial fix that excluded other options

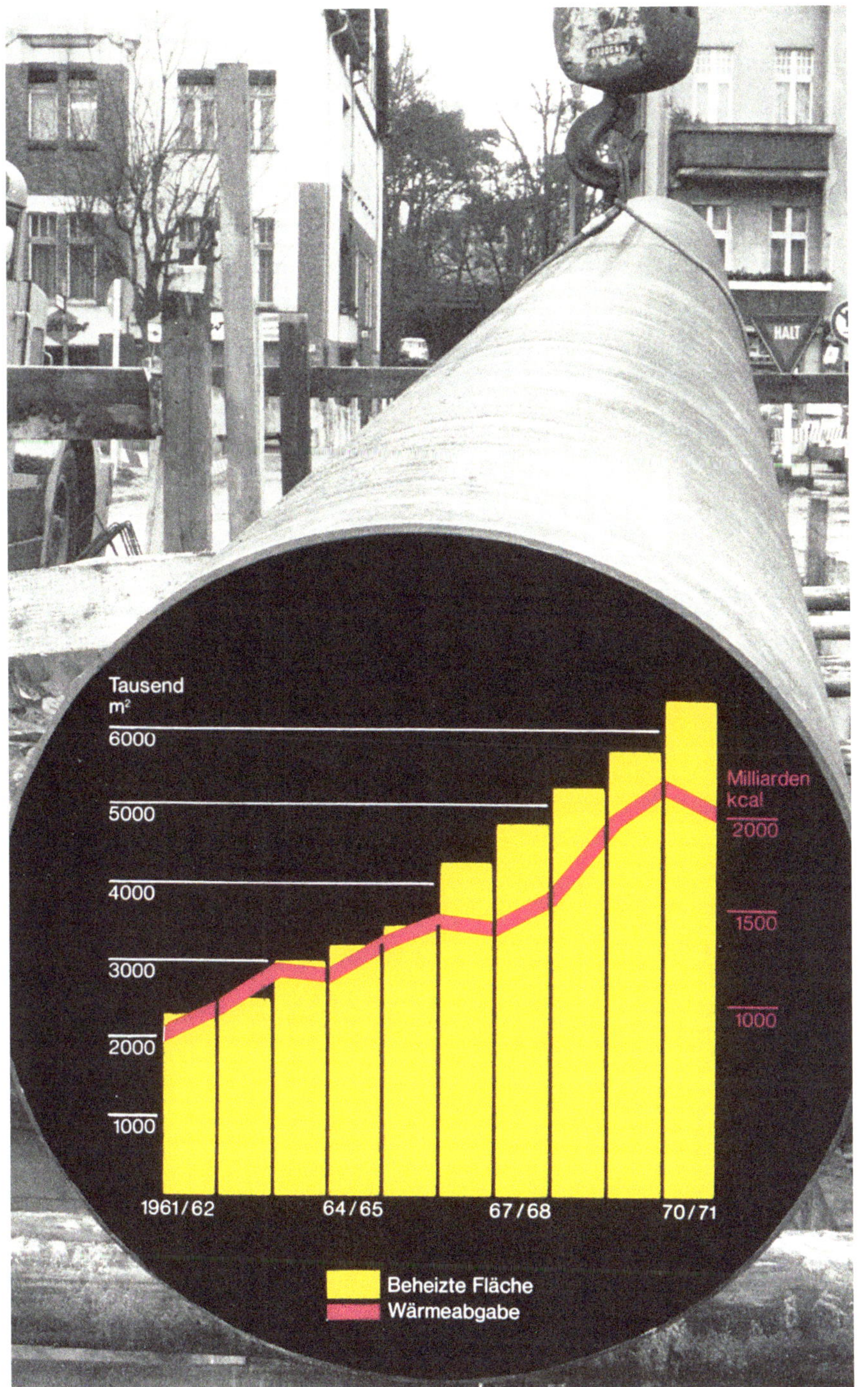

Figure 8.6

The expansion of district heating in West Berlin, 1961–1971

Source: Landesarchiv Berlin (LAB) B Rep. 016, no. 460.

(see figure 8.7). Competition between the city's energy utilities was deftly resolved by the protection of segregated markets. This raised a protest from one of the independent advisers in the working group, who argued in a letter to the senators involved that the report failed to address the potential of renewable energy, dismissed out of hand more efficient block-type CHP plants, ignored emissions from heating plants, and offered no comparison of costs for different heating options.[95] The last point drew on the criticism that Bewag was using its revenue from electricity to cross-subsidize the high costs of district heating and thereby undercut its competitors.[96] This view had sympathizers within

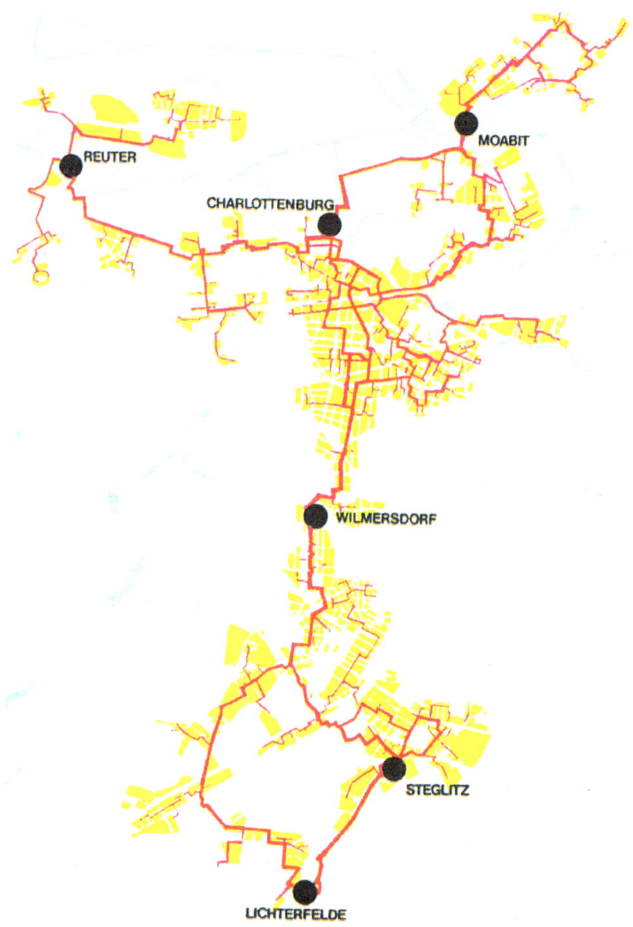

Figure 8.7

Map of Bewag's district heating network, 1977

Source: Berliner Kraft- und Licht(Bewag)-Aktiengesellschaft, *100 Jahre Strom für Berlin*, year 1977. Copyright: Bewag/Vattenfall.

the city government. The Senate Department for Building and Housing actively promoted small-scale, block-type CHP plants, much to the frustration of other senate departments toeing the district heating line.[97] Overall, however, district heating remained the preferred technology of the city authorities. The final report of the working group, submitted in July 1979, recommended building twenty new coal-fired heating plants as well as expanding the gas network for heating purposes.[98] In the Clean Air Plan of 1981 and again in the Heating Concept of 1984 district heating was promoted as the key to improving air quality in the city.[99] With this kind of backing Bewag was planning yet another expansion to its heating network shortly before the Wall fell.[100]

From Local to Imported Gas

Of West Berlin's energy services, gas provision revealed the limits of urban autarky most starkly. Producing all the city's gas needs locally ran up against problems of storage, air pollution, shifting demand, technological adaptation and, above all, costs that would have crippled any city not reliant on external deficit funding.

In the early years of division Gasag was so confident of its ability to meet all West Berlin's gas needs that it rejected outright an offer by the West German Reichswerke in 1951 to supply the insular city with gas via a long-distance pipeline.[101] Resistance to external sources of gas had been a hallmark of Gasag's strategy under the Weimar Republic and Nazi rule, and the bitter experience of forced connection during the war had only strengthened its resolve. The arguments rallied against the offer had, therefore, a familiar ring about them: imported gas would undermine the viability of the city's gas works and cost local jobs the city could ill afford to lose.[102] Above all, the long-distance pipeline would be vulnerable to disruption—this time by the Soviet or East German powers. This line of thinking had the backing of the Berlin senate. The Senator for Transport and Enterprises, Herbert Hausmann, rejected the offer by Reichswerke, telling the company that "Berlin must reckon with the possibility of the Russian and Soviet-German authorities causing us major transportation difficulties."[103]

Without external supplies, the local gas network needed expanding to meet anticipated growth in demand. Old and inefficient gas works were replaced by fewer, larger ones. Largest of all was the new gas works at Mariendorf, which—covering 55 hectares—became West Berlin's largest building site in the early 1950s and a symbol of postwar reconstruction (see figure 8.8).[104] When complete, gas production there increased fivefold, from 300,000 cubic meters a day in 1949 to 1,500,000 cubic meters in 1960.[105] Other gas works, as at Charlottenburg, were also enlarged and modernized. As a result of this infrastructure expansion program gas production increased, although not on the scale of electricity (see table 8.2). Capacity was increased for gas storage as well as

Figure 8.8

Foundation ceremony for the new gas works at Mariendorf, attended by federal president Theodor Heuss, 1956

Source: Landesarchiv Berlin (LAB), F Rep. 290 (07), no. 0047450. Photo by Horst Siegmann, May 29, 1956.

Table 8.2
Gas provision in West Berlin, 1950–1989.

Year	Gas produced by Gasag (million cubic meters)	Gas storage (thousand cubic meters)	No. of homes heated with gas	Per capita gas consumption (cubic meters)
1950	273	700		
1958	401			
1960			1,000	160
1962	377			
1970	509		31,300	230
1980	969	1,500	131,000	491
1987			192,000	594
1989	1,014	590,000*		

* refers to maximum potential underground storage
Sources: Bärthel, *Die Geschichte der Gasversorgung*, 154; Statistisches Landesamt Berlin, *Statistisches Jahrbuch 1952*, 291; Statistisches Landesamt Berlin, *Statistisches Jahrbuch 1959*, 322; Senat von Berlin, *Zweijahresbericht des Senats von Berlin 1961/1962*, 132; GASAG, *... über 160 Jahre Gasversorgung*, 3, Annex; Statistisches Landesamt Berlin, *Statistisches Jahrbuch 1990*, 251.

production.[106] Owing to the limited amounts that could be stored above ground, this had less to do with geopolitical sensitivities than with the need to meet peak loads on an hourly or daily basis.[107]

With demand for gas increasing gradually during the 1950s, Gasag's balance sheet was buoyed by the sale of by-products from town gas production. The production of town gas had always had the additional benefit of creating marketable by-products, in the form of coke, tar, ammonia, and benzene. Gasag's sales of tar, used primarily in road construction, doubled from 15,200 metric tons in 1950 to 31,800 metric tons in 1958. Production of ammonium sulphate, an artificial fertilizer, rose from 1,600 metric tons in 1950 to 7,500 metric tons in 1958. Benzene sales surged from 900 metric tons in 1950 to 6,900 metric tons over the same period. The principal by-product, however, was coke, widely used for heating buildings. Sales of coke increased dramatically from 154,000 metric tons in 1950 to 564,000 in 1957. That year Gasag was supplying 55 percent of all the coke used in West Berlin.

It was at this time, however, that cracks in the system of self-sufficiency began to appear. The market for locally produced coke suddenly weakened, as cheaper coke became available from the Ruhr and consumers switched to oil or district heating.[108] Cheaper, imported sources of tar and artificial fertilizers were also undermining the viability of local gas production. This was alarming for Gasag's directors, who called on the senate to protect its markets from competition that threatened the very foundations of autarkic gas production. Throughout the 1960s they campaigned for a protectionist policy oriented toward maintaining a circular economy of gas and its by-products, using geopolitical arguments to shore up their case.[109] When Gasag learned that its coke was no longer being bought by public agencies, such as police stations or hospitals, it complained to the responsible senate departments, calling on them to show solidarity with the plight of local gas production in the insular city.[110] The Senator for the Interior retaliated, protesting against buildings under his authority having to pay over the market price for coke just to help Gasag.[111] The conflict over Gasag's by-products is revealing about how political division and geographical isolation permeated into the most mundane of resource markets. It also illustrates how urban autarky needed to be constantly shored up, even by enrolling other metabolic flows in the provision of energy.

During the 1960s Gasag was also struggling to keep up with a further challenge: major shifts in demand for gas. In the early 1960s gas consumption in West Berlin actually declined briefly, as a consequence of a shift from gas to electricity in both street lighting and industrial production (see table 8.2). From the mid-1960s onward, however, gas consumption rose once more as a growing number of homes switched to gas heating. Sales of gas nearly doubled in just a decade, between 1970 and 1980. The number of homes in West Berlin heated by gas shot up from a mere 1,000 in 1960 to 192,000 in 1987 (see table 8.2). This growth in gas for heating brought with it fresh problems. As the proportion of gas used for heating rose from 3 percent in 1960 to over 60 percent by 1977, the load curve became increasingly imbalanced.[112] Gas for heating was required at particular times of the day and year. This required higher production capacity capable of dealing with peak evening loads in the winter, but left the same infrastructure largely redundant during the summer. The ratio of summer to winter loads rose dramatically from 1:2.4 in 1960 to 1:8.2 in 1977.[113]

The problem was not just an issue of production capacity, but also of technologies capable of responding to rapid surges in demand. Coal-fired gas works were too cumbersome for this task and consequently had to be replaced in part by facilities that produced gas via the catalytic splitting of oil products, primarily petrol.[114] These oil-based gas works could be fired up quickly and required less space for fuel storage, but they were far more expensive to operate.

In the wake of the oil crisis, the switch from coal to oil as a fuel for gas production weighed even more heavily on Gasag's accounts. Importing costly oil resources to produce town gas containing one-third less energy than natural gas in order to meet excessively high peak loads made for a highly uneconomical business model. The option of raising gas tariffs to cover the financial shortfalls was not open to Gasag, for political reasons. West Berlin's gas tariffs were kept deliberately low so as not to act as a disincentive to business. Nevertheless, the tariff for industrial customers was still around 30 percent higher than the West German average in 1968.[115] The net effect of these factors was financial losses incurred by Gasag every year after 1967 that took on colossal proportions. The utility's annual losses rose from 24 million Deutschmark in 1973, 52 million in 1976, to 134 million in 1981, peaking at 150 million in 1985.[116] These losses were largely a consequence of the political choice to produce town gas locally at artificially low tariffs. How they could get so out of hand at a time when the utility was experiencing a massive growth in gas sales for home heating does, however, raise questions about the capability of its management.

It was on the cusp of this compounded crisis that Gasag's directors Krentz and Restin found themselves in Moscow in the summer of 1970. They had come to realize that resistance to a gas pipeline was a luxury West Berlin could no longer afford and that sourcing natural gas directly from the Soviet Union was probably the best option around. Apart from the pressure to act, two opportunities had recently emerged that made a gas connection to the East appear less risky than in the past. First, political rapprochement between the BRD and DDR from 1969 onward—heralded by the "*Ostpolitik*" of the Brandt government—created a greater sense of reliability in bilateral relations.[117] Second, a geological find opened up the possibility of storing huge quantities of gas underground in West Berlin. Drilling into the city's substrata had originally been conducted in the hope of discovering natural gas or oil reserves.[118] What it revealed, instead, were porous geological layers, between 500 and 860 meters deep, that were covered by a 200-meter-thick dome of clay. Once the water had been pressed out of them, these layers could store up to 1 billion cubic meters of gas (see figure 8.9). Initially, Gasag was skeptical, fearing not only possible interruptions to a transnational pipeline but also the DDR potentially tapping the underground gas store from the border six kilometers away.[119] These concerns were soon overridden by the appeal of being able to store enough gas underground to supply the city for a whole year. With this technology West Berlin could make itself far less dependent on a continuous supply of imported gas and, thereby, on the vagaries of European geopolitics.

Negotiations to supply West Berlin with natural gas from the Soviet Union revealed, nevertheless, a whole gamut of complex geopolitical interests characteristic of the thaw in Cold War relations.[120] Gasag and the West Berlin government remained concerned about security of supply. The Senator for Finance was keen to get a deal that would reduce the cost of insular gas provision. The Federal Ministry of Economics preferred supplying West Berlin with gas from the Ruhr. The Western Allies were insistent that

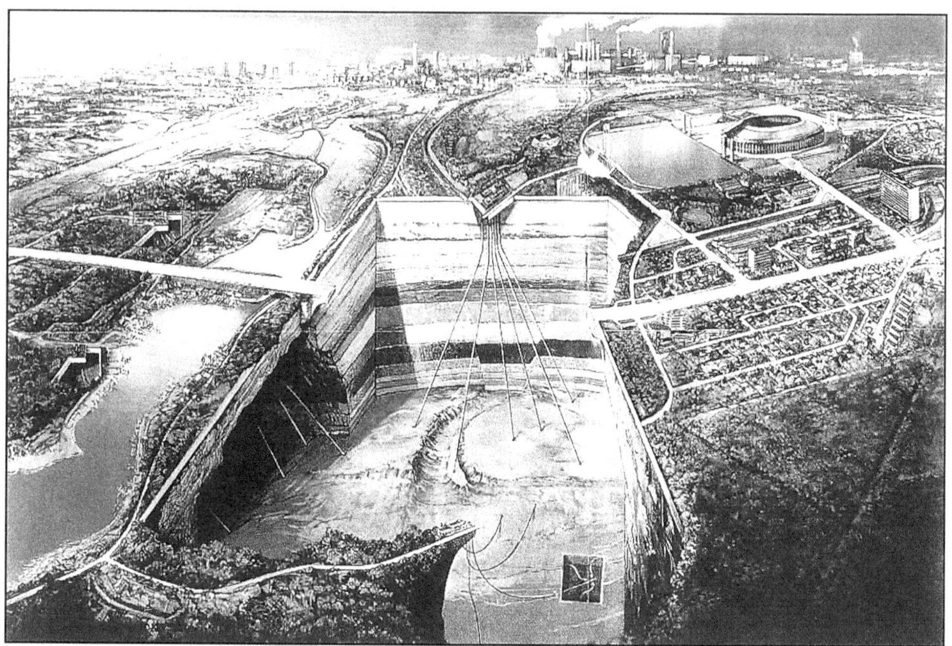

Figure 8.9
Artist's impression of underground storage for natural gas in West Berlin
Source: Bärthel, "Anlagen und Bauten der Gasversorgung," 51. Copyright: GASAG.

the underground storage technology must be proven before agreeing to any deal. The Soviets themselves were keen to sell their gas, but wary of offending their East German partners by conceding too many security assurances to West Berlin. Unsurprisingly, little progress was made in the early negotiation phase of 1969–1971.[121]

It was only on March 30, 1983, that a contract was finally signed for the Soviet Union to deliver natural gas to West Berlin, followed by a further contract between Gasag and Ruhrgas on delivery conditions.[122] By then, assurance had been provided by the DDR that it would allow Soviet gas to pass through its territory unhindered. The final part of the deal was an obligation by West Berlin to buy 650 million cubic meters of natural gas a year.[123] This was a massive amount, representing almost twice the energy Gasag supplied at that time, thus condemning the utility to boost its future gas sales.[124] On October 22, 1984, a section of the Berlin Wall was temporarily dismantled at Buckow to permit the laying of the gas pipeline.[125] On October 1, 1985, the supply of natural gas to West Berlin commenced, ending thirty-five years of insular gas provision.[126] For several years this natural gas needed transforming into town gas at the city's gas works, until the urban network and all appliances could gradually be converted to natural gas. It was only after the fall of the Wall in 1989, therefore, that West Berlin belatedly joined the fold of European cities using natural, rather than town, gas in its homes and businesses.

Closing Urban Water Cycles

The experience of water supply shortages in the early 1950s, when the West Berlin authorities had been obliged to seek help from East Berlin, galvanized the city's water utility, Berliner Wasserwerke (BWW), into developing its own strategy of maximizing self-dependence. Its new technical director, Kurt Hünerberg, strove to achieve this by increasing infrastructure capacity to supply water and securing sources of drinking water in the city.[127] In 1950 West Berlin possessed only seven of the city's sixteen water works that together had a maximum capacity of 500,000 cubic meters a day, far too low to serve its 2.2 million inhabitants (see figure 8.10).[128] A new water works, at Riemeisterfenn in the southwest of the city, was completed in September 1955, but not without having to overcome considerable opposition from residents and the Police President critical of the negative impact on groundwater levels.[129] Subsequently, the utility switched to extending existing water works as a politically less controversial strategy. Supply capacity was expanded at all West Berlin's water works: Beelitzhof, Spandau, Tiefwerder, Jungfernheide, Tegel, and Kladow. It increased from 500,000 cubic meters a day in March 1949 to 603,000 in June 1957 and 850,000 in July 1963 (for an overview of water use in West Berlin see table 8.3).[130] At the same time maintenance to the water mains reduced water losses from leakage sharply, from 11.7 percent of all water supplied in 1950 to just 3.4 percent in 1963.[131] With these extensions to capacity, supply was able to match rising demand, but only after around 1960. This was in part thanks to a decline in demand between 1959 and 1963 as people and businesses left West Berlin during a period of high political volatility.

Water consumption rose again by 3 percent in the 1970s and 8 percent in the 1980s, creating some concern and renewed efforts to extend supply (see table 8.3).[132] Capacity at the water works was increased to 1,140,000 cubic meters a day in 1978.[133] This was to remain peak capacity in West Berlin until the fall of the Wall.[134] Investments by the water utility in capacity expansion were substantial throughout the period of division, but—unlike the gas utility—were not dependent on subsidies from elsewhere. Between 1949 and 1981 they amounted to around 880 million Deutschmark.[135] Despite the constantly high level of investment the water utility was able to produce a profit every year except 1974.[136] At the same time the water utility could keep water tariffs lower

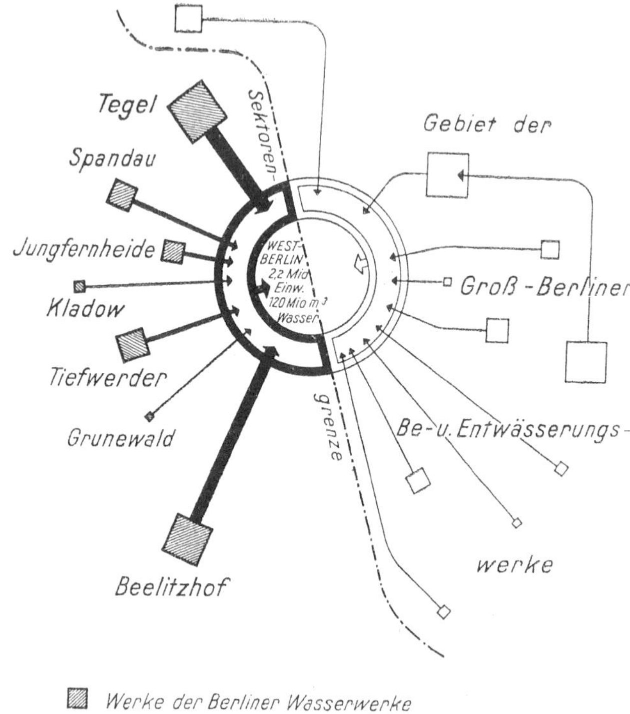

Figure 8.10
Stylized map of Berlin's divided water supply network, 1953
Source: Hünerberg, "Die Berliner Wasserversorgung," 40.

than the West German average.[137] This was partly due to efficiency gains, such as reducing the number of employees from 1,619 in 1955 to 1,268 in 1970, but partly also to Berlin's favorable water resource situation.[138]

Raising the capacity of West Berlin's own water supply network made sense, of course, only if there were enough local water resources to feed this growing infrastructure. Without the ability to influence groundwater aquifers in East Berlin or surface water flowing through the city from upstream areas in East Germany, BWW sought to protect and enrich the water resources on its own territory as part of its resilience strategy. There were two components to this strategy: replenishing groundwater and reducing surface water pollution. In essence, both approaches were oriented toward closing urban water cycles within the confines of West Berlin. Groundwater replenishment was applied systematically to address the annual groundwater deficit in West Berlin of about 45 million cubic meters.[139] By 1978 groundwater resources were being replenished to

Table 8.3
Water supply and wastewater disposal in West Berlin, 1950–1989.

Year	Water supplied (million cubic meters)	Wastewater collected (million cubic meters)	Proportion of wastewater treated in DDR (%)
1950	105	129	
1958	121	140	
1962		145	86
1970	168	175	82
1980	174	175	63
1985		170	53
1989	188	165	

Sources: Statistisches Landesamt Berlin, *Statistisches Jahrbuch 1952*, 292; Statistisches Landesamt Berlin, *Statistisches Jahrbuch 1959*, 323; Berliner Entwässerungswerke, *Bericht über das Geschäftsjahr*, 5; Berliner Entwässerungswerke, *100 Jahre Berliner Entwässerungswerke*, 8; Der Senator für Stadtentwicklung und Umweltschutz, *Planungsdaten für Berlin (West)*, 283–285; Statistisches Landesamt Berlin, *Statistisches Jahrbuch 1990*, 475.

the tune of around 25 million cubic meters per year.[140] The aim was to increase this figure to 50 million cubic meters so as to secure West Berlin's water resources for the future. At the same time, the quality of Berlin's water was improved by reducing nutrient loads. Phosphates emanating from sewage treatment plants upstream posed a serious threat to the quality of West Berlin's lakes and rivers, and, thereby also, its drinking water sources.[141] Phosphate elimination facilities were built at Beelitzhof in 1978–1981 and at Tegel in 1981–1985. By reducing the annual phosphorus load in Lake Tegel from 150 metric tons to just 1.5 metric tons, the plant there effectively solved the nutrient overload problem for the Tegel water works, which supplied around one-third of all West Berlin's drinking water.[142]

Dealing with the consequences of inadequate wastewater treatment in order to shore up drinking water supplies revealed the strong interdependence of water and wastewater management in the island city of West Berlin. It was for this reason, in part, that the two utilities were gradually drawn into an ever closer organizational union. The other reason lay in the structural weaknesses of the wastewater utility. Hünerberg, director of the water utility, was advocating a takeover of the wastewater utility by his own BWW as early as 1958.[143] The poorly veiled ambition behind this initiative prompted an angry rejection from his counterpart at Berliner Stadtentwässerung, Albrecht Cohrs. Only when Cohrs suddenly died was the opportunity hastily seized to create a joint management board for the two utilities in 1962.[144] They remained separate entities but were placed under the overall leadership of Hünerberg's BWW. In 1967 Berliner

Stadtentwässerung became an owner-operated municipal enterprise (*Eigenbetrieb*), like BWW.[145] Only in 1988 were the two utilities finally amalgamated into one organization, Berliner Wasserbetriebe (BWB), with a solution that accommodated the different legal status of water supply and wastewater treatment according to West German law.[146] This process of organizational convergence helped advance a coordinated approach to urban water management that took into consideration not just supply capacity and treatment targets but also the environmental conditions for these to be achieved effectively at all.[147]

The Mutual Passage of Sewage

In the wastewater sector itself the option of going it alone was seriously limited by the sheer volume of sewage passing from West to East and the almost total dependence of West Berlin on sewage treatment at East German facilities. This, however, did not prevent advocates of urban autarky in the senate and the utility from pushing for self-sufficiency even under these most unfavourable circumstances. Within a month of the December 1950 agreement with the East Berlin utility over cross-border sewage flows, referred to in the previous chapter, Mayor Ernst Reuter and the senator responsible for municipal enterprises, Hausmann, were envisaging the rapid construction of sewage treatment plants on West Berlin territory in order to minimize dependence on the East.[148] An initial plan for five treatment plants was subsequently revised downwards to three (see figure 8.11).[149]

In January 1954 the senate agreed to these three facilities, at a cost of 87 million Deutschmark.[150] A report produced by the Senator for Transport and Enterprises on May 10, 1954, to justify the construction program painted a dramatic picture of what would happen if East Berlin decided to shut off the sewers from the West.[151] Pumping stations in the West would have to be shut down, raw sewage would flow into the watercourses, and a public health disaster would unroll. This grim scenario was presented also to the US Deputy High Commissioner for Germany in the hope of leveraging an American loan: "The additional working places and the storing of raw materials and foodstuffs will not be of any use if the power of resistance of the Berlin population should be considerably weakened by epidemics. The proper disposal of sewage is, to a large extent, much more important for building up industries within a large city than the supply of electricity, gas, and water."[152]

The director of the wastewater utility, Cohrs, was also not averse to playing on fears of reprisals from the East. In a letter to the Senator for Transport and Enterprises of April 1954, he provided arguments in favor of the three sewage treatment plants,

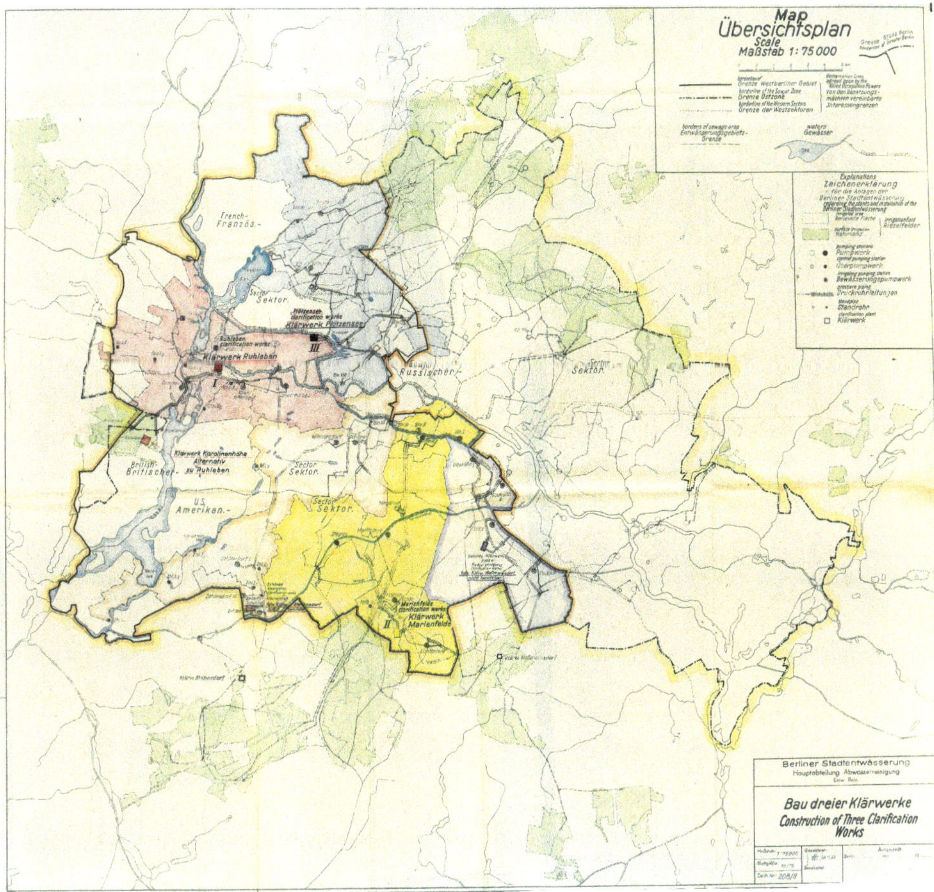

Figure 8.11

Map of planned sewage treatment plants for West Berlin, 1953

Source: Landesarchiv Berlin (LAB) B Rep. 011, no. 30.

concluding that "security can only be assured if West Berlin makes itself self-dependent in sewage treatment as quickly as possible."[153] He subsequently warned that allowing West Berlin's sewage to continue to be irrigated, untreated, on sewage farms in East Germany posed a huge risk to the city's public health, as it would leach back into the watercourses that fed its water supply.[154]

This line of thinking, however, ran up against severe criticism within and beyond the city government. First, it was pointed out that East Germany needed West Berlin's wastewater for irrigating its sewage farms just as much as West Berlin needed its disposal. The relationship between them was, therefore, not as one-sided as the supporters of the planned treatment plants made it out to be. The Senator for Economics and the Chamber of Commerce preferred a solution that sought to maintain, rather than remove, this interdependence.[155] Second, environmental arguments were marshaled to demonstrate that locating sewage treatment plants within West Berlin would not improve, but actually worsen, the water quality of the city's lakes and rivers if they had to take up the treated outflow.[156] The Police President, as local environmental regulator, rejected approval of the initial application on these grounds and proved a persistent opponent to the scheme.[157] Third, the huge cost of building several sewage treatment plants and redirecting urban sewage flows to them was criticized repeatedly.[158] Fourth, some were concerned that construction of the sewage treatment plants might be construed by the Soviets as a provocation, prompting unforeseen reprisals. These criticisms demonstrated an astute awareness of the negative regional implications of a city-centered solution.

The wastewater utility wisely entered into parallel negotiations with the East Berlin wastewater utility to allay fears of a potentially confrontational separation of the sewers.[159] It emerged from this exchange that locating one of the sewage treatment plants at Ruhleben, in the north of West Berlin, would have the least effect on the operation of East German sewage farms. In a further move to appease criticism of pollution to the city's watercourses, it was agreed with the senate that treated wastewater from the new plants should, during the summer months, not be emitted into the Spree and Havel rivers but be pumped into the Teltow Canal and thus away from West Berlin's bathing and drinking water protection zones.[160]

Even though these modifications did not allay all the concerns voiced, the senate finally approved the construction of the Ruhleben plant on July 7, 1956.[161] This first sewage treatment plant on West Berlin territory was officially opened on May 10, 1963, enabling the city to treat 20 percent of its own sewage.[162] It was subsequently extended, increasing its treatment capacity from 150,000 cubic meters to 240,000 per day in 1985.[163] A second treatment plant was built at Marienfelde between 1968 and 1974, capable of treating 125,000 cubic meters of sewage a day.[164] The third plant, planned for Jungfernheide, was never built.[165] By 1986 West Berlin was treating 47 percent of its sewage on its own territory (see table 8.3). This was a far cry from the full self-dependence that had been advocated by some in the 1950s. It represented, rather, a political compromise that acknowledged the advantages to be gained by achieving some degree of independence while maintaining mutual interdependencies around the cross-border passage of sewage (see figure 8.12).

Even partial self-reliance in wastewater treatment came at a high financial cost. Investments in West Berlin's sanitation infrastructure for the whole period of political division, from 1950 to 1989, totaled a staggering 3,794.7 million Deutschmark.[166] The loans needed to fund these investments placed a huge burden on the wastewater

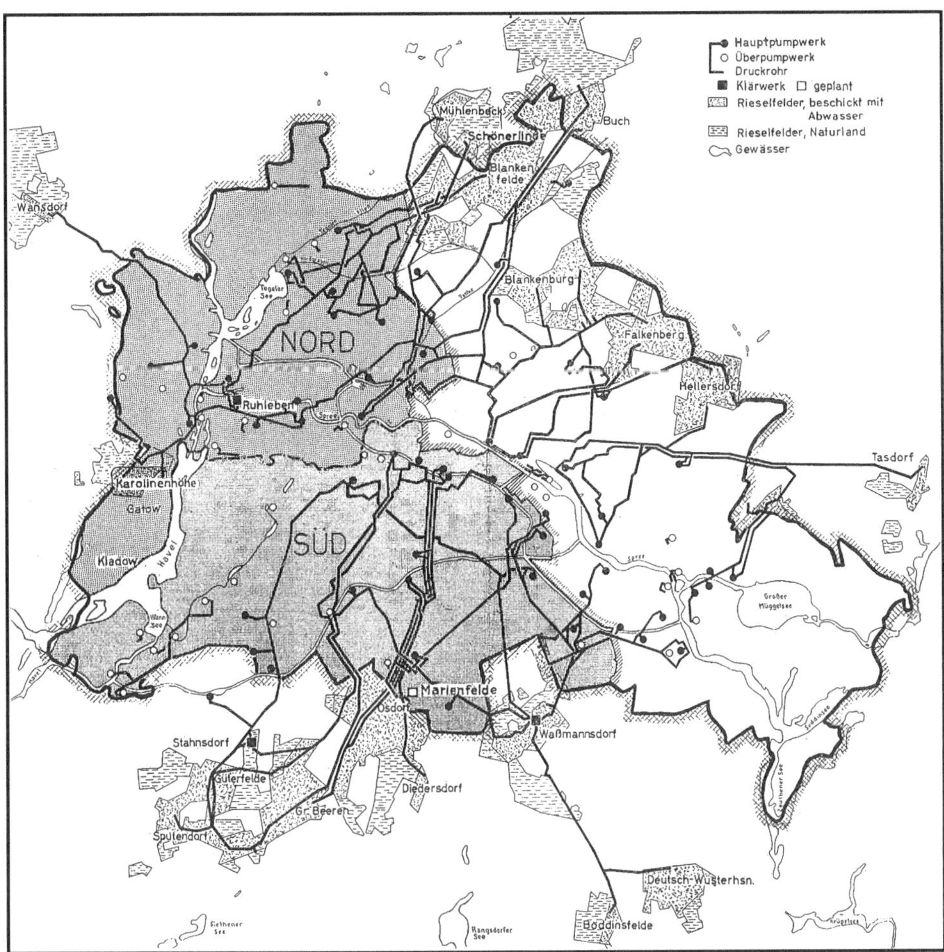

Figure 8.12
Map of West Berlin's sewage treatment in the DDR, 1967
Source: Hünerberg, "Planungen der Berliner Entwässerungswerke," 263.

utility. In 1981 it had to pay 17 million Deutschmark in interest and 15.9 million Deutschmark in debt repayment.[167] In an attempt to cover the costs of investments wastewater tariffs were increased to a greater extent than the water tariff, from 24 Pfennig per cubic meter in 1958 to 57 Pfennig in 1972.[168] The amount of wastewater produced in West Berlin reached a peak—at 175 million cubic meters—in 1970 and declined slightly after a decade, bringing down revenues with it (see table 8.3). It is little wonder, then, that the wastewater utility struggled to avoid making financial losses each year.

Cocoon Culture

West Berlin's isolation from the outside world affected far more than flows of people, material, and energy. Over the years, it exerted a powerful influence on political, business, and social life in the city. Enforced insularity bred a culture of victimization and, with it, a strong sense of entitlement to outside support. After it became apparent that the Allies would always protect West Berlin's political status and the federal government would always pick up the tab to keep the city going, the hard resolve of the early years gradually gave way to complacency. The bubble that secured West Berlin's existence in a hostile geopolitical environment had, in many respects, a stifling effect on life on the inside. Without any real incentive to balance the city's budget, politicians grew liberal in distributing largesse to their clients, businesses became dependent on tax breaks and subsidies, while the population at large came to expect a variety of perks for living in the insular city. This found expression in party patronage, inflated salaries, over-employment, and a predilection for corruption scandals, especially in the construction sector.[169] While no one openly condoned criminal practices, the generosity with which West Berlin's politicians blessed their subjects was widely upheld as a necessity under the city's special circumstances. A mentality of providing for one's own (*Versorgungsdenken*) became an established norm of life.[170]

The utilities were not immune from this dependency culture. On the contrary, as some of the city's largest employers with strong ties to the senate, they embodied many of its core features. At the benign end of the scale, the utilities offered generous employment conditions to their extensive workforce. All of them maintained high levels of employment even during periods of economic dislocation.[171] They paid their staff good salaries and provided social benefits such as recreational activities and subsidized housing. The works council at Bewag could boast that just the threat of a strike would regularly result in its wage demands being met.[172] As such, the utilities fulfilled the role assigned to them by the SPD and trade unions as model employers in the quasi-public sector.[173] In the words of those employed by them, the utilities operated like a big family, caring for its members and protecting them from the harsh outside world.[174] It was common for the offspring of employees—so-called MiKis (*Mitarbeiter-Kinder*)—to be given jobs in the same utility. The problem with this generous approach to employment was that it created jobs "that weren't really needed, requiring bureaucratic procedures to be made more complicated so as to give these people something to do."[175]

Jobs were created not only for the virtuous reason of keeping people employed, but also under the dubious practice of rewarding members of political parties. The utilities all became targets for party patronage, especially for the SPD. In an unhealthy alliance of personnel among party, state, and utilities, the SPD had, by the 1960s, come to dominate staff appointments at all utilities.[176] Not only was the senator responsible for municipal enterprises usually from the SPD, but the supervisory boards of all utilities generally had a strong representation of SPD members. This enabled the appointment of senior posts to be made according to party membership. A former power plant manager recalls: "The SPD was really strong in the power stations. Its political influence was immense in those days. Basically, you didn't get into Bewag if you were not a member of the trade union."[177]

Patronage of this kind was particularly damaging when party membership overrode considerations of qualifications or expertise. Another insider describes how Bewag was renowned for offering jobs to politicians who had to be hidden from public view: "People would get lifted into a job who hadn't a clue about energy; especially those that had to be 'accommodated.' That was a really bad disease in Berlin: anybody who had fallen from grace in the parties would get shoved into one of the utilities. Whether they were competent or not was immaterial."[178]

For all the party-political influence exerted over appointments, the utilities enjoyed relative freedom from political intrusions in their internal management. The intense exchanges over infrastructure strategy between senate departments and utility directors that had characterized the 1950s gave way from the 1960s onward to a more relaxed form of regulatory supervision by the city government. Although the supervisory board of each utility—with the exception of Bewag, owing to its shareholder ownership—was chaired by the senator responsible for municipal enterprises and included four other members appointed by the senate, political influence on utility strategy appears to have subsided considerably.[179]

Kept on a loose rein, the utilities felt even less compulsion to stick to their budgets and willingly overspent on the most modern technology available.[180] They could do so in the confidence that the senate would always be willing to make a special case of their particular needs under insular conditions. Following a series of annual losses by Gasag, the senate institutionalized subsidies for the utility in 1975 on the basis of its "locational disadvantage," according to which Gasag received the difference between its real costs in producing town gas locally and the fictive cost of importing gas from the Ruhr.[181] Cushions of this kind provided no incentive to cut costs or raise efficiency. A special case could be made for huge profits as well as huge losses. Bewag reaped impressive profits each year, enabling it to pay out yearly dividends to its shareholders of between 5 and 9 percent, in addition to the concession fee paid to the city.[182] The company was able to do this thanks not only to growing demand for electricity, but also to its freedom, as a share company, to levy tariffs that were up to 30 percent higher for industrial consumers than the West German average.[183] Bewag countered any criticism of overpricing with reference to the special circumstances of West Berlin. The standard line of argument was, to quote its director, Wilm Tegethoff, "This is the only industrialized city in the world where electricity has to be provided in island mode."[184]

Showcase Consumerism

Consumers of utility services were ascribed a particular role in West Berlin. Beyond using urban infrastructures in a way that was, ideally, conducive to both supply capacity and their own growing needs, consumers became unwitting vehicles of showcase capitalism. In direct competition with the socialist alternative on the other side of the divide, West Berlin set great store on home comforts as a symbol of capitalist supremacy. Electric cookers, gas heaters, and warm-water boilers took on a new significance in the Cold War of consumerism.[185]

Bewag was at the forefront of this offensive. In 1950 it reopened its showrooms and demonstration kitchens in Steglitz, Neukölln, and Spandau, encouraging electricity consumption especially for heating appliances in the bathroom and kitchen.[186] At the same time it reintroduced the Elektrissima hire purchase scheme to great effect. Already by 1956 hire purchase agreements for electrical household goods worth 45 million Deutschmark had been concluded.[187] In 1966 the Elektrissima scheme had half a million customers on its books. Many of these customers were women, at whom much of the advertising was targeted. Gasag also promoted its new gas-fired products for cooking, heating rooms, and supplying hot water, for instance with its "dream kitchen" at the industrial exhibition of 1955. When the utility scaled this up into a whole "dream house" in 1964, the property was visited by 40,000 visitors over just a few days. All these activities had the purpose of not only encouraging or managing demand, but also making West Berlin look an attractive, normal place to live.

Contested Environments

Not all users proved as content with utility services as these showcase activities suggest. From the late 1960s onward, many began to criticize the utilities and their unbending strategy of "build and supply." Unlike in East Berlin, this criticism was not rooted in dissatisfaction with the reliability or quality of service, which was consistently high. It targeted, rather, the negative environmental effects of expanding capacity to secure the island city. The very insularity of West Berlin was creating a concentration of urban infrastructure that was having a detrimental impact on the city's watercourses, forests, parks, and, above all, air. Closing urban resource flows was intensifying local pollution.

Early protests against air pollution from power stations were highly localized and sporadic. Typically, they targeted the clouds of black smoke emitted from chimney stacks when oil-fired turbines were fired up. A former Bewag employee recollects an encounter following such an event in the 1960s: "Shortly afterwards, the housewives in the vicinity wiped their window sills and came to the power station bearing the dirty cleaning rags. As a young engineer I had to deal with them. They said: you're to blame for this, it must stop, and so on. Well, I calmed them down a bit, took the cleaning rags and had them tested. Actually, we found most of the soot was from cars, not the power plant."[188]

Isolated complaints against existing pollution developed into the first organized protest against a new power station in 1969. At that time Bewag was planning the largest power plant in West Berlin, to be located in Lichterfelde in the south of the city. Designed to produce 450 MW of electricity and 600 MW of heat, it was to supply a quarter of all West Berlin's district heating needs.[189] The planned plant aroused opposition not just from local residents, but from a wider community of people concerned at the impact on the urban environment of West Berlin's energy policy. The protests were leveled against the health risk of locating the plant in a densely populated area of the city, the destruction of local landscape features, and the negative impact on property values.[190] Environmentalists were particularly enraged at the choice of crude oil as the fuel, which would exacerbate the already critical problem of SO_2 emissions across the city. The protest around the Lichterfelde CHP plant proved unsuccessful in its immediate objective, as the power station was built in 1972–1974, but it proved to be a formative event in the emergence of citizen activism in West Berlin.[191] It also galvanized the city's regulatory body—the Gewerbeaufsichtsamt—into putting pressure on Bewag to reduce SO_2 emissions at the plant following construction.[192]

This experience should have been a warning to Bewag about the risks of riding roughshod over public opposition to its capacity expansion program. The era in which West Berliners had been willing to accept anything that appeared to provide energy security had, by now, definitely passed. Bewag, however, remained impervious to the critical attention it was attracting. In the mid-1970s, when it launched plans for a huge 1200 MW power plant in Spandau, the utility—accompanied by the Berlin senate sleepwalked into a public relations disaster.

As in the past, Bewag justified the need for yet another power station on the grounds of rapidly increasing demand, the inaccessibility of imported electricity, and limits to generation capacity.[193] Aware, at least, that air pollution was an issue of concern, the utility planned to locate the new plant at the northern periphery of the city, close to the River Upper Havel, where the prevailing winds would take harmful emissions away from West Berlin to the East.[194] A working group of representatives from several senate departments followed this line of thinking and recommended, in March 1976, a site in the forest at Oberjägerweg as the best option.[195]

By this time, there had already emerged strong public protests against the plan, from both local residents and citizens groups (see figure 8.13). Confronted by the combined might of the city government and the power utility, they found inspiration from the antinuclear protests of 1975–1976 at Wyhl and Brokdorf in West Germany.[196] They also gained support from academics of diverse expertise, who began challenging some of the assumptions underpinning Bewag's plans. Urban ecologists sharply criticized the "catastrophic effects on valuable eco-systems," elaborating on the likely impact of the new power station on forestation, groundwater, wildlife, and the urban landscape.[197] These natural assets had a huge significance to daily life in the insular city: their potential loss on a large scale aroused widespread concern.[198] Other experts were questioning the need to expand power-generation capacity at all, calling for a more effective use of reserve plant, energy efficiency options, and renewable energy alternatives.[199] These issues came to a head at a public meeting held in Spandau on June 2, 1976, when representatives from Bewag, three senate departments, and the borough of Spandau were confronted with a four-hour barrage of criticism of the city's energy policy.[200] To the obvious frustration of a senate employee attending the meeting, the whole debate was transmitted by local television and radio stations.

The senate and Bewag responded to this unpleasant exposure of their plans by trying to force them through. The Senator for Economics attempted to have the landscape protection status of the site removed in September 1976.[201] The previous month he persuaded the city mayor to silence criticism of the plan by the borough mayor of Spandau, who—in response to the public protests—had changed his tack.[202] All senate departments were called upon not to deviate from the agreed line to build the power station as planned.[203] Bewag, for its part, tried to block the release of data on future emissions in order to avoid upsetting local residents.[204]

To the outside world the planned power station was, all the while, being presented as existential for West Berlin. As the Senator for Economics, Wolfgang Lüder (FDP), put it to the house of representatives on November 4, 1976: "Without the additional power station the future development and, indeed, viability, of Berlin cannot be assured."[205] In this he was backed by his colleagues in the senate. The Senator for Building and Housing, Harry Ristock (SPD), reiterated to a parliamentary committee on December 8, 1976, that West Berlin's very existence depended on supplying enough electricity to its inhabitants and that any shortfall in supply would cause businesses to leave the city.

Figure 8.13

Poster "The Power Plant at Oberjägerweg Must Not Be Built"

Source: Landesarchiv Berlin (LAB) F Rep. 260–03, no. A 2127.

He was dismissive of citizens groups and their "romantic eccentricity" in believing in reduced energy consumption.[206]

Following the decision by the senate on October 12, 1976, to build a power station at Oberjägerweg of, initially, 600 MW capacity, regular protest actions took place on site.[207] By now the issue had come to focus on the 30–60,000 trees that would have to be felled for the plant to be built. While the protestors called for a one-year moratorium on tree felling until further impact studies had been undertaken, the senate was adamant in opposing such delays. Behind the scenes it supported Bewag's application to circumvent a landscape protection decree in order to commence felling on December 1.[208] This enraged the citizens groups who, following a mass meeting of 6,000 people on November 20, marched to the forest in question and set up a tree camp, effectively occupying the site for weeks (see figure 8.14).[209] Once again, the media was there in full force, attracted by this refreshing contrast to the closed-shop politics characteristic of West Berlin.[210]

The ultimate humiliation of the senate and Bewag came, however, in the courts. Decisions by the Administrative Court in December 1976 and the Higher Administrative Court in May 1977 backed the protestors by prohibiting the felling of trees in advance of a finalized planning procedure. The courts criticized the extent of landscape destruction required by the power plant, disputed the claim that there was no alternative site, and reprimanded the senate for overriding a valid urban development plan.[211] The Higher Court concluded, damningly, that the executive had demonstrated an arrogant disregard for the planning process.[212] Adding insult to injury, it argued that any planning crisis in providing enough electricity was not the fault of opposition to the planned plant, but of the senate and Bewag themselves for failing to address the issue earlier. These judgements were so dismissive that they killed off the Upper Havel project, although not before the senate had appealed unsuccessfully against them.

Instead, Bewag took up a proposal made by the citizens groups themselves to build a much smaller, 100 MW fluidized-bed power plant at Moabit. In the absence of any organized opposition, this plant was built faster than any other in West Berlin.[213] Already in May 1977 Bewag and the Senator for Economics were working on a plan to meet growth in electricity demand by modernizing existing power plant only.[214] This proved perfectly adequate for the next few years. The impending supply crisis conjured up by the city government and Bewag in 1976 to justify building the Upper Havel power station had been proven unfounded. More than this, the tactics used to override legal procedures and political sensitivities had been revealed to be wholly incommensurate with organizations claiming to be vanguards of Western democracy. The Upper Havel case became, as one insider reflects, a "lesson for the whole electricity sector."[215]

Figure 8.14

Occupation of the forest site of the planned power plant at Oberjägerweg, 1976

Source: Landesarchiv Berlin (LAB) F Rep. 260 (03), no. 0194662. Photo by Ludwig Ehlers, November 24, 1976.

It took Bewag some time to digest this lesson, but by the mid-1980s it had agreed to modernize its fleet of power stations to limit significantly emissions of sulphur dioxide, nitrogen oxide, and dust particles. It was prompted to do so by a federal decree on large combustion plants of 1983 that required the installation of flue gas desulphurization units.[216] This milestone in environmental legislation instigated the largest investment program ever undertaken in Bewag's history. The utility invested 3 billion Deutschmark in installing these units in all its plants by 1989, to great effect.[217] Emissions of sulphur dioxide were reduced by about 75 percent and of nitrogen oxide by about 80 percent.[218] Given that two-thirds of sulphur dioxide emissions in West Berlin came from power and heating plants alone, this represented a remarkable improvement. When West Berlin's last new power station, Reuter West, was completed in 1989, it boasted the lowest SO_2 emissions of any power station in Germany.[219]

Alternative West Berlin

Many critics of West Berlin's infrastructure policies were not content with protest, but devised alternative solutions for energy and water use. Inspired by ecological thinking gaining ground across the globe and schooled in the urban ecology, civil engineering, or political science departments at West Berlin's universities, specialists were emerging by the late 1970s with their own, very different visions for utility services in the city. Their approach to energy and water use was framed not by a sense of obligation to meet demand curves with more infrastructure, but by a sense of responsibility to the environment and the limitations it posed for future resource use. This approach challenged the very foundation of conventional infrastructure policy that had been predominant in Berlin—East and West—for decades. Rather than accepting demand as a given and focusing on building up supply capacity to meet anticipated demand growth, it meant critically reappraising the ways energy and water were used so as to conserve natural resources, minimize pollution, and limit disruption to biodiversity. West Berlin posed a particular challenge in this respect because of its insularity. Natural resources were very limited and, thus, highly valued by the city's residents. Saving energy, recycling water, and maximizing use of local energy sources took on a special meaning in the confined city. The alternative solutions proposed and, often, implemented were in some cases counter-models to the conventional infrastructure systems that deliberately avoided any connection to them. In other instances, they set out to reconfigure the existing sociotechnical assemblage in radically new ways.

The alternative water concepts devised for the borough of Kreuzberg during the 1980s fall firmly into the first category. They were oriented toward the design of wastewater systems for single properties that could be largely decoupled from the urban sewer system.[220] This was made possible by reducing water use as far as possible, by means of behavioral change and water-saving technologies, substituting treated rain and gray water for drinking water, for use in washing, and treating black water on site, for instance with reed-bed percolation systems. Developed primarily by university-trained engineers, these concepts were selected as pilot projects in the framework of the International Building Exhibition (IBA) of 1987. This IBA supported many alternative urban development schemes in the city, proving an inspiration for experimental and innovative approaches to engineering and architecture. A notable example, still operative in an adapted form today, is Block 6, part of a new-build apartment block comprising 106 homes located in Kreuzberg.[221] Here, new technologies for saving water and energy and treating waste- and rainwater were tested under real-life conditions. Projects of this kind inspired hydrologists and water engineers in the city to consider broader schemes for recycling water on an urban or regional scale. Such ideas found their way into concept papers but rarely into widespread practice, with the notable exception of local rainwater percolation.[222]

Alternative concepts for home heating that emerged during the 1980s were born out of a critique of district heating. The modernization of heating systems, it was argued here, had come at a huge cost to the environment and household budgets.[223] Energy consumption for centrally heated homes had rocketed since the replacement of coal-fired stoves, in large part because district heating, in particular, did not enable users to regulate heating levels. For the same reason the cost of heating homes had increased substantially, creating serious problems of affordability. Alternative concepts for heating three socially diverse areas of West Berlin—in Kreuzberg, Wilmersdorf, and Neukölln—were developed in a campaign to stop the spread of district heating and advocate solutions based on improving existing structures.[224] Oriented toward the interests of users and the environment, these concepts mapped out ways of helping consumers use less energy for heating. This could entail providing energy advice, improving building insulation, installing thermostats, or retaining coal-fired stoves, depending on a user's circumstances. For new buildings the preferred technology was block-type CHP plants capable of providing heat and power for a single building complex.

The alternative proposals made for electricity provision were geared more to reconfiguring the existing sociotechnical system than to creating a micro-system in parallel. They were based on the need to reduce electricity use for both environmental and economic reasons, drawing on ideas of least-cost planning for modern utility management.[225] At the same time, they were framed by the emergent potential, in the late 1980s, for West Berlin to access electricity and gas from outside. Considering ways of modernizing East Germany's power generation plant became, in this context, a component of an environmentally friendly future for West Berlin's electricity supply.[226] A prominent example of this new thinking was a report produced by the Environmental Policy Research Centre (FFU) at the Free University of Berlin and the Öko-Institut of Freiburg in October 1989.[227] It recommended the transformation of Bewag from an energy provision into an energy service utility. This entailed encouraging customers to use as little electricity as necessary provided by the utility in the most energy-efficient way feasible. To achieve this would require drawing on imported cleaner electricity for the basic load, replacing ageing power plants with modern gas-fired plants and block-type CHP units, and promoting energy saving and efficiency by service users. The report was under no illusion that Bewag would need to be pressured into adopting such measures. It advised the West Berlin senate to reject investment plans that failed to maximize existing infrastructure, to introduce a progressive concession fee requiring Bewag to pay the city more the more electricity it sold, and to exercise its supervisory powers over energy pricing to promote energy saving.

The prospects of such unconventional strategies for urban water and energy services finding their way into government policy were initially very limited. Within the SPD there was some sympathy for a more environmentally oriented approach to energy policy from the early 1970s onward that permeated into public debate without shaking mainstream infrastructure policy. It was not until the emergence of West Berlin's particular brand of green party politics—the Alternative List (AL)—in 1978 and its election to the house of representatives in 1981 that this new way of thinking began to influence the political agenda. The AL was not only dedicated to environmental protection but also sympathetic to experimental modes of living. This made the party a born skeptic of the city's utilities, rejecting their intransigence as much as their environmental performance.

In the early 1980s progress was made in advancing energy efficiency—in provision and use—as an urban policy goal. Instrumental behind this was a series of energy advisory boards, incorporating independent experts alongside specialists from the senate and the utilities. A more high-profile Enquete Commission "Future Energy Policy" was created in 1982 to advise the house of representatives on diverse options for supplying the city with electricity, gas, and heating.[228] One of the recommendations emerging from this and other reports at the time was to improve coordination between Bewag and Gasag as a prerequisite for integrated energy planning. Regular meetings between the two utilities had already been established in 1980, but without much success beyond dividing up areas of the city for either district or gas heating.[229] Threats by the SPD to enforce an amalgamation of the two energy utilities unless they took energy efficiency more seriously did not have the desired effect.[230]

However, when the AL joined the SPD in a coalition government in early 1989 there were signs of a significant shift in energy policy.[231] The new red-green senate set about promoting many of the alternative measures advocated earlier, such as block-type cogeneration plants, renewable energies, and a new concession agreement with Bewag. The environmental spokespersons for both SPD and AL were—they claimed—prepared to "clip Bewag's wings" by introducing greater competition in heat and power provision if the utility did not prove amenable.[232] The company, with the backing of its workforce, tried to block such intrusions, claiming as in the past that these would destabilize West Berlin's energy provision and cost local jobs.[233] The senate, in its new complexion, was no longer cowed by such threats. It began implementing institutional reforms, such as the creation of an energy task force to develop new energy policies, and promoting pilot schemes, such as a contracting model for energy saving, to demonstrate viability.[234] Then, just a few weeks later, the Berlin Wall fell. With this definitive end to West Berlin's splendid isolation, everything was up in the air.

9 Contested Infrastructures in a Reunified Berlin

Anyone who expected the fall of the Berlin Wall to herald an era of stability and tranquility to the city's infrastructure systems was in for a nasty surprise. The restoration of unity and democracy across the city in 1990 had the allure of Berlin returning to the fold of normalcy for the first time since 1933. Instead, the city was about to experience the most volatile period of infrastructure management it had ever encountered. The disruption this time was caused not by regime change but by seismic shifts in the political economy of the city that echoed global trends in urban governance, utility management, and climate politics. Fundamental tenets of urban infrastructure that had served democratic, fascist, and socialist systems alike have, over the past thirty years, been abruptly undermined or rudely questioned. First, the assumption that demand for utility services would always grow was dashed when, within a few years of reunification, water consumption in the city dropped by over a third while electricity use stagnated. Ambitious infrastructure investment programs of the immediate post-unification period had to be jettisoned and flexible responses sought for an unfamiliar phenomenon: overcapacity in the networks. Second, the city's water, electricity, and gas utilities that had been reunified as municipal enterprises in the early 1990s were all privatized—wholly or in part—during the course of the same decade. The promise of short-term financial gain to help relieve an urban debt crisis overrode a century-old ethos of municipal ownership. Third, liberalization of the European energy market in the late 1990s put an end to some territorial monopolies enjoyed by utilities in the past. The Berlin-based utilities Gasag and, in particular, Bewag had to adapt rapidly to competitors offering energy services that were either cheaper or greener. Finally, even Berlin's citizens proved a disruptive force to conventional logics, no longer willing to play their ascribed role of compliant consumer. Opposition to the privatization deals and discontent with the city's climate, energy, and water policies combined to engender a powerful protest movement that prompted policy U-turns toward re-municipalization. Over the past thirty years the reunified city has undergone a series of contested reconfigurations to its infrastructure systems that shows no sign of letting up.

This chapter takes Berlin's infrastructure odyssey up to the present day. The narrative begins with the process of reuniting the city's infrastructure systems—physically and organizationally—and their enrollment in Berlin's post-unification aspiration to become a world city once more. Both factors were instrumental in unleashing a wave of investments in modernizing and extending the city's electricity, gas, heating, water, and wastewater networks during the early 1990s. The chapter then explores the various ways in which this renaissance of municipal expansionism came to be severely challenged. It explores the ambitions and limitations to addressing the whole region, rather than just the city, in reordering Berlin's infrastructures. It examines how efforts to commercialize and diversify the utilities in the mid-1990s distanced them from the reaches of the local state. It describes how, contrary to expectations, demand for water dropped dramatically and for electricity significantly, undermining the utilities' costing models. The chapter then explains why, in response to a severe fiscal crisis, the city government felt obliged to sell off major shareholdings in its electricity, gas, and water/wastewater utilities to private investors during the late 1990s. How privatization affected infrastructure services and their urban governance is addressed in a subsequent section, which is followed by an analysis of competition between the city's utilities through the lens of urban heating. The chapter concludes by describing the emergence of social movements campaigning to re-municipalize the city's infrastructures and assessing their impact on the form and substance of infrastructure governance today.

Reconnecting Networks, Reuniting Utilities

The fall of the Berlin Wall in November 1989 and reunification of Germany in October 1990 radically reordered the political context of the city's infrastructure systems once again. During this year the two halves of the city were de jure run by separate governments, a red-green coalition in the West and—after democratic elections on May 6, 1990—a coalition of Social Democrats and Christian Democrats in the East. In practice, both were working closely to ease formal reunification of the city-state government. The first citywide election to the city parliament since 1946 was held on December 6, 1990, and produced a coalition of Christian Democrats and Social Democrats.

The immediate task of reconnecting the city's technical networks was portrayed at the time in terms of healing the wounds of nearly fifty years of division.[1] This rhetorical flourish glossed over the fact that the infrastructure systems of West and East Berlin had, as described above, developed along quite distinct trajectories. The political scientist Richard Merritt, who conducted research on Berlin's divided infrastructures in the 1960s, had predicted then that territorial separation of the city's technical networks would seriously impede any future reunification process.[2] Did his prophecy prove correct, in retrospect?

Merritt was certainly right in warning that reunifying the city's infrastructure systems would entail more than just reversing the disconnections of the 1950s. In the case of electricity, it meant striking a path between West Berlin's structures of self-generation, embodied by a large number of power-generating units scattered across the city, and East Berlin's orientation toward the national grid, producing only one-third of its electricity demand (see figure 9.1).[3] It also meant dealing with differences in fuel source. While three-quarters of West Berlin's electricity was produced from coal, lignite accounted for over half of East Berlin's power supply. The gas sector was similarly

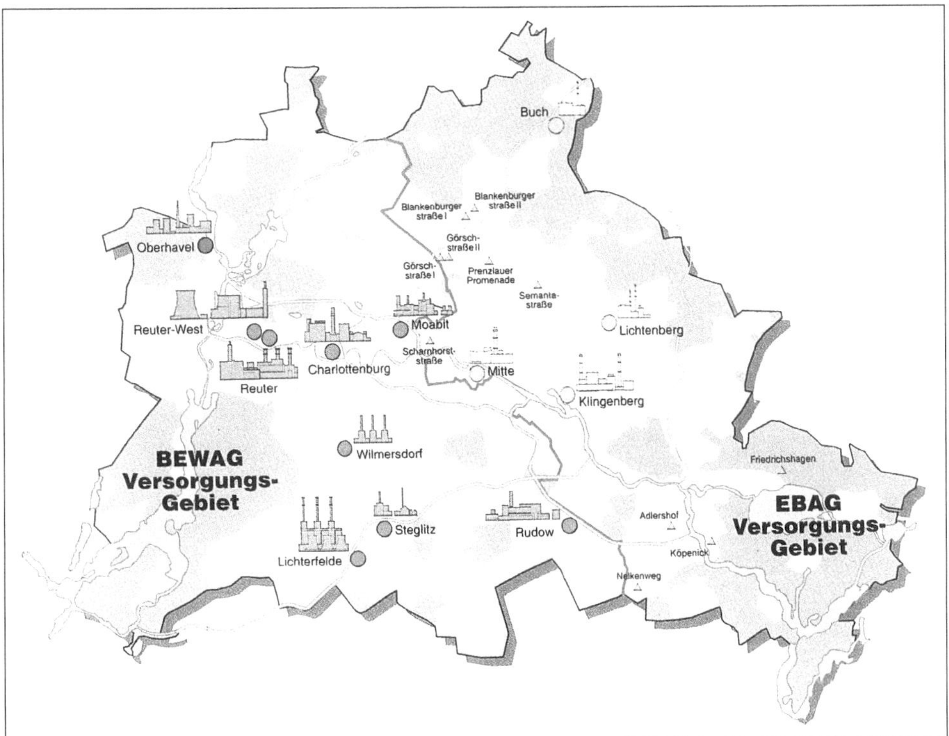

Figure 9.1
Map of power stations in Berlin, 1990
Source: Berliner Kraft- und Licht(Bewag)-Aktiengesellschaft, *Von der Inselversorgung zum Verbund*, 2. Copyright: Bewag/Vattenfall.

characterized by asymmetry between local production in the West and reliance on imports in the East. The West needed to be weaned off its traditional technology of town gas production at urban gas works, a process that was completed only in May 1996.[4] The district heating networks also differed in the two halves of the city. District heating in the West of the city used a three-pipe system and was produced almost wholly in cogeneration, generating electricity as well as heat.[5] In the East, by contrast, only around 30 percent of district heating was produced in cogeneration and a two-pipe system was used that was not interoperable with the Western model.[6] This legacy of division ensured that the two district heating networks have remained largely disconnected to this day.[7] Problems of physical interconnection were less demanding for water supply and wastewater treatment. Although new treatment plant and pumping stations had been built on both sides of the divide to optimize local supply, the systems had remained essentially the same. The wastewater systems, indeed, had remained connected throughout the era of division.

Overall, network connections following reunification did not pose major problems, they just demanded investments in new infrastructure and the decommissioning of unnecessary plant.[8] The border valves on water pipes were reopened immediately and the barriers in the sewers removed. A new 380 kV transmission line was built in December 1994 connecting West Berlin via Spandau to the international electricity grid, as agreed prior to reunification.[9] A cable connecting the two halves of the city became operative in 1996, enabling electricity supply to be balanced across the whole city (see figure 9.2). The concern at the time was not that the legacy of division would jeopardize the reunification process, as Merritt had feared, but that the new infrastructure required for reconnection might exacerbate the problem of excess infrastructure capacity resulting from duplication on each side of the city.[10] It was anticipated, though, that any infrastructural slack would be quickly taken up as the reunited city grew.

More difficult to navigate was the organizational reunification of the city's utilities. Initial meetings between the directors of the gas, power, and water utilities of West and East were held within a few weeks of the Wall being breached. Joint working groups were set up between the gas and the water utilities of both sides in January 1990 to coordinate the reunification process.[11] Reunification meant, in effect, the incorporation of the utility from the East into its partner from the West. In all instances it was very much amalgamation in the Western mold. This did not make it particularly straightforward. The utilities serving East Berlin needed to be restored to ownership by the city of Berlin. The water utility WAB Berlin became a municipal enterprise (*Eigenbetrieb*) of Berlin in August 1990.[12] It was formally amalgamated into Berliner Wasserbetriebe (BWB) of West Berlin on January 1, 1992.[13] The energy utility serving the East of

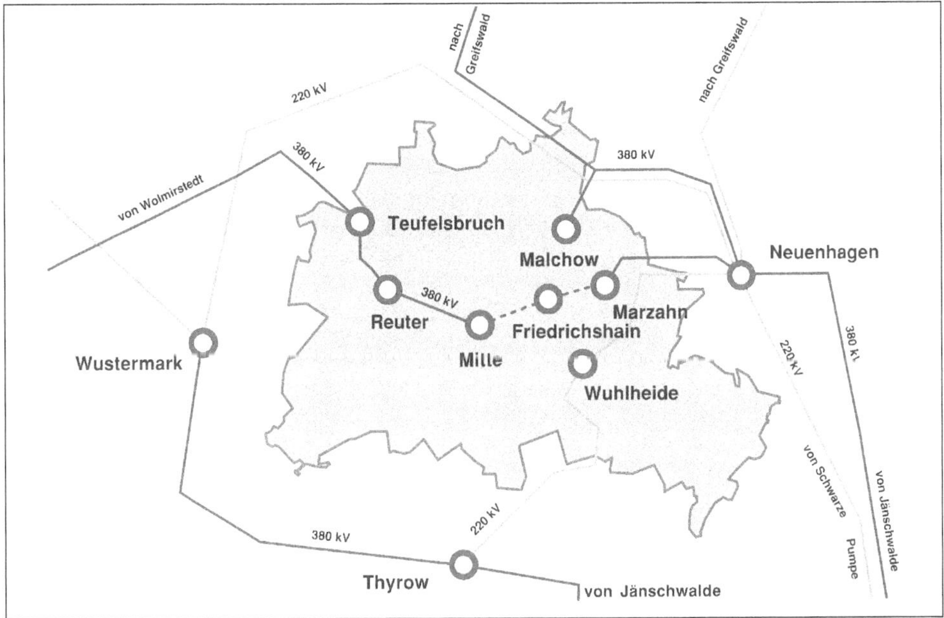

Figure 9.2
Map of power grid connections in and beyond Berlin
Source: Senatsverwaltung für Stadtentwicklung, Umweltschutz und Technologie, *Stadtentwicklungsplan Ver- und Entsorgung*, 18.

the city, Energiekombinat Berlin, was unbundled into a gas company (Berliner Erdgas) and an electricity and heating company (Energieversorgung Berlin) so as to ease integration into Gasag and Bewag respectively.[14] The amalgamation of Energieversorgung Berlin into Bewag was formally completed in July 1994.[15] The case of gas proved trickier because Gasag was a municipal enterprise and Berliner Erdgas a share company. This legal hurdle was overcome by turning Gasag into a share company in June 1992.[16] This opened the way to amalgamating the two gas utilities. It also, however, created an opening for the later privatization of the municipal gas utility.

The way reunification was enacted within each of the utilities revealed the prevalent asymmetry of power relations between West and East. Even before formal amalgamation, the utilities in East Berlin were placed under the supervision of their West Berlin counterparts. The director of WAB Berlin, Stefan Scheusing, was relieved of his duties at the constitutive meeting of his utility and, by October 1990, the heads of department of West Berlin's BWB had taken over all the respective positions in the East Berlin utility. Similarly, Gasag placed its three directors in charge of the corresponding units of Berliner Erdgas in November 1991. When it came to appointing leadership positions in the amalgamated utilities it was generally the Western colleagues who got the posts. Since combining two utilities inevitably meant cutting down on staff to avoid duplication, this left many Eastern colleagues feeling hard done by. They found it frustrating when preference for Westerners was justified by virtue of their experience of a market economy, rather than professional expertise. This was particularly galling at Gasag, where colleagues from the East had far better knowledge about natural gas than their Western colleagues did.[17] On the other hand, many employees from the East had little experience in infrastructure planning, which had been conducted by central planning agencies of the DDR rather than within the utility, and lacked knowledge of the legal regulations governing infrastructure services in a reunified Germany.[18] Cultural differences continued to exist within each utility, with colleagues from the East—having experienced the disruption of reunification first-hand—often proving more flexible than their Western counterparts, who often saw little need to change their ways.[19] As one contemporary at Gasag put it: "with reunification two worlds collided with one another."[20]

For consumers in the Eastern part of the city reunification of the utilities was felt primarily in their pockets. Prices for energy and water services had been notoriously low in the DDR, far below the cost of service provision. Prior to reunification East Berliners had been charged just 0.25 Mark per cubic meter for water and 0.13 Mark per cubic meter for wastewater services.[21] These tariffs were gradually increased until parity was achieved with West Berlin for water—at 2.10 Deutschmark—in October 1992 and for wastewater—at 4.85 Deutschmark—in 1996.[22] Fees charged for electricity and gas were similarly increased in line with West Berlin rates, although this price alignment was primarily at the expense of households rather than industry.[23] Even assuming equal value between the two currencies, this represented massive price hikes that had a significant impact on household incomes and, subsequently, consumption practices.

The Renaissance of Expansionism

Unity within the utilities was aided considerably by the common purpose of modernizing and extending Berlin's technical networks. Reunification of the city, its restored function as national capital, and talk of Berlin becoming once more a world city all seemed to point in one direction: urban growth. The euphoric growth scenarios circulating during the early 1990s were music to the ears of utility managers. This was what they were good at: building up infrastructure capacity to meet anticipated rising demand for their services. Here was the chance to expand the networks without the earlier constraints of a bounded territory (West Berlin) or inadequate funding (East

Berlin). The renaissance of an expansionist infrastructure logic of "build and supply" brought infrastructure managers together in both halves of the city.[24] Urban unification, just as after the creation of Greater Berlin in 1920, inspired powerful sociotechnical imaginaries of growth and progress.

There was plenty to do. First, the networks in the Eastern part of the city were in urgent need of repair and modernization. Poor building materials, underinvestment, and rudimentary maintenance had left East Berlin's infrastructures in a dire state.[25] Inspection of the gas mains there revealed over 63,000 leaks that needed repairing between 1991 and 1995.[26] The district heating network in the East was the biggest headache of the city's energy system, owing to its highly inefficient production plant and distribution network.[27] Several lignite-fired district heating plants had to be closed down, replaced, in part, by new ones.[28] Shortly after becoming director of the unified water/wastewater utility BWB, Heinz Tessendorff listed a litany of problems affecting the Eastern part of the city, ranging from leaking sewers and inoperable water pumps to polluted groundwater aquifers and malfunctioning water meters.[29] All six sewage treatment plants serving the city needed a complete rebuild to meet EU regulations on permitted emissions.[30]

Second, the technical networks needed extending to settlement areas not already served or earmarked for development. In 1990 there were still around 63,000 inhabitants of East Berlin and even 42,000 inhabitants in the Western half of the city who were not connected to the public sewers.[31] Most of these largely peripheral communities were designated for connection to the sewer network as a top priority for reasons of public hygiene and groundwater protection in accordance with the EU Wastewater Directive. New urban developments, such as at Potsdamer Platz and the designated government quarter, called for completely new infrastructures for electricity, gas, heating, water, and wastewater that were expected to meet the highest technical standards of the day.[32] Beyond the city center, housing and commercial developments in Adlershof, Rummelsburger Bucht, Karow, and Spandau also placed new demands on utility services.

Third, and above all, expectations of rapid population growth and economic development called for expansion of the city's infrastructures. In the early 1990s there was a pervasive sense of euphoria that Berlin, now liberated from its shackles, would return to the fold as one of the world's great cities. Nostalgia for past greatness combined with confidence in globalization to persuade the political and business elite in Berlin that the city was on the brink of becoming a bridgehead between West and East, well positioned to benefit from the emerging markets of the former socialist bloc countries.[33] This boosterism translated into ambitious population projections. It was estimated by regional planners at the time—and widely accepted in decision-making circles—that the population of Berlin would grow from 3.4 to 4.0 million by 2010, while the population of the surrounding region would double, from 0.9 to 1.8 million inhabitants.[34] The implications for infrastructure were clear for the Senator for Urban Development and the president of the Berlin Chamber of Commerce: "Berlin is currently experiencing a renewal of its infrastructure the like of which has not been experienced in the history of the city, or probably in any other European metropolis."[35]

Berlin's utilities responded with alacrity to this gargantuan task. In 1992 BWB launched an infrastructure investment program that would total 12.8 billion Deutschmark by the year 2000, with the lion's share allocated to modernizing and expanding the wastewater system.[36] This sum represented five times more than what the company had invested in West Berlin over the previous ten years.[37] Once the extent of repairs become fully known, this figure was increased in early 1993 to an eye-watering 20 billion Deutschmark for the period 1993–2003, only to be reduced to 12.8 billion Deutschmark when it became clear that it was simply not affordable.[38] BWB did, indeed, invest over a billion Deutschmark a year in the early post-unification years, totalling 6.4 billion Deutschmark between 1990 and 1996.[39] The electricity utility Bewag invested nearly 4.5 billion Deutschmark over the same period, mainly in the local grid, power stations, and district heating network.[40] The urban-planning department estimated that Berlin's utilities invested a staggering total of 25 billion Deutschmark in the city's technical infrastructure between 1990 and 1997.[41]

These investments increased infrastructure capacity substantially. Electricity generating capacity grew from 2,603 MW in 1991 to 3,143 MW in 2000, despite the new grid connections enabling the whole city to draw on power generated elsewhere.[42] The expansion of the gas network in line with the conversion to natural gas enabled sales of gas in Berlin to rise by over 50 percent between 1991 and 1996, from 10,529 GWh to 15,915 GWh.[43] Two new sewage treatment plants were built for the city during the 1990s: at Waßmannsdorf with a capacity of 230,000 cubic meters a day and at Wansdorf with a capacity of 40,000 cubic meters a day.[44]

Increasing capacity of water supply was a far harder task, owing to the limitations imposed by relying on local ground and surface water sources. Underpinning the investment programs here was the assumption that total water demand would level off in the Eastern part of the city at a daily average of 250 liters per person a day, in line with West Berlin's consumption curves.[45] Taken together with the population projections, this entailed a growth in water demand by the city from 340 million cubic meters a year to 430 million by 2010. For the metropolitan region it was calculated that water supply capacity would need to be expanded from 456 million cubic meters a year to 578 million. Such projections instilled fear of water shortages among utility managers and environmental regulators alike. A conference entitled "Is Berlin Drying Up?" in

October 1990 discussed various ways of averting a crisis of water supply for the growing metropolis.[46] The subsequent plans devised to address the problem, culminating in the Water Supply and Wastewater Disposal Concept of 1993, all took the projected demand curves at face value and set out measures to build up supply capacity as well as replenish groundwater sources.[47] Even an alternative concept produced by the environmental group BUND Berlin did not challenge the water consumption calculations, but called for more extensive measures to recycle water in the region.[48] In recognition of the city's reliance on its infrastructure, the 1993 concept warned that shortage of water could even jeopardize Berlin's future: "Providing the population with water is getting increasingly uncertain, resulting in water supply becoming an early limiting factor on population and urban development."[49] Echoes from the early 1920s, following the unification of Greater Berlin, are unmistakable.

The financial burden of these huge infrastructure investments could no longer be softened by hefty subsidies from Bonn, as in the days of the Cold War. The federal government had been quick to put an end to any special treatment for a capital city that was expected to be booming within a few years. The costs for infrastructure investments fell, therefore, squarely on the city's consumers. In addition to the major tariff adjustments already being experienced by consumers in the Eastern part of the city, all consumers experienced sharp hikes in the costs of utility services as a consequence of extensive infrastructure investments. For example, in the Western part of Berlin the water tariff almost trebled between 1990 and 1996, from 1.30 to 3.45 Deutschmark per cubic meter, and the wastewater tariff more than doubled over the same period, from 2.30 to 4.85 Deutschmark per cubic meter.[50] This represented an overall price increase for BWB's services of 230 percent in just six years, even before privatization. Again, such price rises—making Berlin's water more expensive than in most other German cities—were bound to affect consumption practices in the future.[51]

Infrastructuring the Sustainable City

The expansionist strategy shaping Berlin's infrastructures in the immediate post-unification era differed from its earlier manifestations across the twentieth century in one crucial regard. It encompassed a new environmentalist agenda that sat alongside and, to some extent, complemented the dominant "build and supply" logic. Provocatively, perhaps, one can speak of the period as one of environmental expansionism. This dualism was to some extent a result of the utilities themselves recognizing the ecological consequences of unrestrained resource exploitation and use as well as the public's disapproval of excessive environmental degradation. Far more significant, though, was the policy of successive city governments to encourage the city's utilities to improve local water and air quality, minimise resource use, use energy efficiently, and protect the global climate. Within the context of broader environmental policy objectives, the Berlin senate enrolled the utilities in "infrastructuring" the sustainable city.

Although the red-green coalition of 1989 in West Berlin turned out to be a brief interregnum, it nevertheless set a yardstick for urban environmental policy that is still admired today. During its year and a half in office, the coalition introduced a series of innovative policies to protect the environment and the climate, first for West Berlin and then, after the fall of the Wall, effectively for the whole city. The ambition was to set up Berlin as a model sustainable city, demonstrating how it was possible to steer urban development along a path that did not equate growth with ever-increasing resource use and environmental pollution. This policy gained wide support not only within the green movement, but also in the SPD and even within the ranks of the conservative CDU. The governing coalition of CDU and SPD formed in early 1991 pursued several of the environmental policies initiated by the red-green coalition, albeit with less determination and perseverance.[52]

In the field of energy, the red-green government had set up the Energy Task Force in the autumn of 1989 as a unit designed to spearhead a new, alternative energy policy. Embedded in the Senate Department for Urban Development and Environmental Protection, its task was to develop an energy concept for the city, promote pilot projects for energy efficiency, and win over other senate departments.[53] In practice, it exceeded initial expectations by generating a number of institutional innovations within the space of just a few years. These included an energy agency helping local businesses to save energy, a council of energy experts advising the city government, and a contracting partnership for energy saving in public buildings that received nationwide acclaim.[54] Most significantly, the red-green coalition managed to push through a pioneering law called the State Energy Saving Act just before the 1990 elections.[55] This required the city-state of Berlin to orientate all its plans and policy measures according to the principle of a resource-efficient, low-cost, and environmentally sustainable energy supply, as well as to adopt a state energy program every four years.[56] With respect to the city's power and gas utilities, the law specified that future concession agreements must address energy saving and environmental pollution abatement.[57] It was followed up with the Energy Concept of Berlin of 1994, developed out of an unusually interactive process of negotiation involving the interested public as well as key stakeholders.[58] It set out steps designed to achieve a 25 percent reduction in CO_2 emissions by 2010, compared to 1990 levels. These included renegotiating the concession agreements with Bewag and Gasag, providing energy advice to households and businesses, building decentral cogeneration plants, initiating energy teams in each of the Eastern boroughs, and promoting solar power.[59] Some 430 million Deutschmark were allocated to implementation for the financial years 1995 and 1996.[60]

How effective did these policy initiatives prove in changing the performance of the city's energy utilities? In terms of air quality improvements, the positive effects were dramatic. As a consequence of Bewag implementing the costliest investment program in its history, used to install catalytic converters in thirteen of its power-generating blocks, flue gas emissions dropped sharply. By contrast, CO_2 emissions could not be addressed with end-of-pipe technology but only by using less fuel and burning it more efficiently.[61] Partly for this reason CO_2 emissions did not fall quite so dramatically. Nevertheless, a drop from almost 14 million metric tons in 1991 to around 11.5 million metric tons in 2001 represented a 25 percent reduction, nine years ahead of the original target.[62] Disputes between both energy utilities and the city government raged over the content of new concession agreements.[63] Bewag also resisted the development of block-type cogeneration plants competing with its own district heating network. This did not stop the number of these decentral cogeneration units from growing substantially to sixty-seven by 1997.[64] Similarly, the number of photovoltaic units in Berlin grew, thanks to public subsidies, to 260 by 1995. In hindsight, the head of the Energy Task Force credits the city authorities with getting Bewag interested in the least-cost planning approach, managing energy demand to suit available capacity as a resource- and money-saving alternative to infrastructure investments.[65] He concedes, though, that they had no effective leverage to block or even question Bewag's investment decisions.[66]

Over new water-management priorities there was a more substantial meeting of minds between the city government and the responsible utility. When the Senator for Urban Development and Environmental Protection, Michaela Schreyer, announced the need to question old tenets of water supply and explore new ways of meeting water-related needs at the October 1990 conference mentioned above, the BWB director, Heinz Tessendorff, agreed with almost all her proposals, ranging from recharging groundwater aquifers to securing water protection zones in the future.[67] The city set out a five-point program in its Water Supply and Wastewater Disposal Concept of 1993: (1) to protect local and regional groundwater resources, (2) to prioritize water protection over other land uses, (3) to extend the existing water supply network, (4) to retain and reuse more rainwater on site, and (5) to reduce water consumption to at least 10 percent below the national average.[68] Over the following years this program of measures was pursued with vigor by the city authorities and selectively by the water utility BWB.

Some measures—like the upgrading of sewage treatment plants to improve surface water quality—were largely consensual. Closing down outdated treatment plants and replacing them with modern ones proved a productive field of joint activity at the interface of wastewater infrastructures and water protection.[69] It was substantiated by a detailed wastewater disposal plan in 2001, which set out a series of measures to fight the eutrophication of Berlin's waterways and protect its drinking water sources.[70] The effect on Berlin's watercourses was impressive: between 1990 and 2006 emissions of ammonium fell by 98 percent, of nitrogen by 79 percent, and of phosphor by 80 percent, while chemical oxygen demand (COD) fell by 56 percent and biochemical oxygen demand (BOD) by 75 percent.[71] There was also agreement between city and utility over the need to secure the region's water sources by replenishing groundwater sources artificially, with new sites in Karolinenhöhe and the Spandau Forest.[72]

More controversial were ideas to recycle water. Talk of a possible water supply crisis in the metropolitan region generated renewed enthusiasm for water recycling projects of various kinds that had been experimented with in West Berlin since the 1980s.[73] At the household scale, these were targeted, for instance, at flushing toilets or watering gardens with rainwater or water from showers and installing separate non-potable water pipes.[74] At the regional scale, they included the reuse of treated wastewater for landscape enhancement and groundwater recharge on former sewage farms.[75] At the urban scale, rainwater and treated wastewater were enrolled in plans to improve local rivers and water-based biotopes.[76] Tessendorff and others at BWB were highly skeptical of these schemes, many of which would require reconfiguring the existing wastewater network. In his opinion, "we should not gamble with the hygienic safety we have achieved on such experimental cravings."[77]

By contrast, the environmental department of the senate was keen to explore these options, taking an early interest in rainwater use and wastewater recycling.[78] Public money was allocated to hydrologists, ecologists, and engineers outside BWB to enable them to test water recycling technologies. This was promoted primarily by a special unit for ecological urban development set up within the Senate Department for Building and Housing, which generated a number of high-profile projects of water conservation and reuse with extensive funding schemes.[79] One recycling technology that did gain increasing support within the water utility was onsite rainwater retention. This was because it helped relieve pressure on rain- and wastewater sewers during stormwater events, when over 160 rainwater overflows emptied untreated effluent into the city's watercourses.[80] A new strategy to retain rainwater locally wherever feasible was implemented in all Berlin's urban development sites of the 1990s, with soakaways and trough-trench systems installed in new settlements at Rummelsburger Bucht, Karow, and Adlershof, as well as Potsdamer Platz (see figure 9.3).[81] An additional attraction of this technology for BWB was, certainly, that it effectively shared responsibility for

Figure 9.3
Stormwater soakaways at Adlershof, 2016
Photo: Timothy Moss.

stormwater collection and disposal with property owners, saving the utility considerable investments in underground rainwater storage.[82]

Promoting decentral solutions for urban technologies was a core feature of another policy initiative of the Berlin administration in the 1990s: the Urban Development Plan on Utility Services (StEP V+E).[83] This was an unusual plan, dedicated solely to urban technology, that was devised to address the very particular challenges of coordinating urban and infrastructure development in a reunified Berlin. It was intended to build a bridge between sectoral plans for energy and water on the one hand and urban zoning and building plans on the other. Comprising a lengthy documentation of existing systems for electricity, gas, district heating, water, rainwater, and wastewater alongside richly detailed maps for each infrastructure sector, the StEP V+E represented a further attempt in Berlin's modern history to integrate infrastructure into urban planning. Echoes of the East Berlin General Plan for Infrastructure of 1970 were not coincidental, as one of the urban planners drawing up the StEP V+E had, twenty-five years previously, worked on the East Berlin plan.[84] However, the ambition of the new plan was much more modest. Rather than prescribe the future development of technical networks, the StEP V+E was limited to providing basic information for urban planners and investors and suggesting optimal solutions with respect to infrastructure capacity and environmental performance.[85]

An impressive document of the urban-infrastructure interface, the StEP V+E nevertheless failed to make much impact on either policy or practice. First of all, it took until 1998 before the plan was finalized and published, by which time many investment decisions had already been taken and much of its data on consumption was out of date.[86] Second, the plan suffered—like many other policy initiatives—from lack of cooperation, or even downright opposition, between different senate departments.[87] Third, the envisaged follow-up to the plan, targeting sustainable innovations to urban infrastructure, never materialized. When the remaining member of the infrastructure planning unit retired in 2008, his post was not replaced. "Technical infrastructure was no longer 'in,'" he reflects today, "when I left, that was it."[88]

Restrained Regionalism

The fall of the Berlin Wall heralded not only the reunification of the two halves of Berlin, but also the restoration of relations between the city as a whole and its surrounding region. High hopes were placed in infrastructure systems as instruments of regional reconnection—physically and organisationally. Already by mid-November 1989 a provisional regional committee had been established as a platform for exchange between representatives from Berlin and the surrounding districts of Potsdam and Frankfurt an der Oder. Water became an emblematic issue of regional collaboration over the following months.[89] The water and wastewater utilities of the Berlin metropolitan area set up, under the auspices of the regional committee, the Working Group on Water as one of the very first collaborative ventures in the region. By 1991, this working group had developed one concept for future water supply in the region and another for wastewater disposal.[90] Both concepts were oriented around a common approach to protecting the region's water resources and exchanging expertise between BWB and the much smaller municipal utilities being reestablished around Berlin. The working group is still operative today, organizing regular events for knowledge transfer between its members.[91] Such a cross-territorial platform for water utilities is unique in Germany and highly valued by those involved. Cooperation between the two states of Berlin and Brandenburg over water protection was also exemplary in the early years, resulting in the Water Management Framework Plan of 1994—the first one of its kind in Germany to cover more than one federal state.

Regional cooperation on technical infrastructure quickly stalled, however. As each state government sought to pursue its own strategic objectives, differences of interest grew increasingly apparent. The asymmetries between a self-confident capital city and a large number of emergent municipalities in Brandenburg generated tension and distrust between the two sides. Already in 1993 political cooperation between the two state governments was poor, hindered by rigid political positions and unconstructive discussions.[92] For this reason, many plans—such as the StEP V+E described above—stopped at the boundaries of the city.[93] When the proposal to amalgamate the two states of Berlin and Brandenburg was rejected in a referendum on May 5, 1996, regional relations took a further knock.

Berlin and Brandenburg have been in conflict over each other's energy strategy since the early 1990s.[94] The issue of contestation has always been electricity generated from lignite in Brandenburg. While Berlin has largely resisted importing this electricity to avoid its negative impact on the city's CO_2 emissions, Brandenburg has consistently accused Berlin of failing to appreciate the economic and social benefits for the region of keeping the lignite mines and their associated power plants going.[95] As a result, there has never been any joint energy planning between the two states, notwithstanding the potential for using biomass from Brandenburg for energy in Berlin or supporting renewable energies in Brandenburg directly.[96]

Despite the stronger interdependencies over water and wastewater flows between Berlin and Brandenburg, differences of opinion have thwarted effective collaboration between the two state governments. One issue of contestation is the high quality of treated wastewater from Berlin's sewage treatment plants demanded by Brandenburg. Another is Brandenburg's sensitivity to Berlin owning land in Brandenburg previously used as sewage farms. A third recurrent conflict is over how best to secure sufficient water flow in the River Spree during hot summers.[97] Brandenburg's ideas to retain more water upstream of Berlin regularly unsettle the city's water managers. Berlin, however, is reluctant to spend huge sums on water retention basins on Brandenburg territory.

The principal mode of cooperation over water infrastructure has been of a commercial nature between the utilities of the metropolitan region. Emanating out of the Working Group on Water, BWB shares ownership of two utilities in the region with local municipalities.[98] One is a jointly owned sewage treatment plant at Wansdorf, the other is a regional company supplying water from BWB's water works at Stolpe to communities North of Berlin. BWB has also concluded contracts to supply water to twenty municipalities and treat sewage for 113 municipalities outside the city limits (see figure 9.4).[99]

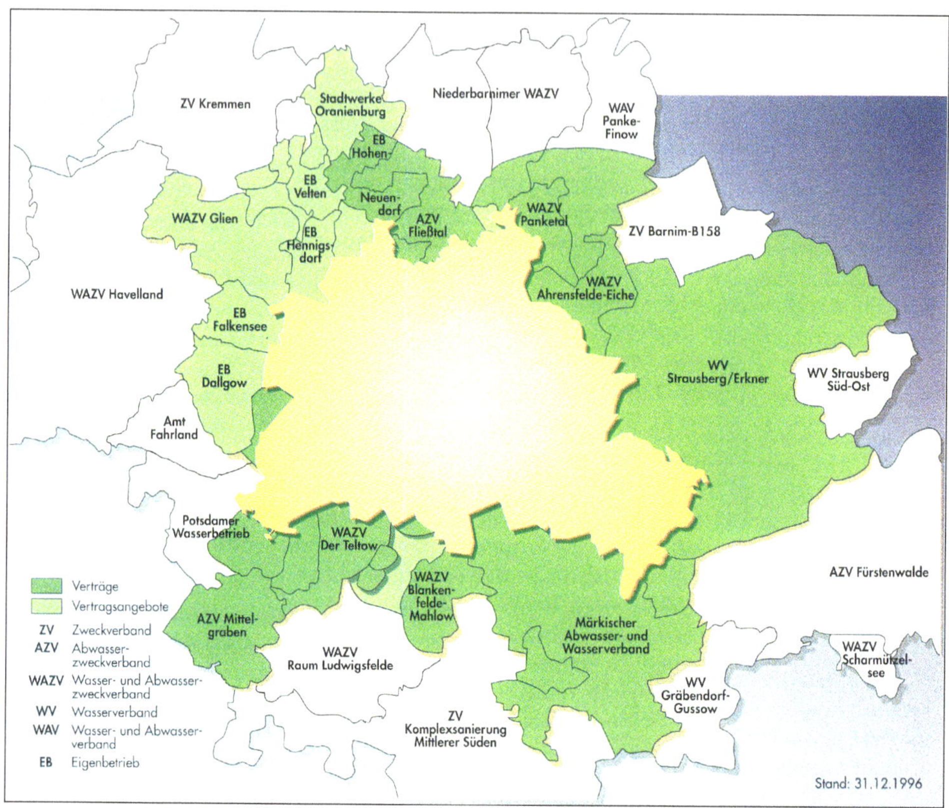

Figure 9.4

Map of contracts for sewage disposal concluded by BWB with neighboring municipalities
Source: Berliner Wasserbetriebe, *Geschäftsbericht 1996*, 19.

Today, BWB provides drinking water to around 80,000 people and treats wastewater for around 593,000 people in Brandenburg.[100] Initially, BWB was keen to gain these additional customers to offset capacity surpluses at its water works and sewage treatment plants. As slack in plant capacity has recently been taken up, however, interest in extending its services in the region has dropped.[101] Regional collaboration no longer has the value or appeal it possessed in the heady days of 1990.

Commercialization and Diversification

Reunification of the city and reconnection to the region were not the only major changes to Berlin's political geography after 1989. The city found itself having to respond to seismic shifts in the global economy and their reception in Germany. As Ross Beveridge and Matthias Naumann have put it: "Policy-making in Berlin in the 1990s is as much a story of urban governance in the context of globalization as it is an account of German reunification."[102] The fall of the Wall marked not an end to the influence of global politics on Berlin's development, merely a reorientation: from the geopolitical game-playing of the Cold War to the lure and threat of globalization. As Germany's capital city, Berlin was expected to play its part in this new global game. Given its geographical position and historical experience, Berlin was believed to be well placed to reap the benefits of market liberalization in Central and Eastern Europe especially. To do this, it was widely held, the city would need to conform to the neoliberal norms of the global economy.[103] This posed a major challenge to a city where, for forty years, one half had been subordinated to state socialism and the other half had been cocooned from the outside world.

Berlin's utilities were acutely aware of their vulnerable position as their protected worlds were gradually undermined by the withdrawal of state subsidies, emergent competition, and threats to their territorial monopolies. At the same time, they saw in the removal of political and market barriers a huge opportunity to transform into commercial enterprises operating beyond the confines of the city and their traditional fields of activity. In danger of becoming victims of neoliberalism, Berlin's water, electricity, and gas utilities were reinvented as its vanguards, in Germany at least. With the full backing of the city authorities, these municipal utilities commercialized their internal management, diversified their business interests, and expanded into new global markets. Their global infrastructure agendas fitted perfectly to Berlin's post-unification aspirations as a world trendsetter in environmental technologies.

It would be incorrect to speak of neoliberal models of liberalization and privatization being simply rolled out across Berlin's infrastructures. Rather, these new global norms of infrastructure governance of the 1990s framed the debate and set the benchmarks for reconfigurations to the city's utilities that were very place- and sector-specific.[104] The electricity utility Bewag was particularly concerned about its unfavorable market position in the event of liberalization, owing to the high costs of modernizing the network in East Berlin, excess generation capacity in the West, and the need to protect district heating from competition.[105] Well before Germany's electricity market was liberalized in 1999, following EU reforms to the internal market, Bewag was optimizing processes and cutting costs to improve its commercial viability.[106] Staff levels were reduced from 12,307 employees in 1991–1992 to 9,482 in 1997.[107] In order to strengthen its hold over the local energy market, Bewag had by 1995 acquired substantial shareholdings in the district heating companies FHW Neukölln (75.22 percent) and EAB Fernwärme (100 percent), the gas utility Gasag (11.95 percent), and the newly created Berlin Energy Agency (33.33 percent).[108] It also ventured into international markets, cooperating with the Moscow energy provider Mosenergo and the real estate sector in Berlin.[109]

While Bewag remained a highly profitable enterprise, Gasag was a huge loss maker in the early 1990s, owing primarily to the exorbitant cost in the past of having to produce town gas in West Berlin. Here, the political response was to sell a minority shareholding in the municipal enterprise so as to acquire the external capital and expertise deemed essential to make it profitable. In 1994, 48.8 percent of Gasag's shares were sold to the national energy giants Ruhrgas, RWE Energie, and VEBA Energiebeteiligungs-GmbH as well as to the city's own Bewag.[110] In the wake of this partial privatization Gasag developed, together with the Boston Consulting Group, its Concept 2000 that set out a strategy geared toward making efficiency gains, attracting customers, and reducing costs.[111] Staff levels were reduced substantially, from 4,102 employees in 1991–1992 to 2,820 in 1996 and, subsequently, to just 1,015 in 2002.[112] The scale of these job cuts reflected not the new commercial rationale alone, but primarily the end to gas production in the city as Berlin converted to natural gas, as well as the duplication of jobs in East and West.[113]

The water/wastewater utility BWB, like Bewag, was a profitable enterprise earmarked for market expansion and diversification well before any talk of privatization.[114] A key step in the commercialization of BWB was its transformation from a municipal enterprise (*Eigenbetrieb*) into a public-law corporation (*Anstalt des öffentlichen Rechts*) in January 1994.[115] While not altering ownership of the utility, BWB's new legal status made it more independent of the city administration. It could in future restructure its internal organization, set levels of investments, raise its own loans, conclude contracts, create subsidies, and set tariffs without consulting the city parliament. Above all, it could now operate beyond the bounds of Berlin. The city government exercised influence over the utility primarily through its representation on the supervisory board. A political appointee—Bertram Wieczorek (CDU)—was made the new chairman of the board of directors at the same time. By 1998 the old guard of civil engineers who had led BWB for decades had been replaced.[116]

The new strategy of BWB, in the words of one of those replaced, was to "create a market-oriented structure for business processes while maximizing the potential for optimization."[117] The talk at the time was to restructure the utility in order to assure its survival in a future characterized by growing competition but also exciting new market opportunities.[118] Payments from BWB to the Berlin budget were portrayed now not as an important contribution to life in the city but as a constraint on the utility's ability to compete effectively in an increasingly global water market. BWB began to invest in infrastructure manufacturers, consultancies, and providers in the Berlin region.[119] In 1995 it branched out into the waste sector by acquiring a company—Sekundärrohstoff-Verwertungszentrum Schwarze Pumpe (SVZ)—with which to produce methanol and other energy products from recycled sludge, plastics, and household waste. BWB invested 320 million Deutschmark in this venture alone between 1995 and 1998.[120] In 1997 BWB launched its own telecommunications company, BerliKomm. Later that year it took over operation of the wastewater disposal system in Budapest, having acquired a 25 percent share in the company together with the French giant Compagnie Général des Eaux.[121] Further service contracts were concluded with Moscow, Baku, and cities in Hungary, Poland, China, Lithuania, and Namibia. By the late 1990s BWB had shareholdings in over fifty companies at home and abroad. The multi-utility to which BWB aspired was distinctly global rather than urban.

A press statement by the utility in August 1997 praised these early intrusions into new markets but compared BWB's diversification strategy unfavorably with those of its perceived competitors in France and the United Kingdom.[122] The high proportion of water-based activities by BWB—at 90 percent—was portrayed as a weakness in a market where sales of water services were predicted to decline. In truth, BWB's ventures outside its traditional realm of competence were to prove highly problematic for the company's viability. SVZ turned out to be a commercial disaster, owing to managerial incompetence and uncompetitive products, that resulted in BWB losing a staggering 1 billion Deutschmark on its investment.[123] Similarly, BerliKomm proved unable to survive competition in the telecommunications market. Few of the international collaborative ventures proved a commercial success. Typical of Berlin's early steps in a globalized economy, not enough strategic thought or sound investment went into substantiating the rhetoric of a commercialized utility.[124] Ironically, it was not the success of commercialization that created a pretext for subsequent privatization of BWB, but its failures that—despite undeniable gains in management efficiency—helped turn a profitable utility into one burdened with heavy debts and insecure investments.

Consumption Curves Defied

The profitability of Berlin's electricity and water utilities was further undermined by overcapacities in their networks.[125] This problem was initially a legacy of the divided city, in which each side had built up its own, largely self-dependent system with—in West Berlin's case—substantial security reserves. Reunification left many power stations and water treatment facilities surplus to requirements. An iconic example of redundant infrastructure was the natural gas storage facility in Spandau that had only just been built as a means of securing West Berlin's gas supply from interruption by the Soviet or DDR authorities.[126] When this plant went into operation in September 1992, its original purpose was obsolete. It continued to be used, instead, to respond to fluctuations in the price of natural gas. As the volatility of gas prices declined and, with it, the market for gas storage facilities, the facility in Spandau was finally taken out of service in 2016, with its future uncertain. Overcapacities like this would, under conditions of territorial monopolies, be an expensive luxury. In the climate of commercialization driving infrastructure strategies in the post-1990 era, they proved a financial liability. If Berlin and its economy had grown as predicted in 1989, this slack may well have been taken up by rising demand for energy and water services. When this boom did not happen and the city even slipped into decline, the consequences for the water utility in particular were severe.

Berlin's population failed to grow in tune with the heady predictions made when the Wall fell. It rose slightly to a peak of 3,475,392 in 1993, only to fall gradually to 3,382,169 in 2000.[127] Rather than being on track to breach the four-million barrier by 2010, Berlin actually had 51,000 fewer inhabitants in 2000 than in 1990. Even more significant for levels of energy and water consumption was deindustrialization. As a further indicator of Berlin's problems in adapting to a market economy, the city lost over 150,000 jobs in the industrial sector between 1991 and 2000.[128] Unemployment rose sharply, from 10 percent in 1991 to nearly 19 percent in 2003, while the proportion of Berliners living off social welfare benefits doubled.[129] Aspirations that the decline in traditional industries would be offset by growth in the service sector were not fulfilled. The few jobs created in the knowledge-intensive economy could not conceal the harsh reality that Berlin lagged far behind other German cities in its economic performance.

Berlin's economic downturn was mirrored in its energy use. Electricity consumption had been predicted to rise sharply following reunification, as we have seen. In fact, the amount of electricity sold in the city declined gradually between 1990 and 2011 (see figure 9.5). It has since grown slightly, in line with population growth, to around 12.4 billion kWh in 2017 (see table 9.1).

Far more serious, however, was the dramatic drop in water use (see figure 9.6). Water consumption in Berlin fell by an astonishing 42 percent between 1990 and 2000.[130] Most of this collapse in demand occurred during the first five years after reunification (see table 9.2). By 2004 water consumption had fallen to a level—just over 200 million cubic meters per annum—at which it remains to this day. Deindustrialization was probably the single most significant cause of this unprecedented decline in water consumption. Water use by industrial consumers fell by 51.3 percent between 1991

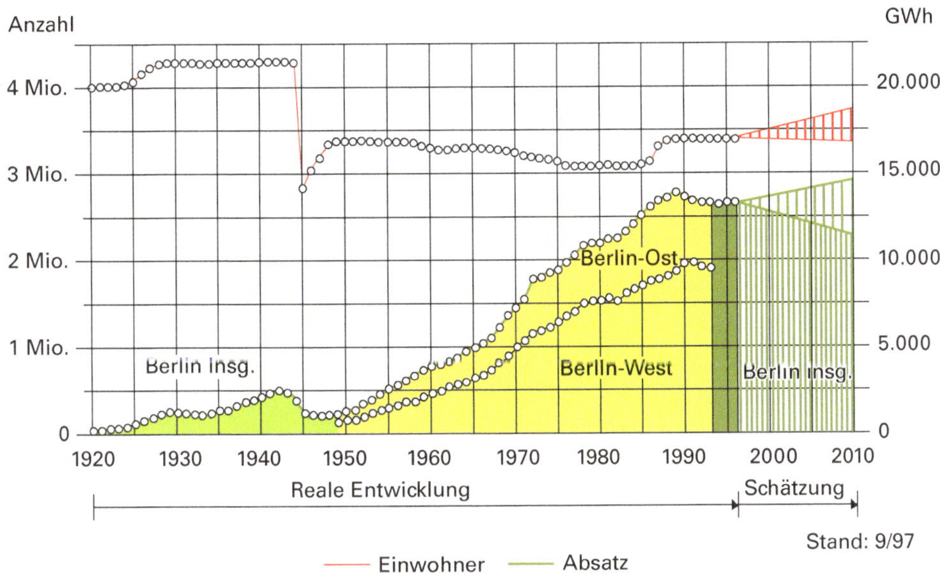

Figure 9.5
Berlin's electricity consumption and population, 1920–1996
Source: Senatsverwaltung für Stadtentwicklung, Umweltschutz und Technologie, *Stadtentwicklungsplan Ver- und Entsorgung*, 20.

Table 9.1
Sales of electricity and gas in Berlin, 1990–2017.

Year	Sales of electricity (million kWh)	Sales of gas (million kWh)
1990	13,439	10,529
1994	13,012	10,925
1997	12,923	14,532
2004	12,810	18,178
2011	11,371	19,444
2016	11,512	21,474
2017	12,366	20,330

Sources: Statistisches Landesamt Berlin, *Statistisches Jahrbuch 1995*, 312–313; Statistisches Landesamt Berlin, *Statistisches Jahrbuch 2005*, 268; Amt für Statistik Berlin-Brandenburg, *Statistisches Jahrbuch 2009 Berlin*, 349; Amt für Statistik Berlin-Brandenburg, *Statistisches Jahrbuch 2018 Berlin*, 390–391. Amt für Statistik Berlin-Brandenburg, *Statistisches Jahrbuch 2019 Berlin*, 382–383.

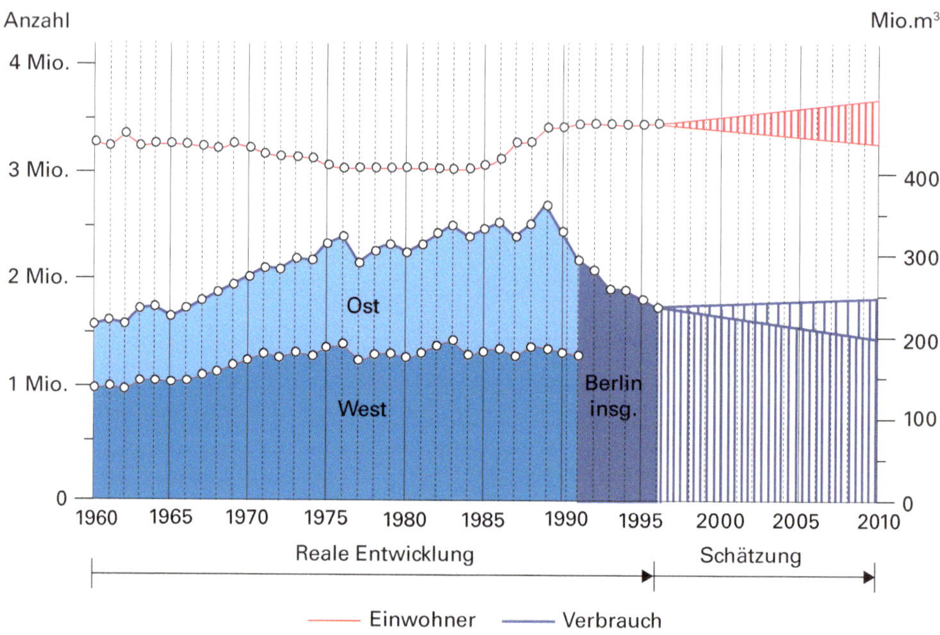

Figure 9.6

Berlin's water use and population, 1960–1996

Source: Senatsverwaltung für Stadtentwicklung, Umweltschutz und Technologie, *Stadtentwicklungsplan Ver- und Entsorgung*, 63.

Table 9.2

Water supplied and wastewater collected in Berlin, 1989–2017.

Year	Water supplied (million cubic meters)	Wastewater collected (million cubic meters)
1989	369	
1990	331	349
1994	261	273
2000	222	227
2004	209	232
2013	207	
2017	201	262

Sources: Statistisches Landesamt Berlin, *Statistisches Jahrbuch 1995*, 610; Statistisches Landesamt Berlin, *Statistisches Jahrbuch 2005*, 526; Amt für Statistik Berlin-Brandenburg, *Statistisches Jahrbuch 2016 Berlin*, 324; Berliner Wasser-Betriebe, *Geschäftsbericht 2017*, 7.

and 1995.[131] A further factor was the sharp decline in household use of water. Whereas in 1990 water use by households had stood at 156 liters a day in West Berlin and 180 liters a day in East Berlin, by 1996 the figure for the whole city had dropped to just 129 liters.[132] Responsible for this dramatic drop were sharp increases in water tariffs, discussed above, and the widespread installation of water-saving appliances. Total water consumption, expressed as an average per inhabitant, declined from 242 liters in West Berlin and 381 liters in East Berlin in 1990 to 192 liters for the whole city in 1996.

Declining water use on this scale resulted in massive overcapacities in the existing infrastructure. These were emerging, ironically, at a time when BWB was extending its water and wastewater networks into peripheral and new urban settlements.[133] As the length of its water mains and sewers grew year by year, the volume of water and wastewater flowing through them was falling sharply. The problems this gave rise to were, first, of a technical nature. The slower flow of water through the pipes compromised the quality of the city's drinking water. The slower flow of wastewater resulted in a sharp increase in blockages to the sewers, with a reported 3,400 cases in 1996 alone.[134] Declining use and overcapacity combined, second, to undermine the utility's revenues. Owing to the high proportion of fixed costs involved in providing water and wastewater services, lower levels of use do not translate into lower costs of provision. The response of BWB has been to raise tariffs—acting as a further disincentive to use water—and to introduce, in 2007, a basic fee immune from shifts in demand alongside the consumption-based tariff.[135] The third challenge was to reduce capacity. The utility closed down seven of its sixteen water works between 1996 and 2001 to reduce costs and improve performance.[136] Although wastewater volumes have declined by less, owing to relatively constant levels of rainwater in the combined sewers, BWB decommissioned sewage treatment plants at Adlershof (1996), Marienfelde (1998), and Falkenberg (2003). This has required pumping large volumes of sewage via expensive new sewers to the remaining operative treatment plants.[137]

BWB's various responses to the underutilization of its water and wastewater infrastructures have generated new problems themselves, bringing the utility into conflict with the environment department of the city government. One consequence of closing down water works and extracting less water has been to allow groundwater to rise to levels that are posing a risk to property. In low-lying areas of the city, especially in the vicinity of decommissioned water works, the groundwater is today so close to the surface that it is rendering cellars permanently damp or flooded.[138] The same problem encountered in the immediate postwar years has re-emerged, this time without the prospect of resolution with a recovering economy. Although a series of court cases has established that affected property owners have no legal right to compensation from either the water utility or the city government, the senate has come under so much political pressure to find a solution that it has obliged BWB, against its will, to resume water extraction at wells close to the affected areas.[139] For years now, BWB has been pumping water from its former water works at Johannisthal and flushing it straight into the nearest watercourse solely to keep groundwater levels low and cellars dry.

A second consequence of decommissioning water works is that it questions the necessity of having water protection zones around them. Owing to the local sourcing of Berlin's water supply, around 25 percent of Berlin's territory—some 230 square kilometers—was designated a water protection zone of one kind or another in 2000. As BWB implemented its plan to close down superfluous water works, the environment department and environmental NGOs grew increasingly alarmed at the consequences for the long-term security of the city's drinking water resources.[140] Here, too, a compromise has been struck, with BWB agreeing to keep the remaining water works open and even reactivating the plant at Johannisthal.

A third challenge of overcapacity is the implications it has for environmental policy to conserve water. The water utility has, understandably, been concerned that measures to reduce water use even more will only exacerbate the problems of underutilization of its networks. BWB has, indeed, sought ways of encouraging greater water consumption—such as introducing the basic fee—arguing that this will prevent them having to raise water tariffs to meet shortfalls in revenue.[141] The environment department disputes this line of reasoning, arguing instead that water conservation continues to be essential to secure the region's water resources in the long term, pointing to climate change as an additional argument. The conflict has revealed in stark relief how the efficient use of water infrastructure can run wholly counter to the efficient use of water resources. Ultimately, the issue of overcapacity has proven so intractable not only because of the multiple problems it has generated, but also because it challenges the very roots of the "build and supply" logic upon which Berlin's infrastructures have been developed over the past century.[142]

Selling the City Silver

The final blow to post-unification euphoria proved the most disruptive of all. By the mid-1990s economic decline, severed subsidies, and failed investments had combined to produce a fiscal crisis for the city government. A public debt of epic proportions created a climate in which desperate solutions were considered unavoidable. Principal among these were plans to privatize the city's utilities to help relieve the fiscal crisis. The prime motive for privatization was not, as in many other countries at the time, to improve the performance of the utilities themselves.[143] Indeed, the privatization negotiations had little to do with energy or water issues and far more to do with providing quick cash for the city coffers. The true precedent was not any contemporary model in Britain or elsewhere, therefore, but Berlin's own history of the Bewag sale in 1931. What resulted was by far the largest infrastructure privatization program in any German city. The stories of the privatization of Berlin's energy and water utilities in the late 1990s have already been ably told in research monographs by Jochen Monstadt (Bewag), Ross Beveridge (BWB), and Frank Hüesker (BWB).[144] The following section draws out and compares the salient points, focusing first on why and how the utilities were privatized and then on how privatization affected utility management and performance.

The fiscal crisis which spawned the wave of privatizations was largely of Berlin's own making. All the attempts to present the city as a victim of past geopolitics and contemporary globalization could not conceal the glaring truth that Berlin itself had contributed significantly to its dire financial state. Apart from its unrealistic ambitions of economic growth, the city government had made massive investments in a series of commercial ventures that quickly revealed catastrophic consequences. Towering over all others was the scandal surrounding Bankgesellschaft Berlin, a large public financial corporation owned by the city that was engaged in speculative real estate bonds in East Germany. When Bankgesellschaft collapsed, it left losses of between 30 and 35 billion euros—twice as high as the annual city budget—to be borne by the Berlin taxpayer.[145] Apart from the political uproar that followed, this scandal was instrumental in pushing up Berlin's public debt from an already high level of 13.1 billion euros in 1992 to 23.7 billion in 1995 and 31.2 billion in 1998.[146]

In an atmosphere of intensifying crisis, the city government was looking for rapid responses that could make a difference. Selling its utilities to private investors seemed to promise immediate relief. In the process of privatizing the electricity, gas, and water/wastewater utilities three points stand out as common driving logics. First, the negotiations were always primarily about maximizing the sale price and hardly at all about creating attractive infrastructures for Berlin.[147] Second, privatization was successfully constructed by its proponents in the city government as an unavoidable measure to help resolve the fiscal crisis.[148] Third, the privatization deals were all packaged as ways of drawing on the external expertise of global players to help Berlin's utilities adapt to the new commercial environment of energy and water service provision.[149]

Bewag, as the shiniest jewel in the municipal crown, was the first to be privatized. Bewag was a highly lucrative enterprise, recording a profit of 157 million Deutschmark in the financial year 1994–1995 and 185 million Deutschmark in 1996–1997, notwithstanding the stagnation in electricity sales and heavy investments described above.[150]

Berlin at this time owned a 50.8 percent share in Bewag, having steadily clawed back its majority since the privatization of 1931.[151] The sale of this shareholding promised a windfall of several billion Deutschmark for the city budget. Bewag's full privatization was initiated in the spring of 1997 under the forceful leadership of the Senator for Finance Annette Fugmann-Heesing (SPD).[152] Although strongly criticized by the opposition green and left parties (Bündnis 90/Grüne and PDS), environmental NGOs, trade unions, and the energy advisory board, the idea was widely supported within the city government. Here it was acknowledged that this was a painful, but unavoidable step to take under the circumstances. Within a short space of time a deal was reached and, in September 1997, Berlin's majority shareholding in Bewag was sold for 2.85 billion Deutschmark to a consortium of private energy companies led by Southern Energy (26 percent shareholding), Bayernwerke (26 percent), and Preußen-Elektra (23 percent).[153] In addition to the sale price, the three principal investors made a number of commitments to invest in the Berlin economy, guarantee jobs, keep the Bewag headquarters in Berlin, and co-fund projects on renewable energy.[154]

The Gasag privatization the following year differed in several respects. First, Gasag was at the time not a profitable enterprise, with company debts totalling 856 million Deutschmark at the end of 1996 and an annual loss of 42 million Deutschmark in that financial year.[155] Unlike Bewag, it was seen as being in urgent need of external capital to help readjust to the challenges ahead. Second, prospects for the gas market in Berlin appeared less uncertain than for electricity, given the anticipated growth in gas-fired heating and the less intrusive form of liberalization of gas markets expected.[156] Third, a minority shareholding in Gasag had already been sold in 1994, so a further sale was subject to less public scrutiny. Indeed, there was little opposition to the second privatization wave, even from environmentalists.[157] Once again, the desire to achieve a high sale price overrode any concerns over the long-term implications of selling the city's silver. In February 1998 agreement was reached to sell Berlin's remaining 51.2 percent shareholding in Gasag for 1.41 billion Deutschmark to a consortium of energy corporations.[158] This resulted in an overall shareholding in the utility of 38.16 percent for Gaz de France, 24.99 percent for Bewag, and 11.95 percent each for Ruhrgas, RWE, and VEBA. There were several supplementary agreements, as with the Bewag deal, including a one-off payment of 15 million Deutschmark, a guarantee to protect jobs, and a commitment to set up an environmental fund.

The privatization of BWB in 1999 proved far more controversial, despite the city retaining a majority shareholding in the company.[159] This was in part because BWB had not experienced any private co-ownership before and in part because water was a far more emotive resource to commodify than electricity or gas. Like Bewag, BWB was a highly profitable enterprise. Despite the sharp decline in water use, increased tariffs had ensured an impressive performance in the mid-1990s. Annual profits of BWB stood at 52 million Deutschmark in 1995, 190 million in 1996, 163 million in 1997, and 65 million in 1998.[160] Unlike Bewag, though, BWB was burdened with liabilities incurred during its diversification drive of the 1990s, notably the debts of the failed recycling enterprise SVZ.

In view of the anticipated opposition to the planned sale, the senate conducted negotiations with potential investors largely behind closed doors and assisted by teams of commercial and legal consultants.[161] This raised concerns at the lack of transparency and political accountability in the decision-making process that were later to erupt into a challenge to the whole privatization contract. It produced at the time, though, a holding model deemed acceptable to a majority in the city parliament. This model was approved and came into force in October 1999. It envisaged a new holding company—Berlinwasser Holding—as a silent partner holding 49.9 percent of the shares in BWB. Berlin retained a 50.1 percent share in both Berlinwasser Holding and BWB, with the remaining 49.9 percent shareholding divided between the multinational utilities Vivendi and RWE (45 percent each) and the insurance company Allianz (see figure 9.7).[162] The sale price of 3.1 billion Deutschmark was widely regarded as high.[163] Since the sale contract included guaranteed high revenues to the private investors, the sale price was effectively a loan to the city to be paid off with future revenues from BWB.[164] As with Bewag and Gasag, the private investors agreed in the contract to a number of concessions. These included no compulsory redundancies, fixed water and wastewater tariffs until 2003, investments of 5 billion Deutschmark in BWB over the following 10 years, a commitment to develop the Berlinwasser group into a competitive company at home and abroad, and the creation of a center of competence for water in Berlin to fund research.[165]

The impact of the three privatization deals on the city's budget—the principal purpose of the whole exercise—was, ultimately, limited. Impressive though the combined sale price of 7.36 billion Deutschmark was, it paled in comparison with the city's debt, which actually increased to 98 billion Deutschmark by 2003. As one contemporary reflects today: "Berlin felt it had to generate these billions of Marks [through privatization], but they just disappeared into a black hole."[166] The windfalls from privatizing the city's utilities did not significantly alleviate the city's debt problem. Yet by selling off such substantial shares the city forfeited annual income from the two profitable utilities. In the case of Bewag this lost revenue amounted to at least 200 million Deutschmark a year: a figure that would have exceeded the sale price over a period of just fifteen years.[167] BWB's private investors received profits from the utility totalling about 670

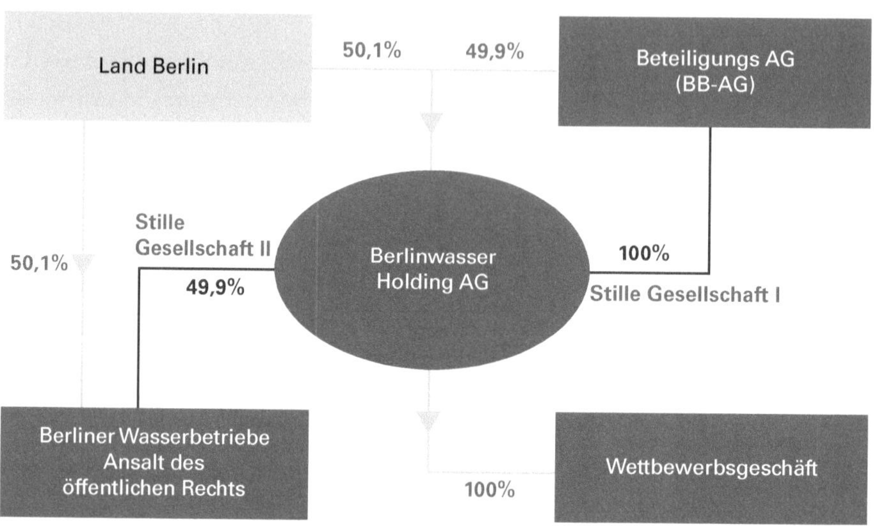

Figure 9.7
Holding model of the Berlin Water Company, 1999
Source: Bärthel, *Geklärt!*, 248.

million euros between 1999 and 2006: that is, one-third of the sale price they had paid after only eight years.[168] Not even fiscally, therefore, did privatization make much sense.

Those who paid the price of privatization—literally and figuratively—were the city's energy and water consumers. The high sale prices were predicated on the ability of the private partners to recoup their investments with increased revenue from the utilities. Bewag's net profits doubled within a year after full privatization, reaching 224 million Deutschmark in 1998 and rising to 246 million Deutschmark in 1999.[169] These figures enabled a return on equity for its shareholders of around 9 percent. Although Bewag had to maintain competitive tariffs for electricity in a liberalized market, it preferred to prioritize its shareholders over its customers when it came to sharing the profits. Gasag also provided its shareholders with increasingly lucrative returns, following internal cost-cutting and a boost in gas sales, which rose from 14,366 GWh at the time of full privatization to 18,178 GWh in 2004.[170] By 2004 the company was showing annual profits.[171] In 2008 it increased gas tariffs by an average 7.5 percent.[172] BWB had been prevented from raising its tariffs initially, as part of the privatization contract. This precipitated a sharp increase—by some 15 percent—on January 1, 2004, when the restriction was lifted.[173] Between 2003 and 2006 tariffs for drinking water were increased three times by a total of 21 percent, while those for wastewater were increased four times by a total of 30 percent.[174] By 2006, Berlin's tariffs for water (2.31 euros per cubic meter), wastewater (2.47 euros per cubic meter), and rainwater (1.53 euros per cubic meter) represented among the highest of Germany's largest cities.[175] Although justified by BWB in terms of falling water sales, the utility was generating at the time increased revenues and profits while reducing staff levels. Profits for the private investors alone rose from a meagre 7.7 million euros in 1999 to 78 million euros in 2002 and 134 million euros in 2004.[176] In June 2012 the Federal Cartel Office rejected BWB's tariffs for being unjustifiably high, prompting a dispute in the courts.

The improved commercial performance of Bewag and BWB in spite of the unfavorable conditions of a competitive electricity market and low levels of water consumption, respectively, can in part be attributed to the new leadership reversing the earlier strategy of diversification. By the late 1990s Bewag had largely disassociated itself from its ventures into the fields of telecommunications, waste management, and real estate, focusing once more on its core business of electricity and heating.[177] This process of restructuring Bewag was accelerated following its takeover by the Swedish conglomerate Vattenfall Europe in 2002, culminating in the disappearance of the Bewag name in January 2006.[178] The holding model for BWB had deliberately been set up to exploit opportunities emerging from deregulated markets for power, heating, gas, waste, and water, as Berlinwasser Holding enthusiastically endorsed in its first annual report of 1999.[179] Just one year later, however, the tone had changed, with calls now for selling off unprofitable activities—such as the disastrous SVZ and BerliKomm—while still retaining the multi-utility ambition and international collaborative ventures.[180] Over the following years these aspirations were also ditched, leaving BWB by 2014 without any activities abroad.[181] The privatization experience in Berlin—for all its faults—is most regularly praised for having purged the utilities of their most expensive habits.[182] It is ironic that the strategy of diversification so lauded by the city-run utilities in the 1990s was jettisoned by the very private investors who embodied this multi-utility ideal once they took control of Berlin's utilities in the 2000s.

Urban Governance of Privatized Utilities

How did privatization affect relations between the utilities and the city administration? What impact did it have on urban policy implementation? Overall, privatization had the effect of distancing the three utilities still further from the reach of public scrutiny. This, however, merely accelerated a process that had emerged during the 1990s as the utilities became more commercialized. The close collaboration between utilities and administration which had characterized the heyday of municipal expansionism in the 1920s, infrastructural resilience in the 1950s, and socialist integration in the 1970s had long since given way to a looser relationship between regulator and contractor. The attempt by the red-green government of 1989 to rein in a self-dependent Bewag had been replaced by a distributive strategy of public subsidies in the early 1990s. From the mid-1990s onward the local state withdrew from active intervention, without either the political will to confront the utilities or the public funds to promote desirable measures.[183] The city government had to rely instead increasingly on voluntary agreements with the utilities, using persuasion rather than legal obligation or financial incentives to get them to implement urban policy.

In the case of Bewag, the city government had lost all its influence as a shareholder over the utility. This was why a number of commitments—such as to co-fund projects on renewable energy—were written into the privatization contract. Yet the city government never assessed the degree to which Bewag, and later Vattenfall, honored its commitments.[184] It appeared, in Jochen Monstadt's view, unable to adapt to the changing environment of privatized and liberalized energy markets, resulting in a "regulatory gap."[185] A number of cooperation agreements have been signed between the city and Bewag as expressions of the loose form of persuasive governance that has characterized the post-privatization era. For instance, in 1997 an agreement was made for Bewag to invest 40 million Deutschmark over four years to promote innovative technologies for renewable energy, cogeneration, fuel cells, and heat pumps.[186] In 2008 Vattenfall entered into a climate protection agreement with Berlin, as part of the city's Climate Alliance, committing to reduce CO_2 emissions by 50 percent against 1990 levels and to undertake measures to extend district heating and increase the use of renewables. In 2009 the company produced its own energy concept for the city, in which it announced it would end the use of lignite at its Berlin power stations by 2020 and set up steps for promoting local cogeneration, smart metering, and bioenergy.

CO_2 emissions in Berlin have declined sharply since 1990. Based on end-energy use, they were down by 32.6 percent in 2011.[187] This well exceeded the 25 percent target set for 2010 in the Energy Concept of 1994 and reiterated in the State Energy Program of 2000. The electricity sector made an above-average contribution to this decline. CO_2 emissions from electricity use in the city halved between 1990 to 2011, from 13.4 million metric tons to 6.7 million metric tons.[188] At least one-third of this reduction, however, is attributable to the collapse of industrial production in the city.[189] Those advocating environmentally sustainable and climate-proof solutions for the city's energy services are critical of Bewag/Vattenfall's performance following full privatization in 1997.[190] They point in particular to the unwillingness of the utility to promote renewable energy in Berlin with any conviction. A study commissioned for Berlin's Energy Concept of 2011 highlighted that only 2.3 percent of the electricity produced in the city was generated from renewables, which produce an even lower proportion of its heating.[191] This figure put Berlin at the bottom of the league table of German federal states.[192] According to the study, Berlin could increase the renewable share of its electricity generation to 17 percent and of its heating sector to 12 percent if a concerted effort was made to promote photovoltaics, heat pumps, and solar thermal as well as biomass.[193]

The influence of the local state over BWB after privatization was greater, of course, owing to Berlin's majority shareholding in the new company. This did not mean that Berlin determined the utility's strategy, however. In practice, decision making on all major issues was reached in consensus between the senate and the private investors.[194] A joint position was generally negotiated in advance at informal meetings between the two sides. Without being able to enrol party political support in open debate, the city government had to rely on making deals with the private partners to retain any influence over the BWB's strategic direction. Officials in the senate department responsible for water management and environmental protection have, though, detected little change in relations with the utility since partial privatization.[195] Indicative of BWB's ability to accommodate urban policy was the Water Supply Concept it developed in 2008 to establish, effectively, which water works would be needed to meet (modest) future water demand.[196] Rather than insisting on a small number of water works to reduce costs for the utility, BWB agreed to keep a larger number open and operative so as to meet the city government's interest in regulating problematic groundwater levels and securing water protection zones. At a meeting of a parliamentary committee to discuss the concept on October 6, 2008, its basic premises were praised even by representatives of the Greens, who criticized only the lack of public participation in preparing the plan and its nonbinding status for the utility.[197]

Silo City: Competing for Heat

If relations between Berlin's utilities and the city government range from the distanced to the consensual, how have relations between the utilities themselves developed since reunification? Berlin remains one of the few cities in Germany where its utilities are not united, to a greater or lesser degree, under the umbrella of a single Stadtwerk. The legacy of providing distinct services by separate organizational entities over the past 100 years has made Berlin, infrastructurally speaking, a "silo city." There are obvious forms of interdependency over the use of electricity to drive water and sewage pumps or the use of water for cooling purposes in power stations. These kinds of interactions, though, form little more than normal provider-customer relations. The utilities also tend to share common membership of networks set up by the city government to advance certain policy objectives, such as the Climate Alliance referred to above or the Smart City Strategy of 2015. Their enrollment in these joint platforms and the voluntary agreements they sign up to are not predicated, however, on the requirement to cooperate with one another. There exists considerable potential for the water/wastewater utility to engage in energy provision, beyond using its own energy by-products from wastewater treatment processes. One example is deriving heat from wastewater, with an estimated potential to provide about 1,000 MW of heat, representing one-third of the city's district heating capacity.[198] Another example is the use of treated wastewater to irrigate energy crops on former sewage farms surrounding Berlin.[199] Projects of this kind, however, are currently at a very early stage of development. The only significant institutional link between any of the utilities has been Bewag's financial stake in Gasag, increased to almost 25 percent in 1998.

One field of service provision that has long been an arena of contestation is heating. In the absence of a united urban energy utility, technological diversity in heating options has resulted in virulent competition between the city's principal electricity and gas utilities, Bewag/Vattenfall and Gasag, that reaches back to the 1960s. This competition is regarded by many directly involved as highly divisive and often counterproductive.[200] An early example of the stand-offs it has generated over urban development in the post-unification era was the plans for heating the redeveloped Potsdamer Platz complex.[201] The original design for decentralized power, heating, and cooling was opposed by an alliance of Gasag, the federal government, and the investor Debis, who favored a central, gas-fired energy unit. Their proposal was then overturned by a consortium of Bewag and the contractor ABB geared to securing demand for power and heat from Bewag's planned cogeneration plant in Mitte.

The crux of the ongoing dispute is that district heating, to be economically sustainable, needs extensive coverage of the heating market in the area accessible to the district heating network. Bewag/Vattenfall has always dominated the district heating market, using heat from its power stations to produce 87.5 percent of all district heating sold in the city.[202] As before reunification, Bewag has tried to protect its district heating market by undercutting prices with profits from electricity sales, binding heating customers with long-term contracts, and pressing for protected district heating zones.[203] Since liberalization, Bewag/Vattenfall's protectionist strategy has, however, been undermined on several fronts. It can no longer block access to the electricity grid, for instance from power generated in gas-fired cogeneration plants. It is not able to cross-subsidize its district heating any more as it needs to sell electricity at competitive prices. The electricity it generates is, indeed, so expensive relative to the competition that it can be sold only

Figure 9.8
Dismantling the Upper Havel power station, 2007
Photo: Timothy Moss.

occasionally when the spot market price is high. This has required some of its power stations to be decommissioned (see figure 9.8) and others to be reduced to producing heat, rather than power. It is ironic, from an historical perspective, that district heating, originally a by-product of local electricity generation, has today become the core business of the power utility Vattenfall in Berlin.[204] Meanwhile Gasag, a company that was burdened with debt in the mid-1990s, has benefited not only from the rapid growth in gas sales since then (see table 9.1 above), but also from its flexibility in being able to provide the fuel for a variety of heating technologies, from the individual boiler to the block-type cogeneration plant.[205] Competition, rather than cooperation, between the city's former municipal energy utilities is frustrating a coordinated urban energy policy.

Re-municipalization from Below

As if network reconfiguration, shifting consumption patterns, privatization, and liberalization had not destabilized Berlin's infrastructure systems enough in the years following reunification, a further novel challenge has recently been posed by popular pressure to re-municipalize the privatized utilities. Since the privatizations in the late 1990s, there has been growing public criticism of their negative consequences for consumers and the environment as well as of the secretive manner in which the contracts with the private investors were concluded. Out of this criticism have emerged networks of activist groups aspiring to re-municipalize the city's energy and water infrastructures who are inspired by the global "right to the city" movement.[206] Berlin is currently experiencing an epoch in which, to cite Antina von Schnitzler, "[i]nfrastructure itself becomes a terrain on which central questions—of civic virtue, basic needs, and the rights and obligations of citizenship—are negotiated and contested."[207]

The re-municipalization campaigns that have come to characterize Berlin's infrastructure politics over the past decade, attracting worldwide attention, are distinctive and original for two reasons. First, they are driven by civil society groups and not local politicians. Unlike many other cities across the world, where municipal governments are trying to regain control of their water or electricity utilities, in Berlin this is re-municipalization "from below."[208] Indeed, ironically, re-municipalization has until recently been actively resisted by successive coalitions in the city hall. Second, the re-municipalization advocated by local activists goes much further than the traditional municipal utility. It is not about a return to the status quo ante of municipally owned, but largely self-dependent utilities pursuing their familiar supply-oriented strategies. It is rather about creating a new genre of municipal utility that is environmentally sustainable, socially responsible, and democratically accountable. Out of the frustration with urban enactments of privatization have emerged alternative models of the networked city. Even more extraordinary, perhaps, these models have today become part of mainstream infrastructure politics, powerfully influencing city government policy.

The dramatic shift in political discourse happened first over the partially privatized BWB.[209] Against the backdrop of a city government deeply discredited by the banking scandal, public protest arose over the sharp increases to BWB's water and wastewater tariffs after 2003. In 2006 the Berlin Water Roundtable (Berliner Wassertisch) was founded as a network of organizations and citizens committed to reversing the privatization deal. Combining environmental and social groups, the network put pressure on the city government to release the secret contracts supplementary to the privatization deal which guaranteed the private investors high dividends at the expense of the water consumer. This was resisted not only by the new owners of BWB but also by the city government itself, then a coalition of Social Democrats and the Left Party (Linke).[210] A campaign to hold a referendum on the issue of releasing the secret contracts eventually overcame legal challenges in the Constitutional Court. In the ensuing referendum, held on February 13, 2011, 98.2 percent of the 660,000 votes cast were in favor of the law proposed by the Water Roundtable to publish the contracts.[211] This overwhelming majority—marking the first successful referendum ever in Berlin—promoted a gradual policy reversal. Both the SPD and CDU came to accept that their own decision to privatize BWB had been a mistake.[212] On November 7, 2013, the city parliament gave its approval to a proposal by the city government for Berlin to buy back all shares in BWB. By then the two remaining private shareholders, RWE and Veolia, had both indicated their willingness to sell and thereby terminate their involvement with a company that was becoming a corporate image problem for them. BWB was fully re-municipalized in December 2013. Extraordinarily, throughout the entire debate on re-municipalization the issue of Berlin's huge public debt—the key argument behind the privatization rationale in the late 1990s—played no role at all.[213] Although Berlin's debt had actually increased slightly over the intervening years, it was no longer being used as a discursive lever. The BWB case has become a salutary lesson in the power of discourse to affect very material change to a city's infrastructures.

The successful campaign to re-municipalize BWB was only the first step in a process designed to make the utility more accountable to its customers. In response to the criticism that the privatized BWB was charging too much for its services, tariffs for water were reduced by 15 percent and for wastewater by 6 percent following re-municipalization.[214] More significant from a governance perspective have been the various moves to open up water infrastructure management to greater public participation and scrutiny. Already during the campaign for the referendum, an open forum for discussing urban water issues (Stadtgespräch Wasser) was established by BWB, its research wing KWB, several environmental organizations, and consultants, with the backing of the city government. Over the past decade this forum has generated public debate on water in the city, deliberately setting out to involve a wide range of viewpoints, from property owners and businesses to environmental NGOs and consumer organizations. It has proved successful, by its own accounts, in creating a cross-party consensus on the importance of water to the city's development and, more specifically, in getting decentral rainwater management embedded in the coalition agreement of 2016.[215]

The Berlin Water Roundtable, by contrast, has focussed its attention on democratizing BWB.[216] Under the slogan "after re-municipalization: democratization," it established in November 2013 a Water Council (Wasserrat) comprising a wide range of water stakeholders entrusted with devising the decision-making powers of a planned Futures Council (Zukunftsrat) to work alongside BWB's senior management.[217] In a Water Charter it sets out its goals for a transparent, socially just, and ecologically sustainable use of water in Berlin. These pose a challenge to the kinds of technical and financial expertise enrolled by the utility in the past. They also reveal how increased transparency can foster new forms of dispute, echoing findings of Andrew Barry.[218] Major differences of opinion have emerged, indeed, within the Water Council and between different groups within the Water Roundtable that are hampering progress on the democratization project. One key bone of contention is whether the Futures Council should be restricted to water experts only, or whether selected or elected water consumers should be included. Putting participatory democracy into practice is proving far harder than agreeing to it in principle.[219]

The re-municipalization campaign on water inspired a subsequent campaign to municipalize the city's electricity and gas infrastructures. In 2010 the Berlin Energy Roundtable (Berliner Energietisch) was founded by activists to press for the creation of a new municipal utility in Berlin producing electricity from renewables and incorporating participatory principles.[220] The following year it expanded into a grassroots coalition of some fifty environmental, leftist, and anti-gentrification groups calling for the re-municipalization of the electricity grid. When this was rejected by the city government it organized a referendum on the issue (see figure 9.9). This referendum was held on November 3, 2013, resulting in 83 percent of the votes cast in favor of the campaign, but narrowly missing the quorum of a 25 percent turnout. Despite this setback, the Energy Roundtable has continued to press for a democratic, ecologically oriented, and socially just "citizens' utility" (*Bürgerstadtwerk*). Alongside the Roundtable, an energy cooperative was launched in 2011 called Citizen Energy Berlin (BürgerEnergie Berlin).[221] It is proposing a different model based not on municipal, but direct collective ownership of a utility. As a cooperative it aims to generate enough capital from its members to be able to purchase the grid-operating utility in collaboration with a pioneering municipal utility from Southern Germany. Citizen Energy Berlin is also committed to ecological and social principles, calling for 10 percent of profits from the grid utility to be earmarked for investments in solar and cogeneration, and advocating energy savings as a means of lowering energy bills. Having amassed only around 12 million euros from its 1,000 members, the cooperative currently falls well short of the amount needed to make a convincing bid for the city's electricity grid.[222]

The renewal of the concession agreement for the electricity grid provided the window of opportunity for both organizations to challenge the position of the incumbent power utility Vattenfall and its subsidiary operating the local grid, Stromnetz Berlin.[223] While the Roundtable campaigned for the city to take on the electricity grid concession in one form or another, the cooperative sought take it on itself in partnership with others. Bowing to popular pressure, the city government created a municipal company, Berlin Energie, in March 2012 to bid for the concessions for both the electricity and gas networks. There ensued a very public contestation between Vattenfall and its opponents over the future of Berlin's power grid. Vattenfall has argued that only it possesses the

Figure 9.9
Poster "Our Stadtwerk. Our Power Grid. Our Berlin," November 2013
Source: http://www.berliner-energietisch.net/materialien.

experience and expertise necessary to run a complex electricity grid. The civil society organizations have countered that only an accountable municipal utility can deliver on policy targets for renewable energy, demonstrating a lack of trust in conventional notions of technical expertise.[224] As the procedure for granting the concession was challenged in the courts, a resolution over who shall operate Berlin's power grid in future has been delayed significantly. A decision made in Berlin Energie's favor in March 2019 was reversed on appeal in November 2019.[225] The local struggle between Vattenfall and urban activists illustrates well how the political possibilities opened up by the (failed) referendum campaign are reconfiguring the trajectory of Berlin's electricity provision.[226]

The concession for the city's gas network also landed in the courts, with Gasag challenging the ability of the city's own utility, Berlin Energie, to operate the gas system.[227] This dispute is putting the spotlight on Gasag, which in the past has always managed to avoid the level of criticism directed at Bewag/Vattenfall. Despite it being wholly in private ownership, Gasag has skillfully branded itself as a local utility, proud of its historical roots and commitment to the city.[228] It has also benefited from using an environmentally cleaner fuel and investing in energy-efficient block-type cogeneration in the city.[229] This, though, may not prove sufficient to ward off interventions by the city government. In May 2015 the senate began discussions with the owners of Gasag about the possibility of them selling their shares to the city of Berlin.[230]

As the dispute over these network concessions suggests, civil society organizations have been successful in shifting the terms of debate on Berlin's energy and water policies. Already in the city elections of 2011, the manifestos of three contenders for government—the SPD, Left Party, and Greens—called for re-municipalizing the energy networks and even creating a municipal utility as core components of Berlin's energy transition.[231] The subsequent governing coalition of SPD and CDU commissioned a cross-party study for the city parliament to make recommendations for the city's energy infrastructures. The final report, published in November 2015, came out strongly in favor of re-municipalizing both the electricity grid and gas network, as well as—notably—making stronger use of the city's rights of self-government in dealing with the utilities.[232]

Most significantly, the city government set up in 2014 a nascent public utility, Berliner Stadtwerke, with the task of promoting renewable energy in the city. Berlin's first-ever nominal Stadtwerk initially bore all the traits of political compromise between an enthusiastic SPD and skeptical CDU. Embedded organizationally within the (recently re-municipalized) BWB and equipped with only a handful of staff and a minute budget, the new utility was derided as a "bonsai Stadtwerk," only able to sell electricity generated by itself. Following the formation of a left-green coalition of SPD, Left Party, and Greens in late 2016, however, the new utility has received strong political backing and significantly more funding to invest. A reform to the Berlin Enterprise Act (Betriebe-Gesetz) in 2017 "liberated" the Berliner Stadtwerke from its legal fetters, enabling it to engage as a full competitor in the market for renewable electricity and heat.[233] The political ambition now is for "a genuine *Stadtwerk* 2.0" (Stefan Taschner, Greens) that will be "a motor for a socially just energy transition" in the city (Jörg Stroedter, SPD).[234] Since 2017 Berliner Stadtwerke has received a 100 million euro capital injection that has helped fund photovoltaic installations for tenant electricity projects and its first wind turbines on former sewage farms.[235] The utility is still a small enterprise and some commentators are skeptical about its future, fearing that there is not the money available to make a serious dent in its local competitors.[236] What is special about Berliner Stadtwerke and Berlin Energie, though, is the vision of municipally-owned utilities pioneering city government policy. With only slim chances of buying back the city's original electricity and gas utilities, Berlin is building up wholly new entities in direct competition with them. Municipalization, as we have noted before, can take many forms.

Change in Form or Substance?

The last ten years of Berlin's infrastructural odyssey have witnessed a radical change in both the style and the terms of debate on energy and water services in the city. Urban infrastructures that had for decades been kept invisible from public scrutiny have become a key point of reference when discussing Berlin's future. The city's energy and water utilities have always been enrolled to a greater or lesser degree in the delivery of urban (and sometimes national) policy in Berlin, but this was until today rarely a matter for open public debate. The agency of civil society groups in actively shaping—rather than just calling for—alternative futures for Berlin's utility services is a distinctly novel phenomenon. These futures are geared toward making the networked city not only more environmentally sustainable, but also more accountable.

How far, though, do these developments represent a change in substance, as well as in form? What impact can be detected of the new political paradigm for infrastructures to serve Berliners and not just Berlin? It is too early to provide a definitive answer in an ongoing process, but some pointers are possible. On the positive side, there is plenty of evidence that both the city government and the utilities are taking a more robust approach to climate protection, environmental sustainability, infrastructure interoperability, and citizen participation. The city's development strategy of 2014 calls explicitly for better intersectoral collaboration between the city's infrastructures: "[v]ia stronger coordination and connection of urban networks (gas, water, electricity) a modern, efficient, and environmentally friendly service infrastructure will emerge."[237]

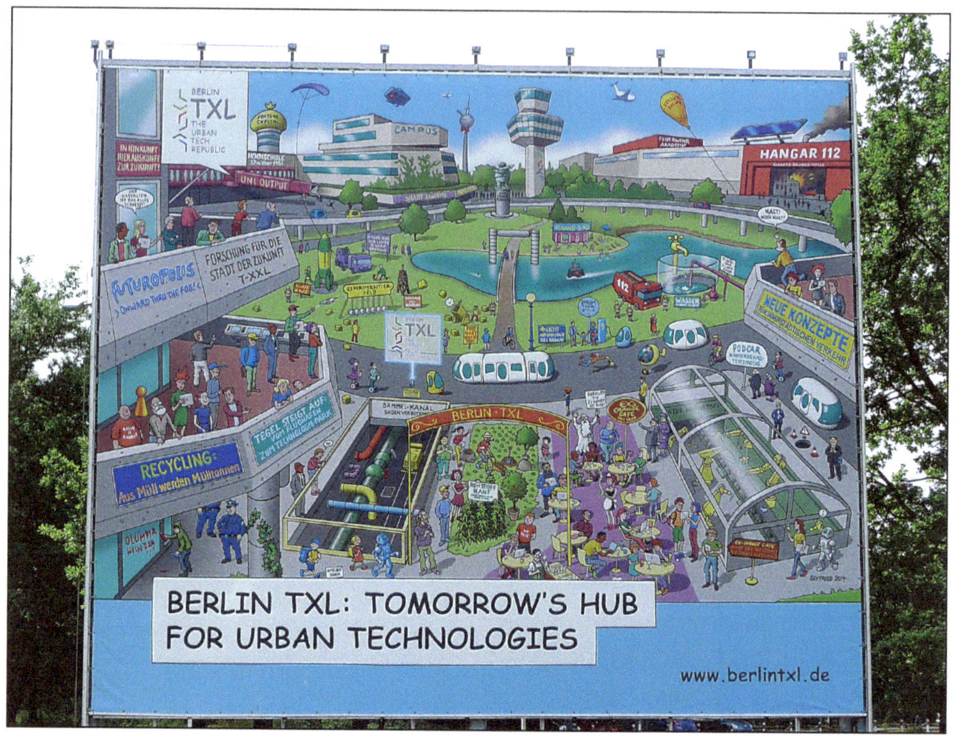

Figure 9.10
Vision of Tegel airport as an urban technology hub, 2015
Photo: Timothy Moss.

The site of Tegel airport is to become a hub for urban technologies and a showcase for Berlin's infrastructural expertise (see figure 9.10).[238] The Berlin Energy and Climate Concept, approved by the senate in June 2017, aspires to make Berlin climate neutral by 2050, requiring reductions in CO_2 emissions (compared to 1990 levels) of 40 percent by 2020 and 60 percent by 2030.[239] These are ambitious targets, given that CO_2 emissions in Berlin have actually been rising since 2008 and are likely to rise further as the population grows, if mitigating steps are not taken.[240] The concept contains 107 measures to achieve this goal, including phasing out coal, expanding gas-fired cogeneration and solar power, as well as promoting heat pumps, geothermal energy, and electricity storage technologies.

In the water sector the city government launched—in conjunction with BWB—a new strategy for localized rainwater management in 2017 that marks a reorientation away from the conventional preference for centralized systems.[241] This is seen within the city administration as a significant policy reversal on rainwater, at least.[242] In May 2018 a rainwater agency was established within BWB, under the supervision of the city's environmental department, with the task of promoting decentralized forms of rainwater retention and use in both new developments and—far harder—existing settlements. While the city administration sees the new entity as a chance to use BWB's huge customer base to interest a wider range of people in the technologies, BWB itself views it as an example of the utility's renewed interest in being a partner of urban development (see figure 9.11).[243]

At the same time, the utilities are keen to portray themselves as vanguards of urban sustainability and promoters of active citizenship. In its sustainability report of 2017 Gasag describes itself as a "driver and motor of Berlin's energy transition" with the aspiration of becoming "ever smarter and greener."[244] Beyond providing customers with contracting models for their heating, cooling, and power requirements, Gasag is active

Figure 9.11
BWB poster "Congratulations: 150 Years of Water for Berlin"
Photo: Timothy Moss.

in urban pilot projects for power-to-gas, wind power, and climate-neutral neighborhood development. BWB is equally proud of its sustainability credentials, highlighting in its 2017 annual report activities not only to protect the region's water resources (for instance, in eliminating nutrients and trace elements from wastewater), but also to mitigate against climate change (for example, using biogas and cogeneration at sewage treatment plants and hosting the Berliner Stadtwerke).[245] Even Vattenfall, the target of so much criticism, presents itself today as a modern, low-carbon utility engaged in innovative green projects across the city. These include using waste heat for its district heating network, investing in power-to-heat technologies to support volatile electricity generation from renewables, home energy management using smart meters, and even—in a nod to alternative Berlin lifestyles—supporting urban gardening on its vacant sites.[246]

Berlin's infrastructure history teaches us, though, to be wary of appearances. It is littered with instances of unfulfilled plans and rhetorical hyperbole. Although recent policy statements and actions are pointing in the direction of more sustainable, equitable, and accountable utility services, experience cautions against high expectations. Several commentators acknowledge the potential to transform the city's infrastructures, but are skeptical whether this is actually happening. They point to the marginal changes to utility practices, the lack of creativity in utility leadership, the limited budgets for new initiatives, and the degree to which utility action is prescribed by legal requirements.[247] The city's water and energy roundtables—the mouthpieces of civil society engagement—are growing increasingly impatient with the pace of progress.

As the centenary of the creation of Greater Berlin approaches, it is self-evident that the remaking of Berlin through infrastructure is by no means complete. From an historical perspective it never will be. From a political perspective it never should be. This is an overarching lesson of Greater Berlin's hundred-year infrastructure history: temporal dynamics and political contestation are not structural weaknesses but the very essence of sociotechnical systems designed to serve the city.

10 Conclusion: Meanings of Berlin's Infrastructure History

> The past is prologue, but it is also a site of memory excavated and reinterpreted in the light of a society's understanding of the present and its hopes for what lies ahead.
>
> —Sheila Jasanoff, 2015

This book has told the history of Berlin from an unusual perspective: through the prism of its piped infrastructures. It has generated one of the first studies to cover the entire century since the city was massively enlarged in 1920. In doing so, it has revealed unknown facets of Berlin's history and given familiar features a fresh, sociotechnical twist. By focusing on urban infrastructures, the book has elucidated their pivotal significance to the city. By conceiving of infrastructures as inherently sociotechnical, it has disclosed the dynamic interplay of their material and nonmaterial components. By looking across five hugely diverse political regimes, it has challenged assumptions about obduracy and transition that underpin many studies of infrastructure. Overall, it has demonstrated the multiple ways in which infrastructure has been both medium and manifestation of the continuous remaking of Berlin. Infrastructure, the book has argued, can tell us a lot about how Berlin has been envisioned, structured, and governed in the past and why this is relevant today.

At the same time, the book has—more broadly—been about the relationship between cities and their infrastructures. Taking the past 100 years of Berlin's history as an exemplar, it has identified long-term trends and multiple shifts in this relationship. The very distinctiveness of Berlin's turbulent past has revealed dimensions to city-infrastructure relations that often remain hidden from view elsewhere. The book has shown, in particular, how the mature phase of urban infrastructures can be more open to change than is commonly assumed. This substantiates recent research that describes sociotechnical configurations as being in a continuous state of consolidation, adaptation, and contestation.[1] It has demonstrated that, in any such configuration, institutional path dependencies can be more powerful than material ones. It has illustrated, furthermore, how the "urban" is inextricably bound up in multi-scalar politics and metabolisms that reach from household energy use and municipal planning to regional resource flows, national policy directives, and geopolitical conflicts. Finally, by comparing five infrastructures sectors, it has revealed important similarities and differences, as well as interdependencies and competition, between them.

This concluding chapter looks across the book to draw out the key findings and highlight their implications. Its purpose is essentially twofold. First, it uses the opportunity of looking back across a century of infrastructure politics, transcending diverse regimes and disruptive events, to expose the most remarkable features of Berlin's sociotechnical history. The task here is to make sense out of the socio-material, temporal, and spatial complexity of infrastructures in modern Berlin. Second, the chapter uses this panoramic tableau to elucidate the book's novel contribution to social research on urban infrastructure histories. This task is about sensitizing STS scholars and historians of technology to the importance of multiple spatialities, urban geographers to the importance of multiple temporalities, and the wider academy to the importance of sociotechnical dynamics. Both lines of thought—empirical and conceptual—are combined in a discussion around each of the five themes of the analytical framework developed in chapter 2. The chapter concludes with reflections on the "usable past" of Berlin's infrastructures and its relevance for urban and infrastructure transitions today.

Infrastructural Traces of Berlin

What has this sociotechnical take on Berlin's recent history revealed that previous histories of the city have not? What, indeed, can an infrastructural perspective bring to urban history in general? On the most superficial level, this book has told the story of how Berlin's energy and water services kept the city going at all times, from the mundane to the momentous. Providing enough electricity, gas, district heating, water, and sanitation in a reliable, safe, and affordable manner has been a tenet of Berlin's development policy across the past century. These services, generally invisible in everyday life, have been exposed as fundamental to the operability of this modern city. The book has traced the myriad ways in which infrastructures have provided the power to drive the urban economy, the gas to warm homes, the water to sustain life, and the wastewater treatment to keep the city healthy. These have ranged from ambitious plans to secure water supplies to restrictions on energy use, from efforts to keep tariffs low in times of hardship to geopolitical negotiations over access to natural gas. The book has thereby rendered visible a dimension of urban modernity that has been widely disregarded in political and cultural histories of Berlin. The advantage of studying Berlin through the lens of its infrastructures is that, by virtue of their general invisibility, they are rarely haunted by ghosts from the past, in contrast to many structures above ground.[2]

On a deeper level, this book has made abundantly clear that there is far more to a city's infrastructures than providing essential services. The work that infrastructures do—and are made to do—for the city reaches way beyond the techno-economic functionality privileged in accounts by engineers and urban planners. In what ways is this political history of Berlin's infrastructures not only unusual, therefore, but also insightful? This is where the sociotechnical approach to infrastructure proves so revelatory. Understanding Berlin's energy and water systems as complex and dynamic assemblages of multiple social and material elements opens up a whole new perspective on their techno-political agency. A host of examples have illustrated this strong relationality of urban infrastructures. These relations can be of a physical nature, as manifested by the water or energy coursing from external sources through the city via the conduits of urban infrastructure. It can be institutional, as reflected in the de-municipalization of the city's utilities under state socialism. It can also be socioeconomic, as when shifts in household income or industrial production during periods of recession had a significant bearing on water and energy consumption. It can even be symbolic, for instance when self-sufficiency in electricity generation became a powerful image of West Berlin's insular resilience. These examples together illustrate that the relationship between a city and its infrastructure is fundamentally bidirectional. Urban development trends can affect infrastructure just as much as infrastructure can affect urban life.

It is no exaggeration, indeed, to assert that infrastructures have helped "remake" Berlin in many ways over the past 100 years. The very contours of today's city were shaped in 1920, in part at least, by acknowledgment of the importance of drinking water sources and water mains infrastructure to the future development of Greater Berlin. The aspiration of a unitary city took material and organizational form during the Weimar years with the unification of municipal utilities, the territorial integration of their technical networks, and the introduction of uniform tariffs across the whole city. Imperfections remained and achievements unraveled in the wake of the Depression, but Berlin's infrastructures were hugely instrumental in enabling urban unity and advancing urban equity. The "remaking" of Berlin by the National Socialists involved subjugating municipal priorities to a nationalist agenda of racial supremacy and territorial aggression. The city's utilities were not the vanguards of this transformation, but they were certainly enlisted in the nazification of the city. This found expression in the political "cleansing" of the city's utilities, the subordination to external supplies of electricity and gas, the enrollment in national autarky plans, and the gradual militarization of utility structures. The debilitation of municipalism during the Nazi era was pursued in a very different vein after the war in East Berlin. The DDR model of socialism required the de-municipalization of infrastructure as a key component of the city's subjugation to party and state. On the other side of the political divide, energy and water infrastructures proved crucial to the very survival of West Berlin during the blockade and formative in sustaining its insular existence throughout the following decades. Reunification in 1990 placed the spotlight once again on infrastructure as a medium of spatial reconfiguration. Reconnecting the cables, pipes, and sewers between the two halves of the city and of West Berlin with the surrounding region became highly symbolic acts of unification. Conduits that had been used as instruments of urban estrangement could recover their role as channels of spatial connectivity.

This is what is meant by "infrastructuring" the city. This book has demonstrated that infrastructures are not just "in" a city (in a locational sense), nor are they just "for" a city (in a functional sense); they are very much "of" a city. That is, they are part and parcel of the urban condition. The Berlin case, being so rich in experience, has shown in stark relief how infrastructures continuously permeate the practices and policies of urban life, whilst at the same time being imbued themselves with the physical, socioeconomic, and political geographies of a city. Understanding processes of "infrastructuring" a city is a promising vein to mine in future research on urban change and sociotechnical transition.

Conjunctions of Continuity and Change

The long-term perspective of this book, spanning 100 years of Berlin's turbulent history, represents a novel longitudinal study of mature infrastructures, but is also distinctive for its fresh take on infrastructural temporality. By unpacking sociotechnical configurations of energy and water over a long period of time, the book has been able to follow which of their components changed, which did not, and why at particular times. This approach is significant for challenging the predominance of path dependence and transitions as frames of analysis and advancing a more nuanced, layered, and nonlinear understanding of change to sociotechnical systems. Obduracy and transformation, Berlin's infrastructure history informs us, are not phenomena that are mutually incompatible, but can be prevalent at the same time within the same sociotechnical configuration. It is important, therefore, to develop an eye for spotting change and continuity to the component parts of urban infrastructures.

Examples from Berlin that substantiate this interpretation are legion. The shift from democracy to fascism in the 1930s is an extreme, but instructive, case in point. On the one hand, there is plenty of evidence to demonstrate radical and disruptive change following the Nazi seizure of power in 1933. Those responsible for urban infrastructure, in the city government and the utilities, were either dismissed from their jobs or cowed into submission. Infrastructure policy was framed no longer in municipal, but in national, terms. Service users were coerced into militarized practices of energy and water consumption. Imaginaries of national autarky reached down into the workings of the city's sewage disposal system. On the other hand, one can point to various aspects of Berlin's infrastructure that remained largely unchanged. For all the rhetoric of radical change, once in power the Nazis failed to induce a strategic reorientation to the city's energy and water systems. The technologies and material structures used to provide energy and water services to Berlin remained largely the same. Plans from the 1920s continued to be implemented, if more slowly. What the Nazi era reveals particularly well is how change and continuity did not simply coexist in different parts of a sociotechnical system, but came together in subtle and often insidious ways. One example of this is the municipalization of the city's utilities. This core policy of the 1920s was pursued by the Nazis after 1933 not as a way of strengthening municipal control, but of ridding the utilities of foreign and non-Aryan influence. A second example is the senior municipal officer responsible for the utilities during the 1920s and 1930s, Bruno Ziethen. Prior to 1933 he had been the chief coordinator of municipal expansionism; after 1933 his loyalty remained to the city, but adapted wholeheartedly to one in the National Socialist image. In both these instances, features of the old coagulated with features of the new to pervert a municipal ideal of infrastructures serving urban citizens.

Just as periods of political disruption did not prove wholly transformational, periods of relative "normalcy" in Berlin's recent history were not eras of strong infrastructural continuity. It is, indeed, intriguing to observe that the two periods when Berlin experienced conditions similar to most comparable cities—during the 1920s and again in the 1990s—were the ones characterized by the greatest changes to its infrastructure systems. Under the democratic Weimar Republic Berlin's urban development was not out of the ordinary for a North European metropolis of the time, yet the sociotechnical configurations of its energy and water systems underwent substantial transformations on several fronts. They were territorially reordered to serve the greatly enlarged city, brought under single municipal ownership, and enrolled in the pursuit of social, economic, and fiscal policies, becoming for the first time a key instrument of integrated municipal policy. When the Berlin Wall fell in 1989, expectations that Berlin's infrastructures would be less susceptible to disruption once the networks of West and East had been reconnected were soon dashed. An unprecedented drop in water consumption created problems of network overcapacity that struck at the very heart of the supply-oriented logic underpinning infrastructure management across all previous political regimes. Berlin's spiraling public debt prompted the sale of shares in all its utilities, reversing a policy that the city government had sought to sustain during earlier times of crisis. Liberalized energy markets removed the territorial monopolies upon which the city's power and gas utilities had always relied. Social movements calling for new models of urban infrastructure have more recently been questioning the ways energy and water utilities are traditionally governed. Overall, these examples drawn from "normal" periods of Berlin's history dispel any assumption that studying the city cannot reveal phenomena of generic interest because of its exceptionality. They also suggest that eras of democratic rule are more capable of radical transformation than is widely assumed.

They demonstrate, further, that research on infrastructural trajectories should not privilege stability as the default setting of sociotechnical systems for energy or water provision. Nor should it be fixated on moments in time when these systems appear to be undergoing radical transition. A focus on path dependence can conceal processes by which the elements of a sociotechnical configuration are being dis- and reassembled, just as a selective orientation toward transitions can overlook long-term forces for continuity. An excellent illustration of this conjunction of continuity and change is the trajectory of the hire purchase scheme Elektrissima. Launched by Berlin's electricity utility Bewag in the mid-1920s, it was initially designed to encourage the sale of household electrical appliances in general by enabling customers to pay for them in installments. When peak electricity loads began to create capacity problems for Berlin's power plants, Elektrissima was modified to promote appliances that used power at off-peak times. During the Depression, when electricity sales to the manufacturing sector collapsed, the scheme was used to shore up household demand, thereby keeping the power stations profitable. The Nazis subsequently adapted Elektrissima to advocate the sale of appliances that helped the war effort, such as electrical fridges. In postwar West Berlin the scheme was reactivated to great effect as a way of stimulating economic growth and showcasing urban consumerism. The case of Elektrissima illustrates well how a sociotechnical configuration survived across very different regimes through adaptation to changing political and economic environments.

Other examples from Berlin's rich history highlight the need to consider nonlinearity when studying trajectories of infrastructure. The physical permanence of many structures characteristic of energy and water provision can mislead observers into presuming continuous progress of the dominant sociotechnical system. If we look carefully, however, it is not difficult to detect evidence of trajectories that do not fit this linear model. The emergence, disappearance and (recent) re-emergence of sewage gas as a vehicle fuel or of nutrient recycling from sewage are two intriguing instances of alternative sociotechnical assemblages that gained traction in the 1930s, fell from favour after the collapse of Nazism, and reappeared after 2000, albeit under a very different political mantle. Echoes from the past are also discernible in the various initiatives to integrate urban and infrastructure planning across the city's history, whether to prevent modernist experiments after the Second World War, to kick-start a socialist infrastructural ideal in the 1970s, or to guide development in the reunified city of the 1990s. Non-linear trajectories should not be dismissed as aberrations, therefore, but embraced as part of the whole story and important indicators of possible alternatives.

A close look at Berlin has revealed how sociotechnical alternatives have often coexisted alongside the dominant system, either complementing or challenging it. Sometimes these new configurations proved very durable, creating long-standing hybrids with existing systems. This was the case with district heating, which emerged in the 1920s as an alternative to coal-fired heating, developed as a by-product of local electricity generation, and became a key component of energy provision in an insular West Berlin. Like many other examples in this book, it demonstrates that a city can host multiple sociotechnical configurations at any one moment in time. Today, for instance, Berlin boasts a large-scale system of combined sewers, but also technologies for stormwater retention at the meso level of select urban neighbourhoods and for gray-water recycling at the micro level of individual buildings. Such infrastructural palimpsests, combining the old and the new, represent a fruitful line of research into a time-sensitive technological urbanism.[3] They can be revealed fully, it should be noted, only with the help of in-depth historical analysis.

On a methodological level, this book has demonstrated that it is feasible, as well as desirable, to analyze sociotechnical assemblages from an historical perspective.[4] Studying how particular configurations get dis- and reassembled does not need to be restricted to a brief point in time, but can equally—and instructively—set these processes in their broader historical context. Historicizing assemblages in this way not only embraces longer-term processes of adaptation, it also opens up the analysis to the multiple temporalities that come together in any sociotechnical configuration. It enabled us, in the case of Berlin, to observe how, for instance, the time frames of infrastructure planning, stretching over decades, were frequently undermined by short-term dips in demand for energy and water during times of hardship. It also permitted analysis of interplay between the past, present, and future. On many occasions in the past, imagined futures for Berlin's infrastructure systems have framed strategies for the present and been re-invoked in later years to justify a particular course of action. This was the case, for example, over Berlin's ambitious plan of the 1920s to harness huge quantities of water from the surrounding region to secure the city's development into a metropolis of twelve million inhabitants by the end of the century. Although not implemented to anything like the full extent, this plan had a lasting impact on the way Berlin's water supply system was conceived in subsequent years, with echoes resonating into the early post-unification days of expansionism. The temporal categories of past, present, and future may appear distinct, but in reality—this book argues—their boundaries are fuzzy and their interdependencies hugely significant.

Urban Politics through Infrastructure

This study of urban infrastructure across five political regimes, ranging from democracy to fascism and state socialism, has provided a unique opportunity to explore the technopolitics of the city through multiple prisms. What difference—if any—did regime change make to the workings of Berlin's sociotechnical systems for energy and water? How did urban politics manifest itself in infrastructure? Conversely, how compliant did the city's infrastructures prove to their political masters?

Our focus on the political history of Berlin's infrastructures has revealed a wide range of political projects in which they were enlisted. Some of these urban functions were a constant across the various regimes ruling twentieth-century Berlin. The city's water and energy utilities were always used to support the local economy and act as model municipal employers. Their tariffs were generally designed to balance the structural demands of infrastructure investment with the social considerations of affordability. The municipal budget was always reliant to a greater or lesser degree on revenue derived from the utilities' profits. Infrastructure was regularly enrolled in modernizing the city's housing stock. At certain times, this supportive role for municipal economic, social, or fiscal policy proved critical in dealing with a crisis, as during the Depression, when Berlin's utilities helped sustain employment levels and social welfare payments.

Other functions performed by utilities for the city were specific to certain political constellations. One obvious example is the way in which infrastructure was used to sustain basic services in both parts of the city following political division in 1948–1949. West Berlin's strategy of maximizing urban autarky was predicated upon becoming self-dependent in the generation of electricity and production of town gas. The spatial reordering of East Berlin's sewers, water pipes, and power lines away from the border with West Berlin was a material manifestation of separation and reorientation around the territory of the DDR. To cite a more recent instance, the brief incursion of Berlin's energy and water utilities into international and multi-utility markets following reunification was a deliberate attempt to use infrastructure as a vanguard of the city in a globalized and liberalized world.

The multiple functions performed by Berlin's infrastructure should not, however, suggest that enrollment in municipal policy was always straightforward or successful. Water and energy infrastructures often proved, to quote Karen Bakker, "uncooperative commodities."[5] Sometimes their physical properties posed major limitations to municipal ambition, as with the local air pollution produced by having so many power stations and gas works concentrated in West Berlin. Sometimes it was their ownership structure, as in the case of the East Berlin branch of the power utility Bewag that for many years still belonged to international shareholders. Sometimes it was the dominant logic of "build and supply" that impeded efforts to promote energy or water conservation. Infrastructure could not be instrumentalized at will, only on the basis of a sound understanding of how it worked and how it could be made to work.

What the Berlin case confirms is that infrastructures are extremely difficult to govern.[6] Utility managers and city politicians may have claimed to have everything under control, but this control was always only partial and often elusive. Maintaining an existing sociotechnical assemblage—let alone trying to establish a new one—required a huge effort of coordination. It involved securing the right combination of technological innovation, political support, investment capital, favorable consumption patterns, regulatory frameworks, natural resources, human expertise, and environmental sinks, to mention just some of the most prominent components. If any one component failed to perform to expectations, it could jeopardize the system, regardless of the human will to succeed. If any component changed as a result of, say, a shift in political regime (as with the Nazi seizure of power), unacceptable levels of environmental pollution (as in 1980s West Berlin), or a shortage of funding (as in East Berlin throughout), the threat of system destabilization was always present.

Looking beyond generic phenomena of infrastructure governance, it is possible to identify distinctive characteristics of infrastructure politics for each era of Berlin's recent history. During the Weimar Republic it was a *politics of redistribution*, in which energy and water utilities helped deliver the unitary city with uniform services at affordable prices. Under Nazi rule it was a *politics of attrition*, marked above all by the erosion of municipal and democratic control. During the 1940s it was a *politics of survival*, keeping the city going with basic services in the face of war and division. In East Berlin it was a *politics of illusion*, characterized by the mismatch between socialist aspirations and realities. In West Berlin it was a *politics of protection*, with infrastructures reconfigured around the political geography of the insular city. Today, it is a *politics of representation* that seems to capture the thrust of infrastructure governance, with diverse visions of the networked city competing for influence.

Which actor groups have proved most influential in governing Berlin's infrastructures? Over the past century recurring figures take center stage. The utility directors have always played a lead role, often seizing the initiative, as with the expansionist plans of the 1920s or the energy autarky strategy for West Berlin. Yet, their influence was generally dependent on the backing of the city government. When the city government, municipal administration, and utility leadership all pulled in the same direction, the urban governance of Berlin's infrastructures proved particularly effective. This occurred during two periods: in the 1920s after the creation of Greater Berlin and in the 1950s in defense of West Berlin. In both instances coordinated action to serve a common good—the city and its citizens—was a powerful way of using infrastructure to the full.

By contrast, when the utilities grew independent of political control (as in the later years of West Berlin), when they were subordinated to state institutions (as in East Berlin), or when infrastructure planning lost political support (as in the reunified city of the late 1990s), infrastructure was far less effective as a force for urban development. The Nazi era epitomizes this finding. Despite all the criticism heaped on municipal infrastructure policy by the Nazis prior to 1933, they had no alternative concept to implement when they came to power. Their governance of urban infrastructure involved subjugating it to the new political order and nebulous national policy but, otherwise, pursuing largely the same technological systems as before.

One actor whose role has changed radically in recent years is the urban citizen. The citizen has traditionally been regarded by those providing energy and water services as a passive consumer. As the book reveals, however passive and uniform utilities might have envisioned their customers, this ideal rarely lived up to reality. Users of energy and water services reminded providers continuously that they were neither an amorphous group with predictable needs nor indifferent to the standards and costs of service provision.[7] Berlin's electricity and gas utilities were confronted with the vagaries of energy demand during the Depression, coming to appreciate the value of household demand at times of declining industrial production. Its water utility grew mindful of the close relationship between water demand and groundwater levels in the city, having to respond to problems of damp in buildings whenever water consumption dropped sharply, as in the aftermath of the Second World War and again in the 1990s. The collapse in water demand by 40 percent in the decade following reunification has, indeed, posed one of the hardest challenges ever for Berlin's infrastructure managers.

Not all urban citizens have been content with their prescribed role as compliant consumers. By the 1970s West Berlin's energy utilities were coming in for growing public criticism of their apparent disregard for air quality, landscape protection, and resource conservation. Protests against the siting and design of new power stations by local residents and environmental groups generated interest in alternative ways of assessing and meeting the city's energy needs. Their success in the courts, challenging the logic of "build and supply" so inherent to Berlin's utilities, inspired a novel environmentalist approach that has since come to influence infrastructure policy significantly. Today's social movements campaigning for urban infrastructures to be more accountable, environmentally sustainable, and socially equitable are standing on the shoulders of those who—in both East and West Berlin—stood up against service providers to articulate alternative visions of sociotechnical configurations. The debates they have unleashed have created not only novel perspectives on energy and water provision, but also engaged publics, opening up new possibilities for democracy in urban energy and water systems.[8] Berlin's infrastructures are increasingly a terrain of contestation. Previously invisible in the public domain, they have become conduits of a politicized urban culture.

A reflection on the book's contribution to technopolitics would not be complete without a discussion of what the Berlin case reveals about the multi-scalar nature of sociotechnical systems. The Berlin case is highly instructive on the relationship between the municipal, national, and even international politics of infrastructure. The insistence on the city as the only territorial unit of concern was always delusory. This applied in the 1920s, when the creation of Greater Berlin nurtured a culture of introversion by municipal politicians, who generally failed to appreciate the extent of resentment in the surrounding region, the erosion of political support for cities in Germany at large, and the impact of the Wall Street Crash on business confidence in the city. It also applied to West Berlin, whose celebrated resilience as an urban bulwark of the free world was predicated upon being protected militarily by the Western Allies and sustained financially by the federal government in Bonn. Municipal self-dependence might have been an aspiration at certain times in Berlin's history, but it was never a full reality. The city could not render itself immune from national strategies of energy and water provision, especially under authoritarian regimes. Examples include the forced connection to the Ruhr gas supply in the late 1930s, the requirement for East Berlin to import electricity from the DDR's lignite mining region, and the vagaries of Soviet policy on delivering natural gas to West Berlin. Berlin's infrastructures, however urban in design and purpose, were subject to forces that reached far beyond the city limits, whether it was foreign loans in the 1920s, Nazi energy policy in the 1930s, military occupation in the 1940s, or Cold War geopolitics in the 1950s. These examples illustrate the need for future research to take far greater account of the broader scalar contexts within which urban infrastructures work.

Infrastructural Interdependence

A further novel contribution of the book to research on urban infrastructures lies in its treatment of five different infrastructure sectors: electricity, gas, district heating, water, and sanitation. Particularly unusual is its long-term analysis of the relationship between these sectors in a single city. What can the Berlin experience tell us about the similarities and differences, interdependencies and contestations between these sectors of piped infrastructure? What attempts have been made to take an integrated, cross-sectoral approach to infrastructure policy and how have these efforts fared?

It is ironic that the creation of Greater Berlin in 1920, an ambitious act of territorial integration, simultaneously institutionalized segregation between the city's infrastructure sectors. The Stadtwerk model of a multi-utility municipal enterprise, which was widespread in Germany and had existed in some of the communities amalgamated into Greater Berlin, was displaced by the organizational structure practiced in the core city: separate utilities for each sector. When these large utilities became share companies in 1923, they developed an even greater sense of independence, not only from the city government, but also from one another. Competition between the city's own electricity and gas utilities was to rage, on and off, throughout the following century. This might have helped keep energy tariffs low, but it effectively blocked all attempts to develop a coordinated energy policy for Berlin. This applied to the late 1920s, as electrification reconfigured the energy landscape, to the 1960s, when district heating from power plants competed with emergent gas heating, and up to the present day when—to frustrate coordination further—the two utilities are now privately owned. By contrast, Berlin did lead the way in Germany by integrating its water and sanitation utilities. These were amalgamated in East Berlin in the 1950s as part of socialist water policy and put under joint management in West Berlin a decade later to assist the heavily indebted wastewater utility.

Organizational fragmentation and competition could not, however, conceal the various interdependencies between infrastructure sectors that have expressed themselves across the past 100 years. Up until the 1950s, coal was the common fuel driving all infrastructure plant, whether power stations, gas works, water pumps, or sewage treatment facilities. This became painfully obvious at times of severe coal shortages, as in the winters of 1946 and 1947 and again for West Berlin during the blockade of 1948–1949. The allocation of extremely limited coal reserves at these times was emblematic of coal's critical significance to the operability of the city's infrastructures. After the 1950s, as most plant became electrified, it was electricity that became the common source of power. This created a new level of dependency of the gas, water, and sanitation utilities on the electricity utility Bewag, which the latter was always able to exploit, financially and politically.

More creative were the cross-sectoral interfaces that emerged from the use of by-products of resource processing. From the late 1920s onward, methane gas derived from sewage treatment was used to power vehicles and generators, fats and oils were extracted from wastewater for use as a fuel, and the residual heat from electricity generation was captured to warm buildings. Some of these alternative technologies—for sewage gas and recycled oils—became associated with the Nazi quest for national autarky and were subsequently ostracized as a result. Others, such as district heating, enjoyed a boom in both East and West Berlin after the war and the division of the city. Today's concerted efforts to exploit synergies between processes of water and energy provision—for instance, deriving gas from waste, heat from wastewater, or energy from biomass on former sewage farms—are unwitting descendants of these historical experiments at infrastructural interfaces.

Cross-sectoral imitation has been a distinctive feature of infrastructure policy and management across the century. A strategy developed for one sector was often copied by another, sometimes without due consideration of the socio-material differences involved. The campaign of the city government to municipalize its utilities fully in the 1920s was born out of a desire to treat all utilities equally in this regard, seeing no principled difference between municipalizing water and, say, gas provision. In West Berlin during the 1950s, self-generation of the city's electricity by its power utility was held up by other utility directors as a model for their own sector, notwithstanding the huge differences between them. In the case of wastewater, the attempt to copy Bewag's model of urban autarky in service provision was revealed to be wholly unrealistic and was soon discarded. Similarly, the privatization drive in the 1990s was characterized by the rationale of selling the utilities to relieve urban debt while making them more commercialized and global in scope, disregarding any differences between them in the kinds of services provided or resources used.

These examples illustrate how disregard for the distinctive features of infrastructure sectors can easily frustrate efforts to enrol them in political projects. These differences can be material, as in the case of wastewater treatment, where reliance on sewage farms outside the city rendered self-sufficiency an illusion for West Berlin. They can also be social, as witnessed by resistance to privatization, which proved far stronger over water than over gas or electricity owing to the emotive significance of this life-giving resource. This points to a promising avenue for future research on multiple infrastructures that explores the socio-material constitution of each sector in any one place and time and how this affects the relationship between sectors.

Infrastructured Metabolisms

The creation of Greater Berlin in 1920 may have unified a city, but it also divided a region. Henceforth, the prime concern for Berlin authorities was internal integration of the enlarged city. The surrounding region was, to Berlin's politicians and utility directors, peripheral: figuratively and physically. Arguably, it has remained like this to the present day, with subsequent threats to the city's integrity—as during the Cold War—only consolidating the notion of Berlin's distinctiveness from its surroundings. Treating Brandenburg as a hinterland serving the metropolis was no better expressed than through the water and energy infrastructures linking the two territories. The areas surrounding Berlin have long acted as source and sink for the metabolic flows needed to keep the metropolis running. At the same time, this material relationship reveals deep dependencies of the city on its regional, national, and even international contexts that the Berlin authorities often chose to ignore.

First and foremost, Berlin has always been dependent for its drinking water on surface and groundwater sources which flow through the wider region. The grand plans of the 1920s to capture ever larger quantities of this water to supply the growing city were devised without any serious consideration of their impact on the region's landscape, environment, or economy. Similarly, Berlin's sewage disposal was almost wholly dependent on the sewage farms—and, later, sewage treatment plants—located outside the city. Berlin, indeed, owned the extensive land in Brandenburg on which its sewage was treated, feeling even less compulsion to consult the local communities over expansionist plans. This attitude found its apogee in the Nazi era, when the land used for sewage treatment was designated for huge settlements of impoverished smallholders providing food for themselves and the metropolis. The wild scheme, born out of an obsession with national autarky, envisaged a reordering of Berlin's metabolisms around nutrient and water recycling in the region alongside the social ordering of the urban poor.

Only when the territory surrounding Berlin came under the tutelage of a major power—the Soviet Union—after the Second World War did the relationship between city and region become more respectful. The agreements reached over the treatment of sewage from West and East during the 1950s are indicative of the mutual recognition that physical interdependencies demanded solutions acceptable to both sides. No such compunctions were held by West Berlin when it came to locating new power stations. These were sited, as a rule, on the edge of the city, preferably where the prevailing wind would take harmful emissions away to the surrounding region. By contrast, the amalgamation of East Berlin's utilities into national and subnational organizations did create greater opportunities for a regional perspective on infrastructure planning. This is visible in the shift of electricity generation from the city to the Lusatia mining region and in the orientation of water management planning around river basins. However, energy and water policy in the DDR were both geared to maximizing resource use to sustain the national economy, resulting in catastrophic damage to the region's ecology.

Examples of this kind have illustrated throughout the book how important infrastructures have been in mediating relations between natural resources, energy sources, and the city. They are witness to the "infrastructured metabolisms" of modern Berlin. Infrastructures have channeled flows of water and energy in and out of the city. In doing so, they have significantly shaped the landscape of both the city and the surrounding region. More than this, they have exerted a powerful influence over the socio-material relations that enable life in a city like Berlin. These relations can appear distinctly urban, as in the schemes to replenish local groundwater resources, build urban gas works, or cross-subsidize social welfare. Often, however, this urban focus masks wider spatial dependencies, such as—in these three instances, respectively—on regional rivers, geopolitical vulnerabilities, and national budget constraints. Many geographies have been co-opted into making Berlin urban.

What the historical panorama of this book has also revealed is that these "infrastructured metabolisms" were often the target of contestation. In the early decades of the twentieth century conflicts over energy and water use were conducted not in the public realm, but between experts. They could, nevertheless, be fierce, as the long-standing dispute over whether and how to treat Berlin's wastewater testifies. At different times the case for reusing wastewater to increase agricultural production was made in the name of resource efficiency, national autarky, and socialist rationalism, provoking strong ripostes from civil engineers on each occasion. Since the 1970s, criticisms of how Berlin's infrastructures mediate resource use have broadened substantially. Environmentalism has transformed public perceptions of the city's utilities. What originally began as popular protests against the siting of power stations within the city limits or against excessive water use has today developed into a fundamental critique of the "build and supply" paradigm that has dominated infrastructure policy for a century. Civic groups, invigorated by the re-municipalization campaigns for water and energy in recent years, are not content to criticize, but are devising alternative visions for urban infrastructure.

Environmental sustainability, social justice, and democratic accountability are cornerstones of these new sociotechnical imaginaries. They are attracting global attention to Berlin as a site of experimentation and a potential model for infrastructure futures.

Usable Pasts of Urban Infrastructure

This book has sought to build a bridge between historical and contemporary research on urban infrastructures. It has, to paraphrase the introductory quote to this chapter, reinterpreted the past in the light of how we see the present. This has entailed telling the history of Berlin's infrastructures up until today, but also framing the historical analysis in terms of concepts being used to interpret ongoing energy and water transitions in cities. Ambitious in thematic scope and temporal scale, the book has nevertheless been strongly focused on the experience of a single city. It is hoped that the approach taken and the insight drawn from this one case can inspire researchers to take a fresh look at urban infrastructure histories. This would involve exploring mature infrastructures for signs of the unusual, considering more than just path dependence or transitions, and studying the dynamics of sociotechnical assemblages over a long period. Above all, it would involve conducting a time-sensitive analysis of technological urbanism in its multiple, place-specific enactments. The case of Berlin may be exceptional, but this has served only to reveal in sharp profile phenomena that may well be waiting to be uncovered in cities that appear more "normal."

What, then, is the overarching significance of Berlin's infrastructure history for urban and sociotechnical transitions today? How can historical knowledge inspire and inform urban futures? Invoking the past to speak to the present is, of course, fraught with potential pitfalls. As Andreas Huyssen warns us in his book on Berlin: "Memory as re-presentation, as making present, is always in danger of collapsing the constitutive tension between past and present."[9] He makes the case, though, for "usable pasts" as a form of productive remembering.[10] Drawing out the "usable past" of a city and its infrastructures from Berlin's recent history is the final task of this book.

Looking back across the past century with the benefit of hindsight, there are three dimensions to a "usable past" that emerge from this study of Berlin. First are the legacies from the past that continue to shape the sociotechnical configurations of infrastructure to this day. In Berlin's case, the physical networks built up to serve each half of the city during the Cold War have resulted in redundancy and overcapacity that weigh heavily on utilities that are today expected to keep costs low. The reliance of both parts of the city on fossil fuels (coal and oil in the West, lignite in the East) is making it hard for Berlin to decarbonize today. The culture of dependency that characterized both West and

East Berlin during the era of division is still discernible in the way the city government expects utilities to follow the urban policy line. The ineffectiveness of past campaigns to encourage households and businesses to use less energy during periods of fuel or electricity shortage has made the city's utilities and regulators skeptical of incentives to reduce energy end-use today. Understanding these kinds of legacy from the past is essential to avoid disappointment when pursuing new ways of enrolling infrastructures in urban futures.

The second way of using the past productively is to challenge historical accounts that are—by accident or design—overly selective, incomplete, or simply inaccurate. We began this book with a stroll around a power station in Berlin to illustrate the limitations of relying on a purely engineering account of infrastructure history. An overarching purpose of this book has, indeed, been to rectify this imbalance by focusing, rather, on the politics of urban infrastructure. It is not only the social that is often missing from earlier histories of Berlin's energy and water systems. There has been huge reluctance to engage with periods of the city's history that are uncomfortable to the collective memory. This applies in part to East Berlin under state socialism, but in particular to the experience of Berlin's infrastructures under Nazi rule. This period of history is avidly avoided in most infrastructure histories. If discussed at all, it is dismissed as an aberration.[11] This historical amnesia has not only hidden alternative technologies, such as around waste-to-energy or wastewater reuse, from closer scrutiny, but has also overlooked how authoritarian regimes provoked contestations over infrastructure which have a pertinence to debates today.

The third value of the past is as a source of inspiration. Berlin's infrastructure history is littered with lessons—positive and negative—on how to derive urban utility from a utility. We have already noted how infrastructure governance was at its most effective when the city government, administration, and utilities worked in unison. The truly integrative approach to urban development and infrastructure policy that characterized Greater Berlin in the 1920s, but also West Berlin in the 1950s, is highly instructive for current attempts to enrol the city's utilities in flagship urban strategies. Understanding how, in those earlier days, a plethora of social and technical elements were brought into association with one another can be immensely helpful in learning how to organize a desirable sociotechnical assemblage today.[12] Conversely, negative experiences in the past, if recognized, can help avert similar mistakes in the future. Given the extraordinary parallels between the privatization of the city's power utility Bewag in 1931 and again in 1997, one can only ruefully reflect on what problems might have been avoided in the late 1990s if the earlier instance had been mustered for critical appraisal at the time.

What practitioners and scholars alike need to appreciate, this book has argued throughout, is how worthwhile it can be to delve into a city's history from the unusual angle of its urban infrastructures. Infrastructures, in their multiple guises, are potent conduits of the urban condition. They channel life-supporting flows through the city, transform natural resources into usable services, enact political aspirations, reflect power relations, and attract contestation. By explicating these dimensions to Berlin's infrastructures, this book has sought to dispel the legendary invisibility of "underground urbanism." Instilling this message in future generations of civil engineers, social scientists, and urban historians is the task in hand.

Notes

Chapter 1

1. See Bruno Latour and Emilie Hermant's online exploration *Paris: Invisible City*, with its discussion of the invisible work performed by the city's engineers and technicians.

2. Hughes, *Networks of Power*; Dame, *Elektropolis Berlin*. The quote by James Joll is cited in Hård and Stippak, "Discourses on the Modern City," 41. In the 1920s Berlin boasted around 135,000 employees in the electrical industry, primarily at the globally renowned electrotechnical companies Siemens & Haske and AEG, see Czada, *Die Berliner Elektroindustrie*, 300, and Binder, *Elektrifizierung als Vision*, 44.

3. Hård and Stippak, "Progressive Dreams."

4. Binder, *Elektrifizierung als Vision*, 44, where she cites the title of Boberg, Fichter, and Gillen, *Exerzierfeld der Moderne*.

5. Friedrich, *Hitler's Berlin*.

6. Cited in Whyte and Frisby, *Metropolis Berlin*, 386.

7. Cochrane, "Making up Meanings," 22. This sentiment is not restricted to Berlin. Latour and Hermant observe that "Paris is constantly obsessed by totalizations that could give meaning to the city in the making," *Paris: Invisible City*, 88.

8. Laak, "Infra-Strukturgeschichte," 389.

9. This is in contrast to other recent books on urban infrastructure which place users at the center of analysis, for instance Sebastián Ureta's study of "human devices" in Santiago's new urban rail network, *Assembling Policy*. For a good analysis of everyday use of electricity in Berlin, see Binder, *Elektrifizierung als Vision*.

10. On Berlin's transportation systems, see Bodenschatz and Polinna, *100 Jahre Groß-Berlin*; Wolf, *Berlin—Weltstadt ohne Auto?*; Merrill, "Identities in Transit"; Porombka, *Medialität urbaner Infrastrukturen*.

11. Huyssen, *Present Pasts*, 49. Berlin's global attraction is reflected in other works by Ladd, *Ghosts of Berlin*, Wise, *Capital Dilemma*, and Till, *New Berlin*.

12. Bernt, Grell, and Holm, "Introduction," 13.

13. Latham, "Berlin and Everywhere Else."

14. Cochrane, "Making up Meanings."

15. Flyvbjerg, "Five Misunderstandings," 229.

16. Summerton, "Introductory Essay," 2.

17. Huyssen, *Present Pasts*, 51.

18. Swyngedouw, "Modernity and Hybridity," 443.

19. Two popular histories of Berlin covering the whole period focus on national, rather than municipal, politics and broader cultural developments, drawing on existing published material only. These are: Large, *Berlin*, published in 2000, and Bisky, *Berlin*, first published in late 2019.

20. See, for instance, Kotowski and Reichhardt, *Berlin als Hauptstadt*; Elkins and Hofmeister, *Berlin*; Schlegelmilch, "Tendenzen der wirtschaftlichen und sozialen Entwicklung Berlins"; Ribbe, *Berlin 1945–2000*.

21. See, for instance, Engeli, *Gustav Böß*; Büsch, *Beiträge zur Geschichte der Berliner Demokratie*.

22. Hachtmann, Schaarschmidt, and Süß, "Einleitung. Berlin im Nationalsozialismus," 11; Wildt and Kreuzmüller, "Stadt und Gesellschaft im Nationalsozialismus."

23. Typically, neither of the two histories covering the whole twentieth century—Large, *Berlin*, and Bisky, *Berlin*—address Berlin's energy or water infrastructures.

24. Wildt and Kreuzmüller, *Berlin, 1933–1945*.

25. Büsch, *Geschichte der Berliner Kommunalwirtschaft*.

26. Hughes, *Networks of Power*.

27. Hoppe and Oevermann, *Metropole Berlin*.

28. Templin, *Wasser für die Volksgemeinschaft*; Bähr and Erker, *Netz-Werke*.

29. Bärthel, *Die Geschichte der Gasversorgung in Berlin*; Bärthel, *Wasser für Berlin*; Bärthel, *Geklärt!*; Bärthel, "Anlagen und Bauten der Elektrizitätserzeugung"; Bärthel, "Anlagen und Bauten der Fernwärmeversorgung."

30. Tepasse, *Stadttechnik im Städtebau Berlins. 1945–1999*; Tepasse, *Stadttechnik im Städtebau Berlins. 20. Jahrhundert*.

31. Dame, *Elektropolis Berlin*.

32. Mohajeri, *100 Jahre Berliner Wasserversorgung*; Eiden, *Versorgungswirtschaft als regionale Organisation*.

33. Thorsten Dame's work is an exception in analyzing municipal processes of negotiation around the architecture of electricity, *Elektropolis Berlin*.

34. Monstadt, *Die Modernisierung der Stromversorgung*; Beveridge, *Politics of Inevitability*; Hüesker, *Kommunale Daseinsvorsorge in der Wasserwirtschaft*; Beveridge, Hüesker, and Naumann, "From Post-Politics to a Politics of Possibility?"; Becker, Naumann, and Moss, "Between Coproduction and Commons."

35. Harvey, Jensen, and Morita, "Introduction," 3.

36. Schnitzler, *Democracy's Infrastructure*, 21.

37. Edwards, "Infrastructure and Modernity," 191.

38. Niewöhner, "Anthropology of Infrastructures," 120.

39. Wittfogel, *Oriental Despotism*; Worster, *Rivers of Empire*.

40. Prominent works include Hughes, *Networks of Power*, and Laak, "Infra-Strukturgeschichte." See also Obertreis et al., "Water, Infrastructure and Political Rule."

41. See van der Vleuten, "Understanding Network Societies"; Högselius, Kaijser, and van der Vleuten, *Europe's Infrastructure Transition*; Engels and Schenk, "Infrastrukturen der Macht."

42. See the special issues of the *Journal of Urban History* in 1979 and 1987 edited by Mark Rose and Joel Tarr.

43. Cronon, *Nature's Metropolis*.

44. Melosi, *Sanitary City*.

45. Schott, *Die Vernetzung der Stadt*.

46. Coutard, *Governance of Large Technical Systems*; Coutard, Hanley, and Zimmermann, *Sustaining Urban Networks*; McFarlane and Rutherford, "Political Infrastructures."

47. Graham and Marvin, *Splintering Urbanism*; Gandy, *Concrete and Clay*; Kaika, *City of Flows*.

48. See, for example, Binder, *Elektrifizierung als Vision*, 37, for the widely held view that infrastructures, once established, lose their interest.

49. Cf. Russell, "Writing Energy History," 34, on the risks of ignoring alternatives to dominant (heating) systems.

50. A notable recent exception is a special issue on interconnectivity between urban infrastructures in *Urban Studies*. See the introduction to this special issue by the guest editors, Monstadt and Coutard, "Cities in an Era of Interfacing Infrastructures."

51. Cf. Farías and Bender, *Urban Assemblages*.

52. A full list of the interviews cited is given at the end of the bibliography.

Chapter 2

1. Till, *New Berlin*, 8.

2. Ladd, *Ghosts of Berlin*; Huyssen, *Present Pasts*.

3. Karen Till's book, *New Berlin*, 196, reveals how "Berlin's materiality is haunted by past visions for the future and contemporary desires for the past."

4. Harvey, Jensen, and Morita, "Introduction," 3.

5. Harvey, Jensen, and Morita, "Introduction," 5.

6. Star, "Ethnography of Infrastructure," 381–382.

7. Hughes, *Networks of Power*; Summerton, "Introductory Essay," 3; Star, "Ethnography of Infrastructure"; Rohracher, "Die Wechselwirkung technischen und institutionellen Wandels."

8. Harvey, Jensen, and Morita, "Introduction," 20–24.

9. Harvey, Jensen, and Morita, "Introduction," 24 (italics in original).

10. Coutard, Hanley, and Zimmermann, *Sustaining Urban Networks*, 1.

11. Engel and Schenk, "Infrastrukturen der Macht," 23–24; Niewöhner, "Anthropology of Infrastructures of Society."

12. Swyngedouw, *Liquid Power*; Laak, "Infra-Strukturgeschichte," 370–373.

13. Edwards, "Infrastructure and Modernity," 186.

14. On the strong path dependence characteristic of infrastructures, see Melosi, "Path Dependence and Urban History." On the sociotechnical imaginaries they often evoke, see Jasanoff, "Future Imperfect."

15. Otter, "Locating Matter"; Anand, Gupta, and Appel, *Promise of Infrastructure*; Swyngedouw, "Modernity and Hybridity"; Gandy, *Concrete and Clay*.

16. Control over infrastructure has always been crucial to modern government. Some scholars have attributed to infrastructures a formative influence on forms of rule, notably Wittfogel, *Oriental Despotism*. Others have observed a correlation between the dominant mode of governance and the organization of infrastructure systems, Mayntz, "Grosse technische Systeme." Gandy, "Rethinking Urban Metabolism," 373, talks of water as "a brutal delineator of social power"; cf. Obertreis et al., "Water, Infrastructure and Political Rule." This does not prevent infrastructures often being presented as being beyond politics, serving some overarching "common good," Laak, *Alles im Fluss*, 21.

17. Edwards, "Infrastructure and Modernity," 185.

18. Graham and Marvin, *Splintering Urbanism*; Gandy, *Concrete and Clay*; McFarlane and Rutherford, "Political Infrastructures"; Monstadt, "Conceptualizing the Political Ecology"; Bulkeley et al., *Cities and Low Carbon Transitions*.

19. Graham and Marvin, *Splintering Urbanism*, 18.

20. Amin, "Lively Infrastructure," 137.

21. Dodson, "The Global Infrastructure Turn."

22. Graham and Thrift, "Out of Order." Cf. Larkin, "The Politics and Poetics of Infrastructure."

23. Williams, *Notes on the Underground*, 52, with explicit reference to Mumford's early work. Vanesa Castán Broto calls infrastructure "an indissoluble part of urban experience," *Urban Energy Landscapes*, 22.

24. Lawhon and Murphy, "Socio-Technical Regimes," 360. The transitions literature is discussed later in this chapter.

25. Shove and Walker, "CAUTION! Transitions ahead"; McFarlane and Rutherford, "Political Infrastructures"; Hodson and Marvin, "Can Cities Shape Socio-Technical Transitions?"; Bulkeley et al., *Cities and Low Carbon Transitions*; Coenen, Benneworth, and Truffer, "Toward a Spatial Perspective."

26. Lees, "Rematerializing Geography"; Latham and McCormack, "Moving Cities"; Bakker and Bridge, "Material Worlds?"; Otter, "Locating Matter."

27. Bakker, *Uncooperative Commodity*; Kaika, "Dams as Symbols of Modernization."

28. Otter, "Locating Matter," 56.

29. Graham and Marvin, *Splintering Urbanism*; Heynen, Kaika, and Swyngedouw, "Urban Political Ecology"; McFarlane, "Assemblage and Critical Urban Praxis"; Bridge et al., "Geographies of Energy Transition."

30. Rutherford, "Rethinking the Relational."

31. Furlong, "Small Technologies, Big Change"; Coutard and Guy, "STS and the City."

32. Bulkeley et al., *Cities and Low Carbon Transitions*; Hodson, Geels, and McMeekin, "Reconfiguring Urban Sustainability Transitions," 8.

33. Rutherford and Coutard, "Urban Energy Transitions."

34. Rutherford, "Rethinking the Relational." Cf. Castán Broto, *Urban Energy Landscapes*, 20.

35. On "infrastructuration," see Ureta, *Assembling Policy*, 15–16.

36. Hughes, *Networks of Power*; Tarr and Dupuy, *Technology and the Rise of the Networked City*; Melosi, *Sanitary City*.

37. Summerton, "Introductory Essay," 1.

38. Sovacool and Hess, "Ordering Theories."

39. An example is Sebastián Ureta's study of a public transportation project in Santiago de Chile, *Assembling Policy*.

40. E.g. Truffer and Coenen, "Environmental Innovation and Sustainability Transitions."

41. Hughes, *Networks of Power*. Cf. LaPorte, *Social Responses*; Summerton, "Introductory Essay"; Coutard, *Governance of Large Technical Systems*.

42. Melosi, *Sanitary City*.

43. Laak, "Infra-Strukturgeschichte," 368.

44. Path dependence has come in for considerable criticism that its periodization of sociotechnical evolution is too linear, it neglects agency beyond the original "system builders," and it focuses only on large technical systems, Joerges, "High Variability Discourse"; Rutherford and Coutard, "Urban Energy Transitions"; Furlong, "STS beyond the 'Modern Infrastructure Ideal'"; Jasanoff, "Future Imperfect." Some of these criticisms are met by more recent research on "path creation" to infrastructure systems that explores the "mindful deviation" from an existing sociotechnical configuration to a new one, Simmie, "Path Dependence," 770, cf. Lovio and Kivimaa, "Comparing Alternative Path Creation."

45. Geels, "Technological Transitions."

46. Geels and Schot, "Typology of Sociotechnical Transition Pathways."

47. Geels, "Ontologies, Socio-Technical Transitions."

48. Coenen and Truffer, "Places and Spaces of Sustainability Transitions"; Späth and Rohracher, "Local Demonstrations for Global Transitions."

49. Geels and Schot, "Typology of Sociotechnical Transition Pathways."

50. Geels, "The Multi-Level Perspective."

51. Coenen and Truffer, "Places and Spaces of Sustainability Transitions."

52. Furlong, "STS beyond the 'Modern Infrastructure Ideal,'" 140.

53. Smith, Stirling, and Berkhout, "The Governance of Sustainable Socio-Technical Transitions"; McFarlane and Rutherford, "Political Infrastructures"; Meadowcroft, "What about the Politics?"; Bulkeley et al., *Cities and Low Carbon Transitions*.

54. Lawhon and Murphy, "Socio-Technical Regimes"; Coenen and Truffer, "Places and Spaces of Sustainability Transitions"; Bulkeley, Castán Broto, and Maassen, "Low-Carbon Transitions." In response to these criticisms transitions scholars have, in recent years, adapted the MLP framework and refined their conceptualization of transition, see Geels et al., "The Enactment of Socio-Technical Transition Pathways."

55. Reference to Fernand Braudel's approach of the *longue durée* is deliberately avoided here, see *Mediterranean and the Mediterranean World*. Although his work also takes a long-term perspective, it was designed to highlight continuity and incremental change and thereby contextualize short-term ruptures and discontinuities as events within broader cycles. My book, by contrast, does not privilege trajectories of inertia, just as it does not privilege disruptive events.

56. Notable exceptions are the works of Melosi, *Sanitary City*, and Gandy, *Concrete and Clay*. A good example beyond urban studies is Timothy Mitchell's book, *Carbon Democracy*, on the age of oil, spanning over 100 years.

57. Bulkeley et al., *Cities and Low Carbon Transitions*; Furlong, "STS beyond the 'Modern Infrastructure Ideal'"; Lawhon et al., "Thinking through Heterogeneous Infrastructure Configurations."

58. Graham and Thrift, "Out of Order"; Dolata and Werle, "'Bringing Technology Back in'"; Hodson et al., "Conclusion"; Moss, "Socio-Technical Change"; Hodson et al., "Reconfiguring Urban Sustainability Transitions."

59. Fuenfschilling and Truffer, "Structuration of Socio-Technical Regimes"; Furlong, "STS beyond the 'Modern Infrastructure Ideal'"; Haarstad and Wanvik, "Carbonscapes and beyond."

60. McGuirk, Bulkeley, and Dowling, "Configuring Urban Carbon Governance," 147; cf. Farías and Bender, *Urban Assemblages*; Collier, *Post-Soviet Social*; Mitchell, *Carbon Democracy*; Ureta, *Assembling Policy*; Schnitzler, *Democracy's Infrastructure*; Bridge, "Map Is Not the Territory."

61. Anderson et al., "On Assemblages and Geography"; Moss, Becker, and Gailing, "Energy Transitions and Materiality."

62. McFarlane, "Assemblage and Critical Urban Praxis."

63. Most notably by Jane Bennett in her pioneering piece on the power blackout in New York City in August 2003, "Agency of Assemblages."

64. De Landa, *New Philosophy of Society*, 12.

65. Maassen, "Heterogeneity of Lock-In"; Schnitzler, *Democracy's Infrastructure*.

66. Bakker and Bridge, "Material Worlds?," 16.

67. Collier, *Post-Soviet Social*, 28.

68. Jasanoff, "Future Imperfect," 31; cf. Müller, "Assemblages and Actor-Networks."

69. Ureta, *Assembling Policy*, 11–13.

70. Latour and Hermant, *Paris: Invisible City*, 70.

71. Cf. Harvey, Jensen, and Morita, "Introduction," 31.

72. Moss, "Socio-Technical Change."

73. Swyngedouw, *Liquid Power*, 163–190.

74. Bulkeley et al., *Cities and Low Carbon Transitions*, 37.

75. Schnitzler, *Democracy's Infrastructure*, 29.

76. Moss, "Discarded Surrogates."

77. Gandy, *Fabric of Space*, 8.

78. Furlong, "Small Technologies, Big Change," 476.

79. Moss, "Socio-Technical Change"; Moss, "Discarded Surrogates"; cf. Geels and Raven, "Non-linearity and Expectations."

80. Graham and Thrift, "Out of Order," 10.

81. Gandy, "Negative Luminescence," 1091.

82. Huyssen, *Present Pasts*, 7, 81.

83. Schnitzler, *Democracy's Infrastructure*, 188.

84. Till, *New Berlin*, 196.

85. Anand, Gupta, and Appel, *Promise of Infrastructure*, in particular the chapters by Appel, Gupta, and Appel, "Introduction," and Gupta, "The Future in Ruins."

86. Schnitzler, *Democracy's Infrastructure*, 7.

87. Huyssen, *Present Pasts*, 11.

88. Jasanoff, "Future Imperfect."

89. On "technopolitics," see Schnitzler, *Democracy's Infrastructure*, 8–11, drawing on work by Gabrielle Hecht and Timothy Mitchell.

90. Star, "The Ethnography of Infrastructure," 379.

91. Schnitzler, *Democracy's Infrastructure*, 107.

92. Barry, *Material Politics*, 1–2.

93. Barry, *Material Politics*, 183.

94. A good example is the Transantiago urban rail project studied as a "policy assemblage" by Sebastián Ureta, *Assembling Policy*.

95. Schnitzler, *Democracy's Infrastructure*; Barry, *Material Politics*.

96. Harvey, Jensen, and Morita, "Introduction," 17.

97. Bakker, *Uncooperative Commodity*; Collier, *Post-Soviet Social*. Cf. for Eastern Europe, Bouzarovski, Sýkora, and Matoušek, "Locked-in Post-Socialism."

98. McFarlane and Rutherford, "Political Infrastructures"; Bulkeley, Castán Broto, and Maassen, "Low-Carbon Transitions."

99. Swyngedouw, *Social Power and the Urbanization of Water*; Gandy, *Concrete and Clay*.

100. Graham and Marvin, *Splintering Urbanism*, 216.

101. Swyngedouw, *Social Power and the Urbanization of Water*; Heynen, Kaika, and Swyngedouw, "Urban Political Ecology."

102. Examples: Furlong, "STS beyond the 'Modern Infrastructure Ideal'"; Silver, "Incremental Infrastructures"; Jaglin and Dubresson, *Eskom*.

103. Bridge, "Map Is Not the Territory."

104. Coutard and Guy, "STS and the City."

105. Collier, *Post-Soviet Social*, 3.

106. Beveridge, *Politics of Inevitability*, 190.

107. Wittfogel, *Oriental Despotism*; Hughes, *Networks of Power*. For a recent overview of historical research on water and political rule, see the special issue in *Water Alternatives*, Obertreis et al., "Water, Infrastructure and Political Rule."

108. Laak, "Infra-Strukturgeschichte."

109. Högselius, Kaijser, and van der Vleuten, *Europe's Infrastructure Transition*.

110. Uekötter, *The Green and the Brown*; Blackbourn, *The Conquest of Nature*. Cf. Brain and Pál, *Environmentalism under Authoritarian Regimes*; Gorostiza and Cerdà, "Unclaimed Latifundium."

111. A notable exception is Hansman et al., "Research Agenda for an Integrated Approach."

112. On water and sanitation in Berlin, see for example Mohajeri, *100 Jahre Berliner Wasserversorgung*. For a recent study on the water-energy nexus from an infrastructural perspective, see Moss and Hüesker, "Politicised Nexus Thinking in Practice."

113. Moss, Naumann, and Krause, "Turning Wastewater into Energy."

114. Monstadt and Coutard, "Cities in an Era of Interfacing Infrastructures."

115. Monstadt and Coutard, "Cities in an Era of Interfacing Infrastructures."

116. Cronon, *Nature's Metropolis*.

117. Cronon, *Nature's Metropolis*, 384.

118. Cronon, *Nature's Metropolis*, xvi.

119. Melosi, *Effluent America*, 130.

120. Heynen, Kaika, and Swyngedouw, "Urban Political Ecology."

121. Gandy, "Rethinking Urban Metabolism," 364.

122. Gandy, *Concrete and Clay*; Kaika, *City of Flows*; Swyngedouw, *Liquid Power*.

123. Bridge et al., "Geographies of Energy Transition," 339. Bouzarovski, Sýkora, and Matoušek, "Locked-in Post-Socialism," 639, talk of how "infrastructural development trajectories are closely integrated with inherited, existing, and evolving urban landscapes."

124. Monstadt, "Conceptualizing the Political Ecology of Urban Infrastructures"; Wolfram and Frantzeskaki, "Cities and Systemic Change for Sustainability."

Chapter 3

Epigraph: Cited in translation in Whyte and Frisby, *Metropolis Berlin*, 348.

1. Repeated efforts to promote greater inter-municipal cooperation had culminated merely in the creation of a weak regional association, the Zweckverband Groß-Berlin, in 1911. This body was purely advisory, with a remit restricted to public transport, urban planning, and forestry, Engeli, *Landesplanung in Berlin-Brandenburg*, 36–39; Büsch, *Geschichte der Berliner Kommunalwirtschaft*, 57.

2. Herzfeld, "Weimarer Demokratie und Nationalsozialismus," 122.

3. Landesarchiv Berlin (LAB) A Rep. 255, no. 93; cf. Bärthel, *Wasser für Berlin*, 156.

4. Engeli and Haus, *Quellen zum modernen Gemeindeverfassungsrecht*, 122; Bisky, *Berlin*, 458–462.

5. Böß, *Berlin von Heute*, 20–21.

6. Böß, *Berlin von Heute*, 20.

7. Engeli, *Gustav Böß*, 118–119.

8. Schmieder, "Wirtschaft und Bevölkerung."

9. Engeli, *Landesplanung in Berlin-Brandenburg*.

10. Langbein, "Die Entwässerung von Groß-Berlin."

11. Böß, *Berlin von Heute*, 21.

12. This represents a prime example of the "recursive" nature of city-infrastructure relations, as elaborated in chapter 2. Cf. Harvey, Jensen, and Morita, "Introduction," 20–24.

13. Büsch, *Geschichte der Berliner Kommunalwirtschaft*, 50ff.

14. See Mayor Böß's defense of the performance of Berlin's gas, water, and electricity utilities in May 1922 against public criticisms in his memo *Maßnahmen zur Verbesserung der städtischen Gas-, Wasser- und Elektrizitätswerke seit der Bildung der Stadtgemeinde Berlin*, LAB A Rep. 255, no. 93, dated May 10, 1922.

15. Böß, *Berlin von Heute*, 53.

16. Adolph, "Normung der Stromverteilung," 435.

17. Adolph, "Normung der Stromverteilung," 434–435; Thierbach, "Die gegenwärtige Versorgung," 1465.

18. Böß, *Berlin von Heute*, 53.

19. Magistrat, *Maßnahmen zur Verbesserung der städtischen Gas-, Wasser- und Elektrizitätswerke seit der Bildung der Stadtgemeinde Berlin*, LAB A Rep. 255, no. 93, 16–17. For an overview of the organizational fragmentation of electricity generation, networks, concessionary agreements, and tariffs within Berlin, see figure 41 in Matschoß, Schulz, and Groß, *50 Jahre Berliner Elektrizitätswerke*, 62.

20. Adolph, "Zum 50jährigen Jubiläum."

21. Bärthel, "Anlagen und Bauten der Elektrizitätserzeugung"; Rehmer, "Der Ausbau," 1.

22. Binder, *Elektrifizierung als Vision*, 328; Thierbach, "Die gegenwärtige Versorgung," 1466.

23. Thierbach, "Die gegenwärtige Versorgung," 1466.

24. Wichmann, "Die Versorgung Berlins mit Fernstrom," 1001; cf. Hughes, *Networks of Power*.

25. Bärthel, "Anlagen und Bauten der Gasversorgung," 38–41; Bärthel, *Die Geschichte der Gasversorgung*.

26. Tepasse, *Stadttechnik im Städtebau Berlins. 20. Jahrhundert*, 103.

27. Bärthel, "Anlagen und Bauten der Gasversorgung," 38–41.

28. Büsch, *Geschichte der Berliner Kommunalwirtschaft*, 70.

29. Tepasse, *Stadttechnik im Städtebau Berlins. 20. Jahrhundert*, 103.

30. Kühne, "Gegenwarts- und Zukunftsprobleme," 426.

31. Cited in Tepasse, *Stadttechnik im Städtebau Berlins. 20. Jahrhundert*, 93.

32. Kühne, "Die Zukunft der Wasserversorgung," 2.

33. Bärthel, "Anlagen und Bauten der Wasserversorgung," 86.

34. The water works closed down were at Heinersdorf, Niederschönhausen, Hohenschönhausen, and Rummelsburg in 1921–1922 and at Rosenthal, Reinickendorf, and Hermsdorf in 1924–1928, Bärthel, "Anlagen und Bauten der Wasserversorgung."

35. Mohajeri, *100 Jahre Berliner Wasserversorgung*, 184–186, 219–221; Bärthel, *Wasser für Berlin*, 157.

36. Bärthel, *Wasser für Berlin*, 154.

37. Büsch, *Geschichte der Berliner Kommunalwirtschaft*, 123.

38. Bärthel, "Anlagen und Bauten der Wasserversorgung," 86.

39. Bärthel, *Geklärt!*, 138; Bärthel, "Anlagen und Bauten der Stadtentwässerung," 145.

40. Bärthel, *Geklärt!*.

41. Langbein, "Die Stadtentwässerung," 351.

42. Langbein, "Die Entwässerung von Groß-Berlin," 93; Langbein, "Die Stadtentwässerung," 351.

43. Bärthel, *Geklärt!*, 138.

44. Bärthel, "Anlagen und Bauten der Stadtentwässerung," 145.

45. Langbein, "Die Entwässerung von Groß-Berlin," 93.

46. Bärthel, *Geklärt!*, 138; Bärthel, "Anlagen und Bauten der Stadtentwässerung," 145.

47. Langbein, "Die Entwässerung von Groß Berlin," 94.

48. Lobeck, *Die Großberliner Stadtentwässerung*, 59–63; cf. Mohajeri, *100 Jahre Berliner Wasserversorgung*, 220.

49. Mohajeri, *100 Jahre Berliner Wasserversorgung*, 221.

50. Ruths, "Stadtgüter und Stadtversorgung," 123.

51. Adolph, "Normung der Stromverteilung," 435.

52. Cited in Tepasse, *Stadttechnik im Städtebau Berlins. 20. Jahrhundert*, 103.

53. Langbein, "Zur Halbjahrhundertfeier der Berliner Stadtentwässerung," 53.

54. LAB A Rep. 001–02, no. 3139.

55. Thierbach, "Die gegenwärtige Versorgung," 1470.

56. Matschoß, Schulz, and Groß, *50 Jahre Berliner Elektrizitätswerke*, 63; Büsch, *Geschichte der Berliner Kommunalwirtschaft*, 107.

57. Adolph, "Zum 50jährigen Jubiläum," 6.

58. "Die neuen Tarife der StEW Berlin," 16–17.

59. Büsch, *Geschichte der Berliner Kommunalwirtschaft*, 109.

60. Adolph, "Normung der Stromverteilung," 436.

61. The situation in Charlottenburg was particularly complex, where voltages of 120 and 130, as well as 3,000 and 6,000, coexisted, Adolph, "Zum 50jährigen Jubiläum," 6.

62. Matschoß, Schulz, and Groß, *50 Jahre Berliner Elektrizitätswerke*, 62.

63. Büsch, *Geschichte der Berliner Kommunalwirtschaft*.

64. Wermuth, *Ein Beamtenleben*, 352.

65. Böß, *Berlin von Heute*, 56.

66. Rehmer, "Die Stromversorgung der Reichshauptstadt," 278.

67. Adolph, "Normung der Stromverteilung," 434–435.

68. Tepasse, *Stadttechnik im Städtebau Berlins. 20. Jahrhundert*, 103.

69. Rudnitzky, *Die Berliner städtische Gaswirtschaft*, 51.

70. See map in Bärthel, *Die Geschichte der Gasversorgung*, 84.

71. On the following, Bärthel, *Wasser für Berlin*, 174–180.

72. LAB A Rep. 255, no. 93; Eiden, *Versorgungswirtschaft als regionale Organisation*, 332.

73. *Erster Verwaltungsbericht der neuen Stadtgemeinde Berlin für die Zeit vom 1. Oktober 1920 bis 31. März 1924*, 37.

74. Bärthel, *Wasser für Berlin*, 174–180.

75. *Stenographische Berichte über die öffentlichen Sitzungen der Stadtverordnetenversammlung der Stadtgemeinde Berlin*, 1925, 595–596.

76. LAB A Rep. 001–02, no. 3181.

77. LAB A Pr. Br. Rep. 030, no. 21249.

78. Kühne, "Übernahme der Wasserversorgung," 555–556.

79. Feilitzsch, "Die Zukunft der Berliner Wasserversorgung," 785–787.

80. Kühne, "Zur Frage der Wasserversorgung."

81. Bärthel, *Wasser für Berlin*, 179–180.

82. Büsch, *Geschichte der Berliner Kommunalwirtschaft*, 73.

83. Statistisches Amt der Stadt Berlin, *Statistisches Taschenbuch*, 208.

84. See the speech by the city treasurer Karding in *Stenographische Berichte über die öffentlichen Sitzungen der Stadtverordnetenversammlung der Stadtgemeinde Berlin*, 1921, col. 1598.

85. LAB A Rep. 259, no. 253.

86. Statistisches Amt der Stadt Berlin, *Statistisches Taschenbuch*, 12–13.

87. Letter from Prussian interior minister Severing to Mayor Böß, August 12, 1923, and letter from Böß to the utility departments, November 15, 1923, LAB A Rep. 001–02, no. 2989.

88. Matschoß, Schulz, and Groß, *50 Jahre Berliner Elektrizitätswerke*.

89. Strikes for higher wages were held on January 21–23, 1919, and November 5–11, 1921; for safer working conditions and workers' rights on October 5–6, 1920, September 12, 1921, and February 5–8, 1922; against the Kapp Putsch on March 13–25, 1920; and against the Cuno government on August 11–14, 1923, Betriebsrat der Berliner Kraft- und Licht(Bewag)-Aktiengesellschaft, *Im Licht der Zeit*, 36–41.

90. Alfred Döblin, "Großstreik in Berlin," *Prager Tageblatt* of November 14, 1922, cited in Tepasse, *Stadttechnik im Städtebau Berlins. 20. Jahrhundert*, 53–54.

91. Betriebsrat der Berliner Kraft- und Licht(Bewag)-Aktiengesellschaft, *Im Licht der Zeit*, 27.

92. Binder, *Elektrifizierung als Vision*, 337.

93. Betriebsrat der Berliner Kraft- und Licht(Bewag)-Aktiengesellschaft, *Im Licht der Zeit*, 46–48.

94. SED-Betriebsparteiorganisation Bewag, *Unsere Kraft. Betriebsgeschichte der Bewag, 1. Teil*, 31.

95. Büsch, *Geschichte der Berliner Kommunalwirtschaft*, 4–5.

96. Engeli, *Gustav Böß*, 165; Rudischhauser, "Die parlamentarischen Debatten."

97. Büsch, *Geschichte der Berliner Kommunalwirtschaft*, 4–5.

98. Büsch, *Geschichte der Berliner Kommunalwirtschaft*, 72.

99. Rudischhauser, "Die parlamentarischen Debatten," 75.

100. Rudischhauser, "Die parlamentarischen Debatten," 76–77.

101. Rudischhauser, "Die parlamentarischen Debatten," 83.

102. Mohajeri, *100 Jahre Berliner Wasserversorgung*, 186.

103. Büsch, *Geschichte der Berliner Kommunalwirtschaft*, 71.

104. Mohajeri, *100 Jahre Berliner Wasserversorgung*, 188.

105. Bärthel, *Die Geschichte der Gasversorgung*, 81.

106. Matshoß, Schulz, and Groß, *50 Jahre Berliner Elektrizitätswerke*.

107. Bärthel, *Die Geschichte der Gasversorgung*, 81.

108. Matschoß, Schulz, and Groß, *50 Jahre Berliner Elektrizitätswerke*, 49.

109. Matschoß, Schulz, and Groß, *50 Jahre Berliner Elektrizitätswerke*, 52.

110. Cited in Matschoß, Schulz, and Groß, *50 Jahre Berliner Elektrizitätswerke*, 50.

111. *Erster Verwaltungsbericht der neuen Stadtgemeinde Berlin für die Zeit vom 1. Oktober 1920 bis 31. März 1924*, 34. The SPD group in the city parliament attributed the retention of Berlin's utilities in municipal ownership during the inflation to its own resolute defense, see Bezirksvorstand der Sozialdemokratischen Partei Deutschlands, *Berliner Kommunalpolitik*, 147–149. This self-confidence was to prove misplaced in 1931, when the SPD agreed to sell a majority shareholding in the city's electricity utility during the Depression (see chapter 4).

112. *Erster Verwaltungsbericht der neuen Stadtgemeinde Berlin für die Zeit vom 1. Oktober 1920 bis 31. März 1924*, 71.

113. Böß, *Berlin von Heute*; cf. Büsch, *Geschichte der Berliner Kommunalwirtschaft*, 70.

114. Cf. Büsch, *Geschichte der Berliner Kommunalwirtschaft*, 38–39.

115. Magistrat, *Maßnahmen zur Verbesserung*.

116. LAB A Rep. 255, no. 116, report of July 1922.

117. LAB A Rep. 255, no. 116, report of July 1922, 4.

118. LAB A Rep. 255, no. 116, memo of September 4, 1922.

119. Engeli, *Gustav Böß*, 138; Rudnitzky, *Die Berliner städtische Gaswirtschaft*, 63–65.

120. Büsch, *Geschichte der Berliner Kommunalwirtschaft*, 75.

121. Matschoß, Schulz, and Groß, *50 Jahre Berliner Elektrizitätswerke*, 53; Rudnitzky, *Die Berliner städtische Gaswirtschaft*, 63–65; Dame, *Elektropolis Berlin*. Transforming utilities into commercial enterprises in municipal ownership was by no means unique to Berlin. In 1928–1929 a study of all municipal gas utilities in Germany revealed that, of the total 1,209 utilities, 159 were organized as share companies (AG) and a further ninety-six as limited companies (GmbH). Nineteen of the 159 gas utilities organized as share companies were in full municipal ownership, like the Berlin gas utility. See Rudnitzky, *Die Berliner städtische Gaswirtschaft*, 58.

122. Cited in Rudnitzky, *Die Berliner städtische Gaswirtschaft*, 68.

123. Writing in 1960, Otto Büsch praised this solution for enabling the de-bureaucratization and depoliticization of the utilities while avoiding their de-municipalization, see Büsch, *Geschichte der Berliner Kommunalwirtschaft*, 75. His analysis sustains the predominant view in the early 1920s that political influence was not essential but potentially detrimental to infrastructure management.

124. Büsch, *Geschichte der Berliner Kommunalwirtschaft*, 18; Bärthel, *Geklärt!*, 138.

125. The separation of water and sanitation services was also detrimental to a holistic management of regional water resources. This was rooted not in sectoral rivalry, but in the different legal status in Germany of water supply (as an economic function) and sanitation (as an administrative function).

126. Engeli, *Landesplanung in Berlin-Brandenburg*, 5.

127. Engeli, *Landesplanung in Berlin-Brandenburg*, 62.

128. Engeli, *Landesplanung in Berlin-Brandenburg*, 35.

129. Bernhardt, "At the Limits of the European Sanitary City," 163.

130. Böß, *Berlin von Heute*, 28.

131. Gudermann, "Die Berliner Abwässer," 153.

132. For a good example, see the report by the Stadtgüter director Ruths, "Stadtgüter und Stadtversorgung."

133. Ruths, "Stadtgüter und Stadtversorgung," 127.

134. Ruths, "Stadtgüter und Stadtversorgung," 128.

135. Gudermann, "Die Berliner Abwässer," 165.

136. Bernhardt, "At the Limits of the European Sanitary City," 167, where he criticizes Berlin's sanitation model as a "colonial metabolic intervention in the hinterland."

Chapter 4

1. Büsch, *Geschichte der Berliner Kommunalwirtschaft*.

2. Cited in Büsch, *Geschichte der Berliner Kommunalwirtschaft*, n.p.

3. Büsch, *Geschichte der Berliner Kommunalwirtschaft*, 21.

4. Böß, *Berlin von Heute*; see the chapters in Brennert and Stein, *Probleme der neuen Stadt Berlin*.

5. Gandy, "The Making of a Regulatory Crisis," 342, 350.

6. Brüggemann, "Berlin arbeitet!"

7. On the "modern infrastructural ideal," Graham and Marvin, *Splintering Urbanism*.

8. Kühne, "Gegenwarts- und Zukunftsprobleme," 432. In reality, Berlin's population in 2000 was—at 3.34 million inhabitants—substantially lower than that of 1925. Even today (2020) the figure stands at only 3.77 million.

9. Tepasse, *Stadttechnik im Städtebau Berlins. 20. Jahrhundert*, 94.

10. Kühne, "Gegenwarts- und Zukunftsprobleme," 430.

11. Hahn, *Denkschrift über die Erhöhung*, 3.

12. Büsch, *Geschichte der Berliner Kommunalwirtschaft*, 10.

13. Schmieder, "Wirtschaft und Bevölkerung," 400.

14. Büsch, *Geschichte der Berliner Kommunalwirtschaft*, 80.

15. Berliner Städtische Elektrizitätswerke Akt.-Ges., *Zur Zukunft der Berliner Elektrizitäts-Versorgung*, 2. Cf. Report of October 1927 by the Bewag directors Rehmer and Adolph in LAB A Rep. 256, no. 250.

16. Bertelsmann, "Die Gasversorgung in der Großstadt," 415.

17. Kühne, "Die Zukunft der Wasserversorgung in Berlin," 6; Tepasse, *Stadttechnik im Städtebau Berlins. 20. Jahrhundert*, 94.

18. Hahn, *Denkschrift über die Erhöhung*, 6.

19. Matschoß, Schulz, and Groß, *50 Jahre Berliner Elektrizitätswerke*; Statistisches Amt der Stadt Berlin, *Berlin in Zahlen 1945*; Tepasse, *Stadttechnik im Städtebau Berlins. 20. Jahrhundert*, 116. On electrification in Berlin, Langguth, "Elektrizität in jedem Gerät."

20. Büsch, *Geschichte der Berliner Kommunalwirtschaft*, 112.

21. Berliner Städtische Elektrizitätswerke Akt.-Ges., *Zur Zukunft der Berliner Elektrizitäts-Versorgung*, 7.

22. Tepasse, *Stadttechnik im Städtebau Berlins. 20. Jahrhundert*, 116.

23. Berliner Städtische Elektrizitätswerke Akt.-Ges., *Jahresbericht der Betriebsdirektion 1926*, 1; Berliner Städtische Elektrizitätswerke Akt.-Ges., *Zur Zukunft der Berliner Elektrizitäts-Versorgung*, 1.

24. Tepasse, *Stadttechnik im Städtebau Berlins. 20. Jahrhundert*, 94.

25. Statistisches Amt der Stadt Berlin, *Berlin in Zahlen 1945*, 335.

26. Letter of Berlin water utility to Berlin press office of September 16, 1929, LAB A Rep. 255, no. 122, 3.

27. Statistisches Amt der Stadt Berlin, *Berlin in Zahlen 1945*, 333.

28. Hughes, *Networks of Power*, 313–319; Binder, *Elektrifizierung als Vision*, 329–340.

29. Leithäuser, *Die unsichtbare Kraft*, 209; Schott, "Empowering European Cities," 176–179.

30. Brüggemann, "Berlin arbeitet!" 26.

31. LAB A Rep. 256, no. 247; Berliner Städtische Elektrizitätswerke Akt.-Ges., *Zur Zukunft der Berliner Elektrizitäts-Versorgung*; cf. Tepasse, *Stadttechnik im Städtebau Berlins. 20. Jahrhundert*, 116.

32. Böß, *Berlin von Heute*, 60–61.

33. LAB A Rep. 259, no. 257; Böß, *Berlin von Heute*, 61–62; Rudnitzky, *Die Berliner städtische Gaswirtschaft*, 129.

34. LAB A Rep. 256, nos. 247 and 250; Berliner Städtische Elektrizitätswerke Akt.-Ges., *Zur Zukunft der Berliner Elektrizitäts-Versorgung*. On Bewag's building programs of 1924–1929, Dame, *Elektropolis Berlin*.

35. Report "Zur Zukunft der Berliner Elektrizitätsversorgung" of May 1925, LAB A Rep. 256, no. 247; Berliner Städtische Elektrizitätswerke Akt.-Ges., *Zur Zukunft der Berliner Elektrizitäts-Versorgung*.

36. Report "Zur Zukunft der Berliner Elektrizitätsversorgung, II. Denkschrift" of October 1927, LAB A Rep. 256, no. 250; Berliner Städtische Elektrizitätswerke Akt.-Ges., *Zur Zukunft der Berliner Elektrizitäts-Versorgung*.

37. Berliner Städtische Elektrizitätswerke Akt.-Ges., *Zur Zukunft der Berliner Elektrizitäts-Versorgung*.

38. Berliner Städtische Elektrizitätswerke Akt.-Ges., *Zur Zukunft der Berliner Elektrizitäts-Versorgung*.

39. Böß, *Berlin von Heute*, 55.

40. Kühne, "Die Zukunft der Wasserversorgung in Berlin," 6; cf. Tepasse, *Stadttechnik im Städtebau Berlins. 20. Jahrhundert*, 94.

41. Kühne, "Die Zukunft der Wasserversorgung in Berlin," 7.

42. Kühne, "Gegenwarts- und Zukunftsprobleme," 430.

43. Kühne, "Gegenwarts- und Zukunftsprobleme," 431; Kühne, "Die Zukunft der Wasserversorgung in Berlin," 8; Tepasse, *Stadttechnik im Städtebau Berlins. 20. Jahrhundert*, 96.

44. Kühne, "Gegenwarts- und Zukunftsprobleme," 432–433; Kühne, "Die Zukunft der Wasserversorgung in Berlin," 9–10.

45. Hahn, *Denkschrift über die Erhöhung*, 19–21.

46. Hahn, *Denkschrift über die Erhöhung*, 21.

47. Hahn, *Denkschrift über die Erhöhung*; Bärthel, *Geklärt!*, 151–152.

48. Hahn, *Denkschrift über die Erhöhung*, 6.

49. Hahn, *Denkschrift über die Erhöhung*, 7.

50. The plants were to be located close to existing sewage farms at Stahnsdorf, Waßmannsdorf, Großbeeren-Osdorf, Falkenberg, Buch-Hobrechtsfelde, and Karolinenhöhe, Hahn, *Denkschrift über die Erhöhung*. Cf. Memo of sanitation utility "Die Berliner Abwasserreinigungsanlagen," dated October 1946, LAB Rep. 255, no. 537.

51. Langbein, "Die Verwertung städtischer Abwässer," 329.

52. Langbein, "Die Verwertung städtischer Abwässer"; "Denkschrift über die zukünftige Gestaltung der Berliner Abwasserreinigung" of September 1932, LAB A Rep. 255, no. 155.

53. Jasanoff, "Future Imperfect."

54. Bärthel, "Anlagen und Bauten der Elektrizitätserzeugung"; Tepasse, *Stadttechnik im Städtebau Berlins. 20. Jahrhundert.*

55. Rehmer, "Der Ausbau," 2.

56. Stahl, 1928, in Whyte and Frisby, *Metropolis Berlin*, 422.

57. Tepasse, *Stadttechnik im Städtebau Berlins. 20. Jahrhundert*, 121.

58. Rehmer, "Der Ausbau," 3.

59. Scholze, "Zu einigen Problemen," 123.

60. Bärthel, "Anlagen und Bauten der Elektrizitätserzeugung," 214.

61. Rehmer, "Der Ausbau," 2.

62. Rehmer, "Der Ausbau," 3.

63. Rehmer, "Der Ausbau," 4; Berliner Städtische Elektrizitätswerke Akt.-Ges., *Jahresbericht der Betriebsdirektion 1926*, 413.

64. Fleischer, "Lastverteilung."

65. Rudnitzky, *Die Berliner städtische Gaswirtschaft*, 83; Büsch, *Geschichte der Berliner Kommunalwirtschaft*, 117.

66. Cited in Brüggemann, "Berlin arbeitet!" 32.

67. Cited in Brüggemann, "Berlin arbeitet!" 41. The length of the water mains was around 4,000 km.

68. Büsch, *Geschichte der Berliner Kommunalwirtschaft*, 123. The following communities were connected to the water mains during this period: Kladow, Gatow, Heiligensee, Schulzendorf, Konradshöhe, Tegelort, Blankenburg, Karow, Malchow, Falkenberg, and Wartenberg, see Mohajeri, *100 Jahre Berliner Wasserversorgung*, 227.

69. Mohajeri, *100 Jahre Berliner Wasserversorgung*, 228; Bärthel, "Anlagen und Bauten der Wasserversorgung," 89.

70. LAB A Rep. 255, no. 370.

71. Report "Die zukünftige Wasserversorgung Groß-Berlins—Bedarf und Befriedigung," dated September 29, 1930, LAB A Rep. 255, no. 370.

72. Bärthel, *Geklärt!*.

73. Bärthel, "Anlagen und Bauten der Stadtentwässerung."

74. Langbein, "Die Stadtentwässerung," 354.

75. Statistisches Amt der Stadt Berlin, *Berlin in Zahlen 1945*, 336; Böß, *Berlin von Heute*, 69–70.

76. Mohajeri, *100 Jahre Berliner Wasserversorgung*, 233–257; Bärthel, *Geklärt!*.

77. LAB A Rep. 255, no. 370.

78. Mohajeri, *100 Jahre Berliner Wasserversorgung*, 249.

79. LAB A Rep. 255, no. 370.

80. Denner and Mösenthin, "Die Grundwasserverhältnisse," 7. Cf. Kühne, "Die Zukunft der Wasserversorgung in Berlin," 1.

81. Denner, "Die wasserwirtschaftliche Bedeutung"; Denner and Mösenthin, "Die Grundwasserverhältnisse."

82. Denner, "Die wasserwirtschaftliche Bedeutung," 463.

83. Hahn, *Denkschrift über die Erhöhung*.

84. Denner, "Die wasserwirtschaftliche Bedeutung."

85. Denner and Mösenthin, "Die Grundwasserverhältnisse," 3; Kühne, *Die Berliner Städtische Wasserwerke*, 70.

86. Eberling, "Chemische Untersuchung."

87. Eberling, "Chemische Untersuchung"; see press reports of flooding events in LAB A Rep. 255, no. 144–01.

88. Rudnitzky, *Die Berliner städtische Gaswirtschaft*, 73.

89. Böß, *Berlin von Heute*, 64.

90. While the water utility Wassag used 35,000 metric tons and the power utility Bewag 400,000 metric tons of coal, the gas utility Gasag consumed over one million metric tons that year, Büsch, *Geschichte der Berliner Kommunalwirtschaft*, 118; Rudnitzky, *Die Berliner städtische Gaswirtschaft*, 73.

91. Tepasse, *Stadttechnik im Städtebau Berlins. 20. Jahrhundert*, 82.

92. Bärthel, "Anlagen und Bauten der Elektrizitätserzeugung," 296.

93. Tepasse, *Stadttechnik im Städtebau Berlins. 20. Jahrhundert*, 86.

94. Langbein, "Die Stadtentwässerung," 358.

95. Langbein and Kroll, "Die Gewinnung und Verwertung," 474.

96. Langbein, "Die Abwasservorkläranlage," 1109; *Die Welt am Abend*, December 7, 1926, in LAB A Rep. 255, no. 144–01.

97. Langbein and Kroll, "Die Gewinnung und Verwertung," 476.

98. Bärthel, *Geklärt!*, 157.

99. Czada, *Die Berliner Elektroindustrie*, 156; Heßler, "Die Einführung elektrischer Haushaltsgeräte," 300; Schott, "Empowering European Cities," 184.

100. Matschoß, Schulz, and Groß, *50 Jahre Berliner Elektrizitätswerke*, 56.

101. Schott, "Empowering European Cities," 182.

102. The housing estate "Heimat."

103. Matzerath and Thienel, "Stadtentwicklung," 182–183; Tepasse, *Stadttechnik im Städtebau Berlins. 20. Jahrhundert*, 55.

104. Bezirksamt Charlottenburg von Berlin, *Stadt unter Strom*, 33.

105. Scholze, "Zu einigen Problemen," 120.

106. Matschoß, Schulz, and Groß, *50 Jahre Berliner Elektrizitätswerke*, 89. Cf. Büsch, *Geschichte der Berliner Kommunalwirtschaft*, 115.

107. Letter of Wassag to the mayor of Berlin of January 19, 1926, in LAB A Rep. 001–02, no. 2801.

108. Bärthel, *Geklärt!*, 141; Büsch, *Geschichte der Berliner Kommunalwirtschaft*, 138.

109. Statistisches Amt der Stadt Berlin, *Berlin in Zahlen 1945*, 329, 332, 335; Büsch, *Geschichte der Berliner Kommunalwirtschaft*, 137–138.

110. Büsch, *Geschichte der Berliner Kommunalwirtschaft*, 15.

111. Rudnitzky, *Die Berliner städtische Gaswirtschaft*, 111–116. Cf. Matschoß, Schulz, and Groß, *50 Jahre Berliner Elektrizitätswerke*, 91.

112. Gasag, for instance, reduced staff numbers from 11,300 in 1923 to 7,800 in 1924, Rudnitzky, *Die Berliner städtische Gaswirtschaft*, 111–112.

113. Rudnitzky, *Die Berliner städtische Gaswirtschaft*, 112.

114. *Vorlagen zu den Sitzungen der Stadtverordnetenversammlung der Stadtgemeinde Berlin*.

115. Trauer and Prüß, *Gutachten der Wirtschaftsberatung Deutscher Städte*, 8.

116. Lange, *Groß-Berliner Tagebuch*, 142.

117. Schmidt, *Die BEWAG-Transaktion*, 12.

118. Matschoß, Schulz, and Groß, *50 Jahre Berliner Elektrizitätswerke*, Appendix: Zahlentafel I.

119. See the unanimous voting for Bewag's investment schemes in the city parliament on March 15 and October 18, 1928, *Stenographische Berichte über die öffentlichen Sitzungen der Stadtverordnetenversammlung der Stadtgemeinde Berlin 1928*, 762. On November 13, 1928, the city parliament approved by a large majority a loan of 12 million Reichsmark for investments in water works

and mains, *Vorlagen zu den Sitzungen der Stadtverordnetenversammlung der Stadtgemeinde Berlin*, 764–765.

120. Schmidt, *Die BEWAG-Transaktion*, 12. By 1932 Bewag had repaid over 20 million Reichsmark of its 223 million Reichsmark long-term loans, Matschoß, Schulz, and Groß, *50 Jahre Berliner Elektrizitätswerke*, Appendix: Zahlentafel I.

121. Lange, *Groß-Berliner Tagebuch*, 142.

122. Böß, *Berlin von Heute*, 59, 67. Cf. Büsch, *Geschichte der Berliner Kommunalwirtschaft*, 124.

123. Böß, *Berlin von Heute*, 55, 67; minutes of a meeting of the joint supervisory board of the three utilities, September 29, 1924, LAB A Rep. 259, no. 253.

124. Büsch, *Geschichte der Berliner Kommunalwirtschaft*, 8.

125. As documented in many debates in the city parliament, e.g., *Stenographische Berichte über die öffentlichen Sitzungen der Stadtverordnetenversammlung der Stadtgemeinde Berlin*, 1926, 403.

126. Büsch, *Geschichte der Berliner Kommunalwirtschaft*, 2.

127. Southerton, Chappells, and van Vliet, *Sustainable Consumption*; Shove, Trentmann, and Wilk, *Time, Consumption and Everyday Life*.

128. Czada, *Die Berliner Elektroindustrie*, 156–157; Rückwardt and Albrecht, "Der gegenwärtige Stand der Elektrizitätsversorgung."

129. Rückwardt and Albrecht, "Der gegenwärtige Stand der Elektrizitätsversorgung," 521.

130. Rudnitzky, *Die Berliner städtische Gaswirtschaft*, 96–97.

131. Czada, *Die Berliner Elektroindustrie*, 157.

132. Bezirksamt Charlottenburg von Berlin, *Stadt unter Strom*, 33.

133. Rehmer, "Der Ausbau und die Betriebsführung," 6.

134. Rudnitzky, *Die Berliner städtische Gaswirtschaft*, 96.

135. Rudnitzky, *Die Berliner städtische Gaswirtschaft*, 98–99.

136. Gasag provided gas for 81 percent of all Berlin's street lamps in 1930, Brüggemann, "Berlin arbeitet!" 35.

137. See the minutes of several meetings of the Bewag executive board in 1929, LAB A Rep. 256, no. 208. Also Böß, *Berlin von Heute*, 63.

138. For a more detailed discussion of electricity demand management in twentieth-century Berlin, see Moss, "Socio-Technical Change."

139. Rudnitzky, *Die Berliner städtische Gaswirtschaft*, 7.

140. Rudnitzky, *Die Berliner städtische Gaswirtschaft*, 92; Brüggemann, "Berlin arbeitet!" 33.

141. Binder, *Elektrifizierung als Vision*, 347.

142. On the following: Binder, *Elektrifizierung als Vision*, 340–351; Tepasse, *Stadttechnik im Städtebau Berlins. 20. Jahrhundert*, 120; Moss, "Socio-Technical Change," 1437–1439.

143. Kauffmann, "Das Abzahlungsgeschäft des Bewag," 82.

144. Matschoß, Schulz, and Groß, *50 Jahre Berliner Elektrizitätswerke*, 76; cf. Tepasse, *Stadttechnik im Städtebau Berlins. 20. Jahrhundert*, 105.

145. Büsch, *Geschichte der Berliner Kommunalwirtschaft*, 34, 48, 114.

146. Binder, *Elektrifizierung als Vision*, 340.

147. Böß, *Berlin von Heute*, 57.

148. Rudnitzky, *Die Berliner städtische Gaswirtschaft*, 91; cf. Brüggemann, "Berlin arbeitet!," 33.

149. Kauffmann, "Das Abzahlungsgeschäft des Bewag," 83.

150. Cited in the report "Zur Zukunft der Berliner Elektrizitätsversorgung, II. Denkschrift" of October 1927, LAB A Rep. 256, no. 250.

151. Report "Zur Zukunft der Berliner Elektrizitätsversorgung, II. Denkschrift" of October 1927, LAB A Rep. 256, no. 250.

152. Berliner Städtische Elektrizitätswerke Akt.-Ges., *Zur Zukunft der Berliner Elektrizitäts-Versorgung*, 10.

153. Lorkowski, "Managing Energy Consumption"; Langguth, "Elektrizität in jedem Gerät."

154. Report "Zur Zukunft der Berliner Elektrizitätsversorgung, II. Denkschrift," of October 1927, LAB A Rep. 256, no. 250.

155. Statistisches Amt der Stadt Berlin, *Berlin in Zahlen 1945*, 335.

156. Mohajeri, *100 Jahre Berliner Wasserversorgung*, 231.

157. Statistisches Amt der Stadt Berlin, *Berlin in Zahlen 1945*, 333. Cf. Tepasse, *Stadttechnik im Städtebau Berlins. 20. Jahrhundert*, 108; Bärthel, *Die Geschichte der Gasversorgung in Berlin*, 91.

158. Büsch, *Geschichte der Berliner Kommunalwirtschaft*, 170.

159. Heßler, "Die Einführung elektrischer Haushaltsgeräte," 300.

160. Rückwardt and Albrecht, "Der gegenwärtige Stand der Elektrizitätsversorgung," 521.

161. Berliner Kraft- und Licht(Bewag)-Aktiengesellschaft, *100 Jahre Strom für Berlin*, 1984.

162. Binder, *Elektrifizierung als Vision*, 340–351; cf. Büsch, *Geschichte der Berliner Kommunalwirtschaft*, 167.

163. Schmidt, *Die BEWAG-Transaktion*, 15.

164. Rudnitzky, *Die Berliner städtische Gaswirtschaft*, 99.

165. Bärthel, *Geklärt!*, 158.

166. LAB A Rep. 001–02, no. 3243. The decision to continue investment followed a controversial debate on Bewag's building program in the city parliament on September 19, 1929, *Stenographische Berichte über die öffentlichen Sitzungen der Stadtverordnetenversammlung der Stadtgemeinde Berlin*, 1929, 775–783.

167. *Stenographische Berichte über die öffentlichen Sitzungen der Stadtverordnetenversammlung der Stadtgemeinde Berlin*, 1932, 353, 475–495.

168. Statistisches Amt der Stadt Berlin, *Berlin in Zahlen 1945*, 329; Büsch, *Geschichte der Berliner Kommunalwirtschaft*, 137–138, 176.

169. Statistisches Amt der Stadt Berlin, *Berlin in Zahlen 1945*, 335.

170. Büsch, *Geschichte der Berliner Kommunalwirtschaft*, 187.

171. Büsch, *Geschichte der Berliner Kommunalwirtschaft*, 190.

172. Büsch, *Geschichte der Berliner Kommunalwirtschaft*, 190.

173. Engeli, *Gustav Böß*, 172–173. Cf. Büsch, *Geschichte der Berliner Kommunalwirtschaft*, 49.

174. See the lengthy debate in the city parliament on November 29, 1929, *Stenographische Berichte über die öffentlichen Sitzungen der Stadtverordnetenversammlung der Stadtgemeinde Berlin*, 1929, 893–911.

175. Böß's memo "Die Reichsbank und die Städte" of November 23, 1929, LAB A Rep. 001–02, no. 1050. Cf. the statement of acting mayor Scholtz to the investigative committee of the Prussian parliament on February 6, 1930, LAB A Rep. 001–02, no. 3293.

176. Engeli, *Gustav Böß*, 209.

177. Council bill to city parliament of January 9, 1930, LAB A Rep. 001–02, no. 3232.

178. See the debate in the city parliament on December 19 and 20, 1929, *Stenographische Berichte über die öffentlichen Sitzungen der Stadtverordnetenversammlung der Stadtgemeinde Berlin*, 1929, 1028, 1048. The KPD later campaigned for a 50 percent reduction in electricity and gas tariffs and free services for the unemployed, see the debate on December 11, 1930, *Stenographische Berichte über die öffentlichen Sitzungen der Stadtverordnetenversammlung der Stadtgemeinde Berlin*, 1930, 1262–1270.

179. LAB A Rep. 256, no. 176 and no. 177; Mohajeri, *100 Jahre Berliner Wasserversorgung*, 232; Bärthel, *Die Geschichte der Gasversorgung in Berlin*, 91; Büsch, *Geschichte der Berliner Kommunalwirtschaft*, 24.

180. Büsch, *Geschichte der Berliner Kommunalwirtschaft*, 174.

181. Rudnitzky, *Die Berliner städtische Gaswirtschaft*, 110.

182. Büsch, *Geschichte der Berliner Kommunalwirtschaft*, 9.

183. On the Sklarek scandal, Engeli, *Gustav Böß*, 226ff. Cf. Bisky, *Berlin*, 519–522.

184. "Mismanagement in the Berlin City Administration" became the title of an investigative committee of the Prussian parliament, set up to examine the charges of corruption. The principal charges were subsequently dropped, but not before the day-to-day management of the municipality had been subjected to at times painful scrutiny, Engeli, *Gustav Böß*, 247.

185. After the district court called for Böß's formal resignation in May 1930, the higher administrative court repealed this verdict, clearing Böß of the most severe charges, although still criticizing his handling of the fur coat issue, Kaeber, "Die Oberbürgermeister Berlins."

186. Dietrich, "Verfassung und Verwaltung," 270; Herzfeld, "Weimarer Demokratie und Nationalsozialismus," 132.

187. As at the disruptive sessions held on January 7 and 9, 1930, *Stenographische Berichte über die öffentlichen Sitzungen der Stadtverordnetenversammlung der Stadtgemeinde Berlin*, 1930, 2–9, 12–22.

188. *Stenographische Berichte über die öffentlichen Sitzungen der Stadtverordnetenversammlung der Stadtgemeinde Berlin*, 1930, 347–350.

189. See letter of Gasag director Alexander to acting mayor Scholtz of December 6, 1930, and his memo of December 13, 1930, LAB A Rep. 259, no. 340.

190. Bärthel, "Anlagen und Bauten der Gasversorgung."

191. Letter from Westphal, director of Thüringer Gasgesellschaft, to general director Franck of Preußen-Elektra of January 19, 1931, LAB A Rep. 259, no. 340.

192. LAB A Rep. 259, no. 340.

193. Memo of director Westphal of March 16, 1931, LAB A Rep. 259, no. 340.

194. Minutes of a meeting between representatives of the city council, Gasag, Thüringer Gasgesellschaft, and Preußen-Elektra on April 10, 1931, LAB A Rep. 259, no. 340.

195. Büsch, *Geschichte der Berliner Kommunalwirtschaft*, 163–165.

196. Matschoß, Schulz, and Groß, *50 Jahre Berliner Elektrizitätswerke*, 69.

197. Lange, *Groß-Berliner Tagebuch*, 158.

198. See the debate on March 26, 1931, *Stenographische Berichte über die öffentlichen Sitzungen der Stadtverordnetenversammlung der Stadtgemeinde Berlin*, 1931, 384–397.

199. On the following, Schmidt, *Die BEWAG-Transaktion*, 124ff. Cf. Dame, *Elektropolis Berlin*, 356–359.

200. Büsch, *Geschichte der Berliner Kommunalwirtschaft*, 170n38.

201. Schmidt, *Die BEWAG-Transaktion*, 138.

202. On Sahm, Sprenger, *Heinrich Sahm.*

203. Writing confidentially to the general director of Preußen-Elektra, director Westphal of Thüringer Gasgesellschaft was dismissive of the way the city had been duped by the consortium over the Bewag deal, see letter (marked "strictly confidential") from Westphal to general director Franck of May 4, 1931, LAB A Rep. 259, no. 340.

204. *Stenographische Berichte über die öffentlichen Sitzungen der Stadtverordnetenversammlung der Stadtgemeinde Berlin*, 1931, 453–460, 471–486.

205. Cited in Schmidt, *Die BEWAG-Transaktion*, 144.

206. Schmidt, *Die BEWAG-Transaktion*, 146.

207. Berliner Kraft- und Licht(Bewag)-Aktiengesellschaft, *75 Jahre Berliner Stromversorgung*, 27; Schmidt, *Die BEWAG-Transaktion*, 147.

208. Büsch, *Geschichte der Berliner Kommunalwirtschaft*, 165.

209. Schmidt, *Die BEWAG-Transaktion.*

210. Büsch, *Geschichte der Berliner Kommunalwirtschaft.*

211. Tepasse, *Stadttechnik im Städtebau Berlins. 20. Jahrhundert*, 123.

212. Bernhardt, "At the Limits of the European Sanitary City," 165.

213. Engeli, *Landesplanung in Berlin-Brandenburg*, 58.

214. On Migge, see the fine biography by David Haney, *When Modern Was Green.*

215. Haney, "Leberecht Migge's 'Green Manifesto,'" 215.

216. On the following, Migge, "Eine Weltstadt kolonisiert!"

217. Migge, "Eine Weltstadt kolonisiert!," 45.

218. Migge, "Eine Weltstadt kolonisiert!," 40.

219. Migge, "Eine Weltstadt kolonisiert!," 73.

220. Migge, "Eine Weltstadt kolonisiert!," 15.

221. Migge, "Eine Weltstadt kolonisiert!," 49.

222. Draft text by Langbein of September 5, 1932, LAB A Rep. 255, no. 155.

223. Büsch, *Geschichte der Berliner Kommunalwirtschaft*, 191.

224. Dietrich, "Verfassung und Verwaltung," 271.

225. Rudnitzky, *Die Berliner städtische Gaswirtschaft*, 67. See the minutes of a meeting of city councillors of June 25, 1931, on the procedural rules for municipal enterprises, LAB A Rep. 001–02, no. 322.

Chapter 5

1. The following is based on the presentations printed in full in the minutes of the meeting, LAB A Rep. 256, no. 216.

2. Schaarschmidt, "In die Höhle des Löwen," 23–26.

3. Fieber and Rockmann, *An der Spitze Berlins*, 61–65.

4. Goebbels, cited in Whyte and Frisby, *Metropolis Berlin*, 595.

5. Reschke and Wildt, "Aufstieg der NSDAP in Berlin."

6. Reschke and Wildt, "Aufstieg der NSDAP in Berlin," 31.

7. Kreutzmüller, "Verfassung und Verwaltung der Hauptstadt," 54–55.

8. Fieber and Rockmann, *An der Spitze Berlins*, 253–255. On Lippert, see Kreutzmüller and Wildt, "Ein radikaler Bürger;" Bisky, *Berlin*, 551–554.

9. Cited in Kreutzmüller, "Verfassung und Verwaltung der Hauptstadt," 55.

10. Kreutzmüller and Wildt, "'Ein radikaler Bürger,'" 26–27.

11. On Sahm under Nazi rule, Fieber and Rockmann, *An der Spitze Berlins*, 43–47; Engeli and Ribbe, "Berlin in der NS-Zeit," 976.

12. Fieber and Rockmann, *An der Spitze Berlins*, 54.

13. Kreutzmüller, "Verfassung und Verwaltung der Hauptstadt," 62; Kreutzmüller and Wildt, "'Ein radikaler Bürger,'" 31.

14. Kreutzmüller and Wildt, "'Ein radikaler Bürger,'" 38; Kreutzmüller, "Verfassung und Verwaltung der Hauptstadt," 65.

15. Dirks, "Einleitung," 16.

16. Engeli and Ribbe, "Berlin in der NS-Zeit," 973.

17. Kreutzmüller, "Verfassung und Verwaltung der Hauptstadt," 60.

18. Fieber and Rockmann, *An der Spitze Berlins*, 256–264.

19. Matzerath, *Nationalsozialismus und kommunale Selbstverwaltung*; Rebentisch, *Führerstaat und Verwaltung*; Bähr and Erker, *NetzWerke*, 107–110.

20. Matzerath, *Nationalsozialismus und kommunale Selbstverwaltung*, 433; Bähr and Erker, *Netz-Werke*, 116.

21. Hildebrandt, "Der Berliner NSDAP-Lokalfunktionär," 41.

22. Kreutzmüller and Wildt, "'Ein radikaler Bürger,'" 32. On the persecution of public employees in Berlin, Dirks, "Einleitung," 15–17.

23. Nolzen, "Die NSDAP im Gau Berlin," 71.

24. Fieber and Rockmann, *An der Spitze Berlins*, 265–273; Kreutzmüller, "Verfassung und Verwaltung der Hauptstadt," 57.

25. Kreutzmüller, "1937–Das letzte Friedensjahr?" 10.

26. Kreutzmüller and Wildt, "'Ein radikaler Bürger,'" 29.

27. On this rivalry, see Kreutzmüller, "1937–Das letzte Friedensjahr?" 10.

28. Kitchen, *Speer*, 57.

29. Werner, *Stadtplanung Berlin*, 44; Schaulinski, "Baustelle Zeichentisch," 111.

30. Kitchen, *Speer*, 57.

31. Kitchen, *Speer*, 58; Donath, "Städtebau und Architektur," 231.

32. Kitchen, *Speer*, 62.

33. Kreutzmüller, "Verfassung und Verwaltung der Hauptstadt," 58.

34. Werner, *Stadtplanung Berlin*, 43–44.

35. See letter from Mayor Sahm to Deputy Mayor Elsas and Treasurer Asch of March 18, 1933, in LAB A Rep. 015, no. 62; memo of Ziethen (Stadtbetriebsamt) of April 14, 1933 in LAB A Rep. 015, no. 62; Berliner Kraft- und Licht(Bewag)-Aktiengesellschaft, *Geschäftsbericht 1933*, 3–4; minutes of supervisory board meeting of Berliner Wasserwerke of June 20, 1933, in LAB A Rep. 255, no. 131.

36. LAB A Rep. 256, no. 173.

37. See memo from Bewag in preparation of the supervisory board meeting of December 15, 1936, in LAB A Rep. 256, no. 164.

38. See statement by Schmidt in A Pr. Br. Rep. 057, no. 1559.

39. See correspondence in LAB A Rep. 259, nos. 259 and 260.

40. Memo of 5 July 1933 in LAB A Rep. 259, no. 259.

41. Dirks and Simon, ... *auf dem Dienstweg*, 90–94.

42. See the press statement of April 1, 1936, on his retirement, LAB A Rep. 255, no. 144–02.

43. See Kühne's press statement of November 14, 1934, in LAB A Rep. 255, no. 131 and his comments in the dispute with the Charlottenburger Wasser- und Industriewerke in LAB A Rep. 015, no. 143.

44. Adolph is listed as a member of the Bewag board of directors in June 1940, LAB A Rep. 256, no. 77.

45. See his speech of May 10, 1936, citing Hitler's *Mein Kampf* in praise of the military value of sport for the German people, *Der Stromkreis* 3, no. 5 (1936): 159.

46. Memo by Ziethen to Deputy Mayor Maretzky of April 24, 1933, LAB A Rep. 015, no. 62.

47. Mecking, "Die Gleichschaltung der städtischen Belegschaft."

48. The same was the case in Munich, see Bähr and Erker, *NetzWerke*, 107–110.

49. Minutes of the Bewag board meeting of April 16, 1934, LAB A Rep. 256, no. 213; *Der Stromkreis* 6, no. 4 (1939): 119–124.

50. On Kasper, Hildebrandt, "Der Berliner NSDAP-Lokalfunktionär."

51. Kasper drew up files on all senior staff in Berlin's municipal enterprises, documenting whether they could be retired or dismissed and replaced by trusted Nazis, Hildebrandt, "Der Berliner NSDAP-Lokalfunktionär," 50.

52. Hildebrandt, "Der Berliner NSDAP-Lokalfunktionär," 51. See the letter from Deputy Gauleiter Görlitzer of October 16, 1936, approving Kasper's appointment as director, LAB A Rep. 015, no. 209.

53. See the minutes of meetings of the board of directors of Bewag in LAB A Rep. 256, no. 168.

54. Letter of Lippert to Görlitzer of December 11, 1936, and subsequent correspondence, LAB A Rep. 015, no. 62.

55. Letter of Lippert to Krecke of August 12, 1937, LAB A Rep. 015, no. 62.

56. Hachtmann and Kreutzmüller, "Arbeiter und Arbeiterorganisationen," 114.

57. A figure given by Director Artelt at the meeting of the Gasag supervisory board on September 28, 1934, LAB A Rep. 259, no. 260.

58. Hachtmann and Kreutzmüller, "Arbeiter und Arbeiterorganisationen," 122.

59. At Bewag, the number of laborers rose from 3,681 in 1933 to 4,309 in 1938, and of clerical staff from 3,074 to 3,777 over the same period. The increases were more modest for the water utility, while employment levels at Gasag were stable. See Statistisches Amt der Stadt Berlin, *Berlin in Zahlen 1945*, 329, 332, 335.

60. Presentation by Director Strassmann in an internal Bewag report on the state of the utility, 1945, LAB C Rep. 101, no. 1185; Gasag report for the rump year 1945, LAB C Rep. 105, no. 4611.

61. This was not unique to Berlin, as similar events in Munich illustrate, Bähr and Erker, *NetzWerke*, 133–134.

62. Heinrich Hauser, cited in Whyte and Frisby, *Metropolis Berlin*, 592.

63. Minutes of the meeting of the Bewag board of directors, May 5, 1933, LAB A Rep. 256, no. 212.

64. Cited in Whyte and Frisby, *Metropolis Berlin*, 592.

65. Tepasse, *Stadttechnik im Städtebau Berlins. 20. Jahrhundert*, 122.

66. Matschoß, Schulz, and Groß, *50 Jahre Berliner Elektrizitätswerke*, 206; *Der Stromkreis* 1, no. 2 (1933): 39.

67. *Der Stromkreis* 3, no. 9 (1936): 246–247.

68. Koch, "Einwirkung der XI. Olympischen Spiele," 718.

69. *Der Stromkreis* 6, no. 5 (1939): 172 and title page.

70. Hachtmann, Schaarschmidt, and Süß, "Einleitung," 17.

71. See his inaugural speech to the Reich Group for Energy in Krecke, "Die Aufgaben der deutschen Energiewirtschaft."

72. Sardemann, "Die deutsche Elektrizitätswirtschaft," 108.

73. Hellige, "Entstehungsbedingungen," 128–131; Ludwig, *Technik und Ingenieure*, 142.

74. Hellige, "Entstehungsbedingungen," 126–147. On how the 1935 Energy Act undermined municipal provision of electricity, Matzerath, *Nationalsozialismus und kommunale Selbstverwaltung*, 398–403; Hellige, "Entstehungsbedingungen," 132–133.

75. See, especially, his ninety-five-page treatise, Krecke, *Die Energiewirtschaft im nationalsozialistischen Staat*; also his speech of November 10, 1936, LAB A Rep. 256, no. 160.

76. *Der Stromkreis* 6, no. 4 (1939): 119–120; circular letter of the Wirtschaftsgruppe Elektrizitätsversorgung of September 11, 1939, LAB A Rep. 256, no. 8.

77. On Karl Kasper as a Nazi careerist, rather than a water utility director, see Hildebrandt, "Der Berliner NSDAP-Lokalfunktionär."

78. Nolzen, "Die NSDAP im Gau Berlin," 73.

79. Cited in Hildebrandt, "Der Berliner NSDAP-Lokalfunktionär," 51.

80. Kasper, "Die Trink- und Brauchwasserversorgung." On the initiative for comprehensive national water resources planning, see Schroeder, "Die wasserwirtschaftliche Generalplanung"; Heiser, "Wasserhaushalt und Raumordnung."

81. Letter from Kasper to the Berlin mayor, Steeg, of July 7, 1943, LAB A Rep. 015, no. 209.

82. Houwink Ten Cate, *Das organisierte Chaos*; Rebentisch, *Führerstaat und Verwaltung*.

83. Berg, "Nazi Rag-Pickers."

84. On the following, Ludwig, *Technik und Ingenieure*; Orland, "Der Zwiespalt zwischen Politik und Technik"; Maier, "Nationalsozialistische Technikideologie."

85. Orland, "Der Zwiespalt zwischen Politik und Technik," 278. See uses of the phrase in Seebauer, "Energiepolitik," 167, and Lawaczeck, "Zur Neuordnung der Elektrowirtschaft."

86. Orland, "Der Zwiespalt zwischen Politik und Technik," 275.

87. Ludwig, *Technik und Ingenieure*.

88. In the words of one lead article, "the spirit of technology will determine the face of the emergent Third Reich," Schmidt, "Der Kampfbund," 47.

89. Minutes of the meeting of the Bewag supervisory board of December 15, 1936, LAB A Rep. 256, no. 170.

90. Bärthel, *Die Geschichte der Gasversorgung*, 92. See Gasag report of August 20, 1933, LAB A Rep. 259, no. 403.

91. Amt für Technik, Gau Groß-Berlin, *Denkschrift*.

92. Amt für Technik, Gau Groß-Berlin, *Denkschrift*, 13.

93. Amt für Technik, Gau Groß-Berlin, *Denkschrift*, 16.

94. See the correspondence between Gasag and the Reich Group for Energy in June and July 1936, LAB A Rep. 259, no. 372.

95. Koch and Kienzle, "Bericht über die Abschlussprüfung"; memos of Gasag dated April 12, 1940, and October 24, 1940, LAB A Rep. 259, no. 189.

96. Memo of Gasag of January 20, 1943, A Rep. 259, no. 190.

97. For instance, Nübling, "Neuzeitliche Fragen der Energiewirtschaft."

98. Lawaczek, "Zur Neuordnung der Elektrowirtschaft"; Matschoß, Schulz, and Groß, *50 Jahre Berliner Elektrizitätswerke*, 79; *Der Stromkreis* 1, no. 6 (1934): 139.

99. *Der Stromkreis* 1, no. 2 (1933): 45–47.

100. Matschoß, Schulz, and Groß, *50 Jahre Berliner Elektrizitätswerke*, 95; *Der Stromkreis* 5, no. 9 (1938): 328.

101. See cartoon images in *Der Stromkreis* 2, nos. 6/8 (1935): 98.

102. *Der Stromkreis* 1, no. 2 (1933): 52; *Der Stromkreis* 3, no. 12 (1936): 358–359.

103. On the national campaign to promote sales, Heßler, "Elektrische Helfer."

104. Heßler, "Elektrische Helfer," 211–213.

105. Statistisches Amt der Stadt Berlin, *Berlin in Zahlen 1945*, 330.

106. Statistisches Amt der Stadt Berlin, *Berlin in Zahlen 1945*, 333.

107. Heßler, "'Elektrische Helfer," 217.

108. Ludwig, *Technik und Ingenieure*, 161; Maier, "'Lauchhammer', 'Döbern' und 'Ragow.'"

109. On autarky in Nazi Germany, Petzina, *Autarkiepolitik im Dritten Reich*.

110. On autarky in other fascist regimes, see Saraiva and Wise, "Autarky/Autarchy"; Gorostiza and Ortega Cerdà, "Unclaimed Latifundium." On the use of alternative fuels in the United Kingdom at this time, see Johnson, Sherry-Brennan, and Pearson, "Alternative Liquid Fuels."

111. Berg, "Nazi Rag-Pickers."

112. Berg, "Nazi Rag-Pickers," 463.

113. See a speech by Krecke on the four-year plan of October 28, 1937, *Der Stromkreis* 4, no. 11 (1937): 378–380.

114. Bärthel, *Die Geschichte der Gasversorgung*, 93–94. Archive documents attest to a keen interest of Gasag in alternative uses for its gas and by-products, LAB, A Rep. 259, nos. 182 and 261.

115. Mohajeri, *100 Jahre Berliner Wasserversorgung*, 229, 260; annual report of the water utility for 1937, LAB A Rep. 255, no. 140.

116. On the following, Moss, "Discarded Surrogates."

117. Heilmann, "Über die biologischen Grenzen," 361.

118. Pallasch, "Reinigung und Verwertung."

119. Heilmann, "Städtereinigung und Vierjahresplan," 323; Pallasch, "Reinigung und Verwertung," 336.

120. This, at least, is the opinion of Mohajeri, *100 Jahre Berliner Wasserversorgung*, 259, footnote 417, who does not provide evidence.

121. Langbein, "Die volkswirtschaftliche Bedeutung."

122. Pallasch, "Reinigung und Verwertung."

123. Imhoff, "Die deutsche Abwasser-Wissenschaft," 67.

124. Mohajeri, *100 Jahre Berliner Wasserversorgung*, 258–261.

125. Weise, "Vorschläge für die Zukunftsentwicklung."

126. Weise, "Vorschläge für die Zukunftsentwicklung," 250.

127. Kölzow, "Neue Gesichtspunkte zur Abwasserverwertung," 108.

128. Sahm's speech is cited in full in *Städtischer Nachrichtendienst* of January 25, 1935, LAB A Rep. 255, no. 157.

129. See a similar speech by Sahm given at the opening of the sewage treatment plant at Waßmannsdorf in June 1935, cited in a twelve-page report, "Die Berliner Abwasserreinigungsanlagen," compiled in October 1946, LAB A Rep. 255, no. 537.

130. Böttcher, "Der Dungwert der Berliner Abwässer."

131. Langbein, "Die volkswirtschaftliche Bedeutung des Abwassers."

132. Uekötter, *Greenest Nation?*, 50–52.

133. According to Karl Imhoff's postwar reflections, hardliners included engineers such as Stein and von Kreutz, whose ideas were welcomed largely by the authorities. The moderates included Heilmann, Pallasch, and himself, Imhoff, "Die deutsche Abwasser-Wissenschaft," 66–67.

Heilmann, however, repeatedly argued against biological treatment for reducing the agricultural value and increasing the cost of wastewater reuse, e.g., Heilmann, "Über die biologischen Grenzen," 359; Heilmann, "Städtereinigung und Vierjahresplan," 16.

134. Langbein, "Die volkswirtschaftliche Bedeutung des Abwassers"; Pallasch, "Reinigung und Verwertung."

135. Böttcher, *Untersuchungen zur Feststellung.*

136. Böttcher, "Geruchsbelästigung durch Abwasser," 104. Böttcher's membership of the NSDAP and SA was raised after the war in conjunction with his reinstatement, see the letter from the water utility director Steppler to Major Bishop of the British military administration of December 5, 1945, LAB A Rep. 254, no. 389.

137. On the initiative of Nazi rulers in Berlin to replace the "wild settlements" on the urban periphery with ordered estates of loyal supporters, Werner, *Stadtplanung Berlin*, 54–63.

138. Weise, "Vorschläge für die Zukunftsentwicklung," 252.

139. Minutes of the meeting of the water utility's supervisory board of February 21, 1935, LAB A Rep. 255, no. 131.

140. Minutes of the meeting of the water utility's supervisory board of June 20, 1933, LAB A Rep. 255, no. 131.

141. Bärthel, *Wasser für Berlin*, 176.

142. See the minutes of the meeting of the water utility's supervisory board of February 21, 1935, LAB A Rep. 255, no. 131.

143. Bärthel, *Wasser für Berlin*, 179; Bärthel, "Anlagen und Bauten der Wasserversorgung," 91.

144. Note from Gasag director Hoffmann to members of staff of March 1, 1940, LAB A Rep. 259, no. 229.

145. Kasper, "Die Vereinheitlichung der Gasversorgung in der Reichshauptstadt," 81–82; see the report "Die Berliner Gasversorgung einheitlich in öffentlicher Hand," LAB, A Rep. 259, no. 320.

146. Engeli and Ribbe, "Berlin in der NS-Zeit," 984; "Die Vereinheitlichung der Stromversorgung," 128.

147. See the correspondence between Lippert, Görlitzer, and Krecke in LAB A Rep. 015, no. 62.

148. Kasper, "Die Vereinheitlichung der Stromversorgung," 128.

149. Letter from Lippert to Krecke of August 12, 1937, LAB A Rep. 015, no. 62.

150. Letters from Mayor Lippert to the Reich economics minister of February 16, 1939, and February 28, 1939, LAB A Rep. 015, no. 76.

151. Letter from Lippert to Minister Funk of February 28, 1939, LAB A Rep. 015, no. 76.

152. Memo by Ziethen of May 10, 1940, LAB A Rep. 015, no. 76.

153. Letter from Ziethen to the Reich economics minister of May 20, 1940, LAB A Rep. 015, no. 76.

154. Memo by Ziethen to City Treasurer Lindig of May 20, 1940, LAB A Rep. 015, no. 76.

155. Memo by the municipal enterprise department to Ziethen of October 18, 1940, LAB A Rep. 015, no. 76.

156. Memo by the municipal enterprise department of April 24, 1941, LAB A Rep. 015, no. 76.

157. Engeli and Ribbe, "Berlin in der NS-Zeit," 983–995; Kitchen, *Speer*, 57–100.

158. Kitchen, *Speer*, 71.

159. Werner, *Stadtplanung Berlin*, 68.

160. Kitchen, *Speer*, 65–71.

161. Werner, *Stadtplanung Berlin*, 68.

162. Kitchen, *Speer*, 73.

163. *Der Stromkreis* 6, no. 1 (1939): 15.

164. Kitchen, *Speer*, 72.

165. Kitchen, *Speer*, 78.

166. Kitchen, *Speer*, 96.

167. Berliner Unterwelten, *Mythos Germania*, 48–50.

168. Annual report of BKL/Bewag 1939/40, LAB A Rep. 256, no. 77.

169. Report "Die Berliner Abwasserreinigungsanlagen" of October 1946, 7–8, LAB A Rep. 255, no. 537; Tepasse, *Stadttechnik im Städtebau Berlins. 20. Jahrhundert*, 41.

170. Report "Die Berliner Abwasserreinigungsanlagen" of October 1946, 8, LAB A Rep. 255, no. 537.

171. Minutes of the meeting of the water utility's supervisory board of May 4, 1939, also January 10, 1939, LAB A Rep. 255, no. 140. Cf. Bärthel, *Wasser für Berlin*, 170.

172. Speech by Director Kasper to the meeting of the water utility's supervisory board of April 10, 1941, 12, LAB A Rep. 255, no. 140.

173. Minutes of the meetings of the water utility's supervisory board of December 17, 1937, and January 10, 1939, LAB A Rep. 255, no. 140.

174. Letter from the water utility to the Inspector General of Buildings of April 19, 1940, LAB A Rep. 015, no. 143.

175. Letter from Speer to the Berlin mayor of September 30, 1940, LAB A Rep. 015, no. 146.

176. The four reports, totaling fifty-six pages, are available in LAB A Rep. 255, no. 480. See the correspondence of around 100 pages between the Berlin water utility and those commissioned to write the reports, LAB A Rep. 255, no. 370.

177. Letter from the Berlin water utility to the Berlin mayor of February 14, 1942, LAB A Rep. 015, no. 146.

178. Memo by Ziethen of the municipal enterprises department of May 28, 1942, LAB A Rep. 015, no. 146.

179. Maier, "'Lauchhammer,' 'Döbern' und 'Ragow.'"

180. Cited in Leithäuser, *Die unsichtbare Kraft*, 217.

181. Wellmann, "Vom Luftschutz der Bewag."

182. Minutes of the meeting of the Bewag board of directors of September 8, 1933, LAB A Rep. 256, no. 212.

183. Koch and Kienzle, "Bericht über die Abschlussprüfung," 70.

184. Article in *Berliner Tageblatt* of June 21, 1938, LAB A Rep. 255, no. 144–02.

185. *Der Stromkreis* 4, no. 4 (1937): 125.

186. See articles in *Der Stromkreis* 5, no. 12 (1938): 470–471 and 6, nos. 8/9 (1939): 289–290. See the letter from the Gestapo, Berlin, to the Berlin mayor of April 28, 1938, warning of sabotage by the KPD targeting the gas, electricity, and water works, LAB A Rep. 255, no. 473.

187. Scholze, "Zu einigen Problemen," 123.

188. Statistisches Amt der Stadt Berlin, *Berlin in Zahlen 1945*, 330.

189. Büsch, *Geschichte der Berliner Kommunalwirtschaft*, 204.

190. Evans, *Third Reich in Power*.

Chapter 6

1. Randzio, *Unterirdischer Städtebau*.

2. Fischer, "Die deutsche Stromversorgung im Kriege."

3. Fischer, "Die deutsche Stromversorgung im Kriege"; Sardemann, "Die deutsche Elektrizitätswirtschaft 1933 bis 1948," 112.

4. Matzerath, *Nationalsozialismus und kommunale Selbstverwaltung*, 409.

5. Matzerath, *Nationalsozialismus und kommunale Selbstverwaltung*, 416–418.

6. Annual report of BKL (Bewag) 1939/49, LAB A Rep. 256, no. 77.

7. Statistisches Amt der Stadt Berlin, *Berlin in Zahlen 1945*, 330; Geschäftsbericht der BKL (Bewag) 1941/42, LAB A Rep. 256, no. 158. Munich experienced a similar sharp increase in electricity and gas sales between 1940 and 1942 as a result of armaments production, Bähr and Erker, *NetzWerke*, 155.

8. Statistisches Amt der Stadt Berlin, *Berlin in Zahlen 1945*, 328.

9. Presentation by the director of the Berlin water utility, Karl Kasper, to the supervisory board, April 10, 1941, LAB A Rep. 255, no. 140.

10. LAB A Rep. 255, no. 140, sheet 6.

11. Bärthel, *Wasser für Berlin*, 181.

12. Director Kasper accused not only industrial users, but also Reich, Prussian, and military authorities in Berlin of using mains water only when their own, illegally extracted sources of water proved inadequate, calling for financial compensation for the major loss of revenue incurred by the utility, LAB A Rep. 255, no. 140, sheet 8.

13. Bärthel, *Wasser für Berlin*, 101.

14. Letter of the Reich Load Distributor Gas to the Load Distributor Gas of Berlin, dated October 6, 1944, LAB A Rep. 259, no. 361.

15. Memo of a meeting at the Inspectorate General for Water and Energy of November 9, 1944, LAB A Rep. 259, no. 361.

16. LAB A Rep. 259, no. 361.

17. Draft annual report of BKL (Bewag), presented to the supervisory board on May 10, 1946, LAB C Rep. 101, no. 478.

18. Presentation by the director of the Berlin water utility, Karl Kasper, to the supervisory board, April 10, 1941, LAB A Rep. 255, no. 140.

19. LAB C Rep. 101, no. 478.

20. Bausch, "Der Zusammenbruch der Gasversorgung 1945," 29.

21. Cf. Similar labor shortages in Munich's Stadtwerke, Bähr and Erker, *NetzWerke*, 150.

22. Memo of Bewag's directors, entitled "Die Organisation der Bewag," dated May 17, 1940, LAB A Rep. 256, no. 191.

23. Eye witness accounts cited in Moorhouse, *Berlin at War*, 36–37.

24. Memo of the Economic Group for Electricity Supply, dated October 30, 1939, LAB A Rep. 256, no. 8.

25. Letter from the Office of Agriculture for the Berlin economic zone to the Armaments Inspection Department of the Army District III, dated November 29, 1941, LAB A Rep. 259, no. 393.

26. Letter from the Load Distributor for Gas to the Office of Agriculture for the Berlin economic zone, dated December 6, 1941, LAB A Rep. 259, no. 393.

27. Letter from the Inspector General for Water and Energy (signed by Fritz Todt) to the District Load Distributors for Electricity and Gas, dated February 5, 1942, LAB A Rep. 259, no. 393.

28. "Energie sparen!" 33; Greiner, "Vom Energiesparen."

29. Ruhstrat, "Wir sparen Energie," 423.

30. Mörs, "Die Aufgaben des Energie-Ingenieurs"; Ruhstrat, "Wir sparen Energie"; Schuster, "Leistungssteigerung"; Hartmann, "Energieeinschränkungen"; cf. Sardemann, "Die deutsche Elektrizitätswirtschaft 1933 bis 1948," 110.

31. "Strom ist kriegswichtig!"

32. Bezirksamt Charlottenburg von Berlin, *Stadt unter Strom*, 48.

33. Memo of Gasag, entitled "Berlin Gas Filling Network," dated May 26, 1942, LAB A Rep. 259, no. 342.

34. Minutes of the meeting of the Berlin Methane Distribution Company of June 9, 1943, LAB A Rep. 259, no. 342.

35. Annual report of the Berlin Methane Distribution Company for 1943, dated April 14, 1944, LAB A Rep. 259, no. 342.

36. Memo of Gasag, entitled "The Sale of High-Pressure Gas for Vehicles in Berlin," dated September 25, 1944, LAB A Rep. 259, no. 342.

37. Annual report of the Berlin Methane Distribution Company for 1943, dated April 14, 1944, and minutes of the meeting of its supervisory board on April 27, 1944, LAB A Rep. 259, no. 342.

38. Memo of the Gasag employee Gückler of October 5, 1944, LAB A Rep. 259, no. 342.

39. Letter from President-Director Hoffmann of Gasag to Director Dominik of the Reich Ministry for Propaganda of October 17, 1944, LAB A Rep. 259, no. 342.

40. See chapter 5. Cf. Steinmann, "Die deutsche Elektrizitätsversorgung."

41. Pohl, "Der Luftschutz."

42. Kasper, "Kriegsaufgaben in der Wasserversorgung"; Bärthel, *Wasser für Berlin*, 183.

43. Kellerhoff, "Luftkrieg um die Reichshauptstadt," 247; Demps, "Berlin im Bombenkrieg," 359.

44. Schieder, "Staat und Wirtschaft," 197.

45. Demps, "Berlin im Bombenkrieg," 360.

46. Demps, *Luftangriffe auf Berlin*, 250.

47. Demps, "Berlin im Bombenkrieg," 367.

48. Sardemann, "Die deutsche Elektrizitätswirtschaft 1933 bis 1948," 112.

49. Overy, *Interrogations*, 136.

50. For examples of damage to utilities in German cities, see Diefendorf, *In the Wake of War*, 16–17.

51. Bärthel, *Geklärt!*, 168; Zabel, "Die Kanalisation Berlins," 172–173.

52. Zabel, "Die Kanalisation Berlins," 172; Vohrer, "Die Kriegsschäden," 70.

53. Bärthel, *Geklärt!*, 168; Zabel, "Die Kanalisation Berlins," 173.

54. Vohrer, "Die Kriegsschäden," 70.

55. Zabel, "Die Kanalisation Berlins," 172.

56. Bärthel, *Wasser für Berlin*, 186–187.

57. Bärthel, *Wasser für Berlin*, 189.

58. Bärthel, *Wasser für Berlin*, 185. See, for example, an overview of bombing damage incurred in three bombing raids in late August and early September 1943 compiled by the Berlin water utility, reporting 950 destroyed water appliances and an estimated loss of 500,000 cubic meters of water, LAB A Rep. 255, no. 488.

59. Bärthel, *Wasser für Berlin*, 185, 187.

60. Memo of the Berlin gas utility, Gasag, dated January 20, 1943, LAB A Rep. 259, no. 190.

61. Bärthel, *Die Geschichte der Gasversorgung*, 101. Bombing of the long-distance pipeline led repeatedly to complete disruption to imported gas supplies, as for example between January 14 and February 1, 1945, and again between February 15 and 19, 1945; see report of the Load Distributor for Gas in Berlin to the Armament Inspection Office III, dated March 5, 1945, LAB A Rep. 259, no. 415.

62. Bärthel, *Die Geschichte der Gasversorgung*, 101.

63. Berliner Gaswerke, *100 Jahre Berliner Städtische Gaswerke*, 22; Bärthel, *Die Geschichte der Gasversorgung*, 102.

64. "Zustand der Berliner Gasversorgung," 90; Berliner Gaswerke, *100 Jahre Berliner Städtische Gaswerke*, 28.

65. Berliner Gaswerke, *100 Jahre Berliner Städtische Gaswerke*, 28.

66. Demps, *Luftangriffe auf Berlin*, 39.

67. Wissell in the report on the state of BKL (Bewag) from May to November 1945 (undated), LAB C Rep. 101, no. 1185.

68. Draft annual report of BKL (Bewag) for 1944–1945, presented to its supervisory board on May 10, 1946, LAB C Rep. 101, no. 478.

69. Wissell in the report on the state of BKL (Bewag) from May to November 1945 (undated), LAB C Rep. 101, no. 1185.

70. Bärthel, *Geklärt!*, 172.

71. See the invoices submitted between 1944 and 1945 by the Berlin water utility in LAB A Rep. 255, nos. 308–01 and 488 and by Bewag in LAB A Rep. 256, no. 185.

72. In April 1943 the authorities responsible for compensation were insisting that each individual affected by bombing damage had to submit their own separate claim, see the memo of the legal department of the Berlin water utility of April 22, 1943, LAB A Rep. 255, no. 308–01.

73. Demps, *Luftangriffe auf Berlin*, 337; Tepasse, *Stadttechnik im Städtebau Berlins. 20. Jahrhundert*, 41.

74. On forced labor in Nazi Germany, Herbert, *Fremdarbeiter*.

75. On the wastewater utility's missing records, Bärthel, *Geklärt!*, 167. A recent study of Hamburg's water and wastewater utilities during the Nazi era encountered similar problems, Templin, *Wasser für die Volksgemeinschaft*, 246–262.

76. Memo of Gasag, dated April 3, 1940, LAB A Rep. 259, no. 385.

77. Memo of Gasag, dated May 31, 1940, LAB A Rep. 259, no. 385.

78. List of Gasag, dated April 1941, LAB A Rep. 259, no. 205.

79. Letter of Gasag to the civil defense unit of local military command (*Wehrkreis* III), June 26, 1941, and letter of Gasag to the mayor of Berlin, October 16, 1941, LAB A Rep. 259, no. 385.

80. Letter of Gasag to the mayor of Berlin, October 16, 1941, LAB A Rep. 259, no. 385.

81. Letter of Gasag to the mayor of Berlin, July 8, 1941, LAB A Rep. 259, no. 385.

82. Letter of the mayor of Berlin to Gasag, July 19, 1941, LAB A Rep. 259, no. 385.

83. Memo by Dr. Cronacher (Gasag) on espionage, dated July 8, 1939, LAB A Rep. 259, no. 400.

84. Manuscript of a speech by director Kiesel (Gasag), dated July 29, 1939, LAB A Rep. 259, no. 400.

85. Letter of the Stadtpräsident of Berlin to the directors of Bewag, Gasag, Wassag, and Charlottenburger Wasser- und Industriewerke of May 29, 1942, LAB A Rep. 259, no. 393.

86. Circular of the Berlin unit of the Gestapo to the mayor of Berlin of August 8, 1942, LAB A Rep. 259, no. 402.

87. List of foreign laborers, compiled by Gasag, dated October 12, 1942, LAB A Rep. 259, no. 205.

88. Beevor, *Berlin*, 1945.

89. Randzio, *Unterirdischer Städtebau*, 61.

90. Bärthel, *Wasser für Berlin*, 189.

91. Cited in Schieder, "Staat und Wirtschaft," 197.

92. Wetzlaugk, *Die Alliierten in Berlin*, 23–28; Ribbe, "Berlin zwischen Ost und West," 1036–1039. The London Protocol was confirmed at the Yalta Conference of February 1945 and came into force as the Berlin Declaration on June 5, 1945.

93. Reichhardt, "Wiederaufbau und Festigung," 7.

94. Schlegelmilch, Hauptstadt im Zonendeutschland, 97.

95. Schlegelmilch, "Tendenzen," 5.

96. Air access was, by contrast, guaranteed under the London Protocol. This was to prove decisive during the blockade of 1948–1949.

97. Bisky, *Berlin*, 638–640.

98. Cited in Reichhardt, "Wiederaufbau und Festigung," 9, and Wetzlaugk, *Die Alliierten in Berlin*, 35.

99. On Werner as mayor, Fieber and Rockmann, *An der Spitze Berlins*, 72–76; Schlegelmilch, *Hauptstadt im Zonendeutschland*, 105–109.

100. The citation is from Fieber and Rockmann, *An der Spitze Berlins*, 73. Werner has also been referred to as a "puppet" of the communists, Ribbe, "Berlin zwischen Ost und West," 1030. He clearly lacked political acumen, Large, *Berlin*, 382.

101. Ribbe, "Berlin zwischen Ost und West," 1030; Schlegelmilch, *Hauptstadt im Zonendeutschland*, 109.

102. Reichhardt, "Wiederaufbau und Festigung," 9; Large, *Berlin*, 382.

103. Reichhardt, "Wiederaufbau und Festigung," 8.

104. Wetzlaugk, *Die Alliierten in Berlin*, 35.

105. Schlegelmilch, *Hauptstadt im Zonendeutschland*, 104.

106. Ribbe, "Berlin zwischen Ost und West," 1040–1042.

107. Reichhardt, "Wiederaufbau und Festigung," 17–20.

108. Large, *Berlin*, 397.

109. Reichhardt, "Wiederaufbau und Festigung," 21–24, Ribbe, "Berlin zwischen Ost und West," 1044–1046.

110. Bisky, *Berlin*, 652–665.

111. On Ostrowski as mayor, Fieber and Rockmann, *An der Spitze Berlins*, 77–81; Ribbe, "Berlin zwischen Ost und West," 1044–1045.

112. Schlegelmilch, *Hauptstadt im Zonendeutschland*, 581.

113. Reichhardt, "Wiederaufbau und Festigung," 28. On Schroeder as acting mayor, Fieber and Rockmann, *An der Spitze Berlins*, 82–87. When Schroeder had to stand down for health reasons for three months in the autumn of 1948 the post of acting mayor was held by Ferdinand Friedensburg (CDU).

114. Bärthel, *Wasser für Berlin*, 189.

115. Bärthel, *Wasser für Berlin*, 191.

116. Senat von Berlin, *Berlin. Kampf um Freiheit und Selbstverwaltung*; LAB C Rep. 101, no. 13. At a meeting held the previous day with the city's utility directors the Soviet Colonel Subawin expressed uncharacteristic praise for the efforts being taken to restore electricity, gas, water, and sanitation services in the city, memo of Bewag, dated June 28, 1945, LAB C Rep. 752, no. 99.

117. Bausch, "Der Zusammenbruch der Gasversorgung," 30.

118. Bausch, "Der Zusammenbruch der Gasversorgung," 30.

119. See, for example, the correspondence between the British military authorities and Charlottenburger Wasser- und Industriewerke between 1945 and 1946, LAB A Rep. 254, no. 389.

120. Diefendorf, *In the Wake of War*, 249–251.

121. Large, *Berlin*, 376.

122. LAB C Rep. 752, no. 155.

123. Leithäuser, *Die unsichtbare Kraft*, 220. See director Witte's detailed reports of May 29, 1945, LAB A Rep. 256, no. 122, and of October 8, 1945, LAB C Rep. 101, no. 422. Complaints by Witte about continuous interventions by the Red Army in the running of the utilities made at a meeting with Soviet Colonel Subawin on June 25, 1945, did not elicit a response, see Bewag memo of June 28, 1945, LAB C Rep. 752, no. 99.

124. Leithäuser, *Die unsichtbare Kraft*, 220.

125. *Zehn Jahre Wiederaufbau der Berliner Stromversorgung*, 1.

126. Bausch, "Der Zusammenbruch der Gasversorgung," 30.

127. This resonates with Stephen Collier's findings on post-Soviet Russia, where the resilience of district heating systems helped sustain life in the disruptive 1990s, Collier, *Post-Soviet Social*, 7–8.

128. Hauptamt für Statistik und Wahlen des Magistrats von Groß-Berlin, *Berlin in Zahlen 1946–1947*, 413.

129. Bärthel, *Wasser für Berlin*, 193; Magistrat von Groß-Berlin, *Berlin 1947*, 136.

130. Report of the Berlin water utility to the British military authorities of August 31, 1946, LAB A Rep. 254, no. 389.

131. Zabel, "Die Kanalisation Berlins," 173.

132. Letter of the Berlin sanitation department to Major David H. Woods of the US High Command, October 26, 1945, LAB A Rep. 255, no. 537.

133. Zabel, "Die Kanalisation Berlins," 173. Undernourishment was a serious concern of staff at Bewag, too, who passed a resolution on July 9, 1947, complaining that they lacked the physical strength to conduct regular work, citing a medical report that 70 percent of the workforce was underweight, LAB C Rep. 101, no. 422.

134. Zabel, "Die Kanalisation Berlins," 174. An article in the newspaper *Tägliche Rundschau* of March 4, 1947 reported that there were still around 30,000 destroyed toilets in the American sector alone, and another 20,000 in the borough of Wedding, LAB C Rep. 118, no. 243.

135. Annual report of Gasag for 1945, LAB C Rep. 105, no. 4611.

136. Senat von Berlin, *Berlin. Kampf um Freiheit und Selbstverwaltung.*

137. "Zustand der Berliner Gasversorgung," 91.

138. Annual report of Gasag for 1946, LAB C Rep. 105, no. 4611.

139. Hauptamt für Statistik und Wahlen des Magistrats von Groß-Berlin, *Berlin in Zahlen 1946–1947*, 412.

140. Hauptamt für Statistik und Wahlen des Magistrats von Groß-Berlin, *Berlin in Zahlen 1946–1947*, 412; cf. Magistrat von Groß-Berlin, *Berlin 1947*, 136; Bärthel, *Die Geschichte der Gasversorgung*, 104.

141. Report compiled on October 8, 1945, LAB C Rep. 101, no. 422.

142. Hauptamt für Statistik und Wahlen des Magistrats von Groß-Berlin, *Berlin in Zahlen 1946–1947*, 411.

143. Hauptamt für Statistik und Wahlen des Magistrats von Groß-Berlin, *Berlin in Zahlen 1946–1947*, 411.

144. Statistical data in LAB C Rep. 752, no. 309.

145. Senat von Berlin, *Berlin. Kampf um Freiheit und Selbstverwaltung.*

146. Electricity rationing was introduced for the first time in Berlin on September 1, 1945. The thirty-day quota for lighting was 15 kWh per household plus 1.5 kWh per person and for cooking 36 kWh per household plus 6.0 kWh per person, Hauptamt für Statistik und Wahlen des Magistrats von Groß-Berlin, *Berlin in Zahlen 1946–1947*, 249.

147. Senat von Berlin, *Berlin. Kampf um Freiheit und Selbstverwaltung.*

148. *Die Sitzungsprotokolle des Magistrats der Stadt Berlin 1945/46. Teil I. 1945*, 708; Senat von Berlin, *Berlin. Kampf um Freiheit und Selbstverwaltung.*

149. *Die Sitzungsprotokolle des Magistrats der Stadt Berlin 1945/46. Teil I. 1945*, 710–714.

150. Magistrat von Groß-Berlin, *Berlin 1947*, 133. The coal reserves on January 16, 1947, were enough to power the station at Klingenberg for eighteen days, but at Rummelsburg for only five, and

at the power stations in Charlottenburg, Moabit, and Wilmersdorf for between one and three days, minutes of a meeting of the Bewag supervisory board on January 17, 1947, LAB C Rep. 101, no. 446.

151. *Die Sitzungsprotokolle des Magistrats der Stadt Berlin 1945/46. Teil I*, 686, footnote 13.

152. *Die Sitzungsprotokolle des Magistrats der Stadt Berlin 1945/46. Teil II*, 772–775, 896–898.

153. Senat von Berlin, *Berlin. Behauptung von Freiheit und Selbstverwaltung.*

154. Report of Bewag, dated January 13, 1947, LAB C Rep. 752, no. 2.

155. Bewag memo of March 17, 1947, LAB C Rep. 752, no. 99.

156. By March 1947 only 1.9 million of the 34 million Reichsmark had been paid, Bewag memo of March 17, 1947, LAB C Rep. 752, no. 99.

157. Minutes of a meeting of the Bewag board of directors, February 6, 1948, LAB C Rep. 752, no. 317.

158. Bewag memo of March 17, 1947, LAB C Rep. 752, no. 99; minutes of a meeting of the Bewag board of directors, February 6, 1948, LAB C Rep. 752, no. 317.

159. In 1946 Elektrowerke provided Bewag with 706 million kWh, compared with the 644 million kWh generated by Bewag itself, letter from Bewag to Elektrowerke, dated January 8, 1947, LAB A Rep. 250-03-07, no. 171.

160. Magistrat von Groß-Berlin, *Berlin 1947*, 135; cf. the agreement between the Soviet and Western Allies of December 1, 1947, LAB C Rep. 752, no. 2.

161. Letter of Allied Military Command to Bewag board of directors, dated March 3, 1948, LAB C Rep. 752, no. 2.

162. Berliner Kraft- und Licht(Bewag)-Aktiengesellschaft, *Inbetriebsetzung des Neubaus Kraftwerk West*, 4.

163. Diefendorf, *In the Wake of War*, 20.

164. Werner, *Stadtplanung Berlin*, 74–99.

165. Moest, *Der Zehlendorfer Plan*, 10; Bonatz, "Der neue Plan von Berlin"; cf. Diefendorf, *In the Wake of War*, 192–193.

166. Memo by a representative of the Berlin water utility on Randzio's presentation to the building committee on May 16, 1946, LAB A Rep. 255, no. 537. Randzio's report was published only later by the Academy of Spatial Research and Planning (ARL) in recognition of its significance to urban planning in post-war Germany, Randzio, *Unterirdischer Städtebau.*

167. Randzio, *Unterirdischer Städtebau*, 15.

168. Randzio, *Unterirdischer Städtebau*, 61.

169. Memo by a representative of the Berlin water utility on Randzio's presentation to the building committee on May 16, 1946, LAB A Rep. 255, no. 537.

170. Randzio, *Unterirdischer Städtebau*, 8.

171. For example, Zabel, "Die Kanalisation Berlins," 174.

172. Werner, *Stadtplanung Berlin*, 78. See also Laak, *Alles im Fluss*, 90.

173. Bonatz, "Der neue Plan von Berlin," 755, 762; Bonatz, "Meine Stellungnahme," 165.

174. Denner, "Der Grundwasserstand"; Pfeil, "Das Wiederansteigen des Grundwasserspiegels"; Denner, "Schutzgebiete."

175. Denner, "Der Grundwasserstand," 59; Pfeil, "Das Wiederansteigen des Grundwasserspiegels"; see letter from the director of CWI to Major Bishop of the British Military Government of January 18, 1946, LAB A Rep. 254, no. 389.

176. Denner, "Der Grundwasserstand"; Pfeil, "Das Wiederansteigen des Grundwasserspiegels"; Denner, "Schutzgebiete."

177. Denner, "Der Grundwasserstand."

178. Ribbe, "Berlin zwischen Ost und West," 1031; Large, *Berlin*, 390–391.

179. *Die Sitzungsprotokolle des Magistrats der Stadt Berlin 1945/46. Teil I*, 190.

180. Annual reports of Gasag, LAB B Rep. 155, no. 119.

181. Betriebsrat der Berliner Kraft- und Licht(Bewag)-Aktiengesellschaft, *Im Licht der Zeit*, 75–78.

182. Letter of Bewag to the city council's department for municipal enterprises, dated September 14, 1945, LAB C Rep. 101, no. 422.

183. Betriebsrat der Berliner Kraft- und Licht(Bewag)-Aktiengesellschaft, *Im Licht der Zeit*, 77–78.

184. Minutes of a meeting of the supervisory board of BKL/Bewag on June 28, 1946, LAB C Rep. 101, no. 1185.

185. Bewag report covering the period May to November 1945, LAB C Rep. 101, no. 1185.

186. Betriebsrat der Berliner Kraft- und Licht(Bewag)-Aktiengesellschaft, *Im Licht der Zeit*, 76.

187. Bewag report covering the period May to December 1945, LAB C Rep. 105, no. 4611.

188. See letter of the director of CWI, Steppler, to US headquarters, dated December 29, 1945, appealing for the early release from detention of key personnel, LAB A Rep. 254, no. 389.

189. *Die Sitzungsprotokolle des Magistrats der Stadt Berlin 1945/46. Teil I*, 104.

190. Senat von Berlin, *Berlin. Kampf um Freiheit und Selbstverwaltung*; *Die Sitzungsprotokolle des Magistrats der Stadt Berlin 1945/46. Teil I*, 352–355.

191. *Die Sitzungsprotokolle des Magistrats der Stadt Berlin 1945/46. Teil I*, 354. A letter from Deputy Mayor Maron to the KPD of December 7, 1945, characterized one of Bewag's directors (Witte) as being sympathetic to the KPD, two others (Wissell and Strassmann) as being SPD members and

the fourth (Nain) as having been a member of the NSDAP, *Die Sitzungsprotokolle des Magistrats der Stadt Berlin 1945/46. Teil I*, 684–686.

192. *Die Sitzungsprotokolle des Magistrats der Stadt Berlin 1945/46. Teil II*, 512–514.

193. Letter of Bewag to the Central German Commission for Sequestration and Confiscation, dated July 30, 1947, LAB C Rep. 752, no. 279.

194. Letter of Bewag (signed Fleischmann) to director Witte of January 10, 1946 and memo of Bewag of February 14, 1946, LAB C Rep. 752, no. 99.

195. Minutes of a meeting of Bewag directors on May 31, 1946, LAB C Rep. 752, no. 317.

196. Bärthel, *Wasser für Berlin*, 179–180.

197. Minutes of a meeting of the supervisory board of the Berlin water utility on December 30, 1954, LAB B Rep. 011, no. 19.

198. A comparison with South Africa in the 1990s is instructive here, Schnitzler, *Democracy's Infrastructure*, 4–5.

199. Reichhardt, "Wiederaufbau und Festigung," 35–38; Schlegelmilch, *Hauptstadt im Zonendeutschland*, 131ff; Large, *Berlin*, 399.

200. Reichhardt, "Wiederaufbau und Festigung," 38–43; Ribbe, "Berlin zwischen Ost und West," 1052–1061.

201. Large, *Berlin*, 401.

202. On the Berlin blockade, see Schlegelmilch, *Hauptstadt im Zonendeutschland*, 536–559; Wetzlaugk, *Die Alliierten in Berlin*, 38–49; Ribbe, "Berlin zwischen Ost und West," 1061–1066. The blockade of West Berlin was never complete: the passage of people and goods remained possible between the Western and Soviet sectors of the city and—thereby—also with the surrounding Soviet zone, Large, *Berlin*, 402.

203. On the following, Moss, "Divided City, Divided Infrastructures." On the economic consequences of the blockade on Berlin, Baar, "Die Berliner Industrie," 147–148.

204. Magistrat von Groß-Berlin, *Berlin 1949*, 76.

205. On June 24, 1948, Senat von Berlin, *Berlin. Behauptung von Freiheit und Selbstverwaltung*.

206. Magistrat von Groß-Berlin, *Berlin 1948*, 52.

207. Magistrat von Groß-Berlin, *Berlin 1949*, 76.

208. Bärthel, *Die Geschichte der Gasversorgung*, 109.

209. Bärthel, *Die Geschichte der Gasversorgung*, 108.

210. Magistrat von Groß-Berlin, *Berlin 1948*, 52. See the correspondence between the Berlin mayor and the Allied commanders on coal shortages for power generation in LAB B Rep. 010, no. 1333.

211. Letters from the French, British, and American military authorities to the Berlin mayor, dated July 9, 1948, LAB B Rep. 010, no. 1333.

212. Magistrat von Groß-Berlin, *Berlin 1948*, 54.

213. Article in *Die Neue Zeitung*, July 3, 1948.

214. This was reported in the press in both parts of the city, see the *Telegraf* of January 9, 1949, and *Berliner Zeitung* of the same day, LAB A Rep. 255, no. 370.

215. Wetzlaugk, *Die Alliierten in Berlin*, 46.

216. Bärthel, *Die Geschichte der Gasversorgung*, 194.

217. Berliner Kraft- und Licht(Bewag)-Aktiengesellschaft, *Inbetriebsetzung des Neubaus Kraftwerk West*, 5.

218. Wetzlaugk, *Die Alliierten in Berlin*, 37; Schlegelmilch, *Hauptstadt im Zonendeutschland*, 577.

219. Ribbe, "Berlin zwischen Ost und West," 1065; Wetzlaugk, *Die Alliierten in Berlin*, 40.

220. Schlegelmilch, *Hauptstadt im Zonendeutschland*, 541.

221. Berliner Kraft- und Licht(Bewag)-Aktiengesellschaft, *Strom für Berlin*, 6.

222. Minutes of meetings of the Bewag board of directors on January 7 and June 14, 1949, LAB C Rep. 752, no. 14.

223. Handwritten translation of an order by the Soviet military authorities to Bewag of June 26, 1948, LAB C Rep. 752, no. 3.

224. Schlegelmilch, *Hauptstadt im Zonendeutschland*, 139–141.

225. Reichhardt, "Wiederaufbau und Festigung," 47.

226. Reichhardt, "Wiederaufbau und Festigung," 49.

227. Letter from Soviet military authorities to Bewag director Witte of December 4, 1948, LAB C Rep. 752, no. 3.

228. Senat von Berlin, *Berlin. Ringen um Einheit und Wiederaufbau*. The Soviet military authorities later appointed a full team of three directors for Bewag (East): Witte (SED), Schlicke (independent), and Mundt (SED), memo of mayor's office, dated March 11, 1949, LAB C Rep. 101, no. 296.

229. Bärthel, *Die Geschichte der Gasversorgung*, 109.

230. Senat von Berlin, *Berlin. Ringen um Einheit und Wiederaufbau*; Bärthel, *Wasser für Berlin*, 195.

231. Bärthel, *Wasser für Berlin*, 196.

232. Memo of the city department for transportation and enterprises, dated April 8, 1949, LAB C Rep. 101, no. 296. Trading deals with the Soviets were not uncommon owing to their dependence on Western manufactured goods, Large, *Berlin*, 410.

233. Letter of (East Berlin) mayor Ebert to Bewag of May 27, 1949, LAB C Rep. 101, no. 296.

234. Magistrat von Groß-Berlin, *Berlin 1949*, 76.

235. Magistrat von Groß-Berlin, *Berlin 1949*, 78.

236. Senat von Berlin, *Berlin. Ringen um Einheit und Wiederaufbau.*

Chapter 7

1. *Generalplan der stadttechnischen Versorgung der Hauptstadt der Deutschen Demokratischen Republik, Berlin*, dated May 1970, LAB C Rep. 107, no. 811.

2. Interview 22.

3. *Generalplan*, LAB C Rep. 107, no. 811, 3.

4. Interview 22.

5. Reichhardt, "Wiederaufbau und Festigung," 69; Ribbe, "Das gespaltene Berlin," 68–69.

6. Large, *Berlin*, 415.

7. Cited in Elkins and Hofmeister, *Berlin*, 49.

8. Large, *Berlin*, 417.

9. Statistical data in LAB C Rep. 752, no. 309.

10. See minutes of meetings of the Energy Commission of Berlin in May 1952 and January 1953, LAB C Rep. 752, no. 38.

11. Musterle, "1955," 2. On the Stalinallee as a showcase for socialist architecture and urban design, see Wise, *Capital Dilemma*, 41–44.

12. Lehmann, "Fernheizung," 194.

13. *Perpektivplan der Bewag*, dated October 16, 1956, LAB C Rep. 752, no. 141.

14. Mampel, "Die politische Ordnung," 55.

15. Elkins and Hofmeister, *Berlin*, 49.

16. Mampel, "Die politische Ordnung," 64–65, 75.

17. Mampel, "Die politische Ordnung," 69.

18. Zschaler, "Die wirtschaftliche Spaltung Berlins," 48.

19. Werner, *Stadtplanung Berlin*, 119.

20. Gropp, "Die Elektrizitätswirtschaft," 159–160.

21. Nöldeke, "10 Jahre Elektroenergiewirtschaft," 436.

22. Letter of Bewag (East) to the mayor Friedrich Ebert, dated December 11, 1953, and an undated memo by the directors, LAB C Rep. 752, no. 157.

23. See the minutes of meetings of Bewag (East) directors, LAB C Rep. 752, no. 20, and the *Perpektivplan der Bewag* of October 1956, LAB C Rep. 752, no. 141.

24. Musterle, "1955," 1; Peters, "Es geht um die Verbesserung," 3.

25. Letter of the water unit of the city council to the finance department of February 26, 1964, LAB C Rep. 106–02, no. 648.

26. Bärthel, *Die Geschichte der Gasversorgung*, 113.

27. Bärthel, *Die Geschichte der Gasversorgung*, 123.

28. Schlegelmilch, "Tendenzen," 14.

29. Zschaler, "Die wirtschaftliche Spaltung Berlins," 68.

30. Casper, "Infrastruktur," 147, 149.

31. Mampel, "Die politische Ordnung," 71.

32. See the speech by the Minister of Coal and Energy, Mitzinger, in Mitzinger, "Gegenwärtiger Stand," 161–162.

33. See, for example, the report of the city council's planning unit on the role of the energy, heating, and water sectors in implementing the second and third five-year plans, dated August 28, 1958, LAB C Rep. 106–02, no. 647. As an example of planning targets, see the twelve-page list of planning data for the VEB Gasversorgung Berlin in 1972, LAB C Rep. 621, no. 70.

34. Collier, *Post-Soviet Social*, 211.

35. Letter from the water and sanitation utility to the city council of March 6, 1959, LAB C Rep. 106–02, no. 647.

36. Papke, "Die Abwasserüberleitung Berlin-Eberswalde," 147.

37. VEB Gasversorgung Berlin, *Betriebskollektivvertrag 1963*.

38. Report of the SED group on urban technology in the city council (*APO-Stadttechnik*) on implementing the five-year plan, dated March 3, 1981, LAB C Rep. 904–059, no. 102.

39. SED-Betriebsparteiorganisation Bewag, *Unsere Kraft. Betriebsgeschichte der Bewag, 2. Teil*, 42.

40. SED-Betriebsparteiorganisation Bewag, *Unsere Kraft. Betriebsgeschichte der Bewag, 2. Teil*, 78.

41. SED-Betriebsparteiorganisation Bewag, *Unsere Kraft. Betriebsgeschichte der Bewag, 2. Teil*, 86.

42. See the many programs of brigades at the Klingenberg power station in 1973, LAB C Rep. 752, no. 222.

43. Augustine, *Red Prometheus*, xi.

44. Cf. Laak, "Infra-Strukturgeschichte," 383; Augustine, *Red Prometheus*, 349.

45. Minutes of a meeting between utility directors and the city council of November 25, 1950, LAB C Rep. 752, no. 20.

46. Minutes of a meeting of the Bewag (East) board of directors of October 25, 1952, LAB C Rep. 752, no. 17.

47. See countless letters from VVB Energieversorgung to Bewag (East) between 1969 and 1972, LAB C Rep. 621, no. 73.

48. Musterle, "Ein Jahr volkseigene Wasserwirtschaft," 1; Musterle, "1955," 1; Haase, "Die Stellung der Wasserwirtschaft," 1–2.

49. Bärthel, *Wasser für Berlin*, 202.

50. Bärthel, *Geklärt!*, 176.

51. Report by the (East) Berlin water and wastewater utility WEW of February 9, 1962, LAB C Rep. 106–02, no. 656.

52. Thalheim, "Verkehr und Versorgungsbetriebe," 154.

53. Most households in the DDR paid for water as part of their rent. It was generally charged according to one collective meter for a whole apartment block. In 1989 the residential water tariff, at 0.25 Marks per cubic meter, was subsidized by up to 1.50 Marks per cubic meter, Stadtfeld, "Die Entwicklung der öffentlichen Wasserversorgung," 669. In other words, sales revenues generated only around one-seventh of supply costs. Any reserves for investments were, under these circumstances, illusory.

54. Reconstruction plan of the (East) Berlin water and wastewater utility WEW of September 15, 1962, LAB C Rep. 106–02, no. 648.

55. Bärthel, *Wasser für Berlin*, 233.

56. Bärthel, *Wasser für Berlin*, 203.

57. Bärthel, *Wasser für Berlin*, 204.

58. Letter from the councillor for urban infrastructure, Hilbert, to all councillors, dated May 20, 1971, LAB C Rep. 101, no. 794.

59. Bärthel, *Wasser für Berlin*, 233.

60. Reconstruction plan of the (East) Berlin water and wastewater utility WEW of September 15, 1962, LAB C Rep. 106–02, no. 648.

61. Bärthel, *Geklärt!*, 179.

62. Bärthel, *Geklärt!*, 179. In February 1969 a confidential report by the river authority for the Upper Spree in Berlin stated that the daily amount of sewage irrigated on the sewage farms was over double the maximum permitted capacity, Schwenk and Weisspflug, *Umweltschmutz und Umweltschutz*, 163.

63. Schwenk and Weisspflug, *Umweltschmutz und Umweltschutz*, 169.

64. Bärthel, *Geklärt!*, 179.

65. Bärthel, *Geklärt!*, 179; Schiemann and Dautermann, "Ist-Stand," 87.

66. Bärthel, *Geklärt!*, 186.

67. Bärthel, *Geklärt!*, 201.

68. Schwenk and Weisspflug, *Umweltschmutz und Umweltschutz*, 169.

69. Sommer, "Die öffentliche Stromversorgung," 100. See the high consumption figures predicted for 1980 and 1990 in a prognosis of March 12, 1968, LAB C Rep. 752, no. 120.

70. VEB Energiekombinat Berlin, *40 Jahre Deutsche Demokratische Republik*, 10.

71. The number of installed gas heaters in East Berlin grew from 45,941 in 1978 to 190,682 in 1988, VEB Energiekombinat Berlin, *40 Jahre Deutsche Demokratische Republik*, 13.

72. Tepasse, *Stadttechnik im Städtebau Berlins. 20. Jahrhundert*, 182. On the significance of district heating in establishing a new pattern of "networked urbanism" in socialist states, see Collier, *Post-Soviet Social*, 21, 102.

73. Report of Bewag (East) of April 14, 1969, LAB C Rep. 107, no. 217.

74. Cited in Bärthel, *Die Geschichte der Gasversorgung*, 116.

75. Report of VVB Energieversorgung of 1976, LAB C Rep. 750–02, no. 7.

76. See reports in LAB C Rep. 101, no. 793.

77. Letter of the Energy Commission of Berlin of October 28, 1952, Senat von Berlin, *Berlin. Chronik der Jahre 1951–1954* (entry for October 30, 1953).

78. Memo of Bewag (East) of October 14, 1954, LAB C Rep. 752, no. 38.

79. Report of the Energy Commission of Berlin of January 11, 1971, LAB C Rep. 101, no. 793.

80. Minutes by the Ministry of Heavy Industry of a meeting on electricity supply in Berlin, dated January 19, 1954, LAB, C Rep. 620–01, no. 66.

81. Letter of the city councillor for urban infrastructure, Hilbert, to the mayor, Fechner, dated March 3, 1972, LAB C Rep. 101, no. 794.

82. The last plan to encompass Greater Berlin was the Gesamtplan of 1955, Ribbe, *Berlin 1945–2000*, 95. For details, see Linke, "Großsiedlungen in Ost-Berlin," 165–166.

83. See planning documents relating to electricity: five-year plan of Bewag for 1951–1955, dated May 1950, LAB C Rep. 752, no. 25; *Perspektivplan der Bewag* for 1956–1970, dated July 1954, LAB C Rep. 752, no. 192; *Perpektivplan der Bewag*, dated October 16, 1956, LAB C Rep. 752, no. 141.

84. Bärthel, *Wasser für Berlin*, 197–199.

85. See, for example, the minutes of a meeting of the Bewag (East) board of directors of May 11, 1951, LAB C Rep. 752, no. 16.

86. Bärthel, *Wasser für Berlin*, 198.

87. Bärthel, *Geklärt!*, 174.

88. Bärthel, *Geklärt!*, 201.

89. Gropp, "Die Elektrizitätswirtschaft," 162; Zimm, *Berlin (Ost) und sein Umland*, 266.

90. See the correspondence in LAB C Rep. 110–01, no. 3598.

91. Holmsten, *Die Berlin-Chronik*, 426; Schlegelmilch, "Tendenzen," 15; Large, *Berlin*, 425.

92. Schlegelmilch, "Tendenzen," 16.

93. Taylor, *Berlin Wall*, 201, 227.

94. Schlegelmilch, "Tendenzen," 17–18.

95. On the building of the Berlin Wall, Taylor, *Berlin Wall*; Large, *Berlin*, 448–456; Bisky, *Berlin*, 711–722.

96. Bärthel, *Wasser für Berlin*, 200.

97. Bärthel, *Geklärt!*, 199–201.

98. Taylor, *Berlin Wall*, 445.

99. Bärthel, *Geklärt!*, 199.

100. Pétery, cited in Castillo, "Nylon Curtain," 47. For everyday exchanges prior to 1961, see Lemke, "Vorwort," 12.

101. Kirchhof, "For a Decent Quality of Life," 3.

102. Bärthel, *Wasser für Berlin*, 196; Reichhardt, "Wiederaufbau und Festigung," 113.

103. On the Quadripartite Agreement on Berlin of 1972 and its implications for Berliners, see Wetzlaugk, *Die Alliierten in Berlin*, 86–88.

104. VEB Gasversorgung Berlin, *Arbeitsordnung*, 3, 5.

105. SED-Betriebsparteiorganisation Bewag, *Unsere Kraft. Betriebsgeschichte der Bewag, 2. Teil*, 86.

106. VEB-Energiekombinat Berlin, *40 Jahre Deutsche Demokratische Republik*, 50.

107. VEB-Energiekombinat Berlin, *40 Jahre Deutsche Demokratische Republik*, 51.

108. SED-Betriebsparteiorganisation Bewag, *Unsere Kraft. Betriebsgeschichte der Bewag, 2. Teil*, 71.

109. See the minutes of a meeting of the board of directors, November 14, 1956, LAB, C Rep. 752, no. 22.

110. Betriebsrat der Berliner Kraft- und Licht(Bewag)-Aktiengesellschaft, *Im Licht der Zeit*, 119.

111. SED-Betriebsparteiorganisation Bewag, *Unsere Kraft. Betriebsgeschichte der Bewag, 2. Teil*, 20.

112. SED-Betriebsparteiorganisation Bewag, *Unsere Kraft. Betriebsgeschichte der Bewag, 2. Teil*, 23.

113. SED-Betriebsparteiorganisation Bewag, *Unsere Kraft. Betriebsgeschichte der Bewag, 2. Teil*, 103.

114. SED-Betriebsparteiorganisation Bewag, *Unsere Kraft. Betriebsgeschichte der Bewag, 2. Teil*, 24.

115. SED-Betriebsparteiorganisation Bewag, *Unsere Kraft. Betriebsgeschichte der Bewag, 2. Teil*, 103.

116. SED-Betriebsparteiorganisation Bewag, *Unsere Kraft. Betriebsgeschichte der Bewag, 2. Teil*, 45.

117. Letter of Bewag (East) of January 10, 1956, LAB C Rep. 752, no. 22.

118. Report of Bewag (East) of March 27, 1968, LAB C Rep. 621, no. 373.

119. Report by the urban technology party unit within the city council, dated September 4, 1974, LAB C Rep. 904–059, no. 73.

120. Report of the SED works organization at the city council of August 12, 1981, LAB, C Rep. 904–059, no. 102.

121. See the *Perspektivplan* of Bewag (East) of June 29, 1963, LAB C Rep. 752, no. 36.

122. Monstadt, *Die Modernisierung der Stromversorgung*, 289.

123. Tepasse, *Stadttechnik im Städtebau Berlins. 20. Jahrhundert*, 207.

124. Tepasse, *Stadttechnik im Städtebau Berlins. 20. Jahrhundert*, 182; Pischl, "Wärmeversorgung in Ost-Berliner Altbauquartieren," 22.

125. In German: *Wurstkocher*, interview 22.

126. Bärthel, *Die Geschichte der Gasversorgung*, 115.

127. Bärthel, *Die Geschichte der Gasversorgung*, 116.

128. Memo of the city council on the second and third five-year plans, dated August 28, 1958, LAB C Rep. 106–02, no. 647.

129. Bärthel, *Die Geschichte der Gasversorgung*, 117–118.

130. See the plans of VEB Gasversorgung Berlin of January 12, 1978, LAB, C Rep. 750–02, no. 6, and of February 17, 1978, LAB C Rep. 750–02, no. 8; Bärthel, *Die Geschichte der Gasversorgung*, 127.

131. Ufer, "Zum neuen Energiekonzept," 323; Stinglwagner, "Die Elektrizitätswirtschaft," 220–222.

132. Casper, "Infrastruktur," 140.

133. Vollrad Kuhn, "Berlin: Rohbraunkohle und Rauchgasentschwefelung in der DDR," *Arche Nova. Forum für Ökologische Gestaltung in Umwelt und Gesellschaft*, no. 1, 1988, in Archiv der Robert-Havemann-Gesellschaft (RHG), PS009/01, no. 1, 23.

134. Mitzinger, "Gegenwärtiger Stand," 161–163.

135. Mehlig, "Thesen für ein neues Energiekonzept," 64; interview 22.

136. See the Energy Commission's program of April 30, 1970, and its report of April 2, 1971, LAB C Rep. 752, no. 57.

137. Reichelt, "Die Aufgaben der Wasserwirtschaft"; Reichelt, "Das neue Wassergesetz."

138. See the five-year plan of 1981–1985, Reichelt, "Wasser rational und sparsam verwenden."

139. Reichelt, "Wasser rational und sparsam verwenden," 41; Reichelt, "Entwicklung der Wasserwirtschaft," 51.

140. Schwenk and Weisspflug, *Umweltschmutz und Umweltschutz*, 156–160.

141. Minutes of the conference "Wastewater Reuse" of July 9, 1953, LAB C Rep. 126–01, no. 5.

142. Schwenk and Weisspflug, *Umweltschmutz und Umweltschutz*, 157.

143. Schwenk and Weisspflug, *Umweltschmutz und Umweltschutz*, 160.

144. Tepasse, *Stadttechnik im Städtebau Berlins. 20. Jahrhundert*, 141.

145. Interview 22.

146. Bärthel, *Die Geschichte der Gasversorgung*; Bärthel, *Wasser für Berlin*; Bärthel, *Geklärt!*.

147. Research report compiled by Hilmar Bärthel, entitled *Beitrag zur weiteren Nutzungsmöglichkeit strukturbestimmender unterirdischer Leitungen im Zeitraum bis zum Jahre 2000*, dated December 29, 1969, Wissenschaftliche Sammlungen des IRS (Leibniz-Institut für Raumbezogene Sozialforschung).

148. Bärthel, *Beitrag zur weiteren Nutzungsmöglichkeit strukturbestimmender unterirdischer Leitungen im Zeitraum bis zum Jahre 2000*, 1, Wissenschaftliche Sammlungen des IRS.

149. East Berlin's population grew from 1,060,000 in 1961 to 1,087,982 in 1971, and 1,165,677 in 1981, Schlegelmilch, "Tendenzen," 28; Elkins and Hofmeister, *Berlin*, 217.

150. Tepasse, *Stadttechnik im Städtebau Berlins. 20. Jahrhundert*, 130.

151. Interview 22.

152. *Generalplan*, LAB C Rep. 107, no. 811, 3.

153. *Generalplan*, LAB C Rep. 107, no. 811, 4.

154. On the following, see the *Generalplan* in LAB C Rep. 107, no. 811.

155. Casper, "Infrastruktur," 154; interview 22.

156. Of the 100 km of the walk-in channel originally planned, only around 12 km were built in total, Tepasse, *Stadttechnik im Städtebau Berlins. 20. Jahrhundert*, 144.

157. Casper, "Infrastruktur," 150.

158. Tepasse, *Stadttechnik im Städtebau Berlins. 20. Jahrhundert*, 146–148.

159. Bärthel, *Geklärt!*, 192.

160. On the following, see the report of the technical infrastructure department of the district planning commission of April 8, 1982, LAB C Rep. 107, no. 1252.

161. Ufer, "Zum neuen Energiekonzept der DDR," 323; Stinglwagner, "Die Elektrizitätswirtschaft der DDR," 220–222.

162. Stadtfeld, "Die Entwicklung der öffentlichen Wasserversorgung," 669. In East Berlin daily water consumption reached 360 liters per capita, interview 22.

163. Schwenk and Weisspflug, *Umweltschmutz und Umweltschutz*, 230.

164. On infrastructural neglect in other socialist countries of Central and Eastern Europe at this time, Bouzarovski, "East Central Europe's Changing Energy Landscapes," 457; Chelcea and Pulay, "Networked Infrastructures," 346.

165. Mehlig, "Thesen für ein neues Energiekonzept," 64; Stinglwagner, "Die Elektrizitätswirtschaft der DDR," 238–239.

166. See the city council's program of January 1966 blaming air pollution on the gas works, power stations, and coal transport, the air pollution maps produced in September 1969 by the district hygiene inspectorate of Berlin documenting high levels of SO_2 and dust particles far exceeding maximum levels, and environmental reports of the Ministry of Environment and Water for 1972 and 1973, Schwenk and Weisspflug, *Umweltschmutz und Umweltschutz*, 207, 214, and 218.

167. SED-Betriebsparteiorganisation Bewag, *Unsere Kraft. Betriebsgeschichte der Bewag, 2. Teil*, 112; Schwenk and Weisspflug, *Umweltschmutz und Umweltschutz*, 207.

168. Schwenk and Weisspflug, *Umweltschmutz und Umweltschutz*, 220.

169. Schwenk and Weisspflug, *Umweltschmutz und Umweltschutz*, 221–222.

170. Schwenk and Weisspflug, *Umweltschmutz und Umweltschutz*, 224.

171. Schwenk and Weisspflug, *Umweltschmutz und Umweltschutz*, 164–167, 174–183.

172. Schwenk and Weisspflug, *Umweltschmutz und Umweltschutz*, 179.

173. Schwenk and Weisspflug, *Umweltschmutz und Umweltschutz*, 233–234.

174. Schwenk and Weisspflug, *Umweltschmutz und Umweltschutz*, 230–231.

175. Report on reducing water losses of the East Berlin water utility of February 9, 1962, LAB C Rep. 106–02, no. 656.

176. Interview 22; cf. *Umweltblätter* of June 1988, RHG, PS 107/23, 21–22.

177. Gromeyer, "Ideologische Grundsätze."

178. Blackbourn, *Conquest of Nature*, 335–345.

179. Schwenk and Weisspflug, *Umweltschmutz und Umweltschutz*, 247–250; Augustine, *Red Prometheus*, 205.

180. Environmental data in the DDR was officially declared confidential in 1983, Kirchhof, "For a Decent Quality of Life," 132.

181. Thoms, "Der Beitrag der Wasserwirtschaft."

182. Reichelt, "Das neue Wassergesetz."

183. Stadtfeld, "Die Entwicklung der öffentlichen Wasserversorgung," 668.

184. Bärthel, *Geklärt!*, 190.

185. Kirchhof, "Structural Strains," 132–134.

186. See the collection of publications in the archive of the Robert-Havemann-Gesellschaft (RHG).

187. Joachim Krause, "Prognosen des zukünftigen Energieverbrauchs—ein glattes Parkett," *Kontakt* September–October 1987, 14–17, RHG, PS 057/04.

188. See the discussion of a study by the (West Berlin) Institut für ökologische Wirtschaftsforschung on an alternative energy strategy for West Berlin and the DDR in Joachim Krause, "Mittelfristige Energieversorgung der DDR mit stark verminderter Luftbelastung und ohne Kernenergie!?" *Arche Nova. Forum für Ökologische Gestaltung in Umwelt und Gesellschaft*, no. 1, 1988, RHG, PS009/01, no. 1, 27.

189. This was, however, relatively rare, Kirchhof, "For a Decent Quality of Life," 3.

190. See RHG, PS 010/03, no. 2, 1.

191. Augustine, *Red Prometheus*, 328–329.

192. Large, *Berlin*, 531.

Chapter 8

1. The following account is related in a confidential letter from the Gasag directors to the Senator for Finance, dated June 24, 1970, LAB B Rep. 155, no. 144.

2. Wetzlaugk, *Die Alliierten in Berlin*, 157; Reichhardt, "Wiederaufbau und Festigung," 65.

3. Wetzlaugk, *Die Alliierten in Berlin*, 158; Reichhardt, "Wiederaufbau und Festigung," 105.

4. Interview 24.

5. Interview 15.

6. Large, *Berlin*, 425–431, 438–442, 448–456.

7. On US aid to West Berlin, see Wetzlaugk, *Die Alliierten in Berlin*, 149–150; Zschaler, "Die wirtschaftliche Spaltung Berlins," 211.

8. Large, *Berlin*, 417; Baar, "Die Berliner Industrie," 147; Schlegelmilch, "Tendenzen," 12; Ribbe, "Das gespaltene Berlin," 71.

9. Ribbe, "Das gespaltene Berlin," 67–68.

10. On the following, Wetzlaugk, *Die Alliierten in Berlin*, 149; Schlegelmilch, "Tendenzen," 12–13; Ribbe, *Berlin 1945–2000*, 100–101; Zschaler, "Die wirtschaftliche Spaltung Berlins," 211.

11. Wetzlaugk, *Die Alliierten in Berlin*, 155.

12. Baar, "Die Berliner Industrie," 148.

13. Taylor, *Berlin Wall*, 528. Despite the influx of nearly a quarter of a million foreigners between 1961 and 1982, the population of West Berlin fell from almost 2.2 million in June 1961 to, at its lowest, 1.8 million in December 1984, Schlegelmilch, "Tendenzen," 30; Elkins and Hofmeister, *Berlin*, 217.

14. Large, *Berlin*, 464.

15. Zschaler, "Die wirtschaftliche Spaltung Berlins," 220.

16. Large, *Berlin*, 464.

17. Elkins and Hofmeister, *Berlin*, 134–135; Presse- und Informationsamt des Landes Berlin, *Perspektiven der Stadtentwicklung*, 151.

18. On power disruptions, Stolpe, "Der Wiederaufbau," 368; Stolpe, "Berlin—Großstadt ohne Verbundbetrieb," 280; Senat von Berlin, *Berlin. Ringen um Einheit und Wiederaufbau*; Merritt, "Political Division and Municipal Services"; Merritt, "Postwar Berlin."

19. Presentation of Bewag director Wissell to a meeting of the supervisory board, April 22, 1955, LAB B Rep. 011, no. 40.

20. See Gasag annual reports of 1951, 1952, and 1953, LAB B Rep. 155, no. 224.

21. On the vulnerability of coal distribution in general, see Mitchell, *Carbon Democracy*, 8.

22. See Gasag annual report of 1955, LAB, B Rep. 155, no. 224. Bewag's consumption was very similar, rising from 413,658 metric tons in 1950 to 666,867 metric tons in 1954, Statistisches Landesamt Berlin, *Statistisches Jahrbuch 1952*, 291; Statistisches Landesamt Berlin, *Statistisches Jahrbuch 1955*, 283.

23. Annual report of the Senator for Transport and Enterprises of 1951, LAB B Rep. 011, no. 14.

24. Minutes of a meeting of the Gasag supervisory board of November 13, 1951, LAB B Rep. 011, no. 19.

25. Bärthel, *Wasser für Berlin*, 196–199.

26. Minutes of a meeting of a special committee on water supply in Neukölln of August 9, 1950, LAB B Rep. 012, no. 17.

27. See the newspaper articles and correspondence between the East Berlin water utility and city council of 1953, LAB C Rep. 124, no. 345.

28. Letter from the Department of Municipal Enterprises of the city council to the deputy mayor Arnold Gohr of July 13, 1953, LAB C Rep. 124, no. 345.

29. Senat von Berlin, *Berlin. Chronik der Jahre 1955–1956.*

30. Senat von Berlin, *Berlin. Chronik der Jahre 1957–1958.*

31. Agreement of December 12, 1950, LAB B Rep. 011, no. 19; Bärthel, *Geklärt!*, 174; Senat von Berlin, *Berlin. Ringen um Einheit und Wiederaufbau.*

32. Berliner Kraft- und Licht(Bewag)-Aktiengesellschaft, *100 Jahre Strom für Berlin*, year 1961; Betriebsrat der Berliner Kraft- und Licht(Bewag)-Aktiengesellschaft, *Im Licht der Zeit*, 117.

33. Annual report of Gasag for 1961, LAB B Rep. 155, no. 225.

34. Tegethoff, in "Energiepreise in Berlin (Podiumsdiskussion)," 16.

35. Memo of the Gasag directors Bausch and Jödicke of July 2, 1951, LAB B Rep. 155, no. 143; letter from Gasag to the city council of January 14, 1950, LAB B Rep. 011, no. 19. The senator responsible for the utilities at the time, Herbert Hausmann (SPD), backed this view fully. See his letters to his colleague Senator Haas of June 22, 1951, and to Reichswerke of May 27, 1952, LAB B Rep. 011, no. 19.

36. Letter of director Cohrs to the Senator for Transport and Enterprises of April 23, 1954, LAB B Rep. 011, no. 32; report of Senator for Transport and Enterprises on wastewater treatment in West Berlin of October 2, 1951, LAB B Rep. 011, no. 19; cf. Tepasse, *Stadttechnik im Städtebau Berlins. 20. Jahrhundert*, 194–195.

37. Tessendorff, "WASSER BERLIN 81," 101.

38. Already in 1950 gas pipelines were being redirected to avoid East Berlin, see minutes of a meeting of the supervisory board of Gasag of September 21, 1950, LAB B Rep. 011, no. 19. For the impact of spatial containment on the city's transport infrastructure, see Carlow, "Limits."

39. Statistisches Landesamt Berlin, *Statistisches Jahrbuch 1952*, 291; Statistisches Landesamt Berlin, *Statistisches Jahrbuch 1959*, 322; Deutsches Institut für Wirtschaftsforschung, *Entwicklung des Elektrizitätsverbrauchs*, 8.

40. Statistisches Landesamt Berlin, *Statistisches Jahrbuch 1990*, 251.

41. Senat von Berlin, *Berlin 1954*, 154.

42. Stolpe, "Der Wiederaufbau," 368; Stolpe, "Berlin—Großstadt ohne Verbundbetrieb," 278.

43. Tepasse, *Stadttechnik im Städtebau Berlins. 20. Jahrhundert*, 204.

44. Senat von Berlin, *Berlin. Chronik der Jahre 1959–1960.*

45. *Zehn Jahre Wiederaufbau der Berliner Stromversorgung*, 12.

46. Holmsten, *Die Berlin-Chronik*, 470; Tepasse, *Stadttechnik im Städtebau Berlins. 20. Jahrhundert*, 205–206.

47. Interviews 21 and 24; Presse- und Informationsamt des Landes Berlin, *Perspektiven der Stadtentwicklung*, 150.

48. As in 1953, Senat von Berlin, *Berlin 1953*, 148. This had reduced to a ratio of 1:3.5 by 1968, Bewag brochure of July 1968, LAB B Rep. 011, no. 141.

49. Bahde et al., "Das Stromversorgungssystem der Bewag," 131; Haase, "Kraftwerks- und Stadtheizungsbetrieb," 427.

50. Presse- und Informationsamt des Landes Berlin, *Energie 1*, 10.

51. Interview 15.

52. Stolpe, "Berlin—Großstadt ohne Verbundbetrieb," 280; Fischer, "BEWAG—vom Inselversorger zum Verbundpartner," 3.

53. The top-priority group included rail transportation and the Allied command, the mid-priority was reserved for industry, leaving households and small businesses as low priority, interview 15.

54. Interview 15.

55. Bahde et al., "Das Stromversorgungssystem der Bewag," 131.

56. Interviews 17 and 21.

57. Interview 24.

58. The problems are summarized in a Bewag brochure of July 1968, LAB B Rep. 011, no. 141.

59. Berliner Kraft- und Licht(Bewag)-Aktiengesellschaft, *100 Jahre Strom für Berlin*, year 1970.

60. On the advantages of oil over coal in minimizing disruption to flows of energy resources, see Mitchell, *Carbon Democracy*, 36.

61. Tepasse, *Stadttechnik im Städtebau Berlins. 20. Jahrhundert*, 206.

62. Presse- und Informationsamt des Landes Berlin, *Energie 1*, 3; Haase, "Kraftwerks- und Stadtheizungsbetrieb," 427; Ziesing, "Strukturelle und sektorale Entwicklung," 237.

63. Ziesing, "Strukturelle und sektorale Entwicklung," 236.

64. Tegethoff, "100 Jahre elektrizitätswirtschaftliche Energiepolitik," 419.

65. Berliner Kraft- und Licht(Bewag)-Aktiengesellschaft, *100 Jahre Strom für Berlin*, year 1959; Senat von Berlin, *Berlin. Chronik der Jahre 1959–1960*.

66. Bezirksamt Charlottenburg von Berlin, *Stadt unter Strom*, 53.

67. Betriebsrat der Berliner Kraft- und Licht(Bewag)-Aktiengesellschaft, *Im Licht der Zeit*, 139.

68. Minutes of the meeting of the working group of the energy advisory council of January 10, 1974, LAB B Rep. 016, no. 461.

69. Interim report of a study for the Federal Ministry for Research and Technology compiled by the Energie-Anlagen Berlin GmbH in September 1975, LAB B Rep. 155, no. 395.

70. On the continued support by the works council, Betriebsrat der Berliner Kraft- und Licht(Bewag)-Aktiengesellschaft, *Im Licht der Zeit*, 142–143.

71. Berliner Kraft- und Licht(Bewag)-Aktiengesellschaft, *100 Jahre Strom für Berlin*, year 1978.

72. Berliner Kraft- und Licht(Bewag)-Aktiengesellschaft, *100 Jahre Strom für Berlin*, year 1979.

73. Minutes of a meeting of the commission to develop an energy saving program of January 24, 1974, LAB B Rep. 016, no. 461.

74. Bill put before the Berlin senate on energy supply, dated September 20, 1977, LAB B Rep. 016, no. 458.

75. Interviews 24, 21, and 17.

76. Resistance came primarily from the Senate Department for Economics and Transport.

77. A popular component of this strategy for Bewag was night-storage heating, encouraged with lower night-time tariffs, Berliner Kraft- und Licht(Bewag)-Aktiengesellschaft, *100 Jahre Strom für Berlin*, year 1962.

78. Memo of the Senate Department for Economics of June 2, 1972, LAB B Rep. 016, no. 462.

79. Minutes of a joint meeting of the parliamentary committees for federal affairs and for urban development of October 7, 1974, LAB B Rep. 016, no. 461.

80. Minutes of October 7, 1974 (as note 79), 2.

81. Minutes of October 7, 1974 (as note 79), 4.

82. Article in *Die Welt* of December 27, 1975.

83. Elkins and Hofmeister, *Berlin*, 135; manuscript for a speech by the Senator for Economics in January 1975, LAB B Rep. 010, no. 2349.

84. Tegethoff, "100 Jahre elektrizitätswirtschaftliche Energiepolitik," 418.

85. Betriebsrat der Berliner Kraft- und Licht(Bewag)-Aktiengesellschaft, *Im Licht der Zeit*, 143.

86. Richert, "Erfahrungen aus Planung," 288–290.

87. Report to the Bewag supervisory board by director Wissell of November 30, 1956; minutes of the meeting of the supervisory board of November 30, 1956, LAB B Rep. 011, no. 40; Tepasse, *Stadttechnik im Städtebau Berlins. 20. Jahrhundert*, 167.

88. Der Senator für Stadtentwicklung und Umweltschutz, *Planungsdaten für Berlin (West)*, 280.

89. Tepasse, *Stadttechnik im Städtebau Berlins. 20. Jahrhundert*, 168; Berliner Kraft- und Licht(Bewag)-Aktiengesellschaft, *100 Jahre Strom für Berlin*, year 1957.

90. On the following, Tepasse, *Stadttechnik im Städtebau Berlins. 20. Jahrhundert*, 166 185; interview 24.

91. In 1985 residents paid 16.34 Deutschmark per cubic meter for district heating from Bewag, but up to 24.69 Deutschmark from other providers, Müller, "Entwicklung der Fernwärmepreise," 202.

92. Tepasse, *Stadttechnik im Städtebau Berlins. 20. Jahrhundert*, 170.

93. See correspondence in LAB B Rep. 010, no. 2079.

94. Minutes of the meeting of the working group of July 20, 1978, LAB B Rep. 010, no. 2079.

95. Letter from Rolf Kreibich to four senators of September 3, 1979, LAB B Rep. 010, no. 2079.

96. Tepasse, *Stadttechnik im Städtebau Berlins. 20. Jahrhundert*, 180; interviewee 24 speaks of "a major disappearance of block-type plants" in the city in the 1980s.

97. Letter of the Senator for Health and the Environment to the Senator for Building and Housing of August 8, 1978, complaining at the latter's projects on block-type CHP plants in Kreuzberg, LAB B Rep. 010, no. 2079.

98. Report of the working group on rational energy of July 31, 1979, LAB B Rep. 010, no. 2080.

99. Tepasse, *Stadttechnik im Städtebau Berlins. 20. Jahrhundert*, 180.

100. Bublitz, "Fernwärme weiterhin im Aufwind," 445; Bublitz, "Ausbau der Fernwärmeversorgung," 488.

101. Tepasse, *Stadttechnik im Städtebau Berlins. 20. Jahrhundert*, 189.

102. Memo of Gasag directors Bausch and Jödicke of July 2, 1951, LAB B Rep. 155, no. 143. Cf. letter of Gasag to the Senate Department of Transport and Enterprises of January 14, 1950, LAB B Rep. 011, no. 19.

103. Letter of Senator Hausmann to Reichswerke of May 27, 1952, LAB B Rep. 011, no. 19.

104. Bausch, "Die Entwicklung der Berliner Gasversorgung," 361.

105. Tepasse, *Stadttechnik im Städtebau Berlins. 20. Jahrhundert*, 190.

106. By 1953 West Berlin had increased gas storage to 830,000 cubic meters, Senat von Berlin, *Berlin 1953*, 146.

107. ÖTV Berlin, *Berliner Gaswerke (GASAG)*, 11.

108. Annual report of Gasag for 1957, LAB B Rep. 155, no. 225.

109. See the correspondence in LAB B Rep. 011, no. 140 and no. 141.

110. Letter of the Gasag directors to the Senator for Transport and Enterprises of April 26, 1962, LAB B Rep. 011, no. 140.

111. See the correspondence between the Senator for the Interior and Gasag between 1969 and 1970, LAB B Rep. 011, no. 141.

112. Bärthel, *Die Geschichte der Gasversorgung,* 144; Aengeneyndt, "Das Erdgas-Versorgungssystem," 181.

113. Bärthel, *Die Geschichte der Gasversorgung,* 145.

114. Tepasse, *Stadttechnik im Städtebau Berlins. 20. Jahrhundert,* 191.

115. Report of the Senate Department for Transport and Enterprises of November 5, 1968, LAB B Rep. 011, no. 141.

116. Annual reports of Gasag, LAB B Rep. 155, no. 245.

117. On the politics of Soviet natural gas sales to Western Europe, see Högselius, Kaijser, and van der Vleuten, *Europe's Infrastructure Transition,* 85–91.

118. Mayrhofer, "Die Erdgasspeicherung in Berlin," 6; Bärthel, *Die Geschichte der Gasversorgung,* 154.

119. Letter of the Gasag directors to the Senator for Finance of August 25, 1969, LAB B Rep. 155, no. 143.

120. See the correspondence in LAB B Rep. 155, nos. 143, 144.

121. See the correspondence in LAB B Rep. 155, no. 146.

122. Holmsten, *Die Berlin-Chronik,* 470; GASAG, *... über 160 Jahre Gasversorgung,* 6; Aengeneyndt, "Das Erdgas-Versorgungssystem," 181.

123. ÖTV Berlin, *Berliner Gaswerke (GASAG),* 14.

124. ÖTV Berlin, *Berliner Gaswerke (GASAG),* 15.

125. GASAG, *... über 160 Jahre Gasversorgung,* 5.

126. Bärthel, *Die Geschichte der Gasversorgung,* 154–155. Already in 1986 West Berlin received 504.7 million cubic meters of natural gas. Dispelling lingering fears, the supply contract was never broken, interview 24.

127. Bärthel, *Wasser für Berlin,* 239.

128. Tessendorff, "WASSER BERLIN 81," 99; Bärthel, *Wasser für Berlin,* 237; Hünerberg, "Die Wasserversorgung von Westberlin," 139.

129. Bärthel, *Wasser für Berlin,* 240.

130. Hünerberg, "Die Wasserversorgung von Westberlin," 139; Bärthel, *Wasser für Berlin,* 279.

131. Annual report of the Berlin water utility BWW for 1963, LAB B Rep. 011, no. 26.

132. Bärthel, *Wasser für Berlin,* 279.

133. Bärthel, *Wasser für Berlin,* 279.

134. Tessendorff, "WASSER BERLIN 81," 99; Pieske, "Wasserversorgung und Abwasserbeseitigung," 2, 4.

135. Tessendorff, "WASSER BERLIN 81," 99.

136. ÖTV Berlin, *Die Berliner Wasserwerke*, 16.

137. In 1961 the water tariff of 31 Pfennig per cubic meter was significantly lower than the West German average of 45 Pfennig, report by BWW of January 13, 1961, LAB B Rep. 011, no. 23.

138. On staff levels, ÖTV Berlin, *Die Berliner Wasserwerke*, 12.

139. Tessendorff, "WASSER BERLIN 81," 100.

140. Tessendorff, "Die Sicherstellung der Wasserversorgung Berlins," 2.

141. On the following, Vogt and Jahn, "Phosphatverringerung in den Berliner Gewässern," 232–233.

142. Bärthel, *Wasser für Berlin*, 276; Tessendorff, "WASSER BERLIN 81," 100.

143. Memo of Director Hünerberg of September 29, 1958, LAB B Rep. 011, no. 22.

144. Minutes of a meeting of the administrative board of BWW of June 18, 1962, LAB B Rep. 011, no. 24. See the report produced to justify amalgamation of April 6, 1962, LAB B Rep. 011, no. 102.

145. Bärthel, *Geklärt!*, 210.

146. Scholz, "Der Querverbund Wasser-Abwasser in Berlin," 44–46.

147. Bärthel, *Wasser für Berlin*, 290. A member of the BWB board claimed, somewhat boldly, that with the new, united utility "instead of thinking in terms of quantities and peak loads, resource protection has become the main issue," Scholz, "Der Querverbund Wasser-Abwasser in Berlin," 46.

148. Noted in a letter from Berliner Stadtentwässerung to the Senator for Transport and Enterprises of July 22, 1955, LAB B Rep. 011, no. 28.

149. Cohrs, "Die Berliner Stadtentwässerung," 809; Tepasse, *Stadttechnik im Städtebau Berlins. 20. Jahrhundert*, 194–195; Bärthel, *Geklärt!*, 203.

150. Memo of the Senator for Transport and Enterprises of January 26, 1954, LAB B Rep. 011, no. 32.

151. Report by the Senator for Transport and Enterprises on the construction of three sewage treatment plants of May 10, 1954, LAB B Rep. 011, no. 31.

152. Letter of the Senator for Transport and Enterprises Ullmann to Mr. Parkman, Deputy High Commissioner for Germany of February 8, 1954, LAB B Rep. 011, no. 35.

153. Letter of Director Cohrs to the Senator for Transport and Enterprises of April 23, 1954, LAB B Rep. 011, no. 32.

154. Letter of Berliner Stadtentwässerung to the Senator for Transport and Enterprises of February 11, 1955, LAB B Rep. 011, no. 32; letter of Berliner Stadtentwässerung to the Senator for Transport and Enterprises of July 22, 1955, LAB B Rep. 011, no. 28.

155. Letter of the Chamber of Commerce to the Senator for Transport and Enterprises of July 1, 1955, LAB B Rep. 011, no. 28.

156. Letter of the Senator for Building and Housing to Berliner Stadtentwässerung of January 10, 1955, LAB B Rep. 011, no. 28.

157. Referred to in a letter from the Federal Minister for Economics to the Federal Minister for Economic Cooperation of January 21, 1955, LAB B Rep. 011, no. 35. The Police President did not enhance his environmental credentials by arguing, instead, for the large-scale reuse of wastewater for agricultural production, see letters of the Police President to Berliner Stadtentwässerung of February 17, 1955, LAB B Rep. 011, no. 28 and of 1 August 1957, LAB B Rep. 011, no. 31.

158. A report commissioned by the Police President argued that the sewage treatment plants would cost nine times more than the current practice of paying the East Berlin utility for dealing with West Berlin's sewage, Tepasse, *Stadttechnik im Städtebau Berlins. 20. Jahrhundert*, 195.

159. See the memo by Berliner Stadtentwässerung of December 20, 1954, reporting on a meeting between the wastewater utilities of West and East Berlin that took place on December 17, 1954, LAB B Rep. 011, no. 28.

160. Senate decision of June 9, 1956, LAB B Rep. 011, no. 31; Tepasse, *Stadttechnik im Städtebau Berlins. 20. Jahrhundert*, 196.

161. Bärthel, *Geklärt!*, 215–216.

162. Hünerberg, "Umstellung der Abwasserreinigung in Berlin," 312.

163. Bärthel, *Geklärt!*, 232.

164. Bärthel, *Geklärt!*, 232.

165. The Ruhleben plant was extended instead, Hünerberg, "Planungen der Berliner Entwässerungswerke," 263.

166. Bärthel, *Geklärt!*, 232; Berliner Entwässerungswerke, *Bericht über das Geschäftsjahr*, 15.

167. ÖTV Berlin, *Die Berliner Wasserwerke*, 5.

168. Berliner Entwässerungswerke, *100 Jahre Berliner Entwässerungswerke 1878–1978*, 111.

169. Large, *Berlin*, 465; Schlegelmilch, "Tendenzen," 35. On the political scandals that rocked West Berlin, see Kotowski, "Vom Vorposten der westlichen Demokratie," 267; Holmsten, *Die Berlin-Chronik*, 478–479.

170. Rotenberg, *Berliner Demokratie*, 565.

171. Bewag employed 6,210 people in 1964, Gasag 3,434 in 1964, Berliner Wasserwerke 1,339 in 1962, and Berliner Stadtentwässerung 1,499 in 1964, Senat von Berlin, *Zweijahresbericht des Senats von Berlin 1961/1962*, 133, 164; Senat von Berlin, *Zweijahresbericht des Senats von Berlin 1963/64*, 165.

172. Betriebsrat der Berliner Kraft- und Licht(Bewag)-Aktiengesellschaft, *Im Licht der Zeit*, 130–131.

173. On the political parties' positions toward the utilities in the 1980s, Röber and Wendt, *Öffentliche Versorgungsunternehmen in Berlin*, 155–161.

174. Interview 18.

175. Interview 18.

176. Interview 24.

177. Interview 15.

178. Interview 24.

179. The relationship between city government and owner-operated municipal enterprises was set down in the Eigenbetriebsgesetz of October 1, 1973, Berliner Entwässerungswerke, *100 Jahre Berliner Entwässerungswerke 1878–1978*, 125–131.

180. Interview 21.

181. ÖTV Berlin, *Berliner Gaswerke (GASAG)*, 23.

182. *Zehn Jahre Wiederaufbau der Berliner Stromversorgung*, 16; Berliner Kraft- und Licht(Bewag)-Aktiengesellschaft, *100 Jahre Strom für Berlin*, year 1954.

183. See criticisms of high electricity tariffs for industrial customers in a report of the Senate Department for Transport and Enterprises of November 5, 1968, LAB B Rep. 011, no. 141.

184. Tegethoff in a podium discussion of November 29, 1988, "Energiepreise in Berlin (Podiumsdiskussion)." His remark was not only brash, but also incorrect. Hong Kong and Singapore also had long traditions of insular electricity provision.

185. On American "exhibition diplomacy" in the design of kitchens in 1950s Germany, see Zachmann, "Küchendebatten in Berlin?"

186. Berliner Kraft- und Licht(Bewag)-Aktiengesellschaft, *100 Jahre Strom für Berlin*, year 1950.

187. Bezirksamt Charlottenburg von Berlin, *Stadt unter Strom*, 46.

188. Interview 15.

189. Holmsten, *Die Berlin-Chronik*, 470; Tepasse, *Stadttechnik im Städtebau Berlins. 20. Jahrhundert*, 205.

190. Betriebsrat der Berliner Kraft- und Licht(Bewag)-Aktiengesellschaft, *Im Licht der Zeit*, 138; interviews 15 and 21.

191. On environmental protests in West Berlin in the 1970s and 1980s, see Kirchhof, "Structural Strains," 133–134; Kirchhof, "'For a Decent Quality of Life,'" 2, 13.

192. Berliner Kraft- und Licht(Bewag)-Aktiengesellschaft, *100 Jahre Strom für Berlin*, year 1974.

193. See the correspondence in LAB B Rep. 016, no. 426.

194. Tegethoff, "100 Jahre elektrizitätswirtschaftliche Energiepolitik," 419.

195. Memo of the Senate Department for Health and the Environment of March 12, 1976, LAB B Rep. 016, no. 426.

196. On the West German protests against nuclear power, see Gross, "Reimagining Energy and Growth."

197. Sukopp, "Zur ökologischen Beurteilung," 169; memo of the Senate Department for Health and the Environment on a meeting of the State Agency for Nature Conservation of March 17, 1976, LAB B Rep. 016, no. 426; letter of Professor Herbert Sukopp, as State Commissioner for Nature Conservation and Landscape Management, to the Senate Department for Health and the Environment of September 24, 1976, LAB B Rep. 016, no. 428.

198. Mielke and Weiß, "Kraftwerksbau," 220–221.

199. Interview 21; letter of Professor Theodor Ebert of the Free University to all members of the house of representatives of December 2, 1976, LAB B Rep. 016, no. 429; Weiß and Mielke, "Kraftwerksbau II," 251.

200. Memo of the Senate Department for Health and the Environment of June 3, 1976, LAB B Rep. 016, no. 427.

201. Letter of the Senator for Economics, Luder, to the Senator for Health and the Environment of September 8, 1976, LAB B Rep. 016, no. 428.

202. Letter of the Senator for Economics to Mayor Klaus Schütz of August 9, 1976, LAB B Rep. 016, no. 427.

203. Memo of the Senate Department for Health and the Environment of a meeting of all senators held on November 23, 1976, LAB B Rep. 016, no. 429.

204. Memo of the Senate Department for Health and the Environment of a meeting with Bewag on November 22, 1976, LAB B Rep. 016, no. 436.

205. Excerpt from the speech by Senator Lüder of November 4, 1976, LAB B Rep. 016, no. 429.

206. Declaration by Senator Ristock to the Committee for Building and Housing on December 8, 1976, LAB B Rep. 016, no. 429.

207. Mielke and Weiß, "Kraftwerksbau," 220; see the senate decision of October 12, 1976, LAB B Rep. 016, no. 428.

208. Letter of Bewag director von Gersdorff to the Senator for Building and Housing of November 2, 1976, LAB B Rep. 016, no. 429.

209. Weiß and Mielke, "Kraftwerksbau II," 251.

210. Interview 21.

211. Weiß and Mielke, "Kraftwerksbau II," 252; flyer of the citizens group Oberjägerweg of December 1976, LAB B Rep. 016, no. 427.

212. See the original judgement of the thirteenth Chamber of the Administrative Court of December 14, 1976, LAB B Rep. 016, no. 436.

213. Interview 21.

214. Memo of the Senate Department for Economics of May 20, 1977, LAB B Rep. 016, no. 431. Bewag was instructed to form a working group to discuss ways of managing peak load in combination with cogeneration, memo of the Senate Department for Health and the Environment of June 7, 1977, LAB B Rep. 016, no. 431.

215. Interview 21.

216. Tepasse, *Stadttechnik im Städtebau Berlins. 20. Jahrhundert*, 150; interview 21.

217. Tegethoff, "Die Berliner Kraft- und Licht(Bewag)-Aktiengesellschaft," 91; Tepasse, *Stadttechnik im Städtebau Berlins. 20. Jahrhundert*, 206.

218. Tepasse, *Stadttechnik im Städtebau Berlins. 20. Jahrhundert*, 206.

219. Berliner Kraft- und Licht(Bewag)-Aktiengesellschaft, *100 Jahre Strom für Berlin*, year 1980.

220. Arbeitsgemeinschaft ökologischer Stadtumbau, *Kreuzberger Wasserkonzepte*; Hahn and Zeisel, *Integriertes Wasserkonzept*; Reichmann, "Stadtökologische Modellprojekte."

221. Hahn and Zeisel, *Integriertes Wasserkonzept*, 6.

222. For a more detailed discussion of water recycling schemes in Berlin, see Moss, "Unearthing Water Flows."

223. Strümpel and Tepasse, *Wärmeversorgung Kreuzberg*.

224. Mauer, *Energiekonzept im Rahmen behutsamer Stadterneuerung*; Prognos, *Erfahrungen bei der Kooperation*; von Grot, "Strukturwandel der Gebäudeheizung in Berlin."

225. Monstadt, *Die Modernisierung der Stromversorgung*, 282–285.

226. Interview 21.

227. On the following, Senatsverwaltung für Stadtentwicklung und Umweltschutz, *Energieagentur Berlin*.

228. Monstadt, *Die Modernisierung der Stromversorgung*, 284.

229. This was the assessment of the audit office in 1981, letter of Bewag to the Senator for Economics and Transport of August 19, 1981, LAB B Rep. 155, no. 258.

230. This threat was contained in energy policy principles agreed by the SPD board, see article in *Berliner Stimme* of September 14, 1979, LAB B Rep. 155, no 146.

231. On the following, Monstadt, *Die Modernisierung der Stromversorgung*, 292–295.

232. Betriebsrat der Berliner Kraft- und Licht(Bewag)-Aktiengesellschaft, *Im Licht der Zeit*, 144.

233. Betriebsrat der Berliner Kraft- und Licht(Bewag)-Aktiengesellschaft, *Im Licht der Zeit*, 144.

234. Interviews 21 and 16.

Chapter 9

1. Senatsverwaltung für Stadtentwicklung, Umweltschutz und Technologie, *Stadtentwicklungsplan Ver- und Entsorgung*, 3.

2. Merritt, "Political Division and Municipal Services."

3. Berliner Kraft- und Licht(Bewag)-Aktiengesellschaft, *Strom für Berlin*, 8; Tepasse, *Stadttechnik im Städtebau Berlins. 1945–1999*, 97; Conrad, Zühlsdorf, and Gerbich, "Strom- und Fernwärmeerzeugung," 707.

4. Bärthel, *Die Geschichte der Gasversorgung*, 168. As imported natural gas began to flow into West Berlin, the proportion of town gas sold there declined from 86.5 percent in 1992 to 27.6 percent in 1994 and ca. 9 percent in 1995. Even today, the two former halves of the city have different gas transfer stations, interview 18.

5. Tepasse, *Stadttechnik im Städtebau Berlins. 1945–1999*, 98.

6. Energieversorgung Berlin AG, *Die Geschäftspolitik der EBAG*, 4.

7. Interview 19.

8. Interview 3; Bärthel, "Anlagen und Bauten der Elektrizitätserzeugung," 246.

9. Fischer, "BEWAG—vom Inselversorger zum Verbundpartner"; Winje, "Integration des West-Berliner Netzes."

10. Interview 1.

11. Bärthel, *Wasser für Berlin*, 291; Bärthel, *Die Geschichte der Gasversorgung*, 157.

12. Bärthel, *Wasser für Berlin*, 292.

13. Bärthel, *Wasser für Berlin*, 294.

14. Bärthel, *Die Geschichte der Gasversorgung*, 157.

15. Bärthel, "Anlagen und Bauten der Elektrizitätserzeugung," 246.

16. Bärthel, *Die Geschichte der Gasversorgung*, 161–162.

17. Interview 18.

18. Tessendorff, "Berliner Wasserbetriebe im Wandel," 556.

19. Interviews 14 and 18.

20. Interview with a leading representative of the Gasag works council in Franz and Giese, *Es werde Licht*, 104.

21. Senatsverwaltung für Stadtentwicklung, Umweltschutz und Technologie, *Stadtentwicklungsplan Ver- und Entsorgung*, 64.

22. Senatsverwaltung für Stadtentwicklung, Umweltschutz und Technologie, *Stadtentwicklungsplan Ver- und Entsorgung*, 64; Senatsverwaltung für Stadtentwicklung, Umweltschutz und Technologie, *Abwasserbeseitigungsplan Berlin*, 42–43; Tepasse, *Stadttechnik im Städtebau Berlins. 1945–1999*, 101.

23. Interview 9.

24. Moss, "Unearthing Water Flows," 69. On the renaissance of infrastructure planning in post-unification Germany, Wilkes, "Die Entwicklung der infrastrukturellen Planung."

25. Interview 4; Pawlowski, "Abwasserentsorgung in Berlin," 1694.

26. Bärthel, *Die Geschichte der Gasversorgung*, 171.

27. Interview 3.

28. Senatsverwaltung für Wirtschaft, Technologie und Frauen, *Energiekonzept 2020*, 45.

29. Tessendorff, "Wasserversorgung und Abwasserbeseitigung," 313.

30. Interview 20.

31. Pawlowski, "Abwasserentsorgung in Berlin," 1694; Bärthel, *Geklärt!*, 251.

32. Tepasse, *Stadttechnik im Städtebau Berlins. 1945–1999*, 93–162.

33. Bernt, Grell, and Holm, "Introduction," 18, talk of "Berlin's megalomania" at this time. Cf. Beveridge, *Politics of Inevitability*, 190.

34. Arbeitsgemeinschaft Brandenburgische-Berliner Wasserver- und Abwasserentsorgungsunternehmen e.V., *Vorschlag zur Abwasserentsorgung*, 8; Berliner Wasser-Betriebe, *Berlin und Umland*, 2; Schreyer, "Erfordernisse einer neuen Qualität des Gewässerschutzes," 9; Böhme, "Berlin auf dem Trockenen?," 39.

35. Senatsverwaltung für Stadtentwicklung, Umweltschutz und Technologie, *Stadtentwicklungsplan Ver- und Entsorgung*, 3.

36. Berliner Wasser-Betriebe, *Berlin und Umland*, 2; Tessendorff, "Berliner Wasserbetriebe im Wandel," 557.

37. Tessendorff, "Wasserversorgung und Abwasserbeseitigung," 314.

38. Berliner Wasserbetriebe, *Geschäftsbericht 1996*, 23; Bärthel, *Geklärt!*, 250; Tessendorff, "Berliner Wasserbetriebe im Wandel," 558.

39. Senatsverwaltung für Stadtentwicklung, Umweltschutz und Technologie, *Stadtentwicklungsplan Ver- und Entsorgung*, 55; Berliner Wasserbetriebe, *Geschäftsbericht 1999*, 6.

40. Senatsverwaltung für Stadtentwicklung, Umweltschutz und Technologie, *Stadtentwicklungsplan Ver- und Entsorgung*, 16.

41. Senatsverwaltung für Stadtentwicklung, Umweltschutz und Technologie, *Stadtentwicklungsplan Ver- und Entsorgung*, 3.

42. Bärthel, "Anlagen und Bauten der Elektrizitätserzeugung," 246; cf. Senatsverwaltung für Stadtentwicklung, Umweltschutz und Technologie, *Stadtentwicklungsplan Ver- und Entsorgung*, 18.

43. Statistisches Landesamt Berlin, *Statistisches Jahrbuch 1995*, 313; Statistisches Landesamt Berlin, *Statistisches Jahrbuch 2005*, 268.

44. Bärthel, *Geklärt!*, 260–272.

45. Tessendorff, "So soll es bleiben," 52.

46. Schreyer, "Erfordernisse einer neuen Qualität des Gewässerschutzes."

47. Arbeitsgemeinschaft Brandenburgische-Berliner Wasserver- und Abwasserentsorgungsunternehmen e.V., *Bericht zur Situation und Entwicklung der Öffentlichen Trinkwasserversorgung*; Arbeitsgemeinschaft Brandenburgische-Berliner Wasserver- und Abwasserentsorgungsunternehmen e.V., *Vorschlag zur Abwasserentsorgung*; Schulze, "Naturnahe Grundwasseranreicherung."

48. BUND Landesverband Berlin e.V., *Konzeption einer ressourcenschonenden Wasserbewirtschaftung.*

49. Senatsverwaltung für Stadtentwicklung und Umweltschutz, *Konzept zur zukünftigen Wasserver- und -entsorgung*, 42.

50. Tepasse, *Stadttechnik im Städtebau Berlins. 1945–1999*, 101.

51. A comparison of water/wastewater tariffs is given in Senatsverwaltung für Stadtentwicklung, Umweltschutz und Technologie, *Stadtentwicklungsplan Ver- und Entsorgung*, 64.

52. Monstadt, *Die Modernisierung der Stromversorgung*, 304.

53. Müschen, "Das solare Regierungsviertel," 73.

54. Interview 16. On the energy agency, Senatsverwaltung für Stadtentwicklung und Umweltschutz, *Energieagentur Berlin*, 4–6; Wicke, "Beiträge der Wissenschaft," 7. On the contracting model for energy-saving partnerships, Leithaus, "Erfahrungsbericht über die Energiesparpartnerschaft Berlin," 3; Kist and Lang, "Energiesparpartnerschaften Berlin," 25–26; Monstadt, *Die Modernisierung der Stromversorgung*, 352–357.

55. Senatsverwaltung für Stadtentwicklung, Umweltschutz und Technologie, *Stadtentwicklungsplan Ver- und Entsorgung*, 22. The law was strongly informed by a report on aims and options for an alternative energy policy for Berlin (West) commissioned by the senate and compiled by energy experts at the Free University and the Öko-Institut.

56. Monstadt, *Die Modernisierung der Stromversorgung*, 303.

57. Cf. Energieversorgung Berlin AG, *Die Geschäftspolitik der EBAG*, 3 and 9–10.

58. Senatsverwaltung für Stadtentwicklung und Umweltschutz, *Energiekonzept Berlin*; Monstadt, *Die Modernisierung der Stromversorgung*, 312–315; Wicke, "Beiträge der Wissenschaft."

59. Senatsverwaltung für Stadtentwicklung und Umweltschutz, *Energiepolitische Ansätze zur CO_2-Minderung*, 33–35; Wicke, "Beiträge der Wissenschaft," 6.

60. Abgeordnetenhaus von Berlin, *Drucksache 12/9154*, 14; Monstadt, "Urban Governance," 330.

61. Winje, "Bewag und Klimaschutz," 790.

62. Monstadt, *Die Modernisierung der Stromversorgung*, 424.

63. Interview 16.

64. Senatsverwaltung für Stadtentwicklung, Umweltschutz und Technologie, *Stadtentwicklungsplan Ver- und Entsorgung*, 23–24.

65. Interview 16. On least-cost planning in Berlin, Winje, "Neue Zielstellungen in der Elektrizitätswirtschaft."

66. Interview 16; cf. interview 8.

67. Schreyer, "Erfordernisse einer neuen Qualität des Gewässerschutzes"; Tessendorff, "So soll es bleiben."

68. Senatsverwaltung für Stadtentwicklung und Umweltschutz, *Konzept zur zukünftigen Wasserver- und -entsorgung*, 44.

69. Interview 25.

70. Senatsverwaltung für Stadtentwicklung, Umweltschutz und Technologie, *Abwasserbeseitigungsplan Berlin*.

71. Berliner Wasser-Betriebe, *Klare Sache*.

72. Schulze, "Naturnahe Grundwasseranreicherung," 220–221.

73. On the following, Moss, "Battle of the Systems?"

74. Nolde, "Greywater Reuse Systems."

75. Ripl and Hildmann, "Zwei in einem Boot."

76. Tepasse, *Stadttechnik im Städtebau Berlins. 1945–1999*, 167–169.

77. Tessendorff, "So soll es bleiben," 41.

78. Interview 10.

79. Reichmann, "Stadtökologische Modellprojekte"; Sommer, "Modellvorhaben." Examples include Block 103 in Kreuzberg and a water conservation project in Marzahn.

80. Senatsverwaltung für Stadtentwicklung, Umweltschutz und Technologie, *Stadtentwicklungsplan Ver- und Entsorgung*, 70 and 85.

81. Tepasse, *Stadttechnik im Städtebau Berlins. 1945–1999*, 101; Moss, "Unearthing Water Flows," 74.

82. On the way rainwater retention schemes reordered actor relations in Berlin, Moss, "Unearthing Water Flows," 76–79.

83. On the following, Senatsverwaltung für Stadtentwicklung, Umweltschutz und Technologie, *Stadtentwicklungsplan Ver- und Entsorgung*. Cf. Interviews 6, 7, and 22.

84. Interview 22.

85. Senatsverwaltung für Stadtentwicklung, Umweltschutz und Technologie, *Stadtentwicklungsplan Ver- und Entsorgung*, 7; interview 22.

86. Schmidt, *Regional Governance*, 210.

87. Rivalry between the senators Volker Hassemer (for urban development) and Wolfgang Nagel (for building and housing) was legendary, interview 6. In the energy sector initiatives of the environmental department of the Berlin senate were frequently blocked by the economics department responsible for supervising the utilities, interview 16; Monstadt, "Urban Governance," 339.

88. Interview 22.

89. Moss and Hüesker, *Wasserinfrastrukturen als Gemeinwohlträger*, 18; Schmidt, *Regional Governance*, 253–254.

90. Arbeitsgemeinschaft Brandenburgische-Berliner Wasserver- und Abwasserentsorgungsunternehmen e.V., *Bericht zur Situation und Entwicklung der Öffentlichen Trinkwasserversorgung*; Arbeitsgemeinschaft Brandenburgische-Berliner Wasserver- und Abwasserentsorgungsunternehmen e.V., *Vorschlag zur Abwasserentsorgung*.

91. Schmidt, *Regional Governance*, 234–236.

92. Interview 2.

93. Interview 7; Schmidt, *Regional Governance*, 252.

94. Monstadt, "Urban Governance," 339.

95. Interviews 3 and 5.

96. Interviews 8 and 16.

97. Interview 12.

98. Schmidt, *Regional Governance*, 229–231.

99. Bärthel, *Geklärt!*, 275.

100. Berliner Wasser-Betriebe, *Geschäftsbericht 2017*, 7.

101. Schmidt, *Regional Governance*, 233; interview 20.

102. Beveridge and Naumann, "Berlin Water Company," 192.

103. Beveridge, *Politics of Inevitability*, 190.

104. On enactments of neoliberal thought in Berlin, see the debate between Allan Cochrane and Alan Latham: Cochrane, "Making up Meanings in a Capital City"; Latham, "Berlin and Everywhere Else." This resonates with Stephen Collier's findings on place-specific forms of neoliberalism in post-Soviet Russia, Collier, *Post-Soviet Social.*

105. Interview 9.

106. Monstadt, *Die Modernisierung der Stromversorgung*, 410–414; Monstadt, "Urban Governance," 332–333. On infrastructure liberalization in Germany, Voß and Bauknecht, "Netzregulierung in Infrastruktursektoren," 112–116.

107. Berliner Kraft- und Licht(Bewag)-Aktiengesellschaft, *Geschäftsbericht 1994/95*, 47; Berliner Kraft- und Licht(Bewag)-Aktiengesellschaft, *Geschäftsbericht 2000/01*, 22.

108. Berliner Kraft- und Licht(Bewag)-Aktiengesellschaft, *Geschäftsbericht 1994/95*, 59.

109. Berliner Kraft- und Licht(Bewag)-Aktiengesellschaft, *Geschäftsbericht 1994/95*, 61.

110. Bärthel, *Die Geschichte der Gasversorgung*, 163.

111. Bärthel, *Die Geschichte der Gasversorgung*, 174.

112. Monstadt, *Die Modernisierung der Stromversorgung*, 418–419; Berliner Gaswerke (GASAG) Eigenbetrieb von Berlin, *Jahresbericht 1999*, 25.

113. Interview 18.

114. Beveridge and Naumann, "Berlin Water Company," 194.

115. Bärthel, *Wasser für Berlin*, 296; Tessendorff, "Berliner Wasserbetriebe im Wandel," 561.

116. Interview 14.

117. Tessendorff, "Berliner Wasserbetriebe im Wandel," 562.

118. See the BWB annual report of 1996, Berliner Wasserbetriebe, *Geschäftsbericht 1996*, 11 and 56.

119. Bärthel, *Geklärt!*, 247.

120. Senatsverwaltung für Stadtentwicklung, Umweltschutz und Technologie, *Stadtentwicklungsplan Ver- und Entsorgung*, 56.

121. Tessendorff, "Die Berliner Wasser-Betriebe als Partner"; Oswald and Pawlowski, "Know-how aus Paris und Berlin."

122. Berliner Wasserbetriebe, *Presseinformation 23/97.*

123. Beveridge, Hüesker, and Naumann, "From Post-Politics," 70; Berliner Wasserbetriebe, *Geschäftsbericht 1999*, 23–24.

124. Interview 14.

125. On the following, Moss, "'Cold Spots' of Urban Infrastructure."

126. On the following, Bärthel, *Die Geschichte der Gasversorgung*, 170; interview 26.

127. Amt für Statistik Berlin-Brandenburg, *Statistisches Jahrbuch 2016 Berlin*, 36–37.

128. Krätke, "City of Talents?"; Krätke and Borst, *Berlin*.

129. Krätke, "City of Talents?" 142; Statistisches Landesamt Berlin, *Statistisches Jahrbuch 2001*, 287, 289.

130. Bärthel, *Geklärt!*, 279. This level of decline was characteristic of Eastern Germany as a whole, see Moss, "'Cold Spots' of Urban Infrastructure."

131. Meißner and Prehn, "Wasserversorgung und Abwasserbeseitigung," 114.

132. Senatsverwaltung für Stadtentwicklung, Umweltschutz und Technologie, *Stadtentwicklungsplan Ver- und Entsorgung*, 63.

133. A senior BWB employee reflects, "It was absurd to be investing gigantic sums in a collapsing market," interview 20.

134. Berliner Wasserbetriebe, *Geschäftsbericht 1996*, 32.

135. Hüesker, *Kommunale Daseinsvorsorge*, 254.

136. Bärthel, *Geklärt!*, 279. Water supply capacity of BWB decreased, as a result, from 1.78 million cubic meters per day in 1995 to 1.14 million in 1998, Bärthel, "Anlagen und Bauten der Wasserversorgung," 109.

137. Decommissioning the treatment plant at Falkenberg required the construction of an 18 km "sewer autobahn" to the plant at Waßmannsdorf, representing BWB's largest investment project since 2000, Bärthel, "Anlagen und Bauten der Stadtentwässerung," 185.

138. Senatsverwaltung für Stadtentwicklung, Umweltschutz und Technologie, and Berliner Wasserbetriebe, "Jahresbericht der Wasserwirtschaft—Berlin," 38; Darkow, "Nachhaltiger Gewässerschutz," 18.

139. Interviews 10 and 12; Darkow, "Nachhaltiger Gewässerschutz," 28.

140. Darkow, "Nachhaltiger Gewässerschutz," 17–18; Hüesker, *Kommunale Daseinsvorsorge*, 310; interview 23.

141. Hüesker, *Kommunale Daseinsvorsorge*, 305.

142. Moss, "Utilities, Land-Use Change," 513; Moss, "'Cold Spots' of Urban Infrastructure," 447.

143. Beveridge, *Politics of Inevitability*, 194; Beveridge and Naumann, "Berlin Water Company," 195.

144. Monstadt, *Die Modernisierung der Stromversorgung*; Beveridge, *Politics of Inevitability*; Hüesker, *Kommunale Daseinsvorsorge*.

145. Krätke, "City of Talents?," 148, 192.

146. Monstadt, *Die Modernisierung der Stromversorgung*, 435. The euro figures are converted from the original values in Deutschmark.

147. Interviews 14 and 20.

148. Beveridge, *Politics of Inevitability*, 190–193.

149. Interviews 13 and 11.

150. Berliner Kraft- und Licht(Bewag)-Aktiengesellschaft, *Geschäftsbericht 1994/95*, 11; Senatsverwaltung für Stadtentwicklung, Umweltschutz und Technologie, *Stadtentwicklungsplan Ver- und Entsorgung*, 16.

151. Monstadt, *Die Modernisierung der Stromversorgung*, 328.

152. On the following, Monstadt, *Die Modernisierung der Stromversorgung*, 328–331.

153. Tepasse, *Stadttechnik im Städtebau Berlins. 20. Jahrhundert*, 208; Moss, "Utilities, Land-Use Change," 520.

154. Monstadt, "Urban Governance," 331.

155. GASAG Berliner Gaswerke Aktiengesellschaft, "Dokumentation über den Verkauf," 6–7; Monstadt, *Die Modernisierung der Stromversorgung*, 331–332.

156. *Berliner Zeitung*, October 16, 1997; interview 18. Following the legal requirement to unbundle services of gas sales and distribution, Gasag still retains a dominant influence over the newly created distribution company NBB Netzgesellschaft Berlin-Brandenburg thanks to an 83.5 percent shareholding, GASAG Berliner Gaswerke Aktiengesellschaft, *Geschäftsbericht 2010*.

157. Monstadt, *Die Modernisierung der Stromversorgung*, 332.

158. GASAG Berliner Gaswerke Aktiengesellschaft, "Dokumentation über den Verkauf," 4; Tepasse, *Stadttechnik im Städtebau Berlins. 20. Jahrhundert*, 193; Bärthel, "Anlagen und Bauten der Gasversorgung," 52.

159. On the following, Beveridge, *Politics of Inevitability*, 107–188; Beveridge, Hüesker, and Naumann, "From Post-Politics," 70ff.

160. Senatsverwaltung für Stadtentwicklung, Umweltschutz und Technologie, *Stadtentwicklungsplan Ver- und Entsorgung*, 55; Berlinwasser Holding Aktiengesellschaft, *Geschäftsbericht 1999*, 6.

161. Beveridge, *Politics of Inevitability*, 147–177.

162. Wolfers, "Privatization of the Berlin Water Works," 117.

163. Beveridge and Naumann, "Berlin Water Company," 195.

164. Interview 14; Beveridge, *Politics of Inevitability*, 61; Beveridge, Hüesker, and Naumann, "From Post-Politics," 70.

165. Berliner Wasserbetriebe, *Geschäftsbericht 1999*, 15; Beveridge, *Politics of Inevitability*, 60. On the center of competence, Schlippenbach and Moss, "Intermediation of Water Expertise."

166. Interview 16.

167. Monstadt, *Die Modernisierung der Stromversorgung*, 332.

168. Hüesker, *Kommunale Daseinsvorsorge*, 261.

169. Speeches by the Bewag chairman of the board, Dietmar Winje, held on December 14, 1998, and December 13, 1999.

170. Statistisches Landesamt Berlin, *Statistisches Jahrbuch 2005*, 268; Amt für Statistik Berlin-Brandenburg, *Statistisches Jahrbuch 2009 Berlin*, 349.

171. Tepasse, *Stadttechnik im Städtebau Berlins. 20. Jahrhundert*, 194.

172. Werle, "Strom teurer—Gas teurer—Wasser teurer," 16.

173. Berliner Wasserbetriebe, *Geschäftsbericht 2004*, 19.

174. Beveridge, Hüesker, and Naumann, "From Post-Politics," 71.

175. Hüesker, *Kommunale Daseinsvorsorge*, 254; Linde, "Teures Wasser," 4.

176. Hüesker, *Kommunale Daseinsvorsorge*, 261. The number of employees of BWB declined from 6,262 in 1999 to 4,986 in 2006, Berliner Wasser-Betriebe, *Klare Sache*.

177. Monstadt, *Die Modernisierung der Stromversorgung*, 417.

178. Monstadt, *Die Modernisierung der Stromversorgung*, 415.

179. Berlinwasser Holding Aktiengesellschaft, *Geschäftsbericht 1999*, 25–26.

180. Berlinwasser Holding Aktiengesellschaft, *Geschäftsbericht 2000*, 2.

181. Interview 20.

182. Interviews 20, 18, and 14.

183. Monstadt, *Die Modernisierung der Stromversorgung*, 321, 477–478; Müschen, "Der Sonne entgegen," 430. Cf. Similar shifts in governance in the promotion of rainwater harvesting in the city, García Soler, Moss, and Papasozomenou, "Rain and the City."

184. Monstadt, "Urban Governance," 331.

185. Monstadt, *Die Modernisierung der Stromversorgung*, 494.

186. Müschen, "Der Sonne entgegen," 428.

187. Amt für Statistik Berlin-Brandenburg, *Energie- und CO_2-Bilanz in Berlin 2011*, 20.

188. Amt für Statistik Berlin-Brandenburg, *Energie- und CO_2-Bilanz in Berlin 2011*, 33.

189. Interview 16.

190. Interviews 16, 21, and 24.

191. Senatsverwaltung für Wirtschaft, Technologie und Frauen, *Energiekonzept 2020*, 43.

192. Harald Wolf (Left Party) in a speech to the city parliament, February 16, 2017, Abgeordnetenhaus von Berlin, *Plenarprotokoll 18/6*, 367.

193. Hirschl et al., *Potenziale erneuerbarer Energien*, 4.

194. Hüesker, *Kommunale Daseinsvorsorge*, 224, 314–315.

195. Interviews 12 and 25.

196. Möller and Burgschweiger, *Wasserversorgungskonzept für Berlin*.

197. Abgeordnetenhaus von Berlin, *Wortprotokoll*, 8–9.

198. Tepasse, *Stadttechnik im Städtebau Berlins. 1945–1999*, 165.

199. Studied in the recent ELaN project, Lischeid et al., *Nachhaltiges Landmanagement*; Moss, Naumann, and Krause, "Turning Wastewater into Energy."

200. Interviews 16, 9, and 18.

201. On the following, Tepasse, *Stadttechnik im Städtebau Berlins. 1945–1999*, 98–100.

202. Senatsverwaltung für Stadtentwicklung, Umweltschutz und Technologie, *Energiebilanz 2005*, 14.

203. Tepasse, *Stadttechnik im Städtebau Berlins. 1945–1999*, 145; interview 18.

204. Interview 15.

205. Interview 18. Gas sales by Gasag have increased substantially since it was fully privatized, from 14,366 GWh in 1998 to 20,593 GWh in 2015, Statistisches Landesamt Berlin, *Statistisches Jahrbuch 2005*, 268; Amt für Statistik Berlin-Brandenburg, *Statistisches Jahrbuch 2016 Berlin*, 371.

206. Becker, Naumann, and Moss, "Between Coproduction and Commons."

207. Schnitzler, *Democracy's Infrastructure*, 107.

208. This echoes the dispositive of "governing through citizenship" in modern Berlin, Lanz, "Be Berlin!," 1309.

209. Beveridge, Hüesker, and Naumann, "From Post-Politics," 71.

210. Beveridge and Naumann, "Berlin Water Company," 197.

211. Beveridge, Hüesker, and Naumann, "From Post-Politics," 72.

212. See the speeches of Stroedter (SPD) and Garmer (CDU) in the debate of November 7, 2013 in the city parliament, Abgeordnetenhaus von Berlin, *Plenarprotokoll 17/38*, 3789, 3792.

213. Beveridge and Naumann, "Berlin Water Company," 198.

214. Daniel Buchholz (SPD) in Abgeordnetenhaus von Berlin, *Plenarprotokoll 17/71*, 7266.

215. Interviews 14 and 23.

216. See https://berliner-wassertisch.net/.

217. See https://www.berliner-wasserrat.de/.

218. Barry, *Material Politics*, 5.

219. See Sebastián Ureta on how democratization can create new challenges of urban governance, Ureta, *Assembling Policy*, 21.

220. On the following, Becker, Beveridge, and Naumann, "Reconfiguring Energy Provision in Berlin"; Blanchet, "Struggle over Energy Transition in Berlin," 248–249; Becker, Naumann, and Moss, "Between Coproduction and Commons," 67–68.

221. On the following, Blanchet, "Struggle over Energy Transition in Berlin," 249; Becker, Naumann, and Moss, "Between Coproduction and Commons," 68.

222. See homepage, https://www.buerger-energie-berlin.de/.

223. On the issues at stake over the concession for the electricity grid, Rocholl and Bolton, "Berlin's Electricity Distribution Grid," 1188–1190.

224. Blanchet, "Struggle over Energy Transition in Berlin," 251–252.

225. The legal uncertainties that have prompted this protracted legal dispute are summarized in Rocholl and Bolton, "Berlin's Electricity Distribution Grid," 1190–1191.

226. Cf. Mitchell, *Carbon Democracy*, 8.

227. Interview 18.

228. Interview 18.

229. Interview 24.

230. Abgeordnetenhaus von Berlin, *Drucksache 18/13649*.

231. Blanchet, "Struggle over Energy Transition in Berlin," 248.

232. The report was entitled "New Energy for Berlin: The Future of Energy-Sector Structures," Abgeordnetenhaus von Berlin, *Neue Energie für Berlin*. See the debate on the report in the city parliament on November 12, 2015, Abgeordnetenhaus von Berlin, *Plenarprotokoll 17/71*, 7262–7273.

233. Ramona Pop, Senator for Economics, Energy, and Enterprises, to the city parliament on February 16, 2017, Abgeordnetenhaus von Berlin, *Plenarprotokoll 18/6*, 371.

234. Speeches in the city parliament on February 16, 2017, Abgeordnetenhaus von Berlin, *Plenarprotokoll 18/6*, 358, 363.

235. Berliner Wasser-Betriebe, *Geschäftsbericht 2017*, 6; Berliner Wasser-Betriebe, *Jahresbericht 2017*, 24; interview 20.

236. Interview 14.

237. Senatsverwaltung für Stadtentwicklung und Umweltschutz, *BerlinStrategie*, 41.

238. Senatsverwaltung für Stadtentwicklung und Umweltschutz, *BerlinStrategie*, 64.

239. Senate Department for Urban Development and the Environment, *Climate-Neutral Berlin 2050*.

240. Senate Department for Urban Development and the Environment, *Climate-Neutral Berlin 2050*, 5. Berlin's population has recently grown from a low of 3.38 million inhabitants in 2000 to 3.64 million in 2018, Amt für Statistik Berlin-Brandenburg, *Statistisches Jahrbuch 2019 Berlin*, 37.

241. Abgeordentenhaus von Berlin, *Drucksache 18/0212*.

242. Interview 25.

243. Interviews 25 and 20.

244. GASAG Berliner Gaswerke Aktiengesellschaft, *Nachhaltigkeitsbericht 2017*, 6, 9.

245. Berliner Wasser-Betriebe, *Geschäftsbericht 2017*, 4–5.

246. See https://sustainablecities.vattenfall.com/de.

247. Interviews 23, 14, 24, and 20.

Chapter 10

Epigraph: Jasanoff, "Future Imperfect," 31.

1. Bulkeley et al., *Cities and Low Carbon Transitions*; Furlong, "STS beyond the 'Modern Infrastructure Ideal'"; Haarstad and Wanvik, "Carbonscapes and beyond."

2. Ladd, *Ghosts of Berlin*; Huyssen, *Present Pasts*; Till, *New Berlin*.

3. On infrastructural palimpsests, see Graham and Thrift, "Out of Order."

4. Collier, *Post-Soviet Social*, 28.

5. Bakker, *Uncooperative Commodity*.

6. See the warning by Susan Leigh Star that "nobody is really in charge of infrastructure," Star, "Ethnography of Infrastructure," 382.

7. For a historically informed critique of common notions of the (water) consumer, see Trentmann, *Making of the Consumer*.

8. Cf. Mitchell, *Carbon Democracy*, 267.

9. Huyssen, *Present Pasts*, 10.

10. Huyssen, *Present Pasts*, 29. On the concept of the "usable past," see Hammersley, "Towards a Usable Past."

11. See the discussion in Moss, "Discarded Surrogates."

12. Cf. Ureta, *Assembling Policy*, 9.

Bibliography

Archival Sources

Landesarchiv Berlin (LAB)

Ca. 250 files from the following series covering the period 1920–1989:

A Pr. Br. Rep. 030 Polizeipräsidium Berlin

A Pr. Br. Rep. 057 Der Stadtpräsident der Reichshauptstadt Berlin

A Rep. 001–02 Magistrat, Generalbüro

A Rep. 015 Magistrat, Stadtbetriebsamt

A Rep. 250-03-07 Elektrowerke AG

A Rep. 254 Charlottenburger Wasser- und Industriewerke AG

A Rep. 255 Berliner Städtische Wasserwerke

A Rep. 256 Berliner Städtische Elektrizitätswerke

A Rep. 259 Berliner Städtische Gaswerke

A Rep. 263 Berliner Stadtgüter

B Rep. 010 Senatsverwaltung für Wirtschaft

B Rep. 011 Senatsverwaltung für Verkehr und Betriebe

B Rep. 012 Senatsverwaltung für Gesundheit

B Rep. 016 Senatsverwaltung für Stadtentwicklung und Umweltschutz

B Rep. 155 Berliner Gaswerke (GASAG)

C Rep. 101 Der Oberbürgermeister von Berlin

C Rep. 105 Magistrat, Abt. Finanzen

C Rep. 106–02 Magistrat der Stadt Berlin, Wirtschaftsrat des Bezirks

C Rep. 107 Magistrat der Stadt Berlin, Bezirksplankommission

C Rep. 110–01 Magistrat der Stadt Berlin, Chefarchitekt—Büro für Städtebau

C Rep. 118 Magistrat von Berlin, Abteilung Gesundheits- und Sozialwesen

C Rep. 124 Magistrat, Erster Stellv. Bürgermeister

C Rep. 124–02 Magistrat von Berlin, Abteilung Kader

C Rep. 126–01 Magistrat von Berlin, Fischereiamt von Groß-Berlin

C Rep. 303 Präsidium der Volkspolizei

C Rep. 308 Deutsche Post

C Rep. 620–01 VBB der Energiewirtschaft Berlin

C Rep. 621 VVB Energieversorgung

C Rep. 752 BEWAG

C Rep. 752–01 VEB Energiekombinat Berlin

C Rep. 750–02 VEB Gasversorgung

C Rep. 904–059 Grundorganisation der SED, Magistrat von Berlin

F Rep. 260 Postersammlung

F Rep. 270 Kartensammlung

F Rep. 290 Fotosammlung

Archiv der Robert-Havemann-Gesellschaft, Berlin (RHG)

Files on the following samizdat newsletters covering the period 1986–1990: *Arche Nova*, *Arche-Info*, *Kontakt*, *Kontext*, *Die Umwelt-Bibliothek*, *Umweltblätter*

Wissenschaftliche Sammlungen des IRS (Leibniz-Institut für Raumbezogene Sozialforschung), Erkner

Reports compiled for the Institut für Städtebau und Architektur, Deutsche Bauakademie der DDR

Statistical Sources

Amt für Statistik Berlin-Brandenburg. *Energie- und CO_2-Bilanz in Berlin 2011. Statistischer Bericht E IV 4–j/11*. Potsdam: Amt für Statistik Berlin-Brandenburg, 2014.

Amt für Statistik Berlin-Brandenburg, ed. *Statistisches Jahrbuch 2009 Berlin*. Berlin: Kulturbuch-Verlag, 2009.

Amt für Statistik Berlin-Brandenburg, ed. *Statistisches Jahrbuch 2016 Berlin*. Berlin: Be.Bra, 2017.

Amt für Statistik Berlin-Brandenburg, ed. *Statistisches Jahrbuch 2018 Berlin*. Berlin: Be.Bra, 2019.

Amt für Statistik Berlin-Brandenburg, ed. *Statistisches Jahrbuch 2019 Berlin*. Berlin: Berliner Wissenschafts-Verlag, 2019.

Hauptamt für Statistik und Wahlen des Magistrats von Groß-Berlin, ed. *Berlin in Zahlen 1946–1947*. Berlin: Das Neue Berlin, 1946.

Statistisches Amt der Stadt Berlin, ed. *Berlin in Zahlen 1945*. Berlin: Das Neue Berlin Verlagsgesellschaft, 1947.

Statistisches Amt der Stadt Berlin, ed. *Statistisches Taschenbuch der Stadt Berlin, N.F.2*. Berlin: n.p., 1926.

Statistisches Landesamt Berlin, ed. *Statistisches Jahrbuch 1952*. Berlin: Kulturbuch-Verlag, 1952.

Statistisches Landesamt Berlin, ed. *Statistisches Jahrbuch 1955*. Berlin: Kulturbuch-Verlag, 1955.

Statistisches Landesamt Berlin, ed. *Statistisches Jahrbuch 1959*. Berlin: Kulturbuch-Verlag, 1959.

Statistisches Landesamt Berlin. *Statistisches Jahrbuch 1990*. Berlin: Kulturbuch-Verlag, 1990.

Statistisches Landesamt Berlin. *Statistisches Jahrbuch 1995*. Berlin: Kulturbuch-Verlag, 1995.

Statistisches Landesamt Berlin. *Statistisches Jahrbuch 1997*. Berlin: Kulturbuch-Verlag, 1997.

Statistisches Landesamt Berlin. *Statistisches Jahrbuch 2001*. Berlin: Kulturbuch-Verlag, 2001.

Statistisches Landesamt Berlin. *Statistisches Jahrbuch 2005*. Berlin: Kulturbuch-Verlag, 2005.

Literature

Abgeordnetenhaus von Berlin. *Drucksache 12/9154*. Berlin: Abgeordnetenhaus von Berlin, 1994.

Abgeordnetenhaus von Berlin. *Drucksache 18/0212*. Berlin: Abgeordnetenhaus von Berlin, 2017.

Abgeordnetenhaus von Berlin. *Drucksache 18/13649*. Berlin: Abgeordnetenhaus von Berlin, 2018.

Abgeordnetenhaus von Berlin, ed. *Neue Energie für Berlin. Zukunft der energiewirtschaftlichen Strukturen. Abschlussbericht der Enquete-Kommission "Neue Energie für Berlin."* Berlin: Abgeordnetenhaus von Berlin, 2016.

Abgeordnetenhaus von Berlin. *Plenarprotokoll 17/38*. Berlin: Abgeordnetenhaus von Berlin, 2013.

Abgeordnetenhaus von Berlin. *Plenarprotokoll 17/71*. Berlin: Abgeordnetenhaus von Berlin, 2015.

Abgeordnetenhaus von Berlin. *Plenarprotokoll 18/6*. Berlin: Abgeordnetenhaus von Berlin, 2017.

Abgeordnetenhaus von Berlin. *Wortprotokoll. Ausschuss für Gesundheit, Umwelt und Verbraucherschutz 16/33*. Berlin: Abgeordnetenhaus von Berlin, 2008.

Adolph, Johannes. "Normung der Stromverteilung." In *Probleme der neuen Stadt Berlin. Darstellungen der Zukunftsaufgaben einer Millionenstadt*, edited by Hans Brennert and Erwin Stein, 434–439. Berlin: Deutscher Kommunal-Verlag, 1926.

Adolph, J. "Zum 50jährigen Jubiläum der Berliner Stromversorgung." *Elektrotechnische Zeitschrift* 55, no. 18 (1933): 434–440.

Aengeneyndt, J. D. "Das Erdgas-Versorgungssystem für Berlin." *Gesundheitsingenieur* 108 (1987): 181–184.

Amin, Ash. "Lively Infrastructure." *Theory, Culture & Society* 31, no. 7/8 (2014): 137–161.

Amt für Technik, Gau Groß-Berlin, Untergruppe Gas. *Denkschrift: Die Zukunft der Berliner Gasversorgung mit besonderer Berücksichtigung des Lieferangebotes der Ruhrgas-A.G. vom Herbst 1933*. Berlin: n.p., 1934.

Anand, Nikhil, Akhil Gupta, and Hannah Appel, eds. *The Promise of Infrastructure*. Durham, NC: Duke University Press, 2018.

Anderson, Ben, Matthew Kearnes, Colin McFarlane, and Dan Swanton. "On Assemblages and Geography." *Dialogues in Human Geography* 2, no. 2 (2012): 171–189.

Appel, Hannah, Nikhil Anand, and Akhil Gupta. "Introduction: Temporality, Politics, and the Promise of Infrastructure." In *The Promise of Infrastructure*, edited by Nikhil Anand, Akhil Gupta, and Hannah Appel, 1–38. Durham, NC: Duke University Press, 2018.

Arbeitsgemeinschaft Brandenburgische-Berliner Wasserver- und Abwasserentsorgungsunternehmen e.V. *Bericht zur Situation und Entwicklung der Öffentlichen Trinkwasserversorgung des Landes Berlin und der Städte und Gemeinden des Landes Brandenburg im Umland von Berlin (Umlandkonzeption Wasserversorgung)*. Potsdam: AG Wasser, 1991.

Arbeitsgemeinschaft Brandenburgische-Berliner Wasserver- und Abwasserentsorgungsunternehmen e.V. *Vorschlag zur Abwasserentsorgung der Städte und Gemeinden des Landes Brandenburg mit Anschluß an die Großkläranlagen der Stadt Berlin und des Umlandes (Umlandkonzeption Abwasserentsorgung)*. Potsdam: AG Wasser, 1991.

Arbeitsgemeinschaft ökologischer Stadtumbau. *Kreuzberger Wasserkonzepte. Konzepte zum behutsamen Umgang mit der natürlichen Lebensgrundlage Wasser in der Stadterneuerung*. Berlin: Bauausstellung Berlin GmbH, 1985.

Augustine, Dolores L. *Red Prometheus: Engineering and Dictatorship in East Germany, 1945–1990*. Cambridge, MA: MIT Press, 2007.

Baar, Lothar. "Die Berliner Industrie nach dem Zweiten Weltkrieg." In *Wirtschaft im geteilten Berlin 1945–1990. Forschungsansätze und Zeitzeugen*, edited by Wolfram Fischer and Johannes Bähr, 137–150. Munich: Saur, 1994.

Bahde, Curt, Manfred Bohge, Klaus Bürgel, and Joachim Schlede. "Das Stromversorgungssystem der Bewag." *Elektrizitätswirtschaft* 76, no. 6 (1977): 129–141.

Bähr, Johannes, and Paul Erker, eds. *NetzWerke. Die Geschichte der Stadtwerke München.* Munich and Berlin: Piper, 2017.

Bakker, Karen. *An Uncooperative Commodity: Privatising Water in England and Wales.* Oxford: Oxford University Press, 2004.

Bakker, Karen, and Gavin Bridge. "Material Worlds? Resource Geographies and the 'Matter of Nature.'" *Progress in Human Geography* 30, no. 5 (2006): 5–27.

Barry, Andrew. *Material Politics: Disputes along the Pipeline.* Chichester: Wiley-Blackwell, 2013.

Bärthel, Hilmar. "Anlagen und Bauten der Elektrizitätserzeugung." In *Berlin und seine Bauten. Teil X, Band A (2) Stadttechnik*, edited by Architekten- und Ingenieur-Verein zu Berlin, 187–250. Petersberg: Michael Imhof, 2006.

Bärthel, Hilmar. "Anlagen und Bauten der Fernwärmeversorgung." In *Berlin und seine Bauten. Teil X, Band A (2) Stadttechnik*, edited by Architekten- und Ingenieur-Verein zu Berlin, 295–318. Petersberg: Michael Imhof, 2006.

Bärthel, Hilmar. "Anlagen und Bauten der Gasversorgung." In *Berlin und seine Bauten. Teil X, Band A (2) Stadttechnik*, edited by Architekten- und Ingenieur-Verein zu Berlin, 21–52. Petersberg: Michael Imhof, 2006.

Bärthel, Hilmar. "Anlagen und Bauten der Stadtentwässerung." In *Berlin und seine Bauten. Teil X, Band A (2) Stadttechnik*, edited by Architekten- und Ingenieur-Verein zu Berlin, 111–186. Petersberg: Michael Imhof, 2006.

Bärthel, Hilmar. "Anlagen und Bauten der Wasserversorgung." In *Berlin und seine Bauten. Teil X, Band A (2) Stadttechnik*, edited by Architekten- und Ingenieur-Verein zu Berlin, 53–110. Petersberg: Michael Imhof, 2006.

Bärthel, Hilmar. *Die Geschichte der Gasversorgung in Berlin. Eine Chronik.* Edited by GASAG Berliner Gaswerke Aktiengesellschaft. Berlin: Nicolai, 1997.

Bärthel, Hilmar. *Geklärt! 125 Jahre Berliner Stadtentwässerung.* Berlin: Verlag für Bauwesen, 2003.

Bärthel, Hilmar. *Wasser für Berlin: die Geschichte der Wasserversorgung.* Berlin: Verlag für Bauwesen, 1997.

Bausch, Herbert. "Die Entwicklung der Berliner Gasversorgung." *Das Gas- und Wasserfach* 97, no. 9 (1956): 357–363.

Bausch, Herbert. "Der Zusammenbruch der Gasversorgung 1945 und Beginn des Wiederaufbaus." In *Feuer und Flamme für Berlin. 170 Jahre Gas in Berlin. 150 Jahre Städtische Gaswerke*, edited by Deutsches Technikmuseum Berlin, 29–31. Berlin: Nicolaische Verlagsbuchhandlung, 1997.

Becker, Sören, Ross Beveridge, and Matthias Naumann. "Reconfiguring Energy Provision in Berlin: Commoning between Compromise and Contestation." In *Urban Commons: Moving beyond State and Market*, edited by Mary Dellenbaugh, Markus Kip, Majken Bieniok, Agnes Katharina Müller, and Martin Schwegmann, 196–213. Basel: Birkhäuser, 2015.

Becker, Sören, Matthias Naumann, and Timothy Moss. "Between Coproduction and Commons: Understanding Initiatives to Reclaim Urban Energy Provision in Berlin and Hamburg." *Urban Research and Practice* 10, no. 1 (2017): 63–85.

Beevor, Anthony. *Berlin: The Downfall 1945*. London: Viking, 2002.

Bennett, Jane. "The Agency of Assemblages and the North American Blackout." *Public Culture* 17, no. 3 (2005): 445–465.

Bennett, Jane. *Vibrant Matter: A Political Ecology of Things*. Durham, NC: Duke University Press, 2010.

Berg, Anne. "The Nazi Rag-Pickers and Their Wine: The Politics of Waste and Recycling in Nazi Germany." *Social History* 40, no. 4 (2015): 446–472.

Berliner Entwässerungswerke, ed. *100 Jahre Berliner Entwässerungswerke 1878–1978*. Berlin: BEW, n.d.

Berliner Entwässerungswerke. *Bericht über das Geschäftsjahr vom 1. Januar bis 31. Dezember 1980*. Berlin: Berliner Entwässerungswerke, 1981.

Berliner Entwässerungswerke / Gewerkschaft Öffentliche Dienste, Transport und Verkehr (ÖTV)–Bezirksverwaltung Berlin. *Arbeit für die Umwelt. Aussichten für ein leistungsfähiges öffentliches Unternehmen*. Berlin: ÖTV, 1983.

Berliner Gaswerke. *100 Jahre Berliner Städtische Gaswerke*. Berlin: Berliner Gaswerke, 1947.

Berliner Gaswerke (GASAG) Eigenbetrieb von Berlin. *Jahresbericht 1999*. Berlin: GASAG, n.d.

Berliner Kraft- und Licht(Bewag)-Aktiengesellschaft [East], ed. *75 Jahre Berliner Stromversorgung*. Berlin: Bewag, n.d.

Berliner Kraft- und Licht(Bewag)-Aktiengesellschaft, ed. *100 Jahre Strom für Berlin. Ein Streifzug durch unsere Geschichte in Wort und Bild, 1884–1984*. Berlin: Bewag, 1984.

Berliner Kraft- und Licht(Bewag)-Aktiengesellschaft. *Geschäftsbericht 1933*. Berlin: Bewag, 1933.

Berliner Kraft- und Licht(Bewag)-Aktiengesellschaft. *Geschäftsbericht 1994/95*. Berlin: Bewag, 1995.

Berliner Kraft- und Licht(Bewag)-Aktiengesellschaft. *Geschäftsbericht 2000/01*. Berlin: Bewag, 2001.

Berliner Kraft- und Licht(Bewag)-Aktiengesellschaft. *Inbetriebsetzung des Neubaus Kraftwerk West am 1. Dezember 1949*. No publication details.

Berliner Kraft- und Licht(Bewag)-Aktiengesellschaft, ed. *Strom für Berlin. Von der Spaltung zur Wiedervereinigung. Berlins Stromversorgung wächst zusammen*. Berlin: Bewag, 1993.

Berliner Kraft- und Licht(Bewag)-Aktiengesellschaft. *Von der Inselversorgung zum Verbund. Berlins Stromversorgung wächst zusammen*. Berlin: Bewag, 1993.

Berliner Städtische Elektrizitätswerke Akt.-Ges. *Jahresbericht der Betriebsdirektion 1926*. Berlin: Bewag, n.d.

Berliner Städtische Elektrizitätswerke Akt.-Ges. *Zur Zukunft der Berliner Elektrizitäts-Versorgung*. Berlin: Bewag, 1928.

Berliner Unterwelten. *Mythos Germania. Schatten und Spuren der Reichshauptstadt. Eine Ausstellung der Berliner Unterwelten e.V.* Berlin: Lehmanns Media, 2008.

Berliner Wasser-Betriebe. *Berlin und Umland*. Berlin: Berliner Wasser-Betriebe, 1992.

Berliner Wasserbetriebe. *Geschäftsbericht 1996*. Berlin: Berliner Wasserbetriebe, 1997.

Berliner Wasserbetriebe. *Geschäftsbericht 1999*. Berlin: Berliner Wasserbetriebe, 2000.

Berliner Wasserbetriebe. *Geschäftsbericht 2004*. Berlin: Berliner Wasserbetriebe, 2005.

Berliner Wasser-Betriebe. *Geschäftsbericht 2017*. Berlin: Berliner Wasser-Betriebe, 2017.

Berliner Wasser-Betriebe. *Jahresbericht 2017*. Berlin: Berliner Wasser-Betriebe, 2018.

Berliner Wasser-Betriebe. *Klare Sache. Die Wasserinfos 2006*. Berlin: Berliner Wasser-Betriebe, 2006.

Berliner Wasserbetriebe. *Presseinformation 23/97*, August 28, 1997.

Berlinwasser Holding Aktiengesellschaft. *Geschäftsbericht 1999*. Berlin: Berlinwasser Holding AG, 1999.

Berlinwasser Holding Aktiengesellschaft. *Geschäftsbericht 2000*. Berlin: Berlinwasser Holding AG, 2000.

Bernhardt, Christoph. "At the Limits of the European Sanitary City: Water-Related Environmental Inequalities in Berlin-Brandenburg, 1900–1939." In *Environmental and Social Justice in the City: Historical Perspectives*, edited by Genevieve Massard-Guilbaud and Richard Rodger, 156–169. Cambridge: White Horse, 2011.

Bernhardt, Christoph. "Wohnungspolitik und Bauwirtschaft in Berlin (1930–1950)." In *Berlin, 1933–1945*, edited by Michael Wildt and Christoph Kreutzmüller, 177–192. Munich: Siedler, 2013.

Bernt, Matthias, Britta Grell, and Andrej Holm. "Introduction." In *The Berlin Reader: A Compendium on Urban Change and Activism*, edited by Matthias Bernt, Britta Grell, and Andrej Holm, 11–21. Bielefeld: Transcript-Verlag, 2013.

Bertelsmann, Wilhelm. "Die Gasversorgung in der Großstadt." In *Probleme der neuen Stadt Berlin. Darstellungen der Zukunftsaufgaben einer Millionenstadt*, edited by Hans Brennert and Erwin Stein, 415–424. Berlin: Deutscher Kommunal-Verlag, 1926.

Betriebsrat der Berliner Kraft- und Licht(Bewag)-Aktiengesellschaft, ed. *Im Licht der Zeit. 90 Jahre Betriebsvertretung bei der Bewag*. Berlin: Betriebsrat der Berliner Kraft- und Licht(Bewag)-Aktiengesellschaft, 1998.

Beveridge, Ross. *A Politics of Inevitability: The Privatisation of the Berlin Water Company, the Global City Discourse, and Governance in 1990s Berlin*. Wiesbaden: VS Verlag für Sozialwissenschaften, 2012.

Beveridge, Ross, Frank Hüesker, and Matthias Naumann. "From Post-Politics to a Politics of Possibility? Unravelling the Privatization of the Berlin Water Company." *Geoforum* 51, January (2014): 66–74.

Beveridge, Ross, and Matthias Naumann. "The Berlin Water Company: From 'Inevitable' Privatisation to 'Impossible' Remunicipalisation." In *The Berlin Reader: A Compendium on Urban Change and Activism*, edited by Matthias Bernt, Britta Grell, and Andrej Holm, 189–203. Bielefeld: Transcript-Verlag, 2013.

BEWAG, ed. *Strom für Berlin. Von der Spaltung zur Wiedervereinigung*. Berlin: Berliner Kraft- und Licht(Bewag)-Aktiengesellschaft, 1991.

Bezirksamt Charlottenburg von Berlin. *Stadt unter Strom. Zur Kulturgeschichte der Elektrifizierung*. Berlin: Heimatmuseum Charlottenburg, 1990.

Bezirksvorstand der Sozialdemokratischen Partei Deutschlands, ed. *Berliner Kommunalpolitik 1921–1925*. Berlin: n.p., 1925.

Binder, Beate. *Elektrifizierung als Vision. Zur Symbolgeschichte einer Technik im Alltag*. Tübingen: Tübinger Vereinigung für Volkskunde, 1999.

Bisky, Jens. *Berlin. Biographie einer großen Stadt*. Berlin: Rowohlt, 2020.

Blackbourn, David. *The Conquest of Nature: Water, Landscape, and the Making of Modern Germany*. New York and London: Norton, 2006.

Blanchet, Thomas. "Struggle over Energy Transition in Berlin: How Do Grassroots Initiatives Affect Local Energy Policy-Making?" *Energy Policy* 78, March (2015): 246–254.

Boberg, Jochen, Tilman Fichter, and Eckhart Gillen, eds. *Exerzierfeld der Moderne. Industriekultur in Berlin im 19. Jahrhundert*. Munich: C. H. Beck, 1984.

Bodenschatz, Harald, and Cordelia Polinna, eds. *100 Jahre Groß-Berlin. Verkehrsfrage und Stadtentwicklung*. Berlin: Lukas, 2018.

Böhme, Martin. "Berlin auf dem Trockenen?" *Stadt + Umwelt* 11 (1990): 39–42.

Bonatz, Karl. "Der neue Plan von Berlin." *Neue Bauwelt* 2, no. 48 (December 1947): 755–762.

Bonatz, Karl. "Meine Stellungnahme zu den Planungsarbeiten für Groß-Berlin, die ich bei meinem Amtsantritt vorfand." *Neue Bauwelt* 2, no. 11 (March 1947): 163–165.

Böß, Gustav. *Berlin von Heute. Stadtverwaltung und Wirtschaft*. Berlin: Gsellius'sche Buchhandlung, 1929.

Böttcher, G. "Der Dungwert der Berliner Abwässer. Untersuchungen aus den Jahren 1935/1936." *Gesundheits-Ingenieur* 60, no. 21 (1937): 330–334.

Böttcher, G. "Geruchsbelästigung durch Abwasser. Bedeutung und Zustandekommen unter besonderer Berücksichtigung der Berliner Verhältnisse." *Gesundheits-Ingenieur* 60, no. 7 (1937): 104–107.

Böttcher, G. *Untersuchungen zur Feststellung des Einflusses der Notauslässe der Stadtentwässerung auf die Berliner Gewässer während der Jahre 1932/1935*. Typescript, Berlin, 1936.

Bouzarovski, Stefan. "East-Central Europe's Changing Energy Landscapes: A Place for Geography." *Area* 41, no. 2 (2009): 452–463.

Bouzarovski, Stefan, Luděk Sýkora, and Roman Matoušek. "Locked-in Post-Socialism: Rolling Path Dependencies in Liberec's District Heating System." *Eurasian Geography and Economics* 57, nos. 4–5 (2016): 624–642.

Brain, Stephen, and Viktor Pál. *Environmentalism under Authoritarian Regimes: Myth, Propaganda, Reality*. London: Routledge, 2018.

Braudel, Fernand. *The Mediterranean and the Mediterranean World in the Age of Philip II*. Berkeley: University of California Press, 1995.

Brennert, Hans, and Erwin Stein, eds. *Probleme der neuen Stadt Berlin. Darstellungen der Zukunftsaufgaben einer Viermillionenstadt*. Berlin: Deutscher Kommunal-Verlag, 1926.

Bridge, Gavin. "The Map Is Not the Territory: A Sympathetic Critique of Energy Research's Spatial Turn." *Energy Research and Social Science* 36, February (2018): 11–20.

Bridge, Gavin, Stefan Bouzarovski, Michael Bradshaw, and Nick Eyre. "Geographies of Energy Transition: Space, Place and the Low-Carbon Economy." *Energy Policy* 53, February (2013): 331–340.

Brüggemann, Heinrich, ed. "Berlin arbeitet! Vortragsreihe des Reichsbundes Deutscher Technik. Ortsgruppe Berlin 1929/39." Special edition of *Technik voran! Mitteilungsblatt des Reichsbundes Deutscher Technik*. Berlin, n.d.

Bublitz, Dietrich: "Ausbau der Fernwärmeversorgung in Berlin." *Elektrizitätswirtschaft* 86, no. 12 (1987): 487ff.

Bublitz, Dietrich. "Fernwärme weiterhin im Aufwind." *Elektrizitätswirtschaft* 83, nos. 9/10 (1984): 441–447.

Bulkeley, Harriet, Vanesa Castán Broto, Mike Hodson, and Simon Marvin, eds. *Cities and Low Carbon Transitions*. London and New York: Routledge, 2011.

Bulkeley, Harriet, Vanesa Castán Broto, and Anne Maassen. "Low-Carbon Transitions and the Reconfiguration of Urban Infrastructure." *Urban Studies* 51, no. 7 (2014): 1471–1486.

BUND Landesverband Berlin e.V. *Konzeption einer ressourcenschonenden Wasserbewirtschaftung für die Region Berlin. Kurzfassung*. Berlin: BUND, 1993.

Büsch, Otto, ed. *Beiträge zur Geschichte der Berliner Demokratie, 1919–1933 / 1945–1985*. Berlin: Colloquium, 1988.

Büsch, Otto. *Geschichte der Berliner Kommunalwirtschaft in der Weimarer Epoche*. Berlin: Walter de Gruyter, 1960.

Carlow, Vanessa Miriam. "Limits: Urban Density and Mobility Networks in West Berlin during the Period of Containment." *Sustainability* 6, no. 10 (2014): 7452–7465.

Casper, Dieter. "Infrastruktur." In *Raumplanung und Raumforschung in der DDR*, edited by Karl Eckart, Gerhard Kehrer, and Konrad Scherf, 137–158. Berlin: Duncker & Humblot, 1998.

Castán Broto, Vanesa. *Urban Energy Landscapes*. Cambridge: Cambridge University Press, 2019.

Castillo, Greg. "The Nylon Curtain: Architectural Unification in Divided Berlin." In *Berlin: Divided City, 1945–1989*, edited by Philip Broadbent and Sabine Hake, 46–55. New York: Berghahn, 2010.

Chelcea, Liviu, and Gergö Pulay. "Networked Infrastructures and the 'Local': Flows and Connectivity in a Postsocialist City." *City* 19, nos. 2–3 (2015): 344–355.

Cochrane, Allan. "Making up Meanings in a Capital City: Power, Memory and Monuments in Berlin." *European Urban and Regional Studies* 13, no. 1 (2006): 5–24.

Coenen, Lars, Paul Benneworth, and Bernard Truffer. "Toward a Spatial Perspective on Sustainability Transitions." *Research Policy* 41, no. 6 (2012): 968–979.

Coenen, Lars, and Bernard Truffer. "Places and Spaces of Sustainability Transitions: Geographical Contributions to an Emerging Research and Policy Field." *European Planning Studies* 20, no. 3 (2012): 367–374.

Cohrs, Albrecht. "Die Berliner Stadtentwässerung." *Das Gas- und Wasserfach* 98 (1957): 804–810.

Collier, Stephen J. *Post-Soviet Social: Neoliberalism, Social Modernity, Biopolitics*. Princeton, NJ: Princeton University Press, 2011.

Conrad, Wolfgang, Klaus Zühlsdorf, and Manfred Gerbich. "Strom- und Fernwärmeerzeugung im Ostteil der Stadt Berlin." *Elektrizitätswirtschaft* 91, nos. 11/12 (1992): 707–725.

Coutard, Olivier, ed. *The Governance of Large Technical Systems*. London and New York: Routledge, 1999.

Coutard, Olivier, and Simon Guy. "STS and the City: Politics and Practices of Hope." *Science, Technology, and Human Values* 32, no. 6 (2007): 713–734.

Coutard, Olivier, Richard E. Hanley, and Rae Zimmermann, eds. *Sustaining Urban Networks: The Social Diffusion of Large Technical Systems*. Abingdon: Routledge, 2005.

Cronon, William. *Nature's Metropolis: Chicago and the Great West*. New York and London: Norton, 1991.

Czada, Peter. *Die Berliner Elektroindustrie in der Weimarer Zeit. Eine regionalstatistisch-wirtschaftshistorische Untersuchung*. Berlin: Colloquium, 1969.

Dame, Thorsten. *Elektropolis Berlin. Die Energie der Großstadt. Bauprogramme und Aushandlungsprozesse zur öffentlichen Elektrizitätsversorgung in Berlin*. Berlin: Mann, 2011.

Darkow, Petra. "Nachhaltiger Gewässerschutz in Berlin." *Wasser und Abfall*, no. 10 (2000): 16–21.

De Landa, Manuel. *A New Philosophy of Society: Assemblage Theory and Social Complexity*. London and New York: Continuum, 2006.

Demps, Laurenz. "Berlin im Bombenkrieg." In *Berlin, 1933–1945*, edited by Michael Wildt and Christoph Kreutzmüller, 357–371. Munich: Siedler, 2013.

Demps, Laurenz. *Luftangriffe auf Berlin. Die Berichte der Hauptluftschutzstelle, 1940–1945*. Berlin: Ch. Links, 2014.

Denner, Julius. "Der Grundwasserstand als Spiegelbild der Entwicklung und Wirtschaftslage Berlins. Beitrag zur Untersuchung der Grundwasserverhältnisse Berlins." *Die Technik* 2 (1947): 59–65.

Denner, Julius. "Die wasserwirtschaftliche Bedeutung der künstlichen Anreicherung des Grundwassers unter besonderer Berücksichtigung der Wasserwirtschaft Groß-Berlins." *Das Gas- und Wasserfach* 77, no. 24 (1934): 413–415, 429–433, 444–447, 462–467.

Denner, Julius. "Schutzgebiete bei Wassergewinnungsanlagen und Hydrogeologie." *Das Gas- und Wasserfach* 90, no. 5 (1949): 106–109.

Denner, Julius, and Friedrich Mösenthin. "Die Grundwasserverhältnisse in Berlin-Innenstadt seit 1870." *Deutsche Wasserwirtschaft* 33 (1938): 1–7.

Der Senator für Stadtentwicklung und Umweltschutz. *Planungsdaten für Berlin (West) 1960 bis 1980. Ein Zahlenwerk des Statistischen Landesamtes Berlin*. Berlin: Der Senator für Stadtentwicklung und Umweltschutz, 1982.

Der Stromkreis. Zeitschrift des Werkvereins der Berliner Städtische Elektrizitätswerke Akt.-Ges. 1, no. 1 (1933) to 6, no. 12 (1939).

Deutsches Institut für Wirtschaftsforschung. *Entwicklung des Elektrizitätsverbrauchs im Land Berlin (West) bis zum Jahre 2010. Gutachten im Auftrag der Berliner Kraft- und Licht(Bewag)-Aktiengesellschaft*. Berlin: Deutsches Institut für Wirtschaftsforschung, 1988.

Diefendorf, Jeffrey M. *In the Wake of War: The Reconstruction of German Cities after World War II*. New York and Oxford: Oxford University Press, 1993.

"Die neuen Tarife der StEW Berlin." *Mitteilungen der Vereinigung der Elektrizitätswerke* 281 (January 1921): 16–17.

Die Sitzungsprotokolle des Magistrats der Stadt Berlin 1945/46. Teil I: 1945. Edited by Dieter Hanauske. Berlin: Arno Spitz, 1995.

Die Sitzungsprotokolle des Magistrats der Stadt Berlin 1945/46. Teil II: 1946. Edited by Dieter Hanauske. Berlin: Arno Spitz, 1999.

Dietrich, Richard. "Verfassung und Verwaltung." In *Berlin und die Provinz Brandenburg im 19. und 20. Jahrhundert*, edited by Hans Herzfeld, 265–277. Berlin: Walter de Gruyter, 1968.

"Die Vereinheitlichung der Stromversorgung in der Reichshauptstadt." *Zeitschrift für öffentliche Wirtschaft* 5, no. 4 (1938): 128–129.

Dirks, Christian. "Einleitung." In *... auf dem Dienstweg. Die Verfolgung von Beamten, Angestellten und Arbeitern der Stadt Berlin 1933 bis 1945*, edited by Christian Dirks and Hermann Simon, 12–22. Berlin: Hentrich & Hentrich, 2010.

Dirks, Christian, and Hermann Simon, eds. *... auf dem Dienstweg. Die Verfolgung von Beamten, Angestellten und Arbeitern der Stadt Berlin 1933 bis 1945*. Berlin: Hentrich & Hentrich, 2010.

Dodson, Jago. "The Global Infrastructure Turn and Urban Practice." *Urban Policy and Research* 35, no. 1 (2017): 87–92.

Dolata, Ulrich, and Raymund Werle. "'Bringing Technology Back in': Technik als Einflussfaktor sozioökonomischen und institutionellen Wandels." In *Gesellschaft und die Macht der Technik. Sozioökonomischer und institutioneller Wandel durch Technisierung*, edited by Ulrich Dolata and Raymund Werle, 15–43. Frankfurt and New York: Campus, 2007.

Donath, Matthias. "Städtebau und Architektur." In *Berlin, 1933–1945*, edited by Michael Wildt and Christoph Kreutzmüller, 229–244. Munich: Siedler, 2013.

Eberling, Georg. "Chemische Untersuchung der Berliner Spree im November und Dezember 1931." *Gesundheits-Ingenieur* 55, no. 16 (1932): 181–186.

Edwards, Paul N. "Infrastructure and Modernity: Force, Time, and Social Organization in the History of Sociotechnical Systems." In *Modernity and Technology*, edited by Thomas J. Misa, Philip Brey, and Andrew Feenberg, 185–225. Cambridge, MA: MIT Press, 2003.

Eiden, Christian. *Versorgungswirtschaft als regionale Organisation. Die Wasserversorgung Berlins und des Ruhrgebietes zwischen 1850 und 1930*. Essen: Klartext, 2006.

Elkins, T. H., and B. Hofmeister. *Berlin: The Spatial Structure of a Divided City*. London and New York: Methuen, 1988.

"Energie sparen!" *Deutsche Technik* 11, January (1943): 33.

"Energiepreise in Berlin (Podiumsdiskussion)." *Mitteilungen. Verein Berliner Kaufleute und Industrielle* 39 (1989): 6–21.

Energieversorgung Berlin AG, ed. *Die Geschäftspolitik der EBAG und das Gesetz zur Förderung der sparsamen sowie umwelt- und sozialverträglichen Energieversorgung und Energienutzung*. Berlin: n.p., 1992.

Engeli, Christian. *Gustav Böß. Oberbürgermeister von Berlin 1921 bis 1930*. Stuttgart: Kohlhammer, 1971.

Engeli, Christian. *Landesplanung in Berlin-Brandenburg. Eine Untersuchung zur Geschichte des Landesplanungsverbandes Brandenburg-Mitte, 1929–1936*. Stuttgart: Kohlhammer and Deutscher Gemeindeverlag, 1986.

Engeli, Christian, and Wolfgang Haus, eds. *Quellen zum modernen Gemeindeverfassungsrecht in Deutschland*. Stuttgart: Kohlhammer, 1975.

Engeli, Christian, and Wolfgang Ribbe. "Berlin in der NS-Zeit (1933–1945)." In *Geschichte Berlins. Zweiter Band: Von der Märzrevolution bis zur Gegenwart*, edited by Wolfgang Ribbe, 927–1025. Munich: C. H. Beck, 1987.

Engels, Jens Ivo, and Gerrit Jasper Schenk. "Infrastrukturen der Macht—Macht der Infrastrukturen." In *Wasserinfrastrukturen und Macht von der Antike bis zur Gegenwart*, edited by Birte Förster and Martin Bauch, 22–58. Munich: Walter de Gruyter, 2014.

Erster Verwaltungsbericht der neuen Stadtgemeinde Berlin für die Zeit vom 1. Oktober 1920 bis 31. März 1924. Berlin: Statistisches Amt der Stadt Berlin, n.d.

Evans, Richard J. *The Third Reich in Power, 1933–1939: How the Nazis Won over the Hearts and Minds of a Nation*. London and New York: Penguin, 2005.

Farías, Ignacio, and Thomas Bender. *Urban Assemblages: How Actor-Network Theory Changes Urban Studies*. London and New York: Routledge, 2010.

Feilitzsch, Alfred von. "Die Zukunft der Berliner Wasserversorgung." *Gesundheitsingenieur* 51 (1928): 785–787.

Fieber, Hans-Joachim, and Thomas Rockmann. *An der Spitze Berlins. Zweiter Teil. Biographisches und Kommunalgeschichtliches zu den Stadtoberhäuptern Berlins von 1871 bis zur Gegenwart*. Berlin: Edition Luisenstadt, 1995.

Fischer, Clemens. "BEWAG—vom Inselversorger zum Verbundpartner." Special edition, *Energiewirtschaftliche Tagesfragen* 12 (1992).

Fischer, R. "Die deutsche Stromversorgung im Kriege." *Elektrizitätswirtschaft* 43, no. 8 (1944): 222–224.

Fleischer, W. "Lastverteilung bei der Berliner Städtische Elektrizitätswerke Akt.-Ges." *Elektrizitätswirtschaft* 28, no. 493 (1929): 502–507.

Flyvbjerg, Bent. "Five Misunderstandings about Case-Study Research." *Qualitative Inquiry* 12, no. 2 (2006): 219–245.

Franz, Markus, and Kai Giese. *Es werde Licht. Ein Lesebuch voller Energie zum 170. Geburtstag der GASAG*. Berlin: GASAG, 2017.

Friedrich, Thomas. *Hitler's Berlin: Abused City*. New Haven, CT: Yale University Press, 2012.

Fuenfschilling, Lea, and Bernard Truffer. "The Structuration of Socio-Technical Regimes: Conceptual Foundations from Institutional Theory." *Research Policy* 43, no. 4 (2014): 772–791.

Furlong, Kathryn. "Small Technologies, Big Change: Rethinking Infrastructure through STS and Geography." *Progress in Human Geography* 35, no. 4 (2010): 460–482.

Furlong, Kathryn. "STS beyond the 'Modern Infrastructure Ideal': Extending Theory by Engaging with Infrastructure Challenges in the South." *Technology in Society* 38 (2014): 139–147.

Gandy, Matthew. *Concrete and Clay: Reworking Nature in New York City*. Cambridge, MA: MIT Press, 2002.

Gandy, Matthew. *The Fabric of Space: Water, Modernity, and the Urban Imagination*. Cambridge, MA: MIT Press, 2014.

Gandy Matthew. "The Making of a Regulatory Crisis: Restructuring New York City's Water Supply." *Transactions of the Institute of British Geographers* 22, no. 3 (1997): 338–358.

Gandy, Matthew. "Negative Luminescence." *Annals of the American Association of Geographers* 107, no. 5 (2017): 1090–1107.

Gandy, Matthew. "Rethinking Urban Metabolism: Water, Space and the Modern City." *City* 8, no. 3 (2004): 363–379.

García Soler, Natàlia, Timothy Moss, and Ourania Papasozomenou. "Rain and the City: Pathways to Mainstreaming Rainwater Harvesting in Berlin." *Geoforum* 89, February (2018): 96–106.

GASAG Berliner Gaswerke Aktiengesellschaft. "Dokumentation über den Verkauf des 51,2%-Landesanteils an der GASAG Berliner Gaswerke Aktiengesellschaft." Unpublished manuscript, 1998.

GASAG Berliner Gaswerke Aktiengesellschaft. *Geschäftsbericht 2010*. Berlin: GASAG, 2010.

GASAG Berliner Gaswerke Aktiengesellschaft. *Nachhaltigkeitsbericht 2017*. Berlin: GASAG, 2017.

GASAG.... *über 160 Jahre Gasversorgung*. Berlin: GASAG, 1987.

Geels, Frank W. "Ontologies, Socio-Technical Transitions (to Sustainability), and the Multi-Level Perspective." *Research Policy* 39, no. 4 (2010): 495–510.

Geels, Frank W. "Technological Transitions as Evolutionary Reconfiguration Processes: A Multi-level Perspective and a Case-Study." *Research Policy* 31, no. 8 (2002): 1257–1274.

Geels, Frank W. "The Multi-Level Perspective on Sustainability Transitions: Responses to Seven Criticisms." *Environmental Innovation and Societal Transitions* 1, no. 1 (2011): 24–40.

Geels, Frank W., Florian Kern, Gerhard Fuchs, Nele Hinderer, Gregor Kungl, Josephine Mylan, Mario Neukirch, and Sandra Wassermann. "The Enactment of Socio-Technical Transition Pathways: A Reformulated Typology and a Comparative Multi-Level Analysis of the German and UK Low-Carbon Electricity Transitions (1990–2014)." *Research Policy* 45, no. 4 (2016): 896–913.

Geels, Frank W., Andy McMeekin, Josephine Mylan, and Dale Southerton. "A Critical Appraisal of Sustainable Consumption and Production Research: The Reformist, Revolutionary and Reconfiguration Positions." *Global Environmental Change* 34, September (2015): 1–12.

Geels, Frank W., and Rob Raven. "Non-Linearity and Expectations in Niche-Development Trajectories: Ups and Downs in Dutch Biogas Development (1973–2003)." *Technology Analysis & Strategic Management* 18, nos. 3/4 (2006): 375–392.

Geels, Frank W., and Johan Schot. "Typology of Sociotechnical Transition Pathways." *Research Policy* 36, no. 3 (2007): 399–417.

Gorostiza, Santiago, and Miquel Ortega Cerdà. "'The Unclaimed Latifundium': The Configuration of the Spanish Fishing Sector under Francoist Autarky, 1939–1951." *Journal of Historical Geography* 52, April (2016): 26–35.

Graham, Stephen, and Simon Marvin. *Splintering Urbanism: Networked Infrastructures, Technological Mobilities and the Urban Condition*. London and New York: Routledge, 2001.

Graham, Stephen, and Nigel Thrift. "Out of Order: Understanding Repair and Maintenance." *Theory, Culture & Society* 24, no. 3 (2007): 1–25.

Greiner, Josef Peter. "Vom Energiesparen. Gedanken zur Propaganda in der Technik." *Deutsche Technik* 10, December (1942): 521–522.

Gromeyer. "Ideologische Grundsätze für die Arbeit in der Wasserwirtschaft." *Wasserwirtschaft—Wassertechnik* 5, no. 9 (1955): 281–283.

Gropp, Fr. "Die Elektrizitätswirtschaft der sowjetisch besetzten Zone Deutschlands, Ende 1950." *Elektrizitätswirtschaft* 50, no. 6 (1951): 159–162.

Gross, Stephen G. "Reimagining Energy and Growth: Decoupling and the Rise of a New Energy Paradigm in West Germany, 1973–1986." *Central European History* 50, no. 4 (2017): 514–546.

Grot, Rötger von, "Strukturwandel der Gebäudeheizung in Berlin." *Gesundheitsingenieur* 108 (1987): 211–218.

Gudermann, Rita: "Die Berliner Abwässer und das Umland (1870–1930)." In *Blickwechsel. Beiträge zur Geschichte der Wasserversorgung und Abwasserentsorgung in Berlin und Istanbul*, edited by Noyan Dinçkal und Shahrooz Mohajeri, 153–169. Berlin: Technische Universität Berlin, Zentrum für Technik und Gesellschaft, 2001.

Gupta, Akhil. "The Future in Ruins: Thoughts on the Temporality of Infrastructure." In *The Promise of Infrastructure*, edited by Nikhil Anand, Akhil Gupta, and Hannah Appel, 62–79. Durham, NC: Duke University Press, 2018.

Guy, Simon, Simon Marvin, and Timothy Moss, eds. *Urban Infrastructure in Transition. Networks, Buildings, Plans*. London: Earthscan, 2001.

Haarstad, Håvard, and Tarje I. Wanvik. "Carbonscapes and beyond: Conceptualizing the Instability of Oil Landscapes." *Progress in Human Geography* 41, no. 4 (2017): 432–450.

Haase. "Die Stellung der Wasserwirtschaft in unserer Volkswirtschaft und die nächsten Aufgaben." *Wasserwirtschaft—Wassertechnik* 5, no. 10 (1955): 313–314.

Haase, Martin. "Kraftwerks- und Stadtheizungsbetrieb." *Elektrizitätswirtschaft* 83, nos. 9/10 (1984): 426–441.

Hachtmann, Rüdiger, and Christoph Kreutzmüller. "Arbeiter und Arbeiterorganisationen in Berlin (1930–1945)." In *Berlin, 1933–1945*, edited by Michael Wildt and Christoph Kreutzmüller, 111–126. Munich: Siedler, 2013.

Hachtmann, Rüdiger, Thomas Schaarschmidt, and Winfried Süß, eds. *Berlin im Nationalsozialismus. Politik und Gesellschaft 1933–1945*. Göttingen: Wallstein, 2011.

Hachtmann, Rüdiger, Thomas Schaarschmidt, and Winfried Süß. "Einleitung. Berlin im Nationalsozialismus." In *Berlin im Nationalsozialismus. Politik und Gesellschaft 1933–1945*, edited by Rüdiger Hachtmann, Thomas Schaarschmidt, and Winfried Süß, 9–18. Göttingen: Wallstein, 2011.

Hahn. *Denkschrift über die Erhöhung der Leistungsfähigkeit der Rieselfelder durch den Bau von Belebt-Schlammanlagen und über die Verbesserung der Wasserverhältnisse der Spree durch künstliche Anreicherung ihres Wasserschatzes*. Berlin: n.p., 1928.

Hahn, Ekhart, and Joachim Zeisel. *Integriertes Wasserkonzept zur dezentralen Abwasserentsorgung durch Pflanzen und zur Trinkwassersubstitution in einer innerstädtischen Wohnanlage. Block 6*. Berlin: Arbeitsgemeinschaft Ökologischer Stadtumbau, 1987.

Hammersley, Martyn. "Towards a Usable Past for Qualitative Research." *International Journal of Social Research Methodology* 7, no. 1 (2007): 19–27.

Haney, David H. "Leberecht Migge's 'Green Manifesto': Envisioning a Revolution of Gardens." *Landscape Journal* 26, no. 2 (2007): 201–218.

Haney, David H. *When Modern Was Green: Life and Work of Landscape Architect Leberecht Migge*. London and New York: Taylor and Francis, 2010.

Hansman, R. John, Christopher Magee, Richard de Neufville, Renee Robins, and Daniel Roos. "Research Agenda for an Integrated Approach to Infrastructure Planning, Design and Management." *International Journal of Critical Infrastructures* 2, nos. 2/3 (2006): 146–159.

Hård, Mikael, and Marcus Stippak. "Discourses on the Modern City and Urban Technology, 1850–2000: A Review of Recent Literature." In *The Urban Machine: Recent Literature on European Cities in the 20th Century. A "Tensions of Europe" Electronic Publication*, edited by Mikael Hård and Thomas J. Misa, 38–59. 2003. http://www.iit.edu/~misa/toe20/urban-machine/completepwd.pdf.

Hård, Mikael, and Marcus Stippak. "Progressive Dreams: The German City in Britain and the United States." In *Urban Machinery: Inside Modern European Cities*, edited by Mikael Hård and Thomas J. Misa, 121–140. Cambridge, MA: MIT Press, 2008.

Hartmann, R. "Energieeinschränkungen und -sparmaßnahmen in der Haushaltsgasversorgung." *Das Gas- und Wasserfach*, 86, no. 18 (1943): 281–282.

Harvey, Penny, Casper Bruun Jensen, and Atsuro Morita. "Introduction: Infrastructural Complications." In *Infrastructures and Social Complexity. A Companion*, edited by Penny Harvey, Casper Bruun Jensen, and Atsuro Morita, 1–42. London and New York: Routledge, 2016.

Heilmann, Adolf. "Städtereinigung und Vierjahresplan." *Gesundheits-Ingenieur* 60, no. 21 (1937): 321–327 and no. 22: 351–366.

Heilmann, Adolf. "Über die biologischen Grenzen der landwirtschaftlichen Verwertung städtischer Abwässer. Eine zusammenfassende und abschließende Betrachtung." *Gesundheits-Ingenieur* 64, no. 25 (1941): 357–361.

Hellige, Hans Dieter. "Entstehungsbedingungen und energietechnische Langzeitwirkungen des Energiewirtschaftsgesetzes von 1935." *Technikgeschichte* 53, no. 2 (1986): 123–155.

Heiser, Heinrich: "Wasserhaushalt und Raumordnung." *Raumforschung und Raumordnung* 2, no. 1 (1938): 31–36.

Herbert, Ulrich. *Fremdarbeiter. Politik und Praxis des "Ausländer-Einsatzes" in der Kriegswirtschaft des Dritten Reichs*. Berlin and Bonn: J. H. W. Dietz, 1985.

Herzfeld, Hans. "Weimarer Demokratie und Nationalsozialismus. Die Weltstadt Berlin (1919–1945)." In *Berlin und die Provinz Brandenburg im 19. und 20. Jahrhundert*, edited by Hans Herzfeld, 117–135. Berlin: Walter de Gruyter, 1968.

Heßler, Martina. "Die Einführung elektrischer Haushaltsgeräte in der Zwischenkriegszeit—Der Angebotspush der Produzenten und die Reaktion der Konsumentinnen." *Technikgeschichte* 65, no. 4 (1998): 297–311.

Heßler, Martina. "'Elektrische Helfer': für Hausfrau, Volk und Vaterland." *Technikgeschichte* 68, no. 3 (2001): 203–229.

Heynen, Nik, Maria Kaika, and Erik Swyngedouw. "Urban Political Ecology: Politicizing the Production of Urban Natures." In *In the Nature of Cities: Urban Political Ecology and the Politics of Urban Metabolism*, edited by Nik Heynen, Maria Kaika, and Erik Swyngedouw, 3–20. London: Routledge, 2006.

Hildebrandt, Antje. "Der Berliner NSDAP-Lokalfunktionär Karl Kasper: eine exemplarische Karriere." *Totalitarismus und Demokratie* 10, no. 1 (2013): 37–59.

Hirschl, Bernd, Astrid Aretz, Elisa Dunkelberg, Anna Neumann, and Julika Weiß. *Potenziale erneuerbarer Energien in Berlin 2020 und langfristig—Quantifizierung und Maßnahmengenerierung zur Erreichung ambitionierter Ausbauziele. Studie zum Berliner Energiekonzept (Anlage 6)*. Berlin: Institut für ökologische Wirtschaftsforschung (IÖW), 2011.

Hodson, Mike, Frank W. Geels, and Andy McMeekin. "Reconfiguring Urban Sustainability Transitions, Analysing Multiplicity." *Sustainability* 9, no. 2 (2017): 299ff.

Hodson, Mike, and Simon Marvin. "Can Cities Shape Socio-Technical Transitions and How Would We Know if They Were?" *Research Policy* 39, no. 4 (2010): 477–485.

Hodson, Mike, Simon Marvin, Harriet Bulkeley, and Vanesa Castán Broto. "Conclusion." In *Cities and Low Carbon Transitions*, edited by Harriet Bulkeley, Vanesa Castán Broto, Mike Hodson, and Simon Marvin, 198–202. Abingdon: Routledge, 2011.

Högselius, Per, Arne Kaijser, and Erik van der Vleuten. *Europe's Infrastructure Transition: Economy, War, Nature*. Basingstoke: Palgrave Macmillan, 2016.

Holmsten, Georg. *Die Berlin-Chronik. Daten, Personen, Dokumente*. Düsseldorf: Droste, 1984.

Hommels, Anique. "Studying Obduracy in the City: Toward a Productive Fusion between Technology Studies and Urban Studies." *Science, Technology & Human Values* 30, no. 3 (2005): 323–351.

Hommels, Anique. *Unbuilding Cities: Obduracy in Urban Sociotechnical Change*. Cambridge, MA: MIT Press, 2005.

Hoppe, Joseph, and Heike Oevermann, eds. *Metropole Berlin. Die Wiederentdeckung der Industriekultur*. Berlin: Be.Bra, 2020.

Houwink Ten Cate, J. T. M. *Das organisierte Chaos: "Ämterdarwinismus" und "Gesinnungsethik": Determinanten nationalsozialistischer Besatzungsherrschaft. Nationalsozialistische Besatzungspolitik in Europa 1939–1945.* Berlin: Metropol, 1999.

Hüesker, Frank. *Kommunale Daseinsvorsorge in der Wasserwirtschaft. Auswirkungen der Privatisierung am Beispiel der Wasserbetriebe Berlins.* Munich: Oekom, 2011.

Hughes, Thomas, P. *Networks of Power: Electrification in Western Society, 1880–1930.* Baltimore, MD, and London: John Hopkins University Press, 1983.

Hünerberg, Kurt. "Die Berliner Wasserversorgung." *Das Gas- und Wasserfach* 96, no. 2 (1955): 39–43.

Hünerberg, Kurt. "Die Wasserversorgung von Westberlin." *Wasser und Boden* 13, no. 5 (1961): 137–142.

Hünerberg, Kurt. "Planungen der Berliner Entwässerungswerke." *Das Gas- und Wasserfach* 108, no. 10 (1967): 262–266.

Hünerberg, Kurt. "Umstellung der Abwasserreinigung in Berlin vom Rieselfeldbetrieb auf biologische Klärwerke." *Das Gas- und Wasserfach* 109, no. 12 (1968): 311–315.

Huyssen, Andreas. *Present Pasts: Urban Palimpsests and the Politics of Memory.* Stanford, CA: Stanford University Press, 2003.

Imhoff, Karl. "Die deutsche Abwasser-Wissenschaft in der Kriegszeit." *Gesundheits-Ingenieur* 68, no. 3 (1947): 65–70.

Jaglin, Sylvy, and Alain Dubresson. *Eskom: Electricity and Technopolitics in South Africa.* Cape Town: UCT Press, 2016.

Jasanoff, Sheila. "Future Imperfect: Science, Technology, and the Imaginations of Modernity." In *Dreamscapes of Modernity: Sociotechnical Imaginaries and the Fabrication of Power,* edited by Sheila Jasanoff and Sang-Hyun Kim, 1–33. Chicago: Chicago University Press, 2015.

Joerges, Bernward. "High Variability Discourse in the History and Sociology of Large Technical Systems." In *The Governance of Large Technical Systems,* edited by Olivier Coutard, 258–290. London and New York: Routledge, 1999.

Johnson, Victoria C. A., Fionnguala Sherry-Brennan, and Peter J. G. Pearson. "Alternative Liquid Fuels in the UK in the Inter-War Period (1918–1938): Insights from a Failed Energy Transition." *Environmental Innovation and Societal Transitions* 20, September (2016): 33–47.

Kaeber, Ernst. "Die Oberbürgermeister Berlins seit der Steinschen Städteordnung." *Jahrbuch des Vereins für die Geschichte Berlins* 2 (1952): 53–114.

Kaika, Maria. *City of Flows: Modernity, Nature, and the City.* New York and London: Routledge, 2005.

Kaika, Maria. "Dams as Symbols of Modernization: The Urbanization of Nature between Geographical Imagination and Materiality." *Annals of the Association of American Geographers* 96, no. 2 (2006): 276–301.

Kasper, Karl. "Die Trink- und Brauchwasserversorgung im Rahmen der deutschen Wasserwirtschaft." *Das Gas- und Wasserfach* 82, no. 24 (1939): 442–444.

Kasper, Karl. "Die Vereinheitlichung der Gasversorgung in der Reichshauptstadt." *Berliner Kommunale Mitteilungen* 11 (1940): 81–83.

Kasper, Karl. "Kriegsaufgaben in der Wasserversorgung." *Das Gas- und Wasserfach* 83, no. 49 (1940): 623–624.

Kauffmann, R. "Das Abzahlungsgeschäft des Bewag." *Elektrizitätswirtschaft* 26, no. 427 (1927): 81–83.

Kellerhoff, Sven Felix. "Luftkrieg um die Reichshauptstadt." In *Berlin 1933–1945. Zwischen Propaganda und Terror*, edited by Stiftung Topographie des Terrors, 242–248. Berlin: Stiftung Topographie des Terrors, 2010.

Kirchhof, Astrid Mignon. "'For a Decent Quality of Life': Environmental Groups in East and West Berlin." *Journal of Urban History* 41, no. 4 (2015): 1–22.

Kirchhof, Astrid Mignon. "Structural Strains und die Analyse der Umweltbewegung seit den 1960er Jahren." In *Theoretische Ansätze und Konzepte der Forschung über soziale Bewegungen in der Geschichtswissenschaft*, edited by Jürgen Mittag and Helke Stadtland, 127–146. Essen: Klartext, 2014.

Kist, Klaus, and Willibald Lang: "Energiesparpartnerschaften Berlin—ein Modellprojekt geht in Serie." In *Energiespar-Contracting als Beitrag zu Klimaschutz und Kostensenkung. Ratgeber für Energiespar-Contracting in öffentlichen Liegenschaften*, edited by Umweltbundesamt, 25–31. Berlin: Umweltbundesamt, 2000.

Kitchen, Martin. *Speer: Hitler's Architect*. New Haven, CT: Yale University Press, 2015.

Koch, E. "Einwirkung der XI. Olympischen Spiele 1936 auf die Verbesserung der Straßenbeleuchtung und den Gasverbrauch in Berlin." *Das Gas- und Wasserfach* 79, no. 40 (1936): 717–718.

Koch and Kienzle. "Bericht über die Abschlussprüfung der Berliner Städtische Gaswerke (Gasag) für die Geschäftsjahre 1938 und 1939 vom 10. März 1942." Berlin: Typescript report, 1942.

Kölzow, H. "Neue Gesichtspunkte zur Abwasserverwertung." *Gesundheits-Ingenieur* 58, no. 8 (1935): 108–109.

Kotowski, Georg. "Vom Vorposten der westlichen Demokratie zur Stadt des Viermächte-Abkommens 1963–1985." In *Berlin als Hauptstadt im Nachkriegsdeutschland und Land Berlin 1945–1985*, edited by Georg Kotowski and Hans J. Reichhardt, 207–313. Berlin and New York: Walter de Gruyter, 1987.

Kotowski, Georg, and Hans J. Reichhardt. *Berlin als Hauptstadt im Nachkriegsdeutschland und Land Berlin 1945–1985*. Berlin and New York: Walter de Gruyter, 1987.

Krätke, Stefan. "City of Talents? Berlin's Regional Economy, Socio-Spatial Fabric and 'Worst Practice' Urban Governance." In *The Berlin Reader: A Compendium on Urban Change and Activism*, edited by Matthias Bernt, Britta Grell, and Andrej Holm, 131–154. Bielefeld: Transcript-Verlag, 2013.

Krätke, Stefan, and Renate Borst. *Berlin. Metropole zwischen Boom und Krise*. Opladen: Leske + Budrich, 2000.

Krecke, Carl. "Die Aufgaben der deutschen Energiewirtschaft." *Deutsche Technik* 2, July (1934): 554–556.

Krecke, Carl. *Die Energiewirtschaft im nationalsozialistischen Staat*. Berlin: Junker und Dünnhaupt, 1937.

Kreutzmüller, Christoph. "1937–Das letzte Friedensjahr?" In *Berlin 1937. Im Schatten von morgen*, edited by Stiftung Stadtmuseum Berlin, 9–15. Berlin: Verlag M—Stadtmuseum Berlin, 2017.

Kreutzmüller, Christoph. "Verfassung und Verwaltung der Hauptstadt." In *Berlin, 1933–1945*, edited by Michael Wildt and Christoph Kreutzmüller, 51–67. Munich: Siedler, 2013.

Kreutzmüller, Christoph, and Michael Wildt. "'Ein radikaler Bürger'. Julius Lippert—Chefredakteur des "Angriff" und Staatskommissar zur besonderen Verwendung in Berlin." In *Berlin im Nationalsozialismus. Politik und Gesellschaft 1933–1945*, edited by Rüdiger Hachtmann, Thomas Schaarschmidt, and Winfried Süß, 19–38. Göttingen: Wallstein, 2011.

Kühne, Carl. "Die Zukunft der Wasserversorgung von Berlin." Special issue *Das Gas- und Wasserfach* 28/29 (1926).

Kühne, Carl. *Die Berliner Städtische Wasserwerke Aktien-Gesellschaft auf der Deutschen Ausstellung Gas und Wasser Berlin 1929*. Berlin: Berliner Städtische Wasserwerke, 1929.

Kühne, Carl. "Gegenwarts- und Zukunftsprobleme der Wasserversorgung von Berlin." In *Probleme der neuen Stadt Berlin. Darstellungen der Zukunftsaufgaben einer Millionenstadt*, edited by Hans Brennert and Erwin Stein, 425–433. Berlin: Deutscher Kommunal-Verlag, 1926.

Kühne, Carl. "Übernahme der Wasserversorgung Schöneberg und Steglitz durch die Berliner Städtische Wasserwerke AG." *Amtsblatt der Stadt Berlin* 1928: 555–557.

Kühne, Carl. "Zur Frage der Wasserversorgung von Berlin." *Das Gas- und Wasserfach* 72, no. 1 (1929): 11–16.

Laak, Dirk van. "Infra-Strukturgeschichte." *Geschichte und Gesellschaft* 27, no. 3 (2001): 367–393.

Laak, Dirk van. *Alles im Fluss. Die Lebensadern der Gesellschaft—Geschichte und Zukunft der Infrastruktur*. Frankfurt am Main: Fischer, 2018.

Ladd, Brian. *The Ghosts of Berlin: Confronting German History in the Urban Landscape*. Chicago: University of Chicago Press, 1997.

Langbein, Fritz. "Die Abwasservorkläranlage auf dem Bölkensberge des Berliner Rieselfeldes Waßmannsdorf als Gaslieferer." *Das Gas- und Wasserfach* 70, no. 46 (1927): 1109–1118.

Langbein, Fritz. "Die Entwässerung von Groß-Berlin und die Organisation ihrer Verwaltung." *Technisches Gemeindeblatt* 23, no. 10 (1920): 93–95.

Langbein, Fritz. "Die Stadtentwässerung." In *Probleme der neuen Stadt Berlin. Darstellungen der Zukunftsaufgaben einer Viermillionenstadt*, edited by Hans Brennert and Erwin Stein, 348–363. Berlin: Deutscher Kommunal-Verlag, 1926.

Langbein, Fritz. "Die Verwertung städtischer Abwässer zum Zwecke der Landeskultur." *Gesundheits-Ingenieur* 53 (1930): 321–330.

Langbein, Fritz. "Die volkswirtschaftliche Bedeutung des Abwassers." *Gesundheits-Ingenieur* 59, no. 19 (1936): 268–272.

Langbein, Fritz. "Zur Halbjahrhundertfeier der Berliner Stadtentwässerung." *Gesundheits-Ingenieur* 51, no. 4 (1928): 49–57.

Langbein, F., and F. Kroll. "Die Gewinnung und Verwertung des Faulgases auf der Berliner Abwasservorkläranlage in Waßmannsdorf." *Das Gas- und Wasserfach* 74, no. 21 (1931): 469–476.

Lange, Friedrich C. A. *Groß-Berliner Tagebuch 1920–1933*. Berlin and Bonn: Westkreuz-Verlag, 1982.

Langguth, Frauke. "Elektrizität in jedem Gerät. Die Elektrifizierung der privaten Haushalte am Beispiel Berlins." In *Haushalts-Träume. Ein Jahrhundert Technisierung und Rationalisierung im Haushalt*, edited by Barbara Orland, 93–102. Königstein im Taunus: Langewiesche, 1990.

Lanz, Stephan. "Be Berlin! Governing the City through Freedom." *International Journal of Urban and Regional Research* 37, no. 4 (2013): 1305–1324.

LaPorte, Todd R., ed. *Social Responses to Large Technical Systems*. Dordrecht: Kluwer, 1991.

Large, David Clay. *Berlin*. New York: Basic Books, 2000.

Larkin, Brian. "The Politics and Poetics of Infrastructure." *Annual Review of Anthropology* 42, October (2013): 327–343.

Latham, Alan. "Berlin and Everywhere Else: A Reply to Allan Cochrane." *European Urban and Regional Studies* 13, no. 4 (2006): 377–379.

Latham, Alan, and Derek P. McCormack. "Moving Cities: Rethinking the Materialities of Urban Geographies." *Progress in Human Geography* 28, no. 6 (2004): 701–724.

Latour, Bruno, and Emilie Hermant. *Paris: Invisible City*. Online book, 2006. http://www.bruno-latour.fr/virtual/EN/index.html.

Lawaczeck, Franz. "Zur Neuordnung der Elektrowirtschaft." *Deutsche Technik* 2, February/March (1934): 270–275, 340–343.

Lawhon, Mary, and James T. Murphy. "Socio-Technical Regimes and Sustainability Transitions: Insights from Political Ecology." *Progress in Human Geography* 36, no. 3 (2011): 354–378.

Lawhon, Mary, David Nilsson, Jonathan Silver, Henrik Ernstson, and Shuaib Lwasa. "Thinking through Heterogeneous Infrastructure Configurations." *Urban Studies* 55, no. 4 (2018): 720–732.

Lees, Loretta. "Rematerializing Geography: The 'New' Urban Geography." *Progress in Human Geography* 26, no. 1 (2002): 101–112.

Lehmann, H. "Fernheizung der Wohnstadt Berlin-Friedrichshain und der Stalinallee." *Energietechnik* 4, no. 5 (1954): 194–202.

Leithäuser, Joachim G. *Die unsichtbare Kraft. Roman der Elektrizität.* Berlin: Safari-Verlag, 1959.

Leithaus, Jürgen. "Erfahrungsbericht über die Energiesparpartnerschaft Berlin." *Gesundheits-Ingenieur* 120, no. 1 (1999): 3–5.

Lemke, Michael. "Vorwort." In *Konfrontation und Wettbewerb. Wissenschaft, Technik und Kultur im geteilten Berliner Alltag (1948–1973)*, edited by Michael Lemke, 7–14. Berlin: Metropol, 2008.

Linde, Christian. "Teures Wasser." *Mieter-Echo* 316 (2006): 4–6.

Linke, Nina. "Großsiedlungen in Ost-Berlin und Wien (1945–1975)." In *Paradigmenwechsel und Kontinuitätslinien im DDR-Städtebau: Neue Forschungen zur ostdeutschen Architektur- und Planungsgeschichte*, edited by Frank Betker, Carsten Benke, and Christoph Bernhardt, 163–178. Erkner: Leibniz-Institut für Regionalentwicklung und Strukturplanung, 2010.

Lischeid, Gunnar, Martina Schäfer, Uta Steinhardt, Timothy Moss, Benjamin Nölting, and Petra Koeppe. *Nachhaltiges Landmanagement durch integrierte Wasser- und Stoffnutzung. Kernaussagen des ELaN-Foschungsverbunds.* Müncheberg: Leibniz-Zentrum für Agrarlandschaftsforschung (ZALF), 2015.

Lobeck, Reinhard. *Die Großberliner Stadtentwässerung.* Berlin: Julius Springer, 1928.

Lorkowski, Nina. "Managing Energy Consumption: The Rental Business for Storage Water Heaters of Berlin's Electricity Company from the Late 1920s to the Early 1960s." In *Past and Present Energy Societies*, edited by Nina Möllers and Karin Zachmann, 137–162. Bielefeld: Transcript, 2014.

Lovio, Raimo, and Paula Kivimaa. "Comparing Alternative Path Creation Frameworks in the Context of Emerging Biofuel Fields in the Netherlands, Sweden and Finland." *European Planning Studies* 20, no. 5 (2012): 773–790.

Ludwig, Karl-Heinz. *Technik und Ingenieure im Dritten Reich.* Düsseldorf: Droste, 1974.

Maassen, Anne. "Heterogeneity of Lock-In and the Role of Strategic Technological Inventions in Urban Infrastructural Transformations." *European Planning Studies* 20, no. 3 (2012): 441–460.

Magistrat. *Maßnahmen zur Verbesserung der städtischen Gas-, Wasser- u. Elektrizitätswerke seit der Bildung der Stadtgemeinde Berlin.* Berlin: Magistrat, 1922.

Magistrat von Groß-Berlin, ed. *Berlin 1947. Jahresbericht des Magistrats.* N.p.: n.d.

Magistrat von Groß-Berlin, ed. *Berlin 1948. Jahresbericht des Magistrats.* Berlin: Kulturbuch-Verlag, 1950.

Magistrat von Groß-Berlin, ed. *Berlin 1949. Jahresbericht des Magistrats.* Berlin: Kulturbuch-Verlag, 1950.

Maier, Helmut. "'Lauchhammer', 'Döbern' und 'Ragow': Imaginäre und reale Verknotungen der Niederlausitzer Landschaft in die Elektrizitätswirtschaft des 20. Jahrhunderts." In *Die Niederlausitz vom 18. Jahrhundert bis heute: Eine gestörte Kulturlandschaft?*, edited by Günter Bayerl and Dirk Maier, 149–195. Münster: Waxmann, 2002.

Maier, Helmut. "Nationalsozialistische Technikideologie und die Politisierung des 'Technikerstandes': Fritz Todt und die Zeitschrift 'Deutsche Technik.'" In *Technische Intelligenz und "Kulturfaktor Technik". Kulturvorstellungen von Technikern und Ingenieuren zwischen Kaiserreich und früher Bundesrepublik Deutschland*, edited by Burkhard Dietz, Michael Fessner, and Helmut Maier, 253–268. Münster: Waxmann, 1996.

Mampel, Siegried. "Die politische Ordnung im Sowjetsektor und ihre Stellung zur Sowjetzone." In *Berlin Sowjetsektor. Die politische, rechtliche, wirtschaftliche, soziale und kulturelle Entwicklung in acht Berliner Verwaltungsbezirken*, edited by Büro für Gesamtberliner Fragen, 54–76. Berlin: Colloquium, 1965.

Matschoß, Conrad, Erich Schulz, and Arnold Theodor Groß. *50 Jahre Berliner Elektrizitätswerke 1884–1934*. Berlin: VDI-Verlag, 1934.

Matzerath, Horst. *Nationalsozialismus und kommunale Selbstverwaltung*. Stuttgart: Kohlhammer, 1970.

Matzerath, Horst, and Ingrid Thienel. "Stadtentwicklung, Stadtplanung, Stadtentwicklungsplanung. Probleme im 19. und 20. Jahrhundert am Beispiel der Stadt Berlin." *Die Verwaltung* 10, no. 2 (1977): 173–196.

Mauer, Willi. *Energiekonzept im Rahmen behutsamer Stadterneuerung. Leitlinien einer bewohnerorientierten und altbaugerechten Wärmeversorgungsplanung am Beispiel Berlin-Kreuzberg*. Berlin: IBA, 1985.

Mayntz, Renate. "Grosse technische Systeme und ihre gesellschaftstheoretische Bedeutung." *Kölner Zeitschrift für Soziologie und Sozialpsychologie* 45, no. 1 (1993): 97–108.

Mayrhofer, Erich. "Die Erdgasspeicherung in Berlin." *Der Energiebote* (1985), no. 19: 5–7 and no. 20: 6–8.

McFarlane, Colin. "Assemblage and Critical Urban Praxis: Part One." *City* 15, no. 2 (2011): 204–224.

McFarlane, Colin, and Jonathan Rutherford. "Political Infrastructures: Governing and Experiencing the Fabric of the City." *International Journal of Urban and Regional Research* 32, no. 2 (2008): 363–374.

McGuirk, Pauline M., Harriet Bulkeley, and Robyn Dowling. "Configuring Urban Carbon Governance: Insights from Sydney, Australia." *Annals of the American Association of Geographers* 106, no. 1 (2016): 145–166.

Meadowcroft, James. "What about the Politics? Sustainable Development, Transition Management, and Long Term Energy Transitions." *Policy Science* 42, no. 4 (2009): 323–340.

Mecking, Sabine. "Die Gleichschaltung der städtischen Belegschaft zur politischen Gefolgschaft. Kommunalverwaltung zwischen Ideologie, Propaganda und Praxis (1933–1945)." In ... *auf dem*

Dienstweg. Die Verfolgung von Beamten, Angestellten und Arbeitern der Stadt Berlin 1933 bis 1945, edited by Christian Dirks and Hermann Simon, 106–123. Berlin: Hentrich & Hentrich, 2010.

Medon, Gustav H. "Das Grundwasser von Groß-Berlin." *Wasserwirtschaft—Wassertechnik* 2 (1952): 39–44.

Mehlig, Johannes Georg. "Thesen für ein neues Energiekonzept." *Energietechnik* 40, no. 2 (1990): 64–67.

Meißner, Ursula, and Jürgen Prehn. "Wasserversorgung und Abwasserbeseitigung im verarbeitenden Gewerbe von Berlin 1995." *Berliner Statistik. Monatsschrift* 51, no. 7 (1997): 114–118.

Melosi, Martin. *Effluent America: Cities, Industry, Energy, and the Environment*. Pittsburgh, PA: University of Pittsburgh Press, 2001.

Melosi, Martin. "Path Dependence and Urban History: Is a Marriage Possible?" In *Resources of the City: Contributions to an Environmental History of Modern Europe*, edited by Dieter Schott, Bill Luckin, and Geneviève Massard-Guilbaud, 262–275. Aldershot: Ashgate, 2005.

Melosi, Martin. *The Sanitary City: Urban Infrastructure in America from Colonial Times to the Present*. Baltimore, MD: John Hopkins University Press, 2000.

Merrill, Samuel. "Identities in Transit: The (Re)connections and (Re)brandings of Berlin's Municipal Railway Infrastructure after 1989." *Journal of Historical Geography* 50 (2015): 76–91.

Merritt, Richard L. "Political Division and Municipal Services in Postwar Berlin." In *Public Policy*, edited by John D. Montgomery and Albert O. Hirschman, 165–198. Cambridge, MA: Harvard University Press, 1968.

Merritt, Richard L. "Postwar Berlin: Divided City." In *Berlin between Two Worlds*, edited by Ronaldo A. Francisco and Richard L. Merritt, 153–175. Boulder, CO: Westview, 1986.

Mielke, H.-J., and Heinrich Weiß. "Kraftwerksbau im Landschaftsschutzgebiet Spandauer Forst." *Berliner Naturschutzblätter* 20, no. 59 (1976): 219–224.

Migge, Leberecht. "Eine Weltstadt kolonisiert! Berlin versorgt sich selbst! Eine Million Berliner siedeln aus!" Unpublished manuscript, 1932.

Mitchell, Timothy. *Carbon Democracy: Political Power in the Age of Oil*. London and New York: Verso, 2013.

Mitzinger, Wolfgang. "Gegenwärtiger Stand und weitere Entwicklung der Energiewirtschaft der DDR." *Energietechnik* 31, no. 5 (1981): 161–166.

Moest, Walter. *Der Zehlendorfer Plan. Ein Vorschlag zum Wiederaufbau Berlins*. Berlin: Verlag des Druckhauses Tempelhof, 1947.

Mohajeri, Shahrooz. *100 Jahre Berliner Wasserversorgung und Abwasserentsorgung 1840–1940*. Stuttgart: Franz Steiner, 2005.

Möller, Klaus, and Jens Burgschweiger. *Wasserversorgungskonzept für Berlin und für das von den BWB versorgte Umland (Entwicklung bis 2040)*. Berlin: Berliner Wasserbetriebe, 2008.

Monstadt, Jochen. "Conceptualizing the Political Ecology of Urban Infrastructures: Insights from Technology and Urban Studies." *Environment and Planning A* 41, no. 8 (2009): 1924–1942.

Monstadt, Jochen. *Die Modernisierung der Stromversorgung. Regionale Energie- und Klimapolitik im Liberalisierungs- und Privatisierungsprozess.* Wiesbaden: VS Verlag für Sozialwissenschaften, 2004.

Monstadt, Jochen. "Urban Governance and the Transition of Energy Systems: Institutional Change and Shifting Energy and Climate Policies in Berlin." *International Journal of Urban and Regional Research* 31, no. 2 (2007): 326–343.

Monstadt, Jochen, and Olivier Coutard. "Cities in an Era of Interfacing Infrastructures: Politics and Spatialities of the Urban Nexus." *Urban Studies* 56, no. 11 (2019): 2191–2206.

Moorhouse, Roger. *Berlin at War: Life and Death in Hitler's Capital, 1939–45.* London: Vintage, 2011.

Mörs, W. "Die Aufgaben des Energie-Ingenieurs für die Energie-Sparmaßnahmen." *Deutsche Technik* 10, December (1942): 528–530.

Moss, Timothy. "Battle of the Systems? Changing Styles of Water Recycling in Berlin." In *Urban Infrastructure in Transition: Networks, Buildings, Plans*, edited by Simon Guy, Simon Marvin, and Timothy Moss, 43–56. London: Earthscan, 2001.

Moss, Timothy. "'Cold Spots' of Urban Infrastructure: 'Shrinking' Processes in Eastern Germany and the Modern Infrastructural Ideal." *International Journal of Urban and Regional Research* 32, no. 2 (2008): 436–451.

Moss, Timothy. "Discarded Surrogates, Modified Traditions, Welcome Complements: The Chequered Careers of Alternative Technologies in Berlin's Infrastructure Systems." *Social Studies of Science* 46, no. 4 (2016): 559–582.

Moss, Timothy. "Divided City, Divided Infrastructures: Securing Energy and Water Services in Postwar Berlin." *Journal of Urban History* 35, no. 7 (2009): 923–942.

Moss, Timothy. "Socio-Technical Change and the Politics of Urban Infrastructure: Managing Energy in Berlin between Dictatorship and Democracy." *Urban Studies* 51, no. 7 (2014): 1432–1448.

Moss, Timothy. "Unearthing Water Flows, Uncovering Social Relations: Introducing New Waste Water Technologies in Berlin." *Journal of Urban Technology* 7, no. 1 (2000): 63–84.

Moss, Timothy. "Utilities, Land-Use Change, and Urban Development: Brownfield Sites as 'Cold-Spots' of Infrastructure Networks in Berlin." *Environment and Planning A* 35, no. 3 (2003): 511–529.

Moss, Timothy, Sören Becker, and Ludger Gailing. "Energy Transitions and Materiality: Between Dispositives, Assemblages and Metabolisms." In *Conceptualizing Germany's Energy Transition: Institutions, Materiality, Power, Space*, edited by Ludger Gailing and Timothy Moss, 43–68. London: Palgrave Macmillan, 2016.

Moss, Timothy, and Frank Hüesker. "Politicised Nexus Thinking in Practice: Integrating Urban Wastewater Utilities into Regional Energy Markets." *Urban Studies* 56, no. 11 (2019): 2225–2241.

Moss, Timothy, and Frank Hüesker. *Wasserinfrastrukturen als Gemeinwohlträger zwischen globalem Wandel und regionaler Entwicklung—institutionelle Erwiderungen in Berlin-Brandenburg*. Berlin: Berlin-Brandenburgische Akademie der Wissenschaften. Interdisziplinäre Arbeitsgruppe Globaler Wandel—Regionale Entwicklung, 2010.

Moss, Timothy, Matthias Naumann, and Katharina Krause. "Turning Wastewater into Energy: Challenges of Reconfiguring Regional Infrastructures in the Berlin-Brandenburg Region." *Local Environment* 22, no. 3 (2017): 269–285.

Müller, Klaus. "Entwicklung der Fernwärmepreise in Berlin (West) ab 1960." *Gesundheits-Ingenieur* 108, no. 4 (1987): 200–203.

Müller, Martin. "Assemblages and Actor-Networks: Rethinking Socio-Material Power, Politics and Space." *Geography Compass* 9, no. 1 (2015): 27–41.

Müschen, Klaus. "Das solare Regierungsviertel im Rahmen des Energiekonzeptes Berlin." In *Das solare Regierungsviertel. Neue Energiepolitik für Berlin, Heft 10*, edited by Senatsverwaltung für Stadtentwicklung und Umweltschutz, 73–74. Berlin: Senatsverwaltung für Stadtentwicklung und Umweltschutz, 1993.

Müschen, Klaus. "Der Sonne entgegen. Förderung regenerativer Energien in Berlin." *BundesBau-Blatt* no. 6 (1997): 427–430.

Müschen, Klaus. "Der Stellenwert regenerativer Energien im Energiekonzept Berlin." In *Modelle für den Klimaschutz: kommunale Konzepte und soziale Initiativen für erneuerbare Energien*, edited by Michael Knoll and Rolf Kreibich, 65–79. Weinheim: Beltz, 1994.

Musterle, Theo. "Ein Jahr volkseigene Wasserwirtschaft, ein Rückblick und Ausblick." *Wasserwirtschaft—Wassertechnik* 4, no. 1 (1954): 1–2.

Musterle, Theo. "1955–Das Jahr der Vorbereitung des zweiten Fünfjahresplans für die Wasserwirtschaft." *Wasserwirtschaft—Wassertechnik* 5, no. 1 (1955): 1–2.

Niewöhner, Jörg. "Anthropology of Infrastructures of Society." *International Encyclopedia of the Social & Behavioural Sciences* 12 (2015): 119–125.

Nolde, Erwin. "Greywater Reuse Systems for Toilet Flushing in Multi-storey Buildings: Over Ten Years Experience in Berlin." *Urban Water* 1, no. 4 (1999): 275–284.

Nöldeke, W. "10 Jahre Elektroenergiewirtschaft in der Deutschen Demokratischen Republik." *Energietechnik* 9, no. 10 (1959): 436–440.

Nolzen, Armin. "Die NSDAP im Gau Berlin nach 1933." In *Berlin, 1933–1945*, edited by Michael Wildt and Christoph Kreutzmüller, 69–80. Munich: Siedler, 2013.

Nübling, R. "Neuzeitliche Fragen der Energiewirtschaft." *Das Gas- und Wasserfach* 77, no. 11 (1934): 161–166.

Obertreis, Julia, Timothy Moss, Peter Mollinga, and Christine Bichsel. "Water, Infrastructure and Political Rule: Introduction to the Special Issue." *Water Alternatives* 9, no. 2 (2016): 168–181.

Orland, Barbara. "Der Zwiespalt zwischen Politik und Technik: Ein kulturelles Phänomen in der Vergangenheitsbewältigung Albert Speers und seiner Rezipienten." In *Technische Intelligenz und "Kulturfaktor Technik". Kulturvorstellungen von Technikern und Ingenieuren zwischen Kaiserreich und früherer Bundesrepublik Deutschland*, edited by Burkhard Dietz, Michael Fessner, and Helmut Maier, 269–295. Münster: Waxmann, 1996.

Oswald, Karola, and Ludwig Pawlowski. "Know-how aus Paris und Berlin für die Budapester Entwässerungswerke." *Korrespondenz Abwasser* 45, no. 10 (1998): 1922–1926.

Otter, Chris. "Locating Matter: The Place of Materiality in Urban History." In *Material Powers: Cultural Studies, History and the Material Turn*, edited by Tony Bennett and Patrick Joyce, 38–59. New York: Routledge, 2010.

ÖTV Berlin. *Die Berliner Wasserwerke. Wasser zum Leben. Von der Wasserversorgung zur Wasserdienstleistung*. Berlin: ÖTV Berlin, 1985.

ÖTV Berlin. *Berliner Gaswerke (GASAG). Erd-GASAG—vom Energieversorgungs- zum Energiedienstleistungsunternehmen*. Berlin: ÖTV Berlin, 1984.

Overy, Richard J. *Interrogations: The Nazi Elite in Allied Hands, 1945*. New York: Viking, 2001.

Pallasch, Otto. "Reinigung und Verwertung gewerblicher Abwässer in Berlin." *Gesundheits-Ingenieur* 60, no. 21 (1937): 334–337.

Papke, Rainer. "Die Abwasserüberleitung Berlin-Eberswalde—wasserwirtschaftliche Vorleistung zur Steigerung der Hektarerträge und Maßnahme zur Verbesserung des Umweltschutzes." *Wasserwirtschaft—Wassertechnik* 32, no. 5 (1982): 147–149.

Pawlowski, Ludwig. "Abwasserentsorgung in Berlin zehn Jahre nach dem Fall der Mauer." *Korrespondenz Abwasser* 46, no. 11 (1999): 1692–1697.

Peters, G. "Es geht um die Verbesserung der Arbeit in den VEB Wasserwirtschaft!" *Der VEB Wasserwirtschaft* 1, no. 1 (1955): 2–3.

Petzina, Dietmar. *Autarkiepolitik im Dritten Reich. Der nationalsozialistische Vierjahresplan*. Stuttgart: Deutsche Verlags-Anstalt, 1968.

Pfeil, Johannes. "Das Wiederansteigen des Grundwasserspiegels in Groß-Berlin und seine schädlichen Folgen." *Haus und Wohnung* 3 (1948): 180–182.

Pieske, Ursula. "Wasserversorgung und Abwasserbeseitigung im verarbeitenden Gewerbe von Berlin (West) 1977–1987." *Berliner Statistik. Monatsschrift* 44, no. 1 (1990): 2–13.

Pischl, Peter. "Wärmeversorgung in Ost-Berliner Altbauquartieren—Erfordernisse zur Umweltentlastung." In *Zukunft der Energieversorgung in Altbauquartieren. Neue Energiepolitik für Berlin. Heft 5*, edited by Senatsverwaltung für Stadtentwicklung und Umweltschutz, 21–35. Berlin: Senatsverwaltung für Stadtentwicklung und Umweltschutz, 1990.

Pohl, M. von. "Der Luftschutz von Wasserversorgungs- und Entwässerungsanlagen." *Gesundheits-Ingenieur* 64, no. 21 (1941): 300–309.

Porombka, Wiebke. *Medialität urbaner Infrastrukturen. Der öffentliche Nahverkehr, 1870–1933.* Bielefeld: Transcript, 2013.

Presse- und Informationsamt des Landes Berlin, ed. *Perspektiven der Stadtentwicklung*. Berlin: Haupt & Kosta, 1974.

Presse- und Informationsamt des Landes Berlin, ed. *Energie 1 (Grundfragen der Energiesicherung).* Berlin: Presse- und Informationsamt des Landes Berlin, 1978.

Prognos. *Erfahrungen bei der Kooperation von Wärmeversorgungsplanung und Stadterneuerungsplanung. Diskussionspapier Nr. 82/19*. Basel: Prognos, 1982.

Randzio, Ernst. *Unterirdischer Städtebau*. Bremen: Walter Dorn, 1951.

Rebentisch, Dieter. *Führerstaat und Verwaltung im Zweiten Weltkrieg: Verfassungsentwicklung und Verwaltungspolitik 1939–1945*. Wiesbaden: Steiner, 1989.

Rehmer, Martin. "Der Ausbau und die Betriebsführung der Bewag seit dem Jahre 1924." Special edition of *Zeitschrift des Vereins deutscher Ingenieure* 78, no. 18 (1934): 539–545.

Rehmer, Martin. "Die Stromversorgung der Reichshauptstadt Berlin." *Elektrizitätswirtschaft* 27, no. 460 (1928): 278–283.

Reichelt, Hans. "Das neue Wassergesetz und die höheren Anforderungen an die Wasserwirtschaft." *Wasserwirtschaft—Wassertechnik* 32, no. 10 (1982): 327–329.

Reichelt, Hans. "Die Aufgaben der Wasserwirtschaft zur Durchführung der Beschlüsse der 9. Tagung des ZK der SED." *Wasserwirtschaft—Wassertechnik* 23, no. 9 (1973): 289–293.

Reichelt, Hans. "Entwicklung der Wasserwirtschaft zwischen dem X. und XI. Parteitag der SED." *Wasserwirtschaft—Wassertechnik* 36, no. 2 (1986): 50–53.

Reichelt, Hans. "Wasser rational und sparsam verwenden." *Wasserwirtschaft—Wassertechnik* 32, no. 2 (1982): 39–41.

Reichhardt, Hans J. "Wiederaufbau und Festigung demokratischer Strukturen im geteilten Berlin 1945–1963." In *Berlin als Hauptstadt im Nachkriegsdeutschland und Land Berlin 1945–1985*, edited by Georg Kotowski and Hans J. Reichhardt, 3–138. Berlin: Walter de Gruyter, 1987.

Reichmann, Brigitte. "Stadtökologische Modellprojekte." *Wasserwirtschaft—Wassertechnik* no. 6 (1998): 12–14.

Reschke, Oliver, and Michael Wildt. "Aufstieg der NSDAP in Berlin." In *Berlin, 1933–1945*, edited by Michael Wildt and Christoph Kreutzmüller, 19–32. Munich: Siedler, 2013.

Ribbe, Wolfgang. *Berlin 1945–2000: Grundzüge der Stadtgeschichte*. Berlin: Berliner Wissenschaftsverlag, 2002.

Ribbe, Wolfgang. "Berlin zwischen Ost und West (1945 bis zur Gegenwart)." In *Geschichte Berlins. Zweiter Band: Von der Märzrevolution bis zur Gegenwart*, edited by Wolfgang Ribbe, 1027–1125. Munich: C. H. Beck, 1987.

Ribbe, Wolfgang. "Das gespaltene Berlin: ein historischer Überblick (1945–1990)." In *Hauptstadtanspruch und symbolische Politik: die Bundespräsenz im geteilten Berlin 1949–1990*, edited by Michael C. Bienert, Uwe Schaper, and Hermann Wentker, 33–96. Berlin: Be.Bra, 2012.

Richert, H. "Erfahrungen aus Planung und Betrieb der Elektro-Wärmespeicherheizung in Berlin." *Gesundheits-Ingenieur* 87, no. 10 (1966): 288–290.

Ripl, Wilhelm, and Christian Hildmann. "Zwei in einem Boot." *Politische Ökologie* 44, January/February (1996): 31–34.

Röber, Manfred, and Heinz Wendt. *Öffentliche Versorgungsunternehmen in Berlin—ihre Strukturen und ihre Beziehungen zu Kunden*. Berlin: Fachhochschule für Verwaltung und Rechtspflege Berlin, 1985.

Rocholl, Nora, and Ronan Bolton. "Berlin's Electricity Distribution Grid: An Urban Energy Transition in a National Regulatory Context." *Technology Analysis & Strategic Management* 28, no. 10 (2016): 1182–1194.

Rohracher, Harald. "Die Wechselwirkung technischen und institutionellen Wandels in der Transformation von Energiesystemen." In *Gesellschaft und die Macht der Technik. Sozioökonomischer und institutioneller Wandel durch Technisierung*, edited by Ulrich Dolata and Raymund Werle, 133–151. Frankfurt am Main: Campus, 2007.

Rose, Mark H., and Joel A. Tarr, eds. Special issue, *Journal of Urban History* 14, no. 1 (1987): 3–139.

Rotenberg, Dirk. *Berliner Demokratie zwischen Existenzsicherung und Machtwechsel. Die Transformation der Berlin-Problematik 1971 bis 1981*. Berlin: Haude & Spener, 1995.

Rückwardt, Hermann, and Carl Albrecht. "Der gegenwärtige Stand der Elektrizitätsversorgung von Haushaltungen in Berlin." *Elektrizitätswirtschaft* 28 (1929): 521–525.

Rudischhauser, Sabine. "Die parlamentarischen Debatten über die Sozialpolitik der neuen Stadtgemeinde Berlin in der ersten Stadtverordnetenversammlung 1920/21." In *Beiträge zur Geschichte der Berliner Demokratie 1919–1933 / 1945–1985*, edited by Otto Büsch, 45–84. Berlin: Colloquium, 1988.

Rudnitzky, Arnold. *Die Berliner städtische Gaswirtschaft*. Berlin: H. S. Herman, 1932.

Ruhstrat, Otto. "Wir sparen Energie." *Deutsche Technik* 10, October (1942): 423–424.

Russell, S. "Writing Energy History: Explaining the Neglect of CHP/DH in Britain." *British Journal for the History of Science* 26, no. 1 (1993): 33–54.

Rutherford, Jonathan. "Rethinking the Relational Socio-Technical Materialities of Cities and ICTs." *Journal of Urban Technology* 18, no. 1 (2011): 21–33.

Rutherford, Jonathan, and Olivier Coutard. "Urban Energy Transitions: Places, Processes and Politics of Socio-Technical Change." *Urban Studies* 51, no. 7 (2014): 1353–1377.

Ruths, Heinrich. "Stadtgüter und Stadtversorgung." In *Probleme der neuen Stadt Berlin. Darstellungen der Zukunftsaufgaben einer Viermillionenstadt*, edited by Hans Brennert and Erwin Stein, 123–128. Berlin: Deutscher Kommunal-Verlag, 1926.

Saraiva, Tiago, and M. Norton Wise. "Autarky/Autarchy: Genetics, Food Production, and the Building of Fascism." *Historical Studies in the Natural Sciences* 40, no. 4 (2010): 419–428.

Sardemann, F. "Die deutsche Elektrizitätswirtschaft 1933 bis 1948. II. Organisation und Steuerung der Energiewirtschaft bis Kriegsende." *Elektrizitätswirtschaft* 48, no. 5 (1949): 107–112.

Schaarschmidt, Thomas. "'In die Höhle des Löwen'. Das ambivalente Verhältnis der NS-Führung zur Millionenmetropole Berlin." In *Städte im Nationalsozialismus. Urbane Räume und soziale Ordnungen*, edited by Winfried Süß and Malte Thiessen, 21–45. Göttingen: Wallstein, 2017.

Schaulinski, Gernot. "Baustelle Zeichentisch—Der Beginn der Neugestaltung Berlins." In *Berlin 1937. Im Schatten von morgen*, edited by Stiftung Stadtmuseum Berlin, 111–119. Berlin: Verlag M—Stadtmuseum Berlin, 2017.

Schieder, Wolfgang. "Staat und Wirtschaft im 'Dritten Reich': Der Weg in die Katastrophe." In *Berlin und seine Wirtschaft. Ein Weg aus der Geschichte in die Zukunft—Lehren und Erkenntnisse*, edited by Industrie- und Handelskammer zu Berlin, 197–221. Berlin and New York: Walter de Gruyter, 1987.

Schiemann, Dieter, and Jacob Dautermann. "Ist-Stand und weitere Entwicklung der Abwasserbehandlung im VEB WAB Berlin." *Wasserwirtschaft—Wassertechnik* 39, no. 4 (1989): 87–88.

Schlegelmilch, Arthur. *Hauptstadt im Zonendeutschland. Die Entstehung der Berliner Nachkriegsdemokratie 1945–1949*. Berlin: Haude & Spener, 1993.

Schlegelmilch, Arthur. "Tendenzen der wirtschaftlichen und sozialen Entwicklung Berlins seit 1945. Gemeinsamkeiten und Unterschiede im Ost-West-Vergleich." In *Wirtschaft im geteilten Berlin 1945–1990. Forschungsansätze und Zeitzeugen*, edited by Wolfram Fischer and Johannes Bähr, 1–44. Munich: Saur, 1994.

Schlippenbach, Ulrike von, and Timothy Moss. "The Intermediation of Water Expertise in a Post-Privatization Context." In *Shaping Urban Infrastructures. Intermediaries and the Governance of Socio-Technical Networks*, edited by Simon Guy, Simon Marvin, Will Medd, and Timothy Moss, 108–123. London: Earthscan, 2011.

Schmidt, Felix. "Der Kampfbund der Deutschen Architekten und Ingenieure (KDAI)." *Deutsche Technik* 1, September (1933): 47ff.

Schmidt, Martin. *Die BEWAG-Transaktion im Jahre 1931. Eine Studie zur Geschichte des deutschen Finanzkapitals*. Berlin: Dietz, 1957.

Schmidt, Martin. *Regional Governance und Infrastruktur. Kooperationen in der Wasserver- und Abwasserentsorgung am Beispiel der Stadtregionen Frankfurt/M, Berlin und Ruhr*. Darmstadt: Rohn, 2013.

Schmieder, Eberhard. "Wirtschaft und Bevölkerung." In *Berlin und die Provinz Brandenburg im 19. und 20. Jahrhundert*, edited by Hans Herzfeld, 389–409. Berlin: Walter de Gruyter, 1968.

Schnitzler, Antina von. *Democracy's Infrastructure: Techno-Politics & Protest after Apartheid*. Princeton, NJ: Princeton University Press, 2016.

Scholz, Ortwin. "Der Querverbund Wasser-Abwasser in Berlin." *Kommunalwirtschaft* (1989): 44–46.

Scholze, Renate. "Zu einigen Problemen der Entwicklung der Elektrizitätsversorgung Berlins von den Anfängen bis 1945." *Jahrbuch für Wirtschaftsgeschichte*, special issue, *Zur Wirtschafts- und Sozialgeschichte Berlins vom 17. Jahrhundert bis zur Gegenwart* (1986): 109–128.

Schott, Dieter. *Die Vernetzung der Stadt. Kommunale Energiepolitik, öffentlicher Nahverkehr und die 'Produktion' der modernen Stadt. Darmstadt—Mannheim—Mainz 1810–1918*. Darmstadt: Wissenschaftliche Buchgesellschaft, 1999.

Schott, Dieter. "Empowering European Cities: Gas and Electricity in the Urban Environment." In *Urban Machinery. Inside Modern European Cities*, edited by Mikael Hård and Thomas J. Misa, 165–186. Cambridge, MA: MIT Press, 2008.

Schreyer, Michaela. "Erfordernisse einer neuen Qualität des Gewässerschutzes." In *Umwelt- und Naturschutz für Berliner Gewässer. Kongreß "Berlin auf dem Trockenen?" Zukunft der Wasserversorgung*, edited by Senatsverwaltung für Stadtentwicklung und Umweltschutz, 7–22. Berlin: Senatsverwaltung für Stadtentwicklung und Umweltschutz, 1990.

Schroeder. "Die wasserwirtschaftliche Generalplanung." *Das Gas- und Wasserfach* 79, no. 17 (1936): 257–259.

Schulze, D. "Naturnahe Grundwasseranreicherung—Ein Beitrag zur Sicherung der Wasserversorgung des Großraumes Berlin." *Wasser + Boden* 45, no. 4 (1993): 220–224.

Schuster, Fritz. "Leistungssteigerung, ein Beitrag des Gasfachs zur Energieeinsparung." *Deutsche Technik* 10, December (1942): 494–495.

Schwenk, Herbert, and Hainer Weisspflug. *Umweltschmutz und Umweltschutz in Berlin (Ost). Auswirkungen der DDR-Umweltpolitik in Berlin*. Berlin: Edition Luisenstadt, 1996.

SED-Betriebsparteiorganisation Bewag, ed. *Unsere Kraft. Betriebsgeschichte der Bewag, 1. Teil 1884–1949*. Berlin: Bewag, 1973.

SED-Betriebsparteiorganisation Bewag, ed. *Unsere Kraft. Betriebsgeschichte der Bewag, 2. Teil 1949–1961*. Berlin: Bewag, 1975.

Seebauer, Georg. "Energiepolitik." *Deutsche Technik* 4, April (1936): 167–171.

Senat von Berlin. *Berlin 1953. Jahresbericht des Senats*. Berlin: Kulturbuch-Verlag, 1954.

Senat von Berlin. *Berlin 1954. Jahresbericht des Senats*. Berlin: Kulturbuch-Verlag, 1955.

Senat von Berlin, ed. *Berlin. Behauptung von Freiheit und Selbstverwaltung 1946–1948*. Berlin: Heinz Spitzing, 1959.

Senat von Berlin, ed. *Berlin. Chronik der Jahre 1951–1954*. Berlin: Heinz Spitzing, 1968.

Senat von Berlin, ed. *Berlin. Chronik der Jahre 1955–1956*. Berlin: Heinz Spitzing, 1971.

Senat von Berlin, ed. *Berlin. Chronik der Jahre 1957–1958*. Berlin: Heinz Spitzing, 1974.

Senat von Berlin, ed. *Berlin. Chronik der Jahre 1959–1960*. Berlin: Heinz Spitzing, 1978.

Senat von Berlin, ed. *Berlin. Kampf um Freiheit und Selbstverwaltung 1945–1946*. Berlin: Heinz Spitzing, 1961.

Senat von Berlin, ed. *Berlin. Ringen um Einheit und Wiederaufbau 1948–1951*. Berlin: Heinz Spitzing, 1962.

Senat von Berlin, ed. *Zweijahresbericht des Senats von Berlin 1961/1962*. Berlin: Statistisches Landesamt Berlin, 1963.

Senat von Berlin, ed. *Zweijahresbericht des Senats von Berlin, 1963/64*. Berlin: Kulturbuch-Verlag, 1965.

Senate Department for Urban Development and the Environment. *Climate-Neutral Berlin 2050. Recommendations for a Berlin Energy and Climate Protection Programme (BEK)*. Berlin: Senatsverwaltung für Stadtentwicklung und Umweltschutz, 2016.

Senatsverwaltung für Stadtentwicklung, Umweltschutz und Technologie. *Abwasserbeseitigungsplan Berlin (Entwurf)*. Berlin: Kulturbuch-Verlag, 1999.

Senatsverwaltung für Stadtentwicklung, Umweltschutz und Technologie. *Energiebilanz 2005 für das Bundesland Berlin*. Berlin: Senatsverwaltung für Stadtentwicklung, Umweltschutz und Technologie, 2005.

Senatsverwaltung für Stadtentwicklung, Umweltschutz und Technologie. *Stadtentwicklungsplan Ver- und Entsorgung*. Berlin: Regioverlag, 1998.

Senatsverwaltung für Stadtentwicklung, Umweltschutz und Technologie, and Berliner Wasserbetriebe. "Jahresbericht der Wasserwirtschaft—Berlin." *Wasser & Boden* 48, no. 7 (1996): 37–42.

Senatsverwaltung für Stadtentwicklung und Umweltschutz. *BerlinStrategie. Stadtentwicklungskonzept Berlin 2030*. Berlin: Senatsverwaltung für Stadtentwicklung und Umweltschutz, 2014.

Senatsverwaltung für Stadtentwicklung und Umweltschutz. *Energieagentur Berlin. Konzeptstudie. Neue Energiepolitik für Berlin, Heft 2*. Berlin: Senatsverwaltung für Stadtentwicklung und Umweltschutz, 1990.

Senatsverwaltung für Stadtentwicklung und Umweltschutz. *Energiekonzept Berlin. Entwurf für die Öffentlichkeitsbeteiligung. Neue Energiepolitik für Berlin, Heft 9*. Berlin: Senatsverwaltung für Stadtentwicklung und Umweltschutz, 1992.

Senatsverwaltung für Stadtentwicklung und Umweltschutz. *Energiepolitische Ansätze zur CO_2-Minderung im Gebäudebereich. Neue Energiepolitik für Berlin, Heft 12*. Berlin: Senatsverwaltung für Stadtentwicklung und Umweltschutz, 1994.

Senatsverwaltung für Stadtentwicklung und Umweltschutz. *Konzept zur zukünftigen Wasserver- und -entsorgung von Berlin*. Berlin: Senatsverwaltung für Stadtentwicklung und Umweltschutz, n.d. [ca. 1992/1993].

Senatsverwaltung für Stadtentwicklung und Umweltschutz. *Nutzung der Sonnenernergie in Berlin. Neue Energiepolitik für Berlin, Heft 3*. Berlin: Senatsverwaltung für Stadtentwicklung und Umweltschutz, 1990.

Senatsverwaltung für Wirtschaft, Technologie und Frauen. *Energiekonzept 2020. Langfassung*. Berlin: Senatsverwaltung für Wirtschaft, Technologie und Frauen, 2011.

Shove, Elizabeth, Mika Pantzar, and Matt Watson. "The Dynamics of Social Practice: Everyday Life and How It Changes." In *The Dynamics of Social Practice: Everyday Life and How It Changes*, edited by Elizabeth Shove, Mika Pantzar, and Matt Watson, 1–19. London: Sage, 2012.

Shove, Elizabeth, Frank Trentmann, and Richard Wilk. *Time, Consumption and Everyday Life: Practice, Materiality and Culture*. Oxford: Berg, 2009.

Shove, Elizabeth, and Gordon Walker. "CAUTION! Transitions ahead: Politics, Practice, and Sustainable Transition Management." *Environment and Planning A* 39, no. 4 (2007): 763–770.

Silver, Jonathan. "Incremental Infrastructures: Material Improvisation and Social Collaboration across Post-Colonial Accra." *Urban Geography* 35, no. 6 (2014): 788–804.

Simmie, James. "Path Dependence and New Technological Path Creation in the Danish Wind Industry." *European Planning Studies* 20, no. 5 (2012): 753–772.

Smith, Adrian, Andy Stirling, and Frank Berkhout. "The Governance of Sustainable Socio-Technical Transitions." *Research Policy* 34, no. 10 (2005): 1491–1510.

Sommer, E.M.K. "Die öffentliche Stromversorgung in der DDR seit 1945 und Tendenzen ihrer weiteren Entwicklung." *Energietechnik* 11, no. 3 (1961): 99–103.

Sommer, Harald: "Modellvorhaben zur Untersuchung der Möglichkeiten der wassersparenden Installation in Plattenbauten des komplexen Wohnungsbaus in Berlin-Marzahn." *Das Gas- und Wasserfach* 137, no. 8 (1996): 427–434.

Southerton, Dale, Heather Chappells, and Bas van Vliet, eds. *Sustainable Consumption: The Implications of Changing Infrastructures of Provision*. London: Edward Elgar, 2004.

Sovacool, Benjamin K., and David J. Hess. "Ordering Theories: Typologies and Conceptual Frameworks for Sociotechnical Change." *Social Studies of Science* 47, no. 5 (2017): 703–750.

Sovacool, Benjamin K., Katherine Lovell, and Marie Blanche Ting. "Reconfiguration, Contestation, and Decline: Conceptualizing Mature Large Technical Systems." *Science, Technology, & Human Values* 43, no. 6 (2018): 1066–1097.

Späth, Philip, and Harald Rohracher. "Local Demonstrations for Global Transitions: Dynamics across Governance Levels Fostering Socio-Technical Regime Change towards Sustainability." *European Planning Studies* 20, no. 3 (2012): 461–479.

Sprenger, Heinrich. *Heinrich Sahm. Kommunalpolitiker und Staatsmann*. Cologne: Grote, 1969.

Stadtfeld, Richard. "Die Entwicklung der öffentlichen Wasserversorgung 1970–1990." *Das Gas- und Wasserfach* 132, no. 12 (1991): 660–670.

Star, Susan Leigh. "The Ethnography of Infrastructure." *American Behavioural Scientist* 43, no. 3 (1999): 377–391.

Steinmann, Heinrich. "Die deutsche Elektrizitätsversorgung unter Berücksichtigung wehrtechnischer und wehrwirtschaftlicher Fragen." *Deutsche Technik* 7, May (1939): 238–242.

Stenographische Berichte über die öffentlichen Sitzungen der Stadtverordnetenversammlung der Stadtgemeinde Berlin. 1920–1933.

Stinglwagner, Wolfgang. "Die Elektrizitätswirtschaft der DDR." In *Die Geschichte der Stromversorgung,* edited by Wolfram Fischer, 217–245. Frankfurt am Main: Verlags- und Wirtschaftsgesellschaft der Elektrizitätswerke, 1992.

Stolpe, Rudolf. "Berlin—Großstadt ohne Verbundbetrieb." *Österreichische Zeitschrift für Elektrizitätswirtschaft* 9, no. 6 (1956): 277–281.

Stolpe, Rudolf. "Der Wiederaufbau der West-Berliner Stromversorgung." *Elektrizitätswirtschaft* 52, no. 14 (1953): 366–369.

"Strom ist kriegswichtig!" *Elektrizitätswirtschaft* 41, no. 20 (1942): 457–459.

Strümpel, Burkhard, and Heinrich Tepasse. *Wärmeversorgung Kreuzberg. Kritik und Alternativen. Ein Gutachten im Auftrag der Bauausstellung Berlin GmbH.* Berlin: Internationale Bauausstellung Berlin, 1982.

Sukopp, Herbert. "Zur ökologischen Beurteilung von Standorten für ein Kraftwerk in Berlin-Spandau." *Berliner Naturschutzblätter* 20, no. 57 (1976): 166–170.

Summerton, Jane. "Introductory Essay: The Systems Approach to Technological Change." In *Changing Large Technical Systems,* edited by Jane Summerton, 1–21. Boulder, CO: Westview, 1994.

Swyngedouw, Erik. *Liquid Power: Contested Hydro-Modernities in Twentieth-Century Spain.* Cambridge, MA: MIT Press, 2015.

Swyngedouw, Erik. "Modernity and Hybridity: Nature, *Regeneracionismo,* and the Production of the Spanish Waterscape, 1890–1930." *Annals of the Association of American Geographers* 89, no. 3 (1999): 443–465.

Swyngedouw, Erik. *Social Power and the Urbanization of Water: Flows of Power.* Oxford: Oxford University Press, 2004.

Tarr, Joel A., ed. Special issue, *Journal of Urban History* 5, no. 3 (1979): 275–408.

Tarr, Joel A., and Gabriel Dupuy, eds. *Technology and the Rise of the Networked City in Europe and America.* Philadelphia, PA: Temple University Press, 1988.

Taylor, Frederick. *The Berlin Wall, 13 August 1961 – 9 November 1989.* London: Bloomsbury, 2006.

Tegethoff, Wilm. "Die Berliner Kraft- und Licht(Bewag)-Aktiengesellschaft." *Zeitschrift für öffentliche und gemeinwirtschaftliche Unternehmen* 11 (1988): 88–94.

Tegethoff, Wilm. "100 Jahre elektrizitätswirtschaftliche Energiepolitik in Berlin." *Elektrizitätswirtschaft* 83, nos. 9/10 (1984): 415–419.

Templin, David. *Wasser für die Volksgemeinschaft. Wasserwerke und Stadtentwässerung in Hamburg im "Dritten Reich."* Hamburg: Dölling und Galitz, 2016.

Tepasse, Heinrich. *Stadttechnik im Städtebau Berlins. 1945–1999.* Berlin: Gebr. Mann, 2001.

Tepasse, Heinrich. *Stadttechnik im Städtebau Berlins. 20. Jahrhundert.* Berlin: Gebr. Mann, 2006.

Tessendorff, Heinz. "Berliner Wasserbetriebe im Wandel der Nachkriegsgeschichte." *Das Gas- und Wasserfach* 136, no. 11 (1995): 555–563.

Tessendorff, Heinz. "Die Berliner Wasser-Betriebe als Partner im West-Ost-Dialog." *Das Gas- und Wasserfach* 134, no. 9 (1993): 541–545.

Tessendorff, Heinz. "Die Sicherstellung der Wasserversorgung Berlins in der Zukunft." *Forum Städtehygiene* 29 (1978): 1–4.

Tessendorff, Heinz. "So soll es bleiben: Berliner Wasser—alles klar!" In *Umwelt- und Naturschutz für Berliner Gewässer. Kongreß "Berlin auf dem Trockenen?" Zukunft der Wasserversorgung*, edited by Senatsverwaltung für Stadtentwicklung und Umweltschutz, 40–55. Berlin: Senatsverwaltung für Stadtentwicklung und Umweltschutz, 1990.

Tessendorff, Heinz. "WASSER BERLIN 81–125 Jahre zentrale Wasserversorgung." *Das Gas- und Wasserfach* 122, no. 3 (1981): 97–102.

Tessendorff, Heinz. "Wasserversorgung und Abwasserbeseitigung—Neue Aufgaben im vereinten Berlin." *Korrespondenz Abwasser* 39, no. 5 (1992): 310–314.

Thalheim, Karl C. "Verkehr und Versorgungsbetriebe." In *Berlin Sowjetsektor. Die politische, rechtliche, wirtschaftliche, soziale und kulturelle Entwicklung in acht Berliner Verwaltungsbezirken*, edited by Büro für Gesamtberliner Fragen, 148–156. Berlin: Colloquium, 1965.

Thierbach, Bruno. "Die gegenwärtige Versorgung der Stadt Berlin und der Provinz Brandenburg mit elektrischer Arbeit." *Elektrotechnische Zeitschrift* 46, no. 39 (1925): 1465–1471.

Thoms, Guido. "Der Beitrag der Wasserwirtschaft zur sozialistischen Landeskultur." *Wasserwirtschaft—Wassertechnik* 20, no. 9 (1970): 289–292.

Till, Karen E. *The New Berlin: Memory, Politics, Place.* Minneapolis: University of Minnesota Press, 2005.

Trauer, Günther, and Max Prüß. *Gutachten der Wirtschaftsberatung Deutscher Städte Aktiengesellschaft über die Berliner Stadtentwässerung.* Berlin: W. & S. Loewenthal, 1932.

Trentmann, Frank, ed. *The Making of the Consumer: Knowledge, Power and Identity in the Modern World.* Oxford: Berg, 2006.

Truffer, Bernhard, and Lars Coenen. "Environmental Innovation and Sustainability Transitions in Regional Studies." *Regional Studies* 46, no. 1 (2012): 1–21.

Uekötter, Frank. *The Green and the Brown: A History of Conservation in Nazi Germany*. Cambridge: Cambridge University Press, 2006.

Uekötter, Frank. *The Greenest Nation? A New History of German Environmentalism*. Cambridge, MA: MIT Press, 2015.

Ufer, Dietmar. "Zum neuen Energiekonzept der DDR." *Energietechnik* 40, no. 9 (1990): 323–325.

Ureta, Sebastián. *Assembling Policy: Transantiago, Human Devices, and the Dream of a World-Class Society*. Cambridge MA: MIT Press, 2015.

VEB Energiekombinat Berlin, ed. *40 Jahre Deutsche Demokratische Republik. 40 Jahre Sozialistische Energiewirtschaft in Berlin—Hauptstadt der DDR*. Berlin: n.p., 1989.

VEB Gasversorgung Berlin. *Arbeitsordnung vom 2. April 1962*. Berlin: n.p., n.d.

VEB Gasversorgung Berlin. "Betriebskollektivvertrag 1963 vom 6. Februar 1963." Unpublished manuscript.

Vleuten, Erik van der. "Understanding Network Societies: Two Decades of Large Technical Systems Studies." In *Networking Europe: Transnational Infrastructures and the Shaping of Europe, 1850–2000*, edited by Erik van der Vleuten and Arne Kaijser, 279–314. Sagamore Beach, MA: Science History Publications, 2006.

Vogt, D., and D. Jahn. "Phosphatverringerung in den Berliner Gewässern." *Wasser + Boden* 41, no. 4 (1989): 231–134.

Vohrer, Eugen. "Die Kriegsschäden an den Anlagen der Berliner Stadtentwässerung und ihre Überwindung." *Wasserwirtschaft—Wassertechnik* 4, no. 2 (1954): 70–72.

Vorlagen zu den Sitzungen der Stadtverordnetenversammlung der Stadtgemeinde Berlin. 1928, 764–765.

Voß, Jan-Peter, and Dierk Bauknecht. "Netzregulierung in Infrastruktursektoren. Der Einfluss von Technik auf den Verlauf von Governance-Innovationen." In *Gesellschaft und die Macht der Technik*, edited by Ulrich Dolata and Raymund Werle, 109–132. Frankfurt: Campus, 2007.

Wagner, Martin, ed. *Das Neue Berlin*. Berlin: Deutsche Bauzeitung, 1929.

Weise, Erich. "Vorschläge für die Zukunftsentwicklung der Berliner Abwasserwirtschaft." *Gesundheits-Ingenieur* 57, no. 20 (1934): 248–252.

Weiß, Heinrich, and H.-J. Mielke. "Kraftwerksbau im Landschaftsschutzgebiet Spandauer Forst II." *Berliner Naturschutzblätter* 21, no. 60 (1977): 251–255.

Wellmann. "Vom Luftschutz der Bewag." *Der Stromkreis* 1, no. 1 (1933): 15–17.

Werle, Hermann. "Strom teurer—Gas teurer—Wasser teurer. Forderung nach Enteignung wird lauter." *Mieter-Echo* no. 326, February (2008): 16–18.

Wermuth, Adolf. *Ein Beamtenleben. Erinnerungen*. Berlin: A. Scherl, 1922.

Werner, Frank. *Stadtplanung Berlin. Theorie und Realität. Teil I: 1900–1960*. Berlin: Kiepert, 1976.

Wetzlaugk, Udo. *Die Alliierten in Berlin*. Berlin: Berlin Verlag A. Spitz, 1988.

Whyte, Iain Boyd, and David Frisby, eds. *Metropolis Berlin, 1880–1940*. Berkeley: University of California Press, 2012.

Wichmann, Rudolf. "Die Versorgung Berlins mit Fernstrom." *Elektrotechnische Zeitschrift* 43, no. 31 (1922): 1001–1003.

Wicke, Lutz. "Beiträge der Wissenschaft für den Klimaschutz in Berlin." In *Energie und Klimaschutz für Berlin. Beiträge der Berliner und Brandenburger Wissenschaft*, edited by Senatsverwaltung für Stadtentwicklung, Umweltschutz und Technologie, 5–9. Berlin: Senatsverwaltung für Stadtentwicklung, Umweltschutz und Technologie, 1995.

Wildt, Michael, and Christoph Kreutzmüller: *Berlin, 1933–1945*. Munich: Siedler, 2013.

Wildt, Michael, and Christoph Kreutzmüller: "Stadt und Gesellschaft im Nationalsozialismus." In *Berlin, 1933–1945*, edited by Michael Wildt and Christoph Kreutzmüller, 7–16. Munich: Siedler, 2013.

Wilkes, Christopher. "Die Entwicklung der infrastrukturellen Planung." *RaumPlanung* 56 (1992): 19–27.

Williams, Rosalind. *Notes on the Underground: An Essay on Technology, Society, and the Imagination*. Cambridge, MA: MIT Press, 2008.

Winje, Dietmar. "Bewag und Klimaschutz." *Elektrizitätswirtschaft* 95, no. 12 (1996): 789–790.

Winje, Dietmar. "Integration des West-Berliner Netzes in den deutschen Verbund." *Elektrizitätswirtschaft* 93, no. 13 (1994): 726–732.

Winje, Dietmar. "Neue Zielstellungen in der Elektrizitätswirtschaft—Demand-Side Management und Least-Cost Planning als Management-Strategien?" *Elektrizitätswirtschaft* 91, no. 17 (1992): 1057–1066.

Wise, Michael Z. *Capital Dilemma: Germany's Search for a New Architecture of Democracy*. New York: Princeton Architectural Press, 1998.

Wittfogel, Karl August. *Oriental Despotism: A Comparative Study of Total Power*. New Haven, CT: Yale University Press, 1967.

Wolf, Winfried. *Berlin—Weltstadt ohne Auto? Verkehrsgeschichte 1848–2015*. Cologne: ISP, 1994.

Wolfers, Benedikt. "Privatization of the Berlin Water Works: A Blueprint for Balancing Public and Private Interests?" *Journal for European Environmental and Planning Law* 1, no. 2 (2004): 116–124.

Wolfram, Marc, and Niki Frantzeskaki. "Cities and Systemic Change for Sustainability: Prevailing Epistomologies and an Emerging Research Agenda." *Sustainability* 8, no. 2 (2016): 144ff.

Worster, Donald. *Rivers of Empire: Water, Aridity and the Growth of the American West*. New York: Pantheon, 1985.

Zabel, A. "Die Kanalisation Berlins nach dem Kriege." *Gesundheits-Ingenieur* 68, no. 6 (1947): 172–174.

Zachmann, Karin. "Küchendebatten in Berlin? Die Küche als Kampfplatz im Kalten Krieg." In *Konfrontation und Wettbewerb. Wissenschaft, Technik und Kultur im geteilten Berliner Alltag (1948–1973)*, edited by Michael Lemke, 181–205. Berlin: Metropol, 2008.

Zehn Jahre Wiederaufbau der Berliner Stromversorgung. Brochure, n.p., n.d. [ca. 1958].

Ziesing, Hans-Joachim. "Strukturelle und sektorale Entwicklung des Energieverbrauchs in Berlin (West)." *Deutsches Institut für Wirtschaftsforschung. Wochenbericht* 52 (1985): 227–238.

Zimm, Alfred, ed. *Berlin (Ost) und sein Umland.* Gotha: Haack, 1988.

Zschaler, Frank. "Die wirtschaftliche Spaltung Berlins. Zu Unterschieden in der Wirtschafts- und Finanzpolitik zwischen den Westsektoren und dem Sowjetsektor (Ende der vierziger, Anfang der fünfziger Jahre)." In *Wirtschaft im geteilten Berlin 1945–1990. Forschungsansätze und Zeitzeugen*, edited by Wolfram Fischer and Johannes Bähr, 47–75. Munich: Saur, 1994.

"Zustand der Berliner Gasversorgung vor dem Kriege, bei Beendigung der Kampfhandlungen und im Februar 1947." *Das Gas- und Wasserfach* 88, no. 3 (1947): 90–91.

Interviews

1. Senior member of infrastructure planning unit, Berlin Senate Department for Urban Development and Environmental Protection, March 17, 1993.

2. Two members of infrastructure planning unit, Berlin Senate Department for Urban Development and Environmental Protection, April 8, 1993.

3. Senior member of energy unit, Berlin Senate Department for Urban Development and Environmental Protection, May 5, 1993.

4. Member of planning unit of Berlin Water Company BWB, June 9, 1993.

5. Senior member of energy unit, Brandenburg Ministry for Economics, Business, and Technology, June 22, 1993.

6. Three members of infrastructure planning unit, Berlin Senate Department for Urban Development and Environmental Protection, October 1, 1993.

7. Two senior members of infrastructure planning unit, Berlin Senate Department for Urban Development and Environmental Protection, October 24, 1995.

8. Member of energy unit, Berlin Senate Department for Urban Development, Environment, and Technology, August 22, 1996.

9. Member of directors' office of Berlin power utility Bewag, August 23, 1996.

10. Member of water unit, Berlin Senate Department for Urban Development, Environment, and Technology, September 6, 1996.

11. Senior employee at Technology Foundation Berlin, October 12, 2004.

12. Senior member of integrative environmental protection unit, Berlin Senate Department for Urban Development, October 21, 2004.

13. Senior member of technology unit, Berlin Senate Department for Economics, October 2004.

14. Water consultant and former BWB employee, June 4, 2018.

15. Former head of a Bewag power station in West Berlin, June 6, 2018.

16. Former member of energy unit, Berlin Senate Department for Urban Development and Environmental Protection, June 6, 2018.

17. Former member of the Institute for Ecology at the Technical University of Berlin, June 13, 2018.

18. Press officer at gas network company NBB, June 21, 2018.

19. Energy researcher, Technical University of Berlin, July 2, 2018.

20. Press officer at Berlin Water Company BWB, July 3, 2018.

21. Energy researcher, Free University of Berlin, July 4, 2018.

22. Former member of infrastructure planning unit, East Berlin administration, July 5, 2018.

23. Water specialist for environmental NGO Grüne Liga, July 5, 2018.

24. Energy researcher, formerly IZT research institute, July 12, 2018.

25. Senior member of water management unit, Berlin Senate Department for Environment, Transport, and Climate Protection, July 16, 2018.

26. Senior member of underground gas storage facility Berliner Erdgasspeicher GmbH, November 22, 2018.

Index